gnoria dequally roma era stata presa fa
etsono comite. Ilcosa tornoe aentroregne. Et
esendo il. pp. ochupato dilauorare odi murare u
risagiendo lacitade. in tanto incontenente che
quinto fabio fue fuori del magistrato onieo
marçio tribuno dela plebe ilcitoe. po che
cotra iluolito dele giunty sera cobatuto g
elly. Allqually elly era mandato panbascia
dove nala morte ildiliberoe de questo iu
dichamento siaponto che grande parte dela
giente credett cheli morise psua volontade.
Come li tribuni dechaualieri gpodere de g
soly fuorono facty.

ublio chornelio scipio. fue entroregne.
q ad preso luy marco furio camillo.
quely fecie tribuni de chaualiery.
gpodere de gsoly. marco valerio publicola.
Lucio verginio. Publio cornellio. Aulo malio.
Lucio emillio. Lucio postumio Intotenente che
liebono cominciata lasignoria. elly seconsiaro
no tuto primamente col senato di reli
gione. Il senato comando tuto primame
te che leconuegne Pelegi dele dodici ta
uole fosono trouate. qintramente risate.
Alcune altre fuorono strate da quele
g publicate al pp. cioe. Et specialme

VENICE & ANTIQUITY

PUBLISHED WITH THE ASSISTANCE OF
THE GETTY GRANT PROGRAM

VIRGILIVS MARO PARENTIBVS MODICIS FVIT:
et precipue patre Marone:quē quidam opificem figulum:plures ma
gi cuiusdam uiatoris initio mercenarium: mox ob industriam ge
nerum tradiderunt: quē quum agricolationi reiqʒ rusticę et gregi
bus prefecisset socer siluis coemundis et apibus curandis reculam au
xit.Natus est.CN. Pópeio magno:et.M. Licinio Crasso primum
consꝶ. Iduum octubrium die in pago:qui andes dicitur:qui est a Má
tua non procul . pregnans eo mater Maia somniauit enixā se lau
reum ramum:quē contacta terra eōsestim cerneret coaluisse: et ex
creuisse ilico in speciem maturę arboris referte uariis pomis et flori
bus:ac Sequenti luce cum marito rus propinquum petens ex itine
re diuertit:atque in subiecta fossa partu leuata est. Ferunt infantem ut fuit editus:nec euagisse:
et adeo miti uultu fuisse: ut haud dubiam spem prosperioris geniturę iam tum indicaret. Et ac
cessit aliud presagium . Si quidem uirga populea more regionis in puerperiis eodem statim lo
co depacta ita breui coaluit:ut multo ante satas populos adequarit:quę arbor Virgilii ex eo di
cta atqʒ consecrata est sum̄a grauidarum et fętarum religione suscipientium ibi et soluentium
uota . Initia ętatis idest usqʒ ad septimum annum Cremonę egit: et .xvii. anno uirilem to
gam cepit illis consulibus iterum quibus natus erat . Euenitque ut eo ipso die lucretius poe
ta decederet.Sed Virgilius a Cremona Mediolanum:et ide paulopost Neapoli transit.Vbi cum
litteris et grecis et latinis uehementissimā operam dedisset: tandem omni cura omnique studio
indulsit medicinę et mathematicis : Quibus rebus cum ante alios eruditior peritiorque esset:
se in urbem contulit statim̄ʒ magistri stabuli equorum Augusti amiciam nactus multos ua
riosqʒ morbos incidentes equis curauit . At ille in mercedem singulis diebus panes Virgili
o ut uni ex stabulariis dari iussit . Interea a Crotōiatis pullus equi mirę pulchritudinis Cę
sari dono fuit missus: qui omnium iudicio spem portendebat uirtutis et celeritatis immensę.
Hunc cum aspexisset Maro magistro stabuli dixit natum esse ex morbosa equa: et nec uiribus
ualiturum nec celeritate: id ꝑ uerum fuisse inuentum est: Quod cum magister stabuli Au
gusto recitasset:duplicari ipsi in mercedem panes iussit . Cum item ex Hispania Augusto
canes dono mitterentur et parentes eorum: dixit Virgilius et animum celeritatemque futu
ram : Quo cognito mandat iterum augmentari Virgilio panes . Dubitauit Augustus O
ctauii ne filius esset an alterius : idꝗ maronem aperire posse arbitratus est: quia canum et
equi naturam parentesqʒ cognorat.Amotis igitur omnibus arbitris illum in penitiorem par
tem domus uocat : et solum rogat an sciat quisnam esset : et quam ad felicitandos homi
nes facultatem haberet . Noui inquit Maro te Cęsarem Augustum et ferme ęquam cum diis
immortalibus potestatem habere : ut quem uis felicem facias : Eo animo sum respondit Cę
sar ut si uerum pro rogatu dixeris:beatum te felicemqʒ reddam. Vtinam ait Maro interrogan
ti tibi uera dicere queam . Tunc Augustus putant alii Me natum Octauio: quidam suspican
tur alio me genitum uiro . Maro subridens facile inquit si impune licenterqʒ quę sentio loqui iu
bes : id dicam . Affirmat Cęsar iureiurádo nullum eius dictum egre laturum: immo non ni
si donatum ab eo discessurum . Ad hęc oculos oculis Agusti infigens Maro:facilius ait in cę
teris animalibus qualitates parentum mathematicis et philosophia cognosci possunt: in ho
mine nequaquā possibile est :Sed de te coniecturam habeo similem ueri: ut quid exercuerit pa
ter tuus scire possim. Attente expectabat Augustus quidnam diceret . At ille quantum ego
rem intelligere possum pistoris filius es inquit . Obstupuerat Cęsar et statim quo id pacto fi
eri potuerit: aio uoluebat. Interrumpens Virgilius:audi inquit quo pacto id coniitio:Cum quę
dā enunciari: predixerim ꝑ quę intelligi scíriqʒ non nisi ab eruditissimis summisque uiris potuis
sent : Tu princeps orbis item et itē panes in mercedem dari iussisti:quod quidem aut pistoris
aut nati pistore officium erat.At deinceps inquit Cęsar non a pistore sed a rege magnani
mo dona feres. Placuit Cęsari facecia: illumʒ plurimi fecit : et Pollioni commendauit. Cor
pore et statura fuit grandi : aquilino colore: facie rusticana : ualitudine uaria. Ná plerunqʒ
ab stomaco et faucibus ac dolore capitis laborabat . Sanguinē et sepius eiecit: cibi uiniqʒ
minimi . Fama est eum libidinis pronioris in pueros fuisse. Sed boni ita cum pueros amas

PATRICIA FORTINI BROWN

VENICE & ANTIQUITY

The Venetian Sense of the Past

YALE UNIVERSITY PRESS
NEW HAVEN & LONDON

Designed by Gillian Malpass
Set in Linotron Bembo by Best-set Typesetter Ltd., Hong Kong
Printed in Singapore

Library of Congress Cataloging-in-Publication Data
Brown, Patricia Fortini
Venice and antiquity/Patricia Fortini Brown.
Includes bibliographical references and index.
ISBN 0-300-06700-3 (cloth: alk. paper)
1. Venice (Italy) – Civilization – Foreign influences.
2. Venice (Italy) – Civilization – Classical influences.
3. Art and history – Italy – Venice.
4. Art, Italian – Italy – Venice – Foreign influences.
5. Art, Italian – Classical influences.
6. Classical antiquities – Conservation and restoration.
7. Civilization, Classical.
8. Venice (Italy) – History – 697–1508.
9. Venice (Italy) – History – 1508–1797.
I. Title.
DG675.6.B7   1997
945'.31 – dc20   96-3196
                                                          CIP

A catalogue record for this book is available from
The British Library

Frontispiece: Master of the London Pliny, frontispiece to Virgilius Maro, *Opera*,
Venice: Antonio di Bartolomeo da Bologna, 14[7]6, f. a2r.
Parchment, 32.8 × 26.6 cm. London, British Library, C.19.e.14.

Page i: Alessandro Leopardi, *The Instruction of Cupid in Architecture, c.*1482–90.
Bronze, diam. 15.2 cm. London, Victoria and Albert Museum.

Endpapers: Detail from f. 129 of Titus Livius, *Ab urbe condita libri I–X,* 1372–3.
Milan, Biblioteca Ambrosiana, Cod. C. 214 inf.

For Walter

Venice, view of the Piazzetta in the late nineteenth century.

CONTENTS

PART V
THE HISTORICAL IMAGINATION:
CONSTRUCTING AN ALTERNATE REALITY

PART VI
THE HISTORICAL ECHO:
CREATING NEW IDENTITIES

ACKNOWLEDGMENTS

A book that was six years in the making incurs many debts, and I should like to express my sincere gratitude to the institutions and individuals who helped me in manifold ways to bring it to fruition. My research was supported by the American Academy in Rome and by the National Endowment for the Humanities, who sponsored my post-doctoral fellowship year there in 1989–90; by the John Simon Guggenheim Foundation for a fellowship awarded in 1989, but taken in 1992–3; and by the Department of Art and Archaeology at Princeton University, which granted me two sabbatical leaves and gave me further assistance from the Ione May Spears Fund and the Publication Fund. I am also greatly indebted to the Rockefeller Foundation's Bellagio Study and Conference Center, where I spent five weeks in 1992 coming to terms with the *Hypnerotomachia Poliphili*, and to the staffs of the libraries where I carried out most of my research: in Rome at the Biblioteca Hertziana and the library of the American Academy; in Venice at the Biblioteca Nazionale Marciana, the Fondazione Giorgio Cini, and the Biblioteca Correr; and in Princeton at the Marquand, Scheide, and Firestone Libraries.

Furthermore, I am most grateful to the co-chairs of the Department of Art and Archaeology, John Wilmerding and John Pinto, and to my other colleagues at Princeton for providing encouragement and a supportive environment during this period. Particular thanks go to the office staff – Marion White, Susan Lehre, Brenda O'Brien, and Glenda Cain – for many small courtesies, too many to enumerate here. I am also indebted to the following individuals who, among many others, have helped me with various aspects of the book: Robert Bagley, Vittore Branca, David Connelly, Brian Curran, Pietro Frassica, Mino Gabriele, Michael Jacoff, Sandy Kalajian, Patricia Labalme, Alison Luchs, Barbara Lynn-Davis, Stefania Mason, Giancarlo Maiorino, Hugo Meyer, Laurie Nussdorfer, John Pinto, Jane Roberts, Annegrit Schmitt, Juergen Schulz, Wendy Stedman Sheard, Alan Stahl, and Marino Zorzi. Emily Hoover, Evonne Levy, Alick McLean, Jacqueline Musacchio, and Madeleine Viljoen were much valued research assistants. Special thanks go to Shari Kenfield for her tireless efforts to obtain photographs and permissions to publish them; to Joann Boscarino who made the map of Giosafat Barbaro's travels (Plate 165); to Elaine Fantham, Glenn Most and Ryan Balot for invaluable help with the Latin translations; and to Giuliano Martin for generously making available to me the precious color transparencies of Giorgione's frescoes in Casa Marta-Pellizzari in Castelfranco Veneto.

I am particularly grateful to Anthony Grafton, Thomas DaCosta Kaufmann, Glenn Most and Debra Pincus for what must rank as the highest act of scholarly generosity: each read the entire manuscript and each offered thoughtful, challenging, and invaluable advice from a variety of perspectives. I am also deeply indebted to Celia Jones who edited the text with insight and intelligence and to Gillian Malpass, who is as much friend and colleague as gifted editor. Her care, encouragement, and good advice have made this a better book.

My greatest debt I acknowledge last. This book is dedicated in heartfelt gratitude to Walter Winslow, whose unqualified support and unshakable optimism provided a safe refuge during the uncertain genesis and daunting course of the project. His blithe spirit allowed me to pursue chimeras and to subdue a text that sometimes took on a willful life of its own. His music remains a silent accompaniment to every page.

Portolan map, first half of the fifteenth century. Venice, Biblioteca Nazionale Marciana, cod. It. IV, 9 (=5090). South is at the top, according to the convention of the time.

PREFACE

This book explores the evolution of a Venetian view of time, of history, and of historical change as the physical and literary remains of pagan and Christian antiquity are encountered and acknowledged in the art, architecture, literature, and cultural life of Venice's "Golden Age" (the thirteenth to sixteenth centuries). It had its genesis in 1987 at a symposium in Rome in honor of Richard Krautheimer and Father Leonard Boyle, where I gave a paper entitled "Jacopo Bellini: Roman Tradition in the Service of Venetian *Istoria*." It was my first serious encounter with the ancient world and, indeed, with Rome itself.

I had just completed the manuscript for my first book, *Venetian Narrative Painting in the Age of Carpaccio* (1988), in which I examined how Venetians wrote their own history and how a Venetian "eyewitness style" of painting functioned in "aesthetic space" to mediate between the ideology and the reality of civic and religious life. It was during this period that I was challenged by the issues raised in David Lowenthal's stimulating and unabashedly eclectic book, *The Past is a Foreign Country* (1985) and became concerned with the further problem of how the *ancient* past was discovered and rendered present to the Renaissance viewer.

I returned to Rome for a sabbatical leave in 1989–90 and began research on a book that was initially envisioned as a comprehensive look at the development of historical consciousness over the span of the Renaissance in all of Italy, bringing together objects and texts. There were few direct models. Although the subject of classical revival in Italy had been treated extensively in both general and specialized studies, these tended to fall into two categories: the primarily literary, dealing with humanism, antiquarianism, and collecting, and the primarily visual or artistic, a category that included monographic treatments of the antique borrowings of various artists (for example, Ghiberti, Donatello, Mantegna, Pinturicchio, Raphael) and catalogues of ancient marbles known in the Renaissance. There were, however, several important attempts at synthetic overviews of the entire period. Following Panofsky's seminal essay, *Renaissance and Renascences* (1960), Roberto Weiss's *Renaissance Discovery of Classical Antiquity* (1969) stands out. But while it deals cogently and percep-

tively with antiquarians and humanists, it touches on the vernacular culture in only a limited way and is little concerned with the artist. For my purposes it was thus a valuable point of departure, but not a model for an integrative study.

Recent tendencies toward the more interpretative approach pioneered by Aby Warburg (*Die Erneuerung der heidnischen Antike, Kulturwissenschaftliche Beiträge zur Geschichte der europäischen Renaissance*, also known as *Gesammelte Schriften*, 2 vols., Leipzig and Berlin 1932), are best exemplified by the essays found in *Memoria dell'antico nell'arte italiana*, three volumes edited by Salvatore Settis (Turin 1984–6). My own book was conceived as part of the discourse set under way in those volumes, most particularly Settis's important essay, "Continuità, distanza, conoscenza. Tre usi dell'antico," which convinced me that art, ideas, and primary texts could, indeed, be brought together in a "thick" cultural interpretation of the Renaissance experience.

Toward this end, I determined to work with three major "deposits" of evidence, weaving them together in a tapestry of words and pictures that would reveal the emergence of a sense of the antique past and its distinctive relationship to the present: the material of vernacular or popular culture in which antiquities were seen simply as by-products, mentioned only in passing, but often in a revealing manner; the more learned, and more self-conscious, material of "high" culture, including humanist literature and antiquarian studies; and finally, but most importantly, the artistic response to this heightened awareness of the past as it was determined by it, interacted with it, and, in turn, re-informed it.

The scope of the project showed no lack of hubris on my part, and after some months in Rome, it became clear to me that to present the topic as more than a superficial overview, I would need to narrow my focus. Because I was interested in an evolving sense of the past, I maintained the diachronic model, but moved onto (to me) a more familiar terrain bordered by the waters of the Venetian lagoon. My previous work on Venetian art and culture had already confirmed to me the validity of claims about Venice's "otherness" in regard to the rest of Italy. It was clear that *venezianità* also informed the special manner in which Venice experienced a Renaissance, which has been largely defined by modern scholars according to a Florentine model. But here, again, scholarly consideration of the problem has tended to be limited in time frame or to focus either on texts or on objects. Indeed, the studies initially most important for my own inquiry dealt on the one hand with Venetian civic historiography (most notably the studies of Gina Fasoli, Antonio Carile, and Agostino Pertusi) and on the other hand with architecture (particularly Otto Demus's paradigmatic essay, "A Renascence of Early Christian Art in Thirteenth-Century Venice" [1955], along with his monograph, *The Church of San Marco in Venice* [1960], and Manfredo Tafuri's *Venezia e il Rinascimento* [1985]. But the bibliography soon lengthened, along with the repertoire of art and artifacts, and came to include a range of literary and visual testimonials that deliberately efface the modern hierarchical distinction between "high" and "low" culture. As with my earlier book, I have been strongly influenced by Michael Baxandall's notion of a "period eye." During the period in question, it was, I would argue, an eye that made few such distinctions.

I began writing the book in January 1993, during a sabbatical year supported by a fellowship from the John Simon Guggenheim Foundation. Two teaching years have intervened since then, and the manuscript was completed in September 1995. Several parts of the book were originally published as conference papers and have been incorporated in an amended form into the chapters indicated here. Complete citations are included in the Bibliography. Chapters 1 and 2 include passages from "The Self-definition of the Venetian Republic"; chapter 6 draws upon "The Antiquarianism of Jacopo Bellini"; chapter 7 incorporates "Ancient Artifacts and the Mercantile Mentality"; and chapter 11 is an expanded version of "Sacrosanct Antiquity: the Pagan Past and the Quattrocento." Segments from "*Renovatio* or *Conciliatio*?: How Renaissances Happened in Venice," a summary statement of one of the major themes of the book, reappear in several places throughout the text.

I would like to stress a few points. This book is about Venice, and Venetians, and a peculiarly Venetian relationship with their own past as well as the classical past. And yet because something was "Venetian" does not make it exclusively so. The first point is the recognition that certain aspects of the Venetian experience were shared by those in other centers in Europe and especially in Italy.

The second point is an acknowledgment that the scope of the topic meant that sacrifices had to be made. Although Padua is given a significant role in the development of Venetian sensibilities, there is less comparative material from other centers than I would like. And even within the Venetian milieu, many favorite images and objects had to be left out of a discussion that deals with art and literature, as well as history, and that spans over three hundred years. It came down to a matter of choice: of choosing the most telling examples, which seem to sum up the sense of things in a given period.

The third point is the problem of voice. I have sought throughout to let Venetians speak for themselves. So, along with a number of extended passages translated from primary sources, there is often a shifting perspective. At times I take the role of critic; at times the role of historian; at times the role of my Venetian protagonist.

Finally, this would have been a far more manageable book had it been confined only to the civic sphere, or to a more restricted period. It was my aim, however, to examine the reciprocal relationship between the public and the private and to follow the trajectory of a negotiation between past and present over the *longue durée*. In order to do justice to both civic and individual concerns and to follow through on certain themes in more depth, I had to depart from a strict chronology occasionally and to double back in time from one chapter to the next. However, each chapter, although woven into a larger whole, should stand more or less by itself.

I

THE HISTORICAL IMPERATIVE: INVENTING A CIVIC PAST

1   Torcello, Santa Maria Assunta. Pulpit staircase.

PROLOGUE

Accept, oh Man, my warning, as I am Life. Would you catch, would you touch, would you hold my hair? Do not abandon yourself to lust and luxury, do not become proud, and do not offend modesty. You see me nude: do not forget the nakedness of death. To my feet are added wheels: beware them, lest they turn hither and yon. My legs are winged: I flee, I escape from you. In my hand I hold the balance: beware its fluctuations. Why do you try to catch me? You will embrace a shadow, you will grasp the wind. Why do you try to catch me? You will grasp only smoke, only a dream, only the wake of a boat [on water].
Receive, oh Man, my warning, as I am Life. You did not catch, you did not touch, you did not hold my hair? But do not be sad, do not despair. I am nude, and having fled from the hands of these, perhaps I will return to you. To my feet are attached some wheels that may return quickly to you. My legs are winged: I may fly to you: I carry the balance, perhaps to your advantage. So do not despair.
      – Theodore Prodomos, Constantinople, early twelfth century[1]

In antiquity, the concept of *occasio* – that transient aspect of Time as Opportunity – was personified by Kairos, an elusive youth who must be seized at the propitious moment. Prodomos's dialogue may well have been inspired by a celebrated bronze figure of Kairos, copied by Lysippus from an original by Polykleitos. Now lost, it is known to us from epigrams by ancient writers.[2] The Byzantine poet reveals, however, that the ancient Kairos would take on a new layer of significance in the Christian Middle Ages, when human life itself would be portrayed as but a fleeting moment.[3]

Although no direct connection can be demonstrated with the poem or with the Lysippan relief, a pictorial counterpart to Prodomos's epigram can be found on an island in the Venetian lagoon. It constitutes our earliest surviving direct visual testimony to a Venetian concern with time, and it comes in humble form. Embedded in the rebuilt pulpit staircase in the Basilica of Santa Maria Assunta at Torcello is a fragment of relief sculpture, datable to the eleventh or twelfth century (Plates 1–3).[4] Here, too, Opportunity appears in the guise of Kairos, fleeing on winged wheels with a balance in one hand and a baton in the other. His flight impeded by the young man to the left who seizes him by the hair, he escapes the grasp of an older bearded man to the right who is accompanied by a grieving woman. But to the far left is the female figure of a wingless Victory (now a separate fragment, kept in the sacristy of the basilica), who holds a palm leaf and proffers a crown.[5]

In both poem and sculpture, the balance scale affirms the ancient Greek concept of time as a judge.[6] While some observers have seen the unhappy figures on the right as Irresoluteness and Repentence,[7] Prodomos's script suggests a more direct opposition. Old Age who has let opportunity pass by is accompanied by Defeat, while Youth, who captures the fleeting moment, is crowned by Victory.[8]

The discovery in 1892 of a second plaque, clearly a pendant to *Kairos*, in excavations of the baptistery in front of the main door of the cathedral revealed that the original program sought to represent a more comprehensive concept of time – and life – than simply the opportune moment.[9] Unlike the allegory of *Kairos*, for which analogies can be found in late antique and Byzantine art,[10] the iconography of the second plaque is unique (Plate 4). The central figure can be identified as Ixion, King of Thessaly and father of the race of centaurs, who had been condemned by Zeus to revolve in Hades throughout eternity bound to a fiery wheel for his attempt to seduce Hera.[11] With figures of Day and Night at the sides, each holding a torch, one raised and the other lowered, the relief as a whole would symbolize in a specific sense the

3   *Kairos (Opportunity)*, detail of pulpit staircase, with a fragment of *Fortuna* (now in the sacristy). Marble relief. Torcello, Santa Maria Assunta.

4   *Ixion*. Marble relief. Torcello, Santa Maria Assunta, choir enclosure.

2 (*facing page*)   Torcello, Santa Maria Assunta. Pulpit staircase.

punishment that awaits one who seizes the wrong opportunity – and in a larger sense, eternity.[12]

Taken together the two allegories thus encompass the two major concepts of time inherited from antiquity: *kairos* (opportunity or the propitious moment) and *chronos* (eternal or ongoing time). While the first depiction offers hope, the second extends a warning. One may observe in them a typically medieval transformation of pagan mythology into a Christian *memento mori*, endowed with the authority of classical antiquity.[13]

The Torcello reliefs raise several issues that may serve as a point of departure for our inquiry into the Venetian sense of the past. Some of these may seem obvious, but commonplaces are often grounded in truth and worth restating as a prologue to a study that aims to maintain a broad focus, from archaeology on the one hand to poetry on the other.

First, as can be observed repeatedly over the course of this book, time in an abstract sense – its nature, its meanings, its effects, its representation, its inevitability, and, not least, its malleability – continues to be a special concern of artists in the Venetian milieu, from the anonymous sculptor or sculptors of the Torcello reliefs, to Jacopo Bellini and Mantegna in the fifteenth century and Giorgione and Titian in the sixteenth. During this period a gradual shift in emphasis is discernable from a concern with time and chronology in a general, teleological, and primarily civic sense, to a fascination with human time in an intimate and personal sense.

Second, with their subjects drawn from classical mythology and their style and iconography probably depending upon Byzantine ivory plaquettes rather than Roman sarcophagi, the Torcello reliefs recall Venice's initial orientation toward the Greek world in a philosophical as well as an artistic and political sense. They are probably the earliest surviving examples of a classicizing tendency, mediated through Greece, in Venetian sculpture.[14]

Third, the reliefs bear witness to the arbitrary nature of survivals: their damaged state suggests a hiatus – a time when the reliefs, although carved in fine white marble, were no longer valued for their imagery or their message – and then rediscovery. Their salvage as spolia – a modern concept referring to the re-used remains of earlier monuments – occurred only as a second and a third thought. The *Kairos* relief was probably re-used immediately, albeit in an unobtrusive location on the new pulpit. Now bereft of its Victory figure as well as a segment of the surrounding frame, its dignity was awkwardly restored with the addition of a braided frieze of a different pattern and scale. The *Ixion* relief fared less well. It was not just broken, but deliberately sawed into four equal pieces, suitable only for building blocks. Some seven centuries later it was discovered and reassembled, not for its beauty or for its religious message, but only because of its uniqueness and its antiquity.

Finally, the restitution of the fragments to a certain degree of wholeness within the larger program calls attention to another recurring, and consummately Venetian, concern: to create a density of time within their major monuments through the employment of rediscovered relics, consisting for the most part of sculpture and architectural components. Along these lines, sumptuously carved slabs of marble were cut up to make a serviceable staircase for the Torcello pulpit proper, almost as if they were rolled off the bolt of a patterned luxury fabric and cut into arbitrary shapes without any regard for the original integrity of their designs.[15] Observable in such cases of re-use is what might be called an aesthetic of discontinuity: wherein the pastiche effect tends to privilege, and to call attention to, the antiquity of an object. At issue is a kind of historical density involving a notion of time that embraces both Kairos and Ixion and that exists both within and outside historical time. It is perhaps here that one comes closest to defining the early manifestations of *venezianità* as it pertained to a distinctively Venetian sense of the past.

THE ABSENCE OF A PAST

The Venetian sense of the past and the formation of a unique civic identity was in good part grounded in a perceived lack: the absence of a Roman foundation. The problem confronting the Venetians is made plain by the *Tabula Peutingeriana*, a fourth-century map of the Roman road system that survives in a thirteenth-century copy (Plate 5).[16] Dominating the province of "Venetia et Histria" at the head of the Adriatic is the great walled city of Aquileia, flanked by the *municipii* of Concordia and Altino and the thermal complex of Fonte Timavi.[17] While the area is already part of a large commercial network, the Venetian lagoon proper is only a sea route, devoid of significant habitation. The nearest site of human activity is marked "ad portum," directly below Altino and now identified as the port of Padua.[18] The point is that Venice was not a Roman city. It did not yet exist as a civic entity and would not exist for another two hundred years.[19]

Indeed, the first contemporary literary evidence of lagoon settlement dates to A.D. 537/8, when the Roman official Cassiodorus had described small settlements of fishermen, where the only abundance was of fish and where rich and poor lived side by side in similar houses.[20] Although in the Renaissance period Venetians would exploit this image of an early golden age of primitive virtue, in the Middle Ages the nobility of the civic lineage counted for more. In those years, as will become clear, the challenge was to earn respect through the creation of a more dignified and ancient heritage.

No longer discernible on the densely built-up island of Rialto in Venice proper, this early Venice can still be imagined on the comparatively deserted outlying islands of the lagoon, like Torcello or Mazzorbo (Plate 6). The oldest epigraphical document of the city can be found close at hand to the reliefs of *Kairos* and *Ixion* in the cathedral at Torcello. A stone slab with an inscription of 639, it records the foundation

5   Northern end of the Adriatic Sea, from the *Tabula Peutingeriana*, thirteenth-century copy of a fourth-century original. Vienna, Österreichischen Bibliothek, Cod. 324, Segment III.

of the church and its dedication to the Mother of God during the reign of the Byzantine emperor Heraclius (Plate 7).[21] Torcello was a provincial backwater at the time, and Venice, still under the domination and protection of Byzantium, did not yet exist as an independent civic entity. The dogate would only be established some sixty years later (probably in 697), and then not on the islands but in the mainland city of Heraclea.[22]

And yet, part of that mainland would eventually be transported into the lagoon in the form of stones such as the Torcello marble, and in one sense, Venice did have a material, if second-hand, Roman substance. For embedded in the foundations of her buildings and sunk into the mud of her canals was a patrimony of ancient stones deriving from the ruins of the same mainland settlements that had produced the earliest immigrants to the lagoon.[23] Most of these were simply anonymous blocks of marble and limestone, but a number of them bore inscriptions that testify to a rich and varied lapidary inheritance drawn from an extensive territory.[24]

Not surprisingly, the nearest sites were the most exploited.

6   View of Torcello in the late nineteenth century.

7   Torcello, Santa Maria Assunta. Inscription of A.D. 639.

A good number of inscribed stones made their way from Aquileia, but according to early chronicles, Altino – considered the direct ancestor of Torcello – was the major quarry for early lagoon construction. Renaissance sylloges (catalogues) of inscriptions tend to confirm this tradition, with more than one hundred stones recorded with an Altinate provenance. These included three altars dedicated to Belenus, a god worshipped in Aquileia during the pagan era, as well as honorary, votive, and sepulchral epigrams.[25]

Imported stones were often subjected to a drastic change in function when they were converted from pagan to Christian use. An altar dedicated to the Sun God by a certain Q. Baienus Proculus of Aquileia, for example, was re-employed in the Baptistery of San Marco where it likely served as a humble support for the altar table. The gravestone of the Roman decurion Lucius Acilius, on the other hand, was brought from Altino to the church of SS. Maria e Donato at Murano. There it was hollowed out and fitted with a drain to make a baptismal font. As Marilyn Perry observes, "the pagan monument to the dead became a Christian means to immortal life."[26] A number of stones commemorated soldiers and public officials, such as the municipal magistrate, a certain Gnaeus Numerius Fronto, whose name remains in continuous public view on a slab embedded in the base of the campanile of San Vidal. With other more powerful figures now long forgotten, the stone stands as a poignant reminder of the capricious nature of chance survival (Plate 8).[27]

8   Venice, San Vidal, base of the campanile, with classical inscription.

Further afield, stones with Latin inscriptions were gathered from the area around Este, some seventy kilometers from Venice, and also from Istria and Dalmatia across the Adriatic. A good number of Greek-inscribed stones were collected from the entire Aegean area, including Crete, Delos, Thrace, and Athens: some by simple acquisition, others as trophies of war and pillage. Even in Venice, such stones continued to migrate. While a few remain in Venetian walls and founda-

tions, many have now disappeared into private hands, or have ended up in museums and public collections. As one scholar put it, they served the Venetians "first for construction, then for antiquarian interest and as ornaments of their houses."[28]

Such stones, often the fruit of necessity rather than vehicles of conscious discourse, are of limited value as witnesses to historical intention. It is difficult to know if they were used because they were antique or simply because they were there. In any event, the translation of the relics of St. Mark from Alexandria to Venice in 828 seems to have prompted a more deliberate attempt at archaeological self-fashioning. It began on a modest scale. When Doge Giustiniano Partecipazio wrote his testament the following year, he requested that stone left over "and whatever is lying around" from the construction of a monastery in Equilo and a house in Torcello, be brought in for the construction of the first Church of San Marco, displacing the just-built *chiesetta* of San Teodoro as the chapel of the doge.[29] By this time a city of stone and brick was well established in the lagoon, with the ducal seat on the island of Rialto.[30] Although little remains of the ninth-century Church of San Marco, modern on-site investigations indicate a centralized Greek-cross plan on the model of the Apostoleion, the Emperor Justinian's sixth-century Church of the Holy Apostles in Constantinople.[31] Consciously retrospective in form, the new church would have constituted a tangible claim to political legitimacy by invoking an authoritative Byzantine imperial precedent.[32] Equally important, it formed the foundation for the new state church centering on the cult of St. Mark.

THE CHALLENGE OF *ROMANITAS*

By the eleventh century the stakes had changed, for the flourishing communes of north and central Italy had become challenging rivals in a competition for honor and reputation. With heightened civic consciousness came a new awareness of the enduring prestige of antiquity in establishing political and cultural pre-eminence. Campaigns of urban renewal often focused on the construction of cathedrals built or rebuilt in the heart of the city, and many of these claimed the authority of *romanitas*.[33]

Pisa is a case in point. In the wake of a series of victories over the Saracens in the early part of the century, the construction of a stunning new cathedral was begun in 1063/4. Embedded in the wall of its south transept and apse are a number of blocks with Roman inscriptions (Plate 9), deliberately positioned so that the letters would be visible, albeit, in several cases, sideways or upside down. Recent studies show that Pisa imported hundreds of such marbles from Ostia and Rome in the eleventh and twelfth centuries, even though there were abundant remains on the site. Displayed as trophies in the fabric of the cathedral, the blocks with their perfectly formed majuscule lettering, no matter how fragmentary,

9 Pisa, Pisa cathedral, exterior wall of the apse, with classical inscription.

implied that Pisa was not only the daughter, but also the successor to Rome.[34]

Similar claims had been made, of course, for a number of cities since late antiquity, when Byzantine writers proclaimed Constantinople as the New Rome and called themselves Romans. But Pisa's stance was particularly characteristic of the Italian experience from the eleventh century on, when civic triumphs were accompanied by numerous claims of rebirth of, succession to, parity with, and even superiority over the cities of the ancient world: most notably Rome and Athens, but also Constantinople and Jerusalem.[35] It was also during the eleventh century that the Florentines began construction of their baptistery. Its marble revetted Romanesque architecture looked so Roman to later observers that Giovanni Villani, writing in the early fourteenth century, was not alone in affirming that it had been built in antiquity as a temple dedicated to Mars.[36]

And yet Venice, built up from nothing on the salt flats of the lagoon with recycled ancient stones, would be more than equal to the task of pressing for its due share of honor among these cities that could boast a Roman imperial, if pagan, past, well rooted in classical antiquity. This was the first historical imperative: to create a civic history. While the dim outlines of such a process already under way are visible well before the eleventh century, it is then that the emergence of a two-pronged strategy of historical invention, the one visual and the other textual, appears in sharper focus.

Iquidem uenetie due sūt. Prima ē illa
que in antiquitatū hystoriis continetur.
que a panonie tīmitus usqȝ ad adda fluuiū
protelatur. cuius et aquilegia ciuitas exti
tit caput. In qua beatus marcus euāgli
sta. diuina gratia plustratus xp̄m ih̄m
d̄m p̄dicauit. Secunda uero uenetia ē
illa quā apud insulas sc̄m que adriatici maris collecta si
nu intē fluentib; undis positione mutabili multitudine
p̄pli feliciter habitant. Qui uidelicet p̄p̄ls quantū ex nōie
datur intellegi. ⁊ libris annalib; c̄oprobatur ex priori uene
tia ducit originē. Q̄d aūt nūc in insulis maris inhabitat.
hec causa fuit. Winilloru qui et longobardoru gens de
litorib; oceani partes septētrionis egressa. cum p multoru
belloru certamina diuersaruqȝ tr̄a circuit tandē ueniffet
pannoniā ultra iam n̄o audens procedere. sedem sibi in
ea p̄petue habitationis instituit. Vbi cum habitaffet qua
draginta duob; annis. tempore quo iustinian gloriosissi
mus augustus romanū impiū apud constātinopolim gub
nabat. directus ab eo est narsis patritius uir eunuchus ad
urbem roma ut exercitū totile regis gothoru q ytaliam
deuastabat. do auxiliante contereret. Qui cum ueniffet pri
mu cu longobardis omnimodam pace instituit. atqȝ deinde
p̄cedens ad bellū uniūsa gothoru gentē tp̄oa q rege to
tilam usqȝ ad internitione deleuit. ⁊ uniuersos ytalie fines
obtinuit. hic narsis pri cartolarius fuit. deinde apt ūtutē
patriciatus honorē p̄meruit. erat aūt uir uirt in religione
catholicus. ī paupib; largus. ī recupandis basilicas satis stu
diosus. uigiliis ⁊ orationib; in tantū studens ut plus sup
plicationib; ad dm p̄fusis quā armis bellicis uictoriam
obtineret. S; cū despolis gentiū quas contriuerat plu
rimū auri siue argenti diuersaruqȝ reru ī n̄sas diuitias
acquisiffet. maximā a romanis p quib; multi contra eoru hostes

10 *Incipit* to Giovanni Diacono, *Chronicon Venetum et Gradense*, first half thirteenth century. Vatican, Biblioteca Apostolica Vaticana, Cod. Vat. Lat. 5269, f. 1.

1

IMPLIED ORIGINS

There are two Venices. One is that of which the ancient histories speak,
extending from the confines of Pannonia up to the river Adda. Its capital is the
city of Aquileia, in which the Holy evangelist Mark, illuminated by divine grace,
preached the gospel of our lord Jesus Christ. The other is that Venice which is
situated in the insular zone in the gulf of the Adriatic, where the water flows
between island and island, in a splendid position, pleasantly inhabited by a
numerous people. This people, from what we know from their name and from
the annals, draws its origin from the first Venice.

— John the Deacon, early eleventh century[1]

Thus begins the earliest surviving Venetian chronicle (Plate
10). Addressing without apologies the delicate question of
Venice's obscure beginnings, the chronicler goes on to explain
that inhabitants of the first Venice, led by the patriarch of
Aquileia and carrying their most holy relics, sought refuge on
the island of Grado at the time of the Longobard invasions in
the sixth century. Migration continued over the next century
to eleven other islands in the lagoon:

> Thus they gave to these islands the name of Venice, from
> whence they came, and those who live in these islands
> today call themselves Venetici. *Eneti*, although in Latin it
> has one more letter, is a name that derives from the Greek
> and signifies "worthy of praise." After these [immigrants]
> decided to establish their residence in these islands, they
> constructed some well fortified castles and cities, and in
> such a way they recreated a new Venice and altogether an
> excellent province.[2]

John the Deacon thereby established a genealogy and an
etymology for the second Venice: probably the only major
city in medieval Italy that could not boast of a Roman
foundation.[3] Its extraordinary mode of settlement matched by
its singular setting, it could now, moreover, trace its ecclesiastical authority directly back to apostolic origins in the person
of St. Mark the Evangelist.

For another three centuries the Venetian sense of time and
space would be dominated by the necessity to invent a civic
past. This demand engendered strategies both textual and
monumental, infiltrating chronicles and histories of the city
and influencing the articulation of the urban environment.

A BORROWED PAST

A major aspect of the monumental approach involved the
fabrication of a web of visual allusions to an antique or early
Christian past. Such a tendency has already been noted in the
thrice-built church of San Marco, constructed in the ninth
century, and reconstructed in the tenth and again in the
eleventh centuries, on the model of the sixth-century
Apostoleion of Constantinople (Plate 11).[4] It is surely no
coincidence that the Venetian doge Domenico Contarini ini-
tiated construction on the third church of San Marco around
1063 during precisely the same period that Pisa, a rival maritime power, began to build its new cathedral. But Venice,
without an equivalent Roman foundation to boast of, looked
back once more to the less ancient, but more pious tradition
of early Byzantium. Contarini's architects would have been
working with a remarkably serviceable model that was by
then five hundred years old. The church is, in the view of
Otto Demus, the earliest still visible instance of a deliberate
architectural archaism in Venice.[5] But it would be misleading
to attribute both echo and re-echoes to the same motivations,
for Venice was still closely tied to the Byzantine Empire in the
ninth century, while two hundred years later she had become
politically and economically independent. It is thus probable
that the first replication was intended primarily to claim political legitimacy (by emulating an imperial palatine model for
the state church) and the later ones to imply antiquity and
ecclesiastical authority (by claiming preeminence in conserv-
ing and continuing the ancient Christian past).[6]

With the growth of a Venetian national church centered at

11 *The Basilica of San Marco with the Clergy*, from *Biblia Latina*, first half fourteenth century. Venice, Biblioteca Nazionale Marciana, Cod. Lat. III, 111 (=2116), f. 165v.

San Marco, St. Mark took on an ever more politically determined role in state iconography. A handful of coins and ducal seals bear mute, but eloquent, testimony to his upward trajectory in civic symbolism. The earliest imagery was impersonal and generic, with a denaro of *c.*855–80 featuring the schematic façade of a church encircled with the inscription "Christe salva Venecias."[7] Only in the period 1056–1125, more than two centuries after the arrival of his relics in Venice, was St. Mark himself portrayed on a coin, now in company with an enthroned Christ on the reverse. By the time of Doge Pietro Polani (1130–48), Mark has replaced Christ as the *dominus* of the city. He sits enthroned on a ducal seal and hands over his *vexillum* to the standing doge. No longer simply a protector and patron, the saint is now an essential figure in the political chain of command with the doge his earthly delegate and standard-bearer.[8]

The remade basilica was decorated during this period with mosaics based on Byzantine imperial models. The twelfth-century mosaic in the presbytery depicting the *Reception of the Relics of St. Mark by the Doge* owes an obvious debt to the sixth-century *Dedication Mosaic of Emperor Justinian* in San

Vitale in Ravenna (Plates 12–13). Such an emulation may be ascribed to the authority of ongoing tradition, or it may be, as Demus suggests, "part of a consciously archaistic political tendency" inspired by the need to create a national past.[9] In all likelihood, it was due neither completely to one nor to the other, but to an intertanglement of both motivations.

In the later eleventh century, two outside observers had already interpreted the Venetian message (whether gained from written or visual sources) in terms of rebirth and filiation. St. Peter Damian proclaimed Venice both "a reborn Aquileia," by virtue of her possession of St. Mark's relics, and a daughter of Rome by reason of affinity between those relics and St. Peter, the prince of the Apostles. Pope Gregory VII expanded on the theme by praising Venice's liberty, which she had received *ab antiqua* from her Roman roots.[10] If the Byzantine character of San Marco was recognized as something alien to the Latin tradition, it posed no hindrance to either writer in reaching back further into the western past and defining the Republic of Venice as a rightful successor to Rome as an apostolic city true and proper.

A PRIMEVAL PAST

And yet, with their fortunes on the ascendant, Venetians were not content with a borrowed past. Venice had begun building her powerful trading empire in the Levant in the eleventh century. She consolidated her position in the twelfth by establishing permanent Venetian colonies on islands throughout the Aegean. These outposts would function in turn as centers for even more rapid expansion following the territorial gains made after the Fourth Crusade and the conquest of Constantinople in 1204.[11] As Venice grew into an imperial power, her ruling class would continue to refine an already impressive civic image and her chroniclers would revise the historical record many times over.

Already in the twelfth century, a new sense of the city's identity had begun to appear in the chronicles in terms of its place in time and of its place in the larger world. John the Deacon's elegant, but austere (and basically accurate) model of lagoon immigration as a consequence of Longobard invasions no longer sufficed. The *Origo civitatum italie seu venetiarum* (also known as the *Chronicon Altinate* and the *Chronicon Gradense*) now offered a more richly articulated and satisfyingly detailed account of a primitive foundation of the city in the pre-Christian *and* pre-Roman past. The *Origo*, whose authors are not known, is as much a process as a single text. Weaving together themes that had appeared in yet earlier chronicles of the ninth and tenth centuries, it appeared in a first redaction around 1081 and underwent at least two revisions by the end of the twelfth century.[12] Giorgio Cracco defines it as a "choral" work, adding that, as such, it may be regarded as "a more faithful mirror of the current mentality of cultivated Venetians."[13]

12 *Reception of the Relics of St. Mark by the Doge*, twelfth century. Mosaic. Venice, San Marco, Cappella San Clemente.

13 *Dedication Mosaic of the Emperor Justinian*, sixth century. Mosaic. Ravenna, San Vitale.

Three themes in the *Origo* are particularly revealing of a developing historical consciousness within the ruling élite. First, Venetian roots push down more deeply into the past – into primeval times when men still lived in woods and caves. The chronicler begins his account with Orpheus, who charmed uncivilized men with his eloquence and taught them how to live together in cities. The first such city was Troy, named for his grandson Troilus. But this intriguing notion, which seems to have no foundation in any classical text, was only a preface to the issue at hand: the revelation that the city of Venice was a direct linear descendent of this most ancient city of all.[14] For the inhabitants of the first Venice were now held to be of noble Trojan ancestry, with a famous founding

father in the person of Antenor, "who had by the shore entered the lagoon with seven galleys, and in that place built the city named Aquilegia, because it was bound by waterways."[15] The tribal name of the freedom-loving Venetici or Eneti – never subject to any foreign power – also received an appropriately expanded etymology; it was now said to be derived from Aeneas.[16] Admittedly, claims of a Trojan heritage were common to many cities in the medieval and Renaissance period.[17] But in the case of Venice, the Trojan myth could serve two particular objectives. On the one hand, with civic roots as deep as civilization itself, Venice was already formulating a paradigm of primeval consensus and harmony – the benefits of the civil life – that would become part of the "myth of Venice." But on the other, with a distinguished Trojan pedigree, the groundwork was also laid for universalist pretensions that would be played out during Venice's rise to empire.[18]

The second theme involves the cultivation of Venice's Christian roots. The destruction of Aquileia and *antiqua Venecia* was pushed back a century and given a richer, if often muddled, chronology. Instead of the Longobards, it was now the "impious pagan named Attila, most savage, with a great army," who had driven the Christian descendents of the original Trojan settlers from their homes in the cities of the terraferma, to take refuge in wood huts on uninhabited islands at the edge of the lagoon.[19] By giving Attila, *Flagellum Dei*, precedence over the Arian Longobards, the chroniclers could now distinguish the Venetians as specifically *Christian* refugees, fleeing unambiguously pagan hordes (Plate 14).[20]

During the historical caesura between the total destruction of Aquileia and the seventh-century foundation of the city of Heraclea as the first political capital of the second Venice, the refugees lived on Grado and the other islands, just as Cassiodorus had seen them: humbly, simply, and by the toil of their hands. With Grado identified as *Nova Aquileia* – an equation that had not been accepted by John the Deacon – the second Venice could rightfully inherit all the jurisdictions, especially the ecclesiastical, from the first. Thus the foundation of the second Venice on the eleven islands of the lagoon was not just a continuation of the migration, but a legitimate rebirth.[21] It was also, according to the *Origo*, divinely sanctioned. The people of Altino, uncertain as to where they should flee, heard a voice from the heavens: "Go up into the tower and look towards the stars." From the tower they saw the island of Torcello, and, taking refuge there, at first called it *Turris* in memory of the vision, and later Torcello.[22]

Finally, these early immigrants now have identities. For the *Origo* places a notable emphasis on lineage, with the founding families themselves given an ancient past and written into the history of the city. While John the Deacon had named only high political and ecclesiastical figures, there are now inventories of several hundred names. Their diverse origins were clearly a source of pride, for each family was listed with its original homeland. The chronicler began with the earliest

whom we are unable to name; they made and built many beautiful churches in all the squares of the island that is now called Malamocco or constructed houses with all their ornament.[25]

The focus then shifts to the new city and to the great landlords who had contributed so much to its spiritual patrimony. For example:

> The Valeressi and the Pipini, having much [wealth], were protectors of the body of St. Martin the Confessor. Joining together with other neighbors, they built a church in his honor; and also through their influence in this church of God [they built] a scuola in honor of St. Michael the Archangel and of St. Vito the Martyr; and in that place [provided] gold and silver for their welfare, for the tithe that they established in perpetuity.[26]

Here is the first vivid sense in Venetian historiography that the city is defined as a community of men.[27] This model of collective genealogy will reappear again and again in Venetian chronicles. With the great compendia of patrician and *cittadino* families of the sixteenth century, it would become an established independent genre in itself.[28] The paradigm is quite different from Florence, where families typically kept their own personal diaries, called *ricordanze*. In Venice, the history of an individual family was typically to be told only in short notices and only in the context of the entire polity. As the eighteenth-century historian Marco Foscarini observed: "Thus it seems that to our ancients it was enough to have that single memory of their ancestors that was conserved in public documents, from which then in these last centuries entire genealogies were composed."[29]

The sense of historical destiny and the ideal of community expressed in the *Origo* had their counterparts in the visual and building arts of the period. Indeed, similar ideas may well have inspired the development of the urban center around San Marco. Begun in the 1160s, and carried out in several phases, the architectural elaboration of the piazza area took a century to complete. But at least two major components were in place before 1204. First, the piazza in front of San Marco was enlarged and linked to the area now called the Piazzetta to the south of the church. The resulting L-shaped space was not only the earliest civic square in Italy, but also the largest by far.[30] Second, a communal palace was constructed on the south side of the doge's residence. Begun under Doge Sebastiano Ziani (1172–8), it would eventually be joined by seventeen others that were built in towns on the mainland over the next forty years. But, like the piazza, the Venetian communal palace was the first of its kind.[31]

Ziani was something of a "new man," whose surname was not listed in the *Origo* among the ancient tribunal families. He had made his fortune in trade and financial dealings and owned considerable real estate in the city.[32] According to Marin Sanudo, writing in the late fifteenth century, Ziani's

14   *Attila Attacking a Mainland City*, miniature from *Cronaca Veneta*, early fifteenth century. Venice, Biblioteca Nazionale Marciana, Cod. It. Z 18 (=4793), f. 53v.

stock, who had settled the mainland territories of the first Venice, presumably along with the descendents of the Trojans. To cite only a few: the Candiani from Candia; the Ystoli from Este; the Barbolani from Parma; the Centranici from Cesena; the Silvi from Bergamo. Others came from Reggio, Garda, Grado, Fano, Forli, Ferrara, Florence, Mantua, Gaeta, Capodistria, Noale, Capua, Cattaro, Pisa, Salerno, Calabria, Adria, Pola, Cremona, Trieste, Bologna, Ravenna, and, of course, Mestre. The inventory continued, extending well beyond the shores of the Italian peninsula.[23] The chronicler concludes: "For all these most ancient and noble Venetici, whom we have named one by one, were from the stock of their men of old, as we have mentioned; but then they came together in *antiqua Venecia* from diverse provinces; building *castra*, there they remained."[24]

This first migration was only a preface to the second, for the lists resume. Accounting for some 115 families, many of them repetitions from the earlier migration, the chronicler observes:

> For all these, whom we have recorded by name, who left Cittanova Eracliana [Eraclea] and Padua, came to live in Malamocco and Rialto, and many other men with them

great wealth had been based upon an archaeological discovery: "he was rich; he found, it is said, a basin of solid gold in Altino."[33] But his finest moment – a triumph that would later be enshrined as one of the iconic events of Venetian history – was his role in the Peace of Venice of 1177, where he served as a mediator between Pope Alexander III and the Emperor Frederick Barbarossa at the signing of a treaty. By the mid-fourteenth century, this episode had grown considerably in the telling, with Venice's participation given a more heroic tone than it deserved.[34] And yet, later hyperbole should not diminish the importance of the moment as experienced in its own time. The *Historia Ducum Veneticorum*, written within the lifetime of witnesses to the event, presented an impressive picture of Venetian diplomatic spectacle. To the unnamed writer of the chronicle, one of its most noteworthy features was the attendance of a great number of dignitaries from throughout Europe. Through her role as mediatrix, Venice was able to proclaim her sovereignty and also to claim a certain equivalence to pope and emperor – the two great world powers. Venice was now playing a role on an international stage, even though such a role was still at this point more ceremonial than substantive. Asserting her spiritual credentials as a faithful daughter of the Roman Church under the special protection of St. Mark, Venice could also establish herself as a lover of peace, appropriate to a direct linear descendent of the pacific Orpheus of the *Origo*.

A STOLEN PAST

The conciliatory moments of 1177 would soon be overtaken by the bellicose events of 1204, when Venice joined with the Franks in the Fourth Crusade (Plate 15). The enterprise had begun in 1201 with the high and holy purpose of regaining the Holy Land from the infidel. But moved by greed and politics, the crusaders ignored a papal ban of excommunication and detoured instead to Constantinople. Their initial aim was relatively limited: to restore the young pretender Alexius IV to the throne, a service for which they would be paid the handsome reward of 200,000 marks of silver. Within six months of his coronation in Hagia Sophia, however, Alexius was deposed and murdered, and the crusaders had been paid only half the promised sum. The crusaders seized the moment. After a savage three-day sack of the city in April 1204, Count Baldouin IX of Flanders was elected the first Latin emperor of Constantinople and a Venetian patriarch was installed at Hagia Sophia.[35]

The illusion of 1177 had become a reality: Venice was now a well grounded imperial power, with dominion over three-eighths of the former Byzantine Empire. By the time the Greeks retook the capital in 1261, an already established Venetian colonial trading empire was further entrenched in the East.[36] Their share of the booty of 1204 estimated at 500,000 marks of silver alone,[37] the Venetians loaded their

15 *Incipit* to Geoffrey of Villehardouin, *Conquête de Constantinople, c.*1320. Oxford, The Bodleian Library, MS Laud Misc. 587, f. 1.

galleys with a fortune in material spoils – marbles, relief sculpture, architectural fragments, mosaic tesserae, reliquaries, and precious objects – with which to enrich the Treasury of San Marco and to embellish the city center. Indeed, the Torcello relief of *Kairos*, the personification of Opportunity, might well be considered the icon of the moment. It was again time to recast the civic image and to rewrite the civic past. A new sense of Venice's place in history and in the world was destined to emerge.[38]

For nearly four decades, our present-day understanding of thirteenth-century Venice has been enriched and, indeed, dominated by two important paradigms: Gina Fasoli's formulation of a "myth of Venice," a compelling image of an ideal republic born and continuing to flourish under divine providence – always free, but secure; wealthy, but pious and just; peace-loving, but also a militant defender of liberty and a faithful daughter of the Roman church;[39] and Otto Demus's compelling thesis of a politically inspired *renovatio imperii christiani* in art and architecture.

Demus's argument centers on the fabrication of a fictive early Christian past for the Basilica of San Marco through the deployment of late antique and early Byzantine elements in its decoration. Some of these elements were re-used spoils true and proper – ill-gotten gains of the Fourth Crusade – but others were newly made imitations. These fictitious historical artifacts, whether extensively reworked originals or clever replicas of fifth- or sixth-century prototypes, ranged from obvious copies to totally convincing fakes.[40]

Given the dependence of the thirteenth-century *renovatio* on imported spolia, the degree of intentionality remains an open question. Was the early Christian look simply a matter of availability of spoils rather than of conscious choice? What objects did the crusaders destroy or leave behind in Constantinople? And what were the criteria for selection and eventual use? Were the imported objects chosen for their utility, for their rarity, for their beauty, for their holiness, for their Christian (as opposed to pagan) iconography, or simply for their antiquity? Or if, as seems likely, all these things mattered, was there a hierarchy of selection? In sum, what was the Venetian sense of this particular past?[41]

Any attempt to answer such questions must begin in Constantinople. There may have been as many as one hundred antique statues of Roman provenance in the city at the time of the Fourth Crusade. To many of the Christian population, even persons of imperial rank, these *simulacra* of bronze and marble were thought to be still inhabited by demons; they were thus to be dealt with cautiously. In times of crisis they could become powerful allies or treacherous opponents, and, as the Byzantine chronicler Niketas Choniates attests, fear could overtake judiciousness.[42] In 1203 as the crusaders' fleet approached the Golden Horn, the citizenry attacked a monumental statue of Athena that had stood for centuries in the Forum of Constantine. Over fourteen meters tall, with her right arm extended, it "appeared to the foolish rabble that she was beckoning on the Western armies." The mob pulled down the statue and smashed it to pieces: "they discarded the patroness of manliness and wisdom even though she was but a symbol of these." And yet, Choniates deplored their actions not because they were motivated by superstition, but because they were based upon a misconception; the goddess, he declared, was looking toward the south and not the west whence the Western armies came.[43]

The Franks and the Venetians would have been no less credulous. After they took the city, "the Latins resolved to overturn the celebrated ancient palladia of the City stationed along the wall and fosse to ward off the enemy . . . especially those which had been set up against their race."[44] With much of the city devastated by wild fires, Choniates painted a succession of scenes of terrible destruction: "Not a single structure was spared by these barbarians who were borne by the Fates and hated the beautiful."[45]

Bronze statues were particularly at risk, not necessarily because they were pagan idols, but because of the preciousness of their material. Among the pieces consigned to the smelting furnace and minted into coins were a bronze Hera, so large

that it took four yokes of oxen to cart away her head; a mechanical device in the shape of a bronze pyramid decorated with laughing Erotes, warbling birds, and bleating sheep and lambs; and a statue of Hercules, "so large that it took a cord the size of a man's belt to go round the thumb, and the shin was the size of a man."[46] Choniates described eighteen bronzes in all that were melted down, but there must have been many more. By 1411 when Manuel Chrysoloras gave his account of Constantinople in the *Comparison of Old and New Rome*, he could remember a number of empty columns that once held statues, but only a handful of surviving sculptures (Plate 16).[47]

Nor were Christian objects exempt. Choniates lamented:

These forerunners of the Antichrist, chief agents and harbingers of his anticipated ungodly deeds, seized as plunder the precious chalices and patens; some they smashed, taking possession of the ornaments embellishing them. . . . [In

16 *Constantinople*, from Cristoforo Buondelmonti, *Liber insularum archipelagi*. London, British Museum, Cod. Cott. Vesp. A XIII, f. 36v.

Hagia Sophia] the table of sacrifice, fashioned from every kind of precious material and fused by fire into one whole – blended together into a perfection of one multicolored thing of beauty, truly extraordinary and admired by all nations – was broken into pieces and divided among the despoilers as was the lot of all the sacred church treasures, countless in number and unsurpassed in beauty.[48]

One sees here the foundation of the Treasury of San Marco.

It is hard to know if Franks and Venetians were equally responsible for the depredations. But Choniates repeated a popular notion that the Venetians – as descendents of the Trojans – destroyed a bronze statue of Helen, "who had enslaved every onlooker with her beauty," in revenge for the burning of Troy: "It was said that these Aeneadae condemned you to the flames as retribution for Troy's having been laid waste by the firebrand because of your scandalous amours." Choniates himself, however, saw greed, not high-minded morality or ancestral piety as the motivation: "But the gold-madness of these men does not allow me to conceive and utter such a thing, for that madness was the reason why rare and excellent works of art everywhere were given over to total destruction."[49]

That the four horses of San Marco, once in the Hippodrome of Constantinople (and possibly the bronze Lion of St. Mark on the column of the Piazzetta), are the only large bronzes to be transported to Venice is thus not surprising. That they survived at all testifies to their powerful effect on the Venetians, where wonder – and perhaps awareness of their symbolic potential in a Venetian setting – overrode greed.[50] But aside from exceptional works such as the horses or the four porphyry Tetrarchs, what else was taken as booty? Apart from relief sculpture and church treasures, the bulk of the spolia was simply building material: marble columns and capitals, glass mosaic tesserae, bits of decorative friezes. If spolia were to be assessed according to their potential as bearers of meaning, political and otherwise, these items might fall into a neutral category – capable of open readings and multiple interpretations. Indeed, many years of profitable trading experience had given the Venetians an eye for quality; they knew that beautiful material in itself had meaning. They thus lost no time in stripping the west façade of Hagia Sophia, the Church of the Wisdom of God, of its exquisite grey and white Proconessian marble revetment. Made up of thin slabs sliced from a single block, its veined patterns formed a series of watery mirror images.[51] At least the church was left standing. Other buildings did not fare so well, for the Venetians found in St. Polyeuctus a convenient alternative source for equally fine marble. The church had been built in the sixth century by the sister of Justinian, the Princess Anicia Juliana (462–528). Probably intended to emulate the Temple of Solomon, it was once the largest and most sumptuous church in Constantinople next to Hagia Sophia, but was already abandoned by the end of the twelfth century. The Venetians

contributed to its demolition, carrying away columns, piers, capitals, and the so-called *pilastri acritani* or Pillars of Acri.[52]

If Choniates is a reliable witness, Byzantines thought of themselves as Romans and to them Constantinople was still the new Rome.[53] There is no evidence to indicate that Venetians thought any differently or that they had a strong sense of the separateness of pagan artifacts from those of the succeeding Christian period. As will be suggested further on, their own claims to historical identity were yet more ambitious. It may well be true that Roman (pagan) stones from the mainland went into foundations, while Byzantine stones were chosen for decorative ensembles,[54] but the reasons for this may be more arbitrary than programmatic. Since Byzantine sculptors specialized in low-relief carving and made few sculptures in high-relief or in the round, most of the architectural elements available for removal such as transennae and structural elements, and useful for recycling in Venice, would have come from Byzantine buildings.[55] And at least to the crusaders, monumental freestanding bronzes may well have been less useful as statues, however antique, than as coins. Thus, the early Christian, rather than antique Roman, look of the Venetian *renovatio* may well have been in large part a matter of availability.

There is precious little talk about aesthetic values in dugento texts, but a sense of priorities emerges with careful attention to later commentators, such as the fifteenth-century chronicler who praised the unnamed galley captains who had transported the monumental columns of the Piazzetta to Venice during the earlier period. To his mind they were typical of all good Venetians: "who when they went on any voyage and saw some beautiful thing or beautiful edifice, or if they could obtain some relic or holy body, they willingly brought it back to their homeland."[56] In such a view, utility, beauty, and holiness, and not antiquity in and of itself, were the primary criteria for such appropriations.

Most of the booty that can still be discerned as such ended up in, on, and around the Basilica of San Marco. Broadened horizons and heightened aspirations gave new impetus to the urban development of the historic center, of which the piazza was the nucleus. According to Juergen Schulz, the scheme began to take on definitive shape under Doge Pietro Ziani (1205–29), who saw through to completion the campaign begun by his father fifty years earlier; and now it was animated by a pronounced taste for things Constantinopolitan. Notices in several sixteenth-century chronicles, certainly apocryphal but possibly based upon some truth, report that this Ziani even proposed moving the city of Venice to Constantinople.[57] Samuele Romanin, the great Venetian historian of the nineteenth century, cautiously discounts the story: "the better [historians] do not make note of it . . . Nonetheless it could be that the idea would have risen in the minds of some, and that it had also been discussed in the Council, but was justly rejected."[58] But if Venice was not to be translated to Byzantium, perhaps the reverse could happen. For Schulz makes a compelling argument for the conscious emulation of the monumental imperial *fora* of antiquity, twelve of which still survived in Constantinople, in the fully elaborated scheme at San Marco. With its arcades, colonnades, rows of shops, palaces, hospices, monumental columns, and connecting street to Rialto, it was completed under Doge Ranieri Zeno in the 1260s with the paving of the great open-air ceremonial space of the piazza (Plate 17). The project was, in Schulz's view, a tangible expression of Venice's own rise to empire, appropriate to a rising republic whose doge was – for a time – "Lord of a Quarter and Half a Quarter of the Byzantine Empire." Pietro Ziani, the first doge to assume that title, could thus be lauded on his tomb as the equal of Roman emperors:

> Rich, honest, patient and in all things straightforward,
> None could be his equal amongst the high-born and wise,
> Not even Caesar and Vespasian were they still alive.[59]

It is probably during this period that the city without walls was given a symbolic gateway, when two monumental columns of red and grey oriental granite were erected at the end of the Piazzetta facing the lagoon (Plates 18–19).[60] Embellished with Veneto-Byzantine capitals and provided with sculpted bases celebrating "those men whom we are unable to name" – tradesmen, artisans, fishermen, butchers, winesellers – the columns would have served as suitable monuments to the communal ideals of participation and association implicit in the *Origo*.[61] By 1293 a bronze lion "of shining gold" was in place atop one of the columns. The lion, of oriental origin and probably part of the booty of 1204, had been fitted up with wings and a book in Venice. Erected on the column, it was further transformed, becoming a highly visible and powerful symbol of the republic itself.[62] According to tradition, the statue of St. Theodore was placed on the second column in 1329.[63] The figure was a pastiche, assembled from fragments: a Greek head, a Roman imperial cuirass, and halo,

17 Jacopo dei Barbari, *View of Venice*, detail of the area around San Marco, 1500. Woodcut. Venice, Museo Civico Correr.

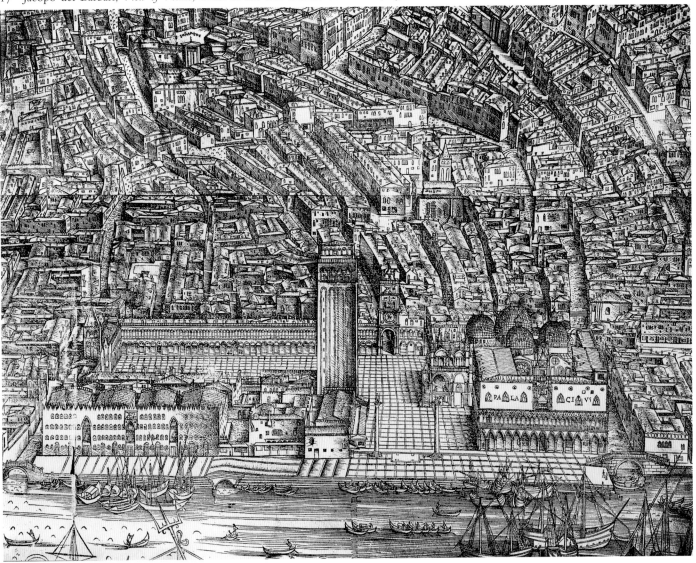

19   *Lion of St. Mark*. Bronze. Venice, Piazzetta.

18   *St. Theodore*. Bronze. Venice, Piazzetta.

limbs, weapons, and crocodile fashioned by a Venetian craftsman.[64] One of the early patrons of the city, the saint had been eclipsed by the arrival of St. Mark's relics.[65] With his Byzantine associations no longer of much consequence, he was now restored to partnership with St. Mark as a powerful guardian of the city. While Venice's two-column entrance is almost unique in Italy (the only parallel is found in Brindisi, where the columns do not support statues), there had once been numerous columns topped with figures in Constantinople.[66] These must have inspired the Venetian ensemble, but, typically, the Venetians reinterpreted the materials and came up with something unique. Providing itself with a monumental gateway to mark its confines and a "monumentum conspicuum" that could be seen from afar, Venice was now protected from dangers both internal and external.[67] But significantly, both St. Theodore and the militant lion turned their backs on potential invaders from the sea and watched serenely over the city.[68]

The piazza as forum was, moreover, a political analogue to San Marco's claim to an apostolic foundation by virtue of its emulation of the Apostoleion.[69] With the basilica itself already an architectural conceit of an early Christian church, Constantinopolitan booty thus simply reanimated a latent impulse that had never been exhausted. In fact, it may be more correct to consider *renovatio* in Venice not so much a revival as a resumption of an ongoing process, albeit one that features an episodic, rather than continuous, engagement with the past. It was also a process that extended beyond the piazza to include private palaces whose arcaded façades flanked by tower blocks betray a debt to Roman villa types, probably by way of the eastern Mediterranean.[70]

San Marco underwent two major structural changes in this period: the extension of a simple narthex across the west front to make a wrap-around atrium, and the transformation of the cupolas from hemispheres to high-profile domes. To this larger and more visible armature, would be applied the stolen wealth of Byzantium. With the interior furnished with new mosaics, marble screens, and revetments, the three visible façades on the exterior were transformed from mural walls of niches and smooth surfaces to plastic ones through an "indiscriminate use of columns."[71] It is estimated that half of the church's six-hundred columns are re-used spolia, of which only fifteen were taken from nearby sites on the Italian mainland.[72] Their integration into the ensemble is so convincing, however, that it is hard to perceive of them as anything other than integral parts of a structure conceived from the beginning as a coherent whole.

There is, however, a small group of objects that were not integrated into the fabric of the church. Trophies true and proper, these exceptional pieces were placed in prominent locations that called attention to their privileged status. The

20   Venice, view of south façade of San Marco in the late nineteenth century.

gilded bronze quadriga installed high above the main entrance is the most obvious example. As spoils of war, the four horses undeniably made a forceful political statement,[73] but they may also have carried an additional spiritual resonance. Michael Jacoff's recent proposal for their identification with the triumph of Christ is compelling. Essentially, he argues that their unusual emplacement on the church was inspired by a conflation of two literary references, one ancient and the other medieval: the four-horse chariot of the Roman triumph and the *Quadriga domini* used as a metaphor for the Four Evangelists by a popular twelfth-century theologian, Honorius of Autun.[74] While the case is not absolutely conclusive, it reinforces Demus's notion of a Christian *renovatio* and would go a long way toward explaining the ingenious solution represented by the Venetian program.

Other objects testifying to Venetian conquest were arranged around the south façade of the church, the first view of San Marco presented to state visitors as they arrived by sea and entered between the great columns on the *molo* (Plates 20–21). Additional mementos from the Fourth Crusade that

fall into the category of "conspicuous trophies" included Byzantine marble reliefs embedded in the outside wall of the church treasury and the two exquisitely carved marble piers, called the Pillars of Acri but actually coming from the church of St. Polyeuktos in Constantinople.[75] Flanking them were two porphyry trophies: two pairs of swordsmen, part of the spoils taken from Constantinople and generally identified as the first Tetrarchy, that were attached to the corner of the Treasury; and the freestanding *pietra del bando*, a truncated column originally used for the reading of Genoese colonial decrees and brought back from the war with Genoa in 1258.[76] Another porphyry trophy – the portrait bust of a Byzantine emperor, probably Justinian (534–8) but popularly called "Carmagnola" – was secured to the railing of the second-story loggia of the southwest corner.[77] Unabashedly booty, these pieces were all the more visible, and symbolically resonant, for being left intact and assembled at the conjunction between state church and palace of state.[78]

★   ★   ★

21   Venice, San Marco, south façade, treasury wall.

A SIMULATED PAST

Such trophies were one of kind, but there is yet another category of spolia that played a central role in the Venetian *renovatio*. Carrying with them aesthetic and formal authority, these objects came to serve as normative models for the counterfeiting of antiquity. Included in this group are the six icons sculpted in low relief that were set into the spandrels of the west façade of the basilica. They functioned as pairs, working from the center out: two military saints, Demetrius (eleventh century) and George (thirteenth century), who flanked the main portal; the Angel Gabriel (twelfth century) and the orant Virgin (thirteenth century); and two figures of Hercules engaged in his heroic struggles, one with the Erymanthean boar (?fifth century) and the other with the Cerynean hind and the Lernean hydra (thirteenth century) (Plates 22–4). Three of the reliefs – the earlier one of each pair – were Byzantine spoils. As the dating indicates, each had a thirteenth-century partner that would have been carved to order in Venice.[79]

In yet another another example of the Venetian ability to seize the opportunity when unexpected treasures came to hand, it is probable that the acquisition of Demetrius would have led to the carving of George, a saint more particularly associated with Venice. This makes a logical pairing, in Demus's view, of guardian saints for the main entrance to the church. But the other two pairs are open to a more historically resonant reading. The linkage of Gabriel and the Virgin may allude to a twelfth-century tradition that Venice had been founded precisely on the feast day of the Annunciation.[80] As will be shown in the next chapter, a firmer historical underpinning would be invented in the fourteenth century for this auspicious conjunction.

The appearance of the pagan hero Hercules in an ecclesiastical context is not as odd as it might seem. While antique reliefs with pagan subjects had long been re-used on the façades of churches in the Byzantine sphere, the Venetians may also have been inspired by twelve reliefs of the Labors of Hercules located at the Golden Gate in Constantinople, where they had served (ineffectively as it turned out) as

22 Venice, San Marco, detail of west façade.

rial antiquity. By creating a palimpsest of chronologically separate, but formally responsive images, the paired icons gave temporal density to the building. The stylistic updating by means of the thirteenth-century replicas – most pronounced in the Hercules reliefs – established continuity between past and present.[85]

In a sense, re-evocations such as these brought the past *into* the present, but there is another level of copying – the deliberate faking of an antiquity – in which the present virtually *becomes* the past. The full range of possibilities was explored in the monumental ducal tombs of the thirteenth century. The double sepulchre of Doges Jacopo (d. 1249) and Lorenzo (d. 1275) Tiepolo, now attached to the façade of SS. Giovanni e Paolo, is the earliest to survive (Plate 25). While the sarcophagus was a medieval type, the lid was an early Christian original, probably made in Ravenna in the fifth

23 Late antique artist, *Hercules with the Erymanthean Boar*, ?fifth century. Venice, San Marco, west façade.

defenders of the city.[81] In a typical Christian reinterpretation of the antique gods, Hercules also appeared as an allegory of salvation on a number of church façades in northern Italy in this period.[82] But his double appearance on the façade of San Marco had a specifically local relevance. A protective deity with deep roots in the Veneto area, he had been the patron of the city of Heraclea – according to tradition, the seat of the first dogate in the lagoon. Demus is surely correct in his interpretation of the Venetian icons as apotropaic images, "holy protectors of the doge and the state."[83]

The talismanic power of certain images was not confined to ecclesiastical settings. Between the eleventh and fourteenth centuries, the façades of Venetian palaces were customarily decorated with *patere* and *formelle* – plaques carved in low relief with Christian, oriental, and classical imagery, as well as with purely ornamental designs. Here, too, images of Hercules and other figures, were, in all likelihood, protective barriers against evil entering the house.[84]

The icons of San Marco, however, had a further resonance, for they also implied Venice's distinguished past in immemo-

century. Some of the reliefs may have been carved in the thirteenth century, but others including the inscription, while archaic in style, were almost certainly added in a later period. And yet the total effect, aside from the coats of arms in the acroteria, is convincingly early Christian.[86]

The tomb of Doge Marino Morosini (d. 1253) in the atrium of San Marco is more problematic, with scholarly opinion divided as to the dating of the two-tiered relief on the front panel (Plate 26). Whether it was a genuine antique made in the fifth century, as some would have it, or an artful thirteenth-century counterfeit as others insist, the relief served as an authoritative prototype for a second relief of the *Traditio legis* in the treasury of the church.[87]

By contrast, the tomb of Doge Ranieri Zeno (d. 1268) in SS. Giovanni e Paolo, of which only the frontal survives, was a monument that featured paleo-Christian iconography but

24 Venetian artist, *Hercules with the Cerynean Hind and the Lernean Hydra*, thirteenth century. Venice, San Marco, west façade.

was of stylistically certain thirteenth-century production (Plate 27). Depicting an enthroned Christ in triumph, his nimbus held by two floating victory-angels, it was one of a group of similar images made in that period that included not only relief sculpture but also spurious antique-looking cameos.

25 Tomb of Doges Jacopo (1229–49) and Lorenzo (1268–75) Tiepolo. Venice, SS. Giovanni e Paolo, exterior façade.

26 Tomb of Doge Marino Morosini (1249–53). Venice, San Marco, atrium.

Defining Venice as a center for the production of cameos, one scholar spoke of "the special aptitude of the Venetians to copy antique models since the Middle Ages, without interpreting them (but not without error at times) . . ."[88] All such imitations represent what Richard Brilliant once characterized in another context as an eclectic and conceptual spoliation. Not spolia in actuality, the newly made objects were still spolia in concept.[89]

Caution is necessary in interpreting these appropriations, for there are important nuances and distinctions. As others have observed, re-used and replicated artifacts have a particularly ambivalent status, being simultaneously past and present with

27 Frontal of tomb of Doge Ranieri Zeno (1253–68). Venice, SS. Giovanni e Paolo, nave.

a commingling (and sometimes confusion) of ancient and modern roles. By their very nature they are incomplete – parts of a once larger whole. But like holy relics, those surviving parts can stand as surrogates for that lost whole. Signifying both a presence (in themselves) and an absence (of their original whole), the spolia of San Marco, both real and conceptual, testified not simply to Venice's early Christian past, but also to her triumphant present.[90]

How, then, should the other "foreign" elements – French Gothic, German, Saracen – that are worked into the Venetian equation, not just at San Marco, but also in secular and ecclesiastical architecture throughout the city, be interpreted? While the many Islamic motifs – arches, patterns, stone grillwork – may simply have been expressions of the aesthetic taste of a trading nation, they might also have been perceived as confirmation of the Christian rather than the Islamic East.[91] Demus thus suggests that the Saracen elements could well have been part of an "authenticating current."[92] Indeed, without excluding references to Byzantium, Staale Sinding-Larsen looks at the same area around San Marco and sees in it an image of Jerusalem. Allowing that many churches in the Middle Ages were compared to the Holy Sepulchre, he cites a claim in the twelfth-century Origo as evidence of Venetian attitudes toward the basilica. Here the chronicler affirms that San Marco had been built "according to the example that he had seen at the temple of our Lord in Jerusalem."[93] With other observers claiming that it was modeled after the Apostoleion, Sinding-Larsen sees the ambiguity as deliberate: "The method of adapting suggestions that avoid declarations that are too explicit appears characteristic for Venice in its ideological attitude: this an attitude of total diplomacy."[94] Before addressing the issue, it is necessary first to turn back to the textual tradition.

A NOBLE PAST

The retrospective current in art and architecture had a counterpart in the chronicles, as historiographical aspirations were heightened to match Venice's new role as an imperial power. The fabrication of a dignified past found its most eloquent literary expression in the third quarter of the century in Martino da Canal's Estoires de Venise. The chronicler, writing between 1267 and 1275, made his intentions plain in the prologue to his work. He had translated the ancient histories from Latin to French, he wrote, "so that all would know the deeds of the Venetians, and who they were, and whence they had come, and who they are, and how they built the noble city that is called Venice, that is today the most beautiful in the world."[95]

Canal's preference for the French language, that "had spread throughout the world, and is more pleasing to read and hear than any other," indicates that romanitas or latinitas were not at the top of his cultural agenda. Indeed, his was the first history to be written in Italy in the volgare, a significant break with tradition even if the language was that of the French court rather than the Venetian marketplace.[96] In all likelihood, Canal wanted to dignify his text, while ensuring its accessibility to a literate upper class. By enriching the historical record, he could sanctify an ennobled civic past and justify an entrepreneurial present. Toward this end he introduced a number of new points concerning Venice's early history. Incorporating the Trojan and Attila traditions recounted in the Origo into the Estoires, he refined and embellished the scenarios with an elevated laudatory agenda. The lore of humble origins was glossed over with the claim that the "noble men and women" who escaped the destruction of Aquileia, had "brought with them gold and silver in great quantities, and so they had beautiful churches and beautiful campaniles and bells constructed, and they built in the major city seventy churches . . . and dispersed through the salt waters, convents in great quantity."[97]

Two politically significant episodes in the legend of St. Mark – the praedestinatio and the apparitio – made concurrent debuts in Canal's Estoires and in the decoration of San Marco. The praedestinatio was the title given a prophetic dream that Mark was said to have experienced during his earlier, supposed ministry in the area of the Venetian lagoon. In it he was visited by an angel who told him that he would find his final resting place on the very site where San Marco would later be built.[98] In support of this claim, a sculpture of the slumbering St. Mark and the Angel was carved and given pride of place in the tympanum of the main entrance to the basilica.[99] The apparitio (or inventio) involved the miraculous recovery of the saint's relics in 1094 after their secret hiding place had been forgotten during a reconstruction of the church. After three days of fasting, prayer, and processions by the patriarch, the bishop, and the entire population of the city, a large stone fell out of a column in the south transept and, as Canal put it, "the Venetians saw the precious remains of the Evangelist" (Plate 28).[100]

Confirming to the Venetians that their city had enjoyed a divinely sanctioned destiny from the time of Christ, the two

28 Paolo da Venezia, *Inventio of the Relics of St. Mark*, detail of the Pala Feriale, 1345. Venice, Museo di San Marco.

prodigious events were important enough to prompt a new campaign of narrative mosaics in the church to augment the cycle of St. Mark's life already in the presbytery. These images were then used as direct visual testimony of the events they depicted.[101]

The thirteenth century was a time of heightened consciousness of civic origins in communes throughout Italy. Nicola and Giovanni Pisano, for example, completed the Fontana Maggiore for the citizens of Perugia in 1278. In a complex sculptural program that has been called an encyclopedia in stone, they gave visual form to Perugia's mythic beginnings, her distinguished past as a Roman city, and her pious Christian present. Among the high-relief sculptures of saints and personifications were the podestà and the *capitano del popolo*, as well as a certain Eulistes, the mythical *pre*-Roman founder of the city.[102] Other cities were equally inventive. Genoa claimed a foundation by Janus, Ravenna by Tubal, Bologna by Felsino with an enlargement by a certain Buono (hence Bononia), Brescia by Hercules, and Turin by Phaeton.[103] The people of nearby Padua were even provided with archaeological evidence for their own founding father in these years. When a huge skeleton was unearthed in 1283 during building excavations, it was immediately identified as that of the mythic

Trojan hero Antenor and honored with a Gothic cenotaph in the center of town.[104] Milan, on the other hand, while claiming a foundation 932 years before Rome, also looked to its glorious present. Bonvesin de la Riva, writing *De magnalibus Mediolani* around 1288 stated that Milan is without equal: "not only worthy to be called a second Rome, but, if it be permitted me to speak my mind without being accused of presumption, it would be right and proper in my judgment that the seat of the papacy and the other dignities should all be transferred here from there."[105]

Canal's *Estoires* may seem modest by comparison, but it was a major contribution to the consolidation of a Venetian civic identity. A generation later the first certain signs of a mature historical sense within the ruling class becomes apparent. In 1291 the Great Council ordered: "that a book should be made in which there may be written all the official proceedings of the Commune of Venice, and especially the Ducate, and every pact, and every privilege that they might make for the governing of the Commune of Venice."[106]

In 1292 another chronicler known only as "Marco" began writing his own history of the city. He edged back civic history further than Canal and claimed that the first Trojan colonists had arrived in the Venetian *lagoon* (and not just Aquileia) immediately after the fall of Troy, while Rome would be founded only 454 years later. "And on account of this," he wrote, "it is well known that the first construction of Rialto preceded the construction of the city of Rome." He also addressed the issue of Venice's priority over Padua, now a troublesome competitor. Perhaps inspired by that city's recent fortuitous discovery, he claimed that Antenor had arrived in Venice after the initial building of the city by an advance guard of his countrymen. Only later, Marco advised, did Antenor found Padua.[107] Then turning to the present, the chronicler produced a prophecy, *ex post facto*, intended to justify Venice's much criticized collaboration in, and profit from, the Fourth Crusade. It concerned no less than the Emperor Constantine, who was said to have predicted at the time of the foundation of Constantinople back in the fourth century that the capital of Byzantium would suffer apocalyptic calamities and destruction "negli ultimi giorni dolorosi." In Marco's view, the crusaders were thus only carrying out the inscrutable will of God, as agents of a divinely sanctioned plan.[108]

A ROMAN PAST

The century ended with yet another allusion to antique origins for San Marco. These were the years immediately after the Serrata, or closure of the Great Council in 1297, a time of heightened civic self-consciousness. The case is instructive, for like the chronicles of Marco and Martino da Canal, it suggests a desire to drive down the civic roots more deeply, beyond the early Byzantine stratum, in this case right into Roman soil.

29 Bronze doors, sixth century. Venice, San Marco, west façade, central portal.

30 Master Bertuccio, bronze doors, *c.*1300. Venice, San Marco, west façade, second portal from the right.

31 Detail of bronze doors, sixth century. Venice, San Marco, west façade, central portal.

32 Master Bertuccio, detail of bronze doors, c.1300. Venice, San Marco, west façade, second portal from the right.

33 . Master Bertuccio, detail of bronze doors with inscription, c.1300. Venice, San Marco, west façade, second portal from the left.

It involved the completion of a set of costly bronze doors for the exterior portals of the west façade. Two pairs had been installed already in the first half of the thirteenth century in the main entrances to the church, one set in the central portal and the other inside the atrium, closing it off from the south entrance in the ante-vestibule (now the Cappella Zen). These were legitimate antiques, datable to the sixth century. Probably booty from the Fourth Crusade, they feature the early Byzantine *opus clatratum* – a latticework pattern – and were apparently adapted for re-use on the basilica by Venetian masters (Plates 29 and 31). In the new sets of bronze doors that were then made at the end of the thirteenth century to fill the lateral portals of the façade (Plate 30), the sculptor followed the general form of *opus clatratum*, but he made it more robust, solid, and regular. Clearly working under the influence of earlier classical models, he reinterpreted the Byzantine motif *all'antica* – in the Roman manner.[109] He also used a new scheme of compartmentation, creating a cross-shaped pattern, that also derives from pagan prototypes. It could now be given a Christian, whilst Roman, interpretation as a Gate of Paradise.[110]

The new doors featured two other important innovations. First, in keeping with the growing self-awareness of artists of this period, the sculptor was no longer anonymous, with the door to the left of the central portal bearing the inscription: "MCCC – MAGISTER BERTVCIVS AVRIFEX VENETVS ME FECIT" (Plate 32). Second, on the corresponding door to the right of the main entrance, each crossbar now featured three large, very Roman looking, female heads flanked by small figures of pagan divinities each holding a cornucopia (Plate 33). These were – in Demus's words – "copies as close to forgeries as possible," cast from molds made from classical originals.[111]

Originality was clearly not at issue, and the borrowing was not accidental. But why, then, would Bertuccio have signed his name so proudly to a counterfeit? Because that may be precisely the point. Bertuccio's pride in his craftsmanship would have been matched by Venetian pride in a costly new set of bronze doors. Deception was not the aim, for the newness of the doors was just as important as their antique look. With this deliberately ambiguous double-play – antique replicas that bore a modern signature – the Venetian sense of the past moves into a new phase, with Bertuccio's doors taking the thirteenth-century *renovatio* one step further. While they allude to an authentic pre-Byzantine Roman past within the Venetian present, they proclaim that present, as well, as something new and unique in itself and perhaps superior to Rome.

★ ★ ★

The Torcello relief of Opportunity has been cited here as an emblem of one aspect of the Venetian approach to time. While the ethos was writ large on the occasion of the Fourth Crusade, as well as in its artistic aftermath in Venice, it was

28

engrained in life as it was lived each day in that mercantile society. In 1309 the Collegio would write a letter to the galley captain Gabriele Dandolo:

> Since our Church of San Marco has need of marbles in fine condition, and since we have heard reports that on the island of Mykonos and also other Roman islands [of the eastern Mediterranean], that there . . . are to be found the most beautiful marbles of every color and type, we ask . . . that when you are in those parts . . . you make inquiries everywhere about those marbles which are whole shafts or pieces thereof, and about medium-sized columns – white, veined, green, porphyry, and every [other] type. And if they are beautiful, you should procure them and load them into our galleys as ballast, [but taking care] not to overload the galleys themselves on this account, nor to put off the affairs of our commune entrusted to you to the detriment of business; and we will provide that those who have labored on this account will be compensated through the Procurators of San Marco, as would be fitting and just.[112]

This was the practical side of the myth of Venice. The pragmatic values and assumptions expressed in the letter were the mundane underpinnings of the thirteenth-century *renovatio*: a product of contingency and calculation. The center was not just supported by, but was constructed from, the material of the periphery. By the fifteenth century, this *modus operandi* of inverse cultural imperialism entered the chronicles as a guarantor of excellence. The *Cronaca Bemba* cites the ninth-century doge who led the Venetians in battle against the Saracens:

> Giustinian [Partecipazio] returned from this victorious enterprise and brought with him many spoils of victory, beautiful columns and other very fine stones of marble . . . and into the construction of [San Marco] he put all the stones and all the marble columns that he had already brought from Sicily.[113]

Referring to the reconstruction of the church under Doge Domenico Selvo (1068), Zorzi Dolfin writes "that he labored to adorn it with the most magnificent columns that could be found and they sent out to search [for them] throughout the world . . ."[114] An anonymous chronicler is more specific: "And many gentlemen and commoners sent out to obtain marbles in Aquileia and Ravenna, and many sent to Constantinople, and others served much with money; thus the church was built very honorably."[115]

Such rhetoric had a distinguished pedigree, which dated back to ancient Rome. In the Byzantine sphere, Eusebius had written in the fourth century that the church of the Holy Sepulchre in Jerusalem was constructed with columns that had been sought out and "conveyed from every quarter; for it is fitting that the most wondrous place in the world should be adorned according to its worth."[116] Two centuries later Procopius would remark on the construction of Hagia Sophia: "The Emperor, disregarding all expense, hastened to begin construction and raised craftsmen from the whole world."[117]

In essence, the special quality of the *renovatio* of the thirteenth century was a *venezianità* grounded in what may be called an "aesthetic of diversity." It rested upon two major principles: accumulation, or aggregation, and incorporation (but not absorption).[118] Tangible works that can be seen and touched – buildings, spolia, icons, mosaics, sculpture, artifacts – were more powerful than texts in creating a civic identity of a reassuring historical density, for they were unmediated testimony: unprovable, thus unchallengeable.

In the fourteenth century came the transition from a communal to a patrician state. With a new and deliberate interpenetration between text and artifact, the civic past would again be edited to conform to current needs.

34 *Antenor founds a City*, from Guido delle Colonne, *Historia Troiana*. Parchment, 27 × 19 cm. Madrid, Biblioteca Nacional, Cod. 17805, f. 28.

2

A DOCUMENTED PAST

A people devoted to God, renowned progeny of the Trojans
  placed their noble walls upon the Illyrian brine
Troy itself was not splendid with such great beauty
  when all Greece sought the ravished bride.
Divine protection, restoring the ruin of Troy
  transported the Trojan gods over the long seas
Aeneas, guided to Latium from the Sicilian waters
  was at last the origin of the race of Romulus.
But Antenor arriving safe on the shores of the Adriatic
  Prudently occupied the pleasant lands of the Illyrian gulf.
Driving out the Euganeans, he settled the Trojans and Venetans,
  and gave the name of the Veneto to both peoples
And when many foundations of the Venetian people were established
  he tried to bring the rights of the sea under his control.
Little by little the city was built up in the middle of the waves
  that would be the head and substance of a new kingdom.
From that time forth she has possessed a name common to many
  and, ruling so many peoples with her scepter, has increased in fame
And now she has grown so much, renowned through the whole world
  that Rome herself is inferior in power to the city of Venice.
                    – Pace da Ferrara, *c.*1300[1]

Just as Magister Bertuccio was incising his autograph on the romanizing bronze doors of San Marco, Pace da Ferrara, a teacher of grammar and Latin in Padua, was completing the first Latin elegy written in praise of Venice. Dedicating the poem to Doge Pietro Gradenigo, he offered the fullest literary treatment to date of the city's Trojan origins. It was no small production, eventually coming to 184 verses in all. Incorporating a large section devoted to the popular Feast of the Maries, the piece was entitled *Descriptio festi gloriosissime Virginis Marie.*[2] Significantly, Pace's poem, like Bertuccio's bronze doors, did not announce a permanent shift toward *romanitas* in Venetian art and literature in the early years of the trecento. For the new hereditary patriciate created by the Serrata of 1297 had its own agenda, with historical interests still narrowly focused on Venice itself.[3]

The city, once a collection of islands, was now a metropolis: one of the largest in Europe with a population of nearly 120,000. The dugento had been a time of feverish building activity facilitated by land reclamation throughout the entire city, as well as in the area around the Piazza San Marco.[4] The coherence of the urban fabric – the *civitas rivoltina* – had been tangibly reinforced in 1264 by the first permanent wood bridge over the Grand Canal at Rialto.[5] The heavily impacted area around it, crowded with government offices as well as commercial and financial enterprises, was refurbished with a new market in the 1280s and would continue to receive government attention throughout the next century.[6] The banning of horses from the Merceria in 1292 (a prohibition that would be extended to the entire city center over the next hundred years) was emblematic of the new phase of self-definition: an assertion that Venice was not just an extension of the terraferma but a city separate and unique unto itself.[7]

★ ★ ★

The movement toward a more insular and cohesive urban structure affected the ways in which historically inclined Venetians regarded – and continued to shape – their civic past throughout this period. While they were not oblivious to the humanistic currents animating the intellectual life of such nearby cities as Padua and Verona, they remained marginalized from them. For the city's separateness had a psychological as well as a geographical dimension. Turning for a moment to the Padua of Pace da Ferrara, a member of a circle of nascent humanists who had fallen under the spell of classical literature, it is possible to get a sense of the differences. That he was the proud owner of a Greek manuscript of Plutarch, which, however, he could not read, is symptomatic of a movement marked by high aspirations and uneven literary skills.[8] Even the learned Lovato Lovati, a jurist and the leading member of the group, was prone to overreach himself when it came to the tantalizing problem of civic origins. It was he who had identified the skeleton unearthed in Padua in 1283 as that of his city's founding father, Antenor.[9] He also oversaw the construction of the Gothic cenotaph in the center of town (Plate 35). The monument and the unclassical Latin inscription that Lovato composed for it typify, as Roberto Weiss puts it, "both the enthusiasm and the weakness of Paduan humanism in its earliest stage."[10]

The growing appetite for a more detailed knowledge of the pagan world may have been driven initially by motives of civic pride, but it soon broadened out and was expressed in a number of ways: in the reclaiming of classical texts, in the copying of inscriptions, in the writing of poetry in the classical manner, in the collecting of antique coins. The ancient ceremony of laureation was revived in 1316, when Albertino Mussato, a member of Lovato's circle, was crowned with a laurel wreath for his compositions of Latin poetry. Civic identification with the classical past reached a high point during those years with the discovery of an ancient tomb inscription with the name "T. LIVIVS HALYS." Although it referred to a freed Roman slave with the cognomen of Halys, in the grand tradition of ambitious but erroneous attributions established by Lovato it was accepted as a genuine relic of the Roman historian Livy – one of Padua's most illustrious early citizens – and embedded in the wall of the church of Santa Giustina.[11]

Before returning to Venice, a brief detour to Verona where early humanism had a different flavor may be in order. Here, even more than in Padua, Rome was still a living material presence. With the Arena, the amphitheater and a number of other ancient structures still surviving and in use, the city boasted more Roman remains than any other city in northern Italy. These physical deposits were augmented by the presence of the huge chapter library whose holdings of classical texts were among the best in Europe; it was here that the poems of Catullus reappeared around 1300.

35   Padua, Tomb of Antenor.

One of the leading beneficiaries of this dual heritage of antique marbles and pagan letters was the historian and antiquarian Giovanni Mansionario. He established the existence of two Plinys rather than one, as was generally believed, and set out to write a *Historia Imperialis* with the biographies of the Roman emperors. The manuscript is notable for its use of illustrations, for Giovanni attempted to reconstruct the sites of historical events, known to him only from written descriptions, with his own crude drawings of antique buildings. But his most significant contribution was the inclusion of profile portraits of the emperors copied by him directly from Roman coins (Plate 36). His is the first demonstrable case of such coins being of interest for their historical information and for their age, and not simply for their rarity or for the value of the metal.[12]

Venice also had its men of letters in the early decades of the fourteenth century, but none with humanist credentials equal to those of their colleagues on the mainland. A certain Venetian indifference to the lure of humanistic studies in this early period can be explained only in part by the lack of a university or of a major monastic library or by the absence of abundant Roman remains. Perhaps the most important causes were not cultural, but political and social. For in Venice, expertise in Latin was a practical thing, the prerogative of commoners – primarily the notaries in the Chancery – and not of the aristocracy. Despite the proximity of Padua and Verona and, later on at mid-century, Petrarch's extended presence and friendship with doges and ducal secretaries, the ruling élite of Venice remained, on the whole, resistant to the attractions of Roman history and Latin letters over its own beloved vernacular tongue. For the deeds of the Romans that were so seductive to their mainland contemporaries were not the deeds of the Venetians. And Venice remained on the periphery of humanistic studies until the last decades of the century. And yet the case should not be overstated. Although an awareness of pagan antiquity played no significant role in Venetian historiography and state art in these years, there are sure signs of a changing historical sensibility, particularly in the private sphere.

36 Giovanni Mansionario, *Historia Imperialis*, early fourteenth century. Parchment, 30 × 23.5 cm. Rome, Biblioteca Apostolica Vaticana, Cod. Chigi I. VII. 259, f. 13.

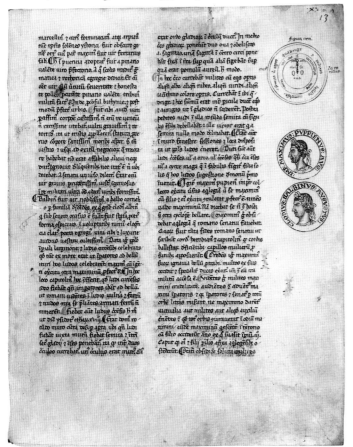

The desire to further document the republic's murky past and to define her singular present may have worked against the perusal of serious classical scholarship in Venice during this period. Venetian attitudes toward the historical record display two significant tendencies, neither limited exclusively to Venice, but strikingly persistent there. The first was a positivist bias toward the eyewitness account or, lacking that, for the document, both written and visual, as an essential element of proof. Such a tendency was already evident in the affirmations of Martino da Canal, who repeatedly challenged his readers to verify his reports through outside witnesses or even through the mosaic images that he regarded as documents of historical events.[13] While not necessarily antithetical to humanist pursuits, such a habit of mind tended to favor local history that could be corroborated by personal testimony or documents, whether genuine or contrived, over the ancient authors. Thus the citizen chronicle in Venice maintained a narrowly insular focus, with modest local events taking on epic importance in the micro-history of the city. The second tendency grew out of the first, and was played out with particular finesse by Venetians: the desire for a mutually confirming interpenetration of text and image culminating in the creation of new historical artifacts.

"*OCCULATA FIDE*": THE NOTARIAL APPROACH

Martino da Canal was an outstanding oddity. It is fair to say that he had no followers and, indeed, no equals in the writing of civic history during the first half of the trecento. But his eyewitness approach was expressed in other ways. A good example is the notarial activity of the Venetian ducal secretary Giovanni Marchisini in 1316. The occasion was the birth of three cubs, "alive and furry," to a pair of lions that had been given to Doge Giovanni Soranzo by Frederick of Aragon, the King of Sicily. The beasts had been placed in a cage under the portico of the Palace of Justice facing the Piazzetta and their mating "was witnessed by a great many people *occulata fide*" – "by the faith of their own eyes." When the pregnant *leonissa* came to term, the Doge ordered Marchisini to be present at the birth and to record the event, "for the eternal memory of persons now living as well as future," in a notarized document in the *Pacta*, one of the most important registers of the Ducal Chancery. The notary reported that as soon as the cubs, one male and two female, were born, "they began to move right away, and to walk through the chamber all around their mother." He further attested that "this was seen by the Lord Doge and almost all the inhabitants of Venice and elsewhere who were in the city that day who flocked together there to see it as though it were a miracle."[14]

But the matter did not end there. Marchisini, a poet and a master of grammar, grasped the moment to illuminate the symbolic resonance of the singular parturition with some verses of his own composition. Dedicating them to the doge, he proposed that the births occurred in Venice because its patron St. Mark had a lion as his emblem. He further suggested that the number of cubs was three, since "a three-fold lineage of races is subject to you, for Venetian, Slav, and even Greek are under your sway."[15] Hoping for an ornate, and preferably oracular, literary response, the doge ordered Marchisini to send copies of the verse to his friend Albertino Mussato, recently *laureato* in Padua.[16] Mussato responded with a poem of his own in the form of a dialogue between himself and the Muse Urania. Allowing that such an event was unusual, but not impossible, the Muse acknowledged that it was, in any case, a good augur for the city.[17]

The doge had hoped for a less tepid and more consequential reaction and ordered the grand chancellor, a certain sier Tanto dei Tanti, to compose a longer poem that would again be sent to Mussato, this time with the explicit request that he address the mystical significance of the event in respect to the destiny of the city. Tanto even supplied the position of the stars in the expectation that Mussato would interpret the horoscope. But the new response was probably no more satisfying than the first. Indeed, Urania forestalled future discussion with her firm reply that the stars are too noble to wish to comment on the prodigies of animals, and that she could foresee great conquests for Venice from the observation of natural phenomena other than the stars (and, one might presume, through interpreting the birth of lions).[18] With the epistolary strategy presumably exhausted, these poems then became part of the historical record, for Soranzo's successor, Doge Francesco Dandolo, had them all transcribed into the official register of *promissioni ducali*.[19] Notices of this sort might be considered documents before the fact. If incorrect they could be conveniently ignored; if borne out in reality, they could be pointed to as proof positive of Venice's providential nature and fore-ordained destiny.

It was also a time to recast cherished episodes of the past into proper historical form. In 1317 the Great Council commissioned Bonincontro dei Bovi, a felicitously named notary in the Ducal Chancery, to write up a new comprehensive account of the Peace of Venice of 1177, that signal occasion when Doge Sebastiano Ziani had played host to the Emperor Frederick Barbarossa and Pope Alexander III for the signing of a peace treaty. Transcribing his account into the *Pacta*, the writer attested: "I, Bonincontro . . . notary and official of the lord doge and the commune of Venice, constructed this honorable history with a clear and distinct epigram for the praise of God and St. Mark and for the perpetual memory of the Venetians."[20] Two years later, the Great Council appropriated funds to paint the Cappella di San Nicolo, located in the Palazzo Ducale compound, "with the history when the Pope was in Venice with the Lord Emperor." These pictorial documents, backed up by the new authoritative text, gave Venetians a firm "documentary" base on which to assert their sovereignty and their devotion to the Roman Church.[21] The dynamic relationship between the paintings and Bonincontro's text may be characterized as parallel, referential, and mutually confirming. While one genre may be complementary to the other, each could generally stand as an independent document of the same series of events.

RINNOVATA PREZIOSA: THE DOCUMENTED ARTIFACTS OF DOGE ANDREA DANDOLO

Yet another permutation of the relationship between image or object and text at the service of historical definition comes to the fore during the dogate of Doge Andrea Dandolo (1343–54), a period that marks the culminating phase of Venice's invention of its own civic past (Plate 37). The greatest Venetian doge of the century, and perhaps of all time, Dandolo had studied law at the University of Padua and remained close to humanist circles until the end of his life. He presided over a Venice that was beginning to free itself from the insular, linguistically limited perspective of a half-century before. Like his grand chancellor, the learned Benintendi de' Ravignani, as well as other members of his chancery, Dandolo had frequent contact with Petrarch through correspondence and direct encounters.[22] Few would have disagreed with Petrarch's own assessment of the doge: "a man distinguished no less for the study of the liberal arts than by the insignia of so high an office."[23]

Dandolo personally pursued an astonishing range of initiatives: the codification of laws and statutes; the compilation of state documents in the *Liber albus* and the *Liber blancus*; and the production of two histories of the city, the *Chronica brevis* and the *Chronica extensa*. All these activities were inspired by a particular vision of the historical mission of the Venetian Republic – its divine origins, its legal basis, the continuity of its institutions – and the doge's crucial role in realizing it.[24]

Dandolo had a special concern for documents, both as privileged testimony of particular laws and as pieces of history in themselves. In the *Chronica extensa*, executed in the Ducal Chancery in the early years of his dogate, he pioneered the insertion of documents into the text of the Venetian chronicle. Transcribed from archives or from older chronicles, a statute or a concession could endow the text with a new precision and a sense of legalistic authority. He drew upon a wide variety of sources and incorporated the most credible items from earlier writers, such as John the Deacon, into his own. But modern scholarship has shown that Dandolo's historical writing is not as reliable as it appears at first view. For like other historians of his time, Dandolo was prone to a selective use of sources with a blurring of the line between fact and forgery.[25] Such habits should be kept in mind when considering his artistic initiatives, for they were directed toward the same ends as his other work: that is, to ground the republic in a legitimate historical past. For Dandolo's was still a Venetian-centered view of history. During his time there was, as yet, little discernible reflection in public art or in

37 *Promissione ducale of Andrea Dandolo*, 1343. Parchment, 34.5 × 25 cm. Venice, Museo Civico Correr, Cod. III, 327.

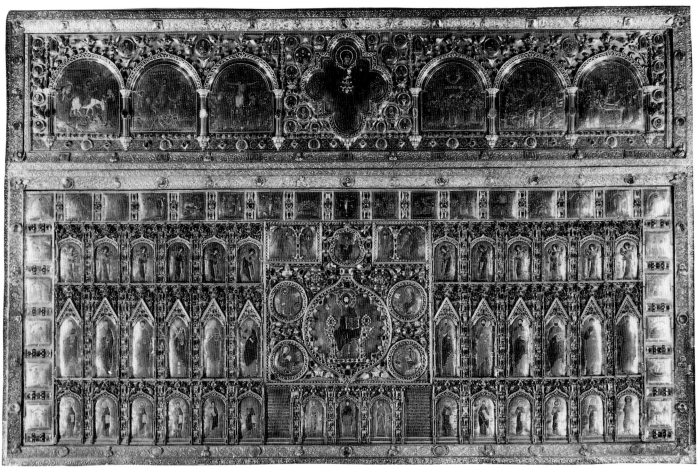

38 Pala d'Oro. Venice, San Marco.

historical writing of Petrarch's call for a reawakening of the Roman past.

Dandolo's first major program of state patronage, and one that may be seen as emblematic, was the complete refurbishment of the high altar of San Marco. The Pala d'Oro, probably the single most precious object in the basilica, was the centerpiece of the campaign.[26] In May 1343, just a few months after Dandolo took office, the procurators asked for an appropriation of the considerable sum of 400 ducats to reset all the enamels and jewels in a new, intricately worked Gothic gold frame.[27] The Pala essentially received its present form at this time: two panels joined by hinges, encrusted with 1,927 pearls and precious stones and inlaid with 255 Byzantine enamels of figures and narrative scenes (Plate 38). Tactilely rich, with tiny compartments of brilliant color unified in a shimmering golden field, it depends on the inconstancy of ever-changing light for its transcendent kaleidoscopic effect. As such, it stands as the supreme example of the Venetian aesthetic at its most costly.

The Pala had already undergone at least one transformation, and several hypotheses as to its earlier aspect have been presented by scholars,[28] but – and this is a key point – the only *textual* evidence regarding its earlier history was provided by Dandolo himself. This took two forms. First, he added two

Latin inscriptions to the remade Pala. And second, he referred to it in several citations in the *Chronica extensa*. Indeed, it is one of the few works of art that is mentioned therein.

According to John the Deacon, writing in the eleventh century, the Pala d'Oro had been preceded by a silver *tabula* ordered as an antependium by Doge Pietro Orseolo (976–8).[29] Dandolo repeated this notice in his *Chronica extensa*, but added another piece of information regarding the Pala d'Oro proper. His notation of a first version made under Doge Ordelafo Falier in 1105 is the earliest written evidence of its existence:

> The doge placed the panel, wondrously made of gold, gems, and pearls in Constantinople, above the altar, for the more abundant glorification of the most holy Mark the Evangelist; which having been augmented by other treasures, remains to this day.[30]

This early Pala, which may actually have been another antependium or altar frontal, probably consisted of a *tabula* the size of the present lower panel.[31] The *Chronica* also records its remaking under Doge Pietro Ziani in 1209: "Angelo Falier, sole Procurator of the ducal chapel, repaired the panel of the altar of St. Mark, having added gems and pearls at the order of the doge . . ."[32] The upper panel was probably added at this time, utilizing Constantinopolitan loot. That the Pala d'Oro

39 Detail of Pala d'Oro. Venice, San Marco.

itself was living proof of Dandolo's claims was not enough, for he also supplied it with an inscription recording the two earlier campaigns of 1105 and 1209:

> In the year one thousand one hundred and five, when Ordelaffo Falier was doge in the city, this pala was newly made most rich with jewels, that was renewed when you, Pietro Ziani, were doge and when Angelo Falier was procurator of the *atti* in the year one thousand two hundred and nine.[33]

This testimony was augmented with a second inscription recording the renewal of 1345:

> In the forty-fifth year of one thousand three hundred, when Andrea Dandolo of great honor among all men was doge, and under the noble procurators of the noble and venerated church of the truly blessed Mark – Marco Loredan and Francesco Querini – this ancient panel was renewed most preciously with gems.[34]

The inscriptions are telling (Plate 39). Supported by the *Chronica*, they provided the artifact with a convincingly documented past and made it the bearer of tradition and historical continuity. Moreover, the inscribed plaques flank three figures who occupy jewel-framed niches directly below the enthroned Christ. The Virgin Orant stands in the center with the Byzantine empress Irene to her left, holding a scepter and identified with an inscription in Greek. To the Virgin's right, in the position of honor, is Doge Ordelafo Falier, now with a Latin inscription and complete with the imperial nimbus and the court costume of a Byzantine *basileus*. It is clear that the doge replaced an earlier image: logically, Irene's consort, the Byzantine emperor Alexius I Comnenus. The change was a drastic one, and, according to Renato Polacco, was yet

another example of Dandolo's historical revisionism. Such a fabrication would only have been possible in Dandolo's time, he argues, when the authority of the Byzantine imperium was diminished.[35] That Irene was allowed to remain on the Pala was a calculated decision, her presence confirming Venice's legacy from Constantinople. As to Dandolo, by putting himself in a sequence of doges, sanctified by both texts and images, he glorified the dogate and implied the continuing permanence of Venice itself.[36]

The renewal of the Pala d'Oro inspired the commission of a painted two-tiered *pala feriale* to cover it on weekdays. It was completed in April 1345 by Paolo da Venezia and his sons, just three days before the feast day of St. Mark (Plate 40).[37] While the holy civic protectors depicted in the upper tier still retain a Byzantine stylistic quality, the narrative scenes of the life of St. Mark below are notable for a Gothic naturalism and vivacity appropriate to their vernacular literary roots in the *Golden Legend* of Jacopo da Voragine. There could be no better testimony of Master Paolo's pivotal role in transforming Venetian painting from an art based upon a Byzantine aesthetic to one that draws its primary vigor from the western tradition. The Pala d'Oro with its precious Byzantine enamels, reset in the Gothic frame with pointed aedicules and curvilinear decorative motifs, demonstrates an analogous – but, as yet, perhaps deliberately unsynthesized – accommodation.

Dandolo's refurbishment of the high altar also included the commissioning of illuminated manuscripts – a sacramentary, an evangeliary, and an epistolary – as service books for the liturgy. Each one a different size, they were specially designed to be bound into three precious Byzantine covers. Encrusted with enamels and jewels like the Pala d'Oro, the covers had been in the treasury since the thirteenth century and may originally have been icons rather than bookbindings. The analogy with the Pala goes even further, for again the old and

40   Paolo da Venezia, Pala Feriale, 1345. Venice, Museo di San Marco.

the new are brought together to make an object that partakes both of venerable antiquity and of sumptuous modernity.[38]

The new unified ensemble at the high altar also included sculpture and other furnishings. When the upper section of the Pala d'Oro was folded down, the Pala Feriale covered it completely. But on feast days the Pala Feriale was pulled up over the back of the Pala d'Oro, which was then opened up by means of an ingenious mechanism of winches, pulleys, and chains attached to two columns of *verde antico* that stood behind it. Atop the columns and visible at all times were marble statues of the Angel Gabriel and the Virgin Annunciate (Plate 41).[39] The choice of sculpture might well have been

41   View of the high altar of San Marco with the Pala d'Oro open and statues of the Angel Annunciate and the Virgin visible atop the columns behind it. Engraving by Padre Vincenzo of Santa Maria delle Scuole Pie, from a drawing by Antonio Visentini. Venice, Museo Civico Correr.

inspired by Andrea Dandolo's sense of Venice's historical mission. As noted earlier, an obscure literary tradition, dating back at least to the twelfth century, claimed the foundation of the city of Venice on the anniversary of the Annunciation. It was only during Dandolo's time, however, that evidence was produced in support of this auspicious birthdate. Recording Venice's foundation at Rialto on March 25, 421, by a group of three Paduan consuls, a document was cited in the chronicle of Jacopo Dondi, a Paduan physician who had moved to Venice in the 1330s and had taken up citizenship.[40] Although the document in question seems to have been lost immediately, Dandolo did not hesitate to incorporate Dondi's welcome discovery into the *Chronica extensa*.[41]

Admittedly, the Annunciation was one of the most popular images in Italian medieval and Renaissance churches, particularly in the framing of chancel arches, and it is not certain that the sculptures behind the Pala d'Oro were intended as a direct allusion to Venice's foundation. But the pervasive presence of the Angel Gabriel and the Virgin Annunciate in public places of the city, both sacred and secular, suggests a deliberate echoing and reinforcement of the popular myth of origins. After Dandolo's death in 1354, for example, their sculpted images were set into shell niches on his tomb, and subsequently became an almost indispensable element of Venetian funerary monuments right through the quattrocento. They were also prominently featured in the decoration of the Great Council Hall of the ducal palace in 1365–8, when the Paduan artist Guariento da Arpo painted the entire east wall with a huge vision of Paradise and flanked it with the Angel Gabriel and the Virgin Annunciate (Plate 42).[42] But their presence in and around the Basilica of San Marco was particularly notable: they were not only part of the dugento program of paired Byzantine (and Byzantinizing) icons on the main façade of the church, but also included in the decoration campaign of the

The translation took place in the terrible plague year of 1348, when the relics were deposited in a tomb in the chapel newly built in the north transept. As with the Pala d'Oro, the artifact provided its own footnotes. For Dandolo's citation in the *Chronica extensa* was confirmed by an inscription located above the tomb of the saint. Thus ratified by the authority of the texts, the story of the saint's life, martyrdom, and translation unfolds in mosaic images and inscriptions on the two side walls and vaults of the chapel (Plate 44).[47] In their vivacious narrative style, in their attention to exotic costumes and types, and in their "popular" tone, the mosaics themselves were intended to convince. They no longer speak Greek, but they do not speak Latin either. Indeed, the program marks the introduction of the *volgare* into Venetian monumental art.[48] It is a figurative language that would have a long life in Venice, culminating at the end of the fifteenth century in the large narrative paintings of the *scuole*, and also presumably the ducal palace, that were likewise intended to convince the viewer of the reality of the event.[49]

Dandolo also took care to tidy up the historical record by

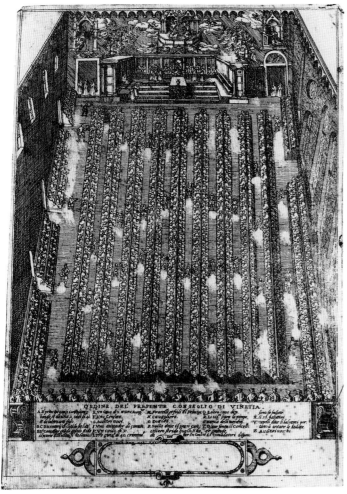

42 *The Great Council Hall before the Fire of 1577*, engraving. Venice, Museo Civico Correr.

43 Jacopo dei Barbari, *View of Venice*, detail of the south façade entrance to San Marco, 1500. Woodcut. Venice, Museo Civico Correr.

late trecento when the roofline would be embellished with a Gothic frosting of pinnacles, aedicules and statues. As in the Great Council Hall, Gabriel and the kneeling Virgin – here full-round sculptures in tabernacles – parenthetically defined the program like acroteria at the upper corners of the façade.[43] Finally, as Jacopo de' Barbari's woodcut view of the city reveals, by the end of the quattrocento a second set of sculptures of the Annunciate pair was also placed above the south entrance portal to the church (Plate 43).

Dandolo's other commissions in San Marco were also shaped by his commitment to defining and documenting the civic past. One of his major projects – the mosaic decoration of the Cappella Sant'Isidoro – was still in progress at the time of his death.[44] According to the *Chronica extensa*, the relics of the saint had been brought back to Venice by Doge Domenico Michiel from Chios in 1124, but their location was forgotten over time.[45] It was Dandolo himself who "rediscovered the body of the most blessed martyr Isidore that had long been hidden in the Church of San Marco, and with great devotion he placed it in the chapel which he then had constructed."[46]

documenting in the *Extensa* the histories of several of the treasures already in the church. The altar mensa of oriental granite in the baptistery, for example, was said to have been found in Tyre by Domenico Michiel in 1124. Identified as a piece of the "stone on which Christ sat outside the city," it was brought back to Venice "cum devotione," along with the relics of St. Isidore.[50] Four relics sent back from Constantinople by Doge Enrico Dandolo in 1204 were also listed: "the miraculous cross framed in gold, which . . . Constantine carried in battle, and the crystal ampoule with the Miraculous Blood of Jesus Christ, and the arm of the martyr St. George, with part of the head of John the Baptist."[51]

The acquisition of the "throne of St. Mark" now in the baptistery, but probably located behind the high altar in Dandolo's time, was credited to the Byzantine emperor Heraclius in the seventh century: "He also brought back with him the cathedra from Alexandria, in which the blessed Mark the Evangelist held the priesthood in that city, that, by a later patriarch, was brought to Venice."[52] The throne bears a roughly incised inscription in Hebrew that seems to have been added in Venice: "the seat of Mark the Evangelist [. . .] they have dedicated it."[53] It is unknown when this textual augmentation would have been carried out, but like the so-called chair of St. Peter in San Pietro di Castello whose backrest is an Arabic gravestone bearing an inscription with quotations from the Qur'an, the "oriental" epigraphy was probably intended to offer proof that the chairs were genuine.[54] It also offers mute testimony of the pious rescue of Christianity from the heathens.[55] An inscription added to the thirteenth-century tomb of Doges Jacopo and Lorenzo Tiepolo was inspired by a similar spirit and has also been dated to Dandolo's time (Plate 25). Debra Pincus observes: "The kind of ducal vision that Dandolo made tangible would appear to have put in motion a deliberate reworking of the past – something the Venetians were *never* reluctant to do."[56]

Although Dandolo had begun the *Cronaca extensa* with St. Mark's early preaching mission in the lagoon area, he was also concerned with the origins of the city of Venice itself. Along with its foundation by Paduan consuls on the day of the Annunciation, there were, in Dandolo's view, two other culminating moments: the legendary Trojan settlement of the first Venice and the lagoon migrations under the threat from Attila. Lacking documentation to support the Trojan myth, he stressed that the story "is contained in old histories." It was even confirmed by writers outside Venice. Most important was Guido delle Colonne, who wrote a *Historia Troiana* in the thirteenth century. In a long list of countries colonized by Trojan refugees, Guido obligingly noted, "That well-known Trojan Antenor inhabited the city of the Venetians."[57] Dandolo went even further, however, and claimed that Antenor and his men had built the very walls of Olivolo, in the present *sestiere* of Castello.[58] The doge may also have given the legend pictorial realization by commissioning an illuminated manuscript, now in Madrid, of Guido delle

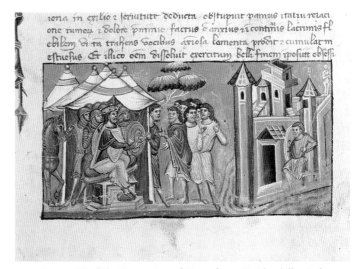

45 *Priam told of the Destruction of Troy*, from Guido delle Colonne, *Historia Troiana*. Parchment. Madrid, Biblioteca Nacional, Cod. 17805, f. 28.

Colonne's *Historia Troiana*. The derivation of its miniatures from the Vienna Genesis, a sixth-century manuscript, has been persuasively demonstrated by Hugo Buchthal (Plates 45–6).[59] The conscious appropriation of its archaizing style and iconography can be considered analogous to the use of the Cotton Genesis as the model for the atrium mosaics of San Marco. In both cases the newly created artifacts served to "document," albeit artificially, an artistic continuity with Christian antiquity. But in the case of the Trojan legend, it was pagan history that was to be served by Christian models.[60]

Some visitors to the city obviously got the message of Trojan beginnings, perhaps more strongly than Dandolo might have intended. The German pilgrim Ludolf von Südheim wrote an account of his journey to the Holy Land in 1336–41. Leaving Constantinople, he sailed to the place:

46 *Isaac and Rebecca with the Philistine King Abimelech*, from the Vienna Genesis. Vienna, Nationalbibliothek, Cod. Theol. Graec. 31, p. 16.

where that most noble city of Troy was once situated, of which no remains are to be seen, except some foundations underwater in the sea and in several places some stones and some marble columns are half-buried, which as soon as they are discovered are exported to other places. About this it should be known, that in the city of Venice there is no stone column or any good piece of cut stone that was not brought there from Troy.[61]

He was just as certain about the foundation of Genoa, on the other hand, which was "totally constructed from the stones of Athens, just as Venice was built from the stones of Troy."[62]

OUTSIDE HUMAN TIME

There was, of course, a certain danger in grounding the republic strictly in terms of temporal and historical accountability. For another strong current observable in Dandolo's writings presented Venice as eternal and outside human time. The issue was also addressed in the mosaic decoration of the

baptistery as Dandolo's burial chamber. Most likely begun in the 1330s when Dandolo was a procurator of San Marco, it was probably completed during his term as doge and at his own expense.[63] Along with images of saints and the celestial hierarchy, these mosaics featured scenes from the lives of Christ and John the Baptist. Most notable from a civic standpoint, however, is the large Crucifixion in the lunette above the altar. In a stylistic disjunction reminiscent of the Pala Feriale, the five holy figures (St. Mark, the Virgin, the Crucified Christ, John the Evangelist and John the Baptist) have Byzantine features, while the three figures kneeling below in a smaller scale and in profile are rendered naturalistically, in accordance with the new western-looking vision (Plate 47).[64] Clearly identifiable from his ducal habit, the doge, presumably Dandolo himself, is given pride of place at the foot of the cross.[65] The identity of the two figures who anchor each end of the composition is not certain, but a grand chancellor, probably Benintendi de' Ravignani (1352–65), is surely on the left,[66] and another magistrate – possibly a ducal councillor or a procurator of San Marco – is on the right.[67] Following this interpretation, the group represents the three major compo-

47   *Crucifixion*, fourteenth century. Mosaic. Venice, San Marco, baptistery.

48 *Julius Caesar, Octavian Augustus, and Titus Vespasianus*, fourteenth century. Venice, Palazzo Ducale, south façade, capital of ground-floor arcade.

nents of the Venetian polity: the doge, the people and the nobility – that is, "a portrait of the state in its workings in present time."[68] But with the mosaic of Christ and the heavenly hosts in the dome above, the temporality of the state is subsumed into the timelessness of the celestial continuum.

For most Venetians, the "antixi" (the ancients) were their own ancestors and not the ancients of the pagan world. And for Andrea Dandolo, for all his humanist qualifications, any antiquarian tendencies that come through in his patronage of art were born of two motivations: the better definition of the civic past and the desire to conserve the relics of that past. In 1353 he wrote:

> And if gratitude for favors should hold any place of praise among mortals, [then] we ought to esteem, as marks of honor, keeping uninjured those things that antiquity has preserved for us in solicitude over a span of years, no less than [we consider as marks of honor] the building of things anew. Thus our authority is exalted, something useful is provided for posterity, and gratitude for the gift received is commemorated . . .[69]

Venetian public art would continue to elaborate on historical themes that were by now well established. The rich exterior decoration of the newly constructed ducal palace, with thirty-six figured capitals in the ground-level arcade just above eye level and three large groups of sculpture on the corners of the walls above, executed over a broad period (*c.*1341–1420), was also universalizing in theme. The program as a whole has not yet been fully explained, but it falls into the broad category of encyclopedic *summae* of the period, like the reliefs on the Florence campanile (begun 1334).[70] It might also be seen as a pictorial analogue of Fra Paolino's *Chronologia magna*, for it offers a similarly comprehensive, and synoptic, view of humankind.[71] The capitals are carved with a motley assortment of subjects, embracing every aspect of human life and

condition from the elevated to the mundane: rulers and sages, knights and ladies, artisans, the ages and nations of man, virtues and vices, allegories of marriage, work and childhood, and fruit, birds, animals, lions and other beasts (Plate 48). In the zone above, a sculpted roundel of Venetia–Justice faces the Piazzetta, and the program is anchored at the ends by full-sized figural groups of the Judgment of Solomon and the Drunkenness of Noah. But, as Salvatore Settis observes, the southwest corner of the building – "the prow of human life" – is the conceptual heart of the program. Standing in front of the portico at ground level one first sees the massive corner column surmounted by a capital carved with the seven planets and the Creation of Man. In the niche directly above it is the figural group of Adam and Eve and the Serpent, signifying the Fall of Man. Further up is a similar arrangement on the second story, now with a more slender column whose capital is carved with the four winds of the earth and the Archangel Michael in the niche above as a symbol of divine justice (Plate 49).[72] Like the baptistery Crucifixion, the sculptural program as a whole set the republic within the larger, meta-historical chronology of God's time.

49 *Archangel Michael* and *Adam and Eve*. Venice, Palazzo Ducale, southwest corner.

Moving inside the ducal palace to the Great Council Hall, God's time again intersected with man's time. At one end of the room, Guariento's fresco of the *Coronation of the Virgin* with all the saints of Paradise covered the entire east wall (Plate 42). When the room was filled with the Venetian patriciate each Sunday afternoon, a community was created where profane business could be conducted under sacred auspices.[73] But the temporal Venetian past was ever present. Painted during the dogate of Marco Cornaro (1365–8) in the lunettes above the heads of the noble members of the Council, and overseeing their deliberations, were portraits of the doges, each with his coat of arms and holding a scroll with an inscription lauding the most important events of his term. The sequence began, curiously, with a certain Doge Beato painted immediately above the doge's throne. He might seem an odd choice. According to John the Deacon, writing in the eleventh century, Beato had risen to the dogate without a vote of the people when his brother, Obelerio, the reigning doge, had arbitrarily made him his consort in a co-dogate at Malamocco (c.804). Then Obelerio turned traitor and fled to France where he promoted a French invasion of Venice. Beato was left to lead the defense of the city in the Battle of Canale Orfano. According to Andrea Dandolo in the *Chronica extensa*, the ducal seat was moved to Rialto immediately after Beato's death, and Agnello Partecipazio (later Badoer) became the first Rialtine doge.

Since Chancery functionaries were well aware of Beato's indeterminate status from Dandolo's *Chronica*, his place of honor at the beginning of the portrait series suggests that the historical record was adjusted to make a point. The inscription on Beato's *breve* in the painting, recorded by later observers, states: "Fratris ob invidiam Rex Pipinus in Rivoaltum venit, Defendi patriam sibi gratificatus" (King Pepin came to Rialto because of the envy of his brother, Satisfying himself by the defense of his country).[74] Spelling out a familiar theme of patriotic rhetoric, the epigram made clear that the good Venetian's duty toward country overrode his duty toward family. It defined Beato, moreover, as precursor of the legitimate succession of the dogate. In any event, the authority of the painted portrait soon vanquished that of the text.[75] The chronicler Nicolò Trevisan, writing around 1366–9, declared that Beato was really to be considered the first doge at Rialto, because "this a famous and distinguished painting already declares."[76] The tradition took hold and would be repeated a century later by Marin Sanudo.[77]

The full succession of ducal portraits also implied the continuing life of the republic, for the program was deliberately left incomplete. Along with the portraits already painted around the room were twenty-two spaces left empty for the doges yet to come. Below them the walls were painted for the second time in the Palazzo Ducale with a cycle of scenes from that most durable and emblematic triumph of Venetian history: the Peace of Venice of 1177.[78]

A brief glance toward the terraferma reveals the uniqueness of the Venetian scheme of decoration in terms of its exclusive *venezianità*. By contrast, other princely palaces throughout Europe during this period were typically painted with heroes and events from ancient and biblical history, as well as from legends and popular romances. By the early fifteenth century, virtually every major court in Italy had its cycle of *viri illustres* drawn from the full spectrum of history. In the early 1330s Giotto painted nine heroes in a "sala dei uomini famosi" for King Robert of Naples in Castelnuovo. The program included two Hebrews (Solomon and Samson) and seven pagans, with an emphasis on the Greeks and the Trojans (Alexander, Hector, Aeneas, Achilles, Paris, Hercules, and Caesar as the single Roman). A similar campaign was undertaken by Azzo Visconti in Milan around 1340. Featuring two Christians – Charlemagne and himself – it also included Attila among the pagan princes. During the period in which Guariento was working in Venice, the Scaligeri of Verona had the great hall of their palace frescoed with scenes of Flavius Josephus's *Jewish War* (c.1370). On the wall above was a row of medallions containing portraits of important political and literary figures of the fourteenth century, including Petrarch as well as the Signori della Scala.[79]

In nearby Padua, Jacopo II Carrara began the decoration of the Reggia Carrarese in 1347 with a Theban cycle. The campaign continued for another sixty-odd years and eventually included rooms dedicated to Nero, Camillus, Lucrezia, and Hercules. The most historically significant component of the decorative scheme was inspired by Petrarch's main historical work, *De viris illustribus*, which contained the biographies of famous Roman statesmen and generals. Commissioned by Francesco il Vecchio da Carrara, the cycle of frescoes decorating the Sala Virorum Illustrium (1367–75), featured full-length portraits of thirty-six Roman heroes from Romulus to Trajan, along with narrative scenes. It seems to have been the only fourteenth-century program to be painted entirely with Roman heroes and Roman deeds.[80]

The appeal of all of these programs to a prince would have been not only exemplary, but also dynastic: to have present the great men of history in one's own court and even to be numbered among them as well. Venice, however, was (as usual) different. Her heroes were not Romans (and again, Venice shows itself resistant to the appeal of Petrarch), but Venetians; and not Venetians as individuals, but as emblems of the ducal dignity.[81] Subject to a strong aristocracy, the elected doge was simply *primus inter pares* and not a Caesar. Sebastiano Ziani, the hero of the Peace of Venice, was honored for his office and not for his person. Venice had its own glorious past, and did not need to borrow Romans to establish one. Taken together, the dogal portraits confirmed the legitimacy and continuity of the dogate and, by natural extension, of Venice itself.[82]

The last major campaign of the trecento in San Marco involved the commissioning of a new marble iconostasis from the Dalle Massegne brothers. Apart from Andrea Dandolo's

50 Jacobello and Pietro Paolo Dalle Massegne, choir screen, 1394. Venice, San Marco.

projects, it was the most important and costly work carried out in the church since the bronze doors of 1300.[83] The front section features a columned arcade supporting a Crucifixion flanked with statues of Christ the Redeemer, the Madonna, and the twelve Apostles (Plate 50). It has been observed that the form and iconography make a clear and intentional reference to the iconostasis of Old St. Peter's in Rome, built under Gregory III in the eighth century.[84] As with so many of the programs in San Marco, it could be argued that the retrospective approach was more than simple conservatism and that Venice was once again re-establishing for herself a venerable past that was now linked directly to Christian Rome. But there is more to it than that. For the inscription reveals a

different world from the bronze doors of Master Bertuccio of a century before. Carved along the architrave in large golden characters is the following message: "1394. This work was made in the time of the eminent lord Antonio Venier, Doge of the Venetians by the grace of God and [in the time] of the noble lords [and] honorable procurators Pietro Cornaro and Michele Steno." And in smaller characters: "The brothers Jacobello and Pietro Paolo of Venice made this work."[85]

It is the confident statement of a secure ruling class. The newly built monument pays due respect to Christian antiquity by observing the authority of its architectural forms, but like the Pala d'Oro it also documents unequivocally the Venetian present.

itaqz Rex Pam quod Antenor ⁊ eneas
celosie fraudibz coecsseiut. Er iter̄ q̄
puisst̄ ano ⁊ argeteu a piamo rege p
cupiut ⁊ in onera frimtaua ero pncta
eoz̄ dednce̅ ad naues ⁊ onerat i erodez.

Ānust̄ n̄o grea couenientes i una
cuz maio denotionis affectu cu
eoz̄ pcessib; secerdotu cu fi
nib; ⁊ alijs neccis trahut equiz ⁊ sa
ad p̄ortas ciutatis edncuc. Noy ei po
tu fuit cute lantidis spaciosa q̄ pei
eaz̄ posset equiis ipe cōmode itrodu
p̄ quod necciis extuit q̄ ex muro et
portu itaiis demolin debet q̄ fiet ad
introductoez̄ eq̄ ipue altitudis ⁊ latiu
diuis spaciosa. Quo fco equiis ipm̄ i
ciuitate Troiam caues cu multo grandio
itroducuc. Sz n̄o e nocui ut extrema
grand̄y luctus occupet cui troiam caues
⁊ maioees ipoz̄ ex eoaos isidiys fca eoa
no eqiiis liue fetu statueiut equin
Sz niotez poa eoz̄ tuscenbz ipssiset.
Iruuscerut ei gr̄a i pdous eqiu quedai
noie Symeouz au gr̄a claues assigna
ueiut ut oportuno caphito tpie apeiut

clansuaz ostuntio i eq̄ ⁊ q̄ imn papa
troaiucz p eoz̄ hospiti cōmdidedo qe
scere iy ipio sozio oastrebiz signa diuei
i flama ignis accesi ut q̄n huutte co
modo̅ posset itraie ⁊ habile posset moi
tuitude cormentez

Aatez aute die q̄a isidiosos qstio
eoaloie unsunt ad panium sc̄ a tro
iu uelle iteede ⁊ aput Tenedon
se uelle osearie u ellena oailte iexe stu
tueiut trmetez si ipaz̄ i traz̄ recepeut ne
forte tumiltuz i exatu ḡroiis isiudeut
s eaz̄ ⁊ ipaz̄ exude morti trudent nec
eet tue q̄ posset eaz̄ sua deffensione tu
eu placueiut ei puiamo uelut iguaio
fictitia illa q̄roiz ca reputas ee ueia
uide ḡreis ipio ascendebiz naues eoz̄
⁊ uelstcatiis a littoubz troianoz̄ troia
uus ecis uidentez ⁊ exude fca leue eq̄a
aput Tenedon applicat puiy aiu sose
occisuz ibiqz eos i multa icaldirate ce
natie supuentez noctis ubraculo oc
se auniz bellias muniteuc ⁊ ad cuuta
te troie se i maḡ sileteo gtuleiut

Smeou
uo postq̄ pcepit claues uisse

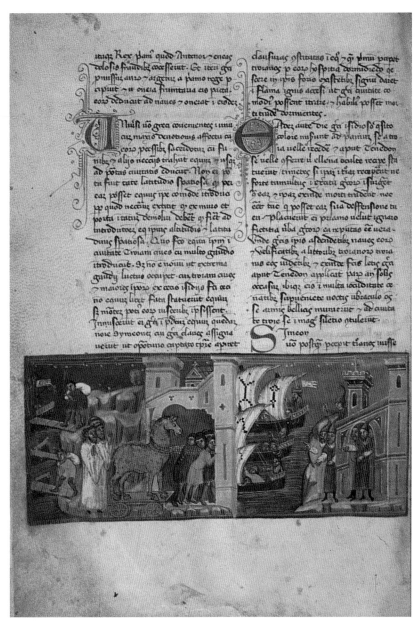

51 Giustino del fu Gherardino da Forlì, *The Trojan Horse brought into Troy*, from
Guido de Columnis, *Historia destructionis Troiae*, c.1370. Parchment, 33 × 22.9 cm.
Geneva–Cologny, Biblioteca Bodmeriana, Cod. 78, f. 73v.

II

THE HISTORICAL PERSPECTIVE: DISTANCING THE PAST

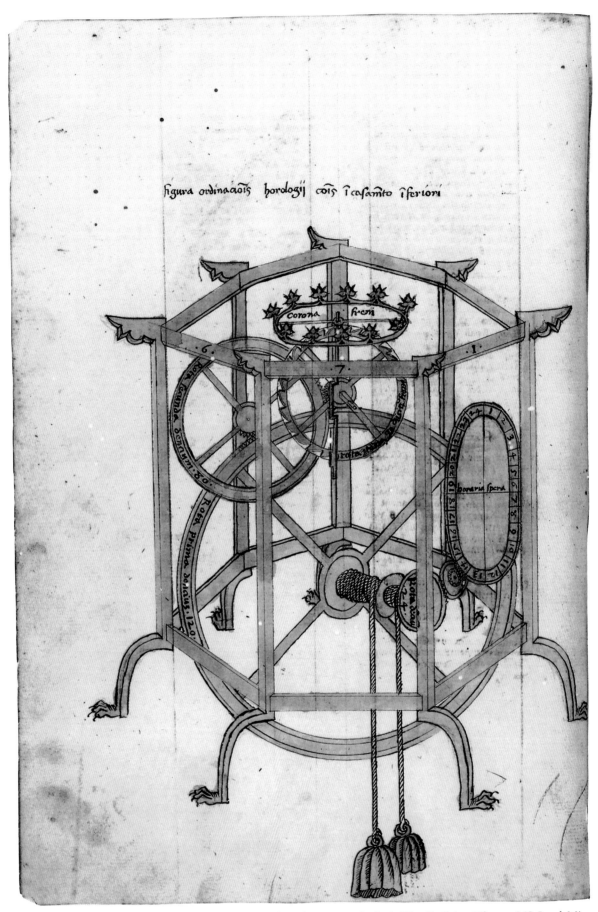

52 *The Astrarium of Giovanni de' Dondi*, drawing, fifteenth century. Oxford, The Bodleian Library, MS Laud Misc. 620, f. 10v.

PROLOGUE

And as in our travels through the remains of a broken city, there too, as we sat,
the remnants of the ruins lay before our eyes. What else may be said? Our
conversation was concerned largely with history which we seem to have divided
among us, I being more expert, it seemed, in the ancient, by which we meant
the time before the Roman rulers celebrated and venerated the name of Christ,
and you in recent times, by which we meant the time from then to the present.
– Petrarch, writing to Fra Giovanni Colonna, 1341[1]

Where there had once been a vast historical continuum stretching without interruption between antiquity and the present day, Petrarch discovered a break: a fracture between "then" and "now". He further explored the fissure and found that it is really a great crevasse, and one that is dimly lit. At the end of his *Africa*, an epic based on the life of Scipio Africanus, he thus addressed the poem itself: "My fate is to live amid varied and confusing storms. But for you perhaps, if as I hope and wish you will live long after me, there will follow a better age. This sleep of forgetfulness will not last for ever. When the darkness has been dispersed, our descendants can come again in the former pure radiance."[2] The new mentality revealed by such attitudes constitutes one of the milestones in the evolution of historical consciousness. As the historian Theodor Mommsen explains: "Antiquity, so long considered as the 'Dark Age,' now became the time of 'light' which had to be 'restored'; the era following Antiquity, on the other hand, was submerged in obscurity."[3] As has so often been observed, the resulting tripartite division of history would eventually become one of the defining paradigms of the Italian Renaissance.

Petrarch lived in the Venetian milieu for much of his adult life, and in the city proper for about six years (1362–8). So it is legitimate to question the extent of his influence there and to ask whether and in what way Venetian attitudes to antiquity were affected by the new ideas. First, however, it will be useful to look briefly at the problem in reverse by asking what factors might have influenced Petrarch to offer a new approach to pagan antiquity that would distinguish him from his humanistically oriented predecessors in Padua, Verona and elsewhere. Although philological studies of classical literature had been flourishing in Padua since the late thirteenth century, with Petrarch a new, more subtle perspective emerges. But it is one that is grounded in paradox: for it involves the melding of a new objectivity *and* a new subjectivity toward both time and space. His concern with time was complex and multifaceted. At once cosmic and personal, time was not simply an abstraction to be captured or to be endured – as with the reliefs at Torcello encountered earlier – but an adversary to be tamed and conquered in his quest for fame.[4]

THE INVENTION OF CIVIC TIME

Time was a concrete presence for Petrarch. His was the first generation to grow up with civic time. Before the invention of the mechanical clock in the last decades of the thirteenth century, time had been the province of the church, and the bells that rang in campaniles throughout Italian cities ordered the day according to the needs of the priest rather than those of the citizen-merchant.[5] Petrarch was only five years old in 1309 when the first public clock in Italy of which there is a record was installed in the campanile of Sant'Eustorgio in Milan.[6] Over the next half-century, devices of varying degrees of sophistication and accuracy were placed in churches, palaces, and public spaces throughout the peninsula. Venice and Padua were in the forefront of horological initiatives. In 1334 Master Mondino di Cremona, a goldsmith working in Venice, sold the King of Cyprus a clock for the considerable sum of 800 ducats. It was, the artisan claimed, of such subtle artifice that its construction had taken the greater part of his life.[7] In 1344 a clock was installed on the entrance tower of the Carrara palace in nearby Padua; it had been designed by none other than Jacopo Dondi, the physician and mathematician who had posited Venice's birth on the day of the Annunciation.[8] In 1360 a Venetian friar constructed a clock to be shipped to the pope in Avignon.[9] But the most famous time-measuring apparatus of the age was a complicated brass astrarium (Plate 52), constructed in Padua in 1364 by Jacopo Dondi's son Giovanni (1330–89).[10] Also a physician, he taught medicine, astronomy, philosophy and logic at the university in Padua and assembled one of the best humanist libraries of his day. He was, furthermore, a close friend of Petrarch, who remembered him warmly in his testament of 1370:

> I have postponed to the last him who deserved to be first, master Giovanni de' Dondi, easily prince of astronomers, who is called dall'Orologio because of the admirable *planetarium* made by him, which the ignorant rabble believe to be an ordinary clock [*orologium*]. To him I bequeath fifty gold ducats for the purchase of a small finger-ring to be worn by him in my memory.[11]

Public clocks were by now not only display pieces for technical virtuosity, but civic necessities. In Venice at the end of the century, government attention was directed to the public clock at Rialto, an area long neglected because of the heavy costs of decades of nearly continuous warfare with Genoa. After a collapse of the belltower of San Giovanni back in 1361, a clock had been installed on the smaller campanile of the nearby church of San Giacomo. With an overly complex mechanism and heavy counterweights, it had functioned badly all along and had occasioned "great and intolerable expense." So in 1394 it was determined to install a new Latin clock with "light counterweights, of beautiful and great mastery, that strikes the hours without difficulty with a sonority triple that of its predecessor."[12] When the campanile of San Giovanni was finally rebuilt in 1408–17, it was fitted with yet another new clock, this one designed by Gasparo Ubaldini of Siena who boasted, "it chimes the hours, and a cock comes out and crows three times an hour."[13]

Whatever the venue and however ingenious, the new iron clocks were devised to ring out objective, secular time: hours of equal length, that could no longer be expanded or contracted according to liturgical needs. Although it would take another three centuries before the calendar of years, months, and days would likewise be organized according to absolute time, the control of the hours was surely an essential feature of Petrarch's psychological formation – an enabling factor that allowed him to think of the historical continuum more objectively in terms of discrete periods with special characteristics of their own.[14]

But what gave Petrarch's engagement with time a potential for going beyond the pages of ancient texts and for directing the attention of his contemporaries to the tangible remains of antiquity was his grounding in the physical world. For many of his writings reveal an acute sensitivity not only to time, but also to place – a factor that was of critical importance in the development of a historical sensibility in Venice and elsewhere. This tendency is perceived most clearly in the precision – exceptional for the period – with which Petrarch endorses his letters to ancient, long dead authors. An epistle to Cicero is signed:

> Written in the land of the living, on the right bank of the river Adige, in Verona, a city of Transpadane Italy, on the sixteenth day before the Kalends of Quintilis [June 16] in the thirteen hundred and forty-fifth year from the birth of that God whom thou never knewest.[15]

In a medieval world with an eye for similitudes, there were few accidental conjunctions, and replicated dates could hold a significance beyond temporal measurement. A letter to Quintilian, for example, concludes:

> Written between the right slope of the Apennines and the right bank of the Arno, within the walls of my own city where I first became acquainted with thee, and on the very day of our becoming acquainted, on the seventh of December, in the thirteen hundred and fiftieth year of Him whom thy master preferred to persecute rather than to profess.[16]

In such instances, a personal relationship is defined in terms of both time and place and a link, as well as a distinction, established between the ancient (pagan) and the modern (Christian) era.

Perhaps Petrarch was particularly sensitive to place because he so rarely felt at home. Born in exile in Arezzo to Florentine parents and raised in Avignon, he remained an outsider throughout his life in a culture where *patria* and family were man's primary allegiances. In his letters he frequently reminds himself that "the homeland for outstanding men is everywhere."[17] The words put a brave face on an implicit sense of isolation, against which antiquity was an antidote and a refuge. As the poet wrote Livy: "thou didst so frequently cause me to forget the present evils and transfer me to better times."[18] He could mentally reconstruct the Roman past whole and entire from its tangible remains and envision it as a physical place because he was so much more at home there. His motives could not be more different from the aims that had inspired the Venetian *renovatio* of the thirteenth century, in which the antique artifacts had meaning only when detached from their original sites and embedded in a continuing Venetian present.

THE CERTAINTY OF MEASURED SPACE

Technological developments may also have played a role in the evolution of Petrarch's sense of place. For alongside clocks, maps were the beneficiaries of the new empiricism and were being produced in the first decades of the fourteenth century with a new scientific rigor and accuracy. With the maritime trade central to Venetian prosperity, it is not surprising that Venice was at the forefront of developments in cartography.[19] This was, after all, the age of Marco Polo, and his *Travels*, written at the end of the thirteenth century, vicariously opened up to Europeans another world well beyond the Mediterranean. Although their own approach to historical writing was still rooted in the Middle Ages, two Venetians, Fra Paolino Veneto (*c.*1270–*c.*1344) and Marin Sanudo il Torsello (*c.*1260–1343), represented an important counter-tendency to the stubbornly insular perspective of Venetian official historiography.[20] As such, they were major contributors to a more accurate and comprehensive view of the physical world. Having spent much of their lives outside the city, each considered geography to be an integral part of history.

Fra Paolino, despite a peripatetic life with travels to central Europe, Rome, Naples, and Avignon, managed to write a number of treatises, including *De Mapa Mundi* and three world chronicles (Plate 54).[21] The literary efforts of Marin Sanudo il Torsello, driven by a special sense of mission, were more focused. Raised in the Venetian colony on the island of Naxos and spending much of his life in the eastern Mediterranean, he called for a new crusade to rid the area of the Muslim presence and to bring it more firmly into Christian–Venetian control under the authority of a newly unified eastern and western church. Toward this end – without success as it turned out – he wrote two treatises on the condition of the states of the Near East under Muslim rule. In 1321 he travelled to Avignon and personally presented two copies of the second work, entitled *Liber secretorum fidelium crucis* to Pope John XXII (Plate 53). Fra Paolino was one of the examiners called in to evaluate it.[22]

The most notable thing about the manuscripts of both authors is a new sense of topography and an extensive use of maps as integral parts of the didactic apparatus. A number of these were the work of Pietro Vesconte, a native of Genoa and the leading cartographer of the time, who was active in Venice in those years. His planisphere was the model for the *mappaemundi* in the manuscripts, and his portolan charts, finely drawn with compass lines and strikingly accurate coastlines, were incorporated into Sanudo's treatise (Plate 55). They also formed the basis for a number of land maps in the works of both writers. This is not yet the modern world, cartographically speaking, for topographical accuracy is erratic and fabulous elements (such as the castle of Gog and Magog) remain. But it is no longer the medieval world either, where moral and religious symbolism took precedence over the testimony of direct visual observation.[23]

The geographical awareness displayed in the manuscripts of Sanudo and Fra Paolino extended into the public life of Venice. On one of his frequent visits to the city, Petrarch would have seen frescoes painted on the back wall of the loggia erected near the foot of the Rialto bridge in the 1320s. The program featured a *mappamundi* surrounded by narrative

53 Marin Sanudo il Torsello, *Liber secretum fidelium crucis*, Venice, before 1321. Parchment, 30.2 × 23.7 cm. Rome, Biblioteca Apostolica Vaticana, Cod. Vat. Lat. 2972, f. 7v.

scenes of the Battle of Canale Orfano and the Rout of Pepin – pictorial documents of one of the "foundation myths" of the republic – thus situating the city both in time and in space.[24] Confirming Venice's central role in the development of geographical science, the frescoes testified as well to the place of the republic in the larger world. That such interests were a natural outgrowth of Venetian mercantile activities was also made plain, for a copy of the *Travels* of Marco Polo was attached to a chain and placed in the loggia for perusal by the public.[25]

A SENSE OF HISTORY

The historian Peter Burke defines three prerequisities for a modern "sense of history" or, to put it another way, for the new historical perspective that is associated with the Renaissance. First, there should be an awareness of anachronism: a sense of the "otherness" of the past. For medieval viewers, ancient ruins (or spolia) were simply part of the inherited landscape and were taken for granted. But for Petrarch, and for the antiquarian movement associated with him, classical

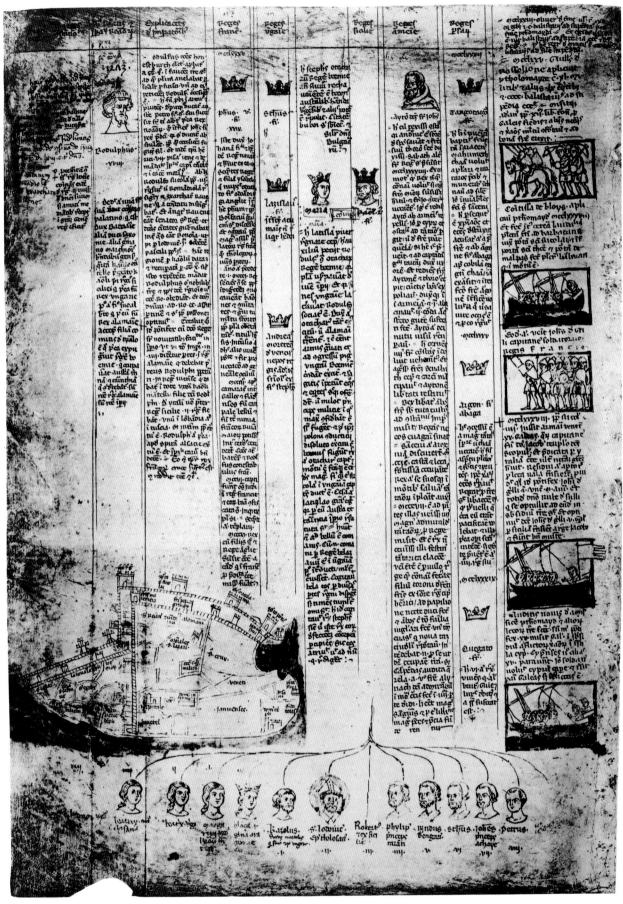

54 Fra Paolino, *Chronologia Magna*, fourteenth century. Parchment, 47 × 35 cm. Venice, Biblioteca Nazionale Marciana, Cod. Lat. Z. 399 (=1610) (after Georgius Martinus Thomas, *De passagiis in Terram Sanctam excerpta ex Chronologia Magna codicis latini CCCXCIX Bibliothecae ad Marci Venetiarum*, Venice 1879).

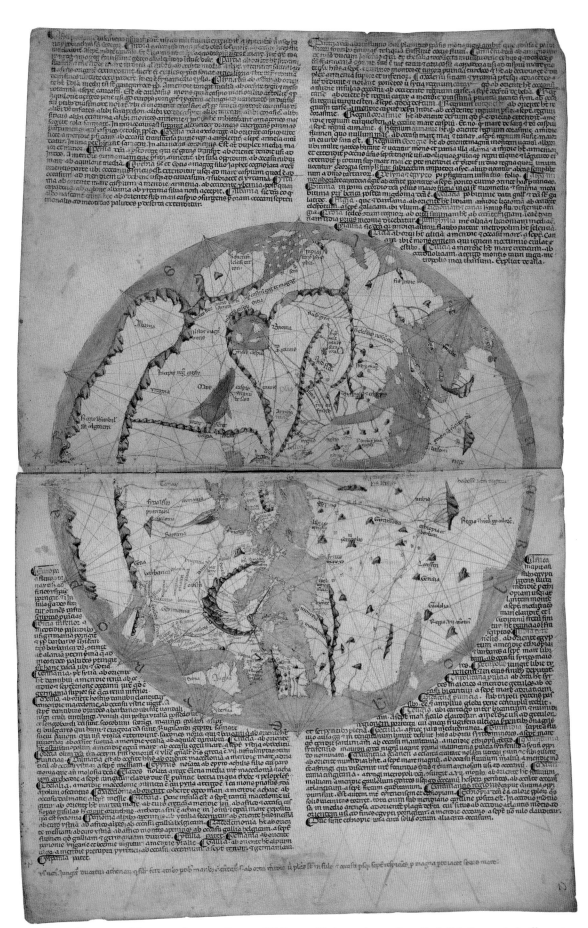

55 Pietro Vesconte, *Mappamundi*, 1320. Rome, Biblioteca Vaticana Apostolica, Cod. Pal. Lat. 1362A, ff. 1v–2r.

remains were gradually noticed and perceived to be alien to the present: fragments of another world that demanded reconstruction, at least in a literary sense, to its former wholeness. The key issue, as Burke points out, is not just ignorance but readiness: "Some information about the differences between past and present was physically available to medieval scholars – but it was not *psychologically* available."[26] Implicit in this new sense of anomaly was an awareness of sequence – of changes wrought by time. It is apparent in Petrarch's complaint to Fra Giovanni Colonna that "nowhere is Rome less known than in Rome," coupled with hope for a better future based upon knowledge of a now distant past: "For who can doubt that Rome would rise again instantly if she began to know herself?"[27]

The second prerequisite is a more critical stance toward evidence. Medieval historiography was characterized on the one hand by a ready, even credulous, acceptance of the equal authority of virtually any written source and on the other by the invention of myths and the forging of documents.[28] Although such an approach was integral to Venetian chronicles and histories right through the end of the quattrocento (and even beyond), with Andrea Dandolo, as well as with Petrarch, one discerns the beginnings of a more skeptical and objective perspective. As Petrarch writes to Colonna: "this is the Septizonium of Severus Afrus which you call the temple of the sun but whose name I find in the form I use written in history."[29]

Finally, a modern sense of history requires an attempt to define causation and motive: that is, an interpretation of the whys and wherefores of an event rather than simply a pure description of it. For medieval historians symbolic connections were more compelling than objective analysis, and moralization often substituted for explanation.[30]

Indeed, many aspects of each of these three prerequisites for a new attitude toward history are visible already in the trecento in Venice, and yet it remains a period with many contradictions. Even though time was increasingly controlled by the civic and the secular, history was still often subject to mystical interpretation. As long as historical causation could be considered not subject to natural law but to supernatural forces, there is still no modern sense of history.[31]

Burke finds the emergence of a new historical perspective to coincide with the discovery of a rationalized pictorial perspective in early fifteenth-century Italy. The discoveries are connected and mutually reinforcing, he suggests, with one based upon an objective awareness of one's own placement in time and the other in space.[32] The idea is credible, but these developments had a lengthy gestation, and it may be more accurate to speak of evolution than of discovery.

In the pages that follow, it is necessary to set aside the dominant Florentine model of the Renaissance revival of antiquity in order to appreciate fully the peculiar flavor of Venetian antiquarianism. It was influenced by at least three fundamental factors: first, and as always, by Venice's unique geographical position and exposure to the East as well as to the West; second, by the dominant patrician ethos of communal solidarity, with the concommitant suspicion of aspirations to individual fame; and third, by the singular capacity for the synthesis and integration of all foreign elements into a new, Venetian whole.

EXPANDED HORIZONS, A HEIGHTENED AWARENESS

> I think that it is not just difficult but impossible without a world map to make [oneself] an image of, or even for the mind to grasp, what is said of the children and grandchildren of Noah and of the Four Kingdoms and other nations and regions, both in divine and human writings. There is needed moreover a twofold map, [composed] of painting and writing. Nor wilt thou deem one sufficient without the other, because painting without writing indicates regions or nations unclearly, [and] writing without the aid of painting, truly does not mark the boundaries of the provinces of a region in their various parts sufficiently [clearly] for them to be descried almost at a glance.
>
> – Fra Paolino Veneto, *De mappa mundi*, c.1321[1]

Just as important as maps themselves in the formation of a modern sense of the past was an awareness of the indivisibility of history and topography. With Fra Paolino, we enter a new era, cartographically and conceptually speaking. Based in Venice for the first fifty years of his life, he was no typical Franciscan friar. A frequent traveler and a voracious buyer of books who had assembled a considerable library, he was criticized for his elegant wardrobe and refined life style, which seems to have included music at meals.[2] His lifelong relationship with Robert of Anjou, also known as Robert the Wise, began with two diplomatic missions to Naples in 1315 as a representative of the Venetian state. By the time he took up his appointment as Bishop of Pozzuoli in 1326, he had traveled to the papal court in Avignon and throughout Italy and also possibly in the East. He remained in Naples as bishop and as a court counselor until his death in 1344, just a year after that of the king. During this period he was part of a cultural community that included Giotto (1328–33) and Boccaccio (c.1328), and also Petrarch, who visited Naples in 1341, before his laureation by Robert on the Capitoline in Rome, and returned there again in 1343.[3]

The salutation of Petrarch's letter to his patron Cardinal Giovanni di Stefano Colonna on the latter visit is emblematic of the times, and could have served as a motto for Fra Paolino as well: "I have known your attitudes for some time; you cannot endure not knowing about things because an implacable desire for knowledge stirs your noble spirit."[4]

AN IMPLACABLE DESIRE FOR KNOWLEDGE

Like his contemporary Marin Sanudo il Torsello, Fra Paolino grasped the essential role of city plans and land maps in conveying a concrete sense of the past. He knew that events took place in a panorama of mountains, valleys, and plains, and in cities linked by roads and rivers; in order to apprehend the drama of history, he maintained, the reader needed to visualize its setting. Two autograph manuscripts of his *Chronologia magna* (one of them joined to the *Satyrica historia*) contain fully realized versions of the earliest surviving plans of Rome conceived as an organic whole. The first manuscript, executed in Venice around 1323, also contains the earliest surviving map of Venice itself, a copy of an early twelfth-century original.[5] The second was made in Naples in 1334–9.[6] The text that accompanies the plans of Rome is based upon a half-century old *mirabilia* – a genre of travel literature, intended as a companion guide to the marvels of Rome for pilgrims and travelers, which first appeared in the twelfth century. But Fra Paolino's plans themselves mark a distinct departure from pictorial traditions for the representation of Rome, which tended to be stylized, schematic, and subordinated to metaphorical demands. In the *Liber Ystoriarum Romanorum*, a late thirteenth-century manuscript, for example, Rome is shown as the Leonine city, its shape and topography grossly, if artfully, distorted to make a figurative point (Plate 56).[7] Here the city is not a place, but a pictogram, albeit one

55

56 *Rome in the Form of a Lion*, from *Liber Ystoriarum Romanorum*, thirteenth century. Hamburg, Staats- und Universitätsbibliothek, Cod. ms. 151 in scrin., f. 107v.

with a certain historical authority. For Honorius of Autun had written in his *De imagine mundi* (first half of the twelfth century), that "It was the custom of the ancients to build their cities in the form of wild beasts. Thus Rome has the form of a lion, because it rules like a king over the other beasts."[8]

Fra Paolino, on his part, conscientiously acknowledges this tradition in a gloss penned on the upper left corner of his own plan of the city: "In Ymagine mundi [Rom]a habet formam leonis."[9] But he also acknowledges the city to be more than just a destination and more than just a metaphor, and makes it a convincing setting for human affairs, past as well as present.

The earlier map, now in Venice, is more accurate than the second and was probably drafted by an artist who had a direct visual experience of Rome (Plate 57).[10] Adopting its oval shape from such medieval models as the Mappamondo of Ebstorf, the city is completely enclosed by the Aurelian walls. These are crenellated in the medieval manner, punctuated with turrets, and pierced with twelve portals. Its unusual

orientation, with "Oriens" or east at the top, instead of south as was customary for maps at that time, may indicate a wish to link Rome to Jerusalem in the east.[11] But it may also have been occasioned by the need to reconcile the vertical format of the page with the desire for completeness of description. The serpentine bed of the Tiber winds through a richly articulated urban terrain that includes recognizable topographical features, such as the Isola Tiburtina, seven prominent hills including the Janiculum, the aqueduct on the Caelian Hill, triumphal arches, monumental columns, obelisks, and a wild animal park.[12]

The emblematic monuments, both ancient and medieval, which came to define the city are all there: the Colosseum in the center, the Capitoline just below it and the Pantheon, labeled "S.M. Rotonda" to the left. Between them stand two fortified towers built by powerful Roman families: the Tor dei Conti, labeled "turris comitis," and the Torre delle Milizie. To the right at the Porta San Paolo is the Pyramid of Cestius, labeled the tomb of Remus, with the Basilica of San Paolo outside the walls. Across the Tiber at the bottom left are St. Peter's and the Castel Sant'Angelo. More mundane,

57 *Map of Rome*, from Paolino Veneto, *Chronologia magna*, *c.*1323. Parchment, 47 × 35 cm. Venice, Biblioteca Nazionale Marciana, Cod. Lat. Z. 399 (1610), f. 98.

58 Detail of the Lateran area from Plate 57.

Direct observation of the city was tempered in at least one instance, however, by the authority of the text. For the artist conscientiously restored the Colosseum to its ancient glory by vaulting it with a huge dome, imaginatively (and erroneously) ascribed to it in the *mirabilia*, where the building was identified as a pagan temple of the sun.[15]

It is worth noting that the golden bull made in 1328 for the coronation ceremony of Ludwig of Bavaria in Rome seems also to have been the work of a Venetian: the goldsmith Leonardo da Venezia or perhaps a follower (Plate 59).[16] The view on the medal is impressive for its commitment to empirical truth, in the details if not in the whole, and features an ideal but credible selection of well-known Roman monuments. Conveying a message of imperial continuity, the Colosseum holds a prominent position on the central axis along with the Palazzo Senatorio on the Capitoline, but now without the enhancement of the invented dome.[17]

59 Golden bull of Ludwig of Bavaria, 1328 (after Frutaz, *Le piante di Roma*, II, Pl. 144).

but perhaps more notable from the standpoint of originality are the street systems in Trastevere, in the Borgo near the Vatican, and in the bend of the Tiber, as well as at the top of the map. Their layouts based at least in part on first-hand visual knowledge, they are lined with anonymous, but often differentiated buildings, and testify to human habitation.[13]

Most telling for our discussion, however, is the group of ancient sculptures then at the Lateran palace, labeled the palace of Nero, that would be moved to the Capitoline in the fifteenth century (Plate 58).[14] All cited with imaginative, if not fabulous, identifications in the *mirabilia* texts, they include the equestrian statue of Marcus Aurelius and the bronze head, hand and sphere of the colossus commonly believed at the time to be a portrait statue of Nero. Their inclusion in Fra Paolino's map is a sign of his "implacable desire for knowledge," for they suggest a new awareness of the antique as something that is no longer complete. Testifying as well to new standards of observation and documentation, they may well constitute the earliest surviving depiction of classical spolia – identifiable pieces and not just generic antique fragments shown in their damaged state – in Italian medieval art.

For all its pictorial novelty, Fra Paolino's map of Rome was accompanied by a didactic text that reveals an unabashedly medieval approach to historiography based upon the *mirabilia* tradition. His marginal commentary tucked into the lower right corner of the folio attempts to account for the present derelict state of the city and telescopes nearly a thousand years of civic history into a seamless and inconclusive litany of calamities:

Rome saw its destruction under Duke Brennus.[18] It was consumed with fire under Alaric. She laments her succes-

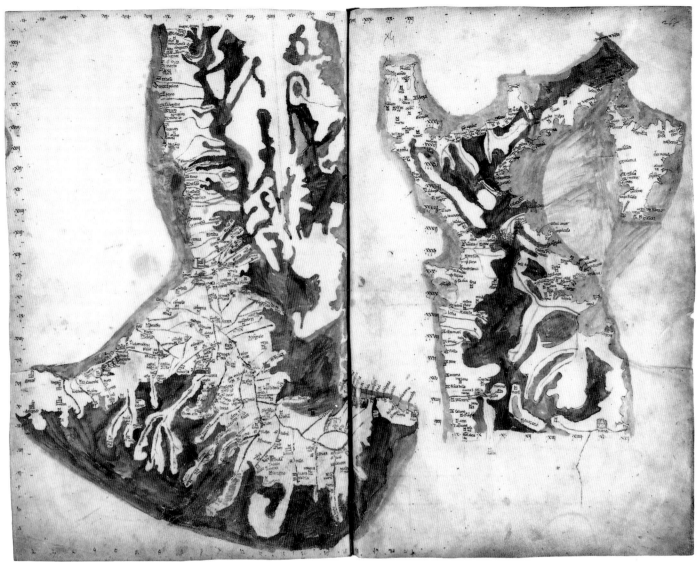

60 The Italian peninsula in two parts, with south at the top, from Fra Paolino, *Chronologia magna* and *Satyrica historia*. Parchment, 44.1 × 28.6 cm. Rome, Biblioteca Apostolica Vaticana, Cod. Vat. Lat. 1960, ff. 267v–268r.

sive and daily collapses of ruins. And like an old man she can scarcely support herself on another man's cane, no longer having any honorable antiquities except a heap of ancient stones and ruinous remains. Among the deeds of St. Benedict, called the high priest of Canossa, because Rome would have been destroyed by Totila, he said, "Rome will not be brought to an end by barbarians, but wither away herself, exhausted by flashing storms, whirlwinds, and earthquakes."[19]

But just as novel as his map of Rome were Fra Paolino's land maps of Italy that accompanied the copies of his *Chronologia* and *satyrica* made in Naples in 1334–9.[20] As crude as they may seem to us now, they may well be considered an early experiment of synthesis, in which the carefully delineated coastline contours of Pietro Vesconte's sea charts take second place to a new circumstantial attention to the land

(Plate 60). The fabric of the world is no longer just a background for the vast network of roads in the *Tabula Peutingeriana*, where cities are little more than way-stations on the itinerary to Rome, but a relief map in color with a rich texture of mountains, cities, towns, and waterways, all laid out in a more or less well defined topographical relationship to one another.[21]

With the maps of Fra Paolino, one enters the cultural world of Petrarch. His knowledge of the ancient world came from texts, but his understanding of its physiognomy came from his own observations. A description written on his first trip to Rome in 1337 reveals his sensitivity to the landscape as a setting for history that went far beyond Fra Paolino in its successful evocation of concrete topography through verbal description:

Humble Capranica is surrounded by illustrious names; on

one side Monte Soracte, famous as the residence of Silvester, but whose praises were sung even before him by poets; next the lake and mountain of Cimino, both mentioned by Virgil; then Sutri, barely two miles away, a place most pleasing to Ceres and said to have been an ancient colony of Saturn. Close to the walls can be seen the plain where it is said that a king from a foreign land planted the very first corn seed to be sown in Italy, and harvested the first crop with his pruning knife . . . The air here, so far as a brief sojourn allows one to judge, is most healthy. On all sides there are numerous hills, easy to get at and to climb, and affording unimpeded views; then, in the valleys between these hills, there are shady hollows with dark caves around them . . . Deep in the valleys sweet springs gurgle; stags, bucks and wild goats, and all the wild woodland animals wander on uncovered hills; birds of every type raise their murmuring voices on the waters or in the branches . . .[22]

According to a later notice, in fact, King Robert and Petrarch had themselves begun a project to make a land map of all Italy, perhaps reflecting the king's political aspirations, but no tangible evidence of the scheme remains. The fact that Fra Paolino seems to have produced the first such maps just a few years earlier and in the same milieu suggests his anticipatory role in the formation of Petrarch's geographical consciousness.[23]

How can one explain the Venetian role in the production of Paolino's map of Rome and the golden bull of Ludwig of Bavaria which together might be considered the two most faithful transcriptions of Roman reality, albeit in two quite different media with different aims, to survive from the first half of the fourteenth century? Four points are worth noting.

First, the weight of a centuries-old craft tradition in Venice may be cited. As seen with Bertuccio's doors and numerous other fictive artifacts at San Marco, as well as with thirteenth-century cameos and gems that still defy attempts to distinguish them from antiques, Venetian artisans were skilled in replication. It would be a distortion to dismiss these tendencies as mere signs of a *retardaire* conservatism.

Second, the new naturalism derives directly from function: didactic in the case of Fra Paolino, who sought to explicate history, and ideological in the case of the medallist, who sought to confirm the imperial prerogatives of his patron in the most convincing manner.

Third, one should look again to Venice's unique setting and her position as the trading power par excellence of Europe. It is no coincidence that the Genoese and the Venetians were at the forefront of developments in cartography. Perhaps more than any population of the time, the Venetian élite were professional travelers, explorers, observers, and diplomats. As sea-going merchants, they knew that their livelihoods and even their lives depended on an ability to read portolan charts and to make accurate observations about to-

pography and to distinguish the salient features of particular landscapes and coastlines. A leading Florentine merchant and man of affairs could have conducted a prosperous business over a lifetime without knowing how to read a map. It would be difficult to say the same of a good number of his Venetian counterparts in that period.

Finally, Venice's self-proclaimed independence from both papacy and empire brought with it a certain distance that may have engendered visual detachment as well.

OMNIA PULCHRA: THE ACQUISITION OF ANTIQUE REMAINS

Venice's unique geographical position between east and west, as well as her mercantile vocation, also ensured her a role in the history of collecting – another major element in the recovery of antiquity and the formation of a new sense of the classical past. As we have seen, the acquisition of antique remains in Venice had begun centuries before through simple necessity, with inscribed marble blocks set into foundations, or through military opportunism, with late antique and Byzantine architectural booty appropriated wholesale for re-use at San Marco and in other public venues.

But there are indications that individuals also acquired antiquities, even in the early period. More often than not, probably, the value of such objects was unrelated to their antiquity *per se*, deriving primarily from the preciousness of material rather than from their rarity or beauty. On the one hand, there is the artifact as treasure. It will be recalled that Doge Sebastiano Ziani was said to have built the family fortune on the lucky discovery of a "basin of solid gold" in Altino in the twelfth century.[24] Whether the legend has any basis in fact, it expresses the popular view of such finds, which often claimed divine intervention in directing the searches of treasure-seekers.[25] On the other hand, the classical artifact could also function as a commodity pure and simple. In 1291, Giacomo Trevisan, a Venetian merchant in Corone, borrowed 200 hyperpyra from another merchant, pledging as security 39 "columpnas marmoreas" including one with a broken capital, 4 smaller columns, and several marble plaques. If he defaulted, the marbles would be transported to Venice at his own expense and offered for sale to pay off the debt.[26]

Alternatively, the antique fragment may be prized solely as a memento or relic of a specific historical event. According to later accounts, Domenico Morosini, the captain of the galley that transported the bronze quadriga of San Marco to Venice from Constantinople after the sack of 1204, was allowed to keep for himself a hind foot that had become detached from one of the horses. It seems to have been passed down in the family, its venue changing with marriages in later generations. Marin Sanudo, writing at the end of the fifteenth century, attested: "And I have seen the said foot on a *modione* [bracket] on a house at Sant'Agostino that belonged to Ser Alessandro

Contarini . . ."[27] When Alessandro's only daughter married Ser Marco Tiepolo, Sanudo reported, the foot was moved to their newly built house at Santi Apostoli where it was again mounted prominently on the exterior. As a modern scholar observes, the trophy was prized not for its beauty nor for its intrinsic worth, but for its commemorative value as a visual emblem of a distinguished family history.[28] Likewise, Lorenzo Tiepolo, hero of the Venetian victory over the Genoese at Acre in 1256, was allowed to keep a large stone foundation block taken from the enemy fortifications. He installed it at the corner of the portico of San Pantaleone as a sign of his military prowess.[29]

But when does fortuitious appropriation turn into collecting true and proper? The attentiveness of thirteenth-century artists to the antique fragment in their skillful replications – copies, if not fakes – of sculptural reliefs dating to much earlier periods has already been observed. To their silent testimony can be added the voice of Ristoro d'Arezzo who wrote a treatise on ancient Aretine vases in that period:

the cognoscenti, when they found [ancient Aretine vases], they rejoiced and shouted to one another with the greatest delight, and they got loud and nearly lost their senses and became quite silly; and the ignorant wanted to throw the [vases] and to break them up. When some of these *pecci* [pieces] got into the hands of sculptors or painters or other *conoscenti*, they preserved them like holy relics, marveling that human nature could reach so high.[30]

The antique *pecci* noted by Ristoro were probably esteemed as treasures pure and simple, or as models of fine craftsmanship for the artisan, and not as documents of a lost but restorable ancient world for the antiquarian. But the reverence with which they were regarded presaged the new cult of antiquity that found its first coherent formulation in the next century with Petrarch. Our earliest certain evidence for the Venetian milieu proper comes in modest form: the well-known shopping list written by the notary Oliviero Forzetta of Treviso. Although composed in mediocre Latin without the ornament of humanist erudition, it displays an intimate familiarity with specific antiquities and works of art available for purchase at that time in Venice. As such, it can well be considered one of the most important documents in the history of Renaissance collecting.[31]

Forzetta begins: "The year 1335. I have to do the following things in Venice." His first entry concerns a house that he had been renting there; it is now to be given up and his household effects shipped back to Treviso. The list continues with a number of specific objects to be purchased in Venice, along with the names of their present owners or locations. The first items are "teste" – sculpted busts or possibly cameos[32] – most of them to be obtained from goldsmiths, who traded in classical sculpture and coins for a select clientele: "bronze heads" – probably medals – from Milan to be ordered from

Ser Giovanni Teutonico, "aurifice" and a marble head from Magister Ognibene. Forzetta further noted that Magister Simeone had promised him fifty "medaias" (coins) and Simeone's nephew Damiano four "pastas" (probably stuccoes or wax medallions) and some ivory chesspieces or a chessboard. While one "bronze head" was to be found at the convent of San Salvador, several of Forzetta's sources seem to have been collectors like himself: a member of the house of Morosini from whom he sought a particular "moneta" (coin) and a "figura brondina" (bronze sculpture); and Guglielmo Zapparin, then deceased, whose widow owned a marble putto and some drawings by an artist named Perenzolo.

In one entry Forzetta reminds himself: "Inquire about the four marble putti of Ravenna, which are sculpted at San Vitale in Ravenna." Now in the archaeological museum of Venice, these putti are the only identifiable works from Forzetta's list that survive today (Plates 61–62). Holding insignia of the god Saturn, the figures were originally part of a series of Roman reliefs datable to the first or second century A.D., in which the thrones of various divinities – Saturn, Neptune, Ceres, Mars, Jupiter, Diana, and Apollo – were flanked by two pairs of putti carrying the symbols of the apposite god or goddess. Whether or not Forzetta was successful in obtaining the sculptures is unknown; in any case, by the fifteenth century they were attached to a house at the end of the Piazza San Marco, above an arcade that led to the Frezzaria, and made frequent appearances in sixteenth-century Venetian art.[33]

Forzetta was also interested in classical texts, seeking them out from booksellers and from Dominican and Franciscan convents in Venice: the complete works of Ovid and Cicero, and manuscripts of Sallust, Seneca, Aristotle, Orosius, and Livy among others, as well as a copy of *Ystoriis Romanis*. By the time of his death in 1373, the notary would amass some 138 volumes, one of the largest libraries in the Veneto.[34] But his interests went beyond antiquities pure and simple, for the memorandum of 1335 also reveals a taste for contemporary art. While he cited tapestry cartoons and other works by Paolo da Venezia and his brother Marco, Forzetta was particularly interested in the paintings, prints, and drawings of two Venetian artists who had died a short time before: Pietro (called Perenzolo) and Gioacchino, both identifiable as the sons of the painter Angelo Tedaldo of the parish of San Canciano.[35] The entire production of all three artists seems to have perished, a particularly unfortunate loss since Forzetta's list cites intriguing subject matter, virtually without reflection in surviving Venetian art of the time:

Item inquire after all the drawings that belonged to Perenzolo, son of Master Angelo, and now are pledges in the possession of Masters Francesco and Stefano of San Giovanni Nuovo, and his sketchbooks, in which there are all kinds of animals and every beautiful thing [*omnia pulchra*] made by the hand of Perenzolo and likewise all of his

61 *Throne of Saturn* (left side), Roman relief from San Vitale, Ravenna, first to second century A.D. Venice, Museo Archeologico.

62 *Throne of Saturn* (right side), Roman relief from San Vitale, Ravenna, first to second century A.D. Venice, Museo Archeologico.

intaglios [incised metal] and drawings, whatsoever would have been left in pledge and on deposit . . .

Item [ask] about the painted head, lions, birds, and horses that Anna, sister of the deceased Gioacchino possesses, which head is crowned by a garland of roses with an ornament [*infula*] . . .

Item [ask] about the stone boy of Guglielmo Zaparino and many other drawings of Perenzolo which his wife has.

And note that Marino de Gallera has lions, horses, oxen, nude men, and engravings [*caelaturas*] of men, beasts and birds by the deceased Perenzolo.[36]

Luciano Gargan suggests that Forzetta's taste for these works was not inspired by a love for contemporary art *per se*, but because the paintings and drawings were themselves antiquities of sorts – conceived in form and content "alla maniera antica." While subjects such as birds and animals might be interpreted simply as early examples of International Gothic naturalism, the inclusion of nude men in the artists' oeuvres implies, instead, that pagan art provided the inspiration. The models could have been classical sculpture or even mythological and still-life compositions of the Hellenistic period, perhaps mediated through later works from the Balkans and the Aegean.[37] One also thinks of late-antique manuscripts such as the Cotton Genesis as well as fragments of mosaic floors, still visible in sites throughout the Veneto.[38] If the possibility of some form of classicism in Venetian secular painting of this period is accepted, then Bertuccio's set of bronze doors of 1300 no longer seems an isolated instance of *romanitas*.

With the pictorial evidence no longer in existence it is not possible to be more conclusive about this "moment of classicism" in the secular art of Venice. But what does seem clear is the existence of a market for antiquities, dominated by

goldsmiths, that served a number of collectors, including Forzetta. The antiquarian interests shared by these figures must have been intense, cutting across lines of class and social status to link artisans and wealthy merchants. Under Scaliger domination at the time, Treviso maintained strong relations with Venice and in 1339 became its first acquisition in the terraferma. Damiano, the nephew of the goldsmith Magister Simeone mentioned above, witnessed a contract for Forzetta in 1338 in the communal palace in Treviso, and his brother Marco was living in the Forzetta home in 1342. The youths were both sons of the goldsmith Leonardo da Venezia.[39] If, as seems possible, this was the Venetian master of the same name who is linked to the golden bull of Ludwig of Bavaria, it would indicate a very intimate circle indeed of artisan-dealers and antiquarian patrons in the Venetian milieu.

It has been observed that Forzetta was not really a collector in the modern sense,[40] for in his testament of 1368, he ordered that all his drawings, paintings, and sculpture be sold upon his death with the proceeds used to endow a dowry fund for poor maidens. His books were to be divided between two convents. The fact that Forzetta made no provision to keep his art collection intact is not all that surprising. Aside from the fact that he died without progeny (despite five marriages), his fortune, like that of his parents, was the result of usurious lending – a heretical activity proscribed by the church and punishable by eternal damnation. But it was a redeemable sin. A long life of profitable dealings and enjoyable collecting could find expiation through a charitable bequest of appropriately substantial proportions.[41]

Forzetta's list is an oddity – an *unicum* – for its time. First published by a priest at the end of the seventeenth century, the autograph original is now lost, but despite the fact that no other such lists survive, its authenticity has never been seri-

63 *Temperance*, fourteenth century. Fresco fragment from a house at San Zulian, 192 × 124 cm. Venice, Museo Civico Correr.

64 *Charity, Constancy, and Hope,* fourteenth century. Fresco fragment from a house at San Zulian, 219 × 221 cm. Venice, Museo Civico Correr.

ously challenged. The same cannot be said, unfortunately, for the inventory of Doge Marin Falier of 1351, the only other Venetian document claimed for the period that reveals similar interests. It was first published by its discoverer, G.M. Urbani de Gheltof, in 1881, but it too disappeared after his death. The writer's unreliability in several other cases, as well as the motley character of the objects noted, has caused some scholars to doubt the authenticity of the list in part or in whole.[42] While it should be viewed cautiously, however, there is no conclusive evidence that it is a forgery, and it should not be dismissed out of hand. It is different in character from

Forzetta's memorandum, for it lists the result rather than the process of acquisition: a wide array of objects, many of them kept in "capse" and "capselete" (chests and little boxes) in a "camera rubea" in Falier's palace at Santi Apostoli.

Inventories of household items were an established genre in this period, but Falier's is notable for the preciosity and variety of the objects – an assortment reminiscent of the princely *Wunderkammer* of the Baroque period that is almost too good to be true. It included "a panel with figures of different nations by the hand of master Thomas the painter";[43] a bronze sphere of the world which belonged to "magister Antonio the astrologer";[44] and a number of objects obtained from Falier's renowned neighbor Marco Polo: "a ring with the inscription '*Ciuble Can Marco Polo*' [From Kublai Khan to Marco Polo],"[45] "a book of travels bound in white leather . . . with many miniatures," and "another volume entitled 'On the lands of the marvelous Tartars,' written in the hand of the stated Marco."[46] But amongst these curiosities are four entries of particular relevance: "a little casket with fifty estimable antique coins";[47] "a sword of wonderful antiquity, with inscriptions";[48] "a bronze sword found in Padua";[49] and "three marble inscriptions found in Treviso."[50]

Falier served two terms as podestà in Treviso, 1339–40 and 1346–7, giving him ample opportunity to make the acquaintance of Forzetta and to acquire the taste for antiquities that could have brought him three inscribed marbles and a casket of coins. But after the unfortunate Falier was convicted of treason and beheaded in 1355, his possessions, including the family palace at SS. Apostoli, were confiscated by the state and none of the items in his inventory is known to survive.[51]

Since public art in Venice showed little humanist influence in the trecento, it would appear that naturalistic tendencies derived more from Gothic than from classical sources. But Forzetta's inventory suggests that art in the private sphere could tell a different story. One intriguing piece of evidence comes in the form of two fresco fragments, now in the Correr Museum, that probably date to the first half of the fourteenth century (Plates 63–64).[52] Characterized by one scholar as "questa rude voce di terraferma," the frescoes were discovered in 1913 in a private house at San Zulian, near San Marco, during a remodeling campaign. They are virtually the only surviving pieces of Venetian domestic mural decoration from the period. The original program would have consisted of a cycle of personified virtues and other allegories painted around the walls of a room. Silhouetted against a black background, the Virtues are seated on thrones beneath an arcade that features gabled arches surmounted by tiny nude figures alternating with aedicules crowned with open cupolas. Flame-like trees behind the arcade imply a garden setting. One fragment shows Temperance, who holds a scroll that bears a moralizing message: "Temperance strengthens your Fortitude." The other piece depicts Charity, Constancy, and Hope, each accompanied by her traditional attribute and an appropriate didactic message. Bearing in mind that such wall paintings may have been the exception rather than the rule, one can still read out of them values toward the antique that were probably typical of the mercantile class of the time.

The Virtues, even in their ruined state, are lively and engaging figures. Charity holds a basket of bread and offers a loaf to a pauper; Constancy gazes at a human face – surely the moon, an ancient symbol of chastity[53] – which she holds in her hand; Hope looks up and stretches out her hands to a tiny saint who descends from the heavens; and Temperance is shown with ewers of water and wine, one held in her lap and the other indicated by her gesture.[54] Modishly dressed in fourteenth-century costume, the Virtues are genteel creatures and decorous in demeanor. But atop the gables, as one scholar observes, "there begins a different and freer life."[55] For here naked figures gambol about devoid of the shame often associated with nudity in medieval art. Whether they are seen as dancers or acrobats inspired by painted Greek vases or Byzantine ivories, as some would have it, or as *droleries* that have escaped from the margins and capital initials of illuminated manuscripts as others suggest, they testify to the playful emancipation – and the disarming – of the pagan idol.[56] Part of their appeal lies in their ambiguous nature: are they animate beings or simply statuettes? And rather than estrangement, the irrepressible figures intimate a cozy familiarity with the alien world of which they were a symbolic part.[57]

PETRARCH AND THE VENETIANS

The accommodation of the pagan aspect of the antiquity to the Christian present would find a less easy fit with Petrarch, for he knew what was at stake. As implied by the valedictions in his epistles to classical authors, he was a man caught between two worlds, dating a letter written to Cicero from the birthdate of "that God whom thou never knewest." Petrarch claimed, furthermore, that the Pantheon, transformed into a Christian church in the seventh century and called Santa Maria Rotonda, was saved from destruction only because of the Virgin Mary, "who sustained that most ancient building by virtue of her name."[58] His ambivalence toward art in general can also be discerned in *De remediis utriusque fortunae*, a treatise on painted pictures and statues. It takes the form of a three-way conversation between Gaudium, Ratio, and himself. Gaudium (Delight), speaking for Pliny, makes the case for the enjoyment of art. He is countered by Ratio (Reason), a thinly-veiled St. Augustine, who cautions against the "seduction of the eyes" by beautiful objects. Just as the reflection in a mirror is inferior to the object reflected, he argues, so too the figurative arts are false and mendacious through intrinsic necessity. Not wholly convinced by either side, Petrarch uses a "yes, but" structure for the often contentious debate. He allows that the enjoyment of sacred images can be a pious act, but suggests that profane images, even though they may elevate the soul toward greater virtue, must not be admired more than is just. His own descriptions of ancient art tend to reflect this ambivalence.[59]

On the one hand, as Petrarch stresses in his account of a meeting with the Emperor Charles IV, the collecting of antiquities has a historical and moral dimension:

> I gave him as a gift some gold and silver coins bearing the portraits of our ancient rulers and inscriptions in tiny and ancient lettering, coins that I treasured, and among them was the head of Caesar Augustus, who almost appeared to be breathing. "Here, O Caesar," I said, "are the men

whom you have succeeded, here are those whom you must try to imitate and admire, whose ways and character you should emulate: I would have given these coins to no other save yourself."[60]

But on the other hand, lacking a connotative vocabulary for art, Petrarch had difficulties in describing such objects. Often he fell back on classical topoi lifted directly from Pliny and Virgil. Foremost among such commonplaces is the durable notion of the "living image" as the highest aim of art. The Roman coin with the face of Augustus "almost appeared to be breathing"; the bronze horses of San Marco, "the work of some ancient and famous artist unknown to us, stand as if alive, seeming to neigh from on high and to paw with their feet."[61]

Or when faced with works of ancient artifice such as the ruins of Baia, he conceded amazement and showed himself to be at a rare loss for words: "The appearance of the place and the labor devoted to its development caused me to marvel."[62] As his elegant descriptions of landscape attest, he was clearly more at ease in dealing with topography than with art objects *per se*. For undercutting an objective assessment of the classical artifact was an inherent bias for the text:

> The gold, the silver, the gems . . . the painted panels . . . all things of this type give a mute and superficial pleasure: books delight instead profoundly, they speak, they counsel, and they are joined to us by a living and speaking custom.[63]

A modern scholar concludes: "This is the point. With books Petrarch can speak, with images not."[64] Petrarch's own artistic efforts seem to have been limited to marginal sketches in his manuscripts, such as the profile head crowned with laurel in the border of his copy of Claudian's *De raptu proserpinae* (Plate 65).[65]

Much has been written about Petrarch's role in Venetian intellectual life and his importance for classical scholarship in Venice. Maintaining a focus on artifacts and images, however, one inevitably asks what effect he had on the way in which Venetians thought about classical remains and how they represented in art the concrete particulars – architecture, costume, personalities – of the classical world. There is little hard evidence, and the case is circumstantial only. Petrarch visited Venice on a number of occasions, sometimes for extended stays. He first passed through the city as a student in 1321 on his way from Bologna to Avignon, but his next visit came nearly three decades later. In 1349 he wrote to a friend of the advantages of living in Padua under Carrara patronage: "And Venice will be close to us, the most marvelous city that I have ever seen – and I have seen almost all those of which Europe is proud."[66] It was during this period that he must have become acquainted with Doge Andrea Dandolo and various members of the Chancery. As Forzetta's activities indicate, Petrarch would also have found in the city dealers in classical texts, coins, and other artifacts.

There were further visits over the next decade when he was living in Milan, and, returning to Padua in the summer of 1361, he decided to take up permanent residence in Venice. The goal was to find "securitatem et quietem" amongst a congenial group of acquaintances. With the help of his friend, the Chancellor Benintendi de' Ravignani, he formulated an ingenious proposal toward this end. In return for leaving all his books to the Venetian government after his death for the express purpose of establishing a public library, he would be provided with a rent-free house described as "non magna sed honesta" – not large, but honorable. The Great Council voted enthusiastically to accept the offer, describing the poet as one "whose fame today in the whole world is so great that, in the memory of man, there has been in Christendom no moral

65 Marginal drawing in Petrarch's hand of a profile head crowned with laurel and a pointing hand, in a copy of Claudian. *De raptu proserpinae*, once owned by Petrarch. Paris, Bibliothèque Nationale, Cod. 8280, f. 4v.

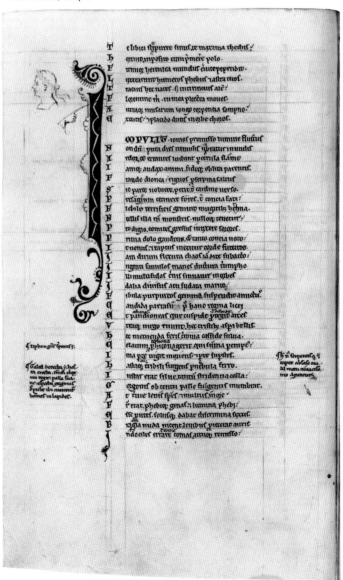

philosopher or poet who can be compared with him."[67] A few days later he moved with his books into the Palazzo da Molin, on the Riva degli Schiavoni, which soon became a meeting place for visiting as well as local literati.[68] The arrangement seems to have suited Petrarch well for the first few years, but he became restless after the deaths in 1365 of both Benintendi and Doge Lorenzo Celsi.

A short time later he was hurt by disparaging remarks made by four younger men whom he had considered close friends. Perhaps envious of his fame, they pronounced him: "certainly a good man but a scholar of poor merit." He responded with a bitter invective that became one of his most acclaimed works: *De sui ipsius et multorum ignorantia*.[69] The offenders, who might be classified as Aristotelians devoted to natural science more than to literature and moral philosophy,[70] were identified in a marginal note on a manuscript copy of Petrarch's treatise: "These were Dominus Leonardo Dandolo [son of Doge Andrea Dandolo], Tommaso Talenti, Dominus Zaccaria Contarini, all of Venice; [and] fourth, Magister Guido da Bagnolo of Reggio: the first a knight, the second a simple tradesman, the third a simple noble, the fourth a doctor of medicine." Following the same order, a second gloss appraised their erudition: "But such that the first had no letters (what I tell you is well known), the second few, the third not many, the fourth I admit quite a few, but disordered and so confused and, as Cicero says, of such frivolity and ostentation, that it would perhaps be better not to have them at all."[71]

Feeling increasingly marginalized and no longer enjoying a central role in the cultural life of the city, Petrarch began spending part of each year in Pavia. In 1368 he packed up his library and moved back to Padua. Two years later he moved again, into a house given him by Francesco Carrara in the tiny village of Arquà in an idyllic setting in the Euganean Hills with a sweeping view of the surrounding countryside. He made his last visit to Venice in September 1373 as an emissary of Carrara in the negotiation of a peace treaty between the two powers. In ill health, he returned to Arquà and died there the following July. His books were dispersed, and the dream of a public library for Venice died with him, at least for the time being.[72] His reputation in the city remained, nonetheless, preeminent. The great Italian critic Ugo Foscolo wrote in the early nineteenth century: "the Venetian Senate made a law against those who purloined his bones, and sold them as relics."[73]

THE IMAGE OF THE PAST

Indeed, it was during the time of Petrarch's visits and residence in Venice that Venetians began to take a more active role in recording the past. Such an interest is documented by the appearance of the first vernacular histories of the city and the proliferation of illustrated historical texts. At the beginning of this period, it may be recalled, the *Historia Troiana* now in Madrid was richly embellished with miniatures based on late antique prototypes. Possibly commissioned by Dandolo himself, the images may have been deliberately "archaized" to imply a similarly venerable lineage for Venice itself.[74] Another manuscript also produced in Venice around 1350 shows a more directly archaeological approach. Now in the Biblioteca Comunale of Fermo, it includes selections from five classical authors, including Suetonius's *Lives of the Caesars*, the Fourth Decade of Livy, and Sallust's Cataline Conspiracy and Jugurthine War. The Suetonius was the most fully illustrated text, with a pen and ink bust-length portrait preceding the life of each of the twelve emperors. These were augmented by four drawings of historical episodes dispersed through the manuscript: the Adlocutio of Julius Caesar, two scenes of homage by barbarian kings, and the Triumph of Marius over Jugurtha.[75] The Fermo manuscript is the earliest known illustrated Suetonius from the trecento and represents a new approach toward illustration that is notably more comprehensive and historically coherent than those of earlier illustrated classical texts.[76] Although the drawing style betrays a trecento hand, it is classical in spirit, and most of the emperors' profiles are remarkably faithful to their numismatic prototypes. The portraits, however, are not simply copies of Roman coins, like those of Mansionario or of Petrarch himself in the marginal drawing in his personal copy of Claudian (Plate 65), for the artist of the Fermo manuscript transcended the restrictive tondo format to depict a half-length figure.[77] He was thus forced to look elsewhere for appropriate models for the armor, dress, and imperial attributes. Nero, for example, was given his lyre on the authority of a coin reverse that portrays him as Apollo Citharoedus (Plate 66). The desire for completeness sometimes overwhelms a strict historicism, with three emperors of the first century given eagle-scepters that first appear on coins only in the third century. But despite anachronisms, the portraits represent a new high level of historical consistency, with Roman figures wearing Roman dress and holding Roman attributes.[78]

The artist was faced with a more challenging problem in working out the narrative scenes. For the composition of the *Adlocutio of Julius Caesar* he looked to a Roman coin type, with Caesar's mount reminiscent of one of the bronze horses of San Marco (Plate 67); but the figures are grouped and interact amongst themselves in an animated trecento manner. The *Triumph of Marius* also depends on numismatic models for the quadriga and the chariot of Marius, but here the artist falls back on fourteenth-century hairstyles and penitential shifts for Jugurtha and his sons (Plate 68).[79]

With both text and images speaking the Latin tongue, the Fermo manuscript is a unique attempt at historical documentation that sought to maintain the linguistic and iconographical unity of the classical world. It is probably no coincidence that it comes out of Petrarch's immediate circle of acquaintances, for the patron was the physician Guido da

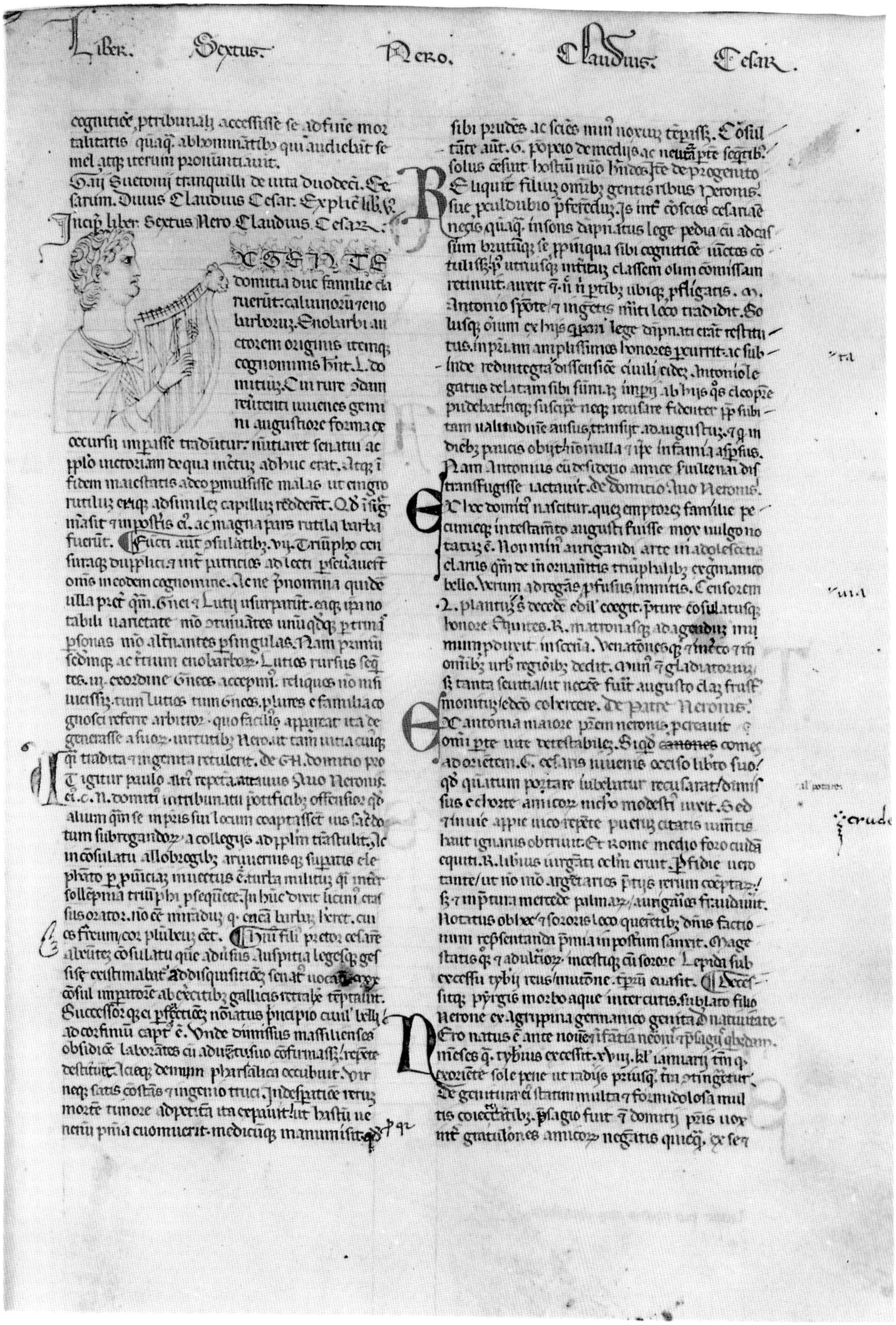

66 *Nero*, from Suetonius, *De vita Caesarum*, *c.*1350. Parchment, 32 × 22 cm. Fermo, Biblioteca Comunale, Cod. 81, f. 35.

67 *Adlocutio of Julius Caesar*, from Suetonius, *De vita Caesarum*, c.1350. Parchment, 32 × 22 cm. Fermo, Biblioteca Comunale, Cod. 81, f. 3.

68 *Triumph of Marius over Jugurtha, King of the Numidians*, from Suetonius, *De vita Caesarum*, c.1350. Parchment, 32 × 22 cm. Fermo, Biblioteca Comunale, Cod. 81, f. 157v.

Bagnolo of Reggio, the most learned of the four "Aristotelians" who had so provoked the poet's ire. Guido had studied arts and medicine at Bologna and lived for a time in the Venetian east, in Cyprus as councilor to the king, and in Nicosia and Modone as a priest. Amassing considerable wealth from his medical practice, he spent large sums on books. During his residence in Venice in the 1360s, he became acquainted not only with Petrarch, Boccaccio, and his three Aristotelian companions, but also with a wider circle of Venetian literati. Among them was the patrician Ludovico Gradenigo, to whom he lent the Fermo manuscript before all the illustrations could be completed. Gradenigo still had the book in his possession when Guido died in 1370. When he himself died in Avignon five years later, his books were shipped back to Venice by Zaccaria Contarini, another of the four "Aristotelians" and then the Venetian ambassador to the papal court.[80]

The classical vision of the Fermo Suetonius was not characteristic of Venetian book illustration in general, however, and Guido da Bagnolo was, after all, an outsider. An abundantly illustrated edition of the First Decade of Livy, dating to 1373 and now in the Ambrosiana library in Milan, reveals the prevailing Venetian mentality far more tellingly. The largest compendium of Venetian drawings of the second half of the fourteenth century, it is the first example in Italy of the complete illustration, chapter by chapter, of this text.[81] The noble patron, Giannino Cattaneo, proudly emblazoned his family arms on the first two pages, but he prefaced the text with a modest disclaimer: "I do not know for certain if I will be doing anything useful in writing the stories of the people of Rome . . ."[82] After 206 abundantly illustrated pages, with minor events often taking precedence over historically more significant episodes, the patron appraises the result in the

explicit, pronouncing it "un notabel libro," worth more than thirty-five ducats. He further attests: "And I Giannino Cattaneo son of Andriolo, son of ser Giovanni of S. Croce made the said book for my own delight and that of certain good friends of mine . . ."[83] Indeed, the book was lovingly illustrated by a number of hands, both professional and amateur, and yet it achieved an extraordinary unity of word and image.

In an early expression of the anecdotal "eye-witness style" that would have a long life in Venice in both the citizen chronicle and in pictorial narrative,[84] the drawings carry the spirit of the Correr fresco cycle of Virtues into the pages of a book (Plate 69). Antiquity is appropriated unselfconsciously for purposes of pleasure (and possibly of instruction) rather than of politics, and historical distance is blithely ignored. When the soldiers of the Roman dictator Furius Camillus kneel before the statue of Juno, displayed in a Gothic tabernacle, after the sack of Veii (Plate 70); when the pagan flamen, or priest, Quirinus, clothed in the habit of a mendicant friar, carries a pagan idol to safety on the Janiculum on the eve of the Gallic invasion and meets a cart full of Vestal virgins dressed like Venetian nuns and holding Gothic triptychs (Plate 71); when the daughters of Marcus Fabius Ambustus engage in a sisterly quarrel in the *androne* of a Venetian palazzo with a characteristic Venetian *pozzo* and door knocker in the courtyard outside (Plate 72); the Roman past is firmly situated in the Venetian present. As one scholar observes: "No precise knowledge of antiquity, drawn from the monuments themselves, disturbs our good Venetians in their visions."[85]

Unlike the artist of the Fermo Suetonius, the illustrators of the Livy needed no classical models. The evocation of historical distance was not even at issue. With the settings, the costumes, the customs, and even the language of the text all

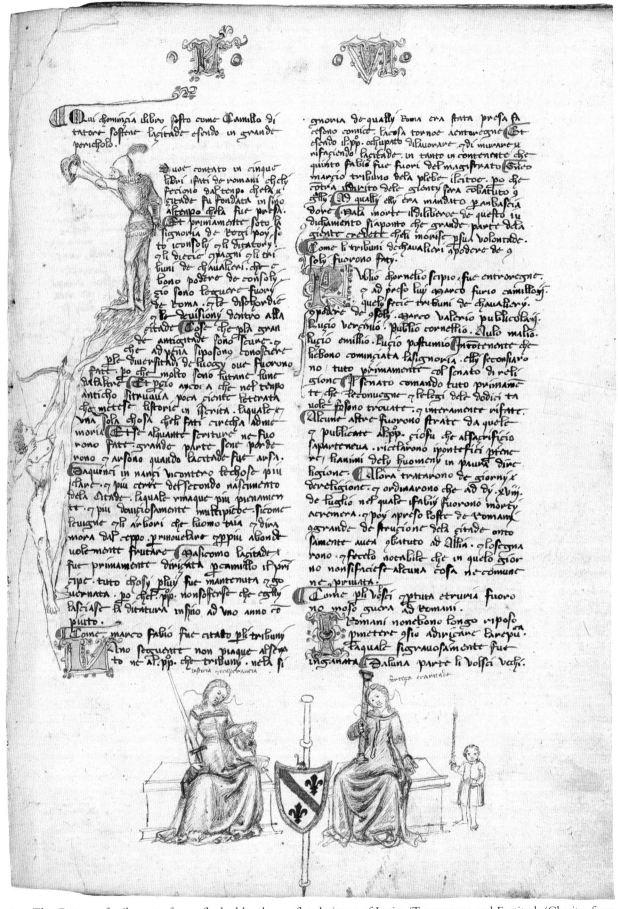

69   The Cattaneo family coat of arms flanked by the conflated virtues of Justice/Temperance and Fortitude/Charity, from *Titus Livius*, *Ab urbe condita libri I–X*, 1372–3. Paper, 35.4 × 28 cm. Milan, Biblioteca Ambrosiana, Cod. C. 214 inf., f. 129.

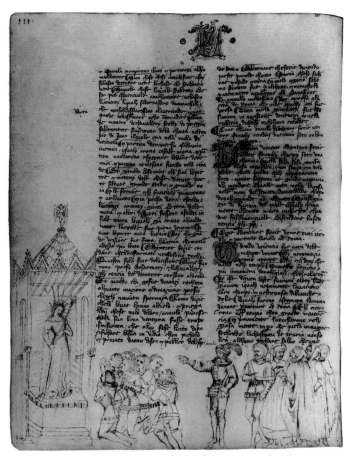

70 *Roman Youths ask a Statue of Juno if she wishes to be taken to Rome after the Sack of Veii by the Roman Dictator Furius Camillus* (Livy v, 22), from Titus Livius, *Ab urbe condita libri I–X*, 1372–3. Paper, 35.4 × 28 cm. Milan, Biblioteca Ambrosiana, Cod. C. 214 inf., f. 110v.

71 *The Romans prepare to defend their City from the Gauls* (Livy v, 40), from Titus Livius, *Ab urbe condita libri I–X*, 1372–3. Paper, 35.4 × 28 cm. Milan, Biblioteca Ambrosiana, Cod. C. 214 inf., f. 118.

Venetian, the manuscript is – in a sense – just as consistent as the Fermo Suetonius. It is as if Livy were sitting with Giannino Cattaneo in a busy *campo* near Rialto and commenting on the life around him.[86]

It was also in the late 1360s that a fresco cycle of the *Story of Alexander III* (or Peace of Venice of 1177) was begun by Guariento in the Sala del Maggior Consiglio. Already painted in the Palazzo Ducale in the Cappella di San Nicolo, this second rendition would be a revised and expanded version of the, by now, emblematic sequence of events.[87] During the same period, the Venetian miniaturist Giustino di Gherardino da Forlì was called upon to illustrate a manuscript version of the story, as well as a volume of Guido delle Colonne's *Historia Troiana*. The manuscripts are now, respectively, in the Correr Museum and the Bodmer Library near Geneva.[88] Both accounts, because mythic, were irrefutable proofs of Venetian sovereignty and liberty from the beginning. Admittedly the Alexander legend was the Venetian elaboration of a real event, but the fabulous Trojan legend was considered civic history as well, its popularity secured by the authoritative statement in Guido's text: "Veneciarum urbem inhabitaverit ille Troyanus

Anthenor" (The well-known Trojan Antenor had inhabited the city of the Venetians).[89]

Not surprisingly, Master Giustino drew upon a common stock of pictorial formulas and often Venetianizing architectural settings for both manuscripts, but the underlying concept was different for each (Plates 73–74). First, the *Story of Alexander III* was more internally consistent. Now translated into the *volgare* for the first time, the episode of medieval Venetian history was recast in a medieval Venetian pictorial *and* linguistic idiom. By contrast, Latin was employed, appropriately enough, for the history of ancient Troy. And yet, here there is an inherent tension between word and image, with a classical story in a classical language in a medieval setting. But secondly, the artist sought to ease this tension in the Trojan manuscript by introducing a sense of historical distance with exotically accoutred protagonists who could not be mistaken for the contemporary Venetians interacting with Alexander III. Their eastern dress, their long hair and beards, and particularly their headgear – broad-brimmed Paleologan hats, oriental turbans, conical caps, and spiked Mongol helmets – define them as alien. A similar sartorial inventiveness had been

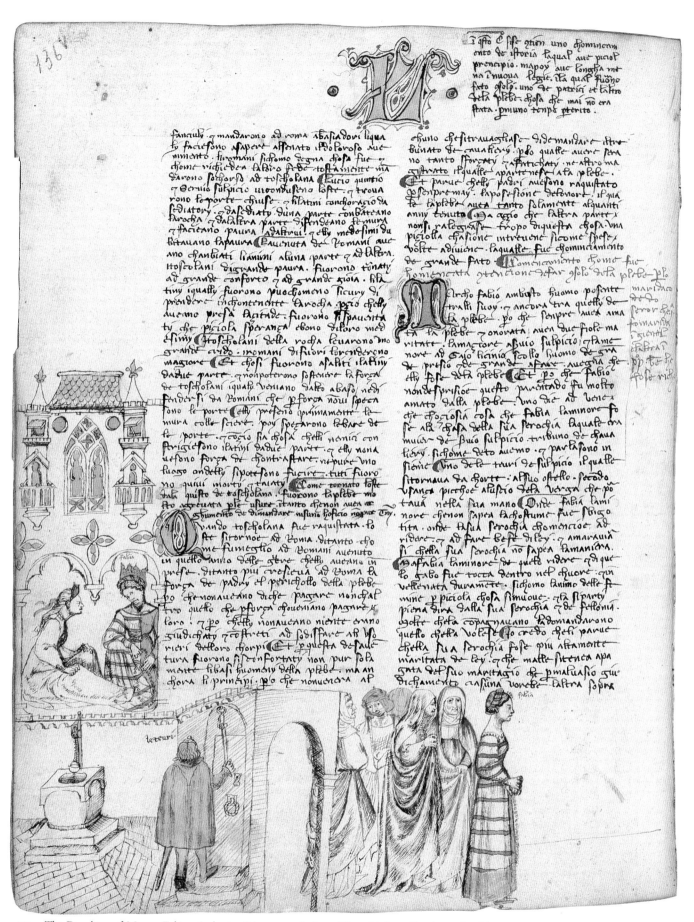

72 *The Daughters of Marcus Fabius Ambustus* (Livy VI, 34), from Titus Livius, *Ab urbe condita libri I–X*, 1372–3. Paper, 35.4 × 28 cm. Milan, Biblioteca Ambrosiana, Cod. C. 214 inf., f. 136v.

Cuies vos morti tradimo 2 nos oms a uestris rembus descendentes/Abstineatis ergo ab hys quo 2 finis est dolo 2 ~ mortis excitatiuus cura te ne prouide et ipm dolcas truncu artne iace transsima osoite tuam excidio tradita 7 omis tuos gladio seuente truncatos ſCu hec oia futura sint it uera si paris in greciam ai ecetu presumat doline ~ his dictis quasi dolens seu propria restituit seruone. ¶Ad Rex igitur uerba Ellem sapietis uacillauit Regis animus ~ titubatoe repletus extitit no modica 2 stupefactus p quod facru est inter oms astantes tractum ex omni potre silentium nec erat aliquis intre eos qui pre timore in uoce 2 smonis erumpere. ¶Tunc ille et troylus ex regis filiis Junior postemo susceptus ut uidit omnes pre multa turbatione sillere Rupto silentio in hec uerba prorupit.

Oun nobiles et mmium bellicosi. Ad quid turbamini area predea pluuisma ad uoce unius pusillanimis sacerdotis no ne est timere proprie sacerdotium: uitrare bella uitare ingressus quos sola pusilla mmitas facit amare delicias et in sola uscedi cabos ~ potius satunitate timescere. Quis ai

die obducantur debitas in armo 2 officium exercere ultiones. Ad quid area eius uerba tum i mate 2 tim smola Rex moliste p turbaris. Jube naui qua soluere ~ in excicatum Ad iter attingere bellicosum cum no sit ferendus oeate 2 io tantus pudor nobis a grecis illatus absq: talione uindicte et suo dictis tiaut troilus eius animo sunt: et deum a astantes ceteri laudiuerunt. et omis ofiliu 2 eius probant. sic g mandante Rege ofilio ipo soluto. predicti Regis filii aim eodem rege piratas mensas appetunt discubentes. ¶Postq; uero Rex priamus prandio celebrato suo sedit in solio in suis proposituis exultans 7 in excitatione ipo 2 important tune totus anellans filios suos pandem et Deyphebum uocauit Ad se et expresim mandauit eisdem ut in panonie prouinciam se ofterant festiuantes delaturos secum milites secum strenuos quos in Grecia aim nauigio secum ferant. Et eodem die idem Rex predes pandem et deyphebum exegit Ad iter. qui statim a rege ipo obtenta licentia recessut. ¶Sequenti uo die idem Rex priamus vniuersos aues troie ad gnale colloquium et quetum entibz illis ſhis est eos smonibz alloquitus.

sapiens potest pro ceito tenere Boni 2 o saen tias ignorates futura posse presare deouum? Non hoc sapientis est credere aut ~ hoc procedit ex sola stulticie leuitate. Pergat igitur Ellenus si timore ocititur in templis et slebrare diuina et siuat alios qui Libe uericu

Colloquiu 2 gnale priami ad Ciues suos Ostideles et dilecti Ciues. Satis e notis uobis quantis fuerimus p greco 2 supeibias multis ob probuosio et dapnio in nu merabilibus lacessiti nec uos latet passos 2 mmuniam aim etiam alieni fabula fecimus

73   Giustino di Gherardino da Forlì, attrib., *The Speech of Priam to the Citizens of Troy* and *Priam in his Council Hall*, from Guido de Columnis, *Historia destructionis Troiae*, *c*.1370. Parchment, 33 × 22.9 cm. Geneva-Cologny, Biblioteca Bodmeriana, Cod. 78, f. 18v.

74 Giustino di Gherardino da Forlì, attrib., *The Emperor and the Pope make Peace in front of San Marco*, from *Storia di Alessandro III*, *c*.1370. Parchment, 33 × 22.9 cm. Venice, Museo Civico Correr, Cod. Correr I 383 (1497).

true of the Madrid manuscript of about twenty years earlier, but in the Bodmer miniatures there is a significant change. Only in this later work are the protagonists consistently distinguished according to nationality: the Greeks wearing Paleologan hats and the Trojans pointed phrygian caps (Plate 75).[90] Thus, even the ancient world was beginning to be viewed in a more subtle and differentiated way. It was a significant, if sometimes bizarre, step beyond the Ambrosiana Livy.[91]

Another new feature in the Bodmer manuscript is a series of portraits of Greek and Trojan leaders and their wives, the heir to the great genealogical compendia in world chronicles such as that of Fra Paolino and the diminutive counterpart of fresco cycles of famous men and women then being painted on walls of private palaces throughout Italy (Plate 76). Antenor, Priam, and Hector are all present and accounted for, confirming in a reassuring way the nobility and antiquity of Venice's own past.

75 Giustino di Gherardino da Forlì, attrib., *Fight between Greeks and Trojans*, from Guido de Columnis, *Historia destructionis Troiae*, *c*.1370. Parchment, 33 × 22.9 cm. Geneva-Cologny, Biblioteca Bodmeriana, Cod. 78, f. 66.

76 Giustino di Gherardino da Forlì, attrib., *Trojan Heroes*, from Guido de Columnis, *Historia destructionis Troiae*, *c*.1370. Parchment, 33 × 22.9 cm. Geneva-Cologny, Biblioteca Bodmeriana, Cod. 78, f. 27v.

77 *Romulus and Remus building the Walls of Rome*, from Petrarch, *De viris illustribus*, *c.*1400. Parchment, 34.1 × 23 cm (entire page). Darmstadt, Hessische Landes- und Hochschulbibliothek, Cod. 101, f. 4v.

All these manuscripts, from the Fermo Suetonius to the Bodmer *Historia Troiana*, display different aspects of a "new realism" that informed Venetian art in this period. It can be seen in the capitals and sculptural groups of the Palazzo Ducale and in the panel paintings of Lorenzo Veneziano and Nicoletto Semitecolo. It can be seen as well in the marginal glosses of the Venetian chancery secretary Paolo de' Bernardo on his copy of the first decade of Livy. At one point he makes a comment about costume and insignia: "Note that from the Etruscans the Romans had lictors, the curule chair, the purple-bordered toga, as it is here, and military insignia, according to Sallust." At another, he is concerned with geography: "Note here and elsewhere, that the Janiculum is the temple of Janus and this Janiculus is a certain hill in Rome."[92] But there was no consistent vision of life in the ancient world articulated in the visual arts; the archeological pretensions of the Suetonius remained the exception in Venice.

To find the semblance of an artistic expression that did justice to Petrarch's vision of a separate Roman world, a Venetian humanist might have looked to the fresco cycles of Roman heroes and deeds in the princely palaces of the terraferma.[93] These paintings have largely vanished, leaving few traces, but one important record remains: an illustrated manuscript now in Darmstadt, of Petrarch's *De viris illustribus* (Plate 77). It is, in all likelihood, a fair copy of the history paintings in the Sala Virorum Illustrium of the Reggia Carrarese in Padua. Attributed to the circle of the Veronese artist Altichiero, it is the earliest surviving example in manu-

script painting of the depiction of Roman historical events with settings based upon actual Roman monuments. Like the golden bull of Ludwig of Bavaria, the drawings appear to be the product of direct visual observation, but with an important distinction. In the manuscript, the monuments are not privileged – plucked out from the ambient and regrouped to form a symbol of the city. Rather, they remain subordinate to the integrity of the landscape, and thus serve as a component of a setting for narrative action. And yet the actors on this Roman stage remain resolutely of the fourteenth century: their garments are the tailored *veste* of Veneto gentlemen and not the draped *togae* of Roman citizens. Even though the life-sized Roman heroes once painted on the walls above, and now destroyed, were probably clad in appropriate dress and armor as in the Fermo Suetonius, it would take another half-century before artists consistently clothed Roman actors in Roman costumes and placed them in a Roman architectural setting in history paintings.[94]

And yet, the Paduan program was an important first step in the realization of Petrarch's vision. What was truly new in his approach to antiquity was his concept of loss, separation, *and* revival. With the classical text as his initial frame of reference, he moved toward a notion of the classical world – most of whose monuments were now in a ruined state – as something that demanded restoration. This attitude, leading first to antiquarianism in the fifteenth century, was a necessary precursor to the scientific archeological approach of the sixteenth.

4

ANTIQUE FRAGMENTS, RENAISSANCE EYES

> Rome, still thy ruins grand beyond compare,
> Thy former greatness mournfully declare,
> Though time thy stately palaces around,
> Hath strewed and cast thy temples to the ground . . .
> Fallen is that city, whose proud fame to reach,
> I merely say, "Rome was," there fails my speech.
> — Hildebert of Lavardin, Archbishop of Tours, *c.*1100[1]

The fascination with ancient ruins associated with Petrarch had a considerable history. But while Hildebert praised the grandeur of what remained, he accepted the finality of its loss. The same was true of the Greek emperor Theodore II Lascaris, who visited the ruins of Pergamon in the middle of the thirteenth century:

> The City is full of theatres, grown old and decrepit with age, showing as through a glass their former splendor and the nobility of those who built them . . . Such things does the city show unto us, the descendents, reproaching us with the greatness of ancestral glory. Awesome are these compared to the buildings of today . . . The works of the dead are more beautiful than those of the living.[2]

In his letter of 1341 to the Dominican monk Giovanni Colonna di San Vito, Petrarch reminisced about their tour of Rome and recalled that they had walked together "through the remains of a broken city."[3] For Petrarch, who abjured the word "ruina" in favor of "vestigia," the classical ruin was more than just a fragment of a vanished, and happily vanquished, pagan world.[4] It was a sign of incompleteness: the vestige of an original intact culture that lay there still, if invisible, beneath the surface. Indeed, his discourse on the Roman past was cast in the present tense: "Here one can still see the wretched Lucretia lying upon her sword and the adulterer fleeing his death, as well as Brutus the defender of violated chastity."[5]

Most importantly, the evocative power of Rome's tumbled down structures also rendered them conceptually open symbols and potentially intact. Like corrupt classical texts, they required exhumation and reconstruction, and from those texts

they would receive a restored population. Petrarch spoke of pagan literature in archaeological terms, of unearthing fragments in order to bring them together in a "laudable act of healing."[6] The emphasis was reversing from the "past in the present" of the Ambrosiana Livy toward a present looking back at an exemplary past as a model for the future.

The emergence of a scientific approach to the past that is now termed archaeological would take at least another two hundred years to realize, the culmination of a lengthy process that had begun well before Petrarch's time. One way to track the evolution of the new mentality is through changing attitudes toward the classical ruin. Medieval writers such as Hildebert of Lavardin had considered the ruins of Rome the inevitable byproduct of the collapse of paganism in the face of Christianity: imperfect because broken and damaged, but valuable because exploitable for building material. Eventually such ruins came to be seen as beautiful in themselves because signs of an original whole. The new vision involved the capacity to look at Rome and to see the ancient ruins as something distinct and different in function, as well as form, from medieval buildings; or to look at medieval buildings and to see the immured antique spolia as extraneous relics of another time.[7]

Although Petrarch's own approach was more textual than visual, no longer was the classical artifact to be regarded as simply a commodity to be exploited or a treasure to be collected (although it remained both of these). From now on it was also a historical document to be recorded and described. Petrarch recognized the traditional equation between classical artifacts and buried treasure in a letter to Francesco Nelli in 1355, but he made an important distinction:

The farmer who while tilling the soil happened to discover under the Janiculum seven Greek and seven Latin books and the tomb of King Numa Pompilius was really doing something else; often there came to me in Rome a vinedigger, holding in his hands an ancient jewel or a golden Latin coin, sometimes scratched by the hard edge of a hoe, urging me either to buy it or to identify the heroic faces inscribed on them; and often while putting in supports for a sound foundation a builder has discovered a golden urn or a treasure hidden in the ground. Which of these with their unusual treasure became famous for his artistry or talent? For these are the gifts of fortune, not the laudable merits of men.[8]

What would change was intent. For high purpose would begin to rival chance and avarice as the motive force of discovery.[9]

THE *NOTABILIA* OF GIOVANNI DONDI

The travel diary of the Paduan physician and inventor Giovanni Dondi dall'Orologio, written during his pilgrimage to Rome around 1375, reveals the new attitude. He is fascinated by ruins: describing the most prominent remains; taking measurements of such monuments as the Pantheon, Trajan's column, and the Vatican obelisk; and copying classical inscriptions. He cites sources and deals with complex structures such as the Colosseum. One cannot but agree with his entry on the Arch of Constantine: "[there] are many sculpted letters, but they are read with difficulty."[10] Most tellingly, Dondi substitutes the term "notabilia" for "mirabilia" (which he never uses).[11] His aim is to record "notable things of the pagans which are to some extent in Rome to this day, and they show how great they were, whose equal is not seen elsewhere . . . ," and adding almost as an afterthought, "beyond which there are churches of Christians and holy relics of saints."[12]

In a letter to a friend, Dondi spoke of the small number of classical objects that still remained and of the high prices paid for them "by those who have a feeling for the matter." That these cognoscenti included artists as well as collectors is suggested by an anecdote in the same letter, which modern scholars often cite as evidence of a new visual, rather than purely literary, approach to ancient remains:

I myself used to know a marble sculptor – a craftsman in this field, famous among those whom Italy then had, particularly in working figures. More than once I heard him discuss the statues and sculptures he had seen in Rome with such admiration and veneration that in his discourse he seemed to be all beyond himself, so full of wonder was the subject. It was said that once he came along with five friends [to a site] where some images were to be seen; he looked and was·so arrested by the wonder of the craftsman-

ship [*artificii*] that he forgot his company and stood there until his friends had gone on a half a mile or more . . .[13]

It is significant that Dondi's activities did not involve the appropriation of the objects themselves, but rather the "paper collecting" of classical inscriptions. Already in the 1340s the Roman notary Cola di Rienzo, friend of Petrarch and thwarted apostle of municipal reform, had been acutely aware of the moral and political authority of classical inscriptions. His anonymous biographer wrote: "Every day he would gaze at the marble engravings which lie about in Rome. He alone knew how to read the ancient inscriptions. He translated all the ancient writings; he interpreted those marble shapes perfectly."[14] Indeed, as objects became more rare and more costly to acquire, inscriptions remained available even to the most impecunious humanist, and epigraphic collections on paper, known as sylloges, would become one of the defining characteristics of the antiquarian movement of the fifteenth century.[15] Thus for a small group of cognoscenti, amazement begins to give way to analysis; the quest is not just for treasure, but also for knowledge; and the search for ancient remains takes on the semblance of scholarly research.

THE *AUTOPSÍA* OF MANUEL CHRYSOLORAS

In the last years of the fourteenth century, the attention of humanists and collectors was directed toward the Greek lands, as witness Coluccio Salutati's invitation to the Byzantine scholar Manuel Chrysoloras to teach Greek in Florence.[16] Not only were Florentine humanists such as Niccolò Niccoli inspired to collect Greek antiquities, but from Chrysoloras they learned a new way to look at remnants of the past. In a perceptive analysis of his *Comparison of Old and New Rome* of 1411, Christine Smith points to the Byzantine habit of mentally reconstructing an original monument from the fragments that remained, and thus "to read the remnant as signifying an ideal whole." As she observes, such refashionings were fundamental to the Renaissance recovery of classical culture.[17]

In a significant step beyond Petrarch, Chrysoloras was explicit in his employment of the ruin to make a full visual reconstruction of Roman culture without the mediation of a text:

Like our own city, Rome uses itself as a mine and quarry, and (as we say to be true of everything) it both nourishes and consumes itself . . . Nonetheless, even these ruins and heaps of stones show what great things once existed, and how enormous and beautiful were the original constructions . . . These remains of statues, columns, tombs, and buildings reveal not only the wealth, large labor force, and craftsmanship of the Romans as well as their grandeur and dignity, if you will, and their ambition, love of beauty, luxury and extravagance, but also their piety, greatness of soul, love of honor, and intelligence . . . They speak of Rome's victories, her general well-being, dominion, dignity, and deeds in war . . . Thus one can see clearly what kinds of arms the Ancients had, what kind of clothes they wore, what the devices of their rulers were, how they formed lines of battle, fought, laid siege, and built encampments . . . Herodotus, and some other historians, are thought to have made useful contributions to our knowledge of such things. But these reliefs show how things were in past times and what the differences were between the peoples. Thus they make our knowledge of history precise or, rather, they grant us eyewitness knowledge [*autopsía*] of everything that has happened just as if it were present [*parousía*] . . .[18]

Ancient images and artifacts were thus superior to the written history of a Herodotus because they offered unmediated testimony – "autopsía" – an attitude that would become one of the fundamental tenets of modern archaeology. And yet, for Chrysoloras, the ruin was still only a metaphor for a lost wholeness, that once restored, would provide a compelling model for the present.

In the early years of the fifteenth century, therefore, two approaches to antiquity and its remains had emerged: the literary or text-based approach formulated by Petrarch and followed by most humanist scholars, and the primarily visual or object-based approach pursued by collectors, by artists such as Donatello and Brunelleschi, and by travelers such as Cristoforo Buondelmonti. The approaches were not necessarily mutually exclusive, and both flourished in a wide range of permutations ranging from the learned Coluccio Salutati, who concentrated on the text to the exclusion of the object, to Poggio Bracciolini, whose impressive erudition was matched by his passion for Roman ruins, classical art, and the codices of ancient texts.[19]

Venice, as usual, was different. Her takeover of the terraferma, consolidated by the end of the third decade of the fifteenth century, ensured a constant exposure to the humanist culture and classical remains of mainland cities of Roman foundation such as Padua, Verona, and Brescia. Her hegemony in the Levant, moreover, remained viable if under increasing strain, even after the fall of Constantinople to the Turks in 1453. Trading activities involved a continuous back and forth traffic with her permanent colonies on Crete and other islands, which were rich in antique ruins.

Venice had its share of humanists and collectors even in the early fifteenth century, but lacking the eloquent empiricism of a Poggio, or a biographer such as Vespasiano dei Bisticci who ensured the lasting fame of Niccolò Niccoli and other Florentines with antiquarian interests, they are easily overlooked. It is a problem of both visibility and focus. During the earlier part of the century, Venetian antiquarians tended to concern themselves with codices and small-scale artifacts such as coins and gems, and it was only toward the end of the

century that the next generation would begin to assemble some of the most important collections of sculpture in Italy.[20]

Humanist writing in Venice, privileging political, religious, and family concerns, favored eloquence over the artifact. And yet, disparate voices can be heard. Venetian humanists were passionate collectors of classical texts, particularly those from the Greek sphere. Francesco Barbaro wrote to Guarino Veronese about his discovery of several Greek codices in a monastery at Frascati in 1426, "that you may know that in this age the good fortune and diligence of one 'barbarian' [Barbaro], unearthed near Rome these treasures of Greek learning which the Roman people allowed to be hidden and buried in squalor and dirt."[21] Other classical objects – coins, seals, gems – were also collected, bought, and sold, but seldom written about until we come to mid-century and the renowned collection assembled by the Venetian cardinal Pietro Barbo, later Pope Paul II.[22]

Indeed, the best information on Venetian antiquarianism in the early quattrocento comes from outside observers such as the Florentine priest Cristoforo Buondelmonti (c.1375 – after 1430), the "worthy predecessor" of that intrepid antiquarian and founding father of Greek archaeology – Cyriacus of Ancona – who will be discussed later.[23]

THE *MARMORA PULCRA* OF CRISTOFORO BUONDELMONTI

Buondelmonti was part of the circle of Niccolò Niccoli in Florence. Inspired by the teaching of Chrysoloras and armed with a first-hand knowledge of Ptolemy's *Geography*, he sailed to Rhodes in 1414 to further his study of Greek and to search for classical texts. Over the next five years he acquired a number of books from monasteries on various islands and shipped them back to Florence: on Crete he found codices of Aristotle, Gregory of Nyssa and Libanius; on Imbros, Plutarch's *Lives*; and on Andros, his most important find, the *Hieroglyphica* of Horapollo.[24] But Buondelmonti's interests were geographical as much as they were textual, and for the next sixteen years or so, he traveled throughout the Aegean exploring dozens of islands. In 1417 he wrote his *Descriptio insule Crete*, based on a twenty-four-day tour by boat and mule of the entire island, and sent the manuscript back to Niccolò Niccoli.[25] Three years later he finished a draft of the *Liber Insularum Archipelagi*, a more comprehensive work, which includes an account of Constantinople and sixty-six islands or island groups of the Aegean.[26] Although Buondelmonti was well versed in the classics, the visual approach is predominant in his accounts. Both itineraries are notable for their liberal inclusion of maps and for their paucity of recorded inscriptions, despite the writer's demonstrated epigraphical interests. The texts of the two treatises underwent several revisions and numerous redactions and are the first examples of the Renaissance *isolario* – a new type of geographical treatise. In a manuscript of the *Liber Insularum* once owned by Pope Pius II, twenty-three of the islands are depicted with classical ruins – among the earliest drawings of the type (Plates 78–80).[27]

Buondelmonti's emphasis on Crete is not surprising. One of the most important of Venice's Aegean colonies, it was called by some her "nazione ultramarina."[28] Despite a short-lived rebellion in 1363–4, the island remained in Venetian hands from 1204 until 1645, when it was captured by the Turks.[29] It is important to stress the intimate relationship that existed in this period between Venice and her Aegean possessions, far closer and more vital than their distance apart would suggest. Frequent changes of officials and an active trade in agricultural products – cereal grain, wine, goat cheese, and sugar cane – ensured a continually renewed presence of Venice in Crete and, vice versa, of Crete in Venice. The Venetian Senate referred to it as "isola nostra Creta copiosa et fertilis biadis" – our island of Crete, copious and fertile with grain.[30] Some of the most prominent and powerful Venetian families

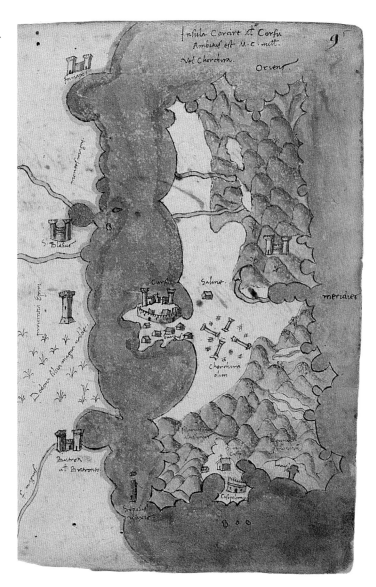

79 *Corfu and Corcyra*, from Cristoforo Buondelmonti, *Liber insularum archipelagi*. Venice, Biblioteca Nazionale Marciana, Cod. Lat. XIV 45 (4595), f. 5 (old f. 9).

78 *Crete*, from Cristoforo Buondelmonti, *Liber insularum archipelagi*. Venice, Biblioteca Nazionale Marciana, Cod. Lat. XIV 45 (4595), f. 34 (old f. 67).

had branches in Crete, and there were frequent visits and relocations. It was not unusual for natives of Crete to move to Venice or, conversely, to be born in Venice and to die in Crete.[31]

Although Buondelmonti was ostensibly searching for codices, he was as susceptible as any humanist of his time to the lure of classical ruins. Tireless in seeking out what remained of Homer's "Crete of the hundred cities," he described a mountainous terrain dotted with great ruined metropolises, Orthodox and Latin churches, and settlements of Venetians and native Greeks. Skirting a shore lined with palm trees and a great number of windmills, his boat approaches the capital city from the sea (Plate 81):

A mile beyond, the walls of the city of Candia, glisten with whiteness. This town, called Ghandaca by the Greeks, has an artificial port. Flanked by walls and towers for protection, it stretches out to give shelter from the wind. It happens, nevertheless, that the arrival of ships is rendered difficult by the violent squalls.[32]

After disembarking, Buondelmonti follows a wide road to the public square:

> To the right of this street in a conspicuous location I observed a majestic portico with steps, inside which sat a group of citizens; in the middle presiding over them were the governors of the entire island sent by the illustrious city of Venice. Offering a welcome in front of this public assembly, the notary Bonaccorsi [Grimani] honored me with these amiable words: "Very dear brother, if you have so much desire to visit this isle, tell me, I ask, so that I can assist you with all the means in my power." Briefly, I told him everything. Then he began to show me the town [saying]: "This does not number among the ancient cities,

but there where you see the port, to the east, there was a small citadel which formerly served to defend a city nearer to it. When the Romans had ravaged that city, what remained of the population retreated into that secure place and made a 'ghandac', that, is an enclave surrounded by houses pressed one against the other. Devastations followed in great number through the centuries. The Venetians bought the entire island and girded Candia with vast ramparts."[33]

The portico cited by Buondelmonti was probably the loggia built in 1325 as an assembly place for the Venetian colonists of the island; it was also the site of official proclamations and a departure point for great processions.[34] In all likelihood, Lorenzo de Monacis, the Chancellor of Crete since 1389, would also have been on hand to greet him. Like Bonaccorsi, Lorenzo was a notary and a native of the city of Venice, to which he returned frequently. A figure of some literary prominence, his role as chronicler of the Venetian Republic will be discussed further in chapter 5.[35]

Buondelmonti's description of Candia is disappointingly terse, but he is more expansive when faced with decaying ruins. Arriving at the summit of Monte di Giove, a mountain consecrated by the ancient Cretans to Zeus Soter, he observes:

> One sees spreading out all around some large villages and verdant vineyards. From a distance this mountain presents the profile of a face. On its brow, I recognized a temple of Jupiter, razed to the foundations. All around, we find dispersed a great number of statues and enormous blocks of stone: we believe that whoever cut them was not [just] a man! After our explorations on the brow of the mountain, we arrived on its nose where we counted three chapels joined together. The first is the church of the Savior because, on this mountain Jupiter was principally worshipped. The second was called Pandon Aghion, that is the church of All Saints, because the universe was governed by numerous gods; the third is consecrated to St. George because in antiquity the dominion of Crete was acquired by the sword.[36]

Near the course of the Massala river Buondelmonti comes upon some ruins at the edge of a plain and identifies them from his Ptolemy as the ancient city of Pollirena:

> From this direction I admired at length a magnificent fountain with enormous blocks of overturned stones. Near the town I had a view of a vast plain surrounded by very rich mountains covered with cypresses. In this plain, the flocks graze on a flowery meadow.[37]

Again, upon reaching the ancient port of Penix, now called Loutro:

> We entered a destroyed city of great antiquity with columns strewn all over the ground. Among them near some peasants' huts I found some sarcophagi made of a very

80 *Tenedos, the Dardanelles, and Troy*, from Cristoforo Buondelmonti, *Liber insularum archipelagi*. Venice, Biblioteca Nazionale Marciana, Cod. Lat. XIV 45 (4595), f. 43 verso (old f. 86).

81   Erhard Reuwich, *View of Candia*, detail from woodcut in Bernhard von Breydenbach, *Opusculum Sanctarum peregrinationum ad sepulcrum Christi venerandum*, Mainz 1486.

white marble where the pigs eat their slops. They forage amidst the magnificent sculptures that adorn the periphery. I saw numerous busts of broken idols, amongst which marble monuments were scattered about. I left this place after having seen vast and innumerable catacombs, and then saw some large towns toward the interior of the island. There I found the remaining members of six families of the ancient Roman nobility who even today are pleased to conserve their titles and coats of arms.[38]

Buondelmonti's reports help us to understand the central role of the *stato da mar* in shaping a peculiarly Venetian perception of the ancient world. The Aegean islands must have seemed like the mountains of Arcady, with sheep and goats wandering amongst the silent and shattered fragments of classical antiquity.[39] Along these lines, one of his most telling observations concerns a Venetian nobleman with cultivated tastes:

Nearby we saw the citadel of Pediada, surrounded by very rich land [Plate 82]. To the north, in a hamlet we saw the [territory of the] bishopric of Chirsonesus, which we visited, and to the south we distinguished in the distance the bishopric of Arcadia. Then continuing toward the east, in a valley, I made the acquaintance of a noble and learned gentleman. He is called Nicolas and descends from the Scipios. He has no heirs and lives in a grove, a *viridarium* like a pleasure garden, that he has constructed and adorned with the most ancient marbles, and whatever pleasure the body finds in trees is found abundantly there. He delights in reading Latin books and occasionally a work of Dante. From the mouth of a marble statue flows a natural spring; to the right and to the left his ancestors had placed the busts of Mark Antony and Pompey. I noticed some beautiful marbles [*marmora pulchra*] that were brought there from other structures.[40]

Nicolas and his forefathers had probably found the pieces of classical sculpture in the nearby ruins of the ancient city of Lyktos. A member of the powerful Cornaro family of Venice who claimed descent from the Roman *gens Cornelia* (that is,

the Scipios), he boasted a distinguished lineage that was later acknowledged in the naming of his great-nephew Scipion, born in Crete in 1462.[41] Although Nicolas's sculpture collection included the busts of two Roman Republican generals, his relationship with antiquity was not only civic and political; it was also intimate, subjective, and personal. It was the private world of the *locus amoenus* that would become one of the defining features of Venetian villa life a century or so later. Of the Cornaro villa, situated in the foothills below the village of Pediados (Plate 83), only the foundations remain today, along with some terraces and bullrushes growing out of the ancient fountain.[42] It was, in all likelihood, not the only Venetian country residence on a Greek island at that time in which a classical ambience was reclaimed with ancient spolia.

If we exclude Petrarch's villa at Arquà, which seems almost suburban by contrast, Buondelmonti's notice may well be the earliest surviving account of a Renaissance re-creation of the pastoral retreat inspired by the evocative descriptions of Pliny and other ancient writers. Without further laboring the point, it seems that the origins of the pastoral tradition in painting lie not only in the foothills of the Italian alps, but also in the Venetian *stato da mar*. The juxtaposition of ancient ruins and

pastoral settings of shady groves and natural springs on islands in the Aegean surely helped to engender the distinctive Venetian concept of antiquity as a world of shepherds, nymphs, and verdant groves.

The milieu was familiar as well to the intrepid Ciriaco de' Pizzicolli, more appropriately called by his Latin name Cyriacus, who would attempt a more systematic restitution of the ancient world.

THE *SIGILLA HISTORIARUM* OF CYRIACUS OF ANCONA

The peripatetic activities of Cyriacus are well known.[43] Armed with such classical texts as Pliny's *Natural History* and Strabo's *Geography* and modern ones such as Buondelmonti's *Liber Insularum* as his guidebooks, he traveled through Italy and the Aegean in search of the monuments and inscriptions of the ancient world. He called these artifacts "relics of sacrosanct antiquity" and "sigilla historiarum": the validating seals of history.[44] And like Chrysoloras he saw the material object as a witness to past deeds, to be given "more faith and notice than books themselves."[45] Cyriacus recorded what he saw – not

CASTEL PEDIADA

82　*Crete, Castel Pediada.* From Francesco Basilicata, *Relazione, 1630, all'ill.mo ed Ecc.mo S.re et Padrone mio Col.mo il S.r Pietro Giustiniano, dignissimo Cap.no Generale nel regno di Candia,* 1614–15. Venice, Biblioteca Nazionale Marciana, 284 D. 39, fol 61, *c.*58.

83　*Crete, Kastelos* (near Skjili). View from the south, with the ruins of Castel Pediada on top of the hill, 1900–02. Venice, Istituto Veneto di Scienze, Lettere ed Arti, Archivio Fotografico della Missione Cretese di Giuseppe Gerola, Lastra 704.

without editing – in annotated notebooks that he called his "commentaria": drawings and descriptions of classical monuments, ruins, bits and pieces of architecture, coins, gems, sculpture, and even exotic animals, as well as numerous inscriptions in Latin and Greek (Plate 84). By the time of his death in 1452, the notebooks had grown to six large volumes.[46] With the exception of a single twenty-four-page gathering bound into a manuscript in the Biblioteca Ambrosiana in Milan that will be discussed later, virtually all the original *Commentaria* seem to have been destroyed by fire in 1514.[47] But vestiges remain; for Cyriacus had often copied out excerpts for his patrons and friends, and many of these found their way into other sylloges that were then recopied at second and third hand.[48] A number of letters also survive, as well as a manuscript account of his life begun by his friend and fellow Anconitan, Francesco Scalamonti, and continued by his disciple Felice Feliciano.[49] It is thus possible to get a proximate sense of a life devoted, as Cyriacus himself put it so well, to "awakening the dead."[50]

Celebrated by the Venetian Jacopo Zeno as "the one and

only liberator and preserver, patron, and parent of antiquity,"[51] Cyriacus has inspired a huge literature that began in his own time. As Scalamonti reports, Cyriacus's aim, "as we often heard from his mouth," was to see for himself, "whatever is left in the world, to the furthest shores of the oceans and all the way to the island of Thule."[52] With the specific goal of understanding more fully Cyriacus's impact on the Venetian sense of antiquity, this study will restrict itself to his relationship to Venetians, whether in Venice itself, the terraferma, or the Levant. Indeed, it was a close and continuous one throughout his life; it is not by chance that Scalamonti's biography of Cyriacus was dedicated to Lauro Quirini – a Venetian humanist.[53]

Born in 1391, Cyriacus first visited Venice at the age of nine with his grandfather. He was to return on a number of occasions, drawn by family ties to the house of Contarini, as well as by the opportunity to renew contacts with numerous friends and clients. These included galley captains and merchants; collectors, antiquarians, and humanists; and clerics of every rank. When he toured the classical ruins of Pula in 1418–19, recording Latin inscriptions that he could not yet read, his guide was the Venetian podestà Andrea Contarini. Scalamonti writes that Cyriacus

> observed that a great part was consumed by age. But he saw the noble vestiges of most of its antiquities. And he saw the excellent gate built by Salvia Postuma, daughter of Sergius the Duumvir and Aedile. And he saw the noble amphitheatre built of huge stones . . . and innumerable sepulchral stones inside the city and outside at the shore, of which the majority had noble inscriptions . . .[54]

In 1421 another Venetian, the Cardinal Gabriele Condulmer, employed Cyriacus to handle the financial arrangements for the reconstruction of the harbor of Ancona.

In so doing, he may well have been the unknowing instrument of Cyriacus's conversion from antiquarianism as avocation to antiquarianism as ruling passion. For it was during this period that Cyriacus subjected the inscription on the arch of Trajan to a close and prolonged scrutiny and thereby realized the importance of epigraphical material as primary historical evidence.[55] He was finally inspired to study Latin and adopted the Trajanic inscription as a personal emblem of sorts. It later became his standard preface for the excerpts of selected inscriptions that he gave to friends.[56] During a forty-day stay in Condulmer's palace in Rome in 1424, Cyriacus seems to have been inspired to begin his first volume of the *Commentaria*, filling it with inscriptions and drawings of ancient monuments. He remained close to the cardinal, even after the prelate's elevation to the papacy as Eugenius IV, and represented him frequently on diplomatic missions.[57]

Between 1425 and 1430, Cyriacus was employed by his Venetian relative Zaccaria Contarini as his agent in Cyprus. Now reasonably competent in Latin – he never reached the level of a Poggio or a Biondo – he began to teach himself Greek. Traveling not only to Cyprus, but also to Constantinople, Rhodes, Beirut, Damascus, Adrianople, and Macedonia, to name just a few of his landfalls, he dealt in virtually every kind of merchandise: carpets, wax, wine, slaves, and textiles, as well as manuscripts, antiquities, coins, and jewels. Chios became his base of operations, where his friendship with the Genoese merchant Andreolo Giustiniani gave him access to the best selection of antiquities in the Aegean to resell to an eager clientele in Italy.[58]

While Cyriacus also traveled extensively in Italy, it was the Greek world that held his fascination. His personal library included texts of Homer, Aristotle, Plato, Plutarch, Herodotus and a Strabo filled with *scholia* – comments and inscriptions in

84   After Cyriacus of Ancona, *Drawing of Ruins of the Amphitheatre at Delos*. Rome, Biblioteca Apostolica Vaticana, Cod. Vat. Lat. 5252, f. 19v–20.

his own hand based on his personal travel observations – in the margins.[59] Not surprisingly, many of his Venetian contacts were made in the Aegean. Around 1429 he is in Damascus with the Venetian Ermolao Donato.[60] In 1435 he is in Epirus "in the house of the magnificent lord Tomaso Venier" – Venetian galley captain and relative of the despot of Arta – where he copies a Greek inscription.[61] In 1436 he is outside Durazzo examining "the noble wall that C. Caesar built against the armies of Pompey in the time of civil war" with the Venetian podestà Fabricio Loredan and "our best friend," the *camerario* Antonio Longo.[63] In 1437 he is in the Venetian colony in Messenia, meeting with the podestà Maffeo Bollani, and his counselors M. Quirini and Bartolomeo Falier, "who received me most kindly," and touring the city with "the learned and generous" M. Calergio of Crete who pointed out "a number of remarkable antiquities."[63] In 1445 he is offshore Crete on the galley of the Venetian Johannes Delphin [Giovanni Dolfin], who showed him his personal collection of Roman coins and gems.[64] Indeed, one might say that Cyriacus brought the Greek east into the drawing rooms and *studioli* of the Latin west, supplying his clients and friends in Italy not only with antiquities, but also – through his inscriptions and excerpts – first-hand eye-witness knowledge of the ancient world. He had been there.

Among Cyriacus's several visits to Venice, two are particularly telling. On the first occasion, he offers an array of classical artifacts to a small, but zealous group of collectors. Ambrogio Traversari, a Florentine humanist and general of the Camaldolensian Order, stayed in Venice for a time in 1432–3 in the monastery at San Michele di Murano and wrote in his *Hodoeporicon*, a travel diary: "Cyriacus of Ancona came to us and showed us many monuments of that antiquity of which he was a *studiosissimus indagator*: *monumenta*, ancient inscriptions, inscribed coins, silver and gold, and seals."[65] Traversari also wrote several letters to Niccolò Niccoli in which he described gold and silver coins with images of Lysimachus, Alexander the Great, and Philip of Macedon, that Cyriacus had acquired in Smyrna (Traversari was dubious of the Macedonian provenance) as well as an effigy of Scipio the Younger incised "in lapide onychino" – an object of "summa elegantia."[66] Traversari also admired several objects already in Venetian collections that were shown him by the owners: Greek codices and silver coins, one of which bore the effigy of Alexander the Great, by the physician and humanist Pietro Tommasi; antique coins by Francesco Barbaro, who gave Traversari two Greek texts; medals and gold coins by Benedetto Dandolo who had collected them in Syria in his youth. Dandolo is perturbed that he had not been given advance notice of Traversari's visit, and the prelate is made to understand that "In fact, many coins of this kind are possessed by most of the nobles, which they would have been happy to show to me."[67] This would have been the milieu in which the young Pietro Barbo, sixteen years old at the time and later to become Pope Paul II, would have formed a taste for numismatics and *anticaglie* that led to one of the greatest collections of antiquities, particularly coins and cameos, of the fifteenth century.[68]

When Cyriacus visited Venice again in August 1436, the city without a classical past itself became an item in his *Commentaria*. He recorded on this occasion thirteen Latin epigrams, mostly in and around San Marco, and subjected the bronze horses above the main entrance of the basilica to close scrutiny. Making careful measurements of one of the horses and calculating its length from withers to tail and its height from rump to hoof, he copied down (correctly) an inscription – possibly a foundry mark – on its raised right hoof.[69] Undaunted by a lack of corroborating evidence, he did not hesitate to establish a Greek provenance for the bronzes, albeit by way of Rome. Reporting on his activities to Eugenius IV, he writes:

> Then after we had looked at all the major sites of the city for three days we finally made our way to the holy and highly decorated temple of St. Mark, where first we were allowed to inspect – not once, but as long as we liked – those four bronze chariot horses which are so splendid a work of art and most elegant design, the noble work indeed of Phidias, and once the glory of the temple of warlike Janus in Rome.[70]

Cyriacus's hosts could only have been pleased, and he continues with an account of his visit to the treasury of San Marco:

> Indeed, afterwards, inside the secret sanctuary of the temple, we saw the most costly and sacred monuments of the Gods and precious objects of gold and stones, and enormous pearls and most spectacular treasures. Amongst those showing all these extraordinary things, the Doge Francesco [Foscari] himself exhibited many precious vases inscribed with Greek letters, and handed them over to Francesco Barbaro and myself, so that we could read them.[71]

Barbaro was an old acquaintance. Fluent in Latin and Greek, he had translated several of Plutarch's *Lives* in 1415; two years later he wrote a treatise on marriage. He might well be considered a typical Venetian humanist: a public man for whom antique culture was most useful as a program for civic life.[72] Cyriacus later wrote of him to a young friend to whom he was giving advice about devising an impresa: "of course, [it should be] a distinguished animal, with some memorable and succinct motto beneath him, that one should wish to emulate, as did our most illustrious knight, Francesco Barbaro, who, bearing the excellent Ermine as an insignia, appended to it the epigram, 'POTIVS MORI QVAM FOEDARI' (Better death than dishonor)."[73]

This is a reminder that Cyriacus was more than simply a merchant and purveyor of rare objects. Indeed, certain of his activities had a profound and long lasting effect on Venetian perceptions about the ancient world. For perhaps his greatest contribution was in teaching others to look: to look beyond the aesthetically accessible remains of the past, such as gems and coins; to look at inscriptions for physical testimony more reliable than manuscript texts; to look at rubble and to discover not just building materials or broken stagesets for Roman history, but monuments resonant with meaning in themselves, and as such, like the classical texts of Petrarch's generation, demanding restoration.

Although Cyriacus's archaeological method may appear to us now to be quaint and grounded in an incongruous amalgam of fact and fantasy, it is not so far from a modern mentality. Driven by a romantic vision, it is informed by direct observation and a hard-headed empiricism. While Cyriacus's Latin transcriptions are far more reliable than the Greek, he aims at accuracy and completeness of description and takes pains to distinguish recorded material from his own emendations. Despite a few misidentifications of important monuments and a tendency toward optimistic attributions, what is truly impressive is how much he does get right.[74]

One of his most important contributions may be in his privileging the object over the literary text, a paradigm shift announced by Chrysoloras but implemented by Cyriacus. Signs of this shift are evident in his account of his first trip to Athens in 1436. He is mightily impressed by the Parthenon, but not so much as to discourage him from making his usual sharp-eyed description:

> I was most pleased to observe that on top of the city's citadel there is a huge, wondrous temple of the goddess Pallas, the noble work of Phidias. It is tall, with fifty-eight columns seven feet in diameter, [and] is decorated everywhere with handsome statues – on both façades, inside on the topmost band of the walls, and outside on the architraves, where a battle of centaurs is seen, marvelous products of the sculptor's art.[75]

That the temple had been transformed long before into a Christian church dedicated to the Virgin, and equipped with a baptistery, altar, and apse, is seemingly not worthy of note.[76]

Cyriacus's description holds three implications pointing toward a new historicism. First, he secularizes the monument, blunting the traditional medieval pagan–Christian antithesis. In so doing, he avoids the conflict still evident in Petrarch, who (it will be recalled) had referred to the Roman Pantheon as Santa Maria Rotonda, whom the Virgin had saved from destruction "by virtue of her name."[77] In Cyriacus's mind's eye, the Parthenon was mentally stripped of its medieval accretions and was reborn as a noble pagan temple.[78] He expresses, moreover, wonder at its beauty and not just its size.

Second, another account, written when he returned to Athens eight years later, reveals that Cyriacus had been able to identify the building and its iconography "from the testimony of Aristotle's words to King Alexander as well as from our own Pliny and a host of other notable authors."[79] Such a comment may seem obvious and unexceptional, but it implies a reversal of Petrarch's priorities. While Petrarch had looked at ruins to illuminate the text, Cyriacus read the texts to illuminate the ruins.

Third, with the classical text placed in service of the rediscovery of the original state of the monument and with a new systematic attitude toward the recovery of antiquity, restoration – conceptual or otherwise – is privileged and the historical caesura of the Middle Ages acknowledged in a material sense.

Another aspect of Cyriacus's new historicism concerns the ability to differentiate styles, an essential element in distancing the past. Cyriacus visited Samothrace in 1444 and hiked up to the ruins of the ancient city of Palaeopolis. He was particularly taken with the great irregular walls that once enclosed it: "They stretched from a high, steep hill a long distance down the slopes that incline toward the sea, and their towers and gates, with their marvelous, varied architectural styles, are partly still extant." Observing the diverse character of the masonry, which varies from ashlar to polygonal and whose relative dating is disputed even today, Cyriacus shows unmistakable signs of a developing critical sense of relative chronology.[80]

Cyriacus's letter to a Venetian friend describing the rock crystal intaglio of Pallas Athene shown him by Johannes Delphin on a galley off Crete one evening in 1445 indicates a considerable gift for visual analysis, even though he misidentifies the subject and gender of the portrait. The survival of the gem, now in Berlin, allows us to share his experience of an object that evoked a response of both reason and delight (Plate 85).[81] Dating the letter, "In the fifteenth year of Pope Eugenius and 1023 years from the foundation of Venice" (he was off by only one year),[82] Cyriacus writes:

And to tell you something really remarkable . . . among other things of the kind, he showed me a noble seal of crystal, of the size of one's thumb; it was engraved in very deep relief by the wonderful skill of the artist Eutyches with the portrait of Alexander of Macedon, helmeted, as far down as the breast; and for an ornament of the polished helmet two heads of rams impressed in front, with twisted horns – the very symbol of his father Jupiter Ammon: and at the very top a tiara is seen to bear on each side Molossian hounds, swift in the chase, of the highest artistic beauty: and under the helmet the prince most delicate with curls on either side, dressed in fine cloth and in a traveller's cloak with elaborate designs at the top seems to have moved his right hand which is bare to the elbow, holding out his clothing becomingly from the upper part of his chest: and his face with a wonderful expression and with royal aspect directing his gaze keenly, truly he seems to show living features from the glistening stone, and also his own heroic grandeur. When you hold up the thick part of the gem

85 *Pallas Athene*, end first century B.C. Rock crystal intaglio, 3.72 × 2.90 × 1.44 cm. Berlin, Staatliche Museen zu Berlin, Preussischer Kulturbesitz, Antikensammlung.

right towards the light, where the breathing limbs are seen to shine out in wondrous beauty with complete solidity, and with luminous crystal shadows in the hollows, we learn who is the maker of so splendid a thing, by the Greek letters – very ancient ones, too – carved above.[83]

Cyriacus's eye was rather more impressive than his hand, for his few surviving drawings are more earnest than eloquent. But one genre should not be separated from the other, for even in the section from his *Commentaria* that is now bound into a larger anthology of epigrams in Milan (Codex Ambrosiano-Trotti 373) there is an essential play between text and image.[84] The account was compiled during his second exploration of the Peloponnese. Beginning in Sparta in the summer of 1447 and armed with the codex of Strabo that he had just obtained in Constantinople, he works his way south down the peninsula.[85] By the end of the year he is back in Mistra where he spends the winter at the court of the despot of Morea Constantine Paleologus, along with the distinguished Greek scholar Gemisthos Pletho. While there, Cyriacus composes in Greek an essay on the Roman calendar and a rendition of the *Bellum Troianum* of Dictys of Crete and writes an ode to Sparta in vernacular Italian.[86]

The pages of the *Commentaria*, of which at least one leaf is missing, are a generous quarto-size (about 23 × 30.5 cm) and contain long narrative passages in Latin that are punctuated by Greek inscriptions. Twelve drawings of monuments are integrated into the text. It is worth noting that Cyriacus typically uses the verb *comperio* for his observations of these artifacts – implying the intellectual processes of discovery, learning, and finding out information – rather than *conspicio* or *video*, which emphasize the cognitive process of seeing. Indeed, his itinerary is nothing so much as a series of discoveries and revelations. He did not try to illustrate every monument that he saw and seems to have aimed for *varietà* – a representative sample of the kinds of things that could be found in the area.

In October, for example, he sailed down the coast of Taenarus and arrived at the village of Dryea:

> Where while remaining for a day we inspected most of the other estates lying in the plain: bountiful with cultivated fields, vineyards and groves of olive trees. Inside this area we examined several ancient monuments of noble illustrious Taenarus, and in the town of Dryea itself we discovered a marble statue of this sort with the ancient costume of an old farmer.[87]

The accompanying drawing conjures up a vision of antiquity that is more Arcadian than aulic (Plate 86).

Still in Taenarum at Porto Quaglio Cyriacus recorded inscriptions written with "Cameis vetustissimis litteris" (very ancient Corinthian letters) and inspected a huge cavern where, according to tradition, Hercules had dragged up Cerberus from the underworld. Despite warnings by local inhabitants about a dragon inside, the intrepid Cyriacus and several reluctant companions entered the cave and peered down into a bottomless abyss. On the way out he discovered and sketched a broken sculpture of a sleeping nymph, a subject that would have a long afterlife in Venetian art (Plate 87). In Nauplia he rendered the masonry of the city walls (Plate 88) and on the Argive plain: "a work of Polykleitos from the ancient shrine dedicated long ago to Hera of Argos and Mycenae and now destroyed, brought to the church of the blessed Virgin by men of later times and our religion as an ornament"[88] (Plate 89). The drawings of Hellenistic tomb reliefs that follow the text are thus set into the proper context, and the separation between the ancient past and the Christian present could not be more distinct.

It was from such pages that Cyriacus extracted choice items to be transcribed and given to friends. These in turn were avidly recopied by others. A scholar observes: "For in these numerous codices we are faced with the work of men who, in their enthusiasm for ancient inscriptions, collected them like stamps from any and every available source."[89]

One of the few surviving examples of an epitome from Cyriacus's own hand is found in the commonplace book of his friend Pietro Donato, the Venetian bishop of Padua. The codex, now in Berlin, is an antiquarian miscellany, containing a congeries of entries on 124 pages of expensive vellum: *De*

86 Cyriacus of Ancona, *Statue of Bacchus-type Figure*, from his *Commentaria*, 1447–8. Milan, Biblioteca Ambrosiana, Cod. Trotti 373, f. 110v.

constructione civitatis Venetiarum, a chronicle beginning with the invasion of Attila the Hun and ending with the foundation of the second Venice; genealogies of Roman families; religious and secular poetry; the epitaph on Petrarch's tomb at Arquà Petrarca; selections from Roman writers; and the ubiquitous classical inscriptions.[90] Cyriacus's personal contribution consists of ten sheets and was probably composed when he was in Padua in 1442–3. Beginning with the emblematic Latin inscription from the Arch of Trajan in Ancona, for the most part it consists of a selection of Greek inscriptions and epigrams, some with Latin translations, recorded on his trip to Athens in 1436. Also included are descriptions and sketches of monuments, passages from Plutarch and Horace, drawings of planets, and Greek and Latin alphabets. Cyriacus's epitome was no passive ornament to be bound into a larger collection and forgotten, for it contains marginal notes in another hand, probably that of Donato himself, such as a quotation from

87 Cyriacus of Ancona, *Sculpture of a Sleeping Nymph*, from his *Commentaria*, 1447–8. Milan, Biblioteca Ambrosiana, Cod. Trotti 373, f. 122.

88 Cyriacus of Ancona, *Walls of Nauplia*, from his *Commentaria*, 1447–8. Milan, Biblioteca Ambrosiana, Cod. Trotti 373, f. 113v.

Vitruvius written next to a drawing of the Temple of the Winds in Athens. In this manner, the sylloges became part of an ongoing and vital tradition.[91]

It is difficult to discern any principle of inclusion or organization other than Cyriacus's own fancy and the perceived interests of the intended recipient. Formally, however, the epitome represents a more sophisticated integration of text and image compared with what we have seen in the Trotti Codex. This higher level of organic unity is noticeable on the page in which Cyriacus's written description provides a backdrop and a frame for a sketch of the Parthenon (Plate 90). While Cyriacus undoubtedly penned the text, if the drawings are compared with those in the Trotti Codex, Degenhart and Schmitt's contention that the building with its pediment and the Panathenaic frieze below it were drawn by other hands is confirmed. In their view, a first unknown artist made the drawings in silverpoint, for which Cyriacus had indicated the

placement in relation to the text, and then a second artist went over the first rendition with pen and ink. In any case, the drawing must be a fair copy of Cyriacus's original sketch in the *Commentaria* made on the spot in Athens.[92] It shows the building stripped of its Christian accretions and conscientiously – if inaccurately – restored to its pristine state. It is surely for other reasons, perhaps the difficulty of rendering them properly in a limited space, that the triglyphs and metopes were also omitted and the pediment sculpture abbreviated.[93]

About forty years later, the Roman architect Giuliano da Sangallo copied Cyriacus's drawing into his sketchbook (Plate 91). Upon first glance it may be concluded that Sangallo has brought a new archaeological rigor to the task, for his drawing looks so much more accurate. But in fact, his Parthenon is no more true to the original than that of Cyriacus. It is simply distorted in a different way. Sangallo not only corrected the

89   Cyriacus of Ancona, *Hellenistic Tomb Relief*, from his *Commentaria*, 1447–8. Milan, Biblioteca Ambrosiana, Cod. Trotti 373, f. 115.

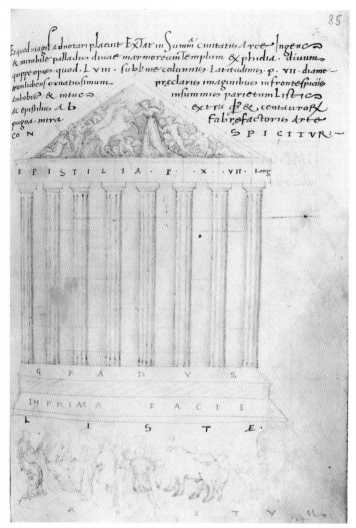

90 Unknown artists, after Cyriacus of Ancona, *Parthenon*, west front and parts of the frieze, from the *Collectanea* of Pietro Donato. Parchment, 25 × 17cm. Berlin, Staatsbibliothek zu Berlin, Preussischer Kulturbesitz, Cod. Hamilton 254, f. 85.

proportions, he also added, gratuitously, an attic story behind the pediment on which he drew the metope reliefs from the south side of the building. These too were probably copied from a separate Ciriacan source, this one unknown today, but now they were rationalized and incorporated by the architect into a completely new and fanciful structure. In fact, it resembles the Pantheon in Rome more than it does the Greek original. In short, Sangallo recast the Athenian monument that he had never seen into a familiar Roman archetype.[94]

Another telling Venetian connection for Cyriacus is indicated by a drawing in sepia ink on parchment of a rather spectacular equestrian monument. Although it bears an inscription with the name of Theodosius, its identification as the statue of Justinian that once stood on a high column in Constantinople is more plausible.[95] The sketch, now convincingly attributed to Cyriacus himself by Degenhart and Schmitt, is bound into a manuscript of excerpts from classical

authors in the University Library in Budapest (Plate 92). The next page — the last in the codex — bears a signature:

IHS

Johannes Darius scripsit atramento nimphirii
per ipsum Kiriaco Aconitano ad scribendum
adducto

(Johannes Darius wrote [this] with the ink of Nimphirius When Cyriacus of Ancona had been persuaded by his [Dario's] advice to draw [it]).[96]

Whether "Nimphirius" is a proper name, a place, or a type of ink (all have been suggested) is not so important as the fact that the entry puts Cyriacus into a close relationship to the merchant and notary Giovanni Dario. Although Dario was born in Crete, where Cyriacus visited three times and where

91 Giuliano da Sangallo, *Parthenon*, west front and parts of the frieze, from his *Book of Drawings*. Rome, Biblioteca Apostolica Vaticana, Cod. Barb. Lat. 4424, f. 28v.

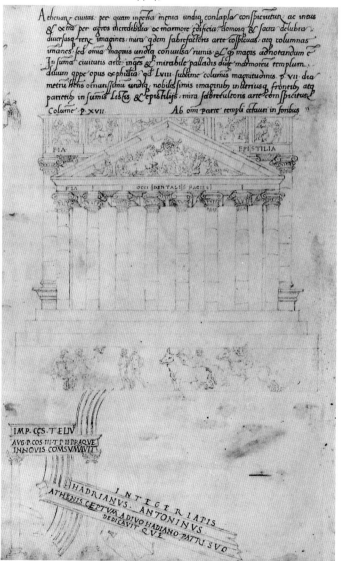

92 Cyriacus of Ancona, *Equestrian Monument of the Byzantine Emperor Justinian*. Drawing. Budapest, Budapest University Library, MS It. 3, f. 144v.

they may have become acquainted, his diplomatic and linguistic skills later carried him to the highest levels of the Venetian Chancery. His most outstanding public achievement would be the negotiation of a peace treaty with the Sultan Mehmed II in 1479 and his most impressive private undertaking the construction of Ca' Dario on the Grand Canal. Dario's earlier acquaintance with Cyriacus, with a shared passion for antiquarian concerns, helps to explain the humanist inscription on his palace façade by a patron whose literary legacy consists only of diplomatic dispatches and not of poetry or philological scholarship.[97]

Cyriacus's drawing may also have played a role in the formulation of a view of Constantinople in a copy of the *Notitia Dignitatum* made in Basel in 1436 for Bishop Pietro Donato (Plate 93). The artist, Perronet Lamy, was working from a Carolingian copy of a late antique text that consisted, for the most part, of a catalogue of high offices of the Roman government. Several of Lamy's illustrations, including the view of Constantinople and a page featuring authentic drawings of the coins of Tiberius, Nero, and Domitian were, however, the artist's own inventions. Notations added to the

end of the volume in Cyriacus's own hand suggest his presence, if not his direct participation, in the fuller elaboration of the manuscript.[98]

Cyriacus's empiricism would have gratified a long-standing Venetian predilection for eye-witness accounts. And yet it is his romantic side, nurtured in the Aegean, that would contribute to the rise of the pastoral vision of classical antiquity in Venetian art at the end of the century. For like Buondelmonti, Cyriacus also viewed antique ruins in the context of *locus amoenus*. Scalamonti describes a visit to Cyprus, where

> he saw the noble ancient monuments of antiquity, walls, columns, statues, bases, and inscriptions in Doric letters . . . He also saw there very pleasant places; he saw verdant meadows, lovely to see, and fruitful royal cedars of paradise and flowering gardens, worthy specimens of the four quarters of the world and of the middle latitude of the *oikumene*.[99]

93 Perronet Lamy, *Constantinople*, from a copy of the *Notitia Dignitatum* commissioned by Pietro Donato. Parchment, 25 × 17 cm. Oxford, The Bodleian Library, Cod. Canon Misc. 378, f. 84.

Despite his high-minded use of Latin and Greek in the *Commentaria*, Cyriacus also wrote vernacular poetry. In an exchange of sonnets, the erudite Leonardo Giustiniani, a Venetian disciple of Guarino of Verona and one of Cyriacus's best clients, responded to him in one passage:

> Your voice renders such a gentle harmony,

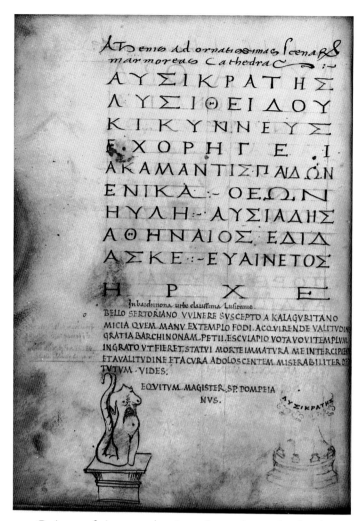

94 Cyriacus of Ancona, drawing of a sculpture in the Agora, Athens, from the *Collectanea* of Pietro Donato. Parchment, 25 × 17 cm. Berlin, Staatsbibliothek zu Berlin, Preussischer Kulturbesitz, Cod. Hamilton 254, f. 88v.

95 Giuliano da Sangallo, detail of a nymph holding a galley, from his *Book of Drawings*. Rome, Biblioteca Apostolica Vaticana, Cod. Barb. Lat. 4424, f. 28r.

one almost believes that the lips of Orpheus, Apollo and
   Amphione
never let free a more beautiful song.[100]

The gentle spirit comes through as well in a whimsical drawing of the nymph Cymodoce – "supreme goddess of the nereid nymphs" and Cyriacus's traditional protectress. Accompanied by three conspicuous dolphins and wearing a dolphin cap, she holds a sixteen-oared galley in one hand.[101] The drawing appears on a page with two views of Hagia Sophia in Constantinople in the drawing book of Giuliano da Sangallo. It is almost certainly a copy of a sketch by Cyriacus that was itself fashioned after his fanciful rendering of one of the giants from the Agora in Athens (Plates 94–5).[102] As one scholar observes, "in the process, the giant had become a giantess."[103] The suggestion that the nymph originally decorated the title-page of a book of excerpts given by Cyriacus to his friend Johannes Delphin, on whose ship he had admired

the rock crystal intaglio of Pallas Athene, is attractive and credible. In a neat visual play on words the sketch would have paid tribute to Delphin and to his trireme, the *Delphinia*.[104] A similar creative imagination is at work in Cyriacus's devotion to Mercury as a tutelary divinity, whom he addresses on more than one occasion as "*Pater alme Mercuri*, Glory of Arts, Mind, Intelligence, and Speech," and prays for "happy auguries" in his "most jocund travels by land and sea."[105]

Cyriacus might have been just another eccentric, if brilliant romantic, as Poggio once charged,[106] were it not for the fact that he was a natural proselytizer. As noted, he not only collected inscriptions, he also actively gave them away. As a result, his most durable scholarly contribution is found in the pages of the *Corpus Inscriptionum Latinarum*, for which the inscriptions collected in his *Commentaria* were the essential foundation.

★ ★ ★

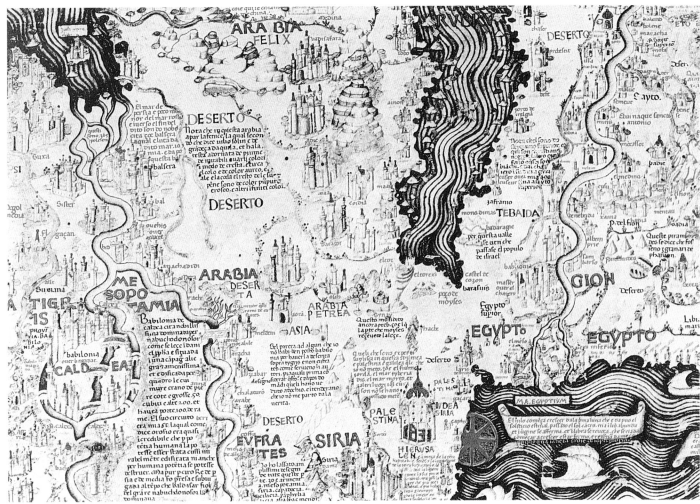

96 Fra Mauro, detail of North Africa from his *Mappamondo*, c.1460. Venice, Biblioteca Nazionale Marciana (after Gasparrini Leporace, *Il Mappamondo di Fra Mauro*, Plate XXIII).

THE *MAPPAMONDO* OF FRA MAURO

The renowned cartographer, Fra Mauro of Venice, was already in residence at the monastery of San Michele at Murano in 1433 when Ambrogio Traversari made the acquaintance there of Cyriacus and the leading collectors of antiquities in the city. By the time of his death in 1459, when he was commemorated with a medal proclaiming him "cosmographicus incomparabiilis," Fra Mauro would create at least three magnificent *mappamondi* on a monumental scale. One of these, made "a contemplation di questa Illustrissima Signoria," remains in Venice in the Biblioteca Marciana. It was probably begun before the fall of Constantinople in 1453 and completed in 1460, shortly after the friar's death.[107] Although the numerous annotations throughout the map attempt to separate the factual from the fabulous, many of them reveal a still medieval respect for scriptural authority over empirical observation. A rubric next to an image of the universe tucked into one of the corners advises: "The number of these heavenly spheres [is] according to the authority of the sacred theologians."[108] But Fra Mauro is also aware of problems of evidence and proof. As he states in an inscription in the region called "Arabia":

> About the confines or borders of these provinces, that is Cirenaica and Libia Marmarica, together with Egypt, one cannot now speak correctly, because it is anything but certain if one follows what the authors write, since the names have been changed and the famous cities destroyed which appear as great ruins in this Africa . . .[109]

At times, however, the images themselves contradict the words, for the numerous towns are indicated by minarets or towers without a ruin in sight (Plate 96).

Much of the visual art of this period is characterized by similar perceptual inconsistencies in relation to the physical remains of the ancient world. And yet Venetian artists and architects strove to overcome these disjunctions with new synthetic statements. On the one hand, they would subsume antique remains and motifs into a more perfect present; and on the other, they would disengage them from that present in order to create internally consistent semblances of the past.

III

THE HISTORICAL SYNTHESIS: ACCOMMODATING THE CLASSICAL TRADITION

97　Venice, San Marco. View of the Cappella dei Mascoli.

PROLOGUE

Then, searching the ancient and the new
    chronicles, and rereading all the histories
    of that land which Neptune caresses,
I do not find any that mention
    that the noble homeland of Rialto
    was exalted by so much glory!
          – Pietro de' Natali, 1381–2[1]

Attempts to create synthetic visions of both past and present that accommodated the new awareness of antique artifacts and monuments are first evident in the Venetian milieu around the middle of the fifteenth century. But before considering these initiatives, it will be useful to travel back in time for a brief visit to late fourteenth-century Venice. The patrician Pietro de' Natali, Bishop of Jesolo and a recognized poet, must have been in his fifties when he concluded a historical work in *terza rima* recounting once again the beloved legend of the Peace of Venice of 1177: that defining moment when Doge Sebastiano Ziani was said to have played a crucial mediating role between Pope Alexander III and the Emperor Frederick Barbarossa.[2] De' Natali's translation of the Latin texts of Bonincontro dei Bovi and Castellano da Bassano into the *volgare* marked the true "venetianizing" of the account. While the two earlier versions had been written by non-noble outsiders, the new text can be seen as the response of an older generation of patricians for whom the language of Dante was still the preferred literary medium.[3] It affirms that the serious study of classical literature had not yet taken hold within the Venetian élite, and that the locus of humanism was still to be found amongst the notaries and scribes of the Chancery, and not with their noble employers.[4] All this was soon to change.

When De' Natali finished his account, Venice had just survived one of the greatest challenges in its history, with a successful defense against Genoa in the costly War of Chioggia (1379–80).[5] During the decades that followed, Venetians would experience a major reorientation of their geophysical universe. With the revival of the sea trade of paramount interest, the republic pursued a cautious diplomatic strategy with the Ottoman Turks and increasingly left the Byzantine emperor to fend for himself. The center of gravity of the Venetian mercantile network in the east thus migrated from Constantinople to the heart of the Aegean. Corfu, Nauplia, Argo, the ducate of Athens, Negroponte, Tines, Mykonos, Naxos, and Andros all became part of the Venetian hegemony in this period.[6]

Class cohesion had become resilient enough by 1381 for the patriciate to welcome into its ranks thirty *cittadino* families who had proven their loyalty with financial support in the War of Chioggia. That done, the doors put in place by the Serrata nearly a century earlier were now essentially closed to new men, and real political power was vested exclusively in a hereditary aristocracy. Internally, the collective mentality that played such a strong role in securing the stability of the state was now mature.[7]

Attention to the sea empire, however, was increasingly diverted by challenges from the terraferma. Since acquiring Treviso and its territory in 1339, the republic had been active in securing trade routes through the Veneto and in preserving vital access to its agricultural products. She satisfied these aims for a time by playing off the various *signorie* against one another – the Carrara of Padua, the Scaligeri of Verona, the Visconti of Milan, and diverse lords in the Friuli – but their growth into larger and more ambitious signorial states put the policy under increasing strain. Thus in the early years of the quattrocento and the dogate of Michele Steno (1400–13), the creation of a mainland empire became part of a conscious Venetian design that was soon to become a reality.[8]

A well-grounded sense of civic and class identity intersected with the expansionist politique toward the terraferma. Young patricians who had been given a humanist education by their learned retainers in and about the Chancery recognized that a new rhetoric was required to celebrate the values of their caste and to articulate and defend their interests to themselves and to the outside world. They found it in Latin eloquence. Margaret King sums up the matter succinctly: "At this critical moment in their history, they intercepted and appropriated the humanist movement."[9]

As King shows so vividly, the first generation of humanists, those who had reached adulthood in the last decades of the fourteenth century, would absorb the classical tradition and adapt it to serve Venetian concerns by grounding it in two imperatives: a detente between a deeply rooted Christian piety and the Aristotelianism that had so offended Petrarch; and a commitment to celebrate Venice and its aristocratic values.[10] King writes:

> Curiously, while deeply conservative at its core, humanism in Venice was in fact generously receptive, incorporating new trends, new persons, new objects, new books . . . Just as an allegiance to traditional intellectual modes colored Venetian humanism, so eclecticism armored it from the thrust of rebellious thought.[11]

Humanists and teachers of the stature of Pier Paolo Vergerio, Guarino Veronese, Gasparino Barzizza, and Vittorino da Feltre – the list is long – maintained close relationships with Venetian patricians and educated their sons throughout lengthy careers both inside and outside the city.[12] It would thus appear that the aesthetic of diversity that had long characterized Venetian art also animated her intellectual life.

The political tenor of humanism in Venice would also determine the ways in which Venetian artists came to respond to the challenge of the classical revival in the arts with a new synthesis of *venezianità all'antica*. However, the reception of antique values in Venice, as elsewhere, was characterized by ambiguities and contradictions, and frequently resulted more in syncretism than true synthesis. Two episodes, both set in Padua, are characteristic of the period and will serve as introductions to the next phase of this exploration of the Venetian discovery of the classical past.

A SHORT-LIVED REVIVAL

With the visual vocabulary of the ancients at the disposal of the Venetian state and a longstanding artisan tradition of crafting antique counterfeits, it might be assumed that the way was open for an early revival of classical art in the civic sphere. But, in fact, such was not the case, for the patrician response was, characteristically, marked with caution, prudence, and a certain reluctance. The revival of the antique medal is a case in point and serves to define the first emblematic moment.

The first Renaissance medals in Italy were struck in Padua to commemorate a Carrara triumph. Francesco I (Il Vecchio) had been chased out of the city by Giangaleazzo Visconti in

1388. His son Francesco II (Novello) took back the city on June 19, 1390, and, perhaps inspired by the numismatic tastes fostered there by Petrarch, ordered three medals to be made on the model of a Roman coin. The obverse of two of the medals carries the profile portrait of Francesco Novello himself, his bull-like neck and bared shoulder giving him a family resemblance to the image of Vitellius on a bronze sestertius of A.D. 69 (Plate 98): a third medal, implying dynastic continuity, depicts his father Francesco Il Vecchio, complete with a Roman toga, draped and tied at the shoulder (Plate 99). The reverse of each piece features the Carrara stemma – a four-wheeled *carro* – thus grafting the glorious Paduan present to a dignified Roman past.[13] The Carrara medals had a long afterlife, with examples circulating north and south of the Alps. But while they reappeared in frescoes and manuscript illuminations, they inspired few imitations as medals *per se*, with the notable exception of a similar revival in Venice.[14]

98 (*top*) *Portrait of Francesco Novello Carrara* (obverse) and the Carrara *carro* (reverse), 1390. Bronze, diam. 3.3 cm. (after Hill, *Corpus*, no. 3).

99 (*above*) *Portrait of Francesco Il Vecchio Carrara* (obverse) and the Carrara *carro* (reverse), 1390. Bronze, diam. 3.6 cm. (after Hill, *Corpus*, no. 1).

Indeed, just three years later, Marco Sesto, an engraver of silver coins at the Venetian mint, struck his own medal *all'antica* (Plate 100). The obverse featured a credibly classical profile portrait bust of the Emperor Galba crowned with a laurel wreath. He was framed by an inscription that pointed to artifice rather than deceit: "MARCUS ✳ SESTO ✳ ME ✳ FECIT:U [UENETUS]:". On the reverse the female figure of Venetia, holding the vexillum, stands on a wheel of fortune. She is surrounded by an inscription – " · PAX · TIBI · UENETIA · 1393"

100 Marco Sesto, *Portrait of the Emperor Galba* (obverse) and *Venetia-Fortuna* (reverse), 1393. Bronze, diam. 3.4 cm. New York, American Numismatic Society.

– essentially co-opting the angelic salutation given to St. Mark many centuries before in the portentous episode of the *praedestinatio*.[15] As David Rosand observes, Sesto's medal typifies a new synthesis of ancient Roman and medieval Christian imagery in a humanist-inspired celebration of the idea of the state.[16]

It also offers an updating of the concept of *occasio*, or opportunity, as represented in the relief of Kairos at Torcello.[17] In later medieval art *fortuna* was often conflated with *occasio*, with a more comprehensive female symbol replacing the male Kairos as an allegory of the caprices of both chance and opportunity.[18] As such, she would seem to defy human control. But Petrarch, upon the authority of Cicero, had cited virtue as a powerful antidote to the vicissitudes of fortune: "Duce virtute comite fortuna" (When virtue leads, fortune follows).[19] Sesto's conflation of Venetia with Fortuna may thus be read as a sign that Venice as the embodiment of civic virtue will maintain its precarious position atop the wheel of fortune, and thus forestall a turn of the wheel that

may also be a Venetia, but one who lacks the ennobling attributes of Fortuna.[22]

The Sesto medals may also have inspired a discreet move to personalize the traditionally generic ducal portrait on Venetian coinage. For the numismatist Alan Stahl recognizes the distinctive, if tiny, bearded profile portrait of Doge Antonio Venier (1382–1400) kneeling before St. Mark on a Venetian silver grosso datable to around 1398–9.[23] However, the idea did not take hold on coins, and only with the lira introduced by Doge Nicolò Tron (1471–4) does one find a true and proper profile portrait bust of a Venetian doge that fills the field like an emperor on a Roman coin. And yet, even at this later date, the experiment would be short-lived. After Tron's death, the type reverted to an anonymous doge kneeling before St. Mark. As a chronicler noted at the time: 'tyrants put their images on coins, not heads of republics.'[24] In an aristocracy where ducal power was monitored and circumscribed, he was to remain *primus inter pares* but not more.

Nor did the pioneering efforts of the Sesto brothers establish a new tradition of classicizing medals in Venice. For the next half-century, only a single additional example can be cited, and it is devoid of specifically Venetian iconography and symbolism. Signed by Alessandro Sesto and dated 1417, it depicts the bust of a monarch, probably Alexander the Great, on the obverse, that is based on a Hellenistic prototype (Plate 102). Unlike the other medals, it features a mythological episode of *abductio mulieris* on the reverse – identifiable as Perseus freeing Andromeda, the Rape of Proserpina, or simply a satyr carrying off a nymph – possibly deriving from a classical gem or an archaic Thracian coin.[25] The next known Venetian medal appears only in the 1450s.[26] Portraying Doge Francesco Foscari it is cast, not struck, and fits into a (by then)

101 Lorenzo Sesto, *Portrait of the Emperor Galba* (obverse) and *Venetia* (reverse), *c*.1393. Bronze, diam. 2.4 cm. (reproduced larger than actual size) (after Hill, *Corpus*, no. 10).

102 Alessandro Sesto, *Portrait of ?Alexander the Great* (obverse) and a mythological episode (reverse), 1417. Bronze, diam. 2.1 cm. (reproduced larger than actual size) (after Hill, *Corpus*, no. 12).

would bring a fall.[20] Along these lines, the image has also been seen as an Apotheosis of Venice.[21]

A similar medal was struck and signed by Marco's brother, also an engraver at the mint: "LAVRENTI SESTO ME FECIT" (Plate 101). Although Lorenzo's medal carries no date, it must have been made somewhat later than Marco's. Here an inscription confirms the emperor's identity: "IMP[ERATOR] S ER[GIUS] GALBA CA[ESAR]." The standing female figure on the reverse

well-established medallic tradition begun by Pisanello at the Este court in Ferrara in the late 1430s (see Plate 107).[27] As a crucial source of honor in a republic whose governing class was made up of an aristocracy of equals, the doge represented the polity on a world stage with princes, kings, and emperors. When classicizing medals eventually became one of the essential elements of princely symbolism in the middle of the quattrocento, it became incumbent upon Venetians to honor their doge in a like fashion. While the profile portrait carried uncomfortably imperial connotations on coins, it was used to depict both ruler and ruled on medals – thus a more acceptable genre.

A FORTUITOUS DISCOVERY

While Venetians were challenged to respond to the political iconography of the courts of northern Italy, they were also intellectually nourished by the established humanist cultures of their own subject cities in the terraferma. By the end of the century, Sanudo listed thirty-nine communities with a Venetian podestà, most of whom served with a captain (*capetanio*) and other officials. Other towns were governed by a castellan or *provedador*.[28] These functionaries, all Venetian patricians, came and went. Bound to limited terms that ensured a regular rotation of personnel, they were the vehicles for a continuing infusion of mainland ideas into Venice itself. Young patricians aiming for a career in terraferma administration, moreover, realized the virtues of a legal education and flooded into the University of Padua in ever greater numbers throughout the quattrocento.[29]

The second emblematic moment is really a small incident, a fortuitous discovery that was of little importance in the larger order of things. But it gives some of the flavor of Venetian participation in terraferma humanism, and it opens up the larger issue of attitudes toward antiquity that will be of concern in artistic representations of the Roman past. In 1413, when Leonardo, brother of Doge Tommaso Mocenigo, was the Venetian podestà of Padua, a skeleton was found in a lead sarcophagus in the graveyard of the monastery of Santa Giustina and enthusiastically identified by the humanist Sicco Polenton as that of the Roman historian Livy. With crowds of sightseers flocking to the site like pilgrims visiting a shrine, a group of university students from out of town went so far as to remove the teeth from the skull 'tum memoria tum reverentia.' Fearing the return of pagan idolatry, an alarmed monk attached to the monastery took a hammer and smashed the skull into bits. Sicco, then the Paduan Cancelliere of the city, wrote off to the Florentine humanist Niccolò Niccoli in outrage: 'that which was conserved for centuries in the bowels of the earth, this man wasted.'[30] But the rest of the bones were rescued from a similar fate. Deposited in a casket draped with laurel branches, they were carried through the streets in a festive, if not solemn, procession like the translation of a holy relic. The entourage included the new Venetian podestà Fantino Dandolo and the captain Zaccaria Trevisan along with Sicco and other prominent citizens. The crowd was so dense, Sicco noted with satisfaction, that the procession could hardly move. It was, moreover, made up not only of humanists, but also of artisans, butchers, and shoemakers – in sum, all the people of the city.[31]

Ambitious plans were proposed for a freestanding monument with an effigy of Livy seated *in cathedra* atop a column with a high three-stepped base, but it was never realized.[32] In 1426 the remains were immured in a niche above the Porta delle Debite, an entrance to the Palazzo della Ragione that had recently been rebuilt after a devastating fire. It was augmented with two portrait reliefs and an epitaph in gold letters composed by Leonardo Giustiniani, the brother of Marco – then the Venetian podestà – and a humanist friend of Cyriacus of Ancona.[33]

These two episodes serve as a reminder that Venetian territorial expansion brought with it new opportunities to reassess time and space. On the one hand, there is a subtle appropriation by Venice of the Roman pasts of her subject cities. On the other, a new 'objectivizing' of antiquity and a growing perception of the distinctions between past and present. Such developments were engendered by a larger vision of civic destiny, which was shaped by the themes of Venetian humanism.[34] This vision would, in turn, define the parameters of a classical revival in Venetian art and architecture. Over the course of the quattrocento, it offered not only a program for governance and a means to create a more perfect present in the public art and architecture of the city; it also provided a matrix for an artistic retreat along Petrarch's intimate path into the lost world of pagan antiquity.

5

A MORE PERFECT PRESENT

Crowned kingdom above kingdoms
    Of the universe, where of Christianity
    In holy baptism
    Your equal in the world is not to be found . . .

You are in the world a living phoenix
    That renews itself and never changes form,
    Just as your custom
    Seems to me transformed into what I speak.

What Alexander, Scipio and Charle[magne]
    Who once ruled, as one finds,
    You see the proof of it
    From the cities that were their seats and mansions.

As they have done, so too the good lion,
    transformed to Mark the Evangelist
    Of whom I speak my view
    Ever more desirous of telling the truth . . .

I speak the truth, I speak of what I love,
    That Troy was never so powerful
    Nor Rome in ancient times
    As Venice, and now it is clearly shown.

You rule in the north and in the south,
    The southwest and the northeast winds, the east and
      the west winds,
    The Scirocco, indeed,
    The mistral without you does not pass.

You were small and now you are so large,
    All around the world kneels down,
    You alone are Queen
    Above every kingdom in the world created.

The great lion has one paw in the meadow,
    The other on the mountain, the third on the plain,
    The fourth is set in the sea
    So as to make a wide passage.

                  – From an unsigned *quartine* addressed
                   to Venice, 1420[1]

A few quatrains extracted from a considerably more lengthy poem give us a sense of how one citizen defined Venice's place in history in the early decades of the fifteenth century. The poet, writing in Venetian dialect, speaks lovingly of a queenly Venice, now more powerful than Troy or Rome in the height of their glory, and mistress of a vast territory of land and sea that can justly be considered an empire.[2] While he might well be considered a less than objective witness, the writer makes four important claims that help us understand the Venetian response to Petrarch's challenge to rediscover the lost radiance of the classical past.

First, unlike the pagan cities of ancient foundation, Venice had been Christian from the very beginning. Furthermore, Venice is superior to Rome. Implicit in civic panegyric from the thirteenth century on, the claim is evident already in the poem of Pace da Ferrara of 1300, although his claims seem modest by comparison. When monumental Venice finally takes on the visual vocabulary of ancient Rome, she will do it not as a successor or daughter but as a moral superior. Beyond that, Venice embraces all things – even the winds of the earth. Such a view lies at the heart of the lingering aesthetic of acquisition, diversity, and reconciliation familiar to us in public art and architecture from the thirteenth and fourteenth centuries.

Finally, the metaphor of the phoenix for a city that constantly renews itself is perhaps the most crucial, if the most elusive, concept to grasp if one is to come close to recapturing a Venetian sense of the civic past. The phenomenon of *renovatio*, discovered in several moments of Venetian history by various scholars, rests on different premises from Petrarch's hope for a restitution of Rome after a dark age. Since nothing was really lost, as it had been with pagan Rome – vanquished by the barbarians as well as by Christianity – the issue in Venice was that of renewal rather than of rebirth or restitution.[3]

This view engendered a Venetian model of historical time that was expressed in a more sophisticated way by the notary Lorenzo De Monacis. Born in Venice to a notarial family in the middle of the fourteenth century, De Monacis rose quickly through the ranks in the Chancery and was soon acclaimed for the eloquence of his poetry. In 1388 he was elected Cancelliere of Crete, the highest Venetian office available to a non-noble *cittadino* aside from that of Cancelliere Grande. It too was a lifetime post, but one that could only be enjoyed by residing permanently outside the city. Well educated in the Latin classics, De Monacis could also read Greek, although he once wrote to Francesco Barbaro that studying it was "un'inutile perdita di tempo." He nonetheless took advantage of his residence in Crete to collect Greek texts and sent Barbaro an *Iliad* as a gift, and perhaps also an *Odyssey*.[4]

Allowed to return to Venice only for short visits, De Monacis was poignantly aware of the homeland from which he was effectively, if most honorably, exiled. Perhaps inspired by the broader perspective that came with geographical distance, he began to collect material for a historical chronicle of the city. Early in 1421, in anticipation of the millenary Jubilee of Venice's foundation that would fall on 25 March of that year, he completed a long oration dedicated to Doge Tommaso Mocenigo. Entitled *Oratio elegantissima ad serenissimum principem et ducem Venetorum in laude et edificatione alme civitatis Venetiarum*, the piece is one of the rare explicit commemorations of the millenary to survive; for no other celebrations or official observances were recorded by the chroniclers of the time.[5] But a portolan map made that year positions Venice, marked by the lion of San Marco on a red and gold banner larger than those of any other city, in the center of the Mediterranean world (Plate 103).

De Monacis's stance was defensive, motivated in part by criticisms of Venice's expansionist policy in the terraferma. He was also responding with a specifically Venetian laudatory agenda to the challenge of a new model for encomiastic literature recently adumbrated by the Florentine Leonardo Bruni.[6] While the piece fits into a longstanding *laus civitatis* tradition common to many cities, it develops in a more elegant manner the essential elements of historical *venezianità* already demonstrated in the *quartine* of 1420 and indicates that such notions were common in Venetian historiography.[7]

Again, De Monacis sets up a spiritual antithesis between Rome and Venice. In contrast to Rome's modest beginnings and corrupting taste for power and luxury as it rose to empire, Venice had been free since its very origins and, because of the sober virtue of her citizens, was entrusted by divine will with the mission of preserving and defending liberty. The providential character of Venice's birth had continued, moreover, with the city enjoying the constant intervention of God throughout her history.

Most importantly, that history was still in process, with the best seemingly yet to come. This notion was demonstrated by a peculiarly Venetian civic variant of a three ages model of historical periodization: *infantia*, a golden age lasting about two hundred years from the city's foundation to the Lombard invasions when men lived simply, without ambition, luxury or treachery; *adolescentia*, another two-hundred-year period, but this one of growth and struggle, during which the nascent republic was ennobled by the patriarchate and new episcopal sees; and *juventus*, an age of robust maturity.[8] This culminating period had been inaugurated with the transfer of the ducal seat to Rialto and the election of the first doge – events that marked the birth of the republic of the present-day, "that having begun at Rialto has been growing for six hundred years and more."[9]

A sumptuous gold-encrusted triptych painted in 1421 by Jacobello del Fiore for the Magistrato del Proprio, one of the six courts of the palace, might well be regarded as a visual counterpart of Lorenzo's message (Plate 104). In the central panel sits a queenly Venetia as Justice, holding a sword and a

103 Francesco de Cesanis, *Portolan*, 1421. Venice, Museo Civico Correr, Portolan no. 3.

104   Jacobello del Fiore, *Venetia–Justice*, 1421. Wood triptych, central panel 208 × 194 cm; *Archangel Michael* (cut at left edge), 208 × 133; *Gabriel*, 208 × 163 cm. Venice, Accademia.

balance and flanked by two living lions implying a solomonic throne, and thus, *sedes sapientae*.[10] She is further framed by two divine counselors, the splendidly adorned Archangels Michael and Gabriel, whose energetic figures animate the side-wings. Reflecting the duties of a judicial body with both civil and criminal jurisdiction, the protagonists engage in a colloquy on the rightful use of civic authority. Each is accompanied by an inscription that makes the erudite message absolutely clear. Proclaiming that "my word announces the virgin birth of peace among men," Gabriel asks Venetia to lead humanity through the darkness. Michael, alluding to the Last Judgment, exhorts her to dispense reward and punishment according to merit and to "commend to me the purged souls with the scales of benignity." She responds, "I abide by the angelic admonition and holy words," and affirms that she is "gentle with the pious, hostile to the wicked, and haughty with the proud."[11] Emphasizing peace and justice as the cornerstones of the state, the inscriptions also allude to the Annunciation, the birth day of Venice.

It is important to note that the painting is resolutely Gothic in both style and iconography, without any discernible classicizing resonance, whether Byzantine or Roman. The figure Venetia–Justice (and some would add Virgin) is vaguely modeled on the trecento tondo of Venetia on the west façade of the ducal palace (Plate 105), but the similarity is confined primarily to her pose and her leonine companions. The Venetia–Fortuna *all'antica* of the Sesto medals was either unknown, ignored, or rejected by the artist and his patrons. It was, as yet, Jacobello's fashioning of the Gothic idiom that represented the newest and most up-to-date style of the moment.

De Monacis went on to write a second more general

105   Giovanni Calendario, *Venetia*, c.1360. Sculptural relief. Venice, Palazzo Ducale, west façade.

historical work on Venice, entitled *De rebus gestis moribus et nobilitate civitatis Venetiarum*. In the opening pages he continues to express a decidedly Venetian concern with time and eternity:

This city alone among all those founded before and after it is unique; and what is admirable, without fields, meadows and vineyards, it has conserved the liberty integral and complete in which it had been founded for more than a thousand years, without ever having changed the mode of government . . . Very few cities fail to lose their liberties after two or three hundred years. Which of them ever endured for more than a thousand?[12]

De Monacis continued writing the chronicle until his death in 1428. During his lifetime he had seen Venice expand toward the west with the addition in 1405–6 of Padua, Verona, and Vicenza to her mainland empire. With further conquests in the 1420s he was able to offer the comforting explanation that the submission of the Friuli was simply the will of God.[13]

Venice's growing empire inspired new initiatives of civic definition through art and architecture. While San Marco was never neglected – the Cappella dei Mascoli comes to mind – the masterworks of state patronage during the quattrocento involved secular buildings and monuments.[14] The first order of business was the completion of the great council hall that was begun back in 1340. During the first two decades of the fifteenth century, the project was finally brought to a successful conclusion. The great *poggiolo* or balcony was added to the south façade in 1400–4 with an elaborate sculptural apparatus consisting of thirteen figures – SS. Theodore and George, seven Virtues, the Doge kneeling before the Lion of St. Mark, and SS. Peter and Paul – and was crowned with a standing figure of Venetia in the form of Justice (Plate 106).[15] In a typically Venetian fusion of the sacred and the secular, the ensemble proclaimed Venice as the just and virtuous daughter of the church, and equivalent, if not superior, to papal Rome.

The painting campaign inside the hall had resumed shortly thereafter, with Gentile da Fabriano and Pisanello, and possibly other artists called upon to complete the fresco cycle of the legend of Alexander III. An imposing new staircase was built and, finally, in 1419 after a campaign of nearly eighty years, the Maggior Consiglio met in the room for the first time.[16] There are indications that the patience (and probably the purses) of the patriciate had been taxed to the limit with these labors. For in the year before his death in 1423 Doge Tommaso Mocenigo proposed the completion of the palace complex with a new palace of justice facing the Piazzetta, and, according to one chronicler, was fined the not insignificant sum of 1,000 ducats for even suggesting further remodeling.[17]

106 Giovanni Grevembroch, *Poggiolo on the South Façade of the Palazzo Ducale*, eighteenth century. Watercolor. Venice, Museo Civico Correr.

THE PRESTIGE OF THE ANTIQUE

The momentum for civic beautification was sufficiently great, however, to sweep aside objections, and the completion of the new wing under Doge Francesco Foscari provided the opportunity to construct the Porta della Carta as an imposing entrance portal to the complex, the first of a series of gateways through which the Renaissance of antiquity entered Venice. Indeed, it is worth noting that aside from the completion of the south and west wings of the ducal palace, and the reconstruction of the doge's apartments after a fire in 1483, the major projects of state patronage in the quattrocento concerned entryways: the Porta della Carta (1438–2/3), the Arco Foscari (1438–early 1480s), the Arsenale portal (1457–60), the Scala dei Giganti (c.1485–93), and the Torre dell'Orologio (1496–9).[18] To these might be added the quasi-civic campaigns of the *scuole grandi*: an entrance *cortile* to the Scuola Grande di San Giovanni Evangelista and the illusionistic façade of the Scuola Grande di San Marco, each with an impressive ceremonial staircase inside the building.[19]

Given Venice's expansionist *politique*, the emphasis on portals and arches reflects a (probably unknowing) congruence with Alberti's view of the triumphal arch as symbols of political and military domination: "the greatest ornament to the forum or crossroad would be to have an arch at the mouth of each road. For the arch is a gate that is continually open. Its invention I ascribe to those who enlarged the empire . . ."[20] Tellingly, Venice – the city without walls – needed no gateways, but built them anyway in the heart of the city.

The ambitious Doge Francesco Foscari was one of the major agents of change, for it was during his term (1423–57) that *romanitas* began to take hold as a visual and verbal cultural ideal in Venetian civic discourse. In this one sees a subtle, but telling difference in viewpoint between outside observers and Venetians. For foreigners, aiming to flatter the ruling élite of the Serenissima and, not comprehending the fine nuances between succession and outright superiority, tended to salute the republic as the new Rome. So Giovanni da Spilimbergo, a grammarian and humanist in the recently annexed Friuli, hailed Venice as a second Rome. Filippo Morandi, a recent arrival from Rimini, proclaimed Doge Francesco Foscari as "dux augustus" in his *Carmen* of 1440–41 and praised Venetian patricians as ideal descendents of the Romans.[21] Porcellio Romano dedicated his *Commentari* to the same doge in 1453 and circumspectly identified the Venetian *pregadi* with the Roman senate in its claims to dignity, "yet not to empire or dominion."[22]

Even before the fall of Constantinople in the spring of that year, Venetians could also lay claim to their city's identity as a perfected version of Athens. The Greek scholar George Trebizond, writing to Francesco Barbaro in 1451, saw the Venetian government as the realization of Plato's ideal state, a regime that combines monarchic, aristocratic, and democratic elements: "your ancestors who have founded your republic have certainly taken from Plato's *Laws* everything that makes the life of a republic long and happy. For it would be quite incredible that things could be so completely identical by accident."[23] An appreciative Barbaro asked Trebizond to include these welcome words in the introduction to his translation of the *Laws* and to dedicate the work to him:

For when our city was because of historical circumstances founded from the remains of other noble cities, and established by great and illustrious men who could find no safety elsewhere, partly by divine, partly by human counsel, and

when in time the city grew so much, our ancestors not without cause turned to Plato and other wise men to understand and learn how to acquire and retain civic liberty, and to increase and amplify public majesty.[24]

The Roman element filtered into Venetian public art and architecture in a similarly ambiguous way. By the 1430s, as indicated by the warm reception given to Cyriacus of Ancona, antique coins and gems were already an important presence in Venetian collections. Portable and still reasonably available, such artifacts also drew the attention of artists in that period, as witness the medals of Antonio Pisanello of Verona. Long active in and around Venice and the courts of north Italy, Pisanello fulfilled the promise offered by the Carrara medals of forty years earlier and reinvented the Renaissance medal. In Ferrara in 1438 during the Council of Ferrara–Florence, he cast his first piece, depicting a profile bust of the Byzantine emperor John Paleologus on the obverse and the emperor on horseback on the reverse. Pisanello's first medals, unlike the earlier ones produced in Padua and Venice, were cast, not struck, and featured neither classical style, iconography, nor epigraphy. Although the inscription was almost invariably in Latin, a credible likeness of the sitter, always in profile and always in contemporary dress, was the primary goal. But beginning with a group of Este medals executed in Ferrara between 1441 and 1444, antique motifs and images began to appear on the reverses, often as nude figures in allegorical scenes.[25]

In an age before the printing press, not to mention the photograph, the possibilities of the medal as a replicative mode were immediately appreciated by princes and *condottieri* eager to propagate an image of authority and cultivated taste or to commemorate a particular event in the manner of the ancients. During the next decade Pisanello celebrated in a similar manner the Gonzaga of Mantua, the Visconti of Milan, the Este of Ferrara, the Malatesta of Rimini, Alfonso of Aragon, and the occasional courtier, humanist, and *condottiere*.[26]

It was only a matter of time before Doge Francesco Foscari would demand a similar distinction. In the early 1450s he, too, was finally celebrated with a proper Renaissance medal, designed by the architect Antonio Gambello (Plate 107). The doge's profile on the obverse, like Pisanello's numismatic portraits, is contemporary in style and costume and lacks any Roman imperial references. The image on the reverse, however, is an imaginative revival *all'antica* of the trecento tondo of Venetia on the west façade of the Palazzo Ducale complex. Lest any observer miss the classicizing intentions, the figure is framed with the inscription "VENETIA MAGNA." The artist was not just copying a motif; he was confirming an ideology.[27]

Old and sick, the once-vigorous Foscari had become increasingly incapable of fulfilling the duties of office. Deposed in 1457 after an unusually acrimonious debate between the Senate and the Maggior Consiglio, he died soon after, and

107 Antonio Gambello, *Portrait of Doge Francesco Foscari* (1423–57) (obverse) and *Venetia–Justice* (reverse), early 1450s. Bronze, diam. 4.74 cm. (after Hill, *Corpus*, no. 410).

a potentially divisive breach remained between the two official bodies. Foscari's successor, Pasquale Malipiero, was elected as a consensus candidate and availed himself of the bronze medium to convey a message of reconciliation. Two pieces were commissioned from the medallist Marco Guidizani. As with Foscari, Malipiero was portrayed in profile, clad in ducal regalia on the obverse of each piece (Plates 108 and 109). But now on the reverse of one medal, Venetia

108 Marco Guidizani, *Portrait of Doge Pasquale Malipiero* (1457–62) (obverse) and *Peace* (reverse), c.1460. Bronze, diam 6.35 cm. (after Hill, *Corpus*, no. 415).

109 Marco Guidizani, *Portrait of Doge Pasquale Malipiero* (1457–62) (obverse) and *Concord* (reverse), c.1460. Bronze, diam. 9.1 cm. (after Hill, *Corpus*, no. 414).

was replaced by Peace, a partly draped female figure who holds a palm branch and stands over a shield and sword lying on the ground. The inscription is clear and direct: "PAX AVGVSTA." The message was even more pointed on the second medal, whose reverse depicted two figures: a male crowned with laurel who holds an olive branch and a woman holding a palm frond. Their hands joined, they are accompanied by an inscription that, again, gives an unambiguous message: "CONCORDIA AVGVSTA CONSVLTI VENETIQVE SENATVS," with the man symbolizing the Senate and the woman the Maggior Consiglio. At the bottom the letters "SVQC" signify, in all likelihood, "Senatus Venetusque Consultus," in a direct appropriation of the SPQR of ancient Rome.[28] One is reminded of the allure of the antique and its power to respond to concerns of the present.

The Istrian humanist Raffaele Zovenzoni wrote a panegyric to Venice and its patriciate for the public celebration of Malipiero's election on the Piazza San Marco. Entitling his work *Epaenodia*, Zovenzoni praised Venice's dominion over land and sea and noted the uniqueness of the city's site and architectural treasures in satisfyingly classical terms:

> What shall I say of the singular city in which, scattered over the surface of the water, stand the holy places of the fathers? Before the walls there, the columns of Hercules meet sailors entering the port.
>
> You perceive here also the temples of the divine Prince, here the tower touching the heavens with its golden top, and here shines the temple built of Parian marble.
>
> To you Mark, whose threshold glistens with doors of bronze: living ivory inside, at the same time you would believe that the bronzes speak.
>
> Here the goddess made by the hand of Scopas and the simulacra made by the great Zeuxis and the great works of the ancient Polykleitos gleam.
>
> Here I pass by the remarkable altarpiece, stiff with gold and gems; here, man of the single *corno*, your statue and ducal mitre, and crowns, heavy with solid adamant.[29]

THE INHERITANCE OF JERUSALEM

While Venice was more than ready to assume some of the political prerogatives of ancient Rome, it was the sacral nature of the city that was emphasized in the mosaic decoration of the Cappella dei Mascoli in San Marco (Plates 110–12). The chapel was built as the Cappella della Madonna by Doge Francesco Foscari in 1430/31, probably as a votive offering after a failed attempt on his life.[30] The mosaics may have been started soon after that, but were only completed around 1451. The program includes the *Annunciation* on the end wall and four episodes from the life of the Virgin disposed in pairs on each side of a barrel vault. In the *Birth of the Virgin* and the *Presentation of the Virgin in the Temple* on the left-hand side, the

110 Michele Giambono, *Birth of the Virgin*, before 1452. Mosaic. Venice, San Marco, Cappella dei Mascoli.

111 Michele Giambono, *Presentation of the Virgin in the Temple*, before 1452. Mosaic. Venice, San Marco, Cappella dei Mascoli.

Virgin is born into a late Gothic world, architecturally speaking. Her palace, featuring both rectangular and pointed windows along with crenellations on the roof, would have been at home on the Grand Canal. Along with the temple, a high-domed pastiche of Byzantine, Gothic, and Renaissance motifs, it would also have been at home in the drawing-books of Pisanello. Positioned at an angle and innocent of Albertian experiments in linear perspective, these structures speak to values of decorative richness and architectural complexity. But moving to the *Visitation* and the *Dormition* on the other side of the vault, one finds the Virgin now grown up and living and dying in a Renaissance world built of rational, measurable architecture.

Confronted with obvious stylistic discrepancies between the two sides of the vault, along with further inconsistencies within the right-hand side, scholars have tried to account for them with a number of possible scenarios. At stake is an understanding of how Venetian artists responded to the challenge of Tuscan aesthetic values in the fifth decade of the quattrocento. Depending on how the realization of this program is interpreted, one may find indifference or resistance, and acceptance or even transcendence.[31]

The main points of general agreement may be summarized as follows.[32] The prominent signature of Michele Giambono, one of the foremost exponents of the International style in Venice, appears on the left-hand side of the vault, where he

was probably responsible for the designs.[33] On the other side of the chapel, however, Giambono's role is clearly much diminished. Here the Florentine artist Andrea del Castagno would have been engaged to design the *Dormition*, probably in 1442 when he was working on frescoes in the Cappella San Tarasio of the church of San Zaccaria. He conceived a boldly three-dimensional centralized triumphal arch with a perspective street view behind it, along with cartoons for Christ in Glory, the recumbent Virgin and two powerfully modeled apostles on the lower left-hand side of the scene. But Castagno must have returned to Florence the next year with the cartoon still incomplete.[34] Giambono would have taken over the remainder of the project, completing it seven or eight years later. He fitted in a group of six saints, not entirely comfortably, in the background on the far right side and added a scroll with the cryptic signature: "fecit." The three apostles in front of them, clearly different in style, as well as all or part of the *Visitation*, would have been the work of Jacopo Bellini.[35]

Whatever the date of Castagno's intervention, his influence on Jacopo Bellini is manifest in the *Visitation*. Inspired by the majestic effect of Castagno's triumphal arch, Jacopo responded in his characteristic manner of stylistic incorporation and reconciliation. Devising a three-part arch of his own, he turned it into a building façade complete with Venetian bifora windows. He also acknowledged the different subject matter

112 Jacopo Bellini, *Visitation*, and Andrea Castagno, Michele Giambono, and Jacopo Bellini, *Dormition of the Virgin*, before 1452. Mosaic. Venice, San Marco, Cappella dei Mascoli.

by transforming the portrait medallions from adults to chubby-faced infants.[36]

The mosaic campaign may well have been an extended one, but it is possible that all the cartoons were realized during the 1440s. Although the *Birth* and the *Presentation* look archaic (and thus earlier) in comparison to the other two scenes, they also include elements that must have been taken from Castagno's cartoon. The knob within a roundel that seems so appropriate in the spandrels of the triumphal arch, for example, becomes a dissonant intrusion in the pediments and *basamento* of the temple. It may well be that this artist, whether Giambono or someone else, could not respond as fully as did Jacopo to the challenge of the Florentine Renaissance style.

In any event, the final result is a strange, and possibly unforeseen one. For in creating a two-part scheme of Gothic and Renaissance forms, it overturns the traditional architectural antithesis of Gothic/positive versus Classical/negative depicted in so many Adorations of the period.[37] Here the values are reversed, with Gothic equated with the old order and Classical with the new. Perhaps inadvertently, perhaps knowingly, the still medieval symbolic system is thus subverted and infused with a different historical sense. And yet, it is not truly a Renaissance sensibility, in which there is a separation between classical past and Christian present. Rather, it may well reflect a specifically Venetian political agenda. In the first two scenes, the Virgin is born into Venice as the new Jerusalem. In the latter two, she fulfills her Christian destiny in Venice as the new Rome, where even Castagno's triumphal arch is surmounted by a parapet lifted directly from San Marco itself.[38] It is thus a Venice that combines the holiness of the one and the power and authority of the other. Indeed, it is precisely during this period that similar values were expressed with a new triumphalist rhetoric in state architecture.

THE AUTHORITY OF ROME

Over the course of some fifty years, the entry to the ducal palace would be developed as a true and proper *via triumphalis*, with the Porta della Carta leading through a covered passageway to the Arco Foscari – a triumphal arch in the midst of the palace complex – and culminating in the Scala dei Giganti.[39] The evolution of the project traces another sort of triumph, as well, in which Roman antique forms and motifs progressively overwhelm the traditional Gothic idiom to create a new Venetian Renaissance architecture.[40]

When the Porta della Carta was built, joining the Palazzo Ducale to San Marco and providing a new ceremonial entrance to the palace complex, it might have looked as if Venetian time had stood still, secured in the flowery foliage of its flamboyant Gothic structure and decorative apparatus (Plate 113). Featuring a pointed central window beneath an oculus,

the portal is surmounted by a figure of Justice, the preeminent civic virtue. With its side tabernacles containing statues of virtues and topped with slender pinnacles, it was both complement to, and critique of, the ecclesiastical-looking tabernacle of the south façade of the palace of four decades before.[41] Indeed, the new portal, commissioned from Giovanni Bon and his son Bartolomeo in 1438, achieves a level of harmony, unity and resolution – a decorative density – that had eluded Dalle Massegne in the earlier window. Originally refulgent in polychrome splendor, with many details painted in red, blue, and gold, it pushes against the outside limits of the Venetian Gothic style. Three winged-victory angels hold aloft a shell tondo that contains the bust of St. Mark in a triumphal epiphany, not only of the patron saint but also of almost-Renaissance forms.

Even the classicizing putti who frolic irreverently in the foliage framing the pinnacle, or who playfully support the coats of arms at the sides, seem aware that if the Venetian decorative vocabulary was to remain a viable and convincing means of communicating the evolving Venetian ideology, its architects and artists had to look for a new idiom.[42] Perhaps spurred on by Venice's new role as heir to the fallen Byzan-

113 Porta della Carta, designed by Giovanni and Bartolomeo Buon, 1438–42/3. Venice, Palazzo Ducale.

114   Venice, Arsenale, portal, 1460.

tium, and responding to the new rhetorical climate, they found it in the Roman ruins of the terraferma. For the same Arco dei Sergii in Pula that had intrigued Cyriacus of Ancona would provide the model for an important portal project executed soon after Foscari's death in 1457.

A new gateway to the Arsenale, dated 1460 on the pedestals, was the first serious attempt to give monumental Venice a plausible Roman presence (Plate 114). While the architect is unknown – he was in all likelihood not Antonio Gambello as has often been argued – credit for the initial idea of the *porta magna* may well be granted in this instance to the patron. As Ennio Concina has shown, responsibility for the commission and its elaboration was vested in a group of prominent humanists who happened to hold office in the government bodies overseeing works in the Arsenale in those years.[43] By using the Roman triumphal arch of the Sergii at Pula as the model, they made a statement that proclaimed Venice's new status as a player on the stage of mainland politics, and also asserted the continuity of Venetian tradition.[44]

The first story of the portal is a credible reinterpretation of

the arch at Pula, with paired Byzantine *cipollino* columns, probably twelfth-century spoils from Torcello, supporting a broken entablature. The upper story, however, is more Venetian than classical, with the Lion of St. Mark framed in an aedicule surmounted by a pediment containing a scallop shell. Some modern observers have attributed the juxtaposition to an unknowing eclecticism, but Ralph Lieberman makes an intriguing case for intentionality rather than incoherence. Regarding the portal as a "historical summary" of Venice's past, he sees it as an imaginative and rational attempt to construct an archaeological artifact *ex novo*. As our eyes work their way from ground level to the top of the structure, he argues, they move from myth to history through the various stages of Venice's past: from a Roman foundation to a Byzantine period and on to a Venetian present.[45]

That the structure was intended to make a bold historical statement is suggested by the dates inscribed in Roman majuscules on the two podia flanking the doorway. Not surprisingly, the date on the right documents the dedication according to the Christian calendar: "x[RIST]I

109

INCAR[NATIONIS]. M.CCCC°.LX.° But the date on the left sets the dedication of the portal into a direct relationship to the legendary foundation of the city in 421: "AB VRBE CON[DITA]. M[ILESIM]O XXX.V.IIII°." Even though Flavio Biondo had recently claimed that Venice was founded instead in 456 and wrote a short treatise on Venetian origins to buttress his case, the weight of tradition was too compelling and his erudite contribution was largely ignored.[46]

With the Arco Foscari, Bartolomeo Bon and the architects who succeeded him were able to achieve a more convincing synthesis. The structure was built in three stages and through its evolution one can document the changing Venetian approach toward the antique over a span of about a half-century.[47] The first campaign, dating to 1438–57, involved the passageway that led into the palace courtyard from the Porta della Carta and the heavy arch with alternating bands of white Istrian marble and pink *pietra da Verona* framing the opening at the opposite end (Plates 115–16). While the polychrome pattern was well grounded in Venetian tradition, the massive arch, carrying triumphal connotations, can be seen as the major vehicle of antique formal values in this phase.[48]

The second campaign was completed after Foscari's death,

115 Arco Foscari, view from the east. Venice, Palazzo Ducale. Begun by Bartolomeo Bon, 1438–71; completed by Antonio Rizzo, 1471–85.

primarily during the term of Doge Cristoforo Moro (1462–71). It was during this time that the east side of the Arco received its definitive two-story architectural structure under Bon's supervision, with a second triumphal arch superimposed on the first. The heavy corner pavilions crowned with crocketed spires and obelisk finials recall the Roman twin-tower gateway, a traditional symbol of political authority.[49] The composite capitals, featuring acanthus leaves and volute forms, are among the earliest Venetian revivals of the genuine antique capital type. *Romanitas* is thus expressed in the Arco Foscari with a renewed commitment to weight but also to assertive individual forms; an integration of the column into the structural system; and a sensitive absorption of such classical motifs as the rosettes, paterae, and capitals into the native Venetian tradition.[50]

The third phase seems to have been completed during the dogates of Nicolò Tron (1471–3) and Giovanni Mocenigo (1478–85). With the addition of the secondary façade facing the courtyard and a program of freestanding sculptures in niches and in the roof zone that celebrate the *virtù* of the doge and glorify ducal rule, it becomes an independent three-dimensional structure and is given a narrative program. Major responsibility for this phase of the campaign can be given to the sculptor-architect and military engineer Antonio Rizzo of Verona. Demonstrating an easy familiarity with and mastery of the antique, he is yet able to subordinate classical elements to harmonize with the preexisting architectural ensemble.[51] The narrative thrust of the sculptural program begins in the lower tier with Rizzo's statues of *Adam and Eve after the Fall*, depicting a human potential for upward movement in its rational and in its sensual aspects.[52] While Eve holds the antique Venus pudica pose, she is, like Adam, decidedly naturalistic and expressive, and polemically unclassical (see Plate 203).[53]

In the second tier, above Adam and Eve, there were originally two ensembles of the doge kneeling before the lion of St. Mark (now removed), one on the main façade and the other on the south side of the arch facing the courtyard. These groups provide the essential link between earth and heaven. For in the celestial realm of the upper tier one finds St. Mark atop the central pinnacle above the main façade, surrounded by putti and adoring angels; and, complementary but subordinate to him, the female personification of *Amor dei*, facing the courtyard. Accompanying them were freestanding figures on spires: seven female allegories, originally the Liberal Arts; and an honor guard of warrior figures, two carrying Tron and Mocenigo arms.

Scanning upward, the attentive viewer could thus take in at a glance a Venetian scheme of salvation and the potential to re-create a new paradise on earth in Venice itself. The pivotal figure in this fulfillment is the doge; the key agents are human will, virtue, and the love of God.[54] As with the trecento sculptural program on the exterior of the ducal palace, which also gave particular prominence to Adam and Eve, the republic is placed in a universal context, outside historical

116 Arco Foscari, view from the south. Venice, Palazzo Ducale.

time. Or to put it another way, the political realm of the *saeculum* is again brought into harmony with God's time.

The gradual absorption of classical ideas in the Arco Foscari is paralleled in the monumental tombs of the Venetian doges.[55] Although they were paid for by the families of the deceased and were located in churches, they have a strong political resonance and should be regarded as public works. The tomb of Francesco Foscari in the Frari was probably built in the late 1460s or even later by Antonio and Paolo Bregno, architects from the Lugano area (Plate 117).[56] Featuring an honorific canopy above a hanging sarcophagus with monumental columns at the sides and a lengthy Latin inscription, it recalls Donatello and Michelozzo's monument of the mid-1420s for Pope John XXIII (Baldassare Coscia) in the Baptistery of Florence. But whereas the Florentine tomb represented an ingenious solution to an architectural necessity, since its flanking columns were part of the building and already in place, the Foscari monument employed the "almost classical columns" not as structural supports, but as framing devices and independent pedestals for sculpture. All seven Virtues, dressed *all'antica*, actively mourn the passing of the defunct, while two warriors in Roman armor attest to the ducal power of the present.[57]

To ask whether the monument should be regarded as simply a transitional work, combining Gothic and classical elements, or as an infelicitous pastiche of ideas taken from other tombs, may not be the point. The issue in such pastiches may well be, as John Onians argues, one of cautious absorption of pagan forms that still need to be balanced, neutralized as it were, by a heavy component of Gothic, and thus Christian elements.[58]

The real breakthrough in ducal tomb design came in the later 1470s with the monuments of Pietro Mocenigo (1476–81) in SS. Giovanni e Paolo and of Nicolò Tron in the Frari. Both feature triumphal arches and both achieve a new unity of architecture and classical detail. The most elaborate sepulchral monuments yet to be built in Venice and featuring, respectively seventeen and twenty-two marble figures, they

117 Antonio and Paolo Bregno, tomb of Doge Francesco Foscari (1423–57), *c.* late 1460s. Venice, Santa Maria Gloriosa dei Frari.

118 Pietro Lombardo, tomb of Doge Pietro Mocenigo (1474–6), 1476–81. Venice, SS. Giovanni e Paolo.

119   Pietro Lombardo, *Hercules and the Hydra*, detail from the tomb of Doge Pietro Mocenigo, 1476–81. Venice, SS. Giovanni e Paolo.

were intended to impress. Neither, however, pretends to be Roman or anything but Venetian. McAndrew's characterization of the Tron tomb can be applied to both: "while the vocabulary is classical, the syntax is not — but neither is it something held over from Gothic. The combination is new, not macaronic, and new also is the portentous scale . . ."[59]

Pietro Lombardo, probably with the help of his sons Tullio and Antonio, was responsible for the Mocenigo tomb (Plate 118). Like the funeral orations honoring doges in this period, it stressed not only the virtues, but also the deeds of the deceased, comparing him to the heroes of antiquity. The doge no longer lies recumbent and lifeless on the bier, but stands upon his sarcophagus, upright and vigilant in full battle armor under his ducal robes, with narrative reliefs on the tomb front commemorating his heroic exploits.[60]

Mocenigo's military prowess in battling the Turks was a matter of particular family pride; the prominent inscription – "EX HOSTIUM MANUBIIS" – proclaims that the tomb was paid for "from hostile booty" and, by implication, not from public or private funds.[61] The epitaph on the base of the monument is flanked by reliefs of military trophies and, significantly, of Hercules with the Nemean Lion and the Hydra in a personal appropriation of the icons that had been immured in the façade of San Marco since the thirteenth century (Plate 119).[62] Surrounding Mocenigo is an honor guard of warriors in antique dress. Those within the arch represent four distinct ages of man: Youth, Prime and Middle Age supporting the casket, and Childhood atop it.[63] As with the republic itself, impotent old age or decrepitude is implicitly rejected.[64]

A concern with human time was also a significant feature of the tomb of Nicolò Tron (Plate 120). Antonio Rizzo's first major commission in Venice, it too was begun in 1476 and completed in the early 1480s. Its development should probably be seen in terms of a reciprocal relationship with the Mocenigo tomb. Rizzo was particularly inventive in his use of imperial coin imagery. The profile heads that decorate the sarcophagus depict the same idealized Roman head at four different stages of life: Youth, Prime, Middle Age and now also Old Age (Plate 121). The standing figures that separate the medallions are drawn from Roman coin reverses – Pax, Abundantia, and Securitas – to form a new set of civic virtues appropriate to the well-governed state. And, significantly, they are connected to a specific ruler whose effigy appears twice on the tomb: alive and standing upright in ducal regalia like Pietro Mocenigo, but also laid out in death on the top of his bier.[65] Were such tombs triumphal portals to the afterlife or ceremonial gateways to the Venetian political present?[66] Perhaps their success may be measured by the degree to which they were both.

The notion of the doge as an ideal, universal ruler is antithetical to Venetian political theory, and the imagery of the tomb in all likelihood comes as a direct response to similar statements by strong rulers elsewhere in Italy.[67] Direct parallels can be found in contemporary orations in which the doge is praised in extravagantly laudatory terms. The patrician Pietro Barozzi thus employed the antique canon to compare Cristoforo Moro to Socrates, Pericles, and Demosthenes – among others – in eloquence, and to proclaim his moral superiority to Romulus, Junius Brutus, Tarquinius, and Gaius Caesar, whose reigns were secured by thieves, pretenders, and parricides. The doge should be understood in such cases in emblematic rather than human terms, summing up in his person the state itself.[68]

Nicolò Tron was particularly susceptible to such paradigms. It was he, it may be recalled, who was criticized for having his bust-length portrait placed on a new lira coin called the Tron.[69] A painting on canvas originally in the Magistrato del Cattaver of the Ducal Palace also uses the telling symbolism of the triumphal arch to make a political point (Plate 122). It succeeds both in exalting Tron the doge and effacing Tron the man, present only in his coat of arms and corno above the architrave. Likewise, the magistrates who commissioned the work are denoted only by coats of arms and by their initials on the podium. The inscription states a fundamental precept of state ideology: "OBSE·LEG·EST·AVG·R·P" (Observare leges est augmentum Rei Publicae – To observe the laws is the enhancement of the Republic). The solid and enduring structure

120 Antonio Rizzo, tomb of Doge Nicolò Tron (1471–3), 1470–*c.* early 1480s. Venice, Santa Maria Gloriosa dei Frari.

121 Antonio Rizzo, detail from the tomb of Doge Nicolò Tron, 1470–c. early 1480s. Venice, Santa Maria Gloriosa dei Frari.

of the state, with its body of laws and procedures, is thus shown to rest on the base of magistrates and is crowned by the doge.[70]

Turning from Venetian architecture to pictorial representation in the middle years of the quattrocento, there is a similar syncretic approach to the past, with Roman elements filtering slowly and erratically into the picture space. But while parallel tendencies of "archaeological contamination"[71] may be observed in paintings, drawings, and sculptural reliefs, the intention of the architect is inherently different from that of the historically minded painter or sculptor. For the former,

122 Venetian School, *Triumphal Arch of Doge Nicolò Tron*, 1471–3. Canvas, 140 × 98 cm. Venice, Accademia.

the aim was to legitimize – indeed, to perfect – the present; for the latter, it was to historicize – indeed, recreate – the ever more distant past.

123   Jacopo Bellini, *Flagellation of Christ*. Ink on detached parchment, 39.6 × 29.1 cm. Paris, Louvre, Cabinet des Dessins (R.F. 427).

6

DISTANT TIMES, NEARBY PLACES

How you may exult, Bellino,
that what your lucid intellect feels
your industrious hand shapes into
rich and unusual form.
So that to all others you teach the true way
of the divine Apelles and the noble Polycleitus;
because if nature made you perfect,
that is a gift from heaven and your destiny . . .
– From a sonnet by Ulisse degli Aleotti, 1441[1]

Jacopo Bellini was the first major Venetian artist to respond to the challenge of Cyriacus of Ancona to "awaken the dead" who inhabited the lost world of pagan antiquity. As the teacher of "the true way" to the next generation of artists, moreover, he played a major role in determining the visual character of the Venetian Renaissance. Although it was once fashionable to compare Bellini unfavorably with his son-in-law Andrea Mantegna for his lack of archaeological sophistication,[2] more nuanced views have emerged in recent years, which take into account differences in age, in patronage, and, ultimately, in intention. As Bernhard Degenhart and Annegrit Schmitt point out in their magisterial study of Bellini, it may be more accurate to view him as a forerunner rather than a competitor of Mantegna.[3] Indeed, in Bellini's work one finds a singular synthesis in which antiquarian initiatives are skillfully embedded in a matrix that preserves traditional Venetian values.[4]

With all his frescoes and most of his panel paintings now destroyed, Bellini's primary artistic legacy consists of two albums of drawings. But these are no small thing: two folio-sized books – one now in the Louvre with ninety-four leaves, all of parchment with the exception of a single inserted leaf of paper, and drawings made in silverpoint or pen and ink, or a combination of the two; the other in the British Museum, with ninety-nine leaves of *carta bombasina*, a heavy drawing paper, with drawings primarily in lead point. While some of the original drawings are known to be missing, the two books still contain, collectively, some 230 drawings, several of which extend across two facing pages.[5] Their original function

uncertain, Jacopo's albums represented something quite new within the established drawing book tradition. The most prevalent form in North Italy at the time, particularly in Lombardy, was the late Gothic model book. It featured individual studies, taken from nature for the most part in accordance with courtly tastes, of exquisitely drawn animals and birds. These were displayed in a clear and visible manner – often in profile and rarely overlapping – in isolation on the page. Such compilations constituted a perfected "reservoir of motifs" to be re-used by the workshop in finished works of art.[6]

By the late 1420s, Gentile da Fabriano was already compiling another type of drawing book, now called a sketch book. Although it too grew out of the court tradition of naturalism, it embraced a wider range of subject matter than the Lombard model book. To the usual birds and animals were now added contemporary figures, architectural motifs, and fragments of compositions, and, significantly, antiquities. While some of the sketches were finely detailed, others were simply spontaneous "first thoughts," rapidly executed and placed on the page in an arbitrary manner. As Gentile's protégé and artistic heir, Pisanello contributed to the early sketch book and made several of his own.[7]

Jacopo's albums feature elements common to both types of drawing books, but there are significant differences. The most obvious concerns their dimensions, for they are more than twice the size of other model and sketch books that survive from the fourteenth and fifteenth centuries.[8] More importantly, while some of the pages of his albums contain isolated motifs suitable for re-use in larger works, a good number of the drawings are *istorie*, well-elaborated narrative scenes with complex architectural or landscape settings. Such compositions have to be regarded as completed works of art in themselves and are probably what Jacopo's widow referred to in her testament as "quadros dessignatos" – roughly translatable as "drawn paintings."[9]

The elevation of the humble drawing into a true and proper work of art in itself, through its incorporation into a larger "corpus," is an innovation of no small significance. As the earliest such compilations known, and the largest produced by any quattrocento artist, the albums can justly be considered one of the major achievements of Venetian Renaissance art. Beyond that, they yield important insights into the ways in which Jacopo participated in the antiquarian movement and incorporated *romanitas* into the culture of *venezianità*. For his "drawn paintings," gathered together into albums, were not only vehicles of artistic discovery. They are also testimony of a particular historical moment in which humanist concerns and artistic sensibilities conjoined in a personal re-appropriation of the classical world.

The dating of Jacopo's albums has been a matter of considerable discussion, and the chronology recently proposed by Degenhart and Schmitt will probably not settle the issue to everyone's satisfaction. In a sweeping revision to earlier scholarly consensus, they place the Paris album first (*c.*1430–1450s), to be overlapped and followed by the London album (*c.*1455–70). They essentially exclude the participation of other artists, such as Jacopo's own sons, who have often been suggested as retouchers of a number of the drawings. Although it is possible to disagree on minor points, the proposal is the most thoroughly argued and most convincing examination of the problem to date. With each drawing assigned its place in a four-decade long artistic evolution, the artist is shown to move from an early period of experimentation within the International Gothic idiom in the precise pen drawings of the Paris album toward larger and simpler Renaissance forms and a freer, broader execution in the lead point drawings of the album in the British Museum. This view of Bellini's development forms the essential foundation for the discussion that follows.[10]

THE ARTIST AS ANTIQUARIAN

Little direct knowledge remains of Jacopo Bellini's participation in the antiquarian movement of his time, and the issue must be approached indirectly and piecemeal, drawing on several kinds of evidence. His widow Anna Bellini wrote her testament in 1471, about a year after her husband's death. In it she leaves to her son Gentile "all the works in plaster, marble and relief, the 'drawn paintings' and all the books of drawings and other things pertaining to painting and the art of painting that belonged to the said late master Jacopo Bellini."[11] The terminology suggests that the artist had assembled a working collection of models that included antique fragments and plaster casts. One of these pieces could well have been the statuette described in the possession of Jacopo's son in the mid-1470s by Raffaele Zovenzoni:

> Any who would wish to see the Venus of Paphos with
>   naked breasts
>   in the ancient marble of Praxiteles,
> Should seek out the shelf of Gentile Bellini where she
>   stands,
>   even though the limbs are cut off, her image lives.[12]

Another piece could have been the "antique bust of Plato with the point of the nose of wax" sold to Isabella d'Este in 1512 by Jacopo's other two sons, Giovanni and Nicolò, after Gentile's death.[13] From the standpoint of both availability and cost, Jacopo would have found it far easier than his sons to obtain such objects, for the growing demand for classical artifacts in the late fifteenth century would have priced them out of the reach of most artists. Indeed, Isabella's ruthless pursuit of antiquities was only a prominent example of a more broadly based phenomenon. What the father could have afforded may well have become too dear for the sons.

Although such citations stand between document and literature, they describe real objects; whether the artifacts cited here might have been part of Jacopo Bellini's collection is at least open to legitimate conjecture. Other literary evidence, favoring classical topoi and tending toward antiquarian hyperbole, has to be treated more cautiously. Ulisse degli Aleotti's sonnet comparing Jacopo to Apelles and Polykleitos was one of two poems that he wrote in 1441 on the occasion of a contest between Jacopo Bellini and Pisanello for the best portrait of Lionello d'Este of Ferrara. In the other verse, he called Jacopo "a second Phidias... for our own dark world."[14] About a decade later, the humanist Angelo Decembrio wrote a dialogue in which Lionello praised both painters as "the finest artists of our time."[15] Such accolades place Bellini within a milieu of humanist patrons, but they may well reveal more about the erudition of the writer than about the classical interests of the artist.

In the last analysis, the most compelling evidence regarding Bellini's antiquarian interests is the unmediated testimony of the drawings themselves. The first important clue is found in his imaginative deployment of antique coins in the earlier compositions of the Paris album. Like Pisanello, Bellini gravitated to them as a major source of artistic inspiration, but he used them quite differently. He was not so much interested in coins as models for a new genre of portraiture, but as pictorial "denotators" of historical authenticity. Enlarging numismatic images into decorative tondi, he applied them to buildings of questionable provenance to give them an antique character. As has often been noted, such works evoke a past that speaks the language of the Venetian present. The Flagellation of Christ, for example, takes place in the spacious palace of

124 Jacopo Bellini, *Presentation of the Virgin* from his *Book of Drawings*, f. 28. Pen and ink over silverpoint on parchment, c.42.7 × 29 cm. Paris, Louvre, Cabinet des Dessins (R.F. 1496/130)

Pontius Pilate, the arcaded façade of which, with projecting balconies, bears a distant kinship to the recently constructed west wing of the Palazzo Ducale (Plate 123). The walls are richly adorned with medallions and reliefs: an enthroned Zeus taken from a tetradrachmon of Alexander the Great; a personification of Africa from a sesterce of Hadrian; Romulus, Remus, and the She-Wolf from a Constantinian seal. In a like manner, no less than eight numismatic motifs – among them one taken from a tetradrachmon of Lysimachos – decorate the Temple of Jerusalem in a drawing of the *Presentation of the Virgin* (Plate 124).[16]

Jacopo's enterprising use of these particular images hints at his familiarity with that circle of Venetian collectors who had gathered around Cyriacus of Ancona on his visit to Venice in 1432–3, and who shared his passion for the ancient world. It was then that Ambrogio Traversari was sufficiently impressed with Cyriacus's gold coins of Lysimachos, Alexander the Great, and Philip of Macedon to write a full report back to Niccolò Niccoli in Florence. The reappearance of two such coins in Jacopo's drawings of the late 1430s is suggestive of an encounter with Cyriacus either on that occasion or at some other time.[17]

Furthermore, the fitful presence of Cyriacus of Ancona can be suggested as a motivating force behind Jacopo's novel decision to assemble and bind together his selected drawings. For the albums share a number of features with the humanist sylloges that Cyriacus did so much to popularize. Among these is the *Quaedam antiquitatum fragmenta* of Giovanni Marcanova, a figure to whom Jacopo seems to have been linked, however tenuously, by bonds of affinity. Venetian by birth, doctor of medicine, and student of antiquities with a long residence in Padua, Marcanova died in Bologna in 1467 with Ulisse degli Aleotti at his bedside. He was, moreover, a close friend of Mantegna's who had married Jacopo Bellini's daughter Nicolosia in 1453.[18] In the preface to his sylloge, Marcanova articulated the high aims of the Renaissance antiquarian:

> Whereas we admire and venerate holy antiquity in all
> things,
>   we think those zealous and diligent investigators
>   worthy of special praise . . .
> Why do you endure the many dangers of sea and land
>   In order to see the ancient monuments of earlier
>   men?
> What you have traveled the whole world to see,
>   now a page sets before your eyes.
> If by chance it brings delight to your mind,
>   do not be reluctant to give thanks to the author.[19]

The wealthy Marcanova was an assiduous and learned collector of inscriptions, but he entrusted the final execution of his sylloge to professional scribes and artists in his *scriptorium* in Bologna. The work went through several redactions. Although the collection of inscriptions was already complete

in 1451, the first version (now in Berne) bears the dates 1457 and 1460.[20] It was followed in 1465 by an expanded version, now in Modena, that features a Cyriacan play between text and image with a similar use of ornament, diversely colored inks, and antiquarian script and includes a section of eighteen full-page drawings of ancient Rome.[21] Two other renditions, now in Paris and Princeton, were copied from it (Plate 125).[22]

The calligraphy of the Modena manuscript is the work of Felice Feliciano. An intriguing figure who liked to call himself "Antiquarius Felix," he was a major force in the revival of Roman epigraphy. He devoted himself to the study of Roman capital letters and designed a new humanist alphabet using the constructive principles of *quadratae litterae*.[23] A native of Verona and, like Marcanova, a friend of Mantegna's, he was one of Cyriacus's earliest and most devout disciples. Indeed, it was the romantically inclined Felice who compiled

125 A tomb monument in Pesaro, from Giovanni Marcanova, *Collectio antiquitatum*, written and illuminated in north-east Italy after 1465. Parchment, 36 × 26.5 cm. Princeton University Libraries, Manuscript Division, MS Garrett 158, f. 146.

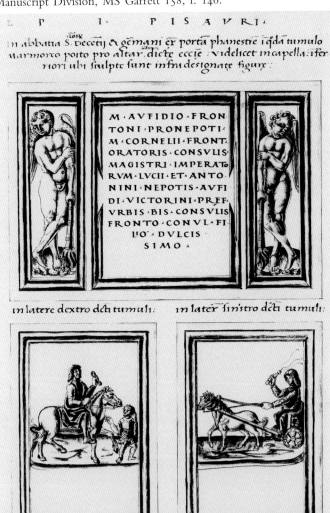

and wrote out the text of Scalamonti's *Vita Kyriaci Anconitani* for his friend Samuele da Tradate.[24] As he did so, he rediscovered on Italian soil those "pleasant and delightful places" that had cast their spell on Buondelmonti, Cyriacus and other travelers to the Aegean islands. If Felice could not experience the "verdant meadows and fruitful regions and cedars of paradise and flowering gardens" at first hand, perhaps he could recreate a similar dreamland closer to home.[25] For it was in this spirit that he wrote his famous – and perhaps imaginary – account of a two-day archaeological expedition around the southern shore of Lake Garda in September 1464.[26] The first day, entitled "MEMORATU DIGNA" – a noteworthy occasion – saw Felice and his friend Samuele (probably the son of the sculptor Jacopino da Tradate) with Andrea Mantegna, exploring the area around Toscolano, site of the ancient Benacum.[27] Felice described the locale *ad viridarios paradiseos*:

> a paradisiacal landscape and gardens, on a most beautiful site beloved of the Muses. Beautiful not only for roses and purple blooms, but also shaded by the leafy branches of orange and lemon trees. We visited the islands and meadows, where water streamed copiously from springs and which were profusely adorned with palms and lofty, old and fruit-bearing laurels. There we saw sundry traces of antiquity . . .[28]

It was in his account of the second day, however – the "IUBILATIO" – that Felice was able to give full expression to a creative imagination inflamed by the seductive vision of Cyriacan prose. He named Samuele, "crowned with myrtle, evergreen ivy, and other foliage," as leader, perhaps as a graceful gesture to him as dedicatee of the manuscript. The group now included Mantegna and a certain Ioanne Antenoreo, probably Giovanni Marcanova, as consuls and Felice himself as *procurante*, along with a "noble band of participants" who followed them "through the dark groves of laurel." After recording several classical inscriptions in churches in the vicinity in "the books we had brought with us," the party "discovered a shrine of the quiver-bearing Diana and other nymphs." They continued the trip "in a large boat, which was adorned with tapestries and all kinds of things and in which we scattered laurel leaves and other noble foliage, and sailed about on the Lake of Garda, that liquid field of Neptune, while the Emperor Samuele played all the time on the lute and sang thereto." The tour concluded with a visit to "the church of the Holy Virgin in Garda, where we sang exultant hymns of praise to the supreme Thunderer and expressed our deepest reverence for his sublime Mother . . ."[29]

As the stones now immured in the campanile of the church of SS. Pietro e Paolo in Toscolano attest, the inscriptions recorded in Felice's sylloges had a basis in concrete reality (Plate 126).[30] The Garda expedition may have taken place primarily in Felice's imagination, but it was grounded in the physical remains of antiquity. In addition to the codex for Samuele, Felice also created epigraphical collections for his

126   Roman inscriptions embedded in the wall of the campanile of SS. Pietro e Paolo, Toscolano (Lago di Garda).

other two companions. Aside from his transcription of *Quaedam antiquitatis fragmenta* for Marcanova, he produced a third manuscript, entitled *Epigrammaton ex vetustissimus lapidibus*, and dedicated it to "the magnificent Andrea Mantegna, Paduan, the incomparable painter."[31] Here, the epigrams had a practical purpose. In his address to Mantegna, "a great lover and student of antiquity," Felice counsels the artist: "If thou wilt read it and read it again, thou wilt reap no little profit from a knowledge of the elegant style of the ancients, and above all thou wilt learn the orthography, to which many are today so indifferent that they must be described as barbarians rather than Latins."[32]

Acknowledging the obvious distinctions between a catalogue of rediscovered texts and a portfolio of original artistic solutions, there are still sufficient analogies between Jacopo Bellini's albums, and Marcanova's sylloges that followed them, to place them in the same visual world. In a sense Jacopo transcended their common model, for in his albums he included the present along with the past. Extending the canon to embrace all the products of the painter's craft, he endowed his own compendium with personal and professional relevance. In it he incorporated a wealth of pictorial revelations, experiments, and solutions: *caxamenti* or architecture; portraiture; sacred and profane *istorie*; perspective studies; mythological vignettes; genre scenes; several groups of lions, foot soldiers, and equestrians; a standing Madonna; festival apparatus; and even a single iris exquisitely rendered in colored inks. Significantly, at least ten pages were prepared with circles to be filled with drawings of antique coins, and two full-page compositions in the Paris album were devoted to re-creations of individual Roman sepulchral monuments complete with antique inscriptions. The latter drawings were cited in an index appended to the volume in the 1470s as: "molti Epitafii

127 Jacopo Bellini, *Roman Monuments*, from his *Book of Drawings*, f. 44. Pen and ink over silverpoint on parchment, 29 × 42.7 cm. Paris, Louvre, Cabinet des Dessins (R.F. 1512).

128 Jacopo Bellini, *Roman Monuments*, from his *Book of Drawings*, f. 45. Pen and ink over silverpoint on parchment, 29 × 42.7 cm. Paris, Louvre, Cabinet des Dessins (R.F. 1513).

altichi romani" and "molti altri Epitafij antichi romani" (Plates 127 and 128).[33]

If Jacopo's albums are compared with three different redactions of Marcanova's sylloges – the Modena codex and the versions in Paris and Princeton that derive from it – some telling points of convergence can be found. In the first place, all the inscriptions on Jacopo's two pages of Roman monuments (save one from Rome) and several of the classical motifs are to be found in the sylloges. The funerary stele of Metellia Prima, once in the church of San Salvatore in Brescia, is the only monument to appear in all four examples bearing its original inscription (Plates 127 and 129–31). If Jacopo's drawing (c.1440) predated those in the codices (1457–65), it may well have been made from direct observation of the monument.[34] The disparities between the four examples indicates the degree of license allowed and taken in such transcriptions. Typically, portrait busts on Roman monuments are positioned in a frontal view, but the artists of the sylloges departed from the classical convention and depicted the busts in canted positions in order to generate the three-dimensional space expected in quattrocento painting. Bellini went even further and added profile portraits as well. It is only in his composition that a psychological connection between the pairs may be observed, as well as variety and unity within the group as a whole.[35]

Each time such a monument was copied it was altered – improved upon, if you will – according to the historical and aesthetic sensibilities of the artist. Jacopo's "romantic" approach to the visual truth of an antique object should thus be viewed within this context of antiquarian emendation. Indeed, if the Modena codex of Feliciano, an expert epigrapher, is accepted as the most accurate in regard to the form of the lettering and word-breaks of the Latin text, it may be concluded that Jacopo was even more faithful to the original

129 *Monument of Metellia Prima*, from Giovanni Marcanova, *Quaedam antiquitatum fragmenta*. Pen and ink on parchment, 36 × 25 cm. Paris, Bibliothèque Nationale, Cod. Lat. 5825 F, f. 133v.

130 Felice Feliciano, attrib., *Monument of Metellia Prima*, from Giovanni Marcanova, *Quaedam antiquitatum fragmenta*, 1460s. Pen and ink with wash on parchment, 34 × 24 cm. Modena, Biblioteca Estense, MS α. 5. 15 (Lat. 992). f. 138v.

Extra Brixiam in pariete eccie Sancti Saluatoris.

METELLIA·PRI
MA·SIBI·ET·P·

VALERIO·P·F·FAB·
INGENVO·
VIRO   SVO·

P·VALERIO·P·F·PRI
MO·
VALERIAE·P·F·FIRMAE·
C·VALERIO·P·F·VITAL·
I·VALERIO·P·F·CELATO
FILIIS   SVIS·
V·   F·

131 *Monument of Metellia Prima*, from Giovanni Marcanova, *Collectio antiquitatum*, after 1465. Pen and ink with wash on parchment, 36 × 26.5 cm. Princeton, Princeton University Libraries, Manuscript Division, MS Garrett 158, f. 127.

model than were the professional scribes of the Paris and Princeton versions.[36]

A second area of consonance with the sylloges can be found in Bellini's building portraits, called *caxamenti* in the index to the Paris album. The Modena and Princeton sylloges each contain a section with full-page compositions of daily life in pagan Rome that are similar in concept and form (if not in style and artistic quality) to several of Bellini's. A scene of pagan sacrifice from the Princeton manuscript features a building façade, isolated and orientated frontally, and the unclassical application of antique ornament familiar from the pages of the Paris album (Plate 132). A *via sacra* lined with fabulous Roman sarcophagi might be regarded as the ultimate

(and perhaps inevitable) synthetic statement that recombines the classical funerary monuments into a reconstituted whole (Plate 133). The point is not that the artist of the manuscript was indebted directly to Jacopo Bellini (the possibility seems most unlikely), but that such scenes were accepted as legitimate components of a humanist sylloge.[37]

In another sylloge related to Cyriacus's *Commentaria*, is a third element that will be taken up in Jacopo's albums: the double-page scene. Cyriacus himself, or a copyist following his example, drew the Trojan horse on one page, the walls of Troy on the other (Plate 134).[38] The structural similarity to Jacopo's *St. George rescues the Princess from the Dragon* and several other paired drawings in the London album, with a large figure on one side and an architectural element on the other may not seem similar at first glance (Plate 135). But it is close enough to suggest some degree of conceptual affinity, even if the subject matter is not the same.[39]

Our fourth point concerns the structure of these collections on parchment and paper. Some sylloges were carefully organized. Marcanova's, for example, devoted separate sections to

132 *Pagan Sacrifice*, from Giovanni Marcanova, *Collectio antiquitatum*, after 1465. Pen and ink with wash on parchment, 36 × 26.5 cm. Princeton, Princeton University Libraries, Manuscript Division, MS Garrett 158, f. 8v.

SACRIFI CIVM

SAC RIFI CIV M

the full-sized drawings of Rome, to inscriptions arranged according to geographical location, and to quotations from classical writers, and concluded with a glossary of Latin abbreviations. Others, however, like the epigraphic collections of Bartholomaeus Fontius, did not follow any particular order of classification. As Fritz Saxl commented: "Who ever had the book was supposed to read in it at random, enjoying one inscription after another."[40] The remark is apposite for Bellini's albums as well. While some scholars have tried to find a conscious program that determined the arrangement of his drawings, any tendencies toward order are undercut by a persistent, even unruly, randomness. Indeed, the very lack of a consistent organizing principle seems to reflect the tensions and ambiguities of the creative process that is played out so eloquently in the drawings as a whole.[41]

Obviously, any parallels between the humanist sylloge and the albums does not constitute an exact equivalence. Jacopo's interests extended well beyond the revival of antiquity, and he included objects and subjects that had little to do with the classical world. But once the artist was inspired to make such

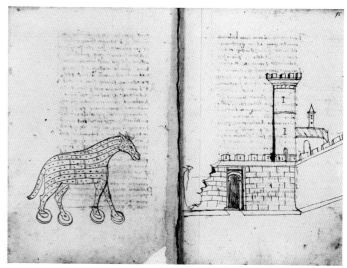

134 Cyriacus of Ancona or follower, *The Trojan Horse before the Walls of Troy*, in a sylloge of inscriptions, first half fifteenth century. Rome, Biblioteca Apostolica Vaticana, Cod. Ottob. Lat. 1586, ff. 94v–95r.

133 *Roman Via Sacra*, from Giovanni Marcanova, *Collectio antiquitatum*, after 1465. Pen and ink with wash on parchment, 36 × 26.5 cm. Princeton, Princeton University Libraries, Manuscript Division, MS Garrett 158, f. 10.

135 Jacopo Bellini, *St. George rescues the Princess from the Dragon*, from his *Book of Drawings*, ff. 6v–7. Leadpoint on paper, 41.5 × 33.6 cm. London, British Museum.

a connective link he could form his own *collectio* according to his personal inclinations.

Finally, moving from form to function, a further analogy may be proposed. The dedicatory inscription of Marcanova's Modena codex, *Quaedam antiquitatis fragmenta*, identifies it as a gift made for Novello Malatesta, Lord of Cesena.[42] In a like manner, Fontius sent his epigraphical compendium to Guillaume de Rochefort, the chancellor of France, in 1489.[43] Collections of classical inscriptions were thus objects of value, suitable pawns of exchange for humanists, princes, and prelates in the elaborate gift-giving and diplomatic protocols of Renaissance society. If Jacopo Bellini's albums are pictorial counterparts to the antiquarian sylloges, then Gentile Bellini's presentation of the volume now in the Louvre to the Ottoman Sultan Mehmed II in 1479, less than a decade after his father's death, becomes quite understandable. Whether or not the albums were originally intended, as some have suggested, to be just "libri studiorum" or a "set of blueprints" to establish an artistic tradition was no longer at issue. At that moment a bound collection of Jacopo's drawings was considered a suitable gift for an oriental potentate, inspired by and akin to the learned sylloges of his humanist contemporaries. The British Museum album remained in possession of the artist's family for another generation before it too left the workshop to enter a private collection, that of the Venetian patrician Gabriele Vendramin.[44]

ANTIQUITY RECONSTRUCTED

The two roles of Jacopo Bellini – as antiquarian and as artist – made, in a sense, for an uneasy alliance. Each required the delicate accommodation of two competing tendencies, both of which can be observed in Marcanova's sylloges: one favoring empirical description and the other aiming at imaginative historical reconstruction. Cyriacus of Ancona had recorded ruins as he saw them and mentally stripped off later additions to recapture the original state of monuments. While he was not above completing partially effaced inscriptions, he also acknowledged the classical fragment as an object of intrinsic interest in itself. The 1430s and 1440s were the formative decades for this approach. It is then that the first attempts to make comprehensive topographical surveys of the city of Rome can be discerned. Alberti sought to represent it in an objective and scientific manner in his *Descriptio urbis Romae*, a measured plan of the city, as well as in a city view.[45] Moved by a similar spirit, the humanist Poggio Bracciolini tried to give a full account of what was left of the ancient city in his *De varietate fortunae* (c.1431–48).[46] He worked from direct observations and aimed for a telling description of antiquities in their fragmentary state along with medieval changes and additions. Opposite the Theatre of Marcellus he noted "numerous marble columns, part of the portico of a temple said to be dedicated to Jove, whose circular arcade is occupied by new buildings and the interior by vegetable gardens."[47] An amphitheatre is observed "with a wall of brick, near the church of Santa Croce in Gerusalemme, that is inserted into new masonry to form part of the circuit of city walls."[48] Using the word "ruina" deliberately, Poggio compared the city of his own time to "a skeleton of a knocked down giant, rotted by the centuries and worn away in every part."[49]

To most working artists, by contrast, damaged classical artifacts demanded reconstruction (as witness the wax tip on Plato's marble nose) or incorporation: physically into architecture as spolia or conceptually into other works as painted, drawn, or sculpted motifs. Similar tendencies animated the humanist Flavio Biondo who sought to present a full reconstruction of the monuments of Rome in his *Roma Instaurata*

(1444–6) and a complementary retrieval of its customs and daily life in the *Roma Triumphans* (1456–60).[50] But both Poggio and Biondo were men of many words and few images, and their descriptions were purely verbal. It would fall to artists like Jacopo Bellini and his contemporaries to open windows into a visually intact, if fictive, classical past; they offered a bewildering range of possibilities.

At one extreme was the manuscript of Ptolemy's *Geography* copied in the original Greek for Cardinal Bessarion shortly after 1453. It features an imaginary portrait of Ptolemy himself, painted by a Venetian miniaturist who, following a long tradition, confused the subject's name with the Ptolemies who were kings of Egypt and accoutered him with a crown and royal robes (Plate 136). Holding an astrolabe, the geographer stands in the open air, surrounded by Gothic architecture of unconstrained many-hued splendor that is totally uncompromised by any archaeologically responsible classical reference. Bessarion, who would leave the volume and the remainder of his library to the Venetian republic in a testamentary bequest of 1468, was a figure of impressive erudition and impeccable humanist credentials. The *Geography* was said to have been one of his most prized possessions. It is worth noting that he was apparently untroubled by any inconsistency between the classical world of the antiquarian sylloges and the fabulous Gothic stage-set inhabited by Ptolemy. For him the ancient world was reachable primarily through texts and perhaps unrealizable through visual images.[51]

The full-page illustrations in Marcanova's sylloges represented an equally fanciful trend, in which a classical past was depicted essentially as that which was other than Gothic. The Baths of Diocletian in the Princeton codex, for example, were constructed of elements that had no place in either the classical or the Gothic architectonic traditions (Plate 137). What the artist did not know, he made up, drawing upon his own experience to represent a rudimentary hydraulic system that would have been more surprising to a Roman than to a quattrocento Italian. Neither the bather peering out the door of the baths nor Bessarion's Ptolemy inhabited a world that was grounded in historical visual reality. By contrast, the reasonably accurate drawings of classical artifacts that accompanied the inscriptions in the main section of the sylloge seem to have been part of another realm, which was not meant to be lived in.[52]

At the opposite pole were Mantegna's boldly classicizing frescoes in the church of the Eremitani in Padua (1448–57): a revolutionary alternative when compared to the exactly contemporary Ptolemy miniature. Mantegna brought a new sense of pictorial decorum to the picture space that was based upon archaeology and antiquarian scholarship (Plate 139). He tried to provide correct Roman costumes and settings for Roman events; and he placed these events in an internally consistent and well differentiated ancient world.[53] He was not, however, Venetian, and his lapidary vision entered Venice only in a well mediated form. One of the major points of dissemination

136 *Portrait of Ptolemy*, from Claudius Ptolemy, *Geography*, c.1453. Vellum, 58.5 × 43.5 cm. Venice, Biblioteca Nazionale Marciana, Cod. Gr. Z. 388 (=333), f. 6v.

graphic expression (Plate 138). Common both to the author of these drawings and to Jacopo is a Gothic feeling for the graceful harmony of the page as a whole. For each artist, the full elucidation of the individual antique figure or object is subordinated, and sometimes sacrificed, to the overall rhythm of the composition.[54] Archaeology, one might say, gives way to art.

138 Gentile da Fabriano (attrib.), drawings after the antique. Brush, pen, and ink over silverpoint on parchment, 21.1 × 15.4 cm. Rotterdam, Museum Boymans-van Beuningen, inv. no. I.523v.

would be the workshop of Jacopo Bellini. For Bellini's drawings represent yet another approach to the past, one that had grown out of the longstanding Venetian tradition of incorporation and accommodation. As will be seen, any new paradigm for Venetian artists would have to take this tradition into account.

Jacopo's immediate artistic past was rooted in the fertile soil of the International Gothic movement. Gentile da Fabriano, one of its foremost representatives, was his most important teacher and mentor. Many of Jacopo's drawings document his efforts both to honor that compelling model and to break free from it and find his own voice. But Gentile himself was more responsive to the antique than his paintings lead one to believe. If a group of figure drawings after antique sarcophagi is correctly attributed to him, then he – like Jacopo Bellini – carried on two stylistic lives in his art: a descriptive approach of circumstantial abundance and rich surface values in painted works, much admired by humanists for its ekphrastic possibilities, and a speculative and classically aware turn of mind in

As has often been observed, Jacopo was particularly skillful at inventing his own perfected assemblages from antiquarian debris. All the inscriptions on his two pages of funerary monuments in the Paris album, save the one from Rome, came from the Veneto. But aside from the monument of Metellia Prima, the epigrams were probably found on stones of little artistic interest, thus prompting Jacopo to acquire suitable motifs from other sources and to recycle them into new constructions of his own design. The dancing nymphs on the monument on the right-hand side of folio 44 (Plate 127), for example, come from a Roman altar now in the Museo Civico in Padua. The base, however, carries an inscription located in the fifteenth century in a garden in Padua belonging to an attorney from Bassano named Alexander. Jacopo went further afield for the corresponding monument on folio 45 (Plate 128). The inscription on top, taken from the base of the Vatican obelisk in Rome, was paired with a second one taken from the Arco dei Gavi in Verona, along with a pictorial motif from its frieze. Whether Jacopo copied the inscriptions directly from the stones themselves or whether he took them from the pages of a sylloge is unknown, but all of them, with the probable exception of the Roman epitaph, were well within his range of personal access.[55]

The specific formal sources of Jacopo's large-scale architectural structures, whether taken from an actual monument or

139 Andrea Mantegna, *St. James before Herod*, *c*.1451. Fresco (now destroyed), w. 330 cm. Padua, Church of the Eremitani, Cappella Ovetari.

from a sylloge, are typically hard to locate.[56] But there is one instance where the invention can be compared with its prototype. The Arco dei Sergii in Pula, once inspected by Cyriacus of Ancona and co-opted for the Arsenale portal by a Venetian architect, drew the attention of Jacopo as well. Embellishing it with a classicizing frieze, he transformed it into the façade of the magnificent palace of Pontius Pilate (Plates 140 and 141). And yet that Roman past is not all that distant from the Venetian present. Looking down the central corridor one sees another façade with the familiar bifora windows, roundels, and crenellations of a typical Venetian palace front.

140   Arco dei Sergii, called the Porta Aurea, in Pula. From I.F. Cassas, *Voyage pittoresque et historique de l'Istrie et Dalmatie*, Paris 1802.

In a second drawing, grandeur gives way to intimacy, with the arch undergoing a further metamorphosis. Here it is reduced to human scale and is made to form the gateway to yet another Venetian courtyard in which Christ's flagellation takes place (Plate 142). Decorative elements are also adjusted to suit the new theme. While the putto holding a torch maintains his position on the keystone of the arch, the winged victories in the spandrels are replaced by roundels with Hercules and the rape of Deianeira by the centaur Nessus. In the time-hallowed tradition of the *Ovide moralisée*, pagan motifs could provide a commentary by analogy on Christian themes.[57]

Jacopo clearly took considerable liberties when recreating the Roman past, but in so doing he was not much different from most of his contemporaries. Just as Giuliano da Sangallo had "seen" Greek architecture through a Roman lens, Jacopo Bellini "saw" the Arco dei Sergii through a Venetian filter. The point was made some years ago by Ernst Gombrich, "that even to describe the visible world in images we need a developed system of schemata . . . Without some initial starting point, some initial schema, we could never get hold of the flux of experience."[58] The known thus becomes an organizing prototype for the unfamiliar.

Although the process of amalgamation in these drawings is almost the reverse of that used in the other *Flagellation* (Plate 123), where antique coin motifs were simply applied to an essentially Venetian building, the underlying assumption is similar: biblical antiquity occupied the interstices between the pagan past and the Christian present. Its built environment, at once retrospective and prospective, thus partakes most logically of both stylistic traditions.

Turning now to Andrea Mantegna, that most archaeological of quattrocento artists, it appears that he too was prone to improve upon the original. In *St. James Before Herod*, completed around 1451, one of the inscriptions from Cyriacus's *Commentaria* has found its way on to the left pier of a triumphal arch (Plate 143). Partially obscured by two soldiers, it replicates exactly the line breaks of the same epigram shown in one of Jacopo's drawings of Roman monuments (Plate 127).[59] Above the inscription in Mantegna's fresco are two roundels containing profile portraits. If Degenhart and Schmitt's dating of Jacopo's drawing to the early 1440s is valid, the adjacent monument of Metellia Prima on the same page may well have provided the young Mantegna – about twenty years old at the time – with a useful prototype for yet another recombination of classical motifs.[60]

While Mantegna's architectural construction looks so much more authentically antique than those drawn by his future father-in-law, it is almost as untenable from a historical standpoint (Plate 138). Although a credible triumphal arch, it functions not as a gateway across a road, but, improbably, as the side wall of a throne room. It is thus just as uncanonical as Jacopo's adaptation of the Arco dei Sergii at Pula. And yet Mantegna's rejection of Jacopo's suave Gothic elegance for a hard, stony style in which to render consistently classical-looking figures, costumes, and motifs would have convinced the quattrocento churchgoer that such a setting could, indeed, have existed in a time both distant and disjoined from his or her own.

Even though both artists used classical details to place the life of Christ and other biblical events firmly in the historical past, the underlying attitude is thus intrinsically different. Bellini's strategy might be labeled as one of inclusion, wherein the *addition* of recognizably antique forms and motifs – coins, inscriptions, reliefs, architectural elements – was enough to re-situate the whole *mise-en-scène* back in antiquity. Mantegna's approach, by contrast, was one of exclusion. He sought to pare away the Gothic elements that might contaminate the Roman integrity of his settings.

In each artist, the empirical values that underwrote both the court tradition of naturalism and antiquarian studies conjoined, but with contrasting results. The difference, to risk summing up a complex issue in a few words, must be explained in part by Mantegna's early formation in Padua. Giotto had laid the foundation for a Paduan school in the first decade of the fourteenth century with his paintings in the Arena Chapel. The pictorial values expressed there – a dramatic narrative style, volume over line, clarity over prolixity, a plastic conception of the human figure, the rational organi-

141 Jacopo Bellini, *Christ brought before Pontius Pilate*, from his *Book of Drawings*, f. 35. Brush, pen and ink on parchment,
42.7 × 29 cm. Paris, Louvre, Cabinet des Dessins (R.F. 1503/39).

142   Jacopo Bellini, *Flagellation of Christ*, from his *Book of Drawings*, f. 8. Brush, pen and ink on parchment, 42.7 × 29 cm. Paris, Louvre, Cabinet des Dessins (R.F. 1476).

zation of the picture space – would remain viable in Paduan painting. Guariento da Arpo, the leading painter in the city in the mid-trecento, thus met the challenge of the emerging International Gothic style by accommodating it to these fundamental aesthetic values. Other major artists active in Padua during the next half-century – the Florentine Giusto da Menabuoi and Altichiero da Zevio of Verona – further translated the Giottesque language into a courtly idiom, but the essential elements remained.[61]

Growing up in Padua just beyond the gravitational pull of Venice, the young Mantegna (born *c*.1431) would also have been exposed early on to the work of some of the most gifted young revolutionaries of the new Renaissance style: most notably Uccello and Fra Filippo Lippi, who both worked there in the 1430s, and Donatello who began a decade of work at the Santo in 1443.[62] According to the sixteenth-century writer Bernardino Scardeone, Mantegna received his earliest training in a school for young painters operated by Francesco Squarcione.[63] An intriguing and still controversial figure, Squarcione was said to have traveled, probably in the 1420s, to Greece, "whence he brought home with him, both in his mind and in drawings, many things worthy of note that seemed likely to promote skill in his art." Attracting no fewer than 137 students from all over Italy to his *studium* during the years that followed, Squarcione was renowned – Scardeone writes – for teaching "from the statues and very many paintings he had, by whose mastery and art he instructed Andrea and the rest of his fellow-pupils, rather than from originals he had executed himself or worked up or from new models provided for copying."[64] Vasari added that Squarcione's teaching collection also included plaster casts "formed from ancient statues."[65] By 1455 the school took up two buildings, one of which was called the "house of reliefs."[66]

Although various scholars have expressed doubts about Squarcione's personal artistic proficiency and the nature and extent of his collection, from all indications he had a profound influence on the course of north Italian painting in the later quattrocento. Ronald Lightbown regards the *studium* as the "earliest known private art-school," perhaps modeled on the new boarding schools run by humanists for the teaching of classical literature, and as such, the ancestor of the modern academy of art.[67] As to Mantegna, it can be suggested that his development as a highly original artist with an independent vision was based upon a prodigious natural talent, the competitive atmosphere of an art school, the proximity of both Venetian and Tuscan art and artists, and the artistic tradition and antiquarian culture of Padua. Aiming at a revival not just of the vocabulary of classical art, but of the classical art of painting in its most ideal form, he set his own uncompromising course away from his early mentors.[68]

Jacopo Bellini's drawings reveal not only a different sense of history from Mantegna's, but also different notions about the purposes of art. Bellini's approach grew out of the aesthetic of diversity and accommodation already evident in Venetian art

143   Andrea Mantegna, *St. James before Herod* (detail of Plate 139).

and architecture of the thirteenth century and in Venetian humanism in the fifteenth. Underlying this aesthetic were assumptions that favored continuity between past and present, that welcomed the incorporation of the new into the old, and that preferred syncretism over true synthesis.[69] Jacopo Bellini, working through images rather than words or objects, sought to satisfy parallel goals of diversity, accommodation, and (ultimately) reconciliation.

PICTORIAL THEMES

The Pagan Past

When an artist moved into the realm of history, peopled by pagans and Christians, his talents for reconciliation could be put to the test. Indeed, men of the time were uncomfortably aware that Petrarch's revolutionary view of the ancient world was grounded in paradox: whether to regard the culture of pagan Rome as a Golden Age whose decline and fall was a tragedy or as an era of spiritual blindness whose passing away should be celebrated. The pictorial theme of the pagan idol crystallizes the dilemma most cogently. In later medieval art, the idol atop a column or an altar was perhaps the quintessential *signum* of pagan antiquity. As such, it typically held negative connotations. While the pagan gods were now vanquished, their supernatural powers, if no longer feared, were still a matter of record. A saint's ability to topple idols from their pedestals and send them crashing to the ground was a sure sign of holiness. Three such episodes are depicted in the Byzantine mosaics of San Marco dating to around 1200. In *St. Philip orders the Destruction of a Pagan Idol*, for example, a pious Scythian is directed to pull down the statue of Mars with a rope (Plate 144).[70] In such a scene, the idol is of secondary interest, serving primarily as an instrument by which the saint can demonstrate his miraculous powers and, by extension, the power of Christianity over paganism.

144 *St. Philip orders the Destruction of a Pagan Idol*, c.1200. Mosaic. Venice, San Marco.

But to medieval observers, single acts of individual saints could not account for the great quantity of fragments and the rarity of intact pieces of Roman sculpture. Although some had surely been destroyed by war and the barbarian invasions, the notion of purposive action by the Roman Catholic Church was a more attractive explanation. By the middle of the twelfth century a tradition had surfaced in which Pope Gregory the Great – that is, the church – was given credit for the wholesale destruction of pagan idols.[71] The ecclesiastical position was articulated in Petrarch's time by Amalricus Augerius, an Augustinian friar and chaplain to Pope Urban V (1362–70):

> [Gregory] resolved and ordered that the heads and limbs of all the images of demons that could be found inside and outside the city of Rome, must be amputated and broken into pieces, so that the palm of ecclesiastical truth would be more fully exalted, with the eradication of the roots of wicked heresy.[72]

It was such views that had led to the act of pious desecration of Livy's presumed remains in Padua in 1413.[73] In response, the issue was addressed by humanists who immediately took steps to amend the historical record. When the remaining bones were finally deposited in the wall of the Palazzo della Ragione in 1426, Sicco Polenton was completing the first version of his *Scriptores illustres latinae linguae*. In it he rejected out of hand the "empty and invented fable" that Gregory the Great was responsible for destroying most of Livy's literary works.[74] But he did not touch on the question of idol destruction, and the matter remained a topic of humanist concern. In 1437, the year when Sicco came out with a second version of his treatise, Guglielmo Capello, writing in Ferrara, composed a commentary reaffirming the old claims: "Pope Gregory broke up the statues in Rome that today one sees almost all without heads. Furthermore, he had many historical books burned such as the works or decades of Titus Livius, which contain the battles and other deeds of the ancient Romans, because they were not Christians."[75]

Jacopo Bellini was also concerned with idols during these years. A double-page drawing in the Paris album, probably datable to the late 1430s, is listed in the fifteenth-century index as "uno tenpio con alguni Idoli che vien roti da zente d'arme" (a temple with some idols that were being broken by soldiers) without further specifics (Plate 145).[76] With its imaginative recombination of classical fragments, the drawing offers yet another example of Bellini's genius for accommodation and stylistic reconciliation. Originally drawn in silverpoint and now barely visible, a female nude statue stands atop a column, the only figure in the composition that was not later reinforced in pen and ink. Like the four male cult statues who stand below her holding cornucopias, she may have been taken from the reverse of a Roman coin. The eight-sided base of the monument, inspired by the polygonal Roman piers flanking the main entrance to the church of SS. Maria e Donato in Murano, is surrounded by foot-soldiers and a horseman clad in both antique and Venetian armor.[77]

The activities of the soldiers appear to be self-directed and unsupervised until one notices an elderly bearded man on horseback all but hidden at the far left side of the verso page. Accompanied by a gesturing soldier, he is greeted with consternation by yet another equestrian, this one in civilian dress. Whether the old man is a ruler initiating an act of pious demolition, or simply an observer, is by no means clear. But the lack of a dramatic center need not mean the absence of specific subject matter. For the relegation to the sidelines of the elderly protagonist followed a strategy of narrative decentralization that was found in many of Jacopo's drawings. Indeed, the two-page composition matches up well enough with the legends of papal iconoclasm, and it is tempting to see the figure as Pope Sylvester or, more probably, as Gregory the Great. If such is the case, the episode would have gained in credibility in the eyes of the Venetian viewer, because it is grounded in the unremarkable activity of ongoing life.[78]

145 Jacopo Bellini, *Soldiers attacking an Idol*, from his *Book of Drawings*, f. 43. Brush, pen and ink over silverpoint on parchment, 42.7 × 29 cm. Paris, Louvre, Cabinet des Dessins (R.F. 1510/1511).

Whether or not Jacopo intended to commemorate a piece of papal history, the moral neutrality of the scene is worth noting. The actions of the soldiers lack firm direction and result in uncertain consequence. The pagan religion is neither good nor bad; it is simply there. Jacopo's ambivalence toward the seductive attractions of pious antiquity set him apart from artists of only a generation earlier. The idols are no longer just symbols of heresy and disbelief. They have become artifacts of history and objects of aesthetic delight, demanding interest, if not respect.[79]

Bellini took up the theme of the pagan idol again in a drawing of the same period listed in the index as simply "uno tempio in piu faze su molti gradi" (a polygonal temple on many steps). Here again the meaning is not easily graspable. It could be argued that the imposing architecture alone was the subject, but the expressions and gestures of the soldiers and the spectators again suggest a narrative situation (Plate 146). In this case, the idol, as far as can be determined, inspires awe

rather than confrontation. Bellini seems to ask: what was it really like to live in a pagan world? With reverence rather than destruction the overriding theme, pagan religion has become a subject for portrayal in itself, in a manner that can even be described as sympathetic.[80]

Bellini was not the only Venetian artist of this period to concern himself with the fate of pagan idols. Four small panels with scenes from the life of St. Apollonia, probably painted around 1450 as part of a polyptych by Antonio Vivarini or one of his circle, also show a certain ambivalence.[81] One panel shows the saint, armed with a hammer, who climbs a ladder with iconoclastic intent (Plate 147). Dwarfed by a splendid column base of luxuriant, if unconvincing, classicism, she is overshadowed by the sensuous nude statue of Bacchus that it supports. Elevated above the crowd on such a magnificent pedestal, Bacchus rather than Apollonia is, arguably, the primary locus of interest in the painting. In contrast to the thirteenth-century mosaic of *St. Philip orders the Destruction of*

146 Jacopo Bellini, *Polygonal Temple with Pagan Idol*, from his *Book of Drawings*, f. 48. Brush, pen and ink on parchment, 42.7 × 29 cm. Paris, Louvre, Cabinet des Dessins (R.F. 1516/153).

147　Antonio Vivarini (attrib.), *St. Apollonia destroys a Pagan Idol*, panel, *c.*1450. Wood panel, 60 × 34 cm. Washington, D.C., National Gallery of Art, Samuel H. Kress Collection.

the Pagan Idol, the idol has now become, effectively, a protagonist equal to the Christian saint. While Vivarini's painting ostensibly sanctioned an act of pious destruction, the devotional message was subverted by its visual elaboration.

The Ruined Past

Even more than the pagan idol, the classical ruin was a mutable sign. As suggested in the first chapters of this book, antique spolia could hold a positive charge, conferring age, authority and aesthetic distinction on contemporary buildings. But the architectural ruin was a different sort of fragment. It was not an intact and possibly perfect part of a once larger whole, such as, for example, the late antique relief of Hercules attached to the façade of San Marco. It was by its very nature imperfect and incomplete: in short, damaged goods. In the pictorial arts the ruin, of whatever style or period, could thus serve as a metaphor of loss and decay. If a classical ruin, it allowed for a multi-valent message with overtones that were not only political and aesthetic, but also moral and religious. This was particularly true when it was juxtaposed not only with perfect wholeness but also with its Gothic successor.[82]

In *The Vision of Augustus*, now in Stuttgart, a building becomes a ruin before our very eyes (Plate 148). Attributed to

148 Venetian School, *The Vision of Augustus*, c.1400. Wood panel, 95 × 79 cm. Stuttgart, Staatsgalerie.

149 Jacopo Bellini, *Baptism of Christ*, from his *Book of Drawings*, f. 24. Pen and ink on parchment, 42.7 × 29 cm. Paris, Louvre, Cabinet des Dessins (R.F. 1492/125).

an artist working in Venice or Padua around 1400, it depicts three miracles that happened on the day of Christ's birth. A heavenly apparition of the Virgin and Child in the disk of the sun dominates the panel, but the expanded spiritual message is played out below. On the left in front of a building with Gothic decorative elements, the Tiburtine Sibyl reveals the vision to the Emperor Augustus. In the center, a fountain begins to gush oil instead of water. And on the right, a Romanesque-style building has developed fissures and begins to fall apart as idols topple from their pedestals. An inscription explains: "The Temple of Peace, built for eternity, crumbled when the Virgin gave birth to a son."[83] It is thus a ruin in progress, a concrete example of divine agency in the triumph of Christianity.

With the drawings of Jacopo Bellini, the awareness of time in both its static and dynamic forms is expressed with a new refinement. In the *Baptism of Christ*, the sacrament is performed in a desolate desert landscape to the accompaniment of an angelic choir (Plate 149). Directly in front of this "narrative core" is an antique column that once held a pagan idol.

Although its base – significantly – remains intact, the ensemble is shattered and lies in fragments on the ground. The capital has fallen nearby, its fastening holes conscientiously recorded in the manner of Cyriacus of Ancona. Here Jacopo used the empirical methods of the latest antiquarian scholarship to convey a Christian message: the new dispensation is inaugurated on the foundation of the old.[84] Salvatore Settis has observed the inevitable tension created by the placement of ruins in a narrative scene: on the one hand there is a sense of necessity, that of the providential and inexorable march of Christian time; on the other there is the paradox of ancient glory – something good – now fallen.[85]

In another drawing, however, the message is extended, becoming at once more subtle and complex. On the day that Christ is led out of Jerusalem on the way to Calvary, the city is undergoing reconstruction (Plate 150).[86] The column monuments rising up behind the high wall identify it as antique and pagan. Workers repair a crumbling wall on the left, while in the foreground a sculptor puts the finishing touches to a classical statue. It is to be set upon a column that

lies ready on the ground. In ironic contrast a Roman soldier and his horse collapse to the right. Now the symbolism is more nuanced and deliberately less clear; indeed, the labors of the artisans may only signify the normalcy of ongoing life surrounding momentous events. But this normalcy is cast in terms of transience: great civilizations must be built up before they can fall. With Jacopo's rendering of imperfect or incomplete antiquity, or antiquity under construction as it were, temporality – the passage of historical time – has been brought into the *istoria*.[87] It is in these small details that the artist's personal, if ambivalent, recognition of detachment from the past may be sensed.[88]

Since nearly all of Jacopo's large-scale narrative paintings have been lost, whether or not they included classical ruins is unknown. But aside from isolated examples in the trecento, they seem to appear all at once in monumental Italian art of the 1450s.[89] Among the earliest to survive are Squarcione's De Lazara Polyptych of 1449–52 and Mantegna's Eremitani fresco of the *Execution of St. James*, now destroyed, but dating to *c.*1454–7 (Plates 151–2).[90]

150   Jacopo Bellini, *Christ on the Road to Calvary*, from his *Book of Drawings*, f. 19. Pen and ink on parchment, 42.7 × 29 cm. Paris, Louvre, Cabinet des Dessins (R.F. 1487/20).

152 Andrea Mantegna, *Execution of St. James*, *c*.1453–7. Fresco (now destroyed), w. 330 cm. Padua, Church of the Eremitani, Cappella Ovetari.

In Italian art throughout the rest of the century, the classical ruin became a standard element of contrast to rusticity in paintings of the Adoration of the Magi and in other scenes of pious regeneration.[91] In all such paintings, the pagan ruins held a negative charge as vestiges of a proud, but rightfully vanquished civilization. They rendered visible the triumph of the church, the positive result of an irreversible process. According to this view, the classical ruin was part of an unrecoverable, because abolished, past. While it was linked to the present, it was to remain just what it was: a fragment.

But there is a further development presaged by Squarcione's use of a crumbling ruin as a classical setting for St. Jerome in the central panel of the De Lazara Polyptych. While it surely carries connotations of Roman decline and Christian triumph, the ruin is not juxtaposed with new architecture but stands by itself. Silhouetted peculiarly against a gold leaf sky above and a blue sky with landscape below, it seems to be caught between a still medieval, symbolizing mentality and the new Renaissance archaeology. This empirical tendency – as yet unassimilated – derived from the separate, but now inter-

151 Francesco Squarcione, *St. Jerome*, detail from the De Lazara Polyptych, 1449–52. Tempera on wood panel, h. 175cm. Padua, Musei Civici.

154 Andrea Mantegna, *The Prayer in the Garden* (detail), *c.*1455. Wood panel, 63 × 80 cm. London, National Gallery. Reproduced by courtesy of the Trustees, The National Gallery, London.

153 Marco Zoppo, *St. Jerome in the Wilderness*, *c.* early 1460s. Wood panel, 82.5 × 67.9 cm. Baltimore, The Walters Art Gallery.

twined, antiquarian concerns of Cyriacus, Poggio, and Biondo. As with a number of Jacopo Bellini's drawings, it is this tradition that informs Mantegna's *Execution of St. James.*

The archaeological approach to ruins perhaps found its fullest realization in Marco Zoppo's painting of *St. Jerome in the Wilderness*, datable to the early 1460s (Plate 153).[92] What had been an isolated element in a stage set now became an ambient. Here the saint is flanked by two imposing masses of ruined Roman architecture – again in juxtaposition to an intact walled city, complete with amphitheatre, on the hill behind – but most of the idols still stand, and monkeys, possibly symbols of vice, prowl through the marble debris. Like Mantegna, Zoppo had been trained in Squarcione's atelier; he would play an important role in the dissemination of an "antique mode" in miniature painting in Venice and Padua during the last half of the fifteenth century.[93]

What is particular to Mantegna is the evocation of historical development through different kinds of stonework and masonry in the wall structures. To a much greater degree than Jacopo Bellini he depicted walls bearing the scars of time. In *The Prayer in the Garden*, also probably painted around the mid-1450s, the city walls of Jerusalem, itself composed of monuments from Rome and Constantinople, show unmistakable signs of damage and repair over successive epochs (Plate 154). Even more than fallen-down ruins, they are metaphors of process and change. Here Mantegna gives visual form to the concerns of Poggio, who had tried to sort out the various phases of a building over time, by analyzing construction techniques, masonry styles, and materials. Given the fact that Mantegna's friend Marcanova owned copies of both Poggio's and Biondo's works, it is not improbable that the artist would have been inspired directly or indirectly by their aspirations and methods.[94] The precise message that Mantegna (and Jacopo Bellini) intended to convey with his patched up walls is uncertain. Some would argue that they were simply the products of an acute empirical sensibility, dedicated to a complete and precise description of the seen world. But the paintings themselves, with their careful attention to decorum and a consistent architectural style, argue for some degree of intentionality.[95] In any event, the habit of observing and recording was an essential skill in the formation of a new historical sensibility detached from moral judgments, in which the past would eventually become separated from the present.

However, one manifestation of a sense of separation was to be found outside history and the sphere of Christian morality in a painted and sculpted mythic past peopled by fauns and satyrs. Although grounded in the empirical study of classical artifacts like sarcophagi and tomb monuments, this was a timeless and – because imaginary and ahistorical – an unchallengeable world. Here, again, both Jacopo Bellini and Mantegna were intimately involved in its earliest formulation. The convincing evocation of an Arcadian past – a topic that will be revisited in Part V – would eventually become one of the most distinctive achievements in Venetian art and literature.

IV

THE HISTORICAL RESTITUTION: ACQUIRING AN ANCIENT PAST

155 Scala dei Giganti (detail). Venice, Palazzo Ducale.

156   Letter of Cardinal Bessarion to Doge Cristoforo Moro and the Venetian
Senate, May 31, 1468. Venice, Biblioteca Nazionale Marciana, Cod. Lat. XIV
14 (=4235), f. 1.

PROLOGUE

From almost the earliest years of my boyhood I strove with all my might, main, effort, and concentration to assemble as many books as I could on every sort of subject . . . But my sense of urgency became the greater after the destruction of Greece and the pitiful enslavement of Byzantium. Since then, all my strength, my effort, my time, my capacity, and my concentration has been devoted to seeking out Greek books. For I feared – indeed I was consumed with terror – lest all those wonderful books . . . should be brought to danger and destruction in an instant . . . Finally, I reflected that my dream would not have been fully realized if I failed to make sure that the books which I had assembled with such care and effort were so disposed in my lifetime that they could not be dispersed and scattered after my death. They must be preserved in a place that is both safe and accessible, for the general good of all readers, be they Greek or Latin.

Next, I came to understand that I could not select a place more suitable and convenient to men of my own Greek background. Though nations from almost all over the earth flock in vast numbers to your city, the Greeks are most numerous of all; as they sail in from their own regions they make their first landfall in Venice, and have such a tie with you that when they put into your city they feel that they are entering another Byzantium.

– Cardinal Bessarion, 1468[1]

In 1468, the Greek prelate Bessarion, a cardinal in the Roman Catholic Church since 1439, left his most priceless possession – an outstanding library of classical texts, eventually comprising over a thousand codices in Greek and Latin – to the Republic of Venice. In these passages from the letter accompanying the deed of donation, he spoke movingly of his mission to save Greek culture from oblivion after the fall of Constantinople to the Ottoman Turks in 1453 (Plate 156).[2] His words are a reminder that the triumphal rhetoric of civic architecture of the later quattrocento in Venice had been played out against a backdrop of crisis and challenge. This cataclysmic event was one of the defining moments of the period: though far away from the Venetian lagoon, it had set up shock waves that would continue to resonate within the Venetian imagination for at least the next half-century.

The parameters of Venice's engagement with the Turks were already drawn up in a letter written by the Venetian Senate to Pope Nicholas V just a month after Mehmed II had taken the Byzantine capital: "if our merciful God, your Sanctity and the other Christian powers do not offer their help against this pestilential evil as soon as possible, all of Christianity will be threated with total annihilation . . ."[3] An eloquent proponent of a new crusade to liberate Constantinople, Bessarion had been sent to Venice in 1463 by Pope Pius II to argue the case before a reluctant Venetian senate. While the Greek cardinal was successful in obtaining a Venetian commitment, his elation was to be short-lived. The pope's death in Ancona in July 1464 while waiting for the arrival of Doge Cristoforo Moro and the Venetian fleet put an end to the grand scheme of a crusade.[4]

The Turkish problem continued to dominate Venetian politics for the rest of the century. Negroponte fell in 1470, Scutari was attacked in 1474, and Venice, eager to normalize trade, made a treaty with Sultan Mehmed II in 1479. Venetian merchants – and with them the republic's economy – thus continued to prosper, albeit under increasing strain, and for a time the Venetian calendar was still defined as much by the periodic departures and arrivals of the great galleys as by the feast days of the saints. But even though the republic was not directly involved, the sea battles continued, and an ever more powerful Ottoman fleet remained a constant threat. Its aggressive designs came to devastating fruition in 1499, when Venetian forces were overwhelmed, and Modone and Corone, the "two eyes of the Republic" in Greece, fell to the Turks. Frederic Lane points to the debacle as "the turning point of Venetian history," when its old maritime hegemony in the East became ever more decisively only a memory.[5]

In *Attila flagellum Dei*, an incunabulum published in Venice in 1477, the unnamed writer found an antecedent for the present state of affairs in Venice's own history. Recounting once again the beloved story of the city's foundation by mainland refugees "fleeing the canine rage" of Attila the Hun, a "persecutor of the Christian faith" who "destroyed the fertile and beautiful Italia," he concluded with an observation on his own time. In the year 1477, he writes, during the reigns of "the high pontiff Pope Sixtus, the Emperor Frederick and the illustrious Doge Andrea Vendramin," other – Greek – refugees would flee the "cruel and abominable persecution of the perfidious Turkish dog... Abandoning their sweet homelands, they came to these islands, on which had been built the most powerful, famous and noble city of Venetia."[6] It was during this period that Donato Contarini drew the profile portrait of Attila the Hun at the bottom of a page of his chronicle of Venice (Plate 157a).[7] Complete with the beard, horns and pointed ears of Pan, the drawing appears to be based upon a medallic image that appeared in the north Italian milieu around the middle of the fifteenth century (Plate 157b). Like the numerous medals of Attila that were struck over the next hundred years, some with reverses depicting the walled city of Aquileia, it would have been yet another artifact that documented in a tangible way an emblematic episode of the civic past.[8]

Paradoxically, Byzantium would become at once more distant and more close during those years: more distant in terms of physical accessibility to Venetians and closer in terms of the Greek presence in Venice itself. Despite passionate (and futile) calls by Bessarion and other western voices for a new crusade to retake Constantinople, the shift was irreversible, its finality underscored by the waves of immigration not only of poor refugees, but also of the most distinguished Greek scholars of the time.[9]

A number of these recent arrivals played a significant role in Venetian cultural life, and some were even included in the narrative paintings of the Great Council Hall. Gentile Bellini had begun the replacement of the trecento fresco cycle of the *Story of Alexander III* with oil paintings on canvas in 1474. Comprising fifteen paintings on the west and north walls, the first phase of the program was completed by 1523 and also involved Giovanni Bellini, Alvise Vivarini, Carpaccio, and Titian.[10]

157b *Attila the Hun.* Bronze, 3.5 × 4.5 cm. (reproduced larger than actual size). Budapest, Hungarian National Museum, fifteenth century.

157a Drawing of a medal of Attila the Hun, from Donato Contarini, *Cronaca veneta sino al 1433*, late fifteenth–early sixteenth century. Vienna, Österreichischen Nationalbibliothek, f. 17.

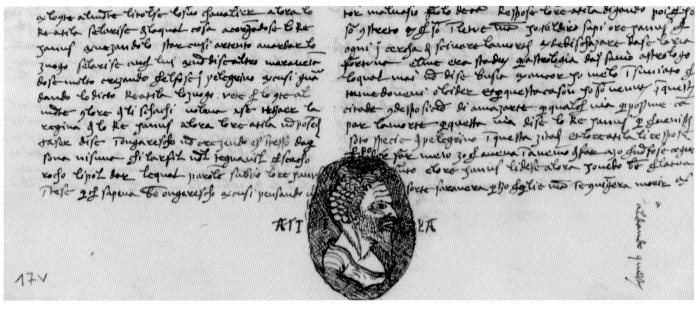

158–62 Engravings by Tobias Stimmer, in Paolo Giovio, *Elogia virorum literis illustrium*, Basel 1577. *Top left: Janus Argyropoulos* (f. 50). *Top center: Demetrius Chalcondyles* (f. 55). *Top right: Manuele Chrysoloras* (f. 41). *Far left: Theodore Gaza* (f. 48). *Left: George Trebizond* (f. 46).

Upon the authority of Francesco Sansovino, writing in 1581, Cardinal Bessarion would have been one of the earliest foreigners so honored. "Dressed in the habit of the monks of San Basilio," he joined Leonardo Giustiniani, "famous for letters and erudition," and Leonardo's son Bernardo, "Procurator of San Marco, who wrote the history of Venice," along with other patricians as witnesses to the *The Presentation of the White Candle* by Pope Alexander III to Doge Sebastiano Ziani.[11] Attributed by Sansovino to Gentile Bellini, the work was probably painted before 1495.[12] But even more conspicuous, and certainly more exotic, was a cluster of scholarly refugees from Byzantium in the crowd assembled behind the three rulers in Carpaccio's *Consignment of the Umbrella*. As Sansovino observed: "Following after them was a group of personages all singular in Greek and Latin letters, and of

recognized erudition. And these were Janos Argyropoulos, Demetrius Chalcondyles, Manuel Chrysoloras, Theodore Gaza, and George Trebizond, all dressed *alla greca* with *capelli in capo*, as in the Albanian style."[13]

The five learned Greeks, active in educating several generations of noble Venetians in the *studia humanitatis*, constituted a virtual chronology of Hellenic studies in quattrocento Italy (Plates 158–62). Their portrayal in the painting was commemorative in nature, since all were deceased by 1511 when Carpaccio was documented at work on the painting, with the possible exception of Chalcondyles who died in that year.[14]

When Chrysoloras, the founding father of Greek studies, had died in 1415, it was Andrea Giuliani, a Venetian patrician and his former pupil, who delivered his funeral oration.[15] As to Argyropoulos, he had traveled from Constantinople to attend the Council of Ferrara–Florence in 1439 and remained to teach for a short time in Padua (1441–4). After a period back in his homeland, he returned definitively to Italy in 1453. Like Chalcondyles, who was Professor of Greek in Padua from 1463 to 1471, he spent most of his time in Italy in Florence and Rome.[16] And it was the contentious George Trebizond, a protégé of Bessarion, who had written to Francisco Barbaro in 1451 claiming that Venice's mixed constitution was based on Plato's *Laws*. After five years in Venice in the early 1460s, where he taught poetry and rhetoric at the School of San Marco, he distinguished himself in Rome as a translator of Greek texts.[17] He was also involved in a polemical debate with Theodore Gaza, one of the leading Hellenists in the Rome of Nicholas V along with Bessarion and Trebizond. Gaza had moved there in 1449 after brief periods of teaching in Mantua and Ferrara and taught the young Ermolao Barbaro in 1462.[18] Finally, it is worth noting that Chalcondyles, who was active in publishing in Florence, was also portrayed in Ghirlandaio's frescoes in the church of Santa Maria Novella in the company of Ficino, Landino, and Poliziano.[19] As the five scholars honored in Carpaccio's painting had spent most of their careers outside Venice, their appearance on the walls of the Great Council Hall has the flavor of an appropriation or, better, an immigration by proxy.

Gentile Bellini turned from Greek to Latin in *The Presentation of the Ring*, where Flavio Biondo was to be found amidst a group of cardinals, prelates, and noble Venetians.[20] Gentile's brother Giovanni did the same in *The Gift of the Sedia to the Doge* which numbers Gregorio Amaseo, Giorgio Merula, and Marcantonio Sabellico amongst the witnesses to the event.[21] When the pope returned to Rome in Giovanni's *Entry to Rome of the Pope, the Doge, and the Emperor*, the Florentine poet Angelo Poliziano was there to greet him along with his Venetian humanist friends, Ermolao Barbaro and Girolamo Donato, the latter "dressed in gold, with a beautiful and rich chain around his neck." They were joined by nine other patricians, including Antonio Cornaro, rector of the Aristotelian School at Rialto for almost fifteen years (1484–98).[22] Cornaro lectured on logic, philosophy, and theology. As his funerary epitaph of 1502 affirmed, "Antenor's Athens [that is, Padua] was wont to be amazed when he taught about the beginnings of things and the Gods."[23] All such portrayals would have confirmed the close and varied associations that had existed between learned Venetians and their distinguished counterparts in other cities.[24]

The loss of the East was thus balanced not only by the inflow of Greek books and minds, but also by the acquisition of the West. It was, however, an unstable equilibrium. As the historian Alberto Tenenti demonstrates most vividly, Venetians of the later quattrocento inevitably began to experience a new sense of their place in the world and indeed, in history.[25] As will be seen, their expansion into the terraferma and their presence in cities of Roman foundation and humanist activity were central to these changes.

THE STILL VISIBLE PAST

... and [the Venetian armada] passed Delos, an island famous for the temple of
Apollo and for the festival that was customarily held there in former times, to
which it was customary for people to travel from the most distant lands to sell
and buy diverse kinds of precious merchandise. One sees many vestiges of the
temple and of the amphitheatre, which is of the whitest and finest marble; some
very beautiful columns, and a great number of statues of the most ancient marble,
and a colossus 15 cubits tall. [Arriving in Smyrna, the Venetian troops burned the
city and] found there among other notable antiquities, the sepulchre of Homer
and his statue in a most beautiful form.

– Domenico Malipiero, *Diario*, 1472[1]

Malipiero's entry on the Venetian armada sailing into battle
against the Turks was emblematic of the times. Antiquities in
the Greek sphere once studied zealously by Cyriacus of
Ancona (Plate 163) were still noticed, but generally only in
passing, and travel to the Aegean area was now, by and large,
motivated as much by military and diplomatic as by mercantile concerns. The handful of surviving accounts written by
traveling Venetians in this period tend toward reportage –
eyewitness description pure and simple – without the need to
reconstruct or to mythologize.

EYEWITNESSES

It was a Venetian subject who wrote the earliest surviving
description of Greece in the Italian language. After residing
for a time in Treviso and Venice, Fra Urbano Bolzanio of
Belluno had traveled to the Aegean and Constantinople,
probably during the period 1475–85, to learn Greek at its
source. In the grand tradition of Cyriacus, he compiled an
Itinerario in Venetian dialect, of which only a fragment
remains.[2]

The text is notable for its circumstantial treatment of the
ruined monuments and antiquities of Athens. With Venetian
forces holding the lower town, the Turks occupied the
Acropolis and had put the Parthenon into use as a mosque.
Fra Urbano could observe the complex only from a distance:

and on the summit of the mountain the fortress is built, and
there is a very strong castle and ancient walls with square
stones . . . and in the castle is a church that was once an
ancient temple of the Romans, most admirable [and] all of
marble with columns around . . . and on the façade in front
are an infinite number of images of marble in relief . . . And
there is also in the castle a most noble ancient palace near
the church, and it is all of marble, built *alla romana*.[3]

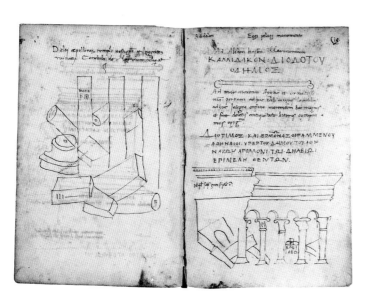

163   After Cyriacus of Ancona, *Ruins of the Temple of Apollo at
Delos*. Biblioteca Apostolica Vaticana, Cod. Vat. Lat. 5252, f. 17v.

Of another building he notes that "the columns are as large as those of San Marco, but they are in pieces."[4] He assiduously copies down inscriptions in both classical languages and ascribes a triumphal arch lying "more than half on the ground" to the Emperor Hadrian on the authority of a Latin epigram, just as Cyriacus had done a generation earlier. Allowing that "the ancient studio of Aristotle" was reputed to be close to the nearby aqueduct, he rejects this location in favor of the Olympeium, a building of which twenty great columns remained: "because it is in the form of a portico open on every side, but it seems, as they say, that it would have been covered with marble and there is not any *scraja* of wall."[5] Of the monument of Lysicrates, he admits: "Why such a building was erected, I could not understand."[6]

The tower of the winds so admired by Cyriacus (Plate 164) is praised as a

building not very large, completely intact with eight faces

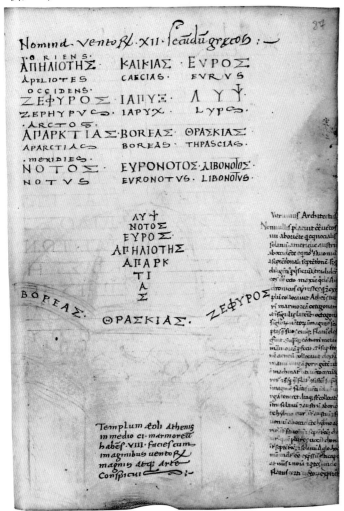

164   Cyriacus of Ancona, *Tower of the Winds at Athens*, from the *Collectanea* of Pietro Donato. Parchment, 25 × 17cm. Berlin, Staatsbibliothek zu Berlin, Preussischer Kulturbesitz, Cod. Hamilton 254, f. 87r.

and a beautiful cupola, and right below the cornice are eight images in half relief, larger than the stature of a man, and they are engaged in diverse actions: they blow the wind, one with a horn, one with the belly, one with the mouth, and above each is written his name: *borea*, etc.; presently it is a church of the Greeks and it is a work very noble, all of marble.[7]

In Fra Urbano's eyes, ancient architecture was *alla romana* pure and simple, even if built in the classical Greek style. And yet, unlike Cyriacus, he distinguished between the pagan temple and the Christian church which replaced it and did not "edit out" the medieval present from the ancient past.

A similar positivistic mentality informed the way in which Venetian merchants of less distinguished antiquarian credentials continued to regard the artifacts and materials of the ancient world. This habit of mind is expressed most vividly in the travel account of Giosafat Barbaro who made two extended trips to Asia Minor in the middle years of the fifteenth century (Plate 165).[8] Venetian patrician, merchant, and diplomat, Barbaro exemplified the tradition of eyewitness documentation for which Venetians were famous.[9] He was seventy-four years old in 1487 when he decided to write his recollections of his travels in the East. He had not done so earlier, he asserted, because his experiences were truly so fantastic and the sights that he had seen so marvelous that no one would believe him anyway. But now, perhaps inspired by the recent publication of the travels of Ambrogio Contarini, he had a change of heart.[10] Barbaro offered three reasons for his own literary undertaking. He was prompted, he said, first by the desire to honor God, second to satisfy the demands of an unnamed friend, and third to provide useful information to pilgrims and merchants who would journey to faraway lands.[11]

With Barbaro one hears another voice that puts the extraordinary vision of a fledgling archaeologist such as Cyriacus of Ancona into a broader perspective – a perspective that includes the "man of affairs" and, as such, gives a more accurate idea of the sense of the ancient past that prevailed in the general vernacular culture in that period. And yet, at the same time, it reveals how a "mercantile mentality" could form an essential foundation for the eventual emergence of archaeology as a scientific discipline.[12]

Barbaro looked back some fifty years to 1436 and his arrival in the distant Venetian colony of Tana on the north shore of the Black Sea near the mouth of the River Don where he would live for the next sixteen years.[13] He writes:

In that region are hills, rivers, and plains: where there are to be seen an infinite number of little hills formed by hand as signs of sepulchres, and on the top of each of them is a great stone with a hole, in which they put a cross of one piece made of another stone.[14]

Barbaro attributed these tombs to the Alani, a Christian tribe whom he learned had been destroyed by the Tartars.[15] As

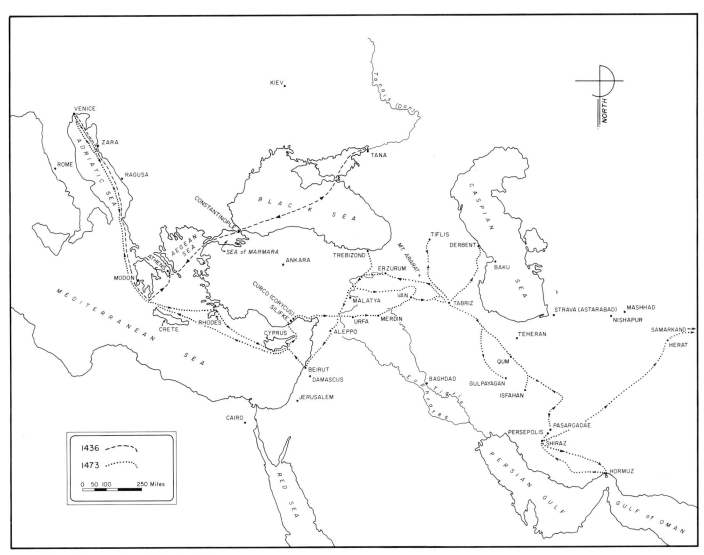

165 Map of the travels of Giosafat Barbaro.

shown in a nineteenth-century print, the area featured a number of burial mounds, among which were the ancient barrows or kurgans of the Scythians and the Sarmatians (Plate 166).[16] Whether Barbaro's tombs were actually these ancient mounds put to re-use, or more recent additions, the intriguing question of their contents came up during a long evening in late November when Barbaro visited the home of his countryman Bartolomeo Rosso. The company included five other Venetian friends whom Barbaro listed with enviable genealogical precision. Aside from Rosso, he named Francesco Cornaro, the brother of Iacomo Cornaro dal Banco; Catarino Contarini, who later carried on his business in Constantinople; Giovanni Barbarigo, the son of Andrea of Candia; Moises Bon, the son of Alessandro of the Giudecca; and Giovanni da Valle, who had manned a *fusta* or bireme along with some other Venetians at Derbent on the Caspian Sea in 1428. With the consent of the local *signore*, da Valle had once pillaged ships coming from Astarabad, or Strava, as Barbaro called it, a city in northern Persia. This latter episode was, in Barbaro's

words, "an almost miraculous thing, which I will leave for now."[17]

Perhaps it was the recounting of such profitable exploits that turned the conversation to a tale of buried riches closer to

166 Perepyaticha kurgan (after Albin Kohn and Dr. C. Mehlis, *Materialien zur Vorgeschichte des Menschen im östlichen Europa*, Jena 1879, Plate III).

167   *The Ruins of Persepolis*, from Cornelius de Bruyn, *Travels into Muscovy, Persia, and Part of the East Indies . . .*, London 1737, II, Plate 119.

hand. For Barbaro continues: "In one of these little hills we were persuaded that there should be hidden a great treasure." The Venetians, as merchants, were not averse to seeking profit even in unfamiliar places. They determined to find the treasure and, in a characteristically Venetian manner, wrote up a contract: "so that we agreed and bound ourselves both by spoken oath and in writing, recorded by Catarino Contarini, the copy of which I still possess, to excavate this hill." According to custom, each of the seven partners would earn a one-eighth share of the profit, with the remainder going to pious works.[18]

The account that follows might well be considered testimony of one of the first systematic archaeological digs on record. The consortium hired 120 local men as diggers for one month at three ducats apiece. It took a week to assemble supplies, including food, weapons, and tools for digging, before the expedition set out. Their destination, sixty Venetian miles (or about 104 kilometers) from Tana, was reached in only a day's travel by sled on the ice of the River Don.[19]

Barbaro made careful note of the dimensions of the site, describing a burial mound about fifty *passi* or paces high (that

is, about eighty-seven meters) and eighty paces in diameter,[20] with a flat top surmounted by a second mound twelve paces high.[21] The huge dimensions of the mound, "circular in form, as if it had been made with a compass," indicate a Scythian tomb, some of which were as large as one hundred meters high.[22] But these men of the sea had not accounted for the effects of winter on the land. For once the workers began to dig, Barbaro writes, "the earth was frozen so hard that neither with mattocks nor with pickaxes could we break it."[23]

Although their efforts were frustrated on this occasion, the Venetians were nonetheless determined to gain the prize.

They returned by barge and boat at the beginning of the following March with an enlarged cadre of diggers, now numbering 150 men. In twenty-two days of work they had made a ditch sixty paces long, eight paces wide and ten paces high. Barbaro described the stratified layers of earth with a precision and analytical eye that would do credit to many a modern archaeologist:

The greatest wonder was that in the first layer next to the grass the earth was black. Then next to that it was all coals, but this is plausible, for there were enough willows so that they might easily build fires on the hill. Under this were ashes a span [that is, about 20 cm] deep. And this is also possible, for having reeds nearby which they might burn, it was no great matter to make ashes. Then were there rinds of millet another span deep, and because of this one might infer that those of that country ate bread made of millet, and would have saved the rinds to put in that place. I would like to know how much millet would have been necessary to cover such a hill of so great a breadth with rinds alone for a depth of one span. Under this layer another span deep were scales of fish such as carp and other similar species, and therefore it may be said that in the river one finds enough carp and other fishes whose scales would suffice to cover such an hill. I leave it up to the judgment of the reader whether this thing could either be possible or plausible. What is certain is that it is true.[24]

However, dirt of whatever color was not what the entrepreneurs were seeking, and the digging continued for another three weeks. Barbaro continues:

Having made this cut and finding no treasure we determined to dig two trenches in the great mound, each measuring four paces in breadth and height. This done we found a white hard earth in which we made steps on which to carry up the barrows. And so going down five paces deeper we found in the bottom certain vessels of stone, some of them with ashes, some with coals, some empty and some full of fish backbones. We also found 5 or 6 *paternostri* as big as oranges made of glazed terracotta and covered with glass such as those that are made in the Marche of Ancona which are tied as weights onto trawl nets. We also found half a handle of a little ewer of silver, made with an adder's head on the top.[25]

When the Monday of Holy Week arrived in mid-April the gusty winds from the Levant began to blow dirt and stones into the faces of the workmen and the excavation came to an end. While such finds after six weeks of digging may seem exiguous, considering the effort involved, Barbaro seems well satisfied, he goes on:

This place was previously called the caves of Gulbedin, but after our digging there it has been called the cave of the Franchi, and is so called unto this day. For the work that we did in those few days was so great, that one might believe that scarcely 1,000 men could have done it in so short a time. We had no certainty of this treasure, but (as much as we understood) if any treasure was there, the reason that Indiabu, Lord of the Alani, had it put there below was because he knew that the emperor of the Tartars was coming against him, and deciding to bury it, so that no one could find it, he feigned to make his sepulchre according to their custom, and secretly had the treasure put there and then had the mound built upon it.[26]

Neither the name of Gulbedin nor that of Indiabu appears in other written sources, ancient or modern, and Barbaro must have been relying on oral – and perhaps apocryphal – tradition.[27]

While the Venetian dig conforms on the whole to the medieval notion of antiquities as buried treasure, a more modern attitude is apparent as well. Barbaro was clearly as fascinated with the process of excavation as with the results. As a "geologist," his common sense making up for a scientific expertise that had not yet been invented, he gave a credible explanation for the distinct character and color of each layer of earth. As an "archaeologist," he used such mundane artifacts as fish scales and grain as primary data from which to make a hypothesis about a lost civilization and adjudged the mound in which he was digging to be a deliberate fake and not a true and proper tomb. As an "historian," he determined the reasons for such a fabrication from his knowledge of the history of the region.

Barbaro returned to Venice in 1462 and pursued a career in public life. Then in 1473 he returned to the East for another five years, this time in an official capacity as Venetian ambassador to negotiate a mutual defense treaty between Venice and Shah Uzun Hasan against the Turks.[28] Barbaro's descriptions of ancient sites on this second trip to the East again reveal his sharp eye and critical faculties. Derbent was, he noted, "a town, so they say, built by Alexander, which is on the sea of Bachu," now called the Caspian Sea.[29] With a mountain behind it topped by a castle, it is protected, he notes, by walls that lead down from the castle into the sea, where, he continues, "they are submerged under the water by a measure of two paces." Examining the masonry, he observes that the walls are built of large stones *alla romana*.[30]

While epigraphical remains also caught Barbaro's attentive eye, he did not share Cyriacus's passion for copying inscriptions (nor that of Fra Urbano). Arriving at the port of Curico, the ancient city of Corycium on the gulf of Cilicia, Barbaro

168 View of royal tombs at Naqshi-i-Rustam near Persepolis. Engraving by Pascal Coste in Eugène Napoléon Flandin, *Voyages en Perse*, Paris 1843–54, vol. 3–4.

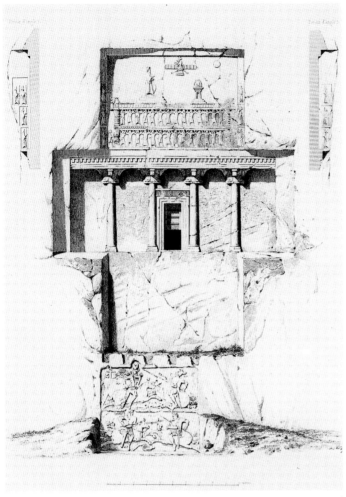

169 (?)Tomb of Darius at Naqshi-i-Rustam. Engraving by Pascal Coste in Eugène Napoléon Flandin, *Voyages en Perse*, Paris 1843–54, vol. 3–4.

observed: "On the principal gates [of a large ruined castle] were engraved certain letters, which seemed very beautiful and similar to Armenian, but, in another form from that which the Armenians use at present: for I had certain Armenians there with me who could not read them."[31]

After further discoveries, Barbaro comes across the impressive ruins of the ancient city of Persepolis atop a plateau near Camarà (Plate 167). He takes note of a site called Cilmynar [Chilil Mīnār] and observes correctly that this "means in our tongue 40 columns, each of which is 20 braccia long and as thick as three men can embrace; but some of them are in a ruined state. Nevertheless, by those which remain it appears to have been a beautiful building."[32] Barbaro's most impressive description was of the royal tombs of the Achaemenid kings at nearby Naqsh-i-Rustam (Plates 168–71):

for, upon this plain there is a mighty stone of one piece, on which are sculpted images of men as great as giants, and above all the rest there is one image like those of ours that represent God the Father in a circle. He holds a globe in his

170 *Submission of Valerian to Shapur I*, relief at Naqshi-i-Rustam. Engraving by Pascal Coste in Eugène Napoléon Flandin, *Voyages en Perse*, Paris 1843–54, vol. 3–4.

hand, [and] under him are other little figures, and in front of him the image of a man leaning on an arch, which they say was the figure of Solomon.[33] Under them are many other small figures, who seem to sustain those that are above them. Among them there is one who seems to wear a pope's mitre on his head, holding up his open hand as though he meant to bless all those who are beneath him, who look at him and seem to be waiting for this benediction [Plate 170]. A little further on there is a great figure on horseback, seeming to be of a very robust man: who they say is Samson. Near him are many other figures dressed *alla francese* and wearing long hair. All these figures are in half relief [Plate 171].[34]

Barbaro was aware that these great images pre-dated the Christian era. Concluding that they must be Hebraic, he

171 *Shapur I on Horseback with Entourage of Foot Soldiers*, relief at Naqshi-i-Rustam. Engraving by Pascal Coste in Eugène Napoléon Flandin, *Voyages en Perse*, Paris 1843–54, vol. 3–4.

cautiously accepted the identifications of both Solomon and Samson on the monument and equated a figure in a tondo – actually the supreme Zoroastrian deity Ahurā Mazdā – to God the Father. What was probably a relief of the Sassanian King Shapur I receiving an act of submission from the Roman emperor Valerian was likened to the pope giving his benediction to his subjects. As he moved on to the ancient ruins of Pasargadae, he observed the tomb of Cyrus. Observing that it had the form of a little church, he noted the Persian cuneiform inscription on its face. It was, he declared, written in Arabic letters and identified the monument as the Mosque of the Mother of Solomon.[35]

Like other Venetian *viaggiatori* of the period, Barbaro is a keen observer of unfamiliar surroundings and an accomplished reporter of full particulars. Although he claims familiarity with classical authors, he does not cite them on the spot as Petrarch or Cyriacus most assuredly would have done. In general, he does not perceive ruined buildings as Roman or Greek antiquities *per se*; to him they are simply castles and ruins. And yet, he shows a certain awareness of period and style, which exceeds that of Cyriacus on one significant point. For Cyriacus, all ruins were either Greek or Roman, but Barbaro made a further distinction and recognized that oriental antiquities like those at Persepolis represented a third, non-classical – and to him, Hebraic – category.

With Barbaro one finds sure signs of a new sense of the past that seems to oscillate between two worlds: one which clings to medieval views of antiquities as commodities (if not as buried treasure), and the other which begins to privilege scientific inquiry, accurate measurement, and objective analysis. Perhaps most significantly, he describes ruins without a hint of Petrarch's need to *repopulate* an imagined intact past or Cyriacus's need to *reconstruct* it. It is this detached, if not necessarily dispassionate, approach – a merchant's view of the past – that was to be joined to the literary and antiquarian views of Petrarch and Cyriacus as a necessary precondition for the birth of a modern archaeology.

THE INCORPORATION OF THE WEST

Turning from the ever more inaccessible lands in the East to Venice's newly acquired territories in the West, we find the young Marin Sanudo approaching the classical past in a different manner. With a larger vision of civic destiny that was shaped by the themes of Venetian humanism, the monumental and the literary approaches to the problem of classical roots (that is, Venice's lack thereof) would now be joined by a third – *topographical* – approach. In a process of cultural appropriation that was both direct and subtle, Venice would now begin to incorporate the Roman pasts of her subject cities into her own history. The process was well along by 1483, when Sanudo wrote an eyewitness account of a newly acquired, historically resonant, countryside:

To begin to describe the lands, castles, towns, villages, lakes, rivers, springs, fields, meadows, and woods that came under the Venetian empire from the mainland territories, would require an intellect, most learned and excellent readers, of more enterprise and maturity than this weak one of mine; and yet, having desired so many times to go to see [these things], and to write about what I have seen with my own eyes, that I would be gifted in describing and that the memory would be eternal may be pleasing to the heavenly Redeemer, through whom all things come . . .[36]

Just seventeen at the time and borrowing heavily from Flavio Biondo's *Italia Illustrata*, Sanudo thus began his account.[37] The occasion was an inspection tour through the terraferma in the company of three Venetian syndics and a notary called Pylades – evidence of a contemporary taste for Greek mythology – whom he addresses as "il mio caro compagno."[38] By Sanudo's time the Venetian hegemony had come to embrace a number of cities of ancient foundation, both large and small. Many are accorded histories that reached back to the distant past and extended into the Venetian present.

The delegation made its first major stop in Padua (Plate 172). Well versed in the local chronicle tradition, Sanudo observes, "We arrived first in the city so beautiful and so delightful that Antenor the Trojan had built and that was our root."[39] Again one hears the familiar litany of not only the Trojan foundation of Padua and Venice, but also that appealing tale of Livy's wandering bones:

And the temple of Santa Justina the Virgin is located on the Prato della Valle, which is the largest in the city, and is where fairs are held. But from what remains, we know that the church is very old; for when it was rebuilt, a casket of lead was found that contained the bones of Titus Livius, and they were placed in the Palace.[40]

Although aware of Biondo's claim to have seen the family sepulchre of Livy, his wife and two sons in Rome, Sanudo preferred accommodation to confrontation. Like his Paduan predecessors, he was not to be discouraged by conflicting evidence. Accepting the misunderstood epitaph of T. Livius Halys as proof of Livy's return to Padua for burial, he reported the eventual translation of the poet's bones back to the church:[41]

In this sacred house of Justina are his body [and those] of S. Maximus second bishop of Padua, of S. Felicita, of S. Luke the Evangelist, of S. Matthew the Apostle, of S. Maximian, S. Brunaldo and S. Prosdocimo, with all the other bodies of saints. But one may be permitted to believe that [the original church building] was the temple of Jupiter where, as Livy narrates in the *Decades*, the booty was brought back from the victory of Padua over the pirates of Cleomenes Lacedaemonius.[42]

172 Francesco Squarcione, *View of Padua*, 1465. Ink and wash on parchment, 117 × 101 cm (entire). Padua, Musei Civici.

In this triumph of hagiography over humanist erudition, given the fact that the Paduan inscription clearly referred to a freed slave and not to the Roman historian, Sanudo finds no inconsistency in commingling the relics of a pagan luminary among those of the Christian saints of the basilica.

To Sanudo the Roman monuments of the city were also to be apprehended in the matrix of contemporary life. As with works of art and architecture of his own time, patronage and location were more important bestowers of value than aesthetic considerations in and of themselves. Buildings are significant because of their owners; tombs are worthy of note not because of their fine craftsmanship or innovative iconography, but because of their relationship to famous men. The designation "anticha" can mean anything before his own time. Sanudo does not regard the Roman arena next to the Church of the Eremitani as a ruined amphitheater as Cyriacus would have done or as a setting for gladiatorial games as Petrarch would have proposed. For him it was simply a palace with a round wall with gardens inside, recently rebuilt by the wealthy Venetian bishop Piero Foscari at a cost of three thousand ducats. As with the Basilica of Santa Giustina, the site "shows by its remains that it is antique and beautiful."[43] Estimating the bishop's yearly income at seven thousand ducats, Sanudo mentions the Arena Chapel, built nearly two hundred years earlier by the Scrovegni family, only in passing

and only as a source of additional revenues to the bishop: "it gives 100 ducats of *jus patronatus*."[44] Of Giotto's frescoes there is nary a word, although later on in his account Sanudo refers to the astrological paintings in the Palazzo della Ragione and to Donatello's bronze equestrian statue of Gattamelata in the Piazza del Santo.[45]

As Sanudo traveled on through the terraferma he interpreted the landscape with the help of classical texts in the venerable tradition of Petrarch. The Euganean Hills south of Padua had a particularly rich literary resonance. Cited not only by Pliny and Lucan, the area had also been acclaimed by Martial: "If before me, Clemens, you shall behold Helicaon's Euganean shores, and the fields decked with vine-clad trellises . . ."[46] The healing powers of the waters at Monteortone had, according to Cassiodorus, been enjoyed by Theodoric, King of the Ostrogoths, Sanudo noted, and were still in use up to the present day.[47] Arquà, the tiny hill town where Petrarch had spent his last days, was "a pleasant and agreeable place" with an intimate historical ambience.[48] After visiting Petrarch's tomb, constructed on the exact model of that of Antenor in Padua, and copying out the epitaph, Sanudo visited the poet's house (Plate 173): "and here he composed, and up to this day his desired laurel remains, and from that time until the present he has never died."[49]

Place names were also telling clues to past circumstance. Approaching Padua by canal he had observed a ruined bridge at Noventa "that was then called *di Graizi*, because the Greeks came here, [but] where the true word is corrupted . . . one allows that it shows some vestige of marble."[50] Monte Ricco near the *castello* of Monselice, the ancient *mons silicis*,

173 Tomb of Francesco Petrarca, *c.*1375. Arquà Petrarca.

is high, most pleasant and full of gentleness and joy, and because all things – grasses as well as fruit, olive trees, and grapevines – are found there and flourish most perfectly, it is called Monte Ricco, also because, as many assert, there were and are found there coins of gold and silver. Of this Pliny in his *Natural History*, in the thirteenth and fourteenth books, says much; [and also] Theophrastus [in his] *Inquiry into plants*; [and] Herodotus; and Apollodorus who wrote *Inquiry into odours*, calls this mountain one of the marvels of the world.[51]

Perhaps moved by the desire to give the terraferma a Greek as well as a Latin heritage, Sanudo took an optimistic – some would say opportunistic – approach to the literary evidence. Aside from his misattribution of Theophrastus's treatise on odors to Apollodorus, the laudatory citations claimed by Sanudo are not to be found in the writings of either figure, nor in that of Herodotus.[52] As far as Pliny is concerned, the thirteenth and fourteenth books *do* deal with botanical subjects but not with the Euganean Hills. The Euganean area and its peoples *are* mentioned in passing in the geographical survey in Pliny's third book, but without the acclaim that Sanudo presumed to find.[53]

Sanudo was on firmer ground when faced with the physical remains of antiquity. For he also took note of Latin inscriptions, copying out the more interesting ones in a separate sylloge in accordance with well-established antiquarian practice. At the bridge over the Brenta near Noventa Padovana, "adorned by houses of our Venetians," he observes: "The most ancient epitaphs are here; I saw and read them all, and the epitaphs are also given in our work *de antiquitatibus et epithafia*: read it if you wish to see them."[54] Believing the Arco dei Gavi in Verona to be a relocated portal to the famous Arena in the heart of the city, he took note of an epigram that was prominently inscribed on its face and, according to tradition, not just once, but twice. While the inscriptions actually indicate that a freedman named Cerdone who was a follower of the famous Roman architect Vitruvius had designed the arch, Sanudo was moved toward a more ambitious inference. He pronounced that it was written "in perfect and good antique letters: *Lucius Vitruvius L. L. (id est Lucij liberti) F. Cerdo Architectus*; thus it appears that Lucius Vitruvius, who wrote about architecture, was Veronese and a most celebrated author, built the Arena, and that he was the founder of it."[55] This recalls the equally optimistic attribution of the inscription of Livius Halys in Padua. It was a time when art – particularly ancient art – was no longer to be anonymous, and when the need to give precise definition to artifacts of the past tended to overwhelm prudence and caution.[56]

Sanudo's observations on the territory around Lake Garda recall the early marriage of antiquarianism and arcadian pleasures portrayed so vividly in the writings of Cyriacus of Ancona and his follower Felice Feliciano. Sirmione, located on the tip of a peninsula jutting into the lake, was "the

homeland of Catullus Veronese, singer of erotic verses. He was a most licentious poet; he loved a maiden named Clodia and called her Lesbia; she died at 30 years. He wrote the epithalamium of Manlius; and here is the cavern where he stayed."[57]

As the delegation traveled along the west shore of the lake on horseback and by boat, Sanudo described a succession of villages that had been founded in Roman times. He illustrated this section of his account with drawings of Riva del Garda and of Salò, the old Roman town of Salodium, situated on a bay surrounded by forested mountains (Plate 174). Moving up

174 Marin Sanudo, drawing of Salò, from his *Itinerario per la terraferma* (1483), ed. Rawdon Brown, Padua, 1847, p. 86.

the coast to the town of Maderno, he noted its "gardens of cedars, orange and apple trees . . . in sum, most pleasant places, gentle and soft, always inhabited [by gentlemen]."[58] In nearby Toscolano and Benaco, a town taking its name from the ancient Lacus Benacus, he saw "an old church that is called Santa Maria de Benaco: There are many antiquities there; one finds under the earth epitaphs with perfect letters and antique; and what I saw placed in the entrance by the door is this recently found [inscription]: *Antonini Pij Hadriani filij*, and his genealogy follows, and many mosaics are dug up."[59] This was the same church visited in 1464 by Mantegna, Felice Feliciano, and other friends of antiquarian inclination on their well-known expedition in search of Roman inscriptions and immortalized by Felice in the *Iubilatio*. Sanudo's description was more circumstantial, if less literary, than his predecessor's:

And the high altar is in the middle of the church with four columns, and upon one [there is] a capital with an idol, that is Jupiter Ammon in the form of Ariete (the Ram). There is an opening in the cupola, through which the smoke of the sacrifices rose; but above the altar there is a stone, which, it is said, runs with sweat three times a year: on Christmas, on Holy Friday and on the day of Our Lady in February . . .[60]

In the margin of his manuscript next to this entry, Sanudo wrote, "Nota mirabilia," and again "miraculum": glosses used throughout his text to call attention to other sites of more conventionally Christian, if equally prodigious, character. One is reminded of the ease with which a well-educated man of the late fifteenth century could reconcile the Christian present with the newly rediscovered Roman past. Most striking is the absence of any necessity to make a moral distinction between the two. This would not always be the case. A century later the "pagan altar" was broken into pieces by order of Carlo Borromeo, Archbishop of Milan, during a pastoral visit. The surviving colonettes were recovered in the nineteenth century and set at the top of a new staircase that leads to a chapel behind the present Basilica of SS. Pietro e Paolo (Plate 175).[61]

The antiquities of the Friuli and Istria were accorded particular attention. "Aquileia, a most ancient city . . . [was] once very powerful and grand; it is now almost abandoned and inhabited by 24 canons who officiate at the cathedral church, and by some fishermen . . ."[62] Aside from the basilica, Sanudo noted the remains of city walls, a theater, and an aqueduct, as well as the monastery of Santa Maria Extra Muros, then inhabited by Benedictine nuns. There he found "a most ancient epitaph around the choir." At first he judged it illegible, but after rubbing it vigorously with water with the help of his companion Pylades, he was able "with great effort" to decipher the letters.[63] In Pula he copied down the inscription from the Arch of the Sergii, just as Cyriacus of Ancona had done some sixty years before. In and around the city itself, he continues, "there are innumerable epitaphs, which I have transcribed in my work *De antiquitatibus Italiae*."[64]

By Sanudo's time the Venetian hegemony had come to embrace a number of cities of ancient foundation, both large and small. Many are accorded histories that reached back to the distant past and extended into the Venetian present. Padua had been a Roman colony, "not like the others, [but] rather more fortunate." The university, long the official organ of higher education for noble Venetians, provided yet another conduit of aggregation by which the best of the outside world was brought into the Venetian domain: "At the Vo, the most celebrated gymnasium in Italy, there are many students in all faculties who come here from every nation, including many gentlemen from north of the Alps; it is supported with great expense by the Venetians."[65]

Verona, Sanudo observes, was "most well-known to the Hebrew writers and was built by Shem, son of Noah" (Plate 176). The city was called "Hierusalem menor" – a "lesser Jerusalem" – he reports, "because to this day, Monte Oliveto, the valley of Calvaria, Nazareth and Bethlehem remain, and are so named, demonstrating its antiquity."[66] In Roman times, Sanudo continued, it was Brennus, general of the Gauls, "a ferocious and bellicose people," who came to Verona after burning Rome and built his fortress on the mountain overlooking the city.[61] More recently, Verona had been ruled by tyrants: Ezzelino Romano, the Scaligeri, the Visconti, and then Francesco da Carrara who had captured it "with great calamity and intolerable damage."[68] This brief but dense pro-

175   The columns formerly of the altar in Santa Maria de Benaco, seen by Sanudo; now removed from the church and placed near the campanile of SS. Pietro e Paolo, Toscolano (Lago di Garda).

file of Veronese history is, however, only a prelude to its altogether more abundant present: "But at last in 1404 it came under the Venetian Empire; through its beneficence and liberty, it has experienced growth and opulence, and day by day it renews itself better still."[69]

Brescia was accorded a less hallowed, but equally venerable foundation, and a precisely equivalent destiny:

> It was built five hundred years before Rome and was called the city of Hercules, and Hercules lived there; and in the old citadel there is an ancient palace where there are many antiquities that still survive; [there are] some marble columns in two rows where there was a street in between and many epitaphs by which its antiquity is shown; but in this time, that is from 1440 on, when it came under the Venetian Dominion, it has experienced admirable growth and opulence.[70]

Above a portal in the city wall of Roveredo, an inscription confirms the now enduring presence of the Serenissima: "Everyone sleep secure; the winged Lion himself, ever vigilant, will protect this city, citizens."[71]

Sanudo's painstaking observations on the notable features of Venice's recently acquired mainland – once the 10th Regione in the time of Augustus – reveal a developing historical imagination in which the sites, artifacts, and texts of Latin antiquity are now incorporated into an expansive history of Venice itself.

Petrarch had looked at the land and saw settings for events of the classical past. Cyriacus of Ancona had found monuments whose original antique forms were to be mentally reconstructed through archaeological investigation. Sanudo looked at many of the same places and saw classical substrata, foundations as it were, for events of the Venetian present.

As attested by his frequent recourse in the *Itinerario* to Latin literature, Sanudo already had a good classical education with a reasonable proficiency in Latin. But even though he would

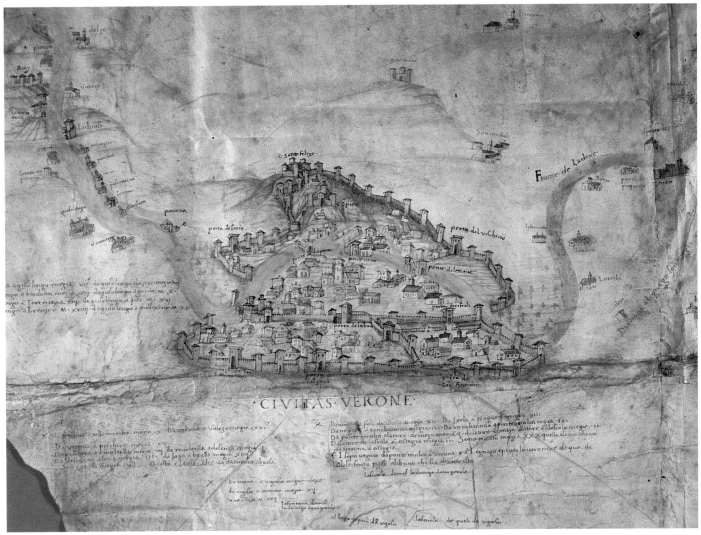

176 *View of Verona*, 1479–83. Venice, Archivio di Stato, Scuola della Carità, b. 36, n. 2530, detail.

eventually amass an impressive library of some 6,500 volumes – unusually large for the times – he was perhaps too much a political creature to be considered a true and proper humanist.[72] It was the life of the city – both public and private – that concerned him more than the life of the mind, and his literary gifts were exercised more in the vernacular than in high-flown Latin rhetoric. While extraordinary in his propensity for first-hand observation and obsessive record-keeping, Sanudo was in many ways typical of other Venetian patricians of the last decades of the quattrocento. Theirs was a culture of merchants, traders, and diplomats that privileged the eyewitness account as a key to prosperity and security.[73] Trained to appraise goods with a dispassionate eye, observers such as Sanudo and Giosafat Barbaro diverted a well-honed visual acuity from the marketplace to the monument.

★ ★ ★

THE DETACHMENT FROM THE EAST

A different approach toward the past is evident in an *isolario* – a type of travel guide dedicated to the Greek islands that had been pioneered by Buondelmonti – that was also written in those years. Offering a "desirous heart" and "ready spirit," the writer introduces himself as the "good Venetian Bartolomeo dalli Sonetti, the true composer" of the work. He affirms that he had written the text himself in sonnet form and painted the maps "with my own hands." The manuscript can be dated to the period 1478–85 from its dedication to Doge Giovanni Mocenigo, whose name was concealed in an acrostic. Bartolomeo identified himself as a galley captain, the veteran of fifteen voyages to the Aegean, and vowed that he intended the book for "the contemplation of sailors and the pleasure of all those who will read my low *volgare*."[74] The reader, he promised, would be shown:

> How many islands there are small and large
> and reefs and shoals and cities and castles

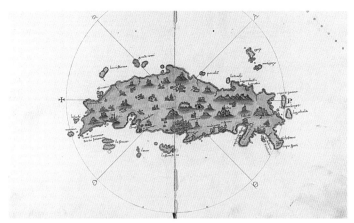

177 Bartolomeo dalli Sonetti, *Map of Crete*, from his *Isolario*: BMV,
Cod. It. IX, 188 (6286), ff. 6v–7.

The places which the sweet waters reach,
   How they once were and how one finds them now
   And what winds blow against their shores.
Which walls are standing and which are fallen down
   All things will be shown you precisely
   I wish that others would be my proof to that effect . . .
One will also see how they were called
   by the ancients and how one calls them now
   and by whom they were and are ruled.[75]

Accompanying each entry with a map painted in watercolor and ink, Bartolomeo then proceeded to treat the islands one by one. Of Crete (Plate 177), he began:

The island held worthy by the great Jove
   Which sits in the middle of the vast sea
   with Mount Ida and 100 cities appears
   as a once great and fruitful kingdom . . .
Here was the kingdom of the most wise Saturn
   son of Uranus (that means the heavens)
   who was the first to strike coins
   and, most learned, to cultivate and sow.[76]

He went on to describe ruined buildings "with mosaics and inscriptions in Greek as well as Latin."[77] Among the ancient cities of the island was Gortyna, once adorned with numerous columns and idols, with its nearby labyrinth, "where the minotaur had resided,"[78] and Mount Ida, with "a building on the summit where Saturn made sacrifices."[79]

Like Sanudo, Bartolomeo was fascinated by place names and their origins. While his descriptions of ruins and topographical features appear to be largely his own, most of his etymological claims are taken directly from Pliny. Of the island of Tenos he writes:

It was earlier called Idrusa by Aristotle the Greek
   and Demosthenes called it Ofiusa;
   each of them calls it according to his own opinion.[80]
On one of the two mountains is the castle, then,

and in the middle a great fruitful valley
that at the time of Alexander was famous
and was almost ruined by the Romans.[81]

Confronted with Delos, then called Schile and the birthplace of Apollo, the poet invoked the God to share his eloquence:

Here I may be permitted to call on Apollo
   in order to observe his poetic style
   to speak of the islets of Delos [Schile]
   where a temple of his was on a hill.[82]

He elaborates:

Here is a great temple of Apollo who was adored
   with gifts and great and worthy sacrifices;
   armed ships came from different countries
   and noble people frequented it.
Here virgin maidens had brought
   images of marble and other devices
   to his temple, showing themselves benign
   To know the future of his state.
Here it is said that Diana was born,
   called Cynthia from Mount Cynthia
   Near which lies a fountain
That when the Nile rises
   the spring of Cynthia rises to spill over,
   [while] all the others remain low.[83]

In stark contrast to Sanudo's *Itinerario*, there is a total absence of Venice and the Venetians from Bartolomeo's account after he has introduced himself. In this he also departed from the Buondelmonti model, which attended to contemporary inhabitants and buildings as well as ancient ruins. Informed by Pliny, as well as Strabo, Pomponius Mela, and other ancient writers, his is still an ancient landscape of temples and pagan idols, but one from which the Gods had fled and where the buildings had fallen apart or had been destroyed. More literary than optical, Bartolomeo's poem implies the separation and isolation of Greek antiquity from his own time – a counter-tendency to Sanudo's will to ground the Venetian present in the Latin past of the terraferma.

A TRAVELER THROUGH TIME

The tension between these two tendencies characterized much of Venetian art and rhetoric in the last quarter of the fifteenth century. Sanudo himself was torn by the need to separate and the desire to connect. In 1485, just two years after writing the *Itinerario*, he transcribed into his commonplace book a copy of a letter sent from Rome by Daniel de San Sebastiano, a Veronese canon, to a fellow citizen of Verona, Jacomo di Maphei. It concerned the discovery of three Roman sarcophagi buried near the via Appia:

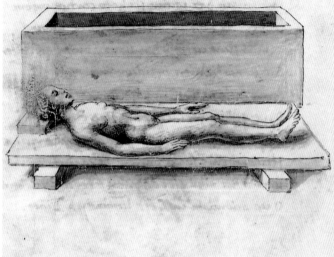

In one of these there was found [the body of] a young girl, complete with all her limbs, embalmed with a coating of thick paste . . . It is judged that this must be made of myrrh, incense and aloe and other worthy substances. One finds a face so agreeable and charming that not many would believe it to be 1,500 years old or more. She seems as if she had been sent [to the tomb] this very same day with her hair arranged on her head in the Roman manner.[84]

The maiden was identified, not surprisingly, as Cicero's daughter Tulliola. With her eyes, eyelids, ears, and nose all intact and seemingly capable of movement as if she were still alive, she was admired by

all Rome, masculine and feminine, who went to see her with the greatest admiration and amazement . . . understanding how much our ancients studied the gentle souls to make them immortal, but also the bodies in which nature to make them beautiful had put all of its genius, that truly, if you had seen this face you would be no less enamored or amazed, and I believe that it will be kept above ground so that everyone will be satisfied and able to see it.[85]

Her image was duly copied by Bartolomeus Fontius into his sylloge of inscriptions (Plate 178).

While the dead could not be reawakened, as Petrarch and Cyriacus would have wished, perhaps modern men could re-enter the ancient world as "time travelers," just as the Roman maiden "Tulliola" had entered their own.

When Giosafat Barbaro, Sanudo, and Bartolomeo dalli Sonetti returned to Venetian soil after their travels beyond the confines of the lagoon, they would confront a growing civic magnificence that was increasingly imbued with the spirit of the antique. And yet, as will become evident, it was an antique that was marked by a pronounced *venezianità* that would have been as alien to Tulliola as she was to them.

178   *Body of a Roman Maiden*, from the sylloge of Bartholomeus Fontius. Oxford, The Bodleian Library, MS Lat. Misc. d. 85, f. 161v.

8

A PERPETUAL EMPIRE

There are many more curious about history who happen to see the city of the Venetians or to hear something about it, and who are wont greatly to wonder at what so novel and unusual a reason for living might have induced men born on the earth, accustomed to meadowlands, to establish a city amidst the swamps.

– Bernardo Giustiniani, late 1470s[1]

As Venice grappled with problems of military threat, economic uncertainty, and a changing sense of identity in the last two decades of the quattrocento, her historians and chroniclers sought to address the problem of repositioning the republic in time and space. The initial response was typically Venetian: to look back to the mythic origins of the city. Although Flavio Biondo had written two short works on Venetian history in the 1450s at the behest of Doge Francesco Foscari,[2] it is only with Bernardo Giustiniani's *De origine urbis Venetiarum*, begun in the late 1470s and published posthumously in 1493, that the first true and proper historian of Venice's civic origins and constitutional structure appears.[3] A disciple of Guarino and Filelfo, Giustiniani appraised the primary and secondary sources with a critical attitude – novel in Venetian historiography – that was worthy of a properly trained humanist scholar. His judicious approach is further revealed in his introductory statement:

> For we see that there are almost always many origins for all things, whether they arise naturally or artificially . . . for it is possible to take as the origin of a city either the older or the more complete beginnings, as it seems best to each man. For any matter placed in the will of the people and the princes is arbitrary.[4]

The modest tone of Giustiniani's work was no match, however, for Marcantonio Sabellico's *Rerum venetarum ab urbe condita libri XXXIII*. With it, a particularly grandiloquent approach to historiography came to fruition in Venice (Plate 179). Commissioned by the Venetian government in 1483 and published in 1487, it was accorded immediate acclaim. Despite the fact that Giustiniani's work was better ordered, more distinguished in a literary sense, and more critical in its use of

179 *Marcantonio Sabellico*, engraving by Tobias Stimmer in Paolo Giovio, *Elogia virorum literis illustrium*, Basel 1577, f. 98.

sources than Sabellico's, it found less favor with the Signoria, who may have counted its high-minded objectivity against it.[5]

Perhaps the times demanded a less equivocal statement. Venice's appropriation of the terraferma had brought with it the growing resentment and hostility of other Italian and European powers. In response, the Venetian debate on civic etiologies – a standard component of the *chronachistica* tradition – was now to be directed toward a particular end: the right to empire. Sabellico's treatise, written in ornate humanist Latin in grand rhetorical style and structured on the model of Livy, was more than equal to the task. In contrast to the measured relativism of Giustiniani, he asks in his own *proemio*:

Who can deny the great and glorious deeds of certain nations that have at some point attained imperial status – at the forefront of whom are the Romans? Before the magnificence and scope of their foreign conquests, we should perhaps yield, but, in the inviolability of its laws, the impartiality of its justice, its integrity and the sanctity of its constitution, Venice shall be not inferior, but indeed far superior.[6]

Perhaps because he was not a native Venetian, Sabellico's was a particularly convincing voice for the traditional notion – already exhaustively explored by John the Deacon back in the eleventh century – that much of Venice's strength came from the diversity of origins of her inhabitants. After drawing upon ancient authority – Polybius, Livy, Cato, Homer, Xenodotus, Cornelius Nepos, Strabo, Pliny – to determine Venice's primordial roots, Sabellico offered "the opinion of the author" about "the true origin of the Veneti":

The Aquileians were Latin inhabitants. The Concordians were Romans. These mixed with the ancient Veneti who stayed in Grado and Caorle when the tumult of the Huns devastated their lands. From all these parts in the course of time, as is known, they came to live in the city that one now sees: from this comes the origin of the Venetians. From Rome, from Italia and from Troy more truly they are descended than from Paphlagonia or Gaul, and this is how much I could narrate in brief of its beginnings and its antiquity.[7]

Marino Sanudo, for his part, observed in his *De origine, situ et magistratibus urbis Venetae*, a manuscript that was essentially completed by 1493, "Those – as I have written – who fled the barbarian persecution, first came to live in these islands around Rialto for its safety and security, and so from time to time new people came, and hence there was variety from the beginning."[8] By the late fifteenth century, these diverse roots might well suggest that the rise to empire was a natural and proper reappropriation of the original homelands of a heterogeneous people. Sanudo, moreover, further echoed a tradition that had prevailed since the time of Martin da Canal when he claimed that Venice had been "founded not by shepherds as Rome was, but by powerful and rich people."[9] And, one might conclude, those who had a natural birthright to empire.

Venetian historiography thus remained, for the most part, defensive, apologetic, celebratory, and acritical.[10] Giustiniani represented this tendency at its most tempered and balanced, Sanudo at its most down to earth and sentimental, and Sabellico at its most pretentious – and influential. In Sabellico's thirty-three books, the republic finally had a literary monument to match its imperial aspirations. It would be complemented in the last decades of the quattrocento with a number of civic projects that provided an analogous message in stone.

A NEW GOLDEN AGE

Construction began during those years on a great ceremonial staircase in the courtyard of the ducal palace (Plates 180–81). With its completion, the *via triumphalis* articulated by the Porta della Carta and the Arco Foscari was brought to a full-blown Renaissance conclusion. Begun by Antonio Rizzo during the term of Doge Marco Barbarigo (1485–6), it was essentially completed around eight years later during the dogeship of Barbarigo's brother Agostino (1486–1501). After Jacopo Sansovino's colossal statues of Mars and Neptune were installed on the top landing in the mid-sixteenth century, it was called the Scala dei Giganti, a title that will be used here before the fact to avoid confusion. The construction of the Scala may have been mandated by a decree of 1485 calling for the public coronation of the doge, but it would actually perform several functions and address several audiences: the doge, the visitor of ambassadorial rank, the senators, the populace – both nobles and commoners – and the intellectual élite among the aristocracy.[11]

The public language of architecture

In its ceremonial role, the Scala served as a monumental plinth for the doge, framing and displaying him in spectacles of state.[12] In the ducal coronation ceremony, the staircase is a goal: the culminating point of a lengthy three-stage ritual. The first stage begins when the doge enters the sacred precinct of San Marco immediately after his election, ascends the porphyry pulpit and is presented to the citizenry by one of his electors. He then descends to the high altar and is invested with the mystical source of ducal authority, the vexillum of St. Mark.[13]

The second stage takes place in the secular space, at once commercial and ceremonial, of the Piazza San Marco. Carried aloft on a platform by sailors from the Arsenal, the doge makes an orchestrated display of ducal largess by tossing coins into the massed crowds of *popolani*. Finally, he is carried through the Porta della Carta, returning to the space of political authority and the administration of justice. He climbs the staircase, whose sides are lined by his electors, and is greeted at the top by his counselors, the grand chancellor and the heads of the Quarantia al Criminale. Here he takes the oath of office, swearing to abide by the provisions of the ducal *promissione*, and is crowned with the *camauro* (a white skullcap) and the jeweled *corno*, the symbol of supreme political authority. While the ritual clearly posits the source of ducal

180 Scala dei Giganti, view from west. Designed by Antonio Rizzo, c.1486–96. Venice, Palazzo Ducale.

181   Scala dei Giganti, view from south. Designed by Antonio Rizzo, *c.*1486–96. Venice, Palazzo Ducale.

prerogatives in the patriciate through its electors, once the power is handed over to the doge during his coronation, the top landing of the staircase is transformed from a place of ritual to a place of rule. It becomes, as one scholar observes, a throne.[14]

It serves, as well, as a stage for the reception of ambassadors. For the visiting diplomat, the visual rhetoric of the Scala is clear and direct, with the expression of state power immediate and unambiguous. Passing from the public space of the Piazzetta through the elegant Porta della Carta, he is drawn into a shaded passageway toward a shining staircase "of the whitest marble." He continues on through the Arco Foscari, more an antechamber than an archway. Re-entering the sunlight, he climbs the broad stairs of the Scala toward the doge who awaits him, silhouetted against the darkness of the larger of three apertures – much like a triumphal arch – that lead into the second-floor loggia of the palace.[15] As he ascends the stairs, the visitor of high rank must be conscious of the inferior position which the architecture has assigned him relative to the Venetian doge. Moving forward in measured steps, with

the requisite pauses and bows of obeisance, he would be aware of the splendour, but perhaps unaware of the particulars, of the niello incrustation decorating each and every riser, and the rich sculptural revetment that covers the walls of the staircase.

In its structural role as the most prominent architectural feature of the palace courtyard, the Scala attracted the eye and organized the space. As Francesco Sansovino later put it:

From the Porta della Carta the staircase looks truly royal, [built] of the whitest marble [and] worked with trophies; standing at the base of the campanile one sees it from top to bottom; and when one enters the palace from the [south] side, one does the same, because of the great visibility of the site; two courtyards are formed by it, the great and common one and the small one of the senators.[16]

By separating the Cortile dei Senatori on its north side from the great public courtyard, the Scala thus underlined the hierarchy of the political order. And although a staircase, its purpose was to control as well as to provide regular access to the doge's palace.[17]

In its ideological role, the Scala expressed the power and the aspirations of the dogate. Using the language of military triumph, it even included a small prison below the staircase in a blunt allusion to ancient custom, wherein the cart of the victorious general was followed by chained prisoners.[18] But while the imposing character of its architectural structure alone carried a triumphal message to all who could see it, the symbolism of its relief decoration – whose iconography was defined by the doges of an individual aristocratic family – spoke a private language that would, in all likelihood, have been understood by only a few.

The private language of relief decoration

In a celebration of the surface values of pattern, color, and texture of which Venetians were so fond, the walls of the staircase consisted of flat panels of veined *marmo africano* framed by a network of white marble pilaster strips carved with a variety of motifs in *schiacciato* relief. The strips themselves – not only carved, but also originally painted in polychrome and highlighted with gilt – were like wide tapestry ribbons in stone, akin to the richly patterned carpets that Venetians hung out of their windows on days of celebration (Plates 182–5).[19]

Seemingly complex, recondite, and esoteric, with multiple layers of superimposed symbolism, the figural reliefs continue to defy a fully satisfactory interpretation. The basic decorative conceit involves the ingenious adaptation of the familiar plant candelabrum motif with the inclusion of a number of objects and emblems – religious, mythological, classical, heraldic, hieroglyphic – that appear to be suspended from the top of each panel and secured by rings and ribbons that link them together in a hanging chain. Some pilasters emphasize instruments of warfare: helmets, armor, and weapons of various types. Others celebrate the benefits of peace. One such arrangement includes a blazon, an S-shaped horn (possibly a type of cornet called a serpent), a ewer, reed panpipes, and an inverted torch, all animated with rippling ribbons (Plate 183).

182 Scala dei Giganti, detail of relief. Venice, Palazzo Ducale.

183 Scala dei Giganti, detail of relief. Venice, Palazzo Ducale.

167

184 Scala dei Giganti, detail of relief. Venice, Palazzo Ducale.

185 Scala dei Giganti, detail of relief with portrait of Doge Agostino Barbarigo (1486–1501). Venice, Palazzo Ducale.

Another ensemble features human busts growing out of urns; acrobatic putti who seem to have escaped from the foliage ornament of the Porta della Carta; and an impressive pair of male busts, probably a helmeted Alexander the Great and a turbaned Aristotle, surely alluding to the wisdom of the prince (Plate 184).[20] Perhaps the most striking feature of the reliefs as a whole is their level of *invenzione*: not one pattern repeats itself, and even the individual motifs are, for the most part, used but once.[21] The closest analogy may lie within the pages of illuminated books of the period, where miniaturists produced imaginative frontispieces of striking originality.[22]

Tucked unobtrusively into many of the pilaster compositions are sets of initials, a classical form of abbreviation that was by now a familiar and beloved genre to humanists of the time. Following the example of Cyriacus of Ancona, a generation of antiquarians was still copying antique epigrams at first-hand from monuments and at second from humanist sylloges. And now, ever more frequently, the most accomplished practitioners went beyond copying and invented their own. On the Scala, some initials proclaim universal princely virtues, such as "L.F.T." (*Liberalitate, Fide, Temperantia*; Liber-

ality, Faith, Temperance). Others are direct adaptations of Roman originals, such as the "S.P.Q.V." (*Senatus Populusque Venetianus*, loosely translated as the Senate and People of Venice) analogous to the "S.V.Q.C." that had already appeared on the medal of Pasquale Malipiero. Or they go beyond them, with the explicit "S.V.D. Ecclesiae" (*Senatus Venetus Defensor Ecclesiae* or The Senate of Venice Defender of the Church).[23]

However, a good number of the inscriptions are more personal, referring directly to the doge. Significantly, Marco Barbarigo is named in only one inscription while Agostino is cited dozens of times as, for example, "A.B.D.V." (*Augustinus Barbadicus Dux Venetiarum*) and, more elaborately, "A.B.D.V.F.F." (*Augustinus Barbadicus Dux Venetiarum Fecit Fieri* or Agostino Barbarigo, Doge of Venice, had it made). His portrait also appears on the corner pilaster of the Cortile dei Senatori, a profile head flanked by the letters "A" and "B" in a tondo carried aloft by two winged lions who rise from the waves of the sea. Above his head is the ducal umbrella, a sign of princely honor, and behind him the rays of the sun of justice (Plate 185).[24]

The winged victories in the spandrels of the supporting arcade may provide further clues to the overall program. One Victory is accompanied by the inscription "ASTREA DUCE" (With Astraea as the leader) (Plate 186). As Wolfgang Wolters points out, the Astraea of Virgil's Fourth Eclogue could be equated with the constellation Virgo located in the heavens between Leo and Libra. In an astrologically literate culture, her appearance here would surely conjure up allusions not only to the lion of Saint Mark, but also to Justice whose essential attribute was the balance scale. With other Victories carrying the ducal *corno*, an olive branch and an apple, a flaming vase and burning torches as symbols of just rule, peace, faith, and triumph, the Venetian patriciate is summoned to follow the doge into a new Golden Age.[25]

Poets of the time were only too ready to give the Barbarigo family a proper Roman lineage. Ventura di Malgrate, writing in Ferrara, sang the praises of Agostino in his *Visione Barbariga*,

Agostino Barbarigo tried to do with the allusive, inaccessible and arcane power of the hieroglyph. However, his glorification of self and family should not be considered an isolated phenomenon. Already in Foscari's reign, tendencies toward ducal exaltation and the personal identification of the doge with the state were becoming all too evident.[28]

The ducal tomb in an age of gold

They were discernible as well in the ever more grandiose funerary monuments of the doges. Little had Andrea Vendramin known when he wrote his will in 1472, ordering a tomb "of a good size and carefully made and well adorned," that he would be elected doge four years later.[29] Nor could he have been aware of possibilities for magnificence that would be realized in the Mocenigo and Tron tombs. His executors, however, had the considerable benefit of hindsight. For only in 1488, twelve years after Vendramin's death, did they finally put the tomb project out to contract. After negotiations with the Florentine sculptor Verrocchio that came to naught with the artist's death, they chose the young Tullio Lombardo. He had worked with his father Pietro on the Mocenigo monument and, even more conspicuously, in the sculptural decora-

186 Scala dei Giganti, detail of relief of *Astraea*. Venice, Palazzo Ducale.

addressing him as "serene doge and prince of new Rome." He called Venice "a mirror to the world of Justice and Faith, whose glory growing every more bright, that if one believes a prophetic spirit, she would be still as Rome was, when the heirs of the great Caesar remained." Her doge was equal to Numus Pompilius, more magnanimous than Tarquinius, a new Scipio in prudence, a new Fabius in wisdom, a Nestor in good council and great understanding, a Ulysses in astuteness and speech, a new Camillus in bringing victory, and a new Brutus in Justice.[26] Another writer drew upon the *Aeneid* to praise the "portal splendid with Barbarigan gold and spoils."[27]

While the elusive visual messages of the Scala may simply have been devised to entertain an intellectual élite who delighted in antiquarian *invenzioni*, they may also have masked ducal aspirations of personal rule inimical to aristocratic values. If so, the program was an extraordinary attempt by a single family to appropriate the prerogatives of political power. Following this line of thought, one might conclude that what Tron was not able to achieve with his image on the coin,

187 Tullio Lombardo, *Sea Creature and Putti*, 1480s. Marble. Venice, Santa Maria dei Miracoli.

tion of Santa Maria dei Miracoli (Plate 187). His high-relief carvings of sea creatures and cherubs for the triumphal arch bases in the church exemplify the ascendence of a competing antique paradigm that was emerging in the last decades of the century with the decoration of the Scala dei Giganti.[30] Already evident in drawings by Jacopo Bellini, this alternate tradition privileges Arcadia over Rome. It puts archaeology in the service not of the state, but in the creation of a romantic

188 Tullio Lombardo, tomb of Doge Andrea Vendramin (1476–8), 1488–93. Venice, SS. Giovanni e Paolo.

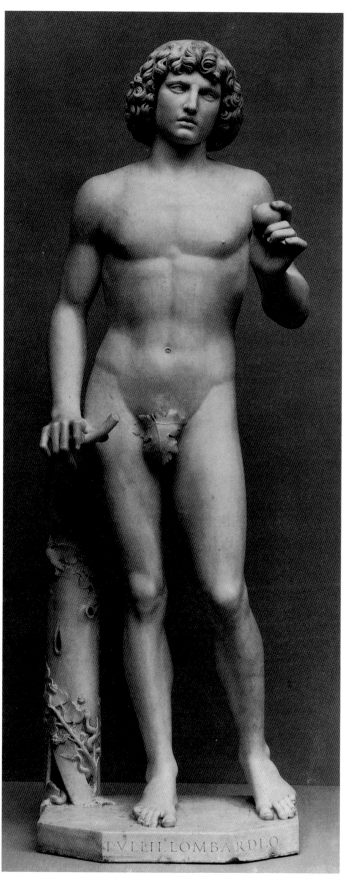

world that exists in an elusive interface between fantasy and nature. The elaboration of this world is played out primarily in the art of private life, but as with the sirens at the top of the Vendramin tomb and reliefs of the Scala, it could also spill out into public space.[31]

The Vendramin monument, virtually complete by 1493, is still impressive, even though it lost some of its figural sculpture when it was moved from Santa Maria dei Servi to SS. Giovanni e Paolo in the nineteenth century: an Adam and Eve from the niches and two Ephebes who hold shields from the top. Of these elements, only Adam, now in the Metropolitan Museum in New York, survives in its original state (Plates 188 and 189).[32] Even the most cursory comparison between it and Rizzo's Adam on the Arco Foscari shows that Tullio's work represents a new level of engagement with the Latin past. Not only is he the most classical of any Venetian artist to date, but he directs his archaeological tendencies toward highly original solutions: the first life-sized marble nude Adam and Eve on a Venetian tomb; the first life-sized soldiers clad in authentic Roman imperial armor (now moved into the niches); the first Virtues portrayed as antique goddesses or Muses; and a new, knowing assimilation of a number of antique styles of carving.[33]

The triumphal arch monument has become, moreover, a freestanding piece of architecture, its three-dimensional

189 Tullio Lombardo, *Adam*, 1488–93. Marble, h. 193 cm. New York, The Metropolitan Museum of Art, Fletcher Fund, 1936 (36.163).

190 *Nessus and Dejanira*, relief, detail of tomb of Doge Andrea Vendramin. Venice, SS. Giovanni e Paolo.

quality heightened by illusionistic carving, and is no longer (as with the Pietro Mocenigo tomb) simply a supporting armature for the sculpture.[34] The roundels of *Nessus and Dejanira* and *Perseus and Medusa*, probably carved by Tullio's brother Antonio on the model of Periclean period relief sculpture,[35] are not so much a borrowing as a critique of the Arch of Constantine in Rome (Plate 190). Several decades later, in a commentary to the first Italian translation of Vitruvius, Cesare Cesariano praised Tullio as one of the most outstanding living practitioners of Vitruvian classical principles.[36]

Not all spectators approved of such display. The German friar Felix Faber of Ulm was shocked during a visit to SS. Giovanni e Paolo, a church of his own Dominican order, to find the ducal tombs "embellished to an unfitting degree with various marbles and sculptures, and with gold and silver." But he directed his most critical comments toward their statuary. Around the images of saints, he charged,

> are arranged with their attributes the images of pagan gods, Saturn, Janus and Jupiter, Juno and Minerva, Mars and Hercules . . . There are also pugilists with naked bodies and with swords and spears in their hands, with shields hanging from their necks and no breastplates, true images of idols. Simple minds believe them to be depictions of saints, and worship Hercules, whom they take to be Samson, and Venus, whom they mistake for Magdalen.[37]

Venetians such as Marin Sanudo had no such reservations, judging the Vendramin tomb to be "the most beautiful on this earth by virtue of the worthy marbles [that] are in it."[38]

Ornaments of humanist culture

The stocking of the Venetian visual vocabulary with archaeological motifs offered an inexhaustible resource for the decoration of state documents. The nobleman Bertuccio Contarini, for example, would have been reminded of Venice's distinguished double heritage of Christian roots and pagan appropriation when he took office as Procurator of San Marco de Supra under Doge Marco Barbarigo (1485–6) and read through his elaborately decorated *giuramento* or oath of office (Plate 192). On the title-page, he solemnly swears to carry out the duties of his office, addressing his pledge directly to St. Mark, "the holy evangelist of God," shown in classical dress next to the letter "I" that begins the text. The oath is carefully written out in Gothic, not humanist, script on a *trompe-l'oeil* sheet of parchment. Its edges appearing to be worn away with age, it overlays a classicizing plaque seemingly carved with a Lombardesque motif of flowers, vines, and tendrils. Historical density is achieved with two medallions featuring profile busts *all'antica* embedded in the foliage, one supported by marine monsters, those ever popular protagonists so well suited to a maritime power.[39]

When Girolamo Cappello was given his commission as podestà and *capitano* of Feltre in 1488 by Agostino Barbarigo, he would find his personal patron St. Jerome and the familiar lion of St. Mark overseeing a cornice adorned with sphinxes, candelabra and bucrania (Plate 191).[40] Such assemblages — unlike the pilaster strips on Barbarigo's Scala dei Giganti — do not appear to demand elaborate decoding. Addressing the eye rather than the mind, they might best be considered ornaments of humanist culture in a well-governed state.

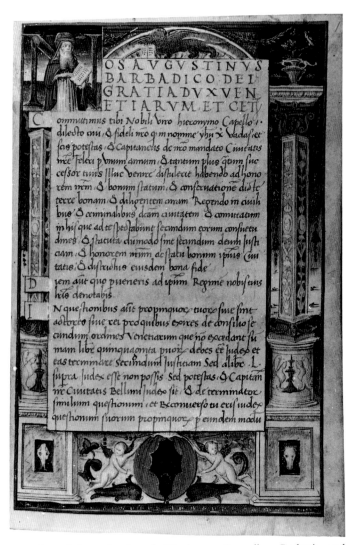

191 *Commissione ducale* of Girolamo Cappello, Podestà and Capitano of Feltre, 1488. Parchment, 23.7 × 15.8 cm. Venice, Museo Civico Correr, Cod. cl. III, 33 (Cicogna 2266).

THE CHRISTIAN REPUBLIC

Like other historians of his time, Bernardo Giustiniani picked up on the providential theme articulated by Lorenzo De Monacis and linked the rise of Venice directly to the decline of Rome:

192 *Giuramento* of Bertuccio Contarini, Procurator of San Marco de Supra, 1485. Parchment, 27.5 × 19 cm. Venice, Museo Civico Correr, Cod. cl. III, 313 (Cicogna 829).

[Venice] was preserved by divine command so that those who excelled in piety or religion, either expelled from home by factions, or tired by lengthy tribulations, might have a refuge to which they could flee with their wives and children, and so that finally, after long misfortunes, they might seek a port of safety for themselves and their holy relics.[41]

For Giustiniani, even Christian Rome of his own day, for all its sacred treasures, was no more impressive than Venice. He had reminded the Venetian cardinals in 1483, "that Venice was their true parent and the Church only a step-mother."[42] Allowing that the republic's power and prosperity had brought her fear and envy from other western powers, he insisted that her greatest foe was still in the Ottoman east. After the fall of Constantinople in 1453, whose ruin had been God's warning to his countrymen, Venice was now the "sea-wall of Christianity" against the Turks. Her own destruction would mark the end of the Christian republic.[43]

If Venice was to be seen as the new Jerusalem as well as the new improved version of old Rome, claims of rightful inheritance that had been implied in the mosaics of the Mascoli Chapel, was it now also to be honored as the new Constantinople? Along with the increased Greek presence in the city and the continuous pressure from the Turks during the latter half of the fifteenth century, signs of a Byzantine revival in Venetian art and architecture have often been remarked upon by modern-day scholars. These signs included not only Giovanni Bellini's icon-like Madonnas,[44] but also, most notably, a group of at least six churches designed by Mauro Codussi and his circle. Deriving from a Byzantine quincunx centralized plan with nine bays and five domes, their basic form is viewed by James Ackerman as "a willed reaction against the Gothic tradition," and "an alternative to an early Renaissance classical style."[45] Sant'Andrea della Certosa, now destroyed, was the first of the series, with the construction of its lower portion datable to 1484–90. Significantly, the neo-Byzantine revivals in Venice were confined to the plan and did not carry through to interior elevations, which generally featured an early Renaissance style in the manner of Brunelleschi and Alberti.[46] And yet even such a devout Latinist as Tullio Lombardo ventured to "carve in Greek" when the occasion called for it. Indeed, the archaic features of his *Coronation of the Virgin* in San Giovanni Crisostomo, one of Codussi's Byzantine revival churches, can best be understood as a conscious reprise of a Byzantine style and iconography (Plate 193).[47]

The nature and meaning of this revival is complex. An early Christian revival in reaction to Albertian classicism in church architecture was under way in Rome at the time under the patronage of Sixtus IV, and to a lesser degree in Florence.[48] Although the square plans were attractive for practical reasons in Venice – compact, easily adaptable, and cheap to build – ideological motivations may also have inspired Venetian

193 Tullio Lombardo, *Coronation of the Virgin*, 1501–2. Marble, c.270 × 200 cm. Venice, San Giovanni Crisostomo.

patrons. Ackerman suggests in the case of Venice that the impulse was born in conservative patrician circles with ecclesiastical connections and populist tendencies and an anti-pagan or even anti-humanist agenda.[49] Manfredo Tafuri, however, characterizes the patrons of San Salvador, the last building of the group (begun 1506/7) and a church with profound civic meanings, as members of a different circle within the patrician élite who had links to Florentine humanism and were involved in philological and antiquarian studies (Plate 194). The church was designed by Giorgio Spavento and built by Tullio Lombardo. In an ingenious accommodation to the restrictions of the site and the joint use of San Salvador as both parish and monastery church, the quincunx module is repeated three times within an overall Latin-cross plan. In the final elaboration of the church, Tafuri argues,

194   Venice, San Salvador. Designed by Giorgio Spavento, 1507–34. Drawing from Cicognara, Diedo, and Selva, *Le fabbriche più conspicue di Venezia*, Plate 96.

they "forced the neo-Byzantine program to speak a humanistic language."[50]

During precisely the same period and within the context of the neo-Byzantine revival, Lionello Puppi sees the recurrence of a Venice–Jerusalem metaphor. It took a number of forms, both experiential and iconographical. Along with the revival of the cults of a number of oriental saints, and of St. Theodore in particular, the accounts of pilgrims passing through the city en route to the Holy Land testify to a public awareness of the urban space of Venice as part of a continuous sacred itinerary that culminated in Jerusalem.[51] Pious travelers such as Felix Faber appreciated the noble Christian origins of the city and recognized the absolute uniqueness of its urban form as proof of its divinely inspired destiny. Faber found the church of San Marco "so surprising to see that, according to common opinion, it seems to be made by angels rather than by men."[52] Venetians themselves referred to their city as "la terra sancta nostra" and "la sancta città." Bringing the Holy Land into the meeting halls of the *scuole* in great cycles of painted histories set in the Orient, they also commissioned biblical scenes in settings that had been refashioned from the urban fabric of Venice itself.[53]

Conversely, the architect Pietro Lombardo made a significant impact on that same fabric by contriving unique solutions for the façades of two of the Scuole Grandi that transmuted the classical vocabulary into something singularly Venetian. The projects were quite different in character, but each was grounded in an illusionism that was intended to create, as well as to breach, spatial and temporal boundaries. In the first project, completed in 1481, Lombardo fashioned a dignified atrium in a small square *campo* that served as a public walkway between the Scuola Grande and Church of San Giovanni Evangelista (Plate 195). He divided the space into two parts, creating a forecourt from the nondescript side walls of the two buildings. This outer vestibule was separated from an inner, more private area by a wall like a choir screen, pierced with a great central portal and two flanking windows. The walls of the forecourt are articulated with Corinthian pilasters to create three bays on each side and unified with a continuous entablature carved with a foliate pattern. The illusory nature of the scheme begins with the wall treatment and extends to the nature of the spaces themselves. The screen or wall is decorated with a rich marble revetment, while the brick side walls, seemingly an integral part of the same scheme, are covered with stucco painted to look like veined marble panels. The outer vestibule, although public space, was embraced by the decorative apparatus of the Scuola; the inner courtyard, although private space, was unadorned and still served as a city street.[54]

Lombardo's other project, the meeting house of the Scuola Grande di San Marco, offered a far greater scope for invention. Called in to replace a previous building that had been completely destroyed by fire, he created – in collaboration with his sculptor sons, Tullio and Antonio Lombardo – an illusionistic

195 Venice, Scuola Grande di San Giovanni Evangelista, atrium. Designed by Pietro Lombardo, 1481.

façade that melded fictive and real architecture (Plates 196 and 197). Its structure inspired by the shape of a Roman triumphal arch, the façade served as a theatrical stage for two sets of relief sculpture: a pair of lions flanking the main portal, and scenes from the life of St. Mark at the sides of the entrance to the *albergo*.[55] In his stocky proportions, his *gravitas*, and his classical dress, St. Mark is not Roman so much as he is early Christian.[56] The reliefs, datable to 1488–90 and carved in *mezzo rilievo*, are radically new in concept and explore a whole range of spatial relationships and ambiguities: between perspective recession and spatial projection; between pictorial and sculptural values; between Roman classicism and monumentality and the Venetian taste for pattern, materials, and surface.[57]

A PLACE IN THE COSMOS

The republic was also to be more firmly situated not just in human, but also in cosmic time, during these years. By the mid-fifteenth century, the groundwork had already been laid

for a precise articulation of Venice's foundation in astrological terms. A manuscript completed in Padua in 1466 contains a horoscope charting the positions of constellations and planets above Venice at midday on March 25, 421 – the feast of the Annunciation and the purported birth-date of the city. Commissioned by Naimerio Conti, the son of a respected astrologer and teacher at the University of Padua, the manuscript contains romantic accounts of his own city's foundation and places Venice within the embrace of Paduan history.[58] But the horoscope, which seems to be a copy of an earlier one, was soon appropriated by Venetian historians as a sign of Venice's own auspicious beginnings. Like Giustiniani, Sabellico did not try to confirm or deny the horoscope, but he pointedly noted the favorable aspect of the heavens for Venice's civic destiny in his *Rerum venetarum ab urbe condita libri XXXIII*, published in 1487.[59] Already symbolically identified with Venice in her persona as goddess, Venus as planet was situated in the sign of Aries, a month that marks the beginning of spring and the birth of a new year. Sabellico also observed that Jupiter and Mercury in the sign of Pisces was a particularly auspicious

196   Venice, Scuola Grande di San Marco, Campo SS. Giovanni e Paolo. Designed by Pietro Lombardo, with reliefs by his sons Tullio and Antonio, 1487–90; crowning of façade completed by Mauro Codussi, 1495.

197   Venice, Scuola Grande di San Marco, detail of façade.

conjunction for a city devoted to commerce.[60] Significantly, both writers elaborated upon the further synchronic implications of Venice's foundation on such a "sacrosanct day." Sabellico observes that

> almost all agree that the city was founded on the 25th of March. Considering the excellent works that have been done on that day, there is no doubt that anything begun then would be abundant and magnificent. For to the perpetual glory of humankind (the sacred scriptures affirm this), on that same day the omnipotent God formed our first Parent. Likewise, the son of God was conceived in the womb of the Virgin. By human genius, this most worthy mystery cannot be explained in words, but only comprehended with intellect. How wisely with love we believe and constantly avow that the divine was with the human conjoined; and the eternal incomprehensible secret combined with the corruptible and the comprehensible . . . And yet some may scorn this as an empty observation, not believing that one day would be any different from another. But we truly esteem such to be the case. Seeing how much nature not once but many times has worked most nobly in that way.[61]

In accordance with Renaissance beliefs in the power of signs and similitudes, Sabellico thus made a link by analogy between the creation of man, the Incarnation of Christ and the foundation of Venice.[62] He also observed: "Some say that where the Church of San Marco now stands was where they first began to build." All such creations – their linkage confirmed by the consonance of date – were similar in their conjoining of the human and the divine.[63]

And there were more to come. Sanudo included a drawing of the horoscope in the manuscript of his *De origine* of 1493, along with a detailed account of the planetary positions. Repeating Sabellico's litany of temporal consonances, he added two more. The first affirmed a longstanding civic tradition. Attesting that "this is the truth," he cited the *figura astrologica* and claimed that "this city was first built on the island of Rialto, and the first foundations were made of the church of San Giacomo – that is presently still in Rialto – in 421 on the 25th of March on the day of Venus [Friday] around the hour of midday . . ." The second coincidence expanded upon the sacred implications of the date: "according to theological opinion it was on this same day that [Christ] was crucified by Jews and placed on the holy cross; it was a day of great ceremony, and so our progenitors wished to choose this day for such a foundation . . ."[64] Some years later in his *Diarii*, Sanudo would add yet another foundation to this compelling chain of resemblances, stating that it was "in 1507 on this day that the first stone was laid for the new reconstruction of the church of San Salvador on this ground. So it is a day much celebrated."[65] The major monuments of Venetian sacred architecture were thus set into a timeless continuity that was rooted in the city's own perfect beginnings.[66]

VENETIAN TIME

As the century ended, the state reaffirmed its control of civic time with the construction of the Torre dell'Orologio – the last of the great quattrocento portals (Plate 198). Built as a tower gateway over the entrance to the Merceria, the twisting commercial street that led to Rialto, the new structure was inserted into the 150-meter long façade of the Procuratie Vecchie that formed the north side of the Piazza San Marco. Sanudo described its unveiling in February 1499 when the doge made his annual procession to the church of Santa Maria Formosa: "the clock was opened and uncovered for the first time . . . [it is] made with great ingenuity and most beautiful."[67] Barbari's view of Venice shows the Torre as Sanudo would have seen it – a four-story tower that occupied a two-bay section of the façade – and before the side wings were added a few years later (Plate 17).[68]

Probably designed by Mauro Codussi, the Torre helped to structure the experience of civic space in at least two impor-

198   Venice, Torre dell'Orologio, Piazza San Marco. Attributed to Mauro Codussi, 1496–9, side wings added by Pietro Lombardo 1500–6 and additional floors by Giorgio Massari in 1755.

tant ways. First, it created a strong focal point for visitors arriving by ship. As they disembarked on the Molo between the great granite columns that marked the urban confines, their eyes would be drawn inevitably to the richly decorated tower of glistening white marble that rose above the buildings on the far side of the Piazza San Marco. It thus provided immediate visual access to the heart of the city. Secondly, it separated the street of commerce from the ritual space of the piazza. Francesco Sansovino would later call it "the gateway through which one goes into the city."[69]

The broad arch forming the lowest tier supports a second story that contains the face of an astronomical clock, complete with zodiac signs, constellations, and a revolving ball that marks the phases of the moon. The aesthetic pre-eminence of San Marco and the Palazzo Ducale is reflected in a rich polychrome decoration of white and pink marbles, blue enamel and gilded bronze, and a gilded sculpture of the Madonna and Child seated inside a classical aedicule in the third tier above reaffirms the sacral character of the city.[70] The wall was covered with a revetment of gold and blue mosaic, a color scheme that was repeated with a different pattern in the fourth tier. Here one finds the ubiquitous lion of St. Mark, originally balanced by the figure of Doge Agostino Barbarigo who knelt before him, marking the street as public domain. On the rooftop a bell was installed and flanked with two bronze giants, soon nicknamed the Moors because of their dark color, who rang the hours.[71]

The clock tower may well be, as Deborah Howard suggests, a Venetian version of the classical watchtower recommended by Alberti as an ornament to the city.[72] The Torre followed a number of his guidelines: the stacked tiers, a 1:4 ratio of width to height, an opening through the center, and "moving dials to indicate . . . the angle of the sun, and the time of day . . ." It conformed, moreover, to his edict that an arch be built "at the point where a road meets a square or a forum, especially if it is a *royal* road . . ."[73] And yet, although many individual components of the Torre are drawn from the classical vocabulary, it is profoundly unclassical in its total effect.

In the last analysis, Venetians had little need to claim their city as a new and improved version of any other civilization. Indeed, they were still confident of Venice's superiority, becoming ever more perfect by taking in the best traditions of the two great civilizations of the classical world. As Sanudo had written in 1493:

One can therefore compare the Venetians to the Romans (who raised such stately edifices) on account of the buildings, both private and public, being erected at the present time. Indeed it can be said, as another writer has done, that our republic has followed the Romans in being as powerful in military strength as in virtue and learning. He writes moreover, Greece was the seat of learning and powerful in arms; now the Venetians are the learned ones, now the lion is strongly armed.[74]

In another short guide to the city published in 1502, Sabellico stressed not only Venice's complete uniqueness of site and condition and its moral and spiritual superiority, but also its enduring permanence. A "stable, perpetual and durable empire" that had by then lasted a thousand years, here too it surpassed Rome.[75] And yet, his tone is as defensive as it is assertive. For all the triumphal aspect of their city and the glory of their past, Venetians were faced with political, military, and economic challenges that offered little room for complacency. Learned Venetians sought respite from the uncertainties of present-day reality in antiquarian activities, and, as will become apparent, engagement with the antique past took on an increasingly privatized dimension.

199 Paduan artist, frontispiece to San Hieronymus, *Vita Malchi monachi; Vita beati Pauli primi eremitae*, c.1460–62. Parchment, 14 × 8.5 cm. Venice, Biblioteca Nazionale Marciana, Cod. Lat. II 39 (2999), cc. 7v–8.

V

THE HISTORICAL IMAGINATION: CONSTRUCTING AN ALTERNATE REALITY

PIV LALTRVI passion ch'el propo Affecto
Publica ilvariar dil nostro stile
Che a satisfar ogni spirto Gentile
Sempre d'un buon servir dimostra effecto
cro se quini Amor in schivo obiecto
Tragr di Ardor vn liquido e sottile
Foco: che hor facci altero: et hora humile
Quel cor che Amando va senza rispecto.
vtto riluce da vn splendor diuerso.
E del oram mar dilesser li Accidenti
Il mondo fan di male e ben consperso.
unque de nostri error vechi e recenti
E di Lopera il dritto et il riuerso
Sia colto il buono. e l'altro posto a venti

200 Allegorical scene, from Francesco Petrarca, *Canzoniere, Trionfi*. Venice: Vindelino da Spira, 1470, f. 145. Venice, Biblioteca Nazionale Marciana, Inc. Ven. 546.

PROLOGUE

...and there were many dances, and many mumij *of gods and nymphs, that would be too long to recount...*

– Sier Ramberto and Sier Giacomo Contarini, 1442[1]

The emerging Venetian sense of the past was shaped only in part by classical artifacts and texts and modern revivals of antique genres of art and architecture. It was also informed – one might say misinformed – by the parallel development of profane theatrical entertainments. Theater provided the means to mix past and present, in which the temporal boundary was ruptured, and the Olympian gods were invited, as it were, into Venetian society. By the end of the century, artists would develop a new mode of visual discourse, deliberately encoded to charge the past with a mysterious elusiveness as antiquity became ever more a retreat from, as well as a model for, the present.

BETWEEN MYTH AND REALITY

Evidence of a playful, free-floating attitude toward the ancient world is already apparent in the letter written by the two Contarini to their brother Andrea, then in Constantinople. The topic was the lavish festivities that were held to celebrate the marriage of their sister Lucrezia to the doge's son, Jacopo Foscari. The youths were all members of a Compagnia della Calza: a group of young Venetian nobles who banded together for a limited period during late adolescence and early adulthood for purposes of celebration and mutual entertainment. Each such group wore a distinctive outfit, typically hose, or *calze*, with each leg a different color: hence their name. While they initially seem to have focused their energies on the wedding celebrations of their members, the companies soon developed into major organizers of Venetian *feste* and staged often sumptuous events to fête visiting dignitaries at the behest of the state.[2] A reflection of such ephemera – although the imagery is, as yet, more chivalric than classical – may be found in Jacopo Bellini's drawing of a knight in contemporary armor, whose galloping horse is transformed into a dragon

with trappings that feature scaly neck armor, wings, and a tail (Plate 201).[3]

Of particular interest in the Contarini letter are the *mumij*, also called *momarie*, *murarie*, and *bombarie* in documents of the time. The term deriving from the Latin *Momus*, these were theatrical productions whose mythological character, with pantomime, music, and dancing, must have been familiar enough to the Contarini brothers to require no explanation.[4] It may be inferred that pagan gods and nymphs were already honored guests in Venetian palaces before mid-century. By the end of the quattrocento, they were frequent participants in open-air pageants, often floating on barges and accompanied by instrumental and vocal music.[5]

Correspondence describing two *feste* held in Venice in 1493 to celebrate the visit of Beatrice d'Este and her mother Eleonora of Aragon portrays a city where classicizing myth had become part of civic reality. The Compagnia of the Potenti, who had recently feted Alfonso d'Este, the Duke of Ferrara, with great success was now given an official commission by the Great Council to organize a banquet, a *momaria*, and a regatta for his wife and daughter.[6] Growing up at the court of Ferrara with a rich dramatic agenda that included revivals of Roman theater, Beatrice was a good observer.[7] Writing detailed accounts back to her husband Ludovico Sforza in Milan, she described a floating theatrical production that presented an allegorical message of classical flavor to the accompaniment of music and dancing. Neptune and Minerva were seated in a boat opposite a make-believe mountain on which were affixed the arms of the pope, the Dukes of Milan and Ferrara, and the Republic of Venice. Following a dance to the shimmery clatter of tambourines, Minerva pierced the mountain with an arrow and pulled out an olive branch; then Neptune plunged his trident into the mountain and retrieved a horse. Each god proposed a name for the city that would be founded on the mountain. A group of judges holding books

201 Jacopo Bellini, *A Knight on a Horse masquerading as a Dragon*, from his *Book of Drawings*, f. 47. Pen and ink on parchment, 29 × 42.7 cm. Paris, Louvre, Cabinet des Dessins (R.F. 1515).

proclaimed the winner to be Minerva who had suggested the name of Athens, the city where, the young Beatrice observed: "there was the foundation of learning, so they say." Her interpretation of the performance shows an awareness – if not a profound understanding – of classical imagery and its power to speak to current political events. She concludes: "With the unity of peace, states are maintained."[8]

An after-dinner event described by Beatrice as "uno bellisimo spectaculo" was directed by a herald. It included a procession of four triumphal chariots, "in one of which was Diana, in another was Death, in another the mother of Meleager, in another were some men holding arms; on these carts there were 4 to 5 persons each; and all were made to represent the life of Meleager, which was represented with dances from his birth to his death most decorously."[9]

The *momaria* performed at the wedding of Lorenzo Pisani del Banco and Maria Pisani in 1497 was only one event of many in a celebration that lasted for an entire month. It included a court composed of both gods and heroes: Jove, Hercules, Venus, Pallas Athene, and Phoebus, as well as Ulysses, Alcinous, Aeneas, and Dido.[10] In the same year,

Sanudo recorded a marine spectacle of a mythological nature with "a *momaria* that was this: men mounted on sea horses, armed to joust . . . many dressed like moors . . . and a king."[11] Such performances were frequent enough in aristocratic circles to reinforce ties between the pagan protagonists and their Venetian admirers and to link the world of myth to the world of present day.

According to Vittore Branca, the structure of the Venetian *momaria* was based upon the dramatic religious *laude*, but with a mythological *fabula* replacing the sacred action and pagan heroes and heroines replacing the saints. Immediately after visiting Venice in 1479–80, the Florentine poet-humanist Angelo Poliziano wrote his *Fabula di Orfeo* on the same model and abandoned, if only in this single work, the neo-Platonism that had animated the triumphs in his *Stanze*. In the *Orfeo*, by contrast, he embraced a north Italian Aristotelian vision of a concrete, if fragile, pagan world. The variety of meters and the sequence of descriptive and lyrical scenes, at once visual and melodic, are exceptional in his oeuvre and are foreign to the Florentine tradition of *sacre rappresentazioni*. Also characteristic of Veneto theater is his alternation of Latin, *volgare*, and local dialects.[12] Branca makes an important point about Venetian dramatic forms in this period that may help to clarify the allusive character of the plastic arts as well: "The sense of a theatricality in which supposed reality is not remote, detached, confined beyond a screen or the frame of a proscenium, but present and immediate, developed on a plane that in respect to distance of places and times comes to collide with the plane in which the life of the spectators take place."[13] In the Venetian *momaria* and in Poliziano's *Orfeo*, myth and everyday reality thus maintain a contiguous, responsive, and precarious balance. A new, more coherent, vision of the past that addressed the enduring themes of nature, love and death would also begin to take shape in the emerging genre of pastoral literature.

Themes of love and death

At the behest of his Venetian host, Pietro Contarini, Poliziano also wrote a *rispetto*: a melodrama in rhyme to be performed with a musical accompaniment. A revival of the ancient Greek poetic genre of the echo, Poliziano's short, exquisite work employs the conceit of a repeated phrase at the end of each verse:

L'Eco

Che fai tu, Ecco, mentre ch'io ti chiamo? *Amo.*
Ami tu duo, o pur un solo? *Un solo.*
E io te solo, e non altri, amo. *Altri amo.*
Dunque non ami tu un solo. *Un solo.*
Questo è un dirmi: I'non t'amo. *I'non t'amo.*
Quel che tu ami, amil tu solo? *Solo.*
Chi t'ha levato dal mio Amore? *Amore.*
Che fa quello a chi porti Amore? *Ah, more!*[14]

The Echo

What are you doing, Echo, While I call to you? *I love.*
Do you love two, or only one alone? *One alone.*
And you alone, and not others, do I love. *Others do I love.*
Then you do not love one alone. *One alone.*
This is what you tell me: I do not love you. *I do not love you.*
He whom you love, do you love him alone? *Alone.*
Who has taken you away from my love? *Love.*
What happens to him to whom you bring love? *Ah, death!*

The poignant role of Echo was played by a gentle and sorrowful young girl. As Branca observes: "It is a dialogue balanced between a nostalgic and abandoned love and the murky shadow of death lying in wait."[15] Published in 1494 with the title *Stanza ingeniosissima*, the poem inspired many imitations and established a popular new genre for dramatic performances in Venetian palaces.[16]

The syncretic tendencies that animated profane theater, as well as the new pastoral literature, made for an easy slippage between past and present. These factors may help to account for the emergence of a romantic – as opposed to a historical – vision of antiquity in Venetian art. The predisposition toward incorporation and accommodation observable in the art and architecture of Venice from the thirteenth century on must have played a role as well. But the essential matrix in which these distinct but intersecting impulses would come together in a peculiarly Venetian sense of the past in the late quattrocento was the lively culture of northern Italian humanism. It was here that the cult of antiquity found its acolytes in artists and poets as well as antiquarians.

THE CULT OF ANTIQUITY

Indirect evidence for close ties between Venetian artists and antiquarian circles can be found in the art itself. The inscription in the lower right-hand corner of the Putti Master's frontispiece to a copy of Livy printed in Venice in 1470 is a case in point (Plate 202).[17] The member of the Priuli family who commissioned the miniature may not have been privy to Marcanova's *Collectio Antiquitatum* or to the drawing book of Jacopo Bellini where the epigram also appeared, but he could well have seen it in the fresco in the Church of the Eremitani in Padua where Mantegna had also painted it onto the wall of Herod's throne room (see Plate 139).[18] The change of venue from a princely audience hall in the fresco to an open-air site of pagan sacrifice and bacchic triumph in the manuscript suggests a straightforward denotative function for such inscriptions; no hidden meaning was intended other than to establish an antique ambience. Commemorating a certain Titus Pullius Linus for at least the third time in a work of art, its presence attests to the continuing appeal of the sylloge of inscriptions in the atelier as well as the humanist's study.

Even more direct evidence of exchanges between artists and intellectuals can be found in the writings of Raffaele Zovenzoni, a humanist from Trieste. Living in exile in Venice in the early 1470s, he addressed ten poems to five Venetian artists in his *Istrias*, a collection of 267 Latin epigrams dedicated to Giovanni Hinderbach, the Bishop of Trento.[19] The verses testify to a virtuosic command of the topoi that humanists were wont to apply to art and artists. Praising the painting of some apples by Marco Zoppo, he judged that they were so true to life that they had deceived his little daughter and that they would, indeed, have fooled Phidias himself.[20] To a certain Laurentino Mentore, *emblematario*, he exclaimed, "Laurentius, your skill captivates me and leaves me stupified, When I see the divine contained within your images."[21] Nor did he hesitate to give voice to the sculptor Antonio Rizzo: "Antonio, looking with wonder at his effigy of Hercules, said, 'I give bodies to the gods; may the gods give a soul to you.'"[22] Zovenzoni then spoke directly to Rizzo's figure of Eve on the

Biblioteca Trivulziana in Milan, where the bound manuscript is also found, and dates it to 1474 (Plate 204).[26] Its immediacy and power belying its tiny size, the miniature measures slightly more than fifteen centimeters square. Even with a false inscription that names the sitter as Zovenzoni's old teacher *Guarinus Veronensis*, it is a remarkably compelling image. Framed by a classical aedicule and flanked by candelabra, the poet Zovenzoni demands the viewer's response. The half a millenium that separates his time from our time is bridged at once with an arresting gaze, and the painted space and our space are linked by the book (most certainly his own) placed before him on the window sill.[27] The three-quarter view and the scrupulous attention to detail, with a meticulous rendering of the stubble of Zovenzoni's beard, may indicate Bellini's awareness of northern models, but such features are even more credibly explained by the influence of Antonello da Messina, who was working in Venice at precisely that time.[28]

The forty-year-old Zovenzoni was not one of the renowned humanists of the day. In Venice he supported

203   Antonio Rizzo, *Eve*, c.1462–70. Marble, h. 204 cm. Venice, Palazzo Ducale, Arco Foscari.

202   Putti Master, frontispiece to Livy, *Historiae romanae decades*, Venice: Vindelino de Spira, 1470, f. 24. Vienna, Österreichische Nationalbibliothek, Inc. 5.C.9.

Arco Foscari (Plate 203): "If your beauty was as it lives in this marble, Eve, who would be amazed if your husband would submit to you?"[23]

Both Gentile and Giovanni Bellini merited Zovenzoni's attention as well. Aside from his admiration of a nude statue of Venus that he had seen in Gentile's studio, he also commended the artist for the lifelike quality of his painted panels, "that exhale the wondrous odor of violets."[24] But his greatest compliment was reserved for Giovanni Bellini. Addressing him as "Bello", in a pun on the artist's name, Zovenzoni not only praised his gifts as a portraitist, proclaiming him "a painter worthy of the prince Alexander," but also commissioned him to paint his portrait.[25]

The miniature, to be bound into the *Istrias* in lieu of Zovenzoni's personal presentation of the work to Hinderbach, was long thought to have been lost. However, Jennifer Fletcher has convincingly identified it on a loose leaf in the

204 (facing page)   Giovanni Bellini, *Portrait of Raffaele Zovenzoni*, c.1474. Cutting on vellum, 15.2 × 15.9 cm. Milan, Biblioteca Trivulziana, p.m. sciolte C 56.

himself by working for several printers and by practising the profession of notary. But his epigrams show him to be a cultivated man: an admirer of poetry, ancient art, and beautiful women, as well as of modern painting and sculpture, and the friend of a number of Venetian patricians. Indeed, educated in Greek and Latin letters in the school of Guarino Veronese in Ferrara and possessed of strong religious convictions, he typified the Christian humanist of the time who sought mightily to reconcile pagan and Christian teaching.[29] In Zovenzoni's poem written to celebrate the opening day of classes in Guarino's school, one scholar sees "master and disciples sealing with the sign of the cross their double cult for Apollo and Jesus":[30]

At the Beginning of Studies

Behold, Apollo smiled favorably on our studies
the kindly day has come to the choral dance of the muses,
the kindly day has come and the harvest
is pressed into new wine:

The kindly day has come to us.
The kindly day has come, now at last the mouths of
the fountains of Bellerophon exhaust themselves: the kindly
day has come.
The kindly day has come:
only let your divine spirit be present,
Jesus Christ, and always the kindly day will come.[31]

A similar habit of mind informed Marin Sanudo's easy negotiation between pagan and Christian artifacts encountered on his trip through the terraferma. It is this syncretic approach, typical of the educated man of the day, that allowed for reliefs of pagan heroes to be sculpted on Christian tombs and for satyrs, harpies, and erotes to decorate the title-pages of a deluxe edition of the Bible. Depending on harmonious reconciliation rather than on moralizing opposition, this philosophical ideal should be distinguished from the medieval tradition of the *Ovide moralisé*, in which pagan figures were identified with Christian counterparts. For the humanists of the late quattrocento, it had become possible to incorporate

205 Antonio da Negroponte, *Madonna and Child*, 1465–7. Tempera on wood panel, 300 × 235 cm. Venice, San Francesco della Vigna.

the beauty of pagan philosophy and poetry into a Christian universe, and yet without removing the substance of its original identity by making it only a symbol for something else.[32]

Possibly the ultimate statement of this heartfelt marriage of past and present can be seen in the engaging altarpiece by Antonio da Negroponte in the Church of San Francesco della Vigna, datable to around 1465–7 (Plate 205). The luxuriant garden imagery deriving from the International Gothic style of Gentile da Fabriano is now enriched with a wealth of classical citations presented in a most unclassical manner.[33]

188

9

ANTIQUITY IN THE MIND

Men were turned into marble
when they looked at the Gorgon:
We are turned into marble
when we look at your marble, Crispo.
– Raffaele Zovenzoni, *Istrias*, 1470s[1]

The ambiguous nature of Felice Feliciano's antiquarian enterprises of the 1460s – at once factual and imaginary – had already pointed to a "shift of interest from antiquity on the site to antiquity in the mind."[2] Zovenzoni's epigram, dedicated to the sculptor Antonio Rizzo, whom he addressed as "Crispo Marmorio Nobilissimo," is a graceful acknowledgement of art's unique capacity to transform and to bring about metamorphosis. It is also evidence for a growing awareness by humanists in the Venetian milieu of the power of the visual arts – as well as that of texts – to bridge the gap between past and present.

STRATEGIES OF DISENGAGEMENT

Renaissance artists tended to follow three basic approaches when representing the personae, the ambients, and the events of the classical world, each implying a different manner of engagement between the past and the present. First, they might recast the past in contemporary terms, thus pulling it into the present and thereby achieving an arbitrary – ahistorical – sort of temporal unity. Second, they could aim at a more modern notion of historical consistency by reconstructing monuments and costumes in an *all'antica* style based upon first-hand observation of classical artifacts; here the past was kept wholly within the past. Finally, they could imply the separateness of the past, but provide access to it from the present, effectively pushing the present back into the past. Appearing in that order over the course of the fifteenth century, all three modes can be found in late quattrocento painting in Venice and elsewhere. But the most significant Venetian contribution was made in the third category, wherein antiquity came to be presented as an alternate world

into which the Renaissance viewer could travel by means of the imagination. These strategies will be discussed in turn.

The present as the past

The "present as the past" approach, the defining mode of a pre-Renaissance mentality, has a long pedigree stretching back into the Middle Ages. It could be observed earlier on in the fourteenth-century manuscript illustrations of the Ambrosiana Livy (Plates 69–72), and it appeared yet again in many of Jacopo Bellini's drawings (for example, Plates 123 and 124). In both cases, episodes from ancient history or mythology are played out in Gothic settings by protagonists clothed in fashions of the fourteenth or fifteenth century. In Florence, this mode remained the standard for *cassone* painting. In Venice, as artists became increasingly aware of the separateness of the past, the strategy took on an increasingly theatrical aspect. Carpaccio's *Theseus receiving the Embassy of Hippolyta, Queen of the Amazons*, datable to the late 1490s, is a case in point (Plate 206). Fetchingly attired in modish Venetian gowns and riding elegantly caparisoned horses, Hippolyta and her entourage approach an outdoor loggia. Although fitted up with columns and adorned with classicizing swags, the structure is draped with oriental carpets like the balcony of a Venetian palace on a feast day. Indeed, its architectural style would surely have been unknown to Vitruvius and disdained by Cyriacus of Ancona. The ladies wear fantastic headgear, moreover, that would have been more appropriate to the *momaria* than to everyday life in the streets of Venice. The aging Theseus is attended by four Venetian youths; their fashionable dress suggesting their association with a Compagnia della Calza, whose members were impresarios of such productions.

Presenting antique subject matter once removed, as trans-

206 Vittore Carpaccio, *Theseus receiving the Embassy of Hippolyta, Queen of the Amazons*, late 1490s. Wood panel, 102 × 145 cm. Paris, Musée Jacquemart-André.

mitted through Boccaccio's *Teseide*, Carpaccio recasts the world of Greek mythology within the idiom of Venetian pageantry.[3] Most of his painted cycles for the *scuole*, from the *Legend of St. Ursula* to the *Life of St. Stephen*, demonstrate a similar contemporizing cast.[4] In accordance with the aggregative approach employed by Jacopo Bellini, classical motifs of varying degrees of archaeological integrity and inscriptions in Hebrew or Latin are introduced to recreate a convincingly ancient *mise-en-scène*. Depending on how one looks at the issue, historical distance is either breached or it is simply ignored. This approach lingered on in Venice – perhaps the epitome of the *societá spettacolo* – even to the end of the sixteenth century, where it animated the great banquet scenes of Veronese.[5]

The past in the past

The "past in the past" strategy in its fully developed form might be considered the Renaissance paradigm proper, where appropriately attired protagonists play out their historical and biblical roles in an archaeologically convincing classical world. Mantegna had set a new standard of historical consistency in his frescoes for the church of the Eremitani in Padua. Here he reconstructed a Roman imperial milieu peopled by the Christian saints and their pagan tormenters based on the direct examination of surviving artifacts of the ancient world. Inserting classical reliefs and epigrams copied from Roman tombstones into painted architectural settings, and attempting to clothe the actors in authentic classical dress, he achieved a new high level of antiquarian credibility. No matter that a triumphal arch was turned on its side to form the wall of an imperial audience hall; the architecture was constructed from a classical and not a Gothic lexicon and spoke a clear and forthright Latin. The ruins littering the mountain landscape behind St. James at his execution were testimony to the decay and imminent collapse of an ancient civilization (see Plate 152).

★   ★   ★

Signs of a more nuanced sense of time, space and the past are recognizable in two new forms of visual expression that appear first in Padua in the milieu of Mantegna and soon find their way to Venice. Each tests the boundaries between reality and artifice, and each is related to the written word.

The cartellino

An early announcement of these forms can be found already in Mantegna's earliest surviving signed work, a painting of *St. Mark* that was completed around 1448–9 while he was working on the Ovetari chapel (Plate 207).[6] Framed by an arch-shaped window with a vaguely classical vocabulary, the saint is a solid material presence, positioned firmly and credibly at the threshold between the tangible and the painted worlds.[7] A scrap of paper – a *cartellino* – is tacked onto the window frame below. Creased with fold lines, it looks like an afterthought: a "casual, temporary ticket of authenticity," as Millard Meiss once put it.[8] But its inscription belies any notion of haste or accident: "INCLITA MAGNANIMI VEN . . ./ EVANGELISTA PAX TIBI M[ARC]E /ANDREAE MANTEGNAE PICTORIS LABOR."[9] The signature is there by design, as much a display

207   Andrea Mantegna, *St. Mark*, *c*.1448–9. (?)Casein on canvas, 82 × 63.7 cm. Frankfurt am Main, Städelsches Kunstinstitut.

of artistic *sprezzatura* as is the masterful handling of perspective and foreshortening and the virtuoso rendering of descriptive detail in the rest of painting. Every element is rationalized and seemingly touchable: the fruit swag, tied together in the center with a jeweled fastener, hangs from golden rings; the book clasps are uncoupled; the *cartellino* can still be detached and taken away. Although nothing is known of the painting's provenance, the civic resonance of the venerable angelic salutation – "PAX TIBI" – suggests a Venetian patron.

Mantegna's *cartellino* is generically related to the medieval banderoles that were still common in late Gothic paintings such as *The Vision of Augustus* in Stuttgart (Plate 148), as well as to the feigned incisions and graffiti painted by Jan van Eyck onto the parapet in his portrait known as *Timoteo*.[10] But it is different from the first in its fragmentary, accidental quality and from the second in its ambiguous status – neither wholly part of the painted nor of the material world.

A precedent for the device, in the form of a seraph holding a placard, appeared in Castagno's fresco of 1442 in the Chapel of San Tarasio in the Venetian Church of San Zaccaria. But Castagno's *cartello* should be regarded as a transitional work in which the banderole motif is simply taken one step further; for the paper is not a fragment, a scrap just unfolded, but something still intact. The distinction is worth noting. Mantegna's shopworn paper tends to undermine the idea of the entire painted surface as a window and thus diminishes the integrity of the picture space as defined by Alberti. Although it creates an illusion, it subverts the totality of the vision. Perhaps for this reason, the *cartellino* never took hold in Florence. But in northern Italy, outside the Tuscan ambient and open to influences from the north, it was embraced and soon became a trademark of the Squarcione atelier. From there it quickly spread to Venetian workshops, particularly those run by the Vivarini and the Bellini families, and remained a commonplace in paintings by such artists as Carpaccio and Cima da Conegliano through the end of the century.[11]

Although the *cartellino* is defined by one scholar as a kind of commercial "trademark" that was invented by the young painters of Squarcione's workshop–academy to identify their individual contributions,[12] it has implications that go beyond mere labeling. Implying both separation and attachment, it defines a relationship between the artist and his work. Perhaps most significantly, it expresses a sense of "layering" in which the distinction between the fictive and the natural world is blurred. Just as St. Mark's elbow, the book, and the swag of fruit are allowed to project into the viewer's world, the *cartellino* below sequences access, as well, back into the painted space. As with any *trompe l'oeil* effect, the observer is never really sure as to what is only feigned and what is really there.

★   ★   ★

The littera mantiniana

A second new form of visual expression is suggested by the lettering of Mantegna's inscription, an early announcement of the *littera mantiniana* that appeared in Padua in the 1450s. Again, the Paduan artist's innovations were preceded by Florentine examples. The *scriptura humanistica* invented by Florentine humanists in the early fifteenth-century on Carolingian models had already undergone a classicizing revision by Donatello. In his signature on the base of *Gattamelata*, he introduced a broader majuscule style featuring more pronounced serifs and a more regular geometry. But again, as with the *cartellino*, the new epigraphical style was greeted with relative indifference back in Florence itself. In the Veneto, by contrast, Mantegna perfected it through the study of Roman imperial epigrams, and artists, miniaturists, and scribes adopted it as an essential part of the classicizing repertory.[13]

The epigraphic interests of Cyriacus of Ancona and Marcanova had created a milieu in Padua that was both responsible for and receptive to Mantegna's palaeographical initiatives. Although it was Felice Feliciano who would write the *Alphabetum Romanum* as the first Renaissance treatise on the proper shaping of Roman letters, it was probably an artist – or perhaps several artists – in the circle of Mantegna who came up with the idea of giving letters a prismatic shape and setting them like freestanding monuments within vegetation. He thus inverted the very essence of the inscription, transforming the negative space of incised letters into concrete objects of bulk and substance. Letters became things, and therefore subject to the new aesthetic rules of perspective and structural clarity. The earliest dated example appears in a manuscript of Ptolemy's *Geographia* dating to 1457 and presented by Jacopo Antonio Marcello to René of Anjou.[14]

A miniaturist known as the Master of the London Pliny, working in Venice in the 1470s, invented a variant of the faceted letter, painting it as if it were made of stone, metal, or crystal.[15] The physicality of the letter comes through even in his frontispiece to a copy of Virgil that he decorated with a pen and ink drawing, augmented with colored washes, instead of the usual tempera and gold (Plate 208).[16] Indeed, for the fullest development of a complex visual play between fiction and reality, one must turn to book illustration.

The frontispiece

The establishment of Padua as a center for the production of humanist manuscripts in the 1450s was followed in 1469 by the introduction of book publishing in Venice. A common – or at least contiguous – visual culture emerged in the two cities, in which the archaeological tradition of the sylloges converged with the taste for illusionism manifest in the *cartellino* and the *littera mantiniana* to create new paradigms for the visual augmentation of the book. Nowhere are ambivalent feelings toward the antique past – at once familiar and distant – more evident than in the frontispieces to manuscripts and printed humanist texts.[17]

In general, during the period between 1450 and 1470, styles in manuscript illumination had tended toward the sculptural and the antiquarian in Padua and toward a more luminous, refined, and impressionistic approach in Venice. During the next two decades the two schools grew quite close together, only to drift apart at the end of the century. Both were receptive to influence from other centers, particularly Lombardy, Emilia, and Ferrara, just as they created their own cross-currents, disseminating the Veneto-Paduan style to Rome and elsewhere.[18]

It is worth noting that these books were as portable as the artists who decorated them. Such mobility makes it difficult to define regional schools precisely. A gifted miniaturist known to us only as the Putti Master illuminated a number of books in Padua and Venice that indicate a first-hand acquaintance with sarcophagi that he must have seen in Rome. An equally talented artist named Girolamo da Cremona worked in Mantua and Siena before coming to Venice, but reveals nothing in his style that can be called Cremonese. The Master of the London Pliny went on to Rome or Naples around 1480 after working for a decade in Venice. Although he had originally decorated the Virgil now in the British Library (Plate 208) for the Agostini, a wealthy Venetian family of merchant-bankers, the book was subsequently owned by a secretary to Cardinal Francesco Gonzaga and by 1520 was in the hands of the artist Giulio Romano.[19]

Likewise, patrons could and did order books from centers outside their own. The earliest known book frontispiece created by the Putti Master was in a Livy printed in Rome in 1469 that bears the arms of the Querini, a patrician family of Venice (Plate 219).[20] Artists, moreover, crossed media boundaries, with painters such as Marco Zoppo, and possibly Mantegna, actively involved in book illustration.[21]

The fluidity of the situation must have been responsible in part for the high level of artifice and originality attained in the best of these miniatures. With artists, patrons, and ideas moving around with ease, a demand was created for the most novel and ingenious pictorial solutions. Another factor was the lack of a strong visual tradition for most of the classical authors other than Livy, Vergil, and Ovid. With humanists generally more interested in texts rather than images, book illumination was often more ornamental than relevant to the text that it augmented. Liberated from the authority of a canon and the demands of narration, a number of gifted artists, many of whose names are unknown to us, rose to the challenge and provided the books with some of the most original visual inventions of the period.

★ ★ ★

208 Master of the London Pliny, Frontispiece to Virgilius Maro, *Opera*, Venice: Antonio di Bartolomeo da Bologna, 14[7]6, f. a2r. Parchment, 32.8 × 26.6 cm. London, British Library, C.19.e.14.

AN ACCESSIBLE PAST

Mantegna's archaeological rigor surely heightened the antiquarian sensibilities of his contemporaries, but it yielded unexpected results in Venice, where it took a willful turn. Indisposed or unable to disjoin the world of classical antiquity from their own, Venetian artists began to create synthetic visions that linked two autonomous realms. The artistic result was a past that was both separate from, and yet still accessible to, the Renaissance viewer: the "past in the present" and the "present in the past."

Mantegna's father-in-law Jacopo Bellini had struggled to address the issue with his fanciful constructions of buildings that were neither Gothic nor classical and with antique ruins or architectural components in varying states of disrepair. He addressed it as well in his drawings of Bacchic themes that were set within generalized landscapes. It is here that the earliest signs of a characteristically Venetian intrusion of the

present into the past can be observed, which might be called "antiquity in the mind." If the result is a confusion of past and present, it seems to be a deliberate one.

Two drawings in the Paris album, dated to around 1440 by Degenhart and Schmitt, illustrate a mythological realm that has nothing to do with inscriptions and pays no respects to the "supreme Thunderer." It is a sensuous, non-textual past inhabited only by Bacchus, Silenus, erotes, and a company of satyrs, fauns and other sylvan deities: naked creatures – half human and half goat – with pointed ears, horns, and split hooves.

In one scene a revel is under way (Plate 209). The god Bacchus, his chariot pulled by a galloping horse, is a visitor to the satyrs' world. Young, middle-aged, and old, they frolic and eat and drink and sleep. Their various actions are bound together by the rhythms of contrapuntal grouping in a skillful paraphrase of their prototypes on classical reliefs. The other scene involves an abduction (Plate 210). Eros, accoutered with spurs tied around his ankles and armed with bow and arrows, has bound a young faun to the back of a horse draped in a rustic caparison of lion skins. Despite the objections of an elderly companion, he carries the creature swiftly away. Bellini added here, atypically, an inscription at the bottom of the page: "Pegasus f[ili]o di P[er]seo che amazo Medusa" (Pegasus, son of Perseus who slew Medusa). Perhaps wishing to display his knowledge of classical literature, he alluded, somewhat incorrectly, to the myth in which the dying Medusa gave birth to Pegasus after she was decapitated by Perseus. But unlike the classical Pegasus whose wings are large and grow from his shoulders, Bellini's horse has little webbed appendages attached to his legs like the fins of a sea-creature. He is, in fact, a figural version of the architectural pastiches that Bellini contrived as stage sets for historical narrative. In antiquity the theme of Pan and Eros could symbolize the contrast between natural and civilized love, but it is hard to find a deep philosophical meaning in Bellini's *scherzo*, which seems to be more erotic fairytale than moralizing allegory.[22]

Jacopo was in constant dialogue with his classical sources. Among the later drawings of the Paris album (c.mid-1450s), he goes back directly to antique models for anatomical studies. A nearly nude figure strains under the burden of a huge marble capital that he carries on his back: a mirror image to a drawing on a single sheet that came out of Bellini's circle if it was not actually by his own hand (Plates 211 and 212). Inspired by the figural realm of the antique sarcophagus, already a source of graphic inspiration to such artists as Gentile da Fabriano, Pisanello, and Squarcione, it is, as yet, a past without an inviting landscape (Plate 213).[23]

The themes of revelry, drunkenness, sleep, and the chase return again in two double-page drawings in Jacopo's London album. Created in the early 1460s, around the time of the purported Garda expedition of Felice Feliciano and friends, these works are suggestive clues to Jacopo's changing sense of the past. The first recasts the Triumph of Bacchus, setting it in

209   Jacopo Bellini, *Triumph of Bacchus*, from his *Book of Drawings*, f. 36. Pen and ink on parchment, 29 × 42.7 cm. Paris, Louvre, Cabinet des Dessins (R.F. 1504/40).

210   Jacopo Bellini, *The Abduction of a Faun*, from his *Book of Drawings*, f. 39. Pen and ink on parchment, 29 × 42.7 cm. Paris, Louvre, Cabinet des Dessins (R.F. 1507/43).

datable to the 1460s, it is one of the earliest panel paintings of a pagan subject by a Venetian artist (Plate 216). As Rona Goffen observes, its meaning is enigmatic and was probably meant to be so. Seated on a block shaped like a classical altar, the ruler patron, clad *all'antica*, accepts the offering of an orb and palm frond from a subject donor who kneels before him. The panel may have been part of a larger program of furniture decoration, and the ritualized gesture of gift-giving could well take on a clearer meaning if still accompanied by other scenes now missing.[25] Giovanni's allegory – if that is what it is – is set in a neutral space, furnished with minimal architecture and lacking a descriptive environment. Almost by default the past remains in the past.

But turning from the profane to the sacred and another of Giovanni's early works, one finds the confrontation of past and present and the beginnings of a more structured relationship between the coordinates of time and space.[26] In *The Blood of the Redeemer*, datable to the early 1460s, Christ stands in the foreground, supporting the cross and displaying his wounds (Plate 217).[27] An angel kneels before him and extends a chalice

211   Jacopo Bellini, *Man bearing a Capital*, from his *Book of Drawings*, f. 79. Pen, ink and metal stylus on parchment, 42.7 × 29 cm. Paris, Louvre, Cabinet des Dessins (R.F. 1547/85).

212   Circle of Jacopo Bellini, *Drawing after the Antique*. Pen and ink drawing on paper, 40.5 × 28.8 cm. Paris, Louvre, Cabinet des Dessins (R.F. 524).

an expansive hilly landscape with a walled city in the distance (Plate 214). The satyrs, now taller and more slender, dance and play the pan pipes, and again one of their number is stretched out on the ground in untroubled sleep. The other composition involves a hunt, again in a rocky landscape, but now more verdant, enhanced with a leafy tree (Plate 215). Two men of the present-day armed with sword and bow pursue a naked satyr astride a lion, while his companions scatter in disarray on the opposite page.[24]

The London drawings represent an intrusion of the present, in the form of architecture or modern dramatis personae, into the mythical past. While they may seem to represent a return to the still-medieval blurring of past and present and, consequently, a step backward from the drawings in the Paris album, the reverse may well be the case. For each scene acknowledges a mythical realm outside the city into which modern men can enter, but only in their imaginations.

Likewise, the *Pagan Allegory* painted by Jacopo's son, Giovanni Bellini, eludes a textual interpretation. Painted in gold on a black background like a manuscript illumination and

213 Francesco Squarcione, *Centaurs and Satyrs*. Pen and ink drawing, with white chalk on grey-green prepared paper, 27.3 × 18.7 cm. Munich, Staatliche Graphische Sammlung.

214 (*top row*) Jacopo Bellini, *Triumph of Bacchus*, from his *Book of Drawings*, ff. 93v–94. Leadpoint on paper, 67.2 × 41.5 cm. London, British Museum.

215 (*bottom row*) Jacopo Bellini, *Hunting a Satyr*, from his *Book of Drawings*, ff. 52v–53. Leadpoint on paper, 67.2 × 41.5 cm. London, British Museum.

216 Giovanni Bellini, *Pagan Allegory*. Wood panel, 31 × 25 cm. Riverdale-on-Hudson, New York, Stanley Moss Collection.

217 Giovanni Bellini, *Blood of the Redeemer*, early 1460s. Wood panel, 47 × 34 cm. London, National Gallery. Reproduced by courtesy of the Trustees, The National Gallery, London.

to collect the blood flowing from his side. They inhabit a precinct set apart by a black and white tile floor: defined as antique by a balustrade decorated with fictive classical reliefs and sanctified by billowing clouds that hover just above the pavement. With figures painted in warm-toned grisaille on a black ground, the reliefs are more painterly than lapidary. Their scenes of pagan sacrifice – in one case partly hidden by Christ's hand – have thus far defied a precise reading. They were surely intended to create a classical ambient and perhaps also, as Fritz Saxl proposes, to make a theological point: that Christ's sacrifice was the second stage of a development prefigured in the pagan rite.[28]

An opening in the balustrade behind Christ leads directly into an expansive landscape recognizable as the artist's present. Two figures clad in monastic habits stand on the right in front of a ruined building. Oblivious to the scene in the foreground, they look out across a broad valley toward a well-built town, while in the distance yet another city covers the lower slopes of a hill. The composition thus features a layered space, with the ancient world of paganism and early

Christianity in the foreground joined to, but separate from, a fifteenth-century background.[29]

The painting's tiny dimensions and Eucharistic subject matter suggest an original function as a tabernacle door.[30] The pious observer would thus be drawn inexorably from contemplation of Christ's sacrificial body back into the familiar landscape of his own time, whose opaque surface concealed the holy blood of Christ and the promise of personal salvation.

PORTALS TO THE PAST

With the groundwork laid within the Paduan circle of Squarcione and Mantegna and the Venetian sphere of the Bellini family for nuanced representations of the complex relationship between past and present, the next conceptual breakthroughs would take place on the hand-painted frontispieces of manuscripts and, most strikingly, of the new printed book. Title-pages, as such, were an invention of the mid-quattrocento. In medieval manuscripts the beginning of each chapter, and of the work as a whole, had typically been distinguished simply by a large capital letter that was followed, indeed surrounded, by the discursive text. While the majuscule initial may well have been sumptuously decorated, it did not function as a proscenium to "frame" and control access to the book.[31] But in Padua in the 1450s, copies of eagerly sought classical manuscripts had become objects as much as texts, and the title of the work or the name of the author was now to be set apart at the front of the volume in an architectural structure of its own. The earliest example, appearing in a manuscript of Solinus's *Polyhistor* copied by Bartolomeo Sanvito in 1457 for the Venetian patrician Bernardo Bembo, betrays its origin as a classical funerary monument (Plate 218).[32] Plucked from a humanist sylloge like that of Giovanni Marcanova, such an artifact would be placed in the center of the page as a support on which the letters of the book's title could be illusionistically inscribed.[33]

The play between illusion and reality became ever more complex and subtle as these frontispiece monuments expanded in size, reaching an apogee of sophistication a decade later with the innovations of the Putti Master, his name an invention of modern scholars who took it from his trademark motif: a putto on a dolphin. Active in Venice between 1469 and 1473, he was perhaps the most classically oriented of the miniaturists. Infusing Paduan antiquarianism and illusionism with Venetian color, he achieved an unprecedented integration between the classicizing *littera mantiniana* and the figurative image.[34] It may be no coincidence that he arrived on the scene in 1469, the same year that Johannes de Spira set up Venice's first printing press. Counting at least a dozen patrician families among his patrons, the Putti Master specialized in providing hand-painted frontispieces and capital letters for the new printed books.[35] Along with the Master of the London Pliny, he would have played a major role in

To recapitulate – a German press in Rome, a Venetian patron, a Florentine drawing, a north Italian print: the work is emblematic of the pan-Italian character of antiquarian culture in this period when images and ideas seemed to circulate throughout the peninsula with lightning speed.

Serving as display pieces of artistic ingenuity, the Venetian architectural title-pages reveal an extraordinary sensitivity to the subtleties of spatial ambiguity. The nature of the medium – flat page, illusionistic image, and text – allowed artists to test the boundaries of visual illusionism to a much greater degree than was possible in monumental religious paintings such as Mantegna's St. Zeno Altarpiece.[38]

In a Bible printed in Venice by Morgan de Spira in 1471, the Putti Master evoked at least three levels of reality, going even further than his efforts in the Livy of two years before. He wished to incorporate into the composition the narrative episode of Shooting at the Father's Corpse, a medieval legend that offered a variant to the familiar Judgment of Solomon

219 Putti Master, frontispiece from Livy, *Historiae romanae decades*, Rome: Sweynheym and Pannartz [*c.*1469]. Parchment, 28.2 × 35.1 cm. Vienna, Graphische Sammlung, Albertina, Inv. no. 2587, detached folio (Part II, f. 167).

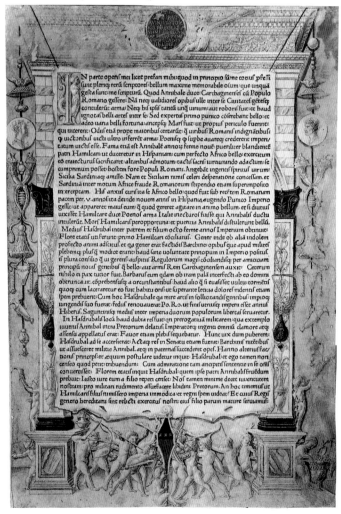

218 Frontispiece from Solinus, *Polyhistor*, 1457. Oxford, The Bodleian Library, MS Canon, Lat. 161, f. 7r.

helping to form a taste for the *all'antica* style in Venice at the end of the quattrocento.

One of the principal users of freestanding faceted letters for initials within the text, the Putti Master gave book illustration not only a new polychrome richness but also a large measure of whimsy and wit. For his title-pages he favored the triumphal arch or a monumental architectural structure from which a text-bearing "parchment," usually with ragged edges, was suspended with strings. His first datable effort on this scale is the frontispiece of the 1469 Livy that was printed in Rome and decorated for the Querini family (Plate 219). The pictorial field is a play-space for putti, who frolic, engage in mock battles and generally belie the serious content of the texts that they introduce. The battling putti motif can be traced to a north Italian print of Hercules and the Giants that was itself copied from Pollaiuolo.[37]

220 Putti Master, *Shooting at the Father's Corpse*, from *Biblia Italica*, Venice: Vindelino de Spira, 1471, f. 3v.
Parchment, 41.5 × 28 cm. New York, The Pierpont Morgan Library, PML 26984.

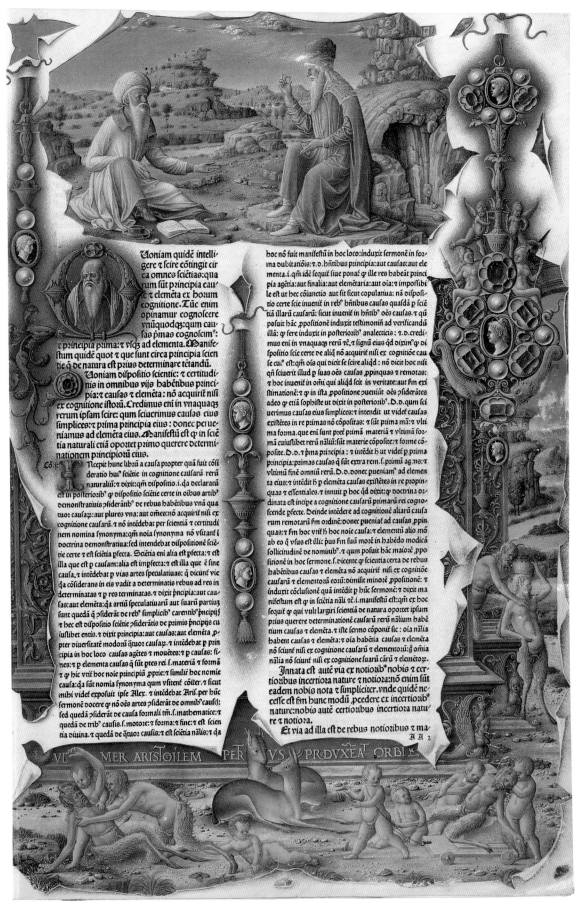

221 Girolamo da Cremona and assistants (attrib.), frontispiece to the *Physics*, from Aristotles, *Opera*, Venice: Torresanus and Blavis, 1483, I, f. 2r. Parchment, 40.9 × 27.2 cm. New York, The Pierpont Morgan Library, PML 21194.

222 Girolamo da Cremona, Antonio Maria da Villafora, and Benedetto Bordon (attrib.), frontispiece to the *Metaphysics*, in Aristotles, *Opera*, Venice: Torresanus and Blavis, 1483, II, f. 1r. Parchment, 41.4 × 28 cm. New York, The Pierpont Morgan Library, PML 21195.

(Plate 220). As the story goes, a judge (sometimes identified as Solomon) commands two rival claimants to an inheritance to shoot at their father's corpse. One refuses out of filial piety and is proclaimed the true heir. Here the Putti Master provided the episode with its own picture frame and putti to hold it and propped it upon the monument with the ripped parchment suspended below it. This painting within a painting is one of the earliest examples of the *quadro riportato*, later used for illusionistic effect by Michelangelo on the Sistine Ceiling, that eventually became a standard part of the Baroque decorative repertory. The larger picture space is a landscape inhabited by putti who carry on their own activities and are oblivious to the parchment text attached to the triumphal arch behind them. They are even less aware of the painted picture that is mounted on top, which represents a step back in time to the patriarchal world of the Old Testament.[39]

Two title-pages in a deluxe edition of a Latin translation of the works of Aristotle, published in Venice in 1483 and now in the Pierpont Morgan Library, explore further possibilities of manipulating the spatial and temporal continuum (Plates 221 and 222). The illuminations, executed for Peter Ugelheimer, a German merchant from Ulm who had business interests in Venice, are generally attributed to Girolamo da Cremona.[40] In the frontispiece to Book I, the torn-paper motif is employed with a new level of artifice. Now the parchment is presented as the original page, which has been ripped apart to reveal the world of myth and philosophical wisdom behind the text. In the lower zone, putti are joined by satyrs and wild deer in a rocky landscape that extends into the far distance. At the top of a monumental structure embellished with harpies and the candelabra motif, Aristotle discourses with another philosopher in a more elevated but equally naturalistic ambient. An apparition as much as a concrete reality, the pair relate to the lower realm in a manner that is perhaps deliberately left ambiguous. By peeling back the vellum covering, the reader is allowed by means of the text to pass through the invisible membrane of time and to penetrate the ancient past. And yet his own space – "real" space – is affirmed as well, for elaborate gold medallions set with pearls and cameos appear to hang from red twine that is knotted into slits deliberately cut into the parchment: the eyewitness punctiliousness that attests to the reality of the mythic.

The frontispiece to Book II of the Aristotle follows a more conventional model, with a text-bearing parchment suspended from a balcony where a monkey is seated. Adorned with a red cape, he appears as an attribute of the pagan world, but as an innocent pet rather than as a medieval symbol of evil and lust. And now the dramatis personae of the human realm are more of the present than of the past. The loggia is occupied by turbanned oriental figures, Greeks wearing fifteenth-century headgear, and a Dominican monk. Possibly St. Thomas Aquinas who wrote a commentary on Aristotle, the latter figure joins the other philosophers as a visitor or tourist;

together they occupy a privileged viewing point from which to inspect the foreign country of Arcadia.

THE NATURE OF ARCADIA

One inevitably asks: what is the nature of that country, glimpsed so tantalizingly near behind the torn parchment of the Pierpont Morgan Aristotle, and where was it to be found? In response to the first question, some general observations can be made.[41] First, as to the setting: the Venetian Arcadia first took shape in the drawing books of Jacopo Bellini as a rocky and arid terrain reminiscent of the sun-baked, deforested parts of the Aegean islands once described by Buondelmonti. A similar ambient is still evident in a more evolved form in the backgrounds of the title pages in the Pierpont Morgan Aristotle. But Arcadia also took on a lush and verdant aspect, at times sylvan and at times bucolic, that eventually materialized in the shady glades of the Giorgionesque *locus amoenus*. Already in 1461–2, the Paduan artist Marco Zoppo painted a frontispiece to Virgil's *Georgics* for the Venetian Morosini family in which Orpheus is shown charming the beasts in a landscape that juxtaposes dense woods and a babbling brook with rocky outcroppings (Plate 225).[42]

Second, as to personae: Jacopo Bellini's Arcadia is essentially a gender-segregated world: perhaps sensual, but not yet sexual. For his satyrs are accompanied neither by satyresses nor by the nymphs and muses who would eventually populate the Venetian pastoral idyll. However, the full-bodied female nude does appear in another context in two double-paged scenes in the London album (Plates 223 and 224).

In the first composition, with women, young girls, and infants shown reclining, sitting, and standing, in unselfconscious display, the mundane activity of bathing provides the pretext for defining a new ideal of feminine beauty based on an antique canon. In the other scene, a crowd of nude females chase an equally naked male off the right-hand page. Although the episode might be interpreted as a straightforward battle of the Amazons, its extension to the left suggests a broader content, for there "the ages of woman" can be seen: a young girl, an old crone supported by a cane and brandishing a stick, and two women in full maturity, one of them a mother seated on the ground nursing her child in the midst of the melée. With one scene depicting a bath and the other a battle, the drawings seem to explore contrasting themes of harmony and strife.[43]

Third, as to the mood of these early Arcadias: it is one of paradox. A place of innocent revels, make-believe battles, dreams, sleep, but also sadness. The melancholy mood of Zoppo's miniature was an early announcement of the contemplative tone that would come to characterize Venetian pastoral art in which innocence and sensuality would eventu-

223 (*top row*) Jacopo Bellini, *Bathing Scene with Female Nudes*, from his *Book of Drawings*, ff. 30v–31. Leadpoint on paper, 67.2 × 41.5 cm. London, British Museum.

224 (*bottom row*) Jacopo Bellini, *Battle Scene with Female Nudes*, from his *Book of Drawings*, 31v–32. Leadpoint on paper, 67.2 × 41.5 cm. London, British Museum.

225 Marco Zoppo, *Orpheus charming the Beasts*, frontispiece to Virgil's *Georgics*, 1461–2. Parchment, 26 × 15.5 cm. Paris, Bibliothèque Nationale, Cod. Lat. 11309, f. 4v.

the paintings of Gentile Bellini. This catholic taste would have been shared by humanistically educated Venetians of the next generation who purchased art with mythological subject matter, but did not supply its iconography nor its intellectual content. Indeed, neither Jacopo Bellini's drawings of mythological themes, nor the Arcadian imagery of the book illuminations, can be linked to specific literary texts or to a scholarly mind. In Jacopo's later drawings, with their binding of mythic past and quotidian reality into a living unity, a textual foundation is even more unlikely. As such, they laid the foundation for the pastoral idyll that was to become one of the distinctive achievements of sixteenth-century Venetian painting.[44]

Illuminating a tension between detachment and approach, these captivating mixtures of the real and the imaginary past reflect two contradictory, but intertwined, tendencies that dominated the art and literature of the period. On one side there is a growing sense of historical distance: that separation of the past and the present that defines a modern sense of history. On the other side, the same impulses that demanded separation also engendered synthesis and the desire to link the lost world of antiquity to the present.[45]

To return to the second question raised at the beginning of this section: where was that Arcadia to be found? During the later fifteenth century in Venice it existed almost exclusively in the realm of what are now considered the minor arts: drawings, book illustration, furniture painting, medals, small bronzes, sculptural decoration, and the ephemeral genre of pageantry.[46] For all that, it would be a mistake to interpret the relegation of classical themes to the "minor arts" as proof of a lack of interest in the antique amongst Venetian patrons.[47] Although we privilege easel painting today, it should be remembered that it was just one mode of visual expression among many in the Renaissance and not necessarily the most costly. In Venice it took Giorgione and Titian to elevate it to a major venue for secular themes. Indeed, following this line of argument, one might grant that the fanciful creatures of pagan myth and modern imagination began to inhabit the most prestigious locales of the Venetian visual world as early as the 1470s and 1480s: in private life, on the richly decorated frontispieces of luxury manuscripts; in religious life, on the towering façades of costly ducal tombs; in public life, on the gleaming white marble pilasters of the Scala dei Giganti, and in open-air dramatic productions that formed an essential, though passing, part of the urban scene.

And yet, Arcadia was also to provide a language of retreat – both visual and literary – from which to construct an alternate reality outside the civic world.

ally be conjoined. In contrast to the lusty bacchanals of Mantegna, those of the Putti Master were particularly genteel affairs.

And a final point: the *all'antica* subject matter of Venetian art was essentially the creation of the artist and not the scholar. Despite Zovenzoni's deft use of classical topoi to compliment the artist, his personal taste in art embraced not only genuine Roman artifacts and Marco Zoppo's paintings of an antiquarian cast, but also works as unclassical as Rizzo's *Eve* and

10

A SPECIAL LICENSE

Do not all of us know, without my saying it, that lovers no less than poets have
a special license to feign things which often are far from any resemblance to the
truth? To give their tongues or even pens new themes which none can rightly
understand, subjects inconsistent with themselves?

– Pietro Bembo, 1495[1]

Bembo's reference to this realm of imaginative invention was offered in defense of lovers and poetry, but it serves equally well for the Venetian evocation of antiquity in the visual arts. A revival of vernacular literature with a pastoral character was already under way in the last years of the quattrocento – a movement, it should be noted, that postdated the Arcadian experiments of Jacopo Bellini and the miniaturists discussed in the preceding chapter. Writing in Naples, Sannazaro had completed a draft of his *Arcadia* by 1489, and Pietro Bembo began writing *Gli Asolani* in the Veneto hilltown of Asolo in 1495. But both works were published only in the early years of the sixteenth century, when pastoral imagery had already migrated from the pages of manuscripts and printed books to animate the canvases of the leading artists of the day.[2]

A few observations made by Paul Holberton are worth restating. First, the literary convention of pastoral upon which Sannazaro's *Arcadia* was based – and which in turn was transformed into visual form by Venetian artists – involved an excursion of a "highly cultivated young man" into the countryside. Thus it was not simply about shepherds, fauns, nymphs, and satyrs; it was about the commingling of mortals, half-mortals, half-gods, and full gods. Second, it was not someplace else; it was a state of mind. The point is that Arcadia was neither only the real world nor only the pastoral one. It was a superimposition of both worlds.[3] As such, it was distant enough to provide escape and close enough to be always accessible.

THE *HYPNEROTOMACHIA POLIPHILI*

Just how accessible an Arcadian world might become is demonstrated by the *Hypnerotomachia Poliphili*: one of the most

intriguing and mysterious – and some would say bizarre – offspring of Renaissance antiquarianism (Plate 226). Published in Venice in 1499, it is the only fully illustrated book to be

226 *Polia and Polifilo view the Ruins of Polyandrion*, woodcut from *Hypnerotomachia Poliphili*, Venice: Aldus Manutius, 1499.

printed by the Aldine Press and the first to be published in the fully perfected roman typeface. In terms of its physical properties alone, it is one of the masterpieces of Renaissance publishing.[4] But the significance of the work in relation to a specifically Venetian sense of the past, is difficult to assess. Its influence on Venetian artists can be traced after the fact, but little is known for certain about its intellectual genesis.

The book has been variously described as "an archaeological rhapsody," "an antiquarian novel," "a dream-allegory," "a philosophical romance," and "an architectural treatise and a love story."[5] Indeed, it is all of these, slipping with ease from alchemy to romance, from scholastic philosophy to neo-Platonic syncretism, from Christian liturgy to pagan ritual, from fantastic buildings to invented hieroglyphs, from grammar to botany, and from dream to actuality. Written in a hybrid language that combines Latin, Greek, and vernacular Italian, with citations in Hebrew, Chaldean, and Arabic, and with a time frame that shifts back and forth between the present and the past, it challenges the reader to a contest of wits where certainty is always just out of reach. Indeed, virtually the only sure thing about it is its publication in Venice in 1499.[6]

The title alone reveals the deliberately labile and elusive quality of the enterprise. Featuring an invented word depending on three Greek linguistic components, *Hypnerotomachia Poliphili* translates at first glance as "Polifilo's Strife of Love in a Dream."[7] But such a reading is not complete: the hero's name can itself be decoded as "Lover of Polia" and that of Polia, in turn, as "Many" or perhaps, as a group of nymphs in the story thought, as "Many Maidens." The subtitle further confirms the intentionally illusory nature of the work: *ubi humana omnia non nisi somnium esse docet* (where he teaches that all human things are nothing but a dream).[8]

This evasiveness applies as well to the identity and provenance of the author, for he did not put his name on the title-page. The text proper is preceded by a dedication to the Duke of Urbino by the Veronese lawyer Leonardo Grassi, who claimed to have paid for the publication of the book himself.[9] As to the author, referred to by Grassi only as "vir sapientissimus," he contrived to reveal himself to the careful reader by concealing his name in an acrostic made up of the first letter of each of the thirty-eight chapters: "POLIAM FRATER FRANCISCUS COLVMNA PERAMAVIT" (Friar Francesco Colonna passionately loved Polia). But assuming that this cipher does indeed unmask the author, who was this Francesco Colonna?

In all likelihood, he was the same person to whom Raffaele Zovenzoni had addressed one of his epigrams:

To Francesco Colonna Antiquario

O Francesco, you derive your surname from the double
    column that the hands of Hercules placed at Cadiz,
on whose lofty summit you have read the prophecy:
– Here for you will be the frontier of the world.[10]

Making a neat play on Colonna's name with a pun coined by Petrarch, Zovenzoni adduced its origins in the columns of Hercules. That he had applied the same metaphor to the monumental columns of the Piazzetta that "formed the walls" of Venice, suggests a double pun: a repetition that might assign a Venetian identity to Colonna himself.[11] A scholarly consensus on this issue, however, has yet to be achieved. According to the traditional view, he was a Dominican priest of Veneto origin who resided in the convent of SS. Giovanni e Paolo in Venice. But two other proposals have received considerable attention in recent years. The first holds that the book's author is not a Venetian priest at all, but the Lord of Palestrina, a Roman nobleman also called Francesco Colonna. The second argues for the writer's identity as a Servite friar, called Fra Eliseo da Treviso.[12] The evidence for the revisionist arguments, while suggestive, is inconclusive and, in any event, not sufficiently compelling to reject the Veneto provenance of the text.[13]

227 Frontispiece, from Herodotus, *Historiarum libri X*, Venice: Joannes and Gregorius de Gregoriis, 1494.

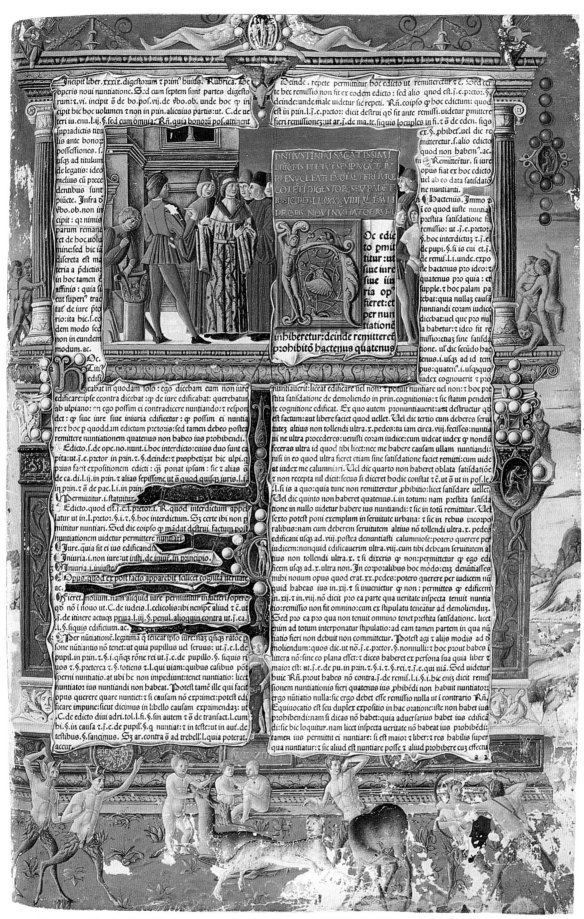

228   Benedetto Bordon, frontispiece, from Justinianus, *Digestum novum*, Venice: Nicolaus Jenson, 1477, f. 2r (a2). Parchment, 42.5 × 28.7 cm. Gotha, Forschungs- und Landesbibliothek, Mon. Typ. 2° 13, Bl. A2a.

The identity of the artists who designed the woodcuts is yet another mysterious aspect of the book. Virtually all the motifs and compositional types have precedents in the Venetian milieu, whether in manuscript illumination, printed books, or in sculptural reliefs.[14] While Colonna's direct participation in the design process is indicated by the close interpenetration of illustrations and text, all that can be said with confidence is that there were probably two artists involved and that they worked in a style characteristic of Venetian printmaking of the period. The frontispiece of a Herodotus published by Gregorio de Gregoriis in Venice in 1494 is almost certainly by one of the same hands responsible for a number of illustrations in the *Hypnerotomachia* (Plate 228).[15] While comparisons between miniatures and woodcuts can be misleading, several painted frontispieces ascribed to the Paduan miniaturist Benedetto Bordone tend to support his candidacy as the lead artist of the *Hypnerotomachia*. A signed folio of a copy of Justinianus, *Digestum novum*, printed in Venice by Nicolaus Jenson in 1477, testifies not only to Bordone's attentiveness to the inventions of Girolamo da Cremona, but also to his own high originality and lively narrative style (Plate 227).[16]

The difficulty in determining whether Colonna was a creature of Veneto humanism or of the Roman academy is significant in itself. With travel frequent in this period and cross-fertilization of artistic models and humanist ideas the norm, clear-cut distinctions between the major centers are difficult to make.[17]

Two assumptions can therefore be made: first, that the *Hypnerotomachia Poliphili* was written by a certain Francesco Colonna who played a major role in planning its illustrations; and second, that whether written by a Venetian friar or not, the book sums up some of the major aspects of Venetian culture that helped to form the sense of the past in the waning years of the quattrocento: the emergence of the city as a major center of printing; the maturing of the antiquarian movement pioneered by Cyriacus of Ancona; the counter-model of antiquity as a sensuous Arcadian (as opposed to a political–historical) world; and the examination of questions of illusion and reality that seem profoundly Venetian in spirit.

Using the literary device of a dream within a dream, the author structured the work in two books.[18] The first is Polifilo's dream-quest, recounted in the first person, in which he falls asleep thinking of his beloved Polia and enters a fantastic lost world of antiquity. The amenities of the site include forests, orchards, gardens, classical ruins, hieroglyphs and inscriptions in arcane languages, gurgling fountains, and elaborate monuments. Although inhabited by the familiar troop of pagan gods, centaurs, satyrs, and putti, it is primarily a female world, with the significant roles – aside from that of Polifilo himself – played by queens, nymphs, goddesses, priestesses, and maidens and matrons of various ages.

Polifilo's experiences in the kingdom of Queen Eleuterilda (or Liberty) establish the metaphysical framework of the book. After bathing with the nymphs of the Five Senses, he is led by the maidens Logistica (or Reason) and Thelemia (or Wish) to three portals where he must choose his own destiny (Plate 229). Each portal bears inscriptions in Arabic, Hebrew, Greek, and Latin that give a universalizing frame to the imperative of choice. Polifilo as Everyman must choose between the Glory of God, the Glory of the World, and the Mother of Love.[19] That he chooses to enter the latter portal provides the rationale for, and determines the trajectory of, the book. Giovanni Pozzi argues that this should not be interpreted as a libertine choice, but a confirmation of the superiority of marriage over the active and contemplative states of human life.[20] In the course of his wanderings, Polifilo encounters Polia (at first disguised as a beautiful nymph), and after a nuptial ceremony in the temple of Venus Physizoa, the lovers sail to the Isle of Cythera where they are joined by a group of nymphs, and by Venus herself, at the fountain of Adonis on the Isle of Cythera.[21] The dream-allegory of the first book thus concludes, and the time frame shifts to the present.

In the second book Polia is given her own voice. Recounting the story of her life and her love affair with Polifilo, she reveals her real identity as a certain Lucrezia Lelli of Treviso. In the end, like Poliziano's Echo, she disappears, crying "Polifilo, my dear lover, farewell." Polifilo awakens to the

229 *Polifilo with Logistica and Thelemia at the Three Portals*, woodcut from *Hypnerotomachia Poliphili*, Venice: Aldus Manutius, 1499.

song of a nightingale, and Polia's story, just like the allegory that preceded it, is revealed to be only a dream. Polifilo responds, "Farewell then, Polia," and relocates himself in real time and space: in Treviso on the first day of May 1467.[22] And again, the author offers up a conundrum, for an analysis of the text indicates that it was in all likelihood written after 1485.[23]

Polifilo was the consummate time traveler. His adventures depend on two central assumptions: that the past could be re-entered, if only through a dream; and that the irreconcilable could be reconciled. For not only could the boundaries of time and space be transgressed, but also those of language, those of image and text, those of archaeology and romance, those of Catholic liturgy and pagan ritual.[24]

With our native tongues

The humanist revival of classical literature had led to a linguistic crisis by the end of the fifteenth century, with impassioned arguments as to the superiority of one language or its variants over another for literary discourse. Colonna's own position was closest to the eclectics, who viewed Latin as a living language: modern, and open to every sort of neologism. Addressing the issue with all the enthusiasm of the erudite amateur, he transferred the same approach to vernacular Italian. His intentions are announced quite succinctly in Grassi's letter of dedication: "One thing in this is to be admired, although he narrates in our native tongue, one needs Greek and Latin as much as Tuscan and the vernacular to understand him."[25]

Colonna literally invented his own language toward this end. For his base language, particularly for syntax, he used the literary *koinè* of northeastern Italy. This was a hybrid form that had developed in the area around Padua in the quattrocento. It has been described as a "continuous oscillation" between proper Tuscan Italian and the local *volgare* or the "dross of common use," as Ariosto would later put it.[26] Onto this already unstable linguistic matrix, Colonna grafted Latin or *volgare* suffixes or prefixes to root words in both tongues and sometimes drew upon Greek as well. Polifilo thus observes "una *percupressata* via de driti et excelsi cupressi" (a cypress-lined road of straight and lofty cypresses).[27] Here Colonna invents a verb by applying the Latin prefix *per-* to the noun *cupressus* and adding the Italian suffix *-ata*. We might think of such unusual and often mellifluous compounds as the lexical equivalents of centaurs or sirens: neither man nor beast but partaking of both.[28]

The aim was to create "thick" description, with lushly evocative nouns, adjectives, and adverbs. Polifilo accordingly describes a triumphal chariot decorated with panels depicting the Rape of Europa (Plate 230):

> El primo degli quatro mirandi et divini triumphi havea le quatro rapide rote di finissima petra de verdissimo smaragdo sycthico, di atomi di colore rameo scintillato . . . Nella

PRIMA TABELLA.

Quella Nympha cófisa la finiftra tabula cótineua, che afcenfo hauea fopra il manfueto & candido Tauro. Et quello qlla p el tumido mare timida, tráffretaua. **SECVNDA SINISTRA.**

Nel fronte anteriore, Cupidine uidi cú inumera Caterua di promifcua géte uulnerata, mirabódi che egli tiraffe larco fuo uerfo lalto olympo. In nel fronte pofteriore, Marte mirai dinanti al throno del magno Ioue, Lamentátife che el filiolo la ipenetrabile thoraca fua egli la haueffe lacerata. Et el benigno fignoree el fuo uulnerato pecto gli monftraua. Et nellaltra mano extenfo el brachio teniua fcripto, NEMO.

230 *The Chariot for the First Triumph, decorated with Scenes from the Rape of Europa*, woodcut from *Hypnerotomachia Poliphili*, Venice: Aldus Manutius, 1499.

dextera tabella mirai expresso una nobile et regia nympha cum multe coaetanee in uno prato, incoronante gli victoriosi tauri di multiplici strophii di flori; et un adhaerente ad essa multo peculiaremente domesticatose.[29]

(The first of the four admirable and divine triumphs had four rapid wheels of the finest stone of the most green Scythian emerald, with colored bits of sparkling copper . . . On the right panel I saw portrayed a noble and queenly nymph with many companions in a meadow, crowning the victorious bulls with multiple garlands of flowers; and one remaining by her very peculiarly domestically.)

Any reader familiar with Ovid would immediately understand the implications of this very peculiar domesticity.

Colonna also ascribed emotions to inanimate objects: "la facinorosa coronice . . . pugnacissime petre . . . uno insolente arbuscolo di cinabarissimo coralio . . ." (the riotous cornice . . . the most obstinate stones . . . an insolent sprig of the most cinnabar coral . . .).[30] But Colonna's linguistic inventions were not simply *bizzarrerie* for their own sake. When examined together with the 171 woodcuts distributed throughout the text, they suggest a more ambitious agenda. By inverting the parallel tasks of diachronic and synchronic communication normally performed, respectively, by the word and by the image – that is, to narrate and to describe – he attempted to create a parallel, interdependent and complementary discourse. The primacy of one mode over the other was determined by his poetic intention. When he wanted to narrate, usually the function of a text, he often let the drawings carry the weight of the discursive message. When he wished to describe, he let the text take on the duties of full elaboration. The word thus becomes a linguistic equivalent to the image.[31]

This reversal of roles takes as its point of departure the *paragone* between painting and poetry, in which painting is ennobled by its association with writing. Accordingly, Renaissance painters vied with poets by transforming poetry into pictures: *ut pictura poesis*.[32] Colonna, in effect, stood the *paragone* on its head. He began with the image and created static verbal pictures that shared its synchronic properties. The result is quite different from the *ekphrasis* so beloved to humanists of the time, for the *ekphrasis* was discursive and tended to narrativize the static image by roaming through it. By contrast, Colonna's model was, as Pozzi puts it, "an antidynamic conception of language, that for him has no pace, has no rhythm, but [simply] is. His language does not possess the 'quid' of music that is the unfolding, the birth and the death of the elements of discourse, but the 'quid' of painting, understood as a composition of varied colors, of lights and of shadows."[33]

Colonna sought altogether to efface the boundaries between the image and the text with two other devices that appear in the book: the *technopaegnia* and the hieroglyph. The *technopaegnia* derives from the Greek tradition of figured poetry (Plate 231). Here the block of type is given the shape of the object under discussion, such as a vase, a box, or an altar, and the text effectively *becomes* the image. One such ideogram had appeared in the volume of Theocritus printed by Aldus in 1495, surely inspired by examples in Greek manuscripts. It seems probable that it drew the attention of Colonna, given his concern with the relationship between the graphic and the verbal, when he participated in the production of his own book.[34]

Le quale vetustissime et sacre scripture

In the case of the hieroglyph, the signifying process is reversed, with the drawing replacing the word. Humanists had

231 *Broken Pediment from Polyandrion*, woodcut from *Hypnerotomachia Poliphili*, Venice: Aldus Manutius, 1499.

been fascinated with hieroglyphs ever since Buondelmonti discovered the *Hieroglyphica* of Horapollo on the island of Andros in 1419 and brought it back to Florence. They saw the symbols not only as a key to the mysteries of the ancients, but also as a universal language that could express any idea or metaphysical concept, at least to the initiate. Alberti praised the Egyptians for adorning their buildings with inscriptions in a secret sign language that "could be understood easily by expert men all over the world, to whom alone noble matters should be communicated."[35] Colonna took Alberti at his word and designed his own hieroglyphs to inscribe on his imaginary monuments.

For Colonna, as for Alberti, such signs were more than mere decoration. In the course of his adventures Polifilo comes across a great elephant of stone "more black than obsidian," that is pierced with an obelisk of green stone topped with a golden sphere (Plates 232 and 233). Its base is inscribed on three sides with "Egyptian letters." Assembling fourteen signs of "the most ancient and sacred writings" in a box, Colonna provides the reader with a key to their edifying message: "Sacrifice your toil generously to the God of nature. Little by little you will then subject your soul to God, and He will take you into His firm protection, mercifully govern your life and preserve it unharmed."[36]

Colonna invented his hieroglyphic symbols without the benefit of genuine Egyptian models. Some of them were based upon real classical motifs, such as those taken from the ancient temple frieze once immured in the Roman church of San Lorenzo Fuori le Mura.[37] Including objects such as rosettes, a bucranium, vases, and ship rudders, they were generally, if incorrectly, accepted at the time as genuine Egyptian hieroglyphs and were well known to artists. Mantegna had already used the frieze as a model for the entablature of the triumphal arch in the final, ninth panel of his *Triumph of Caesar*, and Bernardo Parenzano incorporated it in his frescoes in Santa Giustina in Padua, datable to 1492–8.[38] Piero Valeriano would later include a number of Colonna's hieroglyphs in his great compendium, *Hieroglyphica*, published in 1556, but, alas, as anonymously as they had appeared in *Hypnerotomachia* itself. Valeriano says only that they were "inventa iuniorum" (inventions of more recent people).[39]

Although arguments have been made for a strong neo-Platonic element in the *Hypnerotomachia*, it is unambiguously evident only in the sacred status ascribed to hieroglyphs. The most telling example can be seen in Polifilo's encounter with

232 *Elephant with an Obelisk*, woodcut from *Hypnerotomachia Poliphili*, Venice: Aldus Manutius, 1499.

233 *Hieroglyphs on the Base of the Elephant*, woodcut from *Hypnerotomachia Poliphili*, Venice: Aldus Manutius, 1499.

another enigmatic obelisk, but even there the treatment does not suggest a very profound philosophical involvement in neo-Platonism. Guided by the lady Logistica, Polifilo comes upon a golden obelisk supported on three sphinxes who sit on a three-part stacked base (Plate 234). This consists of a white chalcedony cube inscribed with the word "Inscrutable"; a squat red cylinder engraved with a sun, a rudder, and a lamp; and a black triangular prism decorated with nymphs holding cornucopias. The obelisk is inscribed on each face with a Greek letter inside a circle; taken together, they signify past, present, and future. The monument as a whole, Logistica explains, embodies divine harmony and is dedicated to the infinite Three-in-One. She adds, significantly, that man cannot clearly recognize past, present, and future at one and the same time.[40]

★   ★   ★

also Herodotus and Lucretius; among the moderns, Flavio Biondo, Felice Feliciano, Alberti, Filarete, Niccolò Perotti, Mantegna, Carpaccio, and the Lombardi.[42]

In the shifting perspectives characteristic of the book as a whole, Polifilo moves back and forth between dream and reality and between an antiquity that was at times integral and at times in a ruinous state.[43] With clear echoes of Dante, Polifilo falls asleep dreaming of Polia in the opening pages of the book and finds himself lost in a dark wood. Terrified, he finally emerges near a stream and falls asleep once again beneath an oak tree. The account that follows is thus a dream within a dream. Frightened once again, now by a wolf, Polifilo comes upon a plain scattered with the marble ruins of an ancient city and a soaring *structura antiquaria* in the distance. As is typical, Polifilo's exuberant description of the classical remains far exceeds the detail offered in the accompanying woodcut (Plate 235):

235 *Polifilo in a Valley with Ancient Ruins*, woodcut from *Hypnerotomachia Poliphili*, Venice, Aldus Manutius, 1499.

arboſcelli,& di floride Geniſte,& di multiplice herbe uerdiſſime, quiui uidi il Cythiſo,La Carice,la commune Cerinthe. La muſcariata Pana- chia el fiorito ranunculo,& ceruicello,o uero Elaphio,& la feratula,& di uarie aſſai nobile,& de molti altri proficui ſimplici,& ignote herbe & fio ri per gli prati diſpenſate. Tutta queſta læta regione de uiridura copioſa- mente adornata ſe offeriua. Poſcia poco piu ultra del mediano ſuo,io ri- trouai uno fabuleto,o uero glarcoſa plagia, ma in alcuno loco diſperſa- mente,cum alcuni ceſpugli de herbatura. Quiui al gliochii mei uno io- cundiſſimo Palmeto ſe appræſento,cum le foglie di cultrato mucrone ad tanta utilitate ad gli ægyptii,del ſuo dolciſſimo fructo fœcunde & abun- dante. Tra lequale racemoſe palme,& picole alcune, & molte mediocre, & laltre drite erano & excelſe, Electo Signo de uictoria per el reſiſtere ſuo ad lurgente pondo. Ancora & in queſto loco non trouai incola, ne altro animale alcuno. Ma peregrinando ſolitario tra le non denſate, ma inter- uallate palme ſpectatiſſime,cogitando delle Rachelaide, Phaſelide,& Li byade,non eſſere forſa a queſte comparabile. Ecco che uno affermato & carniuoro lupo alla parte dextra,cum la bucca piena mi apparue.

234 *Obelisk of the Triune God*, woodcut from *Hypnerotomachia Poliphili*, Venice: Aldus Manutius, 1499.

Holy antiquity

As the third architectural treatise to be printed in the Renaissance (after Alberti and Vitruvius) and the first of these to be illustrated, the *Hypnerotomachia* has drawn considerable attention for its unconventional architectonic amalgam of the romantic and the scientific.[41] Colonna's monuments are products of the mind and the eye, with their components taken from both written and figurative sources. Virtually all his architectural inventions can be explained by literary sources and by images and objects available in the Veneto: among the ancient writers, primarily Pliny and Vitruvius, but

Here then so many noble colonnades I found of every figuration, line [*lineamento*][44] and material; one could examine these very well: part broken, part still in place, and part remaining undamaged; with epistyles and capitals, most excellent in contrivance and with embossed carvings, cornices, friezes, arched beams; great statues, overthrown and broken asunder, their exact and perfect members seeming to be of hollow brass; niches and conches and vases, both of numidian stone and of porphyry and of various marbles and ornaments; great baths, acqueducts, and almost infinite other fragments of noble sculpture, far different and inferior to what they had once been when whole and now totally detached and almost reduced to their first unshaped forms, being fallen and cast down upon the earth from which they had been taken. Above and among the overgrown ruins was much wild vegetation and especially the unshaking anagre, and mastic trees of two kinds, and bear's foot [*branca ursina*] and dog's head [*cyncephalo*], and spotted ivy [*spatula fetida*] and coarse smilax and centaury, and many other plants growing among the ruins . . .[45]

Colonna's botanical expertise was based in large part on Pliny, but also on Boccaccio, Perotti's *Cornucopiae*, and the Herbal of Niccolò Roccabonella. The latter work was on public display in the Venetian pharmacy Testa d'Oro from about 1479 to the early sixteenth century.[46]

Polifilo admired antiquity even in its most devastated state, but he was equally concerned to imagine the wholeness that he still perceived in the shattered remains. As he observes at another point in his story:

> Insatiably, then, looking now at one, now at another beautiful and delicate work, he said quietly: "If the fragments of holy antiquity, both broken and ruined and whatever manner of particles, provoke such great admiration and such great delight to gaze upon them, what greater wonder would their wholeness reveal?"[47]

Such desires would be amply fulfilled when Polifilo approached the monument framed between two mountains that closed the end of the valley (Plate 236). Inspired by Pliny's description of the Mausoleum of Halicarnassus and various notions of the great Pyramid of Cheops, he described a massive structure – measuring over 1,000 meters in length and breadth and 3,200 meters high – built without mortar from blocks of white Parian marble.[48] Resting on "a huge and solid plinth" was an "adamantinely sharpened and most prodigious pyramid: so that with reason I judged that not without inestimable thought, time and the greatest multitude of mortals would they have been able to devise and erect such an incredible artifice."[49]

A great obelisk surmounted the pyramid; its mirror-like sides were, not surprisingly, "incised most excellently with Egyptian hieroglyphs."[50] Polifilo finds an inscription at the base of the obelisk that names its architect as a certain Lychas

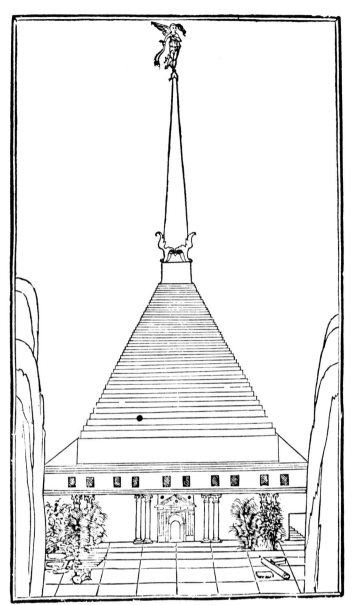

236   *The Great Pyramid and Obelisk surmounted by a Weather-vane in the Guise of Fortuna–Occasio*, woodcut from *Hypnerotomachia Poliphili*, Venice: Aldus Manutius, 1499.

of Libya and states that it is dedicated to the sun.[51] It was crowned with an elegant weather vane: a winged nymph in a flowing gown who held a cornucopia in one hand and covered her bare breasts with the other. Balancing precariously with one foot on a sphere as she turned in the wind, she can be identified as the familiar figure of Fortuna. But her striking hairstyle – a forelock of long flowing tresses and the back of her head almost bald – reveals a dual persona based on a conflation of Fortuna with Occasio or Opportunity:

> This statue was turned around with every blast of wind and moved about with such trembling and tinkling inside the metal device, such that one would never have heard in the Roman treasury; and when the foot of the figure turned

237 School of Mantegna, *Fortuna–Occasio*, *c.*1495. Detached fresco, 168 × 146 cm. Mantua, Palazzo Ducale, Soprintendenza per i Beni artistici e storici di Mantova.

about on the base, the scraping gave off such a jingling sound [*tintinabulo*] that had never been heard at the magnificent baths of Hadrian nor at the five pyramids standing upon the square [the labyrinth of Porsenna described by Pliny].[52]

A far cry from the Kairos relief at Torcello, Polifilo's Fortuna–Occasio has two immediate precedents in the north Italian milieu: a fresco painted on a palace fireplace in Mantua by a follower of Mantegna (Plate 237), and – perhaps more pertinently – a relief by Pietro Lombardo on the portal of the Scuola Grande di San Marco (Plate 238). Here three putti dance around a fountain crowned with a clearly recognizable figure of Fortuna who appears to hold a rudder instead of a cornucopia.[53] A "marriage of classical antiquity and quattrocento actuality," the figure is transparently emblematic of the syncretic tendencies of the period.[54]

In the pages that follow, Polifilo inspected, measured, and analyzed one monument after another. His impressive command of architectural terminology, if uncritical and often confused, reveals a familiarity not only with Vitruvius but also with Alberti, whose *De re aedificatoria* had been published only in 1485. He must also have had access to a copy of Filarete's treatise on architecture, which was acquired for the convent library at SS. Giovanni e Paolo in 1490.[55] Like Francesco Colonna, Filarete had been intrigued with Vitruvius's description of a *macchina* in human form that turns in the wind, and several of his monuments seem to be reflected in the *Hypnerotomachia*.[56]

Colonna's erudition in architectural matters, however unrigorously it may have been applied, reveals his serious intentions. Like Alberti he wanted to recover the theoretical background of classical architecture. But in reframing his analytical model to a polarity between *lineamento* and *prattica* – that is, beween the mental and the physical activities involved in building – he provided a critique of Alberti as well.[57]

Toward this end, Colonna also drew upon musical theory. Making a close analogy between the working method of the architect and that of the composer, he went further than Alberti and Francesco di Giorgio, who had observed a correspondence between musical harmonies and the geometrical proportions used in building design. Colonna often speaks of music and dance directly and is sensitive to the distinctive qualities of the Dorian, the Phrygian, and the Lydian modes. Applying a similar model to the classical orders, he finds a credible architectural equivalent for musical *intonatione*. He draws, furthermore, upon the Vitruvian glossary of column spacing, such as pycnostyle, diastyle, and araeostyle, and defines the colonnade as a structural equivalent to *mensurato tempo* or measured time. With the tempo of the building determined by the spacing of the columns, musical rhythms are created that reinforce the literary message of the book. The tempo of the colonnades thus quickens as the lovers approach the physical consummation of their relationship, and architecture thereby takes on the expressive capacity of language itself.[58] Accordingly, *Hypnerotomachia* may be defined as a manifesto of an expanded *paragone* that embraces the four arts: poetry and painting, architecture and music.[59]

The highest carnal pleasure

Polifilo's passionate response to buildings is expressed with a descriptive vocabulary of voluptuously gendered terms. By his own account, he looks at them with "frenetic pleasure and cupidinous frenzy," and is filled with "the highest carnal pleasure" and "burning lust."[60] But the eroticization of architecture is only one example of the sensuality that runs through the book. In the treatment of the personae, artifacts, and rituals of the ancient world, Apuleius, Ovid, and Boccaccio replace Pliny and Alberti as major literary influences, with alluringly libidinous results.[61]

The transmutation of Petrarch's chastely moralizing triumphs into celebrations of sexuality and fertility is a case in point. During their wanderings, Polifilo and Polia witness six triumphal processions, each celebrating carnal love. As in pageants of the time, the personae of the triumphs have expanded well beyond the canon established by Petrarch (Love, Chastity, Death, Fame, Time, Eternity). In the *Hypnerotomachia*, four triumphs commemorate Jupiter's affairs with mortal women: Europa and the bull, Leda and the swan, Danaë and the shower of gold, Semele and a fiery thunderbolt. The fifth triumph, featuring Vertumnus and Pomona as the patrons of fruits and harvest, is followed by a ritual sacrifice by the nymphs of a donkey to Priapus, whose effigy is set on an altar under a leafy cupola: "On the top of that

238 Pietro Lombardo, *Putti and a Fountain surmounted by Fortuna–Occasio,* c.1490–95. Venice, Scuola Grande di San Marco, portal relief.

venerated altar, rigidly rigorous, projected the rude simulacrum of the protector of gardens with all his seemly and appropriate insignias" (Plate 239).[62] The accompanying woodcut which unflinchingly depicts the god with his "rigidly rigorous" attributes, is effaced in many surviving copies of the book.[63]

Polia and Polifilo then proceed to the temple of Venus Physizoa where they are united in a ceremony featuring a sacrifice to the goddess. Sailing to the island of Cythera, they

disembark and march in the final procession, the triumph of Cupid, whose chariot is pulled by two dragons (Plate 240).[64] Venus welcomes the lovers, Cupid pierces them with a single arrow, and the first book ends at the fountain of Adonis with Polia about to tell her story to the Cytherean nymphs.

Venus is a recurring presence in the story, primarily in the text, but also in a number of woodcuts. The sculpture of a sleeping fountain nymph proved to be a seductive paradigm of tranquillity – and discovery – which Venetian artists would

find hard to resist (Plate 241). Reclining half-draped on her back with her right arm supporting her head, the nymph is unveiled by a satyr "in lascivia pruriente et tutto commoto." Accompanied by two baby satyrs, he both reveals and protects, holding back a drapery to view her and pulling down a tree branch to give her shade. Polifilo was captivated as well. Judging that even the Venus of Praxiteles did not equal this nymph who seemed more of flesh than of stone, he particularly admired her breasts, each of which emitted a fine jet of water: boiling hot and salty from the left and icy cold and fresh from the right. He noted approvingly that the right breast was at precisely the right height so that the thirsty could drink from it directly. The nymph's identity appears to be deliberately veiled. An inscription located just below the base of the fountain in the woodcut would appear to offer the key. Polifilo writes: "I saw sculpted this mysterious saying of excellent Attic characters: ΠΑΝΤΩΝ ΤΟΚΑΔΙ" (To the Parent of All). Lucretius's characterization of Venus as *genetrix omnium* immediately comes to mind.[65]

The visual source for the woodcut is unknown. Several Roman sarcophagi and sculptures have been proposed, but perhaps the artist went no further than an antiquarian sylloge. Cyriacus of Ancona's drawing of a buxom sleeping nymph in the Ambrosiana-Trotti Codex, complete with a nude male who stands near her feet, is a suggestive prototype that might well have been known, if not directly, then in a copy (Plate 87) The fact that the codex was in the possession of Leonardo Botta, Milanese ambassador to Venice in the 1470s, is more than suggestive of a connection.[66]

In another episode, Polifilo describes the Venus depicted in a two-part sculptural relief of coral colored stone that deco-

239 *Sacrifice to Priapus*, woodcut from *Hypnerotomachia Poliphili*, Venice: Aldus Manutius, 1499.

240 (*below*) *Triumph of Cupid*, woodcut from *Hypnerotomachia Poliphili*, Venice: Aldus Manutius, 1499.

rated the portal of the great pyramid, showing the education of Cupid and Vulcan forging Cupid's wing. Supplying no woodcut and deliberately relying on words alone, he leaves no question as to her identity as Venus: "that same lady, with the divine nude form, on the slender chest of whom two breasts thrust out (unshaking in their firmness and roundness), and with ample thighs . . ."[67] In the first scene, a winged Venus is described holding Cupid in front of an anvil where Vulcan fashions "a small pair of glowing wings." Also present are two figures: a helmeted male warrior in armor, who wears a breastplate adorned with the Medusa head that is usually associated with Minerva, and a young man "dressed in thin cloth."

In the second part of the sequence Venus holds an empty quiver and bow and gives the newly winged Cupid to

Mercury who shows the child three arrows, "and to what use he might put them one could easily conjecture." Here there were a warrior and a helmeted woman who carried a trophy topped by a winged sphere inscribed: "NIHIL FIRMUM" (nothing permanent). The extended passage is so detailed that Colonna must have felt that no woodcut was necessary to augment it.[68]

An invention of the late quattrocento, the story does not come from a classical text. A good case has been made for its broader interpretation as a neo-Platonic allegory of the progression of the soul. With the winged Eros a metaphor of the Soul, he acts as a median element between Man and God and ascends to the celestial realm. The theme proved to be popular among Veneto artists and was illustrated a number of times. At least two examples depicting the same two-part theme described by Polifilo can be placed in Venice in the 1490s: a bronze plaque by Camelio and a relief painted as an *all'antica* wall decoration in Carpaccio's *Return of the Ambassadors* in the St. Ursula cycle (Plates 242 and 243).[69] The relationship of these works to the *Hypnerotomachia* raises issues not only about Colonna's mechanics of visualization, but also about the depth of his understanding of neo-Platonic imagery.

Both images are far more summary than Colonna's enthusiastically discursive text, but the greater detail of the plaque indicates that it preceded the painting. If the plaque served as Colonna's model, then he must have written the first half of the *Hypnerotomachia* in Venice itself, probably in the early 1490s. He seems to have recognized most of the protagonists of the allegory (although not without confusion), and also its general theme, but he narrativized it without grasping some of its finer neo-Platonic nuances. A shift of focus between plaque and text is apparent. On the plaque, Vulcan makes each wing separately – one signifying the intellect and the other desire –

241 *Nymph of the Fountain*, woodcut from *Hypnerotomachia Poliphili*, Venice: Aldus Manutius, 1499.

ΠΑΝΤΩΝ ΤΟΚΑΔΙ

Per laquale cosa io non saperei definire, sila diuturna & tanta acre sete pridiana tolerata ad bere trahendo me prouocasse, ouero il bellissimo suscitabulo dello instruméto. La frigiditate dil quale, inditio mi dede che la petra mentiua. Circuncirca dunque di questo placido loco, & per gli loquaci riuuli fioriuano il Vaticinio, Lilii conuallii, & la floréte Lysimachia, & il odoroso Calamo, & la Cedouaria, A pio, & hydrolapato, & di assai altre appretiate herbe aquicole & nobili fiori, Et il canaliculo poscia

242 Camelio (Vettor di Antonio Gambello), *Education of Cupid*, early 1490s. Bronze, 17.5 × 25 cm. London, Victoria and Albert Museum. By courtesy of the Board of Trustees of the Victoria and Albert Museum.

243 Vittore Carpaccio, *Return of the Ambassadors* (detail), *c*.1499. Canvas, 297 × 527 (entire). Venice, Accademia.

with Catholic liturgy and terminology, along with a consistent use of scholastic terms and modes of description are strong evidence for his identity as a priest.[73] Here again the blurring of boundaries allows Colonna to fabricate a profane romance from the substance of the Christian mysteries. For example, he constructs his account of the nuptial ceremony of Polia and Poliphilo from an amalgam of Christian and Jewish rituals and pagan terminology. Six virgins file in at the outset, bearing liturgical objects (Plate 244). Four of them carry implements cited in classical texts that have nothing to do with Roman marriage ritual: two finely embroidered vestments and two crimson skullcaps; holy brine in a golden vase; a sacrificial knife with an oblong ivory handle, a hyacinth vase full of spring water. The other two hold items – a golden bishop's miter studded with gems and a ritual book – that are patently Christian. Swans and doves are sacrificed, water and blood are mixed, and the priestess strikes the altar three times: all distant echoes of Old Testament protocols. A rose tree bearing fruit grows out of the altar in the manner of the flowering verge of

rather than as a pair as called for in the text, and Mercury holds a book instead of three arrows. Both differences are important for a neo-Platonic reading of the plaque. Those elements of Plato's cosmology that do appear in Colonna's text, moreover, such as the inscription on Minerva's sphere, could have been obtained simply by a reading of Aristotle.[70]

As for Polifilo, the sensuous possibilities of the relief tend to overwhelm its transcendent meaning. He observes that Venus is "so delicately expressed that I do not know why the onlooking statues there were not excited by her, but were uniformly devoting themselves to their work."[71] Given the boundary-crossing tendencies of the book as a whole, it is probably futile to seek in it a consistent philosophical stance. And nowhere is the "strife of love," with its confusion of the sacred and the profane, more evident than in its inventions of pagan rituals.

Sacrifices with wonderful rites and worship

In the preface to the *Hypnerotomachia*, the author promises to describe "a marvelous temple . . . where there were performed sacrifices with wonderful rites and worship."[72] His familiarity

244 *Nuptial Ceremony*, woodcut from *Hypnerotomachia Poliphili*, Venice: Aldus Manutius, 1499.

Joseph in the apocryphal account of the betrothal of the Virgin. But the priestess joins the nuptial pair in eating the miraculous fruit in a ceremony that can only vaguely be linked to a re-enactment of the Fall of Man. The pagan objects described in the text are taken from such writers as Varro, Festus, and Nonius Marcellus, rather than from classical images, and are authentically antique, but none relates to Roman nuptial rites.[74]

Colonna's debt to a Christian liturgical model is even more striking in the prayers and recitations that constitute the script of the marriage rites. Not only does he draw upon the ceremony of baptism, but also upon rarely performed ceremonies

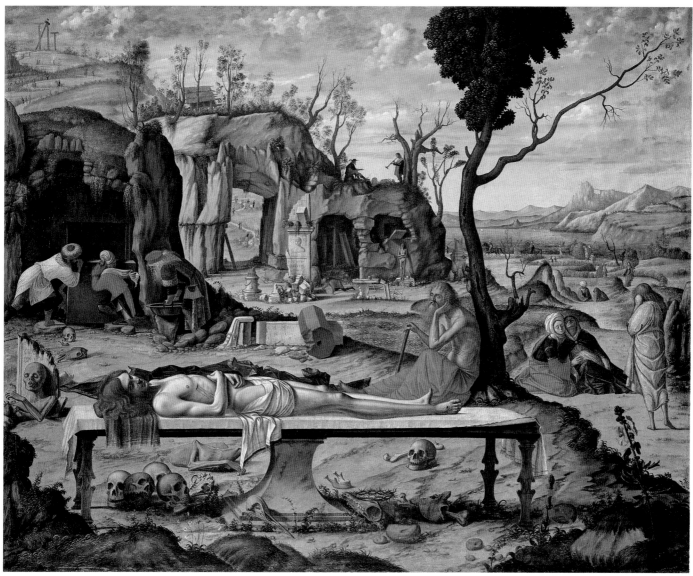

245   Vittore Carpaccio, *Entombment of Christ*, c.1505. Oil on canvas, 145 × 185 cm. Berlin, Gemäldegalerie, Staatliche Museen zu Berlin, Preussischer Kulturbesitz.

like the consecration of churches, for linguistic inspiration. As Pozzi observes, the patent contaminations of pagan and Christian rites were so obvious as to make the author even more vulnerable to charges of sacrilege than to those of obscenity.[75]

A PLACE OF ESCAPE

The classical past of Polifilo and Polia can be entered only in a dream. It is a world concluded – a landscape of evocative fragments that will never be reassembled. The past of the *Hypnerotomachia* has become truly a foreign country: a tourist destination that is a place of escape – not a model for the present and even less for the future.

The critical reception of Colonna's book in Italy shows a sharp distinction between the good fortune of the images

(which were seminal for a number of Venetian pictorial themes of the sixteenth century) and the misfortunes of the text (which seems not to have been read much, if at all). Indeed, most of the books were still unsold in 1509, when the financial sponsor Leonardo Grassi asked for his copyright period to be extended for another ten years, during which time others should not be allowed to reprint or sell the book in Venetian territories. He claimed that the unsettled times, including war "and other urgent causes", had prevented the proper distribution of this "very useful and fruitful work, of the greatest elegance," and that he was faced with the loss of many hundreds of ducats.[76]

While no other writer or artist of the time exercised "a special license" to quite the degree that Colonna did, a similar shifting time frame and capacity for unlikely synthesis is found in some of the masterpieces of early sixteenth-century

221

246 Detail of Vittore Carpaccio, *Entombment of Christ* (Plate 245).

Venetian painting. Carpaccio's painting of the *Entombment of Christ*, datable to around 1505, is a case in point (Plate 245).[77] Here, within a single picture space, the most conservative and the most modern attitudes toward pagan antiquity can be seen. A circumstantial rendering of the broken classical artifacts reveals Carpaccio's keen eye and his debt to the antiquarian sylloge. But unlike the woodcuts of the *Hypnerotomachia*, his painting preaches a moralizing sermon. The pagan ruins, resulting from the earthquake that occurred at the time of Christ's death, are part of the history of the church.[78] In the tradition of Mantegna's frescoes in Padua, they seem at first glance to represent a culture superseded and no longer accessible to men of the present.[79]

And yet there is an anomaly in Carpaccio's painting that reveals a new perception of the classical past that is not entirely dissimilar from that of Francesco Colonna. In the deep background, high on a mound with a flock of sheep, are two figures of Carpaccio's own time (Plate 246). One figure leans against a dead tree, playing a pipe; the other sits on a rock, gesturing in silent discourse. As in the *Hypnerotomachia*, their inclusion tends to "contemporize antiquity."[80]

This vignette comes curiously close to a notion of Christian antiquity as itself a retreat into a world of arcadian melancholy. Like Polifilo and Polia, these time travelers are voyeurs – intruders in a past of which they will never be a part. With them, too, a new age of historical awareness and of historical nostalgia emerges, in which there is a manifest concern for Time in its various aspects and a widening gap between the public and the private in Venetian life.

222

VI

THE HISTORICAL ECHO: CREATING NEW IDENTITIES

PROLOGUE

> Painted grotesques, spoils, spectacles, arrows, and weapons,
> Triumphs, arches, theaters, and beautiful sculptures,
> Trophies, tombs, epitaphs, and poems,
> Colossi, amphitheaters, deeds, paintings,
> Victories, torsos, gilded marbles,
> Ploughs, pick-axes, ploughshares, stakes,
> Those things that do not suffer mortal death,
> Are swiftly conducted to their end by Time.
>
>   – Pietro Aretino, 1512[1]

Just twenty years old, Pietro Aretino, the cobbler's son and future "scourge of princes," was in Venice in 1512 for a short visit to see his first book through the press: a slim, derivative volume of undistinguished verses, whose title promised, nonetheless, *strambotti, sonetti, capitoli, epistole, barzellete,* and a *desperata*.[2] Five of the *strambotti*, including the one cited here, were devoted to the theme of Time.

THE SENSE OF TIME

Aretino's poem is organized around two emblematic clusters of artifacts: products of human genius, such as antique monuments and works of art, that are symbols of triumph; and agricultural tools that allude to mankind's present state of daily toil and labor. From the contrast between the splendor of the ruined past and the modest lot of the present comes the idea of mortality and decline, and thus of Time, which is the true subject of the poem.[3]

Although the verses had been written outside Venice and expressed a general societal concern with the destructive powers of time and the transience of all earthly things, they were particularly apposite to the republic's situation in that period.[4] Indeed, for all its triumphal and prosperous aspect, it was faced with challenges to its very survival from both the sea and the land. Venice's position in the Aegean had remained irreversibly weakened from the Turkish offensives that followed the Fall of Constantinople in 1453. Despite the peace treaty of 1479 with Mehmed II, the very fear of Turkish

aggression, as much as the reality, tended to curtail new trade initiatives and to dampen the robust maritime activity that had underwritten Venetian prosperity for centuries.[5]

After the loss of Modone and Corone to the Turks in 1499, the naval battles continued for another four years, but the worst was yet to happen. Venice's increased military involvement in Italy itself, albeit "less a choice than a necessity" with the invasion of the French king Charles VIII in 1494, had been viewed with growing suspicion by other European powers. The League of Cambrai of 1508, in which the pope and the Holy Roman Emperor joined the French and Spanish monarchies to counter Venetian expansionism, resulted in the second devastating military encounter in a decade with Venice's defeat at Agnadello in May 1509. With the boundaries of the terraferma virtually pushed back to the shores of the lagoon, the old sense of invulnerability was gone, and even Venice's fabled virginity was at risk. This shattering event was, in the view of Alberto Tenenti, a culminating moment that brought about a fundamental restructuring of the Venetian sense of time and of space.[6]

Thoughts such as those expressed so transparently in Aretino's *strambotto* were a constant, painful presence to the Venetian diarist Girolamo Priuli. But in a certain sense, he saw time as an ally rather than a threat. Writing in his diary a few years after the loss of Modone and Corone, he called for a truce as the only hope for Venetian survival in the *stato da mar*: "such a republic, recognizing its manifest ruin, must gain time, and then come what God wills."[7]

The fear of decline coupled with a hope for survival were

writ large in the diary entries that followed the defeat at Agnadello. Priuli tried to make sense of the situation: "Even now, considering that all things made or procreated would, by necessity, come to an end, thinking furthermore of the great Roman lords who were rulers of the world, and finally they too came to an end after many persecutions and travails."[8] But even so, the frail hope that Venice as a republic would be exempt from this law of nature underlies his every word: "Time does much for republics, because they never die."[9] With Venice's commitment to the preservation of liberty as the source of her strength and longevity, her first imperative in the present bleak situation was simply to endure: "It was necessary to do what one could, putting time in the middle, and to let pass these contrary celestial signs and to free the Venetian Republic from peril, and hoping that with time that all should result in some good arrangement and resolution."[10] He concludes: "And finally one must do everything, whether one wishes to or not, in order to live and not to die, if at all possible; because who has time, has life."[11]

If there were challenges from without, there were also uncertainties within. The fabric of Venetian social and economic life was subjected to the same strains that were evident in city-republics throughout the peninsula in that period: the hardening of class structures, the growing disparities of wealth, the consolidation of power in the hands of ever fewer families. The years around the turn of the century in Venice were marked by higher taxes and tariffs, forced loans to the government, and a series of commercial failures. By 1500, the banks of the Garzoni, the Lippomano, and the Pisani had collapsed, and only that of the Agostini remained in operation.[12] And yet, these were the years in which Venice was described by visitors in the most triumphant terms. As in any complex society, there was no single mind-set and no typical experience with which the period can be characterized. There were, in a way, many Venices. There was the prosperous Venice of pageantry, palace building, and abundance in the marketplace; there was the Venice of recurring pestilence, economic retrenchment, and famine in the countryside. Not least of Venice's many incongruities was an ever-decreasing mobility within an increasingly stratified society and a disjunction between social rank and economic level.[13]

Any Venetian man of affairs who opened Aretino's book would have been struck with the peculiar relevance of his second *strambotto* on the theme of Time to the immediate civic past:

> With time the strong ship sinks into the sea
> With time every great state falls
> With time every earthly design disappears
> With time every desire will be shattered
> With time the worthy man is humbled
> With time every great mountain is flattened
> With time the strong iron becomes powder
> With time everything is dissolved into earth.[14]

As Carpaccio's *Entombment* affirms, artists had become quite adept in religious painting at expressing similar sentiments relative to pagan decline and Christian eschatology. But Aretino's second poem reminds us that Time also had a personal dimension. If decay and ruin came inevitably to the artifacts of great civilizations, such sad ends were also the ultimate destiny of all living beings.

Aretino's use of a repetitive technique that begins each line with the phrase "Col tempo" immediately brings to mind Giorgione's painting of *La Vecchia* who holds a scroll bearing the same message (Plate 248). The point is not that the poet would have influenced the artist or the artist the poet; it is, rather, that both were participating in a discourse that drew upon a common language and that addressed a common concern. In fact, the term "col tempo" was widely diffused in Italian literature in the late fifteenth and early sixteenth century.[15] Even Sanudo employed it in a hopeful way with reference to his great historical work on the lives of the doges: "which, God willing, with time [*col tempo*], will be published."[16]

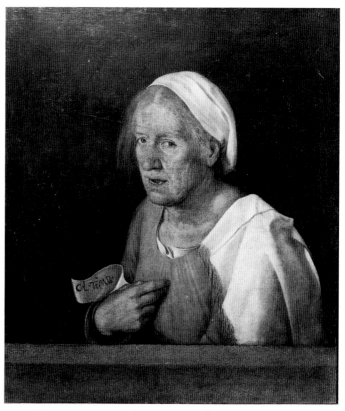

248 Giorgione, *La Vecchia*, c.1510. Oil on canvas, 68 × 59 cm. Venice, Accademia.

Already in 1494, Carpaccio had depicted a member of the Compagnia della Calza with an emblem embroidered on his cloak consisting of a siren with two tails and the motto "Col Tempo."[17] If the siren signifies Pleasure or Luxuria, as Cesare

226

Ripa later counseled in his *Iconologia*, then the message is clear: the seductive siren song of love is ephemeral and – to put a moralizing slant on it – will lead, with time, to ruin.[18]

As to Giorgione's *La Vecchia*, the painting was first recorded in a 1569 inventory of the collection of Gabriele Vendramin as simply "the portrait of the mother of Zorzon by Zorzon."[19] But Panofsky found a more complex allegorical meaning in the work. Emphasizing the didactic message of the scroll, he saw the figure not just as a *memento mori*, but also as a *memento senescere*.[20] But whether or not she carries an additional moralizing connotation of *vanitas* is ultimately less significant than her existential presence. She is, rather, a reminder – like the verses of Aretino – of the implacable and impartial forces of nature. Virtuous or not, *La Vecchia*, like all mortal creatures, will return to dust. As one scholar puts it, she personifies a state of being: that of Old Age – a tangible reminder of the destiny that inevitably awaits all who endure the vicissitudes and insults of time.[21] Her time-ravaged face may be considered a pendant, in a conceptual sense, to the dozens of beauties portrayed by Venetian artists in that period.[22] Like them, she simply is.

Considering these responses to Time and its processes, the paradox is obvious. On the one hand, the republic will endure if only time can be gained (or held back); on the other, everything mortal and beautiful must age and pass away. The visual arts, with their capacity to transcend ambiguity and paradox, helped to articulate these concerns and to resolve the dissonance. For it is precisely in this period that a number of nuanced responses to the theme of transience can be seen in Venetian painting. Such works helped to articulate a private sphere that was becoming ever more a romantic retreat from the intractable problems of public life.

THE FLUX OF NATURE

A group of three small furniture panels, attributable to Giorgione or to an artist close to him, includes an enigmatic work now in the Phillips Collection. Featuring a bearded astrologer holding an hour glass and a youth playing a lira da braccio, it depicts a moment that is neither past nor present (Plate 249).[23] The time is twilight with the setting sun just disappearing behind the mountains. As David Rosand observes, the work is typical of the pastoral mode: its dimensions are modest, the aheroic figures are dominated by the landscape, and it is open to allusive readings of greater or lesser complexity.[24]

The preference for depicting a transitional time of day is what might be called a phenomenological response to the problem of time. Leonardo's drawings of flowing water, cata-

249 Circle of Giorgione, *The Hour Glass*, *c.*1505. Oil on wood, 12 × 19 cm. Washington, D.C., The Phillips Collection.

clysmic deluges, and geological formations in process are the forerunners of a new artistic sensitivity to a natural world in constant movement. At issue is a paradigm shift of profound significance. Artists would no longer be content with depicting *natura naturata*: nature as a static, completed reality. They would now seek to imitate *natura naturans*: a dynamic nature constantly in flux.[25] In Venice such artistic initiatives tended to be carried out in the realm of light and shadows. While Giovanni Bellini had laid the groundwork for a new Venetian aesthetic of luminous energy, it is in the paintings of Giorgione that the first successful attempts to seize the flux of nature by capturing the elusive quality of light may be observed. Twilights and sunsets were favored times of day on his canvases, but his most dramatic achievement in meteorological interpretation is the bolt of lightning in *The Tempest*: possibly the first such depiction in naturalistic terms in the history of art (Plate 250).[26] Accompanying this momentary apparition of time in the picture space is an immemorial

251 Venetian medallist, *Portrait of Paolo Dedo* (obverse) and *Allegory of the Ages of Man* (reverse), 1507. Bronze, diam. 4.5 cm. (after Hill, *Corpus*, no. 529).

250 Giorgione, *The Tempest*, c.1510. Oil on canvas, 68 × 59 cm. Venice, Accademia.

density of time implied by the broken columns. Without getting into the fine particulars of a further overlay of allegorical meaning for both columns and lightning, it may simply be noted that it is articulated with a wholly natural vocabulary.[27]

Turning from time in a cosmic sense to time as a biological imperative, a certain Paolo Dedo ponders the old theme of the Ages of Man in a portrait medal of 1507 (Plate 251). The

reverse features a curious four-faced bust depicting the life cycle from infancy to old age. A variant on the *tricipitium*, an image that found its way into a number of Venetian venues in this period, from Antonio da Negroponte's altarpiece of the *Madonna* (Plate 205) to the *Hypnerotomachia Poliphili* (Plate 240) to palace facade decoration, it is framed by an enigmatic inscription: "SOL · PER · CHE · TROPPO · GLIE." Translatable as "Only because there is too much," the message seems to be a personal motto the meaning of which is difficult to grasp without more knowledge of the patron. Taken together with the image, it appears to express a concern with the phased sequence of human time and perhaps the traditional Venetian regard for prudence.[28]

Titian offered a new perspective on the problem with *The Three Ages of Man* (Plate 252). To Vasari, the subject of the picture was obvious: "a naked shepherd and a country girl who is offering some pipes for him to play, with an extremely beautiful landscape."[29] But there was more to the picture than that. Vasari does not mention the ugly trunk of the dead tree at the right which mars the "extremely beautiful landscape" nor the two infants slumbering in innocent embrace at its base. Clambering over them, but unseen and unfelt, is a winged cupid (or is it a funerary genius?) who grasps the tree trunk as he protects their sleep. Nor does Vasari cite the bearded old man in the middle ground who meditates on not one, but two skulls. The erotic charge of the musicmaking lovers may simply have been taken for granted, but it is here

252 Titian, *The Three Ages of Man, c.*1512–15. Oil on canvas, 106 × 182 cm. Edinburgh, Duke of Sutherland Collection, on loan to the National Gallery of Scotland.

253 (*below*) Giovanni Bellini with assistance, *Fortune, c.*1504–5. Wood panel, 27 × 19 cm. Venice, Accademia.

that the essential meaning of the painting resides. For as Panofsky has observed, Titian depicts three stages of the life cycle and invokes a threat as well as a promise: the threat is death and the promise to overcome it is love. Through human generation and re-generation, Time can be transcended.[30]

THE VICISSITUDES OF FORTUNE

Another artistic response to time was to symbolize its uncertainties through depictions of Fortune, a concept that was given visual form in several aspects by Venetian artists in this period. We have already seen Occasio-Fortuna as weathervane, atop the great pyramidal structure in the *Hypnerotomachia Poliphili*. Giovanni Bellini, perhaps with assistance, painted an earth-bound allegory of fortune on a small panel that would probably have decorated a *restello*, a piece of furniture intended to hold objects of *toilette* (Plate 253). Depicting a winged and blindfolded harpy balancing precariously on two spheres in front of an expansive landscape, he made a witty comment on the often arbitrary vicissitudes of fortune. Traditionally, Fortune personified holds one full and one empty amphora to indicate her ambiguous nature. But Bellini's figure holds two amphorae at an angle with their contents as yet unspilled. The implication is one of even greater uncertainty: the possibility that she might continue to hold them both upright, thus bringing only good luck or the equal possibility that she might empty both out, thus bringing only misfortune.[31] The point would not have been missed by the learned patron who may have ordered the work in contravention to sumptuary laws banning the production of such luxury

229

254 Titian, *Cupid with the Wheel of Fortune*, *c*.1520. Oil on canvas, 66 × 55 cm. Washington, D.C., National Gallery of Art, Samuel Kress Collection.

objects. Articulating a popular German theme that was elaborated more than once by Dürer, Bellini's creature, half-woman and half-beast, was Venetian in style and ultimately classical in inspiration.[32]

In his *Cupid with the Wheel of Fortune* (Plate 254), Titian addressed the issue with the optimistic attitude already apparent in *The Three Ages of Man*. The work, datable to around 1520, is Titian's only independent painting that is entirely in monochrome: the color of marble, but with nothing marmoreal about it. Here Cupid grasps a great wheel and attempts to hold back its inexorable progress toward the right, where the skull of an animal hangs from a tree. His swirling drapery, blown to the left as well as to the right, indicates that he has stopped abruptly.[33] Again it is Cupid who is the motive force, but now he holds back time rather than allow its biological process to work itself through. An old interpretation of the painting by Wilhelm Suida is still the most convincing. According to him, the animal skull symbolizes decline, but offers hope: "Love arrests for you the precipitate wheel of fortune."[34]

While Titian's painting addresses time in the most personal sense, it parallels the concerns expressed by Priuli in the public sphere and reminds us of the infinite capacity of the visual lexicon of antiquity to address issues of the Venetian present. Like Bellini's harpy who served as a metaphor for fortune, Titian's Cupid was a distant memory, but a memory nonetheless, of images that would have had their genesis in classical reliefs.

A NOBLE BLOODLINE

> For Marcello, of Roman probity, name, and family, illustrious both at home
> and abroad, both in peace and in war, has brought back to life his ancestors'
> memorable deeds. It would be proper to say that whatever good fortune, virtue,
> and excellence once shone among all the Roman Marcellos now blaze forth
> among the Venetians in the one Jacopo Antonio.
>
> – Michele Orsini, 1462[1]

The humanistically educated Orsini, Venetian prior of the convent of San Antonio di Castello, was writing a heated rebuttal to Francesco Filelfo who had claimed Gallic origins for the Venetians.[2] The civic panegyric of Sabellico and Sanudo thus had its private side, with numerous patrician families now claiming a distinguished Roman lineage. These mythologies of family origins were rooted in the medieval chronicle tradition of lists of surnames and origins, but they took on an increasingly classical flavor.[3]

ROMAN ROOTS

The genealogy of Jacopo Antonio Marcello was by now well established (Plate 255).[4] About ten years earlier the Hungarian poet Janus Pannonius, then a student of Guarino's in Ferrara, wrote a panegyric extolling the military triumphs of the "noble Marcello from the race of the toga-clad Roman fathers, strong column of Venetian destiny."[5] While other writers would compare Marcello favorably to Hannibal, Xerxes, and Scipio,[6] Pannonius also measured Jacopo's achievements against his illustrious supposed forefather Marcus Claudius Marcellus. Noting that Marcus Claudius had never transported a fleet of ships over the Alps as Jacopo had done and observing that it had taken the ancient Roman three years to capture Syracuse while the modern Venetian took Verona in only three days, Pannonius could only conclude: "If you compare the deeds of the two Marcellos, the Venetian son vanquishes in glory his Roman ancestor."[7]

Admittedly, noble families throughout Italy were pressing claims to similar grandeur in this period, but the Venetian situation had a different flavor. In Venice individual claims to

255 Andrea Mantegna (attrib.), *Portrait of Jacopo Antonio Marcello*, from *The Passion of St. Maurice*, 1453. Tempera on vellum, 18.7 × 13 cm. Paris, Bibliothèque de l'Arsenal, MS 940, f. 38v.

ancestral glory were constrained by the longstanding communal ethos that defined the patriciate as a nobility of equals. Such assertions were thus typically expressed privately in panegyrics and epigrams or, if publicly, in funeral orations. Speaking at the obsequies for the vastly wealthy and powerful Marco Cornaro, the father of Caterina Cornaro, in 1479, Pietro Contarini duly noted the Roman origins of the deceased.[8] According to the sixteenth-century genealogist Marco Barbaro, the Cornari could also claim founding father status in regard to Venice itself, as one of the twenty-four families called *i lunghi*.[9] He declared: "I found it written that they are descended from the Roman Cornelii . . . [and] they were the first who came to live at Rivoalto after the construction . . ."[10] The Contarini, Barbaro advised, had "descended from the Aurelian Emperor, and at Rome they were then of the Aurelii"; but he added judiciously that other writers held that the Contarini had once been counts in Germany and had gone to live in Rome from whence they were sent in 420 to govern Concordia.[11]

Even non-noble *cittadino* families could cautiously claim well-seasoned roots. According to a chronicle written in 1555,

> The house of Dardani, that for nobility and antiquity holds first place among the families of Venetian *cittadini*, as one can rightly say, is descended and had its origins, as one can conjecture from the name, from those Trojans, who with Antenor after the fall of Troy came to build Padua; they were those who descended from Dardanus who, as Virgil affirms, was the first king of Troy.[12]

Just as in public oratory about the origins of the republic, such claims had an ambivalent quality: pride in ancient roots was coupled with assertions of Venetian superiority. Although an ancestral share in the foundation of Venice proper was still a matter of pride, even more ancient antecedents would be sought and proclaimed with varying degrees of subtlety. With this one sees the appropriation of the ancient past for private purposes, and, as with civic identity, personal identity would begin to acquire a classical flavor.

IMPERSONATIONS *ALL'ANTICA*

Indeed, others who could not establish their Roman lineage by orthography could imply it through images alone. The self-fashioning of the medallist Zuan Boldù is a case in point. In 1458 he cast two medals portraying himself. He appears on the obverse of the first example as a young Marcus Aurelius, his shoulders heroically nude and his curly hair bound *all'antica* with an ivy leaf wreath (Plate 256). An inscription written in imperfect Greek identifies him as "Ioannis Boldù, Painter of Venice." On the reverse the artist plays a role in his own humanist *memento mori* as he sits in an attitude of despair opposite a winged putto who rests on a huge skull and holds a flame in his left hand. The putto, inspired by classical

256 Zuan Boldù, *Self-Portrait* (obverse) and *Allegory of Death* (reverse), 1458. Bronze, diam. 8.5 cm. Washington, D.C., National Gallery of Art.

funerary genii, must symbolize death; the skull represents the human body between death and resurrection; and the flame alludes to the immortal soul.[13] While Boldù would have found a precedent for the putto as the genius of Death on an earlier medal by Pietro da Fano, he seems to have been inspired by Roman imperial coins minted in Greece for the composition as a whole. In a fine example of a Renaissance appropriation of the past for purposes of the here and now, official imperial imagery was transumed into a personal quattrocento medita-

Faith, or possibly Hope, raising a chalice toward the sun and by Repentence wielding a scourge. Now resignation – but, significantly not elation – supplants dispair as the Christian promise of redemption supplants the finality of pagan death.[15] Taken together, the two medals are emblematic of the delicate rapprochement between humanist ideals and Christian values in this period. It is as if they were two sides of the same conflicted self.

257 Zuan Boldù, *Self-Portrait* (obverse) and *Allegory of Faith and Penitence* (reverse), 1458. Bronze, diam. 8.7 cm. Washington, D.C., National Gallery of Art, Samuel H. Kress Collection.

tion on mortality, albeit one that was presumably intended for public view in medallic form.[14]

Boldù's second self-portrait medal returns him to the Christian present (Plate 257). Now dressed in contemporary clothing on the obverse, he frames his portrait bust with an inscription in Hebrew, the language of the holy rather than the secular: "Iohanon boldu meveneziya zayyar" (Giovanni Boldù of Venice, painter). He depicts himself once more on the reverse, but here he is flanked by the winged figure of

258 North Italian artist, *The Young Emperor Caracalla* (obverse) and *Allegory of Death* (reverse), 1466. Bronze, diam. 9 cm. (after Hill, *Corpus*, no. 423).

Boldù's allegory had a long afterlife. Another artist was so impressed with its classical appearance that he used it eight years later for the reverse of his own facsimile of a Roman medallion depicting the laureate head of the young Emperor Caracalla (Plate 258). But now he adds an inscription to make the meaning even more explicit: "I SON FINE" (I am the end, or I am finished).[16] The motif reappeared in several other contexts toward the end of the century, including a marble relief on the Certosa of Pavia. There, significantly, the inscription was changed to "innocentia e memoria mortis." With the putto now signifying purity instead of death, the meaning has become more complex and profound: that the thought of death and the awareness of its inevitability makes one virtuous for fear of punishment and thus brings about a return to a state of guiltlessness.[17]

The medallist Camelio had yet another approach to classical self-presentation. Born Vettor di Antonio Gambello, he had Latinized his surname, Venetian dialect for *camelus* (camel), to Camelius: a protocol of humanist self-fashioning that was spreading into the milieu of the artist as well.[18] The hopes for personal transformation that caused such a man to reject his Christian birth name for a more edifying Roman equivalent are revealed by Janus Pannonius in an epigram written in Ferrara in the late 1450s:

On the Changing of His Name

I had been Joannes, now I sign myself Janus,
In order that you do not deny that you were warned,
    dear reader,
I did not despise so noble a name out of disdain,
None has resounded with an equal fame within the
    universe.
The golden Thalia compelled me, though I was
    unwilling,
To change my name, when she bathed me in the
    Aonian lake.[19]

And yet, in another epigram, he also expresses his fears that such a "baptism" might not bring the hoped-for happiness:

On a Transformation of His Life

It is enough for anyone to change his earlier condition
    once;
Happy for whom it turns out for the better![20]

Camelio, on his part, was the son of an architect-sculptor and enjoyed a long career as an engraver and medalist at the Venetian mint.[21] While Boldù had grasped the forms of antiquity, Camelio – perhaps inspired by the transforming powers of Thalia – embraced its spirit as well. He too made two medals portraying himself *all'antica*, but here they were struck and not cast, and were made some years apart. The earlier medal is signed but not dated and portrays on the obverse a young man with thick curly hair (Plate 259). The reverse features a nude male figure in the posture of the Ludovisi

259   Camelio (Vettor di Antonio Gambello), *Self-Portrait* (obverse) and *Figure in Pose of the Ludovisi Ares* (reverse), late fifteenth century. Struck bronze, diam. 2.9 cm. Washington, D.C., National Gallery of Art, Samuel H. Kress Collection.

260   Camelio (Vettor di Antonio Gambello), *Self-Portrait* (obverse) and *Pagan Sacrifice* (reverse), 1508. Struck bronze, diam. 3.7 cm. Washington, D.C., National Gallery of Art, Samuel H. Kress Collection.

Ares, seated in profile and facing a winged caduceus and the implements of war.[22] The later medal carries the date 1508, and portrays the same distinctive profile of the artist, now in middle age (Plate 260). On the reverse a group of animated figures gathered around an altar is augmented by inscriptions that can as easily be given a Christian as a pagan reading: "FAVE FOR[TUNA] SACRIF[ICIO]" (May sacrifice bring fortune).[23] Taken together, the two medals document the artist's personal journey over time as viewed through the idealizing lens of a distant classical perspective.

But these *all'antica* impersonations by artists were the exception in late quattrocento Venetian portraiture. In the case of medals, the vast majority portrayed the sitters in modern clothing and hairstyle. Clues to character in the form of classical allegories were common, but were usually confined to the reverses.

In general, the antique paradigm was acknowledged in the painted portrait only in the preference for a bust-length format and the ubiquitous parapet inscribed with classical looking epigraphy. Again, classical dress was the rare exception.[24] But by the first decade of the sixteenth century, efforts to endow the sitter with Roman roots had become more subtle and more complex. Titian's portrait of the woman now called *La Schiavona* thus draws upon the antique not only to transcend time, but also to offer a telling contribution to the *paragone* debate (Plate 261).[25] The name of the sitter is not known, although her attire and her demeanor connote respectability. She faces us in dignified equanimity from behind a feigned marble parapet that is incised with the artist's initials

261　Titian, *La Schiavona*, c.1510. Oil on canvas, 117 × 97 cm. London, National Gallery. Reproduced by courtesy of the Trustees, The National Gallery, London.

– T.V. – and sculpted with a low-relief profile portrait of the sitter in the guise of a Roman matron.[26]

Titian proclaims the superiority of painting through a multifaceted dialectic: by reproducing sculpture in the two-dimensional medium of paint; by mimicking its three-dimensionality with two views of the sitter; and by challenging nature in its representation of both colored flesh and monochrome marble. But perhaps the most powerful assertion lies in the realm of time. By portraying the sitter as she is, Titian gives her a present; by portraying her *all'antica* on the parapet, he gives her a past; by portraying her together with her own funerary monument, he gives her a posthumous future. David Rosand puts it well, when he concludes that *La Schiavona*, more than any other portrait of the time, "reveals a very special awareness of the competition between nature and art, between life and death, between the lost past and living memory."[27]

AS ANTIQUE AS POSSIBLE

The most traditional instrument for giving visual expression to genealogical concerns was the funerary monument: a genre that occupies a space between the public and the private. Products of individual largesse and filial piety, sepulchres and cenotaphs are trans-generational undertakings by their very nature. While testaments typically provided for tombs to be built from funds in the estate, it was usually the duty of heirs to carry out the instructions, if any, of the deceased for their actual construction. Here too, in Venice as elsewhere, the antique idiom was becoming the preferred vehicle for family, as well as personal, definition.[28]

The renowned humanist Ermolao Barbaro recognized the exemplary importance of such memorials, both literary and marmoreal. Upon hearing that the family of Bernardo Giustiniani had honored his wishes for a modest burial without eulogy, he protested:

> I have heard that in his last will he ordered that his remains be placed in a simple and ordinary tomb near the holy remains of his uncle. But how, for that reason, can you allow the bones of such a great man to lie without the honor of a marble [monument], without the witness of any eulogy? . . . Such [commemorations] are not for the dead, especially those whom not stones or columns consecrate the memory but monuments of deed and character; they are prepared for the living, they are directed towards posterity. . .[29]

In late fifteenth-century Venice, the most impressive and the most classicizing tombs, aside from those of the doges, were inhabited not by humanists but by military heroes. The evolution of three phenomena may be observed in them: the assimilation of classical formal values into a new Venetian aesthetic; the appropriation of state iconography for purposes

262 Tomb slab of Ludovico [Alvise] Diedo, *c.*1466. Venice, SS. Giovanni e Paolo, right aisle.

of self-presentation; and the tendency toward more assertive statements of familial pre-eminence that tested the boundaries of the old tradition of egalitarianism within the patrician caste.

Two such monuments, probably constructed in the 1460s, reveal the infiltration of Tuscan–Paduan classicism into Venetian tomb design and stand at the beginning of these changes: the tomb slab of Ludovico (also known as Alvise) Diedo in SS. Giovanni e Paolo (Plates 262 and 263) and the cenotaph of Federico Cornaro in the Frari.[30] The Diedo gravestone, the more modest of the pair, is set into the pavement of the right-hand aisle of the Dominican basilica.[31] While not imposing, it is a work of considerable artistry and originality and is possibly an invention of the young Pietro Lombardo, who had recently arrived in Venice.[32] Finely crafted with niello inlay work, the slab consists of two parts, the one figurative and the other epigraphic, enclosed by a foliate-patterned frame. The inscription contains a concise, but pithy biography of the deceased, declaring that it was beautiful to die for the republic and ending with the custom-

236

ary declaration that he had ordered the tomb for his heirs and himself.[33] It also records the high point of his career, a heroic moment in 1453 when he led a flotilla of Venetian merchant galleys out of the port of Constantinople to safety just after the city had fallen irrevocably to the Turks.[34]

Although Diedo's career was not primarily a military one, it is that aspect of his life that was emphasized not only in the inscription but also in the figural iconography of the tomb. It features two putti standing on a tiled floor in a three-dimensional space defined by a coffered archway. Together they support the Diedo coat of arms, with each holding a standard topped by a battle helmet decorated with luxuriant foliage. One of these is crowned with a marine monster with a bearded human face and the other with an armillary sphere. The paired emblems suggest man's power to transform himself and to overcome fate predestined by the stars.[35]

The Cornaro monument was a far grander affair. Federico Cornaro had died in 1378 and left funds for the construction of a family chapel dedicated to San Marco in the Franciscan church of Santa Maria Gloriosa dei Frari (Plate 264). The structure was built from the ground up on the west side of the nave and was actually an addition to the church – an unusual

263 Tomb slab of Ludovico [Alvise] Diedo (detail), *c.*1466. Venice, SS. Giovanni e Paolo.

264 Cenotaph of Federico Cornaro (d. 1378), *c.*1460s. Marble and fresco. Venice, Santa Maria Gloriosa dei Frari, Cappella Cornaro.

undertaking in Venice, where family chapels were rare. The project would have been finished by Federico's son Giovanni no earlier than the 1450s. But as sumptuous as the decorative ensemble came to be – with the cenotaph by Jacopo Padovano featuring fine carving, elegant roman uncial lettering, and fresco decoration with a mature classical vocabulary of putti, swags, and profile coin portraits – the actual references to Federico Cornaro and his family on the monument is confined to the epigram. Although the deceased had offered his wealth and sacrificed an arm in defense of the republic in the War of

Chioggia, his effigy does not occupy the central tabernacle. It is filled instead with a more than life-sized angel of a striking classical beauty.[36] As in the case of Diedo, Cornaro was commemorated epigraphically only in terms of his service to the republic and his contribution to the public good.[37]

Across the Frari in the opposite transept, a striking change in tone can be observed. A triumphal arch of white marble frames the doorway to the sacristy. But it is more than a doorframe; surmounted by a sarcophagus, it features a pedimented tabernacle that contains a full-sized standing effigy of Benedetto Pesaro, holding a general's standard and dressed in battle armor (Plate 265).

Pesaro had been elected *generalissimo da mar* in 1500 and charged to lead the Venetian fleet in the resumed Turkish wars. After winning a number of naval victories, he died on his galley in Corfu at the age of seventy and left 1,000 ducats in his will for a tomb to be built of "noble marble." Military heroes had always been allowed a larger measure of personal aggrandizement in funerary display in Venice, but Pesaro's would be, perhaps, the most grandiose monument constructed to date for an individual who was neither doge nor cardinal.[38] More importantly, it reappropriated for personal, if not private, use the iconography of the state. Its similarity to the portal of the Arsenale, with the paired attached columns and a distinctive tabernacle, would not have been missed by the attentive contemporary observer. Nor would the displacement of the lion of St. Mark in the tabernacle by Pesaro himself (see Plate 114). He is flanked, furthermore, by full-sized nude statues of Neptune and Mars, Venice's pagan protectors, who were prominently featured just a few years earlier in Jacopo dei Barbari's view of Venice of 1500. On the piers of the arch below are trophies, placards proclaiming Pesaro's deeds, and two roundels with the lion of St. Mark, whose angelic salutation of peace – "Pax Tibi Marce Evangelista Meus" – would have been concealed within a closed book.[39] Here the entire visual and epigraphical apparatus of civic classicism is employed to glorify not only the state, but also the individual who had served it so well.

The classical vocabulary was by now a *sine qua non* for tomb design. When the Venetian cardinal Battista Zen wrote a codicil to his will in 1501, he specified that his sepulchre be made "with the most beautiful artifice and mastery, that should be as antique as possible."[40] For Marcantonio Sabellico, neither a prelate nor a military man, a tomb monument *all'antica* offered the opportunity for introspection and a statement of personal philosophy. Recently retired on a state pension after years of service as a professional humanist – as a teacher at the School of San Marco and as a historian of the republic – Sabellico took no chances on his posthumous image. He supervised the design of his own tomb slab, and it was already in place in Santa Maria delle Grazie when he wrote his will in 1506 (Plate 266).[41]

Ascribed to Antonio Lombardo, the monument features a classicizing tabernacle that frames two mourning putti flanking

a Roman cinerary urn. At the top of the ensemble, a phoenix arises from the flames in front of a banderole inscribed in Greek: "From death comes life." On the base of the slab, the Latin inscription advises: "This small urn contains Coccio, the writer whom neither the events of history nor the whole of time limits." Forsaking his Latin pseudonym in this, his final statement as a mortal, Sabellico returns to Coccio, his given surname. Like Janus Pannonius he seems to have second thoughts about his re-baptism by the Muses.

Here too the tomb betrays a divided heart. While the symbol of the reborn phoenix rising from the ashes was classical in origin, it had long been incorporated into Christian (and, in the case of Venice, into civic) iconography.[42] And yet the Christian Church had long opposed the ritual of cremation, and the Latin inscription leaves no doubt as to the pagan character of the funerary urn that emblematically contained Sabellico's ashes. As Ruth Chavasse rightly observes, "Sabellico, it would seem, saw no incongruity between the classical and Christian memorials, the former provided for in marble, the latter in the customary rites and ceremonies of the Church as detailed in his will."[43] Indeed, by embracing both the pagan and Christian traditions, he is able to fulfill the hope expressed in the epitaph: to defy and conquer time by transcending it.

Just a few years earlier, Sabellico had written a funeral oration for another humanist, Benedetto Brugnolo, whom Sanudo described as "most learned in Latin and Greek and in humanistic studies." Brugnolo's tomb monument was erected in the Frari in 1505 and paid for by a grateful disciple, the patrician Giovanni Querini (Plate 267). Designed in an austere classical style, its most significant features are Brugnolo's portrait bust, probably a death mask, in the lower zone and three stacks of books arranged around the sarcophagus.[44]

Indeed, as with medals, high relief and full-round sculpture was particularly suitable for *all'antica* self-presentation. Inspired by the Roman *imago clipeata* – a bust set on a shield – Mantegna had designed a bronze portrait head of himself around 1480. It would later be set on a porphyry disk framed in white Istrian stone in his funerary chapel in Sant'Andrea in Mantua (Plate 268).[45] His long, unruly hair and bare chest recall the medallic self-portraits of Boldù and Camelio and suggest a developing notion of unbridled artistic genius. The laurel wreath, like that of Boldù, would seem to press the artist's claim to equivalence with the poet; and the scowling expression associates the artist not only with courage and determination, but also with a melancholy temperament.[46] The antique idiom thus serves as a vehicle to express new ideas about the nature of creativity and the unique qualities of the artist.

Sculpted busts were quite rare in Venice before the end of the quattrocento, but there are a few notable exceptions. Tullio Lombardo made two extraordinary "double portrait" marble reliefs in the 1490s, each intentionally truncated to suggest the fragmentary character of ancient monuments.[47]

265 Lorenzo Bregno and Baccio da Montelupo, tomb monument of Benedetto Pesaro (d. 1503). Marble. Venice, Santa Maria Gloriosa dei Frari, right transept.

266 Antonio Lombardo, tomb monument of Marcantonio Sabellico (d. 1506). Marble. Venice, Museo Civico Correr.

267　Tomb monument of Benedetto Brugnolo, 1505. Marble. Venice, Santa Maria Gloriosa dei Frari, right aisle.

And yet the works were not intended to masquerade as genuine antiques, for they contain contemporary elements as well. One of these pieces, now in Ca' d'Oro, bears an epigram declaring that "TVLLIVS LOMBARDVS" made it, and may well be the sculptor's own marriage portrait (Plate 269). Such an identification is suggested by its function as prototype for a woodcut in the *Hypnerotomachia Poliphili* where the accompanying text recounts the fate of a certain Ser Tullius and his bride who tragically died on their wedding night (Plate 270). The name of the bridegroom replicates that of the sculptor himself in contracts of the time.[48] But the maiden in Tullio's relief is clothed in a quattrocento dress that is tailored to display her bare breasts, in a reprise of the Roman tomb monument of Metellia Prima as re-invented by Jacopo Bellini in his Paris album (Plate 127). Even allowing that the object would have resided in private space, such a display would have been most exceptional for a Venetian bride – a breach of decorum inspired by the authority of the antique. Tullio's synthesis of the contemporary and the classical in the relief suggests an even earlier example of time travel than that of Polifilo and, indeed, the transcendence of time.[49]

By the second decade of the sixteenth century, individual portrait busts would become a popular mode of self-definition in Venice with a revival of the Roman custom of setting up ancestor busts in palace atria.[50] The Florentine sculptor Simone Bianco, who moved to Venice around 1512, built a career on the practise, producing busts in both marble and bronze (Plate 271). Much of his activity seems to have centered on retouching actual antique busts to render the details more legible and more suggestive, and through these labors he absorbed the spirit of the classical style. Although his own works are very naturalistic, they show considerable expressive power and drew admiration even from the acid-penned Pietro Aretino.[51] That Simone typically signed his Roman replicas in Greek is a reminder of Fra Urbano's travel account of Greece, where all classical monuments were defined as Roman.[52] With the necessity – or capacity – to distinguish between the two traditions seemingly absent, a stylistically aware sense of the ancient past was yet to be achieved.

268　Andrea Mantegna, *Self-Portrait*, before 1506. Bronze, porphyry, and Istrian stone, h. 47 cm. Mantua, Sant'Andrea.

Two such works in bronze by an unnamed artist representing the recently deceased Doge Antonio Grimani and his son Cardinal Domenico were recorded by Sanudo in 1526. He described them as part of a special decorative apparatus set up by the parish priest in the church of Santa Maria Formosa for vesper services attended by Doge Andrea Gritti, distinguished visitors and the entire Pregadi.[53] That Sanudo

269   Tullio Lombardo, *Double Portrait*, 1490s. Marble relief, 47 × 50 cm. Venice, Ca' d'Oro.

did not name a sculptor suggests that artistic attribution was of less importance to him than the fact of the objects themselves.

PERSONAL RESTITUTIONS

Toward the end of the fifteenth century, one encounters in Girolamo Donato a learned patrician who understood the special power of artifacts, both classical and classical-looking, to craft for himself a distinctive personal identity. Born in Venice around 1456 and educated in Padua, Donato was one of the outstanding humanists and diplomats of his generation. An active correspondent with the major humanists of his time, he can be compared to Bernardo Bembo and Ermolao Barbaro in terms of his erudition and literary achievements. He was also the friend of Aldus Manutius and an author of many works in Greek and Latin. He translated important texts of Alexander of Aphrodisias and John Chrysostom from Greek

242

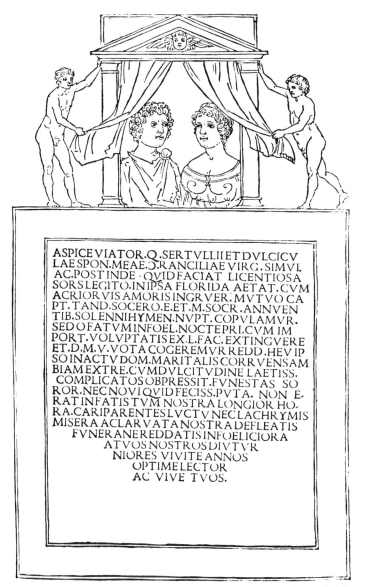

ASPICE VIATOR. Q. SERTVLLII ET DVLCICV
LAE SPON. MEAE. GRANCILIAE VIRG. SIMVL
AC. POST INDE · QVID FACIAT LICENTIOSA
SORS LEGITO. IN IPSA FLORIDA AETAT. CVM
ACRIOR VIS AMORIS INGRVER. MVTVO CA
PT. TAND. SOCERO. E. ET. M. SOCR. ANNVEN
TIB. SOLENNI HYMEN. NVPT. COPVLAMVR.
SED O FATVM INFOEL. NOCTE PRI. CVM IM
PORT. VOLVPTATIS EX. L. FAC. EXTINGVERE
ET. D. M. V. VOTA COGEREMVR REDD. HEV IP
SO IN ACTV DOM. MARITALIS CORRVENS AM
BIAM EXTRE. CVM DVLCITVDINE LAETISS.
COMPLICATOS OB PRESSIT. FVNESTAS SO
ROR. NEC NOVI QVID FECISS. PVTA. NON E-
RAT IN FATIS TVM NOSTRA LONGIOR HO-
RA. CARI PARENTES LVCTV NEC LACHRYMIS
MISERA A CLARVATA NOSTRA DEFLEATIS
FVNERA NE REDDATIS INFOELICIORA
ATVOS NOSTROS DIVTVR
NIORES VIVITE ANNOS
OPTIME LECTOR
AC VIVE TVOS.

270 *Sertullius and Rancilia*, woodcut from *Hypnerotomachia Poliphili*, Venice: Aldus Manutius, 1499.

271. Simone Bianco, *Male portrait bust*. White marble, h. 45 cm. Stockholm, Nationalmuseum.

into Latin and was later praised by the Florentine historian Francesco Guicciardini as a "uomo dottissimo."[54] If Baldassare Castiglione can be considered a reliable source, Donato was also a man of wit. His transposition of a passage from Ovid is cited in *The Courtier* as a particularly artful example of the play on words so beloved of Renaissance literati:

And messer Geronimo [Girolamo] Donato, while visiting the stations at Rome in Lent along with many other gentlemen, met up with a company of beautiful Roman ladies; and when one of the gentlemen said "Your Rome has as many girls as the heaven has stars," he replied at once: "Your Rome has as many satyrs in it as the meadows have lambs," pointing to a company of young men coming from the other direction.[55]

Following a decade of important diplomatic assignments,

Donato was sent to Rome in 1491 as Venetian orator to the papal court. During his tenure there he made several significant acquisitions. The most notable item was a holy relic of early Christianity: a fragment of the titulus attached to the True Cross that had, according to legend, been brought to Rome by St. Helen. The relic had just been rediscovered that year in the church of Santa Croce in Gerusalemme, and a piece of it was presented to Donato by Pope Innocent VIII himself.[56]

When Donato returned to Venice in 1492, he gave the relic to the church of Santa Maria dei Servi. He commissioned at his own expense a cruciform reliquary of oriental jasper within a silver casket to protect it, a costly altar with a tabernacle to enshrine it, and an inscribed plaque to document its provenance. In a possibly calculated choice in favor of a historicizing Paduan *romanitas* over a romanticizing Venetian classicism, he chose the sculptor Andrea Riccio to design a door for the tabernacle and four reliefs with scenes from the Legend of the True Cross that were set into the altar, all in costly gilded bronze (Plate 272).[57] Donato's epigram of dedication recording his gift of the "precious work" was one of the few socially well-sanctioned modes of self-glorification open to a Venetian patrician.[58]

Donato had no sooner returned from his mission to Rome in 1492 than he was sent as podestà to Ravenna where the city was experiencing a renewal under beneficent Venetian rule. Civic buildings were being repaired or constructed anew

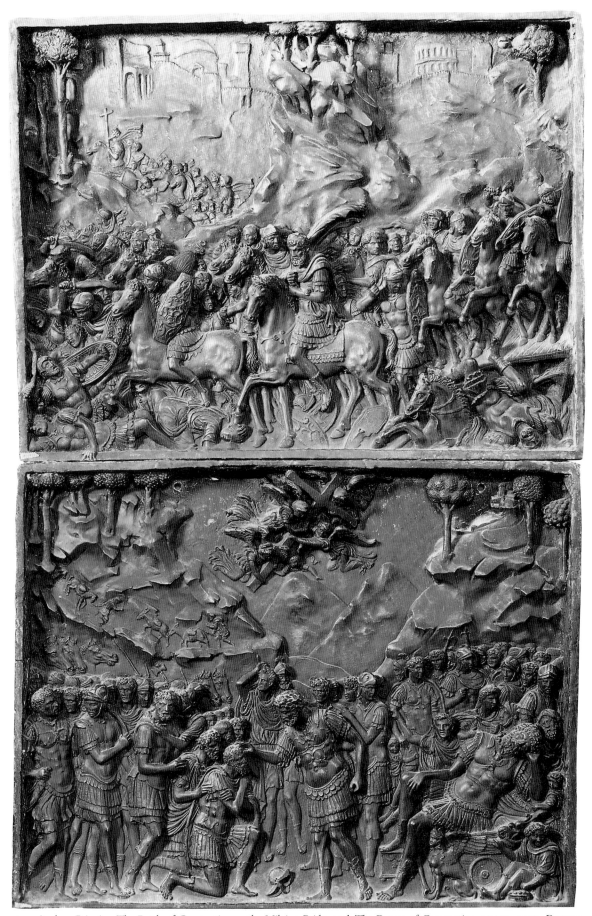

272   Andrea Riccio, *The Battle of Constantine on the Milvian Bridge* and *The Dream of Constantine*, c.1495–1500. Bronze, parcel-gilt, 38.5 × 50.5 cm. each. Venice, Ca' d'Oro, Galleria Giorgio Franchetti.

and ancient monuments rediscovered and refurbished.[59] Bernardo Bembo, who served as podestà in 1483, had sponsored two such projects of historical rehabilitation that would later inspire Donato to perform similar service. Bembo's first commission was an act of humanist *pietas*: a new marble sepulchre for Dante's remains to be made by Pietro Lombardo, Venice's leading sculptor.[60] His second project was an act of civic *pietas*: the erection of two monumental columns in the Piazza del Popolo in front of the Palazzo Communale. Following the model of the Piazzetta of Venice, statues of St. Mark, symbol of the Serenissima, and St. Apollinaris, the patron saint of Ravenna, were installed atop the columns. Lombardo carved their stepped bases with bas-reliefs of allegorical figures, portraits and signs of the zodiac. The sign of Aquarius was given particular local relevance, for he modeled it after Ercole Orario, a colossal Roman statue then in another part of the city near an ancient temple of Hercules. Popularly called *Conchincollo*, it consisted of a nude

273 *Ercole Orario*, from G. Simeoni, *Illustratione de gli Epitafi et Medaglie antiche*, Lyon, 1558, p. 80.

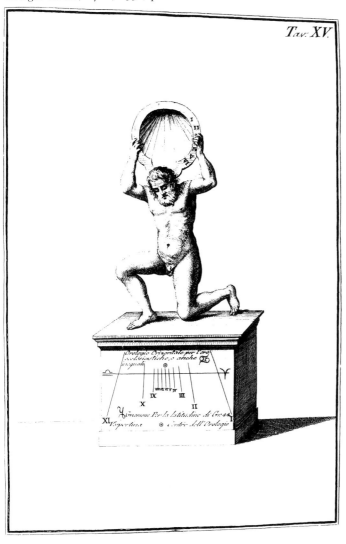

figure who kneeled on one knee and supported a solar quadrant on his head (Plate 273).[61]

When Girolamo Donato assumed the office of podestà in 1492, he seized the moment, so to speak, and accorded the ancient statue of Ercole Orario, then in poor condition, further attention. He had it moved to the Piazzetta dell'Aquila, the old *foro asinario* that was connected to the larger Piazza del Popolo by a passageway through the ground floor of the Palazzo Communale.[62] There it was installed on a base made from a Roman altar and provided with an inscription that recorded its restoration:

Hierony[mus] Do
natus praes[es]
[H]erculis Horarii r[e]
[li]quias ex Herculana[e]
[r]egionis angiportu
[i]n for[um] transtulit et
[Rav]ennatium antiquit[ati]
d[ono] d[edit][63]

(Girolamo Donato, Podestà, transported the remains of Ercole Orario from a narrow street in the quarter of Ercolana to the forum. And he gave it as a gift to [honor] the antiquity of the people of Ravenna)

In all likelihood, it was Sixtus IV's transfer of the antique bronzes from the Lateran to the Capitoline in 1471, along with his plaque dedicating them to the *Romanus populus*, that had inspired Donato toward a similar act of restitution.[64] With the meridian of Ercole Orario equipped with a gnomon to cast a shadow from both the sun by day and the moon by night, Donato's deed could be seen as a gift of time itself.

HOLY THEFTS

Donato acquired objects for private use as well as for public munificence. His service in Rome in 1491 yielded two Roman epigraphs that were later recorded in his house in Venice by Sanudo: pagan equivalents to the Christian titulus on the True Cross. Both inscriptions had been observed on the Via Appia just outside Rome by Fra Giocondo a few years before. One referring to the Tullii and the other to the Terentii, they seem to have been key pieces of evidence for the confident identification of the Roman maiden discovered in the area in 1485 as Tulliola, the daughter of Cicero.[65]

While such epigrams were prized for their immediate historical resonance, Donato possessed others that he would have cherished for more personal reasons. Two stones later recorded in his home in Venice had been discovered in 1502 in Padua. Inscribed with the names "L. Cossius Donatus" and "Q. Nunnius Donatus," the surnames would have offered archaeological – and irrefutable – certainty to family claims to a noble Roman past.[66]

Girolamo's underlying motivations for his forays into the ancient world, whether through the reading and translation of books or through the acquisition and restitution of objects, may be revealed in a portrait medal designed for him by Riccio (Plate 274). The reverse shows two genii stealing books of wisdom from a sleeping female figure. The Greek inscription beneath the figures proclaims: ΣΕΜΝΗ ΚΛΟΠΙΑ – Holy theft.[67]

274   Andrea Riccio, *Portrait of Girolamo Donato* (obverse) and *Allegory of Holy Theft* (reverse). Bronze, diam. 5.2 cm. (after Hill, *Corpus*, no. 530).

Other such thefts, both material and intellectual, were becoming ever more obvious in the Venetian domestic environment. By the end of the fifteenth century, the old aesthetic of incorporation was being transmuted into a new model driven by a passion for collecting and informed by a more knowing connoisseurship.[68] A panel that was once part of a polyptych painted by an artist close to Giovanni Bellini suggests the new mentality (Plate 275). It depicts the saintly tenth-century Doge Pietro Orseolo I and his wife Felicita Malipiero at prayer in a loggia whose peeling brick wall is adorned with a nude marble torso, a classical relief, and a marine sarcophagus.[69] While the doge and his consort were especially revered for their sanctity, the display of classical artifacts in the picture would seem to have more to do with "an escalating taste for collecting such items" than a consciously moralizing message about the triumph of Christianity over the art of the pagans.[70]

Returning once more to the pious Girolamo Donato, it may be noted that he did not return home empty-handed from his term as podestà in Ravenna. A Roman statue of a male figure in a toga still stands to this day in a niche in the courtyard of the Donà family palace at San Stin (Plate 276). Furthermore, according to a history of Ravenna written in 1572, Donato also took with him an "equestre simulacrum e marmore" – an equestrian statue of marble – thought to represent Attila, that once stood near the Basilica Ursiana. But such an object, if it ever existed, has vanished without a trace.[71]

Scattered notices also suggest that the market for Greek *anticaglie* that would flourish in sixteenth-century Venice was already well established by the last decade of the quattrocento.[72] When Poliziano visited Zaccaria Barbaro in 1492, he wrote back to Lorenzo de' Medici that "the said

275   School of Giovanni Bellini, *Doge Pietro Orseolo I and his Wife Felicita Malipiero at Prayer*, c.1490. Wood panel, 19.5 × 30.2 cm. Venice, Museo Civico Correr.

Zaccaria showed me a most beautiful and most ancient vase of clay this morning, that had recently been sent to him from Greece." Zaccaria wanted to present the vase to Lorenzo as a gift, and Poliziano agreed to transport it. His letter continues: "I believe that you do not have one so beautiful of this type; it is nearly three spans high and four wide."[73] Zaccaria knew well the binding power of a gift in that world of patronage, returnable favors, and reciprocal obligations.

Two interrelated phenomena suggest that classical artifacts were now becoming a programmatic part of a new aesthetic environment that embraced the religious as well as the secular, and the private as well the public world: the restoration of damaged, but genuine, antiquities; and the counterfeiting of

276   Giovanni Grevembroch, *Roman statue brought from Ravenna by Girolamo Donato*, in his *Monumenta Veneta*, eighteenth century. Venice, Biblioteca Correr, Cod. Gradenigo 228, *c*.43.

277   *Muse of Philiskos*, antique fragment from the late Hellenistic period with restorations by Tullio Lombardo. Marble, h. 109.5 cm. Venice, Museo Archeologico.

classical objects by modern artists. We have already heard about the "nose of wax" that had been added to the Bellini family's bust of Plato.[74] An even more ambitious undertaking involved the total refurbishment by Tullio Lombardo of a Hellenistic sculpture of a Muse, now in the Archaeological Museum in Venice (Plate 277). Drawing upon medal reverses for inspiration, the sculptor added not only an arm, a foot, and parts of the drapery, but also the entire head, and equipped the figure with attributes that changed her into a Cleopatra. As Debra Pincus observes, the result was more transformation than restoration, and the resulting style, while quite convincingly antique, is "curiously neither Greek nor Roman but partakes of the flavor of both."[75]

278 Venetian artist, *Scene of Leavetaking*, Renaissance imitation of classical relief. Marble, *c*.1520. Vienna, Kunsthistorisches Museum.

As Simone Bianco's portrait busts attest, marble sculptors were no less ingenious than medalists in crafting objects *ex novo* with a distinct and perhaps deliberately misleading *all'antica* appearance. Half-sized statues of a nude Venus and an Apollo that had been carved by the Milanese sculptor Cristoforo Solari were inspected in 1494 by a visitor to the Venetian home of the galley captain Giorgio Dragan. The first work was compared favorably with the Cnidian Venus of Praxiteles and the second with the Apollo Belvedere, which was then in the garden of Cardinal Giuliano della Rovere in Rome.[76]

Another gifted forger carved a credible imitation of a classical Greek relief by augmenting two figures copied from an authentic Attic stele with another pair freely adapted from Michelangelo's *David* and *Risen Christ* (Plate 278). Deliberately chiseling off part of the leg and foot of the seated man, the sculptor left the top edge and right side unfinished to look as if the plaque was worn away over time. Panofsky concludes that the deception depended on the fact that neither the artist nor his patrons could distinguish between the ancient and the modern "classical" styles, but perhaps such an insight misses the point. Indeed, Marcantonio Michiel's sharp awareness of fakes such as this suggests that clever imitations were recognized, admired, and collected for what they were.[77]

AN ANTIQUE AMBIENCE

Inevitably, the same classical objects and motifs that proved so irresistible to artists and patrons in monumental art in public space and in small-scale genres such as medals and book illustration in the private sphere would begin to transform the Venetian family palace. A growing number of patricians – well traveled and more than conscious of the importance of material goods for personal identity – wanted their living spaces to be decorated "in the antique manner." Such tastes are expressed in a letter describing a mission to Rome in 1505 where Girolamo Donato, Bernardo Bembo, and Andrea Gritti attended a dinner described by Sanudo as "luculentissimo" in the palace of Cardinal Domenico Grimani.[78] There the visitors were privy to an early showing of one of the great Venetian collections of Roman antiquities of the century.[79] The writer's aesthetic preferences were clear in his admiring account of the "antique festoons," a door frame with "white columns, capitals, and bases worked in the antique manner," vases of silver and gold "nobly crafted in the antique manner, in form as well as in foliage reliefs and carving."[80] The cardinal conducted the Venetian orators to his private chamber where he showed them his library, "stocked with the greatest quantity of the most beautiful books, and a great number of figures of marble, and many other *cosse antiche*, all found at his *vigna* under the ground, while excavating for the construction of his palace, that is being built there."[81] Domenico Grimani's collection had its nucleus here, an eventual Roman legacy to Venice that had been retrieved directly from Roman soil. Domenico's nephew Giovanni Grimani would, however, exceed him in the breadth of his collection, which came to comprise an important corpus of Greek as well as Roman antiquities.[82]

Two paintings depicting aristocratic interiors, admittedly idealized, provide a sense of decorating conventions in Venice itself at the turn of the century: Carpaccio's *Dream of St. Ursula* (1495) and Mansueti's *The Healing of the Daughter of Ser Benvegnudo of San Polo* (*c*.1506) (Plates 279 and 280). Each example indicates a partial assimilation of classical elements into the prevailing Gothic aesthetic without sacrificing the rich ornamentation of gold and color that was so beloved by Venetians. Cusped windows are now replaced with round-headed openings, and pilasters, balustrades, and wainscoting are carved with the familiar Renaissance-style foliate forms of the Lombardi. While each room contains a traditional icon of the Virgin illuminated with a votive lamp, and the fireplace in Mansueti's painting features two figures in modern dress, there are distinctive classicizing intrusions in the form of small nude figurines which stand on the doorway lintels.[83]

Carpaccio's *St. Augustine in his Study* yields a few more objects of interest, as befits the *studiolo* of a humanist (Plate 281). Arranged on a cornice below a shelf full of books are some ceramic vases in the geometric style of Puglia, two bronze figurines – a female nude and a horse – and several small slender objects that could be *calchi* – plaster casts of antique coins and medals.[84] Some of these pieces were surely *anticaglie*, as a wide range of classical artifacts and curiosities were called.

279   Vittore Carpaccio, *Dream of St. Ursula*, 1495. Canvas, 274 × 267 cm. Venice, Accademia.

Marcantonio Michiel's inventories of aristocratic rooms written a few decades later suggest that genuine antiques brought a higher price because of rarity, but he reveals little sense of an aesthetic hierarchy that privileged classical objects over modern, or that separated one from the other in their actual display. Antonio Pasqualino owned a modern "marble head of a woman with her mouth open" – a description suggestive of Tullio's portrait busts – that he had received from Gabriele Vendramin in exchange for an antique marble torso.[85] Andrea Odoni's groundfloor courtyard held the marble heads of Hercules and Cybele by the contemporary sculptor Antonio Minello along with two antique marble

280　Giovanni Mansueti, *The Healing of the Daughter of Ser Benvegnudo of San Polo* (detail), *c.*1506. Canvas, 359 × 296 cm. Venice, Accademia.

busts, the headless figure of a walking man, and also a number of fragments. Most of the latter were classical, but one was intentionally manufactured: "The entire marble foot upon a base was executed by Simone Bianco."[86]

Marin Sanudo, that voracious collector of facts, both momentous and trivial, satisfied his acquisitive urges with a novel collection that expressed his ethnographic interests. Not a wealthy man, he assembled, among other things, a series of *quadri* with depictions of the fashions of the principal European nations and the variety of human races living in the ancient and in the recently discovered New World. Federico da Porto of Vicenza visited the palace and praised a satisfying density of clutter, exclaiming: "And here we entered a new sea of things; nor can a wall be seen anywhere: not any part is empty." He adds: "Whoever wishes to understand the sea, the earth and the vast world, Should behold this house of yours, learned Marino."[87]

In his *Ricordi* published in 1546, Sabba da Castiglione advised that some gentlemen

> decorate their houses with antiques, such as heads, torsos, busts, and ancient marble or bronze statues. But since good ancient works, being scarce, cannot be obtained without the greatest difficulty and expense, they decorate it with the works of Donatello . . . or with the works of Michelangelo . . . or other modern artists.[88]

Himself a knight of the Order of Rhodes and but "a poor gentleman," Sabba decorated his own "little studio" with a marble head of John the Baptist by Donatello, a terracotta figure of St. Jerome by another artist, three intarsia panels of religious subjects, and "an ancient urn of oriental alabaster, with some veins of chalcedony; it is certainly not inferior to any vase of alabaster that I have seen to this moment, although I have seen many in Rome and other places . . ."[89] The

281　Vittore Carpaccio, *St. Augustine in his Study* (detail), *c.*1502–3. Oil and tempera on canvas, 141 × 211 cm (entire). Venice, Scuola di San Giorgio degli Schiavoni.

VICTOR
CARPATHIVS
FINGEBAT

282 Andrea Mantegna, *The Introduction of the Cult of Cybele in Rome*, 1506. Canvas, 73.5 × 268 cm. London, National Gallery. Reproduced by courtesy of the Trustees, The National Gallery, London.

centuries-old Venetian aesthetic of incorporation was now being transformed into a modern paradigm of ambience.

PAINTED FRIEZES

While objects of a classical character had thus begun to invade the Venetian home by the early sixteenth century, little is known about mural decoration. Writing in the seventeenth century, Carlo Ridolfi cited major works – probably canvases – by Giovanni Bellini that have vanished without a trace: "In Venice in Ca' Grimani at San Marcuola [Bellini] painted in the Sala two large pictures of *Cosmografia* with the figures of Ptolemy, Strabo, Pliny, and Pomponius Mela, and he signed them with his own name."[90]

However, portions of two important projects do survive: a cycle of scenes from Roman history commissioned by the wealthy Francesco Cornaro for his family palace in Venice; and frescoes depicting the Liberal and the Mechanical Arts still *in situ* in a modest house in Castelfranco Veneto – admittedly outside Venice proper, but a revealing indication of a new mentality that many Venetians would have shared. Consisting of painted friezes about seventy-five centimeters high that run along the walls just below the ceiling, they might be considered domesticated versions of the narrative painting cycles in the meeting rooms of the *scuole*.[91] But there the similarity between the two programs stops; for each draws upon the classical tradition in different ways: with different media, different subject matter, different ends, and, ultimately, different artistic visions.

The dignity of the Cornelian line

Upon his formal entry into Verona as bishop in 1504, the Venetian patrician Marco Cornaro was greeted with familiar and altogether satisfying words of welcome by the humanist Hieronimo Avanzi:

> Neither shall we celebrate in a fashion worthy of its dignity the Cornelian line, which as Sextus Pompeius Festus asserts, is ancient and noble above all the other families of Europe and is rich in splendid deeds performed in every age. Famous forever is he [Scipio Africanus] who, as Cicero writes, compelled Hannibal, till then unconquered, to depart from Italy and return to Africa . . . Another of your race [Publius Cornelius Scipio the Younger] is adorned with extraordinary glory because he razed two cities utterly hostile to the Roman power, Carthage and Numantia. L. Cornelius Nasica was adjudged the best of all men known from the beginning of time.[92]

The oration, in which the virtues of the Cornaro family of the present day were linked directly to their illustrious Roman forebears, could have served just as well as a program for the cycle of four paintings commissioned from Mantegna by Marco's brother Francesco just the next year. But the artist finished only one canvas before his death in 1506, *The Introduction of the Cult of Cybele in Rome* (Plate 282).[93] It would have been then that Cornaro turned to Giovanni Bellini who, with the help of his workshop, completed *The Continence of Scipio*, possibly from a drawing by Mantegna (Plate 283).[94] Each work celebrates the private virtues of an ancient member

252

of the *gens Cornelia* as these were expressed in his public deeds.[95]

Mantegna's painting depicts an episode that took place during the Second Punic war in 204 B.C.[96] Upon consulting the Sybilline Books, the Romans learned that they could ensure victory by bringing the Mother Goddess Cybele from Mount Ida to Rome where she was to be received by the worthiest man. By a vote of the Roman senate, this honor was bestowed upon Scipio Nasica, "not yet of an age to be quaestor" and a cousin of Scipio Africanus. Mantegna chose the moment of reception to epitomize this chain of events. On the left a priest and three acolytes rush in with a litter bearing a bust of the goddess, and the young Scipio Nasica demonstrates his singular virtue by falling to his knees before her. Two tombs in the background bear inscriptions of other Cornelii who died heroically in Spain – one honoring Scipio Nasica's father, Gnaeus Scipio, and the other his uncle Publius Scipio the Elder – that leave no doubt as to the genealogical tenor of the work.[97]

The formal terms had been set by Mantegna; with his demise, Giovanni Bellini may well have been faced with a challenge that was not to his liking. That he would not have been eager to take on such an assignment is suggested by his refusal to paint an allegorical painting for Isabella d'Este a few years earlier. He stated at the time that he did not want to compete with the artistry of his brother-in-law Mantegna and resisted, moreover, rigid specifications. As Pietro Bembo commented, "Very precise terms do not suit his style, being accustomed, as he says, always to roam at will in paintings."[98] And yet perhaps moved by a sense of filial duty (or an awareness that Mantegna would never see the finished product), Giovanni took on the task of painting *The Conti-*

nence of Scipio, an episode from the life of another Cornaro ancestor, Publius Cornelius Scipio Africanus. The work depicts Scipio addressing a group of Iberian hostages after the fall of Cartagena. Among them was a beautiful maiden whom Scipio could have taken for himself by right of conquest. But when told that she was of good family and already engaged to be married, he demonstrated his virtue not only by allowing her to return to her fiancé unharmed but also by restoring to her dowry the gold brought by her parents as ransom.[99]

As high drama is countered with poetic prose, Giovanni's placid handling of the theme as a quietly unfolding procession sums up the essential difference between Mantegna's dynamic view of the past and his own.[100] To Mantegna, the Paduan, antiquity is a challenge; to Bellini, the Venetian, it is a retreat.

Time the devourer, virtue the vanquisher

If the Cornaro program is the portrayal of a family's place in history in a biographical, if exemplary, sense, the painted frieze in the Casa Marta-Pellizzari (or the so-called Casa di Giorgione) in Castelfranco Veneto is the portrayal of man's place in history in a metaphysical sense. The fresco, running along the two long sides of the room, features a sequence of objects in *trompe l'oeil* that epitomize the life of the mind and the life of action: implements of the liberal and the mechanical arts, plaques and *cartellini* that bear edifying mottoes, and medallion heads of wise men and emperors.[101]

A classicizing decorative vocabulary embracing objects of learning and war was by now well established in the Venetian milieu in virtually every artistic medium: on book frontispieces, in the *Hypnerotomachia Poliphili*, in intarsia inlay work, in the low relief sculpted friezes on the Scala dei Giganti, and on the frescoed surrounds of funerary monuments.[102] Although the Giorgionesque spirit of the work in Castelfranco has long been recognized, no contemporary documents survive to identify either the patron or the artist. Several mistakes in the Latin suggest that the former was a man of limited erudition, but the intellectual interests and ideas expressed by imagery are characteristic of Veneto humanism.[103] As to the artist, the influences of Mantegna, Rizzo, and the Lombardi come together in the frieze through the brush of an original artist with a capacity for synthesis. Most writers now associate the program with the young Giorgione.[104]

The *concetto* of the Castelfranco frieze is rooted in two fundamental ideas: an awareness of the transience of man with the limits that finite time imposes on him; and the capacity of individual virtue to overcome those limits. The cycle has an expository character that recalls Aretino's *strambotti* on time. Beginning with an initial premise, it offers a number of examples and finally comes to a resolution. The primary ethical theme is announced by two mottoes in the first tableau of the cycle (Plate 284). Flanking a medallion of a bearded elderly man wearing a turban, perhaps Averroes, they warn:

283 Giovanni Bellini, *The Continence of Publius Cornelius Scipio*, shortly after 1506. Canvas, 74.8 × 356.2 cm. Washington, D.C., National Gallery of Art. Samuel H. Kress Collection.

"Our time is only the passing of a shadow," and "Only virtue is held to be luminous and eternal." Significantly, the first phrase is taken from the Bible and the second from the pagan author Sallust.[105]

This portion of the frieze is concerned with the liberal arts. Flanking the mottoes are instruments of scholarship, philological studies, and scientific measurement. After two epigrams counseling reason as an antidote to fortune, the frieze continues with symbols of the active life and military virtue, such as helmets, halberds, and spears. It returns to the arts with an assortment of musical instruments celebrating the humanist ideal of harmony and concludes on this wall with the apparatus of the painter: an easel, plaster casts of antique gems, pens, brushes, colors, a perspective treatise, and even a panel with a sketch of a satyr or satyress and a putto. A plaque offers further counsel that the prudent man should look toward the future.[106]

Moving across the room, there is a shift in emphasis and a change in tone (Plate 285). The mechanical arts take their place alongside more intellectual pursuits, and the mood darkens, with emblems of war and death more tightly juxtaposed with emblems of love, harmony, and creativity. Military armor and weapons and a collection of musical instruments are divided by cartouches with messages of despair and of hope: "Time wastes all things," and "Virtue vanquishes all things."[107]

The focus then turns to symbols of the mechanical arts and of the secret power of love. In a much damaged section of the frieze, a cartouche carries the drawing of a female nude and an erote, perhaps Venus and Cupid. Another placard nearby holds a motto taken from Publilius Syrus: "The lover knows what he desires, he does not see what he should be wise in."[108] At the end of the frieze, the face of death is painted on a pallet, and a cartouche counsels the wise man to "consider [the end of] all things."[109] The cycle is grounded in paradox. Man's works are ephemeral, and yet it is only through these works and his own virtue that he can approach immortality.[110]

The Castelfranco frieze and the Cornaro canvases offer differing views of time, of history and, most significantly, of the role played by virtue in human affairs. In the frieze, virtue is the personal means by which man can transcend time; in the Cornaro paintings, virtue is an inherited quality that legitimizes present privilege.

Few paintings were so obviously genealogical as those commissioned by Francesco Cornaro. However, Giorgione's Dresden *Venus*, which seems to have been painted for the marriage in 1507 of Girolamo Marcello to Morosina Pisani, may have been a more graceful and less direct reminder of even more ancient roots. According to a Marcello family tradition, the line could be traced back not just to a Roman progenitor, but to Venus herself. Other paintings of the time whose veiled meanings are elusive now may well have been inspired by similar motives of family pride.[111]

PATRICIAN MAGNIFICENCE

The Venetian aesthetic of diversity allowed for the antique to be appropriated in its various forms for private pleasure inside palace walls, but a consistent classical style was curiously slow to take hold in palace architecture. Aside from the difficulties of fitting symmetrical, regularly ordered structures into exist-

ing Venetian sites, ideological considerations may have engendered resistence to a new Roman architectural vocabulary in private buildings. At stake was the cherished principle of *mediocritas* – the equality *ab origine* of the patriciate. Sanudo stated the foundation myth in his *De origine* of 1493, writing that the early inhabitants of the lagoon had

> attended to trade with their *barchette*, carrying salt and fish to nearby shores; they were not proud nor did they esteem riches, although they were rich, but piety and innocence. They did not dress ornately, nor did they seek honor, but assembled and chosen for the good of the Commune, they entered government; there was not any difference [between them], and Cassiodorus wrote this in his epistle: The poor live here with the wealthy under equality . . .[112]

Manfredo Tafuri has proposed that the ideal of *aequalitate* could accommodate the well-established Gothic style in palace architecture, no matter how ornate, but was threatened by the novel Albertian classical style, no matter how austere, because it was associated with Rome.[113] In any event, a broadly accepted theory of magnificence similar to that which was developing in Florence would not emerge in Venice until the later sixteenth century.

It was still possible, however, to celebrate the family with the help of carefully chosen and historically resonant architectural details, and classical elements began to appear piecemeal on palace façades by the middle of the fifteenth century. The family palace of Vettore Dandolo, rebuilt in 1475 in the traditional Gothic style, featured an epigraphical approach. Demolished at the beginning of the nineteenth century, the structure was still an imposing presence near the church of San Pantalon in the Barbari *View of Venice* of 1500. For the

inscription in the architrave above the main portal, Dandolo borrowed the two systems of dating that appeared on the recently constructed classical portal of the Arsenale:

FALETRAS DOMOS VETVSTATE COLLAPSAS VICTOR D[ANDOLO]
BENEDICTI. LOB. MEMORIAM MVNERI MATERNI AMPLE RESTITVIT
ANNO SALVAT[ION]IS MCCCCLXXV AB VRBE CONDITA ML.IIII

Dedicating the project to the memory of his mother Cristina Falier (Faletro), Dandolo made transparently clear the family's place in the history of the city: *ab incarnatione* (1475) and *ab urbe condita* (1054), the latter date calculated from the mythic foundation of 421. According to the document purportedly discovered by Giovanni Dondi back in the fourteenth century, an Albertus Falerius or Faletrus was one of the three Paduan consuls present at Rialto on that momentous occasion. Any of Vettore Dandolo's compatriots with even the most superficial knowledge of civic history would have read the inscription and immediately understood the allusion.[114]

Inscriptions in the antique mode also served to rationalize construction that was either untraditional in style or ostentatious in scale. Giovanni Dario, the wealthy *cittadino* and secretary to the Council of Ten, had often been praised in state documents for his prudence and discretion. When he built a striking new palace on the Grand Canal, resplendent with polychrome inlays on the model of Pietro Lombardo's new church of Santa Maria dei Miracoli, he demonstrated his diplomatic skills as well (Plate 286). The monumental epigram in good classical Latin and proper Roman characters that runs across the lower part of the façade serves as his personal deed of gift: "VRBIS GENIO IOHANNES DARIUS" (To the genius of the city, Giovanni Dario).[115]

The Trevisan family followed suit on the façade of their

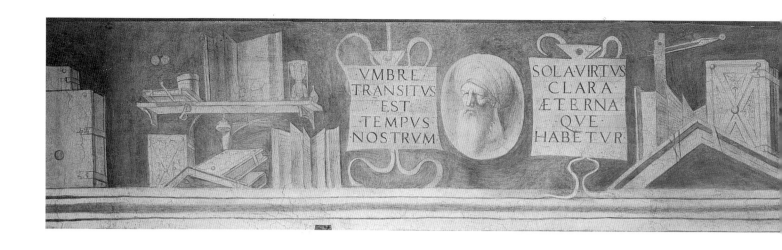

UMBRE
TRANSITVS
EST
TEMPVS
NOSTRVM

SOLA·VIRTVS
CLARA
ÆTERNA
QVE
HABETVR

FORTVNA
NEMINI
PLVS
QVAM
CONSILIVM
VALET·

FORTIOR·QVI
CVPIDITATEM
VINCIT
QVAM
QVI
HOSTEM
SVBIICIT·

LIVS
ANT

SI
PRVDENS
ESSE
CVPIS
IN·FVTVRA
PROSPICIVM
INTENDE

QVI IN
SVIS ACTIBVS
RATIONE DVO
DIRIGVNTVR
IRAM CELI
EFFVGERE
POSSVNT

E PE
RTVS
IN
OSTE
VDATVR

VER
DV
MV

284   Giorgione, frieze with attributes of the Liberal Arts, c.1500. Fresco (east
wall), 78 × 1588 cm. Castelfranco, Casa Marta-Pellizzari.

285 Giorgione, frieze with attributes of the Liberal and Mechanical Arts, *c.*1500. Fresco (west wall), 76 × 1574 cm. Castelfranco, Casa Marta–Pellizzari.

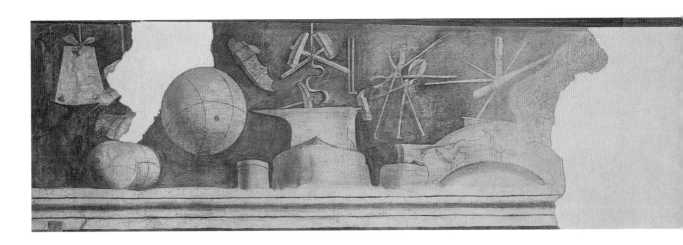

AMANS·QVID·
CVPIT·
SIT·
QVID·SAPIAT·
NON·
VIDET

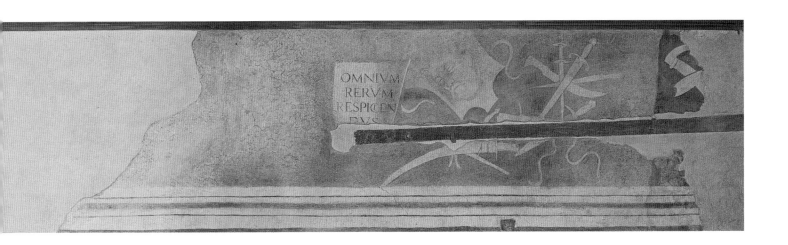

OMNIVM·
RERVM·
RESPICEN
DVS

superimposed Corinthian orders and follows Albertian precepts, but the wall surfaces are encrusted with colored marbles for a restrained and subtly sumptuous effect. A prominent inscription was in order: "NON NOBIS D[OMI]NE, NON NOBIS" (Not unto us Lord, Not unto us). And now it required the spectator to complete it from his knowledge of the scriptures: "But unto Thy name be the glory given" (Psalms 115). In the Venetian context, all such avowals would have had less to do with religious piety pure and simple than with the desire to fend off charges of extravagance and uncollegial vainglory.[118]

Among the figurative elements employed in the new *all'antica* decorative mode, the inexhaustible repertory of Roman portrait heads again proved its utility. For Carpaccio, profile portraits in roundels were sure signs of classicizing *dignitas* in his narrative paintings for the *scuole*,[119] but classical busts also appeared occasionally on real palace façades, such as Ca' Bembo at Campo Santa Maria Formosa. Reconstructed by the Trevisan family in the early years of the sixteenth century, it features a symmetrical elevation with classical orders in a central block, polychrome encrustation and a much admired white marble façade. Decorating the cornice just below the roofline are eight tondi containing heads in the mode of Roman cameos (though no longer in profile) that, significantly, flank a medallion with the monogram of the Holy Name of Christ: "IHS" (Plate 287).[120]

Perhaps the most programmatic use of genuine Roman portraiture for façade decoration is found on Ca' Zorzi-Bon. Here an antique Roman bust, probably of the Emperor Lucius Verus, occupies a niche high on the façade between the ogival arches of a trecento bifora window of the third

286   Pietro Lombardo, attr., Ca' Dario, 1487. Venice, Grand Canal.

marble encrusted palace built around 1500 behind the ducal palace on the Rio della Canonica. Enjoying full patrician status, they drew upon the New Testament (1 Timothy 1: 17) to present their building activity as an act of civic *pietas*: "SOLI DEO / HONOR ET GLORIA" (To God alone, Honor and Glory).[116] When Mauro Codussi built a palace for the patrician Andrea Loredan (now the Palazzo Vendramin-Calergi) at San Marcuola on the Grand Canal during the following decade, he achieved the most thoroughgoing synthesis to date of Venetian tradition and classical principles in residential architecture (Plate 288).[117] The entire façade is articulated by three

287   Ca' Bembo, detail of façade, early sixteenth century. Venice, Campo Santa Maria Formosa.

story. In the manner of St. Theodore on the Piazzetta column, the bust was transformed into St. George, the tutelary saint of the Zorzi family, with the addition of a halo, an arm holding a lance, and a crusader's shield.[121]

288 Mauro Codussi, Palazzo Vendramin-Calergi, 1500–9. Venice, Grand Canal.

Classical erudition, if not lineage, could also be evoked in paint. Although the lost frescoes of the Fondaco dei Tedeschi painted by Giorgione and Titian in 1508–9 have received a good amount of scholarly attention, they were not unique. Indeed, Venice was already becoming an *urbs picta* by the end of the fifteenth century. In 1495 on a trip along the Grand Canal, Philippe de Commynes had observed: "The palaces are very large and tall, and of good stone, and the old ones all painted."[122] The earliest such decorations highlighted parts of buildings with feigned masonry or festoons, tapestries, and carpets, but figurative motifs and grotesques of an antique character – vegetal, animal, and human – became increasingly popular over time. Unlike façade paintings in Florence and Rome, which tended to be in grisaille, the Venetian frescoes were typically painted in polychrome. Sixty-eight such palace façades are recorded, seven of them attributable to Giorgione, who painted them with such mythological figures as Bacchus,

Venus, Mars, and Mercury, as well as with poets, musicians, and female nudes.[123]

One of the most renowned programs was the palace façade painted for the wealthy Flemish merchant Martino d'Anna by Pordenone in 1531–2.[124] Anton Francesco Doni advised a visitor in 1549 to see in Venice only "the four divine horses; the works of the painter Giorgione da Castel Franco; the history painting of Titian, a most excellent man, in the Palazzo [Ducale]; the façade of the house painted by Pordenone on the Grand Canal; an altarpiece by Albrecht Dürer in San Bartolomeo," and few other things.[125] A surviving drawing, probably by Pordenone's own hand, records a scheme in which the architectonic articulation of the façade as a whole serves as a framing system for an elaborate program of *historie* and allegorical figures (Plate 289). It included Marcus Curtius and the Rape of the Sabines on the lower floor, with the Rape of Proserpina above the entrance

289 Giovanni Antonio Pordenone, *Façade of Palazzo Martino d'Anna*, preparatory drawing for fresco program. Pen and brown ink, 41.2 × 55.9 cm. London, Victoria and Albert Museum. By courtesy of the Board of Trustees of the Victoria and Albert Museum.

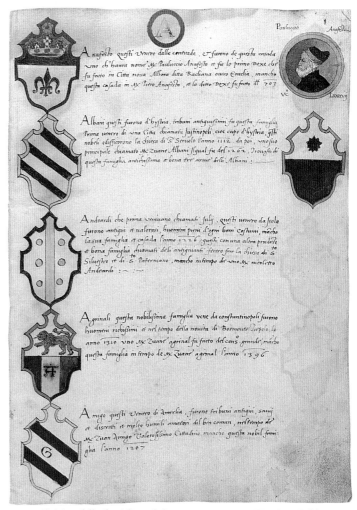

290 *Origine delle famiglie nobeli venete*, 1559–67. Venice, Biblioteca Nazionale Marciana, Cod. It. VII 105 (7732), *c*.1r.

portal; two mythological scenes and four figures of the arts on the piano nobile; and allegories of Time and Fame in the attic zone.[126]

By 1537, Sebastiano Serlio was aware of the "deconstructive" side of this chromatic urban spectacle, and criticized painters who were so intent on creating a rich coloristic effect that they ignored the integrity of the architectonic structure: "for those things break up the building, and transform a solid, material form into a transparent one, without strength, like a ruinous and imperfect building."[127] Although one might imagine that few Venetians would have agreed with such an aesthetic judgment, Time itself was the final arbiter. As Vasari observed, the frescoes began to deteriorate as soon as they were painted in the damp Venetian climate.

The events of the early sixteenth century, particularly the Wars of Cambrai, put the communal ethos to the test. Those who maintained that Venice's prosperity and security lay in maintaining the primitive virtue of her citizens were increasingly challenged by the *Primi*, a small group of families with ties to Rome who sought to consolidate their own power at the expense of the time-honored principle of patrician equality. A rigorous sumptuary law passed in 1512 as part of the austerity measures occasioned by the war seems to have been largely ignored, if not defiantly flaunted. Doge Leonardo Loredan confessed that even he had had the *lanziera di arme* – the traditional patrician display of weaponry in the *portego* –

dismantled in his palace in order to make room for tables for more lavish banquets.[128]

Rivalries were also played out in a new literary genre that appeared in this period: the illustrated genealogy (Plate 290). When Pietro Bernardo wrote his testament in 1515, he ordered an elaborate tomb of marble that should cost 600 ducats and "a book of 800 verses [that would celebrate] the glories of the Bernardo family."[129] Following the model of the citizen chronicle, where family history was recounted in the context of the history of the city, many of these new compilations appended a list of the entire patriciate, each represented by its coat-of-arms, to the history of the individual family.[130] Although some aristocratic families were clearly more equal than others in wealth, all were – in theory – equal in nobility.

12

A NEW TRIUMPHAL VOCABULARY

This city, amidst the billowing waves of the sea, stands on the crest of the open main, almost like a queen restraining its force . . . As another writer has said, its name has achieved such dignity and renown that it is fair to say it may deservedly be called the "Pillar of Italy," of the races of Christianity [and] of the Christian nations. For it takes pride of place before all others, if I may say so, in prudence, fortitude, magnificence, benignity and clemency; everyone throughout the world testifies to this. To conclude, this city was built more by divine than human will . . .

– Marin Sanudo, *Laus urbis Venetae*, 1493[1]

By the end of the fifteenth century, Venetians no longer needed to invent a civic past. The nascent themes articulated by John the Deacon back in the eleventh century, and further elaborated in visual, as well as in literary, terms in the centuries that followed, had long ago come to fruition in the "myth of Venice."[2] And yet, further refinements were possible. As Sanudo's reference to divine agency suggests, efforts continued to position Venice within a majestic, all-embracing teleology.

The problem now was one of redefinition, as Venice's power base shifted from East to West. As already seen, two responses were deployed in tandem: a conceptual appropriation of the Byzantine East, just as it was slipping away, and a strengthened identification with the West, along with claims of Roman prerogatives and legitimacy. By the early years of the cinquecento, new initatives in self-presentation were played out in a reaching back to the imagery of the classical world to expand the temporal and spatial parameters of the republic, in assertions of continuity in both human and political terms, and in restatements of the age-old principle of strength through diversity.

OLYMPIAN PROTECTORS

An expanded *all'antica* cosmology had already been presaged by the enthusiastic response of Venice's historians to the recently calculated civic horoscope.[3] It was announced, as

well, by the mythological personae who had come to inhabit tomb monuments and civic architecture of an ever more classicizing cast. Perhaps inevitably, Venice's pantheon of heavenly protectors was coming to include the pagan gods who took their place alongside the Virgin, St. Mark, and St. Theodore.

Nowhere is this appropriation expressed more eloquently than in Jacopo de' Barbari's *View of Venice* of 1500. According to Anton Kolb, the German merchant who had sponsored the publication of the huge twelve-sheet woodcut "principally for the *fama* of this illustrious city of Venice," it was a labor of the highest difficulty and had taken three years to complete. Just as the map itself is the physical embodiment of the state, the powerful nude figures of Mercury and Neptune are incarnations of its secular spirit (Plate 291).[4]

Seated on a cloud in the skies above Venice, Mercury, the patron of commerce and trade, looks down into the heart of the city and promises: "I Mercury shine favorably on this above all other emporia." It is no accident that Rialto and the Piazza San Marco complex – the most important centers of commercial, political and civic-religious life – are directly on axis beneath him. Looking up to Mercury as if his partner, Neptune sits astride a dolphin and rides the waves of the lagoon below, directly in front of the Palazzo Ducale. He holds a trident with a placard that bears his own pledge of protection: "I Neptune reside here, smoothing the waters at this port." Augmented by the eight winds from the various parts of the world which provided the source of energy for

291 Jacopo de' Barbari, *View of Venice*, detail with Mercury and Neptune, 1500. Woodcut. Venice, Museo Civico Correr.

292 Andrea del Verrocchio (horse and rider) and Alessandro Leopardi (base), equestrian monument to Bartolomeo Colleoni, 1496. Marble. Venice, Campo SS. Giovanni e Paolo.

the great galleys, these powerful protectors of *marchadantia* were the optimum tutelary spirits of a great trading nation with imperial ambitions.[5]

Venice's marine hegemony was again reasserted in the decoration of three bronze flagpole bases or pedestals in front of the Basilica of San Marco, the first major project of civic art patronage of the new century.[6] The sculptor of the pedestals, Alessandro Leopardi, was the bronze-caster who had cast

Verrocchio's equestrian statue of Bartolomeo Colleoni and installed it on a high base of his own design in the Campo SS. Giovanni e Paolo. Completed in 1496, the monument gave Leopardi immediate acclaim and the nickname "Alessandro del Cavallo." While he may have earned borrowed credit for Verrocchio's horse, the base was no small feat in itself (Plate 292). It was crafted from an elegant combination of polychrome marbles and featured a classical entablature originally decorated with a gilded bronze frieze. Designed with a nonpedantic and imaginative classicism, it included the *tabula ansata*, *rinceaux*, and displays of trophies that were beloved components of the Venetian *all'antica* vocabulary. The bold design of the base attests to Leopardi's originality and ability to respond to the challenge of a novel project. It almost earned him a commission to design historiated bronze doors for the Porta della Carta, a project that was announced by the Council of Ten in January 1496 – perhaps as part of the Byzantine revival of those years – but never carried out. He was granted, nonetheless, a salary and worked on several state projects before taking on the assignment for the pedestals of the Piazza San Marco.[7]

Harbingers of the eventual transformation *all'antica* of the Piazzetta area with Jacopo Sansovino's architectural projects four decades later, the pedestals were shaped like monumental antique candelabra (Plate 293). Each consisted of four tiers: at the bottom, a cylindrical base decorated with a frieze in the manner of a Roman altar and featuring a continuous file of marine figures; then a concave unit with three protomes of a luxuriantly winged lion of St. Mark; above that an urn-shaped section decorated with foliate and figural reliefs; and finally a crowning element with a swelling, cushion shaped receptacle to hold the flagpole.[8]

Sanudo recorded the unveiling of the first pedestal on the fifteenth of August in 1505: the feast of the Assumption of the Virgin celebrated each year by the attendance of the doge at Mass in San Marco along with the foreign orators in residence.[9] The day was obviously a well-considered choice and, it would appear, an astrally favored one as well:

> it was the day of Our Lady. And it should be known that yesterday evening there was an eclipse of the moon at two hours of night. And this morning the installation was completed in the Piazza San Marco of the bronze pedestals – that is, the one in the middle – made by Alessandro di Leopardi to hold the standards [banners]. The other two are still being made. And the Collegio appointed Ser Daniel di Renier to oversee the making of the standards. The Procurators of the Church [of San Marco] were sier Polo Barbo, sier Nicolò Trevisan, and sier Marco Antonio Morosini, the cavalier.[10]

That the pedestal was unveiled on a civically resonant Marian feast day was man's design; but the lunar eclipse was a sign from the heavens. Although Sanudo did not make a point of it, the conjunction of astral phenomenon and civic event must

program of the pedestals survives, Pietro Contarini included a detailed interpretation in his *Argoa voluptas*, published in Latin in 1541 and in Italian translation as *L'Argoa volgar*, probably the following year. His description is credible, and may well be a copy of the original program.[13] According to Contarini, the two pedestals at the sides featured a continuous file of sea creatures moving around the base in a counter-clockwise direction: nereids, tritons, and sirens who had seemingly floated out of the pages of Ovid and Virgil. Or, closer to hand, they might be considered the ideal realization of the mythological protagonists of a Venetian *momaria*.[14]

On the north pedestal, toward the newly erected Torre dell'Orologio, were the "Lords of the Sea": Thetis, Glaucus who supports Scylla on his tail whilst caressing her thigh, Peleus and Palemon, and Phorkys and his daughter Euriale

294 Alessandro Leopardi, north flagpole base, detail with Glaucus and Scylla, 1506. Bronze. Venice, Piazza San Marco.

(Plate 294). Most of the other figures hold baskets, cornucopias, or seashells filled with fruits of the land and the sea.[15]

The pedestal on the south, toward the Campanile, included Galatea, Galena, the nymph who calms the seas, Nereus, Amphitrite and, according to Contarini, "the lord of the Sea, Ennosygeo [Neptune], who has black hair, and brandishes the great trident in his right hand, [and] who commands the gods that they should take all the fruits of the sea to sell in the Venetian forum . . ."[16]

The friezes on the two flanking pedestals were, however, only a frame for the central one, for in Contarini's view, it displays the defining conceptual theme of the program:

The one in the middle shows three ships coming from the high seas. On the stern of the first ship one sees the golden Virgin of the Pole [i.e. Astraea, goddess of justice], who having been exiled by the wicked world, has fixed her abode in Venetian waters. In her right hand she has the

293 Alessandro Leopardi, central flagpole base, 1505. Bronze. Venice, Piazza San Marco.

have spoken for itself, and would not have gone unnoticed.[11] The two remaining pedestals were installed on July 4 of the following year. The great standards were almost completed by that time as well. Made of red silk with gold trim and measuring eighteen braccia long, they were designed by the painter Benedetto Diana who executed them in profitable collaboration with Lazzaro Bastiani. The two artists received the considerable sum of 210 ducats for each banner and promised to gild the crowning elements for the flagpoles – either small spheres or crosses – that the Collegio was selecting at that time.[12]

Although no contemporary account of the iconographical

honoured sword, but in the left she holds the head of a convicted traitor. A merman guides her golden vessel; the prow bears the balanced scales. An elephant carries the ship on his shoulders into the beautiful city. A robust triton helps her to tow it and goes along sounding a horn for pleasure.[17]

Astraea, who had appeared as an airborne winged victory on the Scala dei Giganti, has now descended to her proper home in the Venetian lagoon, thus inaugurating a new Golden Age (Plate 295). Her debut on the day after a lunar eclipse may well have seemed a particularly apposite confirmation of such a prodigious occurrence.

The cortege continues toward the left, now in a clockwise movement, with a second boat towed by a singing nereid, Cymothoe. Escorted by a dolphin, the vessel carries Ceres, "the Mother of the Granaries," who holds a sheaf of wheat and a horn of fruit (Plate 296). She is followed by a third boat, this one accompanied by marine horses. It contains "happy Victory in a white dress," who holds a palm branch in her right hand and spoils of the enemy in the left (Plate 297).

While Contarini's account corresponds remarkably well to the visual evidence, he adds a line that confuses the issue and that suggests a certain fluidity in the symbolic meaning of such images. After describing the three boats and their occupants

295–7 Alessandro Leopardi, central flagpole base, 1505. Bronze. Venice, Piazza San Marco. *Above left:* detail with Astraea; *above right:* detail with Ceres; *below:* detail with Victory (or Peace).

he continues: "In the middle, in the honoured vessel, the city of Venice is drawn along through the calm sea by snow-white horses. Portumnus, the god of ports, from whose chin hangs a green beard, assists her." Contarini's identification of "the city of Venice" appears to refer to the figure of Victory. And yet Astraea, holding a sword and vanquishing a figure of discord, appears to be a graceful metamorphosis of the trecento relief of Venetia–Justice in the roundel on the west wall of the Palazzo Ducale (Plate 105). In either case, both Victory and Astraea may be seen as open symbols, each capable of serving as a metaphor for the abstract idea of Venice itself. They were also open to further commentary.

In his *Venetia nobilissima* of 1581, Francesco Sansovino offers an interpretation that differs from Contarini's. It seems to be based upon his understanding of similar iconography in the sculptural decoration of the Loggetta, designed by his father Jacopo and built 1537–46 (Plate 307).[18] In Francesco's view, "these pedestals signify freedom and liberty coming from God and God alone, and not from any prince. It is also said that they represent the three Kingdoms of Venetia, Cyprus, and Candia."[19] To him, all three female figures on the central pedestal added up to a representation of Venice as, perhaps, the sum of the civic virtues of Justice, Abundance, and Peace.[20]

As was customary in public art, each of the flagpoles bore an inscription with the names of the reigning doge, Leonardo Loredan, and the three procurators of San Marco responsible for the project. Also customary were the reliefs of San Marco *in moleca*, a lion rising out of the waves, on the urn-shaped elements of the north and south pedestals. But what was not customary at all were the three profile portraits of the doge that decorated the corresponding portion of the central pedestal. The display of ducal portraits outside the Palazzo Ducale was forbidden by law.[21] Although Agostino Barbarigo had discreetly defied the ban by inserting his own profile portrait on the capital of a pilaster adjacent to the Scala dei Giganti, that image was all but hidden in the larger architectural complex and could easily be overlooked.[22] The same was not the case with Loredan's portraits, which were located in one of the most visible locales of Venetian civic life. That Sanudo took no note of them may be a sign of a growing acceptance of princely prerogatives of office and the erosion of the ideal of *mediocritas* within the aristocracy.

THE WISDOM OF THE ANCESTORS

The primary statement of the pedestals was, in any event, similar to that of the Barbari map: the essential role of the sea and the *stato da mar* in Venice's fortunes. Luigi da Porto, a Vicentine nobleman, recorded a speech to the Great Council in July 1509 by Doge Loredan himself that passionately restated this long cherished truism. He was speaking during one of the lowest points in the history of the republic, just two months after Venice's disastrous defeat at Agnadello. Loredan spoke bitterly, with the benefit of hindsight, against Venice's involvement in mainland politics. Citing the heavy investment in land armies as the high price of freedom, he deplored Venice's dependence on foreign mercenaries and added:

> But this does not happen with affairs at sea, since there we are masters over all, and we conduct our own affairs alone, with true zeal. Nor does one know what stupidity ever drew us away from the sea and turned us to the land, for navigation was, so to speak, an inheritance from our earliest ancestors and has left us with many reminders and warnings that we should remain intent on it alone.[23]

As Loredan acknowledges, for all the rhetoric about divine beginnings, Venice was ultimately a creation of men. His respect for the wisdom and prudence of the founding fathers of the republic was a sentiment that ran through Venetian historical writing and public oratory of the period. It would be a mistake to dismiss it as a pious commonplace. At stake was the natural destiny, and even the survival, of the republic. As Bernardo Giustiniani had put it two decades earlier, "this city was built from the sweat and industry of mortals, and so it must be zealously preserved in the same way."[24]

The insistence upon faithful adherence to original principles and customs has a basis in Aristotelian political theory that would have been well known in the period: that the destiny of a city was contained in the seeds that were planted in its foundation. The persistence of three claims regarding the quality and character of the early Venetians that continued to resound in the histories seems to be motivated by such a notion: perpetual liberty, as proven by its Trojan ancestry; the nobility of the founding fathers; and a diversity of origins implying a heritage of imperial proportions. That such qualities were present at the beginning would have confirmed that they were a natural right and integral to Venice's destiny.[25]

Present-day Venice was thus the product of her own beginnings. While the Venetian constitution would ensure that men were given a proper framework in which human affairs and customs could be contained within rightful boundaries, the transmission of her culture depended upon the generations of men who inculcated the principles of the ancestors in the young who would, in turn, pass them on again in a continuous and unending succession.[26] The principle of continuity is well stated by Sanudo. Recalling a conversation of 1498, he wrote in his diary some years later about the decoration of the Senate chamber, a room in the Palazzo Ducale that had been built in the early years of the trecento:[27]

> One day in the Sala dei Pregadi [the Procurator Federico Cornaro] said to me: "Marin, my son, do you see how this hall is painted? It was made at the time of Doge Pietro Gradenigo. Do you see those trees: large, medium-sized, and small? They are like those who take up posts in this Senate for the governing of the state: the small ones learn, then they become middle-sized and then large; and thus are the three ages: young, middle-aged and old, and in this manner one governs well-instituted republics."[28]

And yet, the commitment to ancestral tradition by the patriciate did not impede the reception of new attitudes toward antiquity so much as it helped to shape them. For Venice was neither isolated nor insulated from the rest of Europe and the eastern Mediterranean.

DISTINGUISHED SOJOURNERS

Indeed, cutting against the conservative tendencies that were the natural consequence of cherished principles of continuity was the dynamic character of Venice's diversity. The Greek migration of the late quattrocento was only one aspect of a recurring phenomenon, for Venice continued to attract enough visitors, both temporary and permanent, to warrant the well-known comment of Philippe de Commynes in 1495: "Most of their people are foreigners."[29] Their contributions were not only welcomed; they were also officially sanctioned by the state. In a *parte* of 1474 the Senate had observed that "in this city, because of its grandeur and bounty, men converge from diverse shores and of the most acute genius, able to excogitate and to discover various ingenious artifices."[30] Recognizing the value of technological innovation to the state, the Senate responded with patent protection for new inventions. None would be more important for Venetian cultural life than the printing press. The industry was dominated well into the sixteenth century by immigrants – in the early years by Germans and after 1480 by Italians from towns outside Venice.[31] The exclusive privilege for printing in the city that had been granted to Johannes de Spira in 1469 expired with his death in 1470. In the next five years, fifteen firms would establish themselves and print over 130 editions, a tally that would rise to around 3,500 by the end of the century.[32] These businesses served as centers of cultural exchange. The shop of Aldus Manutius, for example, was a gathering place for Greek expatriates, distinguished sojourners such as Erasmus, and Venetian intellectuals, both noble and commoner. It was also, as the printer complained half-seriously on one occasion, a place where "tedious interlopers" dropped by "because they have nothing better to do."[33]

Philosophers and poets

Although most of the printing firms contributed to the dissemination of classical literature, the Aldine Press seems to have played a particularly important role in shaping a new relationship to the ancient past in the civic sphere. Indirect evidence for this role is found in Titian's canvas of *The Humiliation of the Emperor before the Pope* in the Great Council Hall. A number of distinguished scholars had already been honored through their inclusion as witnesses to historical events in earlier paintings in the program.[34] In a like manner, Titian's work, painted between 1516 and 1523 and the last

canvas in this phase of the campaign, was well stocked with personae from the Aldine circle. The scene included, among other figures: the young Gasparo Contarini before he became a cardinal; Marco Musurus of Crete, who held the chair in Greek in Padua (1503–9) and in Venice (1512–17); the Ferrarese poet and dramatist Ludovico Ariosto, whose *Orlando Furioso*, a chivalric romance with humanistic overtones was published in 1516; Jacopo Sannazaro, author of *Arcadia*, so important for the Venetian visual imagination; the Venetian historian, Andrea Navagero, celebrated for his elegant Latin prose; Pietro Bembo, whose literary productions were written in both Latin and the *volgare*; and the architect-theoretician Fra Giocondo, who had published the first illustrated Vitruvius in Venice in 1511.[35]

Unlike the Greek scholars in Carpaccio's painting of *The Consignment of the Umbrella*, whose contributions to Venetian culture had been made in the previous century, these were men of the present. That they would have been portrayed in the Great Council Hall, the epicenter of political power, suggests that the most influential group within the patriciate was neither resistant to change nor hostile to humanistic culture. Once strikingly visible, but – as it happened – ephemeral since they were destroyed by fire in 1577, the paintings would have mirrored, albeit as static reflections, a panoply of intellectual exchanges that were grounded in the real, everyday life of the city. Many of these visitors were only passing through, few came to stay; but through their inclusion in the paintings in the Great Council Hall, they became part of Venice's history and of her newly emerging cosmopolitan identity.

Ariosto was already an Aldine customer in 1498, and Sannazaro an Aldine author in 1514 when his *Arcadia* was reprinted by the press. Pietro Bembo, Andrea Navagero, and Fra Giocondo were all members of the Aldine Neakademia, an association formed in 1502 to publish classical texts and to promote the teaching of Greek.[36] By the time of his death in 1515, Aldus had published some fifty-five texts in Greek (thirty-one of them first editions), sixty-seven in Latin and six in Italian.[37] One of his greatest achievements was the conjoining of *otium* and *negotium* – the world of the scholar and the world of the man of affairs – and not only in his workshop, but also with his books. His introduction of small octavo-sized volumes with italic script and more words per page allowed for mass production in editions up to three thousand.[38] They were, he claimed, beautiful and convenient.[39]

The emphasis on Greek philologists in the Great Council Hall paintings suggests that the republic had added yet another, more ancient, correlative to her claims to be an improvement on Rome or an heir to Byzantium. Shortly after Marco Musurus was appointed to his public professorship in 1512, Aldus Manutius appended an epistle to the first volume of the Aldine *Rhetorum Graecorum Orationes* (dated 1513), praising the Grand Chancellor Francesco Faseolo for his support of the appointment:

(*following pages*) Philosophers, detail from Plate 222.

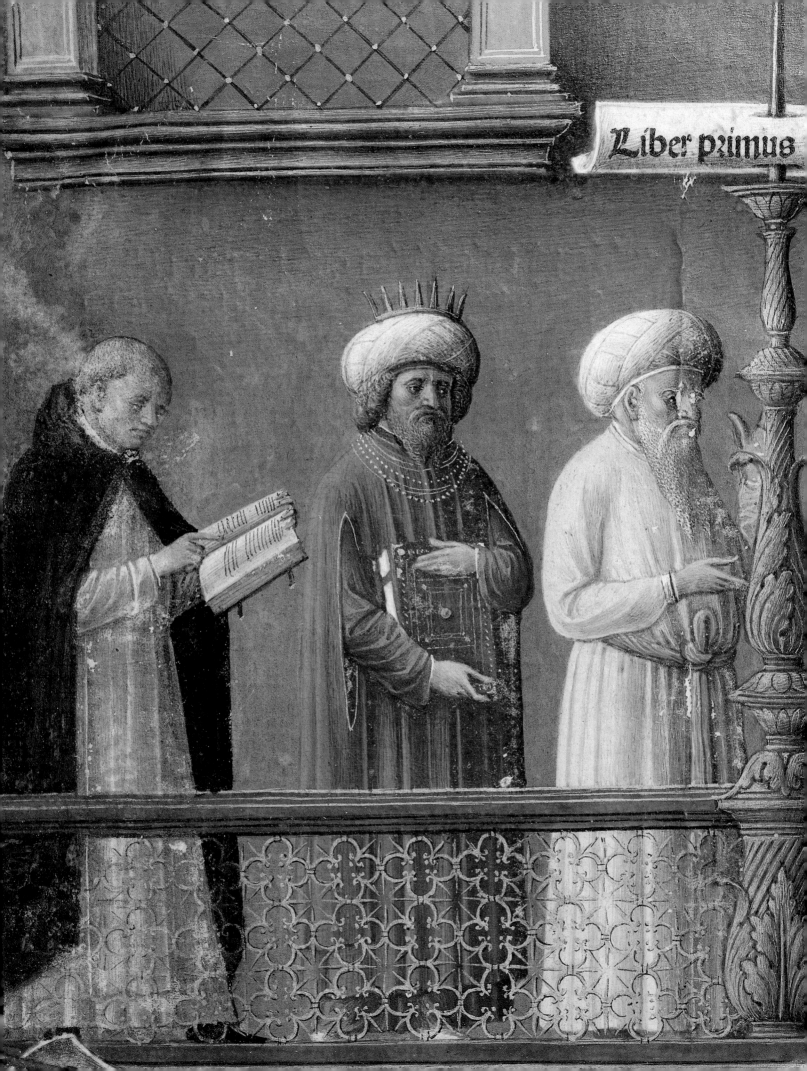

Liber primus

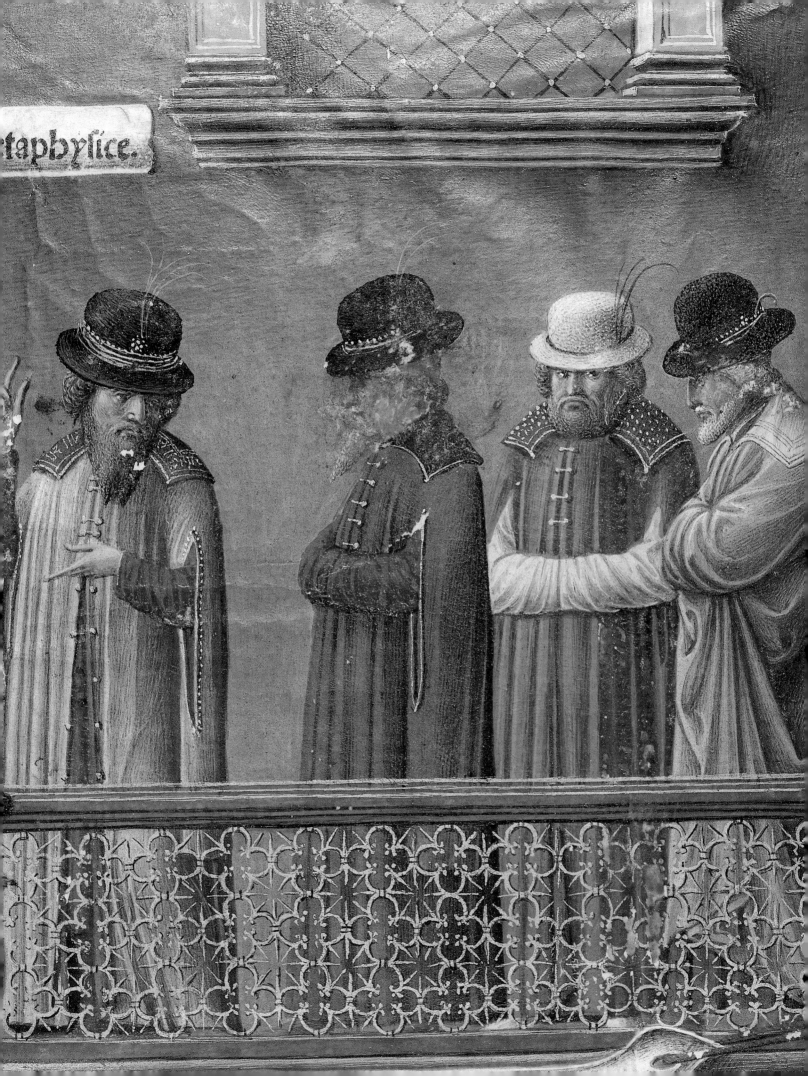

Venice at this time can truly be called a second Athens [*Athenae alterae*] because students of Greek letters gather from everywhere to hear Marcus Musurus, the most learned man of this age, whom you have zealously brought by public stipend, and to whom you show many favors.[40]

The Greek presence was also articulated in small works of art, as well as in manuscripts. A bronze plaquette by Ulocrino, a Venetian sculptor close to the circle of Andrea Riccio, depicts Aristotle seated beneath a tree and addressing Alexander of Aphrodisias (Plate 298). A peripatetic philosopher active in the early third century A.D., Alexander was respected as one the most able commentators on the works of Aristotle. His writings were rediscovered only in the late fifteenth century. Girolamo Donato, who appeared in the previous chapter, had translated Alexander's *De anima*, published in Venice in 1495, and the complete works would follow between 1513 and 1527. In all likelihood, the relief was inspired by one of these projects.[41]

298   Ulocrino, *Aristotle and Alexander of Aphrodisias*, early sixteenth century. Bronze, 72 × 55 mm. National Gallery of Art, Washington, D.C., Samuel H. Kress Collection.

Scientists and theoreticians

The printing industry, in close proximity to the University at Padua, attracted not only philologists and poets; it also drew some of the best theoretical minds of the time. A brief look at three of the most influential figures – Luca Pacioli, Pomponius Gauricus, and Fra Giocondo – suggests that they helped to raise the Venetian consciousness of visual form to a new level of sophistication.

Luca Pacioli, a disciple of Piero della Francesca, was one of the leading mathematicians of the period. His *Summa de arithmetica, geometria, proportione et proportionalità* was published

in Venice in 1494. Although the treatise was concerned primarily with practical arithmetic, Pacioli's dedication names Gentile and Giovanni Bellini and Hieronimo Malatini, a Venetian expert in *prospectivo disegno*, among the artists with whom he had discussed perspective.[42] *Divina proportione*, a second treatise completed by Pacioli in collaboration with Leonardo da Vinci in Milan in 1498 and published in Venice in 1509, emphasized theory as much as practice. Focusing on the theme of ideal proportion, it contains appendices on measure in architecture and the proper formation of letters and is illustrated with woodcuts based upon drawings by Leonardo. Pacioli's influence on Venetian artists and printers was already evident in Carpaccio's paintings of the 1490s and in the script of the *Hypnerotomachia Poliphili*, published by Aldus in 1499. The capital letters used in the book were designed according to the antiquarian proportions initially prescribed by Felice Feliciano and later codified by Pacioli.[43] Pointing to a knowledge of proportion as the key to excellence in the arts and sciences, Pacioli lectured on the fifth book of Euclid's *Elements* in the Venetian church of San Bartolomeo in 1508 to overflow crowds that included Aldus and Fra Giocondo.[44]

Pomponius Gauricus, born around 1482 in Salerno to a grammarian father who named two of his other sons Agrippa and Pliny, must have been destined from the beginning for an intellectual career. By 1501/2 he was studying in Padua and remained in the area at least until 1505 and perhaps 1509. He had a number of Venetian friends, including Giambattista Ramusio and Piero Valeriano. Although his *De sculptura* was published in Florence in 1504, it would have been a product of his experiences in the Padua–Venice milieu. In it Tullio Lombardo is granted the highest praise, but the sculptor of the Colleoni monument at SS. Giovanni e Paolo, unnamed in the treatise, is criticized for his excessive realism and lack of delicacy: "he has rendered the horse in such a crude manner, it is said, that it may be seen as nothing other than the flayed image of a horse."[45]

Fra Giocondo had come to Venice in 1504 as military engineer to the republic. Also a classical scholar, he brought with him notes on a number of Roman texts that were eventually published with his active collaboration by the Aldine Press.[46] He also brought a new rigor to a beloved antiquarian genre: the sylloge of inscriptions. By separating those known from personal examination from those obtained only at second hand, by arranging them topographically, and by thinking of them in terms of a comprehensive corpus and not just a collection of scattered fragments: he contributed to a new detached perspective on the ancient past in scholarly circles.[47] His study of antiquities in Rome and his combined expertise in philology and in architectural drawing culminated in the first illustrated edition of Vitruvius's *De architectura* in Latin, published in Venice in 1511.[48] Interest in Vitruvius had already been stimulated by the *Hypnerotomachia*, and Fra Giocondo's authoritative edition laid the theoretical groundwork for the Venetian *renovatio alla romana* that would be implemented by the next generation.[49]

But few projects were undertaken in the difficult years following the Wars of Cambrai, and as influential as all these transient intellectuals were for Venice's engagement with classical antiquity, they remained outsiders. Fra Giocondo's lack of success in the competition to rebuild Rialto after the devastating fire of 1514 is a case in point. According to the later testimony of Vasari, Fra Giocondo laid out an ideal plan for a Greek forum to balance the Latin forum at San Marco. It consisted of a double row of buildings in the form of a perfect square, rather on the model of the Fondaco dei Tedeschi, but one that would cover the entire Rialtine island. Surrounded by a canal on all four sides, the complex featured a large piazza in the center, which was framed by porticoed buildings. A rigid, but logical, hierarchy of locales was envisioned, with foodstuffs relegated to the external area and luxury goods and financial institutions confined to the privileged innermost zone. There were to be four principal portals, one in the center of each side. Following a rigorous geometry, with ancient principles of symmetry and the harmony of parts, it was to be a complete and perfect city in itself, which was inserted, nonetheless, inside the bend of the Grand Canal.[50]

Fra Giocondo's plan was one of ten that were submitted to the Provveditori, but after careful consideration it was rejected in favor of a more traditional project by the architect Antonio Scarpagnino. It is not difficult to imagine reasons for the lack of enthusiasm for the friar's project. Sanudo described it as *serato* or closed.[51] As Tafuri points out, its self-contained harmony inevitably alienated it from the city that surrounded it. By ignoring longstanding property lines, moreover, it challenged the constituted order of medieval ownership. In short, it violated Venetian principles of continuity in both a temporal and a spatial sense. Sanudo observed that "one [model] was made by Fra Giocondo, who is not from here and does not understand the place."[52]

THE MIRROR AND LIGHT OF ALL ITALY

But change was inevitable. While it may have seemed that the gods had forsaken Venice in the dark years after the Wars of Cambrai, cultural life quickly rebounded and the republic would regain most of her terraferma possessions by 1517.[53] The shape of the future, and a new sense of the past, can be seen in two decisions of the mid-decade. The first involved the fate of the manuscripts bequeathed by Cardinal Bessarion to the republic in 1468. For more than four decades they had been stored in crates in government offices: largely inaccessible to serious scholars and subject to unauthorized borrowing, pilferage, and deterioration. In May 1515, after extended debate, the Senate passed a decree calling for the construction of a new library to house the books.[54] The text, transcribed by Sanudo, put a good face on a dismal record.

Most importantly, it is a manifesto of the new universalist ethos that would culminate in Sansovino's projects at San Marco:

Libraries are often used to celebrate and add special lustre to well-founded cities. Such was the custom in Rome, Athens, and other ancient wealthy cities. For, beyond providing an ornament, [libraries] also encourage [men's] minds to learning and erudition whence good morals and other virtues are wont to arise. Therefore, when the former Most Reverend Cardinal Nicenus who was so gracious to our republic gave, now some time ago, to our government the gift of about 800 Greek and Latin books of great beauty and value, we deemed there was no place in our city which could [accommodate] a gift of such great splendor. But now it is at last fitting to erect [a building] to hold this most precious treasure which has been almost hidden from the vicissitudes of time, especially since the Procurators of our Church of San Marco have willingly donated a place in the piazza itself for the new structure. There could be no lovelier location in this city, nor one more convenient to the learned [community]; because once the library has been finished, it will be a perpetual monument to our heirs and the mirror and light of all Italy.[55]

The patrician Andrea Navagero was appointed librarian the following January and charged with the responsibility of securing the books in their temporary location. He came with impressive practical credentials. An expert Latin editor, he had collaborated with Aldus Manutius on the texts of Cicero, Quintilian, Lucretius, Virgil, and Ovid. Aldus dedicated a volume of Pindar to him in 1513, wishing the book "to come from our Academy under your name."[56] Armed with an apostolic letter that threatened excommunication to those who did not surrender volumes in their possession that had been "borrowed" from the Bessarion collection, Navagero was eventually successful in recovering a number of missing texts.[57]

At the same time as Navagero's appointment as librarian, the Council of Ten made a second decision. Determining that the turbulent events of the present should be recounted in the proper light, they also named him public historian of the republic. The position had remained vacant for nine years after the death of Sabellico, and the choice of Navagero over Sanudo – who had hoped for it himself – indicated that form was to weigh ever more heavily over substance in the fashioning of a new triumphalist image of the republic:

Considering the fact that reputation is one of the principal foundations of every State, something which greatly influences all matters of both peace and war, it has always been a universal principle of all the kings, princes and republics of the world to endeavor to conserve it by every means, and not only through the splendid and memorable deeds themselves, but also to posterity through the memory of those things, perpetuating it not by means of compendious, unreliable, varied and rude chronicles and annals, but by reliable, authentic, elegant and florid histories . . . adorned with elegance and eloquence . . .[58]

The young Navagero was an obvious choice. He was described in the *parte* as "endowed with exceptional Latin and Greek grammar and with a writing style such that in the opinion of all the learned men, neither inside nor outside Italy does he have an equal."[59] And yet, however distinguished his work in editing ancient texts may have been, he had never written history on his own. And, as it turned out, he never would. For the rest of his life, he continued to devote himself to letters, poetry, and the editing of Latin texts, as well as to ambassadorial assignments. When he died in France in 1529, his heirs claimed that he had burned his manuscript of Venetian history because he judged that it did not meet the high standards that the task deserved.[60]

In fact, Navagero's appointment was significant only as a demonstration of a heightened awareness of the importance of interpreting current history amongst the ruling class. For the crisis in public historiography after Sabellico's death was to be resolved outside the official political arena during the next decade when three writers stepped forward to recast the Venetian "myth" in response to the needs of the present.

The first attempt was the most ambitious and had the least success. Tommaso Diplovatazio, born in Corfu and trained in the law in Padua, had arrived in Venice only in 1517, where he had connections with the large Greek community. His *Tractatus de Venetae urbis libertate et eiusdem Imperii dignitate et privilegiis* was presented to the Council of Ten in 1524.[61] Dedicating the work to Doge Andrea Gritti and the Council of Ten, Diplovatazio stated that his aim was to celebrate the "authority and splendor" of the city, its original liberty, the amplitude of its possessions, and its foundation in justice and law. The treatise was a peculiar combination of juridical erudition, philological rigor, religious inspiration, and uncritical celebration with well-worn topoi. Not only was Venice the ideal mixed republic commended by Aristotle and predestined for glory by St. Mark, he argued; it had also been announced by prophets of the Old Testament. Using the longstanding medieval practice of biblical exegesis by antetype and an imaginative use of paraphrase and inversion, he was able to find authority for Venice's miraculous foundation in a number of texts ranging from Ezekiel (Here, the Lord God said, is the city of perfect beauty, situated in the heart of the sea)[62] to Jeremiah (Here is what is called the throne of God, just like Jerusalem).[63]

Building a bridge to the present, Diplovatazio also cited authorities closer to his own time. His precise quotation of the already much cited letter written by Petrarch in 1364 to celebrate Venice's conquest of Crete was perhaps to be expected. In it, Venice is described as "rich in gold but richer in fame, built on solid marble but standing more solid on a foundation of civic concord, surrounded by salt waters but more secure with the salt of good council."[64]

But just as richly evocative was Diplovatazio's citation of the prophecies of Joachim da Fiore (c.1135–1202), the abbot from Calabria whose millenarian visions still had great appeal in the sixteenth century. Joachim was said to have seen in a vision:

> the similitude of a girl dressed in a gown of silk and gold of diverse colors, girdled with precious stones of every type, in whose sight were men of every nation of the world, and they showed reverence to her; at her feet was that gentle lion with two feet in the sea and two on the land. As he admired the virgin, she said to him: "Make known to Joachim that I am a virgin and I sit in judgement as a queen, that I am not a widow nor will I live to see my mourning."[65]

Interest in Joachim enjoyed a resurgence in Venice precisely during this period. An Augustinian preacher, Silvestro Meuccio of Santo Cristoforo della Pace, published no less than five collections of Joachimite and pseudo-Joachimite prophecies between 1516 and 1527.[66] In his dedicatory letter in the *Super Esiam*, Meuccio recounted a longstanding and widely known legend that Joachim had given detailed instructions for certain mosaics in the church of San Marco. Most notable were the figures of Sts. Dominic and Frances, complete with halos and appropriate monastic habit, above the entrance to the sacristy. Since these mosaics were thought to have been made long before their elevations to sainthood, they were regarded as prophetic signs, foretelling the emergence of the two great mendicant orders.[67] The story had first appeared in the fourteenth century in Dominican and Franciscan circles and was later disseminated to a secular audience by quattrocento preachers including St. Bernardine of Siena and St. Anthony of Florence. It was still being repeated with conviction – and considerable embellishment – by Venetian chroniclers through the end of the sixteenth century. Indeed, in 1566 the procurators forbade the destruction of any mosaic or inscription without making an exact record of it, "so that those same works and prophecies, which it is said were ordered by St. Joachim, can be worked on and returned."[68] Padre Giovanni Stringa wrote in the revised edition of Sansovino's *Venetia nobilissima* in 1604: "There is no doubt that the inventor of these figures would have been that venerable man called Abbot Giovanni Gioachino."[69]

Nor did Diplovatazio ignore the classical writers. Citing Strabo and Vitruvius on the uniqueness and healthy climate of the lagoon situation, he passed over the beloved Trojan legend and drew upon Cassiodorus for his account of the early settlement. He even included in the autograph manuscript a large double-page watercolor painting of a tract of the Grand Canal near Rialto, with an imaginary view of the primitive wooden dwellings with thatched roofs that Cassiodorus had praised for their egalitarian simplicity (Plate 299).[70] Earnestly

299 Tommaso Diplovatazio, *View of Early Venice near San Lio*, from his *Tractatus de Venetae urbis libertate et eiusdem Imperii dignitate et privilegiis*. Venice, Biblioteca Nazionale Marciana, Cod. Lat. XIV 77 (2991), ff. 22v–33r.

rendered in its particulars, even with a caption identifying the church of San Lio, the image may be considered an early, unique display of historical erudition that aims at archaeological reconstruction.[71]

Alas, for all his passionate commitment to the mythic nature of Venice – which he called *Roma junior* – Diplovatazio found it hard to leave anything out. Aside from scriptural citations and lengthy borrowings from Venetian chronicles, he included, as well, extended passages from astrological, hermetic, and otherwise esoteric texts.[72] Herein lay his problem. Venetians wanted a single, unified vision that linked up their hallowed civic past to their providential present; Diplovatazio tried to do too much and ended up with a pastiche of fact and legend that pleased no one completely. When one member of the Ten moved to suppress the text, the secretary noted judiciously:

although one could either add or subtract, according to the diversity of opinions of our doctors, for there have been contrary and discordant views among them on many issues contradicting each of the conclusions made by him, the

book is no less valuable for all that, because just as it is easy to replace or to revise things said by others, so it is impossible in principle to compose a work that would be perfect in every part.[73]

Donato Giannotti, a Florentine of Savonarolan persuasions, completed another treatise in 1526, *Della Repubblica dei Venetiani*, but his aims were those of an outsider whose primary interest was to vindicate the short-lived republican experiment in his own city.[74] It took a true and proper Venetian patrician, Gasparo Contarini, to strike the right tone with his *De magistratibus et republica Venetorum* completed in 1524 (Plate 300). Drawing upon the familiar themes of liberty, continuity, peace, and the rightness of the social and political hierarchy, he was able to subsume the existing state into the mythic state and to articulate the image of an ideal Venice, not just of the past, but also of the present.[75] Indeed, to Contarini, Venice was the exemplary city not just in his own day but for all time:[76]

It is clear that there were some republics which had a vast

275

300 *Gasparo Contarini*, engraving by Tobias Stimmer in Paolo Giovio, *Elogia virorum literis illustrium*, Basel 1577, f. 184.

Procuratie Vecchie on the north side of Piazza San Marco in 1512 and Rialto in 1514. Even though the state coffers were depleted because of military expenses, the practical – and symbolic – importance of these areas demanded their restoration at soon as possible.[79] As Scarpagnino's austerely functional plan for the Fabbriche Vecchie at Rialto was nearing completion in 1523, it was decided to restore the undamaged Palazzo dei Camerlenghi – housing the magistrates in charge of the state treasury – that bordered the area on the Grand Canal.[80] Largely confined to cosmetic improvements of the façade with a new revetment of Istrian stone and decorative friezes, the project broke no new ground, architecturally speaking (Plate 302). In fact, as the last civic building constructed in the Lombard style of the late fifteenth century, the Palazzo dei Camerlenghi, completed in 1525, marked the end of an era.[81]

The Procuratie Vecchie, a far more ambitious project, was completed the following year by Bartolomeo Bon (Plate 301).

301 Bartolomeo Bon, Procuratie Vecchie (detail), completed 1526. Venice, Piazza San Marco.

state and empire and more military glory than Venice, but there are none who, for institutions and laws accommodated to live happily and well, could be comparable to ours . . . If, then, someone will compare this city of ours with the most famous ancient cities, he will see that in the writings of the most illustrious philosophers, who imagined republics according to their desires, there are not any so well imagined and organized.[77]

The drive toward universalism was not without its sacrifices. As suggested by the criticism of the *rude cronice et annali* in the *parte* appointing Navagero as public historian of the republic, even the beloved Venetian dialect was at risk. By 1525, Pietro Bembo could write: "Tuscan words sound better than Venetian ones; their sound is sweeter and more pleasing, lively and fluent . . . They are not so loose and languid; they have more regard for rules, tenses, numbers, articles, and persons."[78]

As the literary and historiographical vocabulary began to adapt to a unitary vision of an enduring Venice as "a mirror and light of all Italy," the architectural vocabulary was changing as well. Civic patronage in the 1520s was largely focused on two areas that had been badly damaged by fire: the

302   Guglielmo dei Grigi, Palazzo dei Camerlenghi, completed 1525. Venice, Grand Canal near Rialto.

As Deborah Howard observes, it was the "first major public building in Venice to be erected in a purely classical style."[82] And yet, like so many things in Venice, the implications of this revival – or survival – are both more and less than they appear at first glance. The building features a three-story elevation that might be considered a visual metaphor of Venetian society: at ground level, a long arcade occupied by shops of artisans, some of a very modest sort, and above, two storeys of expensive apartments. Bon's building followed the pre-existing ground plan and rhythm of the façade arcades of its twelfth-century predecessor, while thoroughly updating the Byzantine-Gothic decorative vocabulary with Renaissance forms. According to Sanudo, the building had been designed by a Tuscan architect called "Il Celestro" about whom little is known. In any event, inspired by local Veneto-Byzantine models rather than by ancient Roman monuments, the building's classicism was deeply rooted in the city's own past.[83]

★   ★   ★

A REALIZED UTOPIA

The final phase of romanization began in 1527. Andrea Gritti provided the will, the Sack of Rome served as the catalyst, and the diaspora of intellectuals and artists – including Sebastiano Serlio and Jacopo Sansovino, who joined the previously arrived Pietro Aretino – supplied the agents of change. As André Chastel observes, "the honor of Italy was now in Venice."[84] Gritti, who possessed the characteristic Venetian ability to exploit unexpected "spolia" toward civic ends, was determined to bring about a *renovatio urbis* that would make Venice a second Rome.[85] The Peace of Bologna of 1529 ushered in a period of stability that allowed for huge expenditures on public works. Venice's primary goal in these years was not expansion, but peace, security, and prosperity; her strategy was neutrality and a defensive conservatism; the price was Habsburg domination of Italy. It was, a later writer observed, a time of "universal quiet."[86] A portrait medal

277

better proceed in this profound [science] of Architecture by order and know how to distinguish the genres of buildings, that is Tuscan, Doric, Ionic, Corinthian, and Composite."[88] The drawings, already executed "with laborious zeal and the highest diligence," seem to have been Serlio's own inventions based upon his examination of antiquities in Rome (Plate 304). Although couched in the adulatory language of civil discourse, the appeal has a critical edge, suggesting that

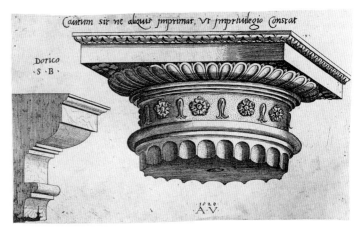

303 Venetian medallist, *Doge Andrea Gritti* (1523–38) (obverse) and *Venetia* (reverse), *c.*1538. Bronze, diam. 6.8 cm. (after Hill, *Corpus*, no. 456).

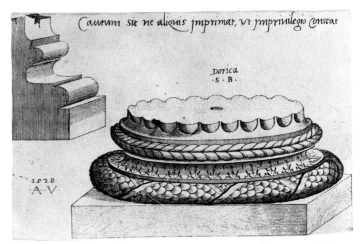

304 Agostino Veneziano after Sebastiano Serlio, *Doric Frieze, Capital and Base*, 1528. Engraving, Bartsch XIV, nos. 525–7. Vienna, Österreichischen National Bibliothek.

probably struck at the time of Gritti's death in 1538, features the familiar figure of Venetia holding the scales of justice on the reverse, but in a new comprehensive statement of civic *virtù* and abundance (Plate 303). Holding a cornucopia, she is seated not in the militant frontal pose of the Venetia on Francesco Foscari's medal of the 1450s (Plate 107), but in a relaxed and graceful profile. Although she wears a cuirass, arms are piled up behind her and Venetian galleys – the source of Venice's economic prosperity and military power – ride the waves in the background.[87]

One of the first documents of the new universalizing ethos in architecture comes in mundane form: an application for a copyright from the Venetian Senate in 1528 by Sebastiano Serlio and the engraver Agostino Veneziano. Praising the magnificence of public and private buildings in the city, the artists requested copyright protection for a series of nine engravings of bases, capitals, and friezes: "So that one could

Venetians would benefit from a more authoritative modern interpretation of the classical rules of architecture.[89] According to their petition, the two artists also intended to publish drawings of "various buildings in *perspicientia* and various other ancient things delightful to all."[90]

What was new about the present architectural *renovatio* in comparison to earlier classical revivals was its theoretical basis. Fra Giocondo had laid the groundwork with the publication of his illustrated Latin *Vitruvius* in 1511. The work had excited much interest and came out in Italian translation five years later. Most importantly, it provided a rational model from which a normative architecture could be developed in the decades to come.[91] Serlio's own treatise on the orders would offer an extended analysis and practical critique of Vitruvian principles. Comprising both text and illustrations, it came out in Venice in 1537 as the Fourth Book – although it was the first published volume – of his *Regole generali di Architetura sopra le cinque maniere de gli edifici, cioe, Thoscano, Dorico, Ionico, Corinthio, et Composito, con gli essempi dell'Antiquita, che, per la magior parte concordano con la dottrina di Vitruvio*. The circumstantial title attested to the author's scientific exactness, while his copyright petition announced his didactic, universalizing intentions. In it, he declared that the treatise would be published in both Italian and Latin "so that more nations could share in it, [and] for these things to be of utility to all."[92] Dedicating the volume to Ercole d'Este, Duke of Ferrara, Serlio suggests that Venice's architectural promise, alluded to in his earlier petition of 1528, was now being fulfilled. For this he credits Doge Andrea Gritti, "who has taken into the service of his illustrious republic these singular men – Sansovino, Scarpagnino, and Sanmicheli – who make so stupendous this city of noble and *artificiosi* edifices."[93]

The penetration of a classical aesthetic into the most venerated events of the civic past can also be seen in the narrative canvases painted for those bastions of conservatism, the Venetian *scuole*, in these years. Paris Bordone's *Presentation of the Ring*, installed in the Scuola Grande di San Marco, depicts an episode that took place in fourteenth century Venice (Plate 306). In it, the doge is enthroned in a portico with columned architecture in the background that already – if anachronistically – proclaims Venice's impeccable classical credentials.[94] Conversely, in Titian's *Presentation of the Virgin* in the Scuola Grande di Santa Maria della Carità, the Temple of Solomon in Jerusalem is modeled on the Gothic Palazzo Ducale of Venice (Plate 305). But it also includes classical topoi, such as the obelisk, the columned portico behind the Virgin, and the fragment of a classical statue, to embed the event in Roman history.[95] It would not be long before reality came to match these pictorial fictions.

In 1535, the Senate articulated a vision of Venice as a Utopia realized, and confirmed the historical rationale for its transformation into exemplar for all Italy:

> Our ancestors have always striven and been vigilant so as to . . . provide this city with most beautiful temples, private buildings and spacious squares, so that from a wild and uncultivated refuge . . . it has grown, been ornamented and constructed so as to become the most beautiful and illustrious city which at present exists in the world.[96]

During the next two years, commissions were granted to Jacopo Sansovino for the new Library of St. Mark, the Zecca or new mint, and the Loggetta. Speaking from a Venetian pulpit in 1539, with all three buildings already under construction, the Sienese friar Bernardino Ochino proclaimed: "I look

305   Titian, *Presentation of the Virgin*, 1539. Oil on canvas, 335 × 775 cm. Venice, Accademia.

306　Paris Bordone, *Presentation of the Ring to the Doge*, c.1535–45. Oil on canvas, 370 × 300 cm. Venice, Accademia.

307 Jacopo Sansovino, Loggetta, 1537–46, and corner of Biblioteca Nazionale Marciana, 1537–88. Venice, Piazzetta.

everywhere, but there is no longer a castle nor a city in Italy that is not perturbed. Only your city really remains standing, so that it seems to me that you contain in yourself the whole of Italy."[97]

Two years later, Pietro Contarini did not hesitate to invite men of the ancient past to visit the triumphal present. These time travelers would be forced to admit, he argued, that even Leopardi's pedestals at San Marco – now thirty-five years old – were equal to the finest sculpture of their own time:

> If some worthy man from ancient times could behold these sacred towers of the sea he would swear that they were the product of Phidias's genius, but he who has sculpted [them] is Alessandro Lionpardo, the new glory of our age, who shines like a star upon the Venetian waters.[98]

The Loggetta was already receiving its sculptural decoration when Contarini's book appeared, and within five years the campaign was completed with Sansovino's bronze figures of Minerva, Apollo, Mercury, and Peace.[99] Its façade modeled after a Roman triumphal arch, the Loggetta employed an antique vocabulary and was designed according to Vitruvian principles so as to endow the republic with a new all-encompassing historical dimension (Plate 307).[100]

Construction on the library and the Zecca proceeded apace,

but over a much extended period. While the Loggetta had spoken the language of triumph, the adoption of a classical basilica form for the library created a complementary metaphor for the wisdom and justice of the state. The building was complete enough by 1553 for the painting of twenty-one ceiling roundels by seven different artists to begin. By 1564 Bessarion's bequest was at last moved into its permanent home.[101] The Zecca was probably completed about two years later. Its rusticated façade with a Doric order was likened to a fortress "for precious gold" by contemporary observers, and, as Serlio had already noted in 1537, the ancient Romans had employed similar combinations to suggest strength and impregnability. Taken together, the three buildings document Venice's acceptance of her Roman legacy and her rightful inheritance of Roman *virtù* (Plate 310).[102]

A NEW CEREMONIAL LANGUAGE

It was perhaps inevitable that Venetians would wish to extend the classical architectural vocabulary to civic spectacle. Around 1560, as part of an ambitious plan to redesign the Bacino of San Marco, Alvise Cornaro proposed a permanent theater *all'antica* to be built on a mudflat at the mouth of the

308 *Roman amphitheater at Pula*, engraving from *Almanacco Istriano*, II. Venice, Museo Correr.

Giudecca Canal opposite the Piazzetta. A realization in brick and stucco of the ephemeral floating "theaters of the world" that had been constructed on barges for special theatrical events since the 1490s, it would have featured the standard elements of a Roman theater with a permanent stage and a *cavea* with seats elevated in tiers "of large and comfortable stones."[103]

A perfect world in itself, Cornaro's theater had a moral and civic dimension that was quintessentially Venetian. For the tiered seating provided that "everyone would have his place and step, as though God had given it to him" – an arrangement that reflected the prevailing patrician view of the social hierarchy of the well-ordered republic. As a microcosm of the urban universe, such a theater was not only an arena for

spectacle; as Tafuri observes, it was also a spectacle in and of itself – a "visual utopia" – when viewed from the Piazzetta. Alas, the theater was not an idea whose time had come. Cornaro was more visionary than engineer, Venice was already utopia to her ruling oligarchy, and such extraordinary measures would have been too drastic a violation of the urban fabric.[104] Perhaps for similar reasons an ambitious, and quixotic, proposal to move the Roman amphitheater from Pula to Venice in 1583 – if one is to trust an undocumented, but persistent tradition in Istrian historiography – was quashed by the Venetian senator Gabriele Emo (Plate 308).[105]

But parity with land-bound cities demanded that Venetians find a way to employ the *trionfo all'antica* for diplomatic and political purposes. Serlio had dealt with the matter in his Fourth Book, offering a model for a triumphal arch featuring the Corinthian order that was based upon the Arch of Trajan in Ancona. The accompanying text, transcribed here in the English translation of 1611, introduces the topic with an observation:

> Although in these our dayes, men make no Arches Tryumphant of Marble or of other stones, neverthelesse, when any great personage entereth into a Towne, they use to make Arches trymphant for to welcome him in, which they set in the fayrest places of the Towne, adorned and painted in most curious maner.[106]

Palladio had designed several such arches in Vicenza as part of the temporary apparatus for civic receptions to welcome new bishops in 1543 and again in 1565. Descriptions suggest

309   Andrea Vicentino, *The Arrival of Henry III at the Lido in 1574*. Oil on canvas, 367 × 791 cm. Venice, Palazzo Ducale, Sala delle Quattro Porte.

310 (*facing page*)   Canaletto, *Piazzetta and Bacino of San Marco* (detail), 1745–46. Oil on canvas, 69 × 94 cm. Munich, Alte Pinakothek.

that these were elaborate devices, decorated with paintings and sculpture, that marked stations on the parade route.[107] But Venice, whose processional itinerary was situated in the lagoon, was at a certain disadvantage with limited opportunities for erecting such structures within the city.[108] Palladio rose to the challenge with a lavish stage set built on the Lido for the entry of Henry III, the future King of France, in 1574 (Plate 309). Consisting of a triumphal arch made of wood and built on the model of the arch of Septimius Severus in Rome, it was decorated with figures, trophies, and history paintings of signal events of the king's life painted by Veronese and Tintoretto. Behind it was a loggia featuring ten Corinthian columns and a compartmented ceiling painted with four winged victories holding palms and crowns.[109] Detached from the urban center, it did not violate the physical fabric of the city itself. Henry III's initial impression of the city, from his viewing point from across the lagoon, would have been that of a city already perfected.

And yet it was also a city that was capable of further perfection as long as principles of prudence and continuity were maintained. For the Venetian aesthetic had no underlying notion of the completed whole. It had no boundaries; it was open-ended, and continuous, just like the republic itself. Thus the eclectic character of Venetian art and architecture was neither the product of unknowing indifference nor of deliberate ambiguity, but rather a conciliation: the appropriation of both the alien and the familiar in a new all-encompassing synthesis.[110] Perhaps the real triumph of Venice lay in her ability to appropriate, to transform and to transcend her past. For hers was a renewable perfection.

EPILOGUE

I have sought in this book to look at Venice's engagement with the past over a long period and, in particular, to examine the ways in which Venetian artists, antiquarians, and the educated class in general participated in the Renaissance revival of antiquity. The inquiry began with the Kairos relief on

the pulpit at Torcello, an artifact that addressed the problem of time directly and that raised issues of survival, revival, and reuse. It is appropriate to conclude with another sculptural group, this one a creation of the mid-sixteenth century, that reflects similar concerns (Plates 311–12).

We find it high on the wall of Ca' Bembo, a Gothic palace overlooking the Campiello Santa Maria Nuova in Canareggio. Awkwardly wedged into the cramped space between two vertical courses of tall ogee windows of the second and third floors, the assemblage consists of several parts: an austerely classical aedicule, complete with pediment, constructed in the Doric order of white Istrian stone; a shell niche inside, containing the statue of Chronos or Saturn in the form of a *homo silvanus* holding a solar disc; an inscribed plaque below, which is supported by a relief sculpture of three male heads carved in high relief; and, implausibly supporting the entire ensemble, a small console carved in the florid gothic style.[1]

The pastiche is not one of the masterpieces of the Venetian Renaissance, but in a curious and silent way it sums up the Venetian experience. The aedicule is a newly constructed product of the mid-sixteenth century, but the wild man, about 1.22 meters tall and carved from Greek marble, appears to date from the late fourteenth century. The relief, also made of Greek marble, may be even earlier. It is badly eroded and may have been recarved, but the ethnographic diversity of the heads – the one on the right has distinctly Tartar features – suggests a date as early as the mid-trecento.[2]

The assemblage was the invention of the patrician Giammatteo Bembo. The erudite nephew of Cardinal Pietro Bembo and a man of affairs active in political life, he composed it as a personal impresa, adding the inscription:

DVM. VOLVITVR. ISTE

IAD. ASCR. IVSTINOP. VER.

SALAMIS. CRETA. IOVIS.

TESTES. ERVNT. ACTOR.

PA. IO. SE. M^V

311 Ca' Bembo in Campiello S. Maria Nuova, Venice, with the sculptural group of *Chronos* (or Saturn) affixed to the wall between the second and third floors.

312 Detail of Plate 311.

(As long as this [the sun] rotates, the cities of Zara [IADRA], Cattaro [ASCRIVIVM], Capodistria [IVSTINOPOLIS], Verona [VERONA], Cyprus [SALAMIS], Candia [CRETA IOVIS] will give testimony to his actions)

The cities are those in which Giammatteo had served as podestà or *capitano*, and the four initials at the end indicate the names of Paulus Iovius and Sebastianus Munsterus, two historians who had recorded his deeds.[3]

We are still in a pre-Copernican universe that is defined by Venetian territories in the terraferma, Dalmatia, and the Aegean. We are also in a world in which the authority of Roman antiquity and the long-standing Venetian capacity for aggregation and incorporation overcomes any disjunction between the hirsute creature of medieval fantasy, his classical receptacle, and the Gothic architectural setting. Venice is the center of this world – and personal identity is still closely tied to civic definition.

As we have seen, such definition was the product of a continuous process of self-fashioning that was based upon certain constants, consistently articulated in the chronicles and implied in the art and architecture of the city.

First, Venice is a creation *ex novo*: an amalgam of people and building stones, all of which came from somewhere else. And yet, the politique of incorporation that would serve the Venetians socially, culturally, and aesthetically over the life of the republic did not produce a melting-pot so much as an accumulation. An empire of fragments, it drew its strength from the diversity of its constituent parts.

Second, Venice is unique. By virtue of its site, the product and cause of that tension of will and energy to survive, it is like no other city. By virtue of its origins, which were grounded in paradox: because of the two Venices, the city could claim a foundation before that of Rome and, at the same time, a foundation that was from the outset always Christian.

Finally, Venice is eternal. As long as the sun rotates, it will endure. That Venetian history is continuous was confirmed when the second Venice was reborn from the first, in a legitimate succession, after the caesura of the Barbarian invasions. It was reconfirmed in the *apparitio*, when St. Mark revealed his enduring civic presence. It was validated, and re-validated, in a retrospective public art and architecture, which was a built up palimpsest of layer upon layer, with later ones replicating or adhering to earlier ones.

Ultimately, the referent is always Venice itself: not Rome, not Florence, not Constantinople, not Athens, not Jerusalem. Asked in 1561 to name those things about the city that pleased him most, Francesco Sansovino responded: "l'antichità delle cose della Città" – the antiquity of the things of the city.[4] The "mirror and light of all Italy," Venice absorbed and transcended her models.

APPENDIX 1

A NOTE ON THE *HYPNEROTOMACHIA POLIPHILI* AND THE IDENTITY OF FRANCESCO COLONNA

The identity of the author of the *Hypnerotomachia Poliphili*, published in 1499 by the Aldine Press, has puzzled scholars for centuries. The commentary to *Le Songe de Poliphile*, a French edition published by J. Kerver in Paris in 1546, stated that the author's name was to be found in the book itself in an acrostic made up from the first letter of each of the thirty-eight chapters: "POLIAM FRATER FRANCISCUS COLVMNA PERAMAVIT" (Friar Francesco Colonna passionately loved Polia).[1]

Francesco Colonna's authorship of the book is also supported by a passage that is printed in a single surviving variant copy of the 1499 Italian edition (Berlin, Deutsche Staatsbibliothek: Inc. 4508). The insertion is signed by a certain Matteo Visconti of Brescia. It consists of a piece of Latin prose and a dedication in Italian, where the key phrase is found in the last two lines: "Mirando poi Francisco alta columna / Per cui phama immortal de voi rissona."[2] Although a minority view holds that the acrostic refers only to the hero of the romance and not to the author, there is a general consensus among scholars that the book was, indeed, written by a certain Francesco Colonna.[3] The name was not an unusual one in fifteenth-century Italy, and the author's precise identity has remained an open question.

The first reasoned argument for Colonna's identity as a Franciscan friar attached to the convent of SS. Giovanni e Paolo in Venice was made by Tommaso Temanza in 1778, who treated him as the first Venetian architect in his book on the lives of the most celebrated Venetian architects and sculptors.[4] In 1959, M.T. Casella and Giovanni Pozzi published a carefully researched study in support of Temanza's claim.[5] It was followed in 1968 by a critical edition of the *Hypnerotomachia Poliphili* by Pozzi and Lucia A. Ciapponi in which the argument was reaffirmed. This edition in turn was reprinted in 1980 with an updating of the literature and a response to alternate proposals for authorship that had surfaced in the intervening years.[6]

In addition to the Visconti citation, which does not,

however, include the terms "Frater" or "Venetus," Pozzi's studies used as their point of departure three contemporary documents that appear to connect a Friar Francesco Colonna of SS. Giovanni e Paolo with the printing of an unnamed book.

1. A letter dated June 5, 1501, from the Master General of the Dominican order Vincenzo Bandello in Rome to Matteo Graziano at SS. Giovanni e Paolo ordering him to collect the monies advanced by the order to Magister Francesco Colonna "for the printing of books" (occasione libri impressi).[7]

2. A citation in a book by Leandro Alberti, historian of the Dominican Order, *De viris illustribus Ordinis Praedicatorum libri sex*, Bologna 1517, f. 154v, referring to two writers: "Thomas Mattei of Florence and Francesco Colonna Venetus, one of whom composed a huge volume of poems in the vernacular tongue . . . the other truly by his genius produced a certain book published in the mother tongue of literature and various and manifold things."[8] Pozzi understands the latter phrase to refer to Colonna.

3. A citation by the scholar Apostolo Zeno in 1723, reporting that a member of the Dominican order, G.B. de Rossi, had told him about a copy of the *Hypnerotomachia* preserved in the observant Dominican convent on the Giudecca that contained a hand-written marginal note dated June 20, 1512. Zeno transcribed the note, which states that the true name of the author was Franciscus Columna Venetus of the Dominican order who had been in love with a certain Hippolyta of Treviso who was called Polia in the book. It also states that Colonna presently lived in the convent of SS. Giovanni e Paolo.[9] Unfortunately, the book in question no longer survives, and there seems to be some doubt as to whether Zeno actually saw it himself.[10]

Casella and Pozzi then constructed a biography for the Venetian preacher, drawing heavily upon Dominican archival material. They estimate that he was born around 1433 and offer evidence that he was attached to a convent in Treviso from 1465 to 1477, with brief visits to Venice, that he was granted a bachelor's degree at the University of Padua in 1473, and that he resided at SS. Giovanni e Paolo more or less continuously from 1481 to 1500 (with short periods outside the city) and from 1512 until his death in 1527. The existence of this Francesco Colonna is abundantly documented, although in some cases the documents may refer to a homonym. The question is whether or not he was the author of the *Hypnerotomachia Poliphili*.

Aside from archival research on Colonna himself, Pozzi provided a detailed analysis of the language of the book along with a broader examination of the north Italian cultural context in which he proposes it was produced. While a number of place-names from the Treviso area are included in the book, one of its most troublesome features is the predominance of Tuscan vernacular and the slight presence of Veneto dialect in the text. Pozzi argues that this is the result of a deliberate attempt to purify the vernacular in an attempt to elevate it to the same dignity as classical Latin. He also points to a number of revealing words and place-names of Veneto origin that appear in the text, perhaps inadvertently. Among the words are "altana," "folpo," "russare," "tequa." Place-names that would probably have been familiar only to a Veneto native include (among others) the tiny villages of Quinto, Casacorba, and Morgano, and water-courses called Musestre, Storga, and Botteniga.[11]

Several scholars have taken issue with Casella and Pozzi's attribution, but none more energetically than Maurizio Calvesi. His revisionist proposal, first aired in 1965 in an article, is further elaborated in a book of 1980 and a number of essays. Citing the absence of consistent traces of Veneto dialect in the text, Calvesi questions whether a preacher and theologian could have produced such a paganizing, erotic, and even heretical text.[12] Then he attacks the integrity of Pozzi's primary documents. Judging the letter of 1501 and Leandro Alberti's citation of 1517 to be too vague, he claims that Apostolo Zeno's report was a deliberate falsity. It was not unusual in the eighteenth century, he asserts, for eminent scholars simply to invent documents.[13]

But if not the Dominican friar at SS. Giovanni e Paolo, who, then, was responsible for the *Hypnerotomachia*? Accepting the acrostic as a valid signature of the author, Calvesi follows up on an assertion in the French edition of 1546 that the author was a member of the noble Roman Colonna family. He finds a likely candidate in another Francesco Colonna, born around 1453 and from 1484 the Lord of Palestrina. This Colonna had overseen the construction of the present Palazzo Barberini on a hemicycle plan above the remains of the upper temple of the great sanctuary of Fortuna Primigenia at Palestrina. An inscription above the portal documenting the campaign uses an Ovidian form for Colonna's name that is, in Calvesi's view, strikingly close to many words found in the *Hypnerotomachia*: "Vastarunt toties quod ferrum flamma vetustas Francisci instaurat cura Columnigeri 1498." Calvesi

argues that the classical remains of the sanctuary stimulated Colonna's archeological interests and inspired much of the architectural discussion in the book. He argues, furthermore, that the botanical nomenclature in the text comes not just from Pliny, but from real plants growing at Preneste.[14]

Calvesi also develops a parallel argument in which he attempts to reconstruct the literary and humanistic culture of the Roman Colonna. He explains the term "Frater" found in the acrostic by suggesting that the Roman Colonna belonged to the Accademia Romana of Pomponio Leto, whose members saluted each other as "fratres." Allowing that the epigram of the Triestine humanist Raffaele Zovenzoni dedicated to a Francisco Columnae Antiquario may very well refer to the author of the *Hypnerotomachia*, he asserts that the language is more appropriate for a noble Roman than for a plebeian Venetian.[15] He also produces two epigrams by Angelo Colucci dedicated to a "Francesco Colonna romano" that refer to the writing of poetry and prose. It is also noted that Francesco's uncle was Cardinal Prospero Colonna, who was passionate about archaeology and who had commissioned Alberti in 1446 to raise the Roman ships sunk at the bottom of Lake Nemi.[16]

However, Calvesi's argument at this point remained at the circumstantial level, for he produced no documents linking the Roman Francesco Colonna to Venice or to the writing of a book. Moreover, his exposition as a whole is marred by a tendency to over-prove the issue by bringing in a good amount of extraneous material. For example, Petrarch's documented relationships with several members of the Colonna family is cited as evidence for the archaeological interests of this Colonna who lived 150 years later. Similarly, a good part of Calvesi's supporting material dates from the middle of the sixteenth century, such as Paolo Giovio's invention of an impresa for Stefano Colonna (either the son or grandson of the Francesco in question) using a two-tailed siren illustrated in the *Hypnerotomachia*.[17] This after-the-fact invention proves little, since the same siren is also found on the capitals of the ducal palace in Venice as part of the late quattrocento complex surrounding the Scala dei Giganti, in book illustrations made in Venice in the 1470–80s, and as an impresa embroidered on the cloak of a member of the Compagnia della Calza in Carpaccio's *The Healing of the Possessed Man*, painted for the Scuola Grande di San Giovanni Evangelista in 1494.[18]

Pozzi's refutation of Calvesi's thesis in the 1980 reprint edition of the *Hypnerotomachia* is further supported in a detailed review by Edoardo Fumagalli that came out the following year. He finds Pozzi's arguments for a Venetian provenance to be "assolutamente persuasivo." Allowing that Calvesi makes some good points, Fumagalli finds that his hypotheses go further than warranted by the evidence and are often improbable.[19] Likewise, Carlo Roberto Chiarlo attacks Calvesi's presentation as "disarticolato e frammentario." Noting that it is based primarily on material from the sixteenth century, he too finds it unconvincing.[20] Giorgio Patrizi affirms, as well, that

> the Veneto origin sustained by Pozzi appears on the whole the most solid and convincing. The hypothesis of Calvesi is entirely supported by inferences and interpretative propositions on which it is certainly possible to elaborate an edifice of attribution, but that do not have, at least for the most important claims, the character of objectivity.[21]

However, two subsequent publications by Calvesi call for another look at his thesis to determine if the weight of evidence is now falling more heavily in the Roman direction. In the first of these, Calvesi continues his investigation into the Roman Francesco Colonna's literary activities and family connections.[22] He claims that "the definitive clarification of the Francesco Colonna question is now at hand," and promises new documentary evidence to support his stand. Much of the essay goes over old ground. The mythological origins claimed by or imputed to the Colonna family are further discussed, but Calvesi's claims that Zovenzoni's epigram contained heraldic references to the Roman Colonna family remains unconvincing. The language of panegyric is notoriously hyperbolic in this period, and even plebeian families in Venice claimed Roman – even mythological – ancestors.[23]

Again Calvesi weakens his own case by encumbering it with material that he has already published and by buttressing it with notices taken from mid-sixteenth- and even seventeenth-century texts. However, he raises several new issues. Three pieces of evidence are introduced that appear to place the Roman Colonna within a humanistic literary context: a letter written by the noted Roman humanist Nicola Della Valle to a Francesco Colonna, who may well be the Lord of Palestrina; and, more significantly, two letters by Paolo Porcari that are definitely addressed to the Lord Francesco Colonna of Palestrina. One of these refers to him with the suggestive label of *docte poeta*.[24]

But the most important finding in the article relates to new archival discoveries that suggest a family relationship between the Roman Francesco Colonna and the Veronese lawyer, Leonardo Grassi, who had underwritten the cost of printing the *Hypnerotomachia*. More precisely, Grassi's brother, Francesco, a condottiere who had died in 1496 in the service of Guidobaldo da Montefeltre, was married to Francesca, daughter of Deiphobo dell'Anguillara and Caterina Colonna. Calvesi cites a document of 1484 that refers to this Caterina Colonna as the sister of the "reverendus pater dominus Franciscus de Columna sedis apostolicae prothonotarius." Assuming that the apostolic protonotary and the Lord of Palestrina are one and the same person – although it should be stressed that no corroborating evidence is presented to document such an identification – then the case for the Roman Colonna's authorship of the *Hypnerotomachia* would be very strong indeed.[25] For Leonardo Grassi's dedication of the work

to the Duke of Urbino, Guidobaldo da Montefeltro, could well be seen as a memorial to his dead brother Francesco, who was related to the author by marriage. Calvesi sees the entire scenario – marriage, frequent trips back and forth, printing of a book – as symptomatic of the close relationships between Rome and Venice in that period.[26]

The family connection remains Calvesi's most promising argument for a Roman provenance of the work. But even if further evidence is drawn from the archives to support his almost single-handed resuscitation of the Lord of Palestrina's claim to authorship, the mysteries of the author's imaginative approach to antiquity still remain. Calvesi's attempts to develop the figurative dependence of the woodcuts on Roman monuments are less than convincing. In an essay of 1989, he returns to the visual argument. Central to the discussion is his proposal that the great mosaic of the Nile in the Temple of Fortuna at Palestrina, first recorded at the end of the sixteenth century, was actually visible, at least in part, in the late fifteenth century. It would, of course, help to strengthen Calvesi's thesis, if it could be shown that Francesco Colonna himself was inspired by the imagery of a mosaic in his own palace at Palestrina.[27]

Calvesi cites as evidence a number of motifs and figures in Pinturicchio's frescoes in the Borgia apartments of the Vatican Palace (as well as other works in Rome) for which he claims derivation directly from the mosaic. He also finds reflections of the mosaic in the woodcuts of the *Hypnerotomachia* and argues they are further proof of the Roman provenance of Francesco Colonna.

Calvesi's case here has two major flaws. First, the Nile mosaic was badly damaged when it was moved to Rome in the seventeenth century. Only small fragments of the original work remain, and the remainder is a restoration.[28] Unfortunately, Calvesi does not provide illustrations of the fragments and it is difficult for the reader to pick out what is original and what is restored. It can be even be argued that the restoration was itself based on Pinturicchio's work. The argument thus becomes quite circular.

The second problem arises with the narrow focus of the figurative argument. For example, Calvesi likens the *Procession of Apis*, painted by Pinturicchio in the Borgia Apartments, to a similar cortege in the Nile mosaic, with the implication of a direct borrowing. The comparison is suggestive at first glance, but in fact, Pinturicchio's image can also be explained by a quite similar scene on the Arch of Titus, visible in the Roman forum.[29] Even if we accept the dependence of the artists of the *Hypnerotomachia* on such Roman images as Pinturicchio's frescoes (and I do not find this compelling), given the portability of drawings and the mobility of artists, we do not come closer to a Roman provenance for the author of the text. Indeed, virtually all the *Hypnerotomachia* woodcuts cited by Calvesi for their suggestive resemblances to the Nile mosaic or to paintings by Pinturicchio and others in Rome can be explained by Venetian prototypes.

For example, Calvesi calls attention to an arch-shaped garden pergola that appears both in the mosaic and in the woodcuts.[30] But as Jacopo de' Barbari's *View of Venice* of 1500 demonstrates, several such structures were standing at the time in gardens on the Giudecca and were already part of the Venetian landscape. They appear, as well, in illustrations for incunabula printed in Venice before the *Hypnerotomachia*. Another example of a "false friend" is found in the comparison of Pinturicchio's fresco of the Libyan Hercules posed "equilibristico" with a fountain featuring a "putto pisant" in the *Hypnerotomachia*. The motif had appeared already in a breviary illustrated by the miniaturist Petrus V in Venice about 1478.[31] Likewise, the fountains, the candelabra, the triumphs, and the trophies of the *Hypnerotomachia* all have their prototypes in Venetian art: the drawings of Jacopo Bellini, the Scala dei Giganti, tomb imagery, numerous frontispieces of books.[32] In the last analysis, without a rigorous comparison between the surviving original sections of the Nile mosaic and the Roman works that are said to derive from it, no firm judgments can be made about its visibility at the time.

Another candidate proposed for the authorship of the *Hypnerotomachia* is Fra Eliseo da Treviso. The name was already put forward by Fra Arcangelo Giani in 1618 in the *Annali* of the Servite order,[33] but was largely ignored over the years until Alessandro Parronchi called attention to the citation in 1963.[34] Pietro Scapecchi supported the attribution with archival material that documented the friar's presence in Florence in 1450 and in Treviso 1502–6.[35] Parronchi then identified this figure with a Fra Eliseo Ruffini of Lucca.[36] Aside from the original notice of Giani, however, no new evidence has been produced to link this friar with the *Hypnerotomachia*.[37]

It is difficult, moreover, simply to dismiss the early references to a Venetian friar named Francesco Colonna. To those already cited above, can now be added the handwritten notes and emendations in two copies of the *Hypnerotomachia* cited by Edoardo Fumagalli. One exemplar, now in Cambridge University Library, contains a sonnet written by Sisto Medici, a sixteen-year-old novice in the Venetian convent of SS. Giovanni e Paolo, that praises the book and names its author

as "Francesco de virtù ferma colo[n]nula." The other incunabulum, now in the Biblioteca Comunale of Siena, contains marginal glosses written in two hands that date to the period immediately after the publication of the book. Appearing to work in tandem, at least in the first part of the book, they correct, amplify, and give allegorical interpretations to numerous passages throughout the book. They also give the impression of an intimate acquaintance with the author. In fact, the second hand calls attention to the acrostic, long before it was announced in the French edition.[38]

To my mind, Colonna's identity and the cultural climate in which the book was conceived can only be satisfactorily explained by a closer examination of the language of the text. Among a number of such studies, a recent contribution by Marco Mancini, published in 1989, is illuminating on this point. After a detailed analysis, he judges that the book would have been written in northern Italy, with its linguistic roots grounded in a form of literary Italian that had developed in the area around Padua in the quattrocento. Significantly, he discovers no signs of the idiomatic language of Latium, the area around Rome. His findings, he concludes, "constitute a good support for the hypothesis of a Veneto birthplace for Francesco Colonna, a hypothesis that, in contrast to the others, reconciles the stylistic sense of the polifilesque artifice with its imaginary and ideological context."[39]

A new critical edition of the *Hypnerotomachia* with an Italian translation now being prepared by Professors Mino Gabriele (University of Udine) and Marco Ariani (University of Rome III) may provide even more conclusive answers. They will offer a new commentary that focuses on classical sources, both textual and figurative, and on the allegorical significance of Polifilo's journey. Gabriele finds Pozzi's identification of the Venetian Francesco Colonna to be the most convincing and well-documented case to be made thus far. In any event, he affirms that the genesis and execution of the work should be placed in the Venetian sphere: "I am convinced, because of the language utilized and because of the iconological references present in the HP, that the work would have been conceived and realized . . . in a Veneto ambient, with 'Venetian' preeminence."[40]

APPENDIX 2

Opera nova del fecundissimo giovene Pietro Pictore Aretino, zoe Stramboti, Sonetti, Capitoli, Epistole, Barzellete et una Desperata, Venice, Nicolo Zopino, Jan. 1512 [BMV, Misc. 2441,2, f. 4v–5v: unique example].

De tempore

Grotesche spoglie ludi strali e armi:
    Triumphi: archi: theatri: e bel scolture:
    Trophi: sepulchri: epitaphi: e carmi:
    Colossi: Amphiteatri: gesti: picture
    Victorie: tronchi: aurati marmi:
    Arastri: zappe: vomeri: e ficture
    Quel che non senten le mortal ruine
    Dal tempo in brieve son condutte alfine.

Col tempo in mar sumerge il forte legno
    Col tempo ogni gran stato cade in basso
    Col tempo mancha ogni terren disegno
    Col tempo ogni disitio va in fracasso
    Col tempo torna vil lhom tanto degno
    Col tempo si dispiana ogni gran masso
    Col tempo il forte fer divenin polve
    Col tempo el tutto in terra se risolve.

Torna ogni tempo a chi il tempo specta
    Ritorna lhom ala patria col tempo
    Col tempo vien ogni giusta vendecta
    Il fier nimico in carcer stia col tempo

Surge de lacqua la debil barchetta
    E vien tranquillo a lei spectato il tempo
    Col tempo torna ogni obscuro in luce
    E il tempo ogni desio alfin conduce.

Sil tempo da catena il tempo scioglie
    Sil tempo servitu liberta dona
    Sil tempo da martir il tempo gioglie
    Sil tempo mala sorte il tempo bona
    Sil tempo dona foco il tempo il toglie
    Sil tempo reo destin fama risona
    Sil tempo mha conducto in lacci enfoco
    Il tempo mi sciotta apoco apoco.

Hor sia che vol agliocchi dice il core
    Da che vol la fortuna diance pace
    Non per tuo fiume mi cessa lardore
    Ne per mio focho tuo acqua si sface
    Andiam la sorte placando e lamore
    E sopportando quelche piu ci spiace
    Spectiamo tempo miglior stella e fato
    Cha pace ogni nimico e destinato.

ABBREVIATIONS

ASV	Venice, Archivio di Stato
BMV	Venice, Biblioteca Nazionale Marciana
Cappellari, *Campidoglio veneto*	Cod. It. VII 15–18 (=8304–8307), Girolamo Alessandro Cappellari Vivaro Vicentino, *Il campidoglio veneto*, 4 vols.
Casella and Pozzi, *FC*	Casella, M.T., and Pozzi, Giovanni, *Francesco Colonna, Biografia e opere*, 2 vols., Padua 1959
Choniates, *Annals*	Choniates, Nicetas, *O City of Byzantium: Annals of . . .*, trans. Harry Magoulias, Detroit 1974
C.I.L.	*Corpus Inscriptionum Latinarum*, v: 1–2, *Inscriptiones Galliae Cisalpinae Latinae*, ed. Theodor Mommsen, Berlin 1872 and 1877
Colonna, *Hyp. Pol.*	Colonna, Francesco, *Hypnerotomachia Poliphili*, ed. Giovanni Pozzi and Lucia A. Ciapponi, 2 vols., Padua (1968) 1980
Dandolo, *Chronica extensa*	Dandolo, Andrea, *Chronica per extensum descripta aa.46–1280 d.C.*, ed. Ester Pastorello, in *Rerum Italicarum Scriptores*, n.s., XII:1, Bologna 1938
Degenhart and Schmitt, *Corpus: Jacopo Bellini*	Degenhart, Bernhard, and Schmitt, Annegrit, *Corpus der italienischen Zeichnungen, 1300–1450. Teil II. Venedig, Jacopo Bellini*, 4 vols., Berlin, 1990
Degenhart and Schmitt, *Corpus, Teil II: Venedig*	Degenhart, Bernhard, and Schmitt, Annegrit, *Corpus der italienischen Zeichnungen, 1300–1450. Teil II. Venedig. Addendu zu Süd- und Mittelitalien*, 3 vols. Berlin 1980
Giorgione. Atti	*Giorgione. Atti del Convegno Internazionale per il 500 centenario della nascita 29–31 Maggio 1978*, Castelfranco Veneto 1979
MCV	Venice, Biblioteca del Museo Correr
Petrarca, *Fam.*, trans. Bernardo	Petrarca, Francesco, *Rerum familiarum libri*, English trans. Aldo S. Bernardo, 3 vols., Albany 1975–85
Sanudo, *Vitae*[1]	Sanudo, Marin, *Vitae Ducum Venetorum*, ed. L. Muratori, in *Rerum Italicarum Scriptores*, o.s., XXII, Milan 1733
Sanudo, *Vite*[2]	Sanudo, Marin, *Le vite dei dogi*, ed. G. Monticolo and G Carducci, in *Rerum Italicarum Scriptores*, n.s., XXII:4, Città di Castello and Bologna, 1900–2

NOTES

PART I
PROLOGUE

1 Muñoz, *Studi d'arte medioevale*, 14, citing Migne, *Patrologia Graeca*, 133, 1419: "Alla vita rappresentata in figura – Accogli o uomo come ammonitore me che sono la vita. Trovasti, toccasti, ritenesti i miei capelli? Non ti abbandonare alla lussuria e alle mollezze, non insuperbire e non offendere la modestia. Tu mi vedi nudo, non ti dimenticare della nudità del mio fine. Ai miei piedi sono aggiunte delle ruote: temile, che non si volgano di qua e di là; le gambe sono alate, fuggo, mi sottraggo a te. Nella mano ho la bilancia, temine le fluttuazioni. Perchè mi prendi? Abbraccerai l'ombra terrai il vento. Perchè mi prendi? Terrai il fumo, il sogno, la traccia della nave (sull'acqua). Ricevi o uomo come ammonitore me che sono la vita. Non trovasti, non toccasti, non ritenesti i miei capelli? Ma non ti addolorare, non disperare. Son nudo, e sfuggito dalle mani di questi, forse ritornerò a te. Ai miei piedi sono attaccate delle ruote che si volgeranno a te velocemente. Le gambe sono alate: volo a te: porto la bilancia, forse in tuo vantaggio. Perciò non disperare."

2 Ibid., 90, citing epigrams by Posidippus, Callistratus, and Ausonius.

3 See Mango, "Antique Statuary," 73; and John Rupert Martin, *The Illustration of the Heavenly Ladder of John Climacus*, Princeton 1954, 50–52, pl. XIX, 72.

4 Cattaneo, *Architecture in Italy*, 334, dates it to *c*.1008, when the church was renovated. Polacco, *Sculture paleocristiane*, 138–42; and idem, *Cattedrale di Torcello*, 35–8, also dates the Kairos plaque and its companion (see below) to the eleventh century as manifestations of the "Macedonian Renaissance" of Byzantine art. For a dating to the second half of the twelfth century see Grabar, *Sculptures Byzantines*, 115–17; and Świechowski, "Les Courants classicisant," 203–9.

5 Cattaneo, *Architecture in Italy*, 334, reported that he found the fragment with the Victory figure in a stonecutter's shop in Venice in 1887.

6 See Whitrow, *Time in History*, 37ff.

7 Panofsky, "Father Time," 69–72. See also O.M. Dalton, *Byzantine Art and Archaeology*, Oxford 1911, 158–9.

8 See Muñoz, *Studi d'arte medioevale*, 8–9, for the later, more pessimistic epigram of Manuele Philes, who lived at the imperial court in Constantinople from the end of the thirteenth to the beginning of the fourteenth century.

9 Selvatico, *Sulla architettura e sulla scultura*, 17, saw the *Kairos* relief as a Roman fragment, possibly from Altino, dating to the third century, and suggested that the scene alluded to the cult of Mercury. Venturi, *Storia*, I, 522–3, states incorrectly that both reliefs were discovered in fragmentary state during excavations of the baptistery, "pochi anni fa." Giulio Lorenzetti, *Torcello*, Venice 1939, affirms only that the plaque of *Ixion* was discovered in the 1892 excavation. Cattaneo, *Architecture in Italy*, 334–6; and Polacco, *Sculture paleocristiane*, 138–42, cite the generally accepted view that the reliefs were probably part of the original pulpit of the cathedral and were transferred to the present site when the choir was rebuilt in the twelfth or thirteenth century. But see idem, *Cattedrale di Torcello*, 35–8, where Polacco proposes that the reliefs were originally part of the Doge's tribune in San Marco and would date to the period immediately after a 1063 reconstruction of the Basilica. According to this hypothesis, they were transferred to Torcello in 1418–26 during renovations in both churches.

10 Giacomo De Nicola, "Sarcophago con motivi della Nekyia di Polignoto," *Bollettino d'Arte*, II, 1908, 88–91, cites five examples, including the Torcello relief. See also Robert von Schneider, "Ueber das Kairosrelief in Torcello und ihm verwandte Bildwerke," in *Serta Harteliana*, Vienna 1896, 279–92; Muñoz, *Studi d'arte medioevale*, 15; and Grabar, *Sculptures Byzantine*, 115; and references in n. 3 above. The earliest example, in the Cairo Museum, is datable to the third to fourth century A.D.: I. Strzygowski, "Koptische Kunst," in *Catalogue général du Musée du Caire*, II, 1904, fig. 159 (no. 8757).

11 Ovid, *Metamorphosis*, 4.461; Virgil, *Aeneid*, 6.599–620. Ixion is not often represented in art and is typically depicted stretched out across the wheel, and not around it. See, for example, Panofsky, *Renaissance and Renascences*, 91–2 and fig. 59. The Ixion relief is now affixed to the inside of the choir enclosure behind the pulpit.

12 Grabar, *Sculptures Byzantines*, 116.

13 See the old classics on this issue, well worth re-reading: Panofsky, *Renaissance and Renascences*, 83–100; Panofsky and Saxl, "Classical Mythology in Mediaeval Art," 228–79; and Seznec, *Survival of the Pagan Gods*, 84–121. Cf. Mango, "Antique Statuary," 72–3, who states that Panofsky's "principal of disjunction" is not characteristic of Byzantine art.

14 Świechowski, "Courants classicizant," 203–9.

15 See the similar observation of Ruskin, *Stones of Venice*, 81–3.

16 Bosio, *Tabula Peutingeriana*; Annalina and Mario Levi, *Itineraria picta. Contributo allo studio della Tabula Peutingeriana*, Rome 1967, 21–3; and Konrad Miller, *Itineraria Romana. Römische Reisewege an der Hand der Tabula Peutingeriana dargestellt*, Stuttgart 1916. For a good facsimile edition see *Tabula Peutingeriana: Codex Vindobonensis 324*, Graz 1976.

17 Bosio, *Tabula Peutingeriana*, 98, 168–9.

18 Mambella and Sanesi Mastrocinque, *Le Venezie*, 31–2; and Forlati Tamaro, "Le iscrizioni," 291. Cf. Marzemin, *Origini romane*, whose claims that *ad portum* referred to Venice are largely discredited.

19 For Roman habitation on Torcello, see Crouzet-Pavan, "Venice and Torcello," 419. Recent archaeological investigations have yielded the remains of a boat and a waterside structure, datable by radiocarbon dating to *c.* A.D. 425–550, on San Francesco del Deserto, a tiny island northeast of the city. Excavations near the churches of S. Pietro del Castello and S. Lorenzo have produced remains dating to the sixth and seventh centuries A.D. The earliest material excavated in the Piazzetta area near San Marco is datable to the seventh or eighth century. For a full account, see Ammerman et al, "More on the Origins of Venice," 501–10; and idem, "New Evidence on the Origins of Venice," 913–16. Cf. Marzemin, *Origini romane*; Alberto Francesconi, "Una città sommersa tutta da scoprire," and Adriana Martini, "'Imperiale' per vocazione," both in *Marco Polo*, no. 89, June 1991, 12–13 and 14–16, respectively; and Dorigo, *Venezia origini*; and the caveat by Schulz, "Urbanism in Medieval Venice," 419–20, n. 2.

20 Cassiodorus, *Variarum libri XII*, 12.24. Cf. n. 19 above.

21 Forlati Tamaro, "Le iscrizioni," 291–8. The stone is thought to record the transfer of the bishopric of Altino to Torcello at the time of the Longobard invasions (*c.*635 or 639). For a good summary, see Sartor, *Altino*, 53–6.

22 The epigram was discovered in excavations of 1895 at the base of the semicircular wall of the presbytery. Damaged during removal, it was subsequently embedded in the left wall of the presbytery. For a transcription and Italian translation, see Carile and Fedalto, *Origini di Venezia*, pl. IV, and 352ff. See also Agostino Pertusi, "L'iscrizione torcellana dei tempi di Eraclio," *Bollettino dell'Istituto di storia della società e dello stato veneziano*, IV, 1962, 9–38.

23 Greenhalgh, "Discovery of Roman Sculpture in the Middle Ages," 157–64. As noted by Rodolico, *Le pietre*, 194–204, the early dependence on secondhand stone eventually gave way to brick for much large-scale construction, and to newly quarried Istrian limestone for architectural ornament.

24 Forlati Tamaro, "Le iscrizioni," 291–8. See also Polacco, "Venezia e l'arte antica," 597–616; Perry Caldwell, "Public Display," 9; and Marzemin, *Origini romane*, 213ff.

25 Forlati Tamaro, "Le iscrizioni," 292.

26 Marilyn Perry, *The Basilica of SS. Maria e Donato on Murano*, Venice 1980, 64. See also Giovanni Diacono, *Cronaca Veneziana*, 58.

27 Forlati Tamaro, "Le iscrizioni," 294.

28 Ibid., 293–7: "stanno a dimostrare con quale larghezza i Veneziani si servissero del materiale di terraferma, prima per le costruzioni, poi per interesse antiquario e quale ornamento delle loro case." The major epigraphical collections in Venice are in the Museo Archeologico, the Seminario Patriarcale and the Galleria Giorgio Franchetti (Ca d'Oro).

29 For the full text, see Cessi, *Documenti*, I, 93–9, no. 53. The church of S. Teodoro, about which little is known, was constructed after 775, according to Cessi, *Origo*, 67. See Carile and Fedalto, *Le origini*, 398–9; and Polacco, *San Marco*, 9–17.

30 For a succinct description of the early city, see Schulz, "Urbanism," 419–22.

31 Polacco, *San Marco*, 9–47, particularly 46 n. 93; and Dorigo, *Venezia origini*, 567. Cf. Demus, *Church of San Marco*, 90–100.

32 Demus, "Renascence of Early Christian Art," 348–61; idem, "Oriente e Occidente"; and idem, *The Church of San Marco*.

See also Kitzinger, "The Arts as Aspects of a Renaissance," 637–70.

33 From a rich literature, see Cracco Ruggini and Cracco, "Changing Fortunes," 463–75; Le Goff, "L'immaginario urbano," 5–43; and Frugoni, "L'antichità," 5–72.

34 Gustina Scaglia, "Romanitas pisana tra XI e XII secolo. Le iscrizioni romane del Duomo e la statua del console Rodolfo," *Studi Medievali*, XIII, 1972, 791–843; Giuseppe Scalia, "Il carme pisano sull'impresa contro i Saraceni del 1087," *Studi di filologia romanza offerti a Silvio Pellegrini*, Padua 1971, 597 (565–627); Peter Classen, "*Res Gestae*, Universal History, Apocalypse: Visions of Past and Future," in Benson and Constable, *Renaissance and Renewal*, 394–5; and Greenhalgh, "'Ipsa ruina docet'," 134–8. For spolia as agents of civic competition, see Esch, "Spolien," 52–4. For the use of spolia in late antique buildings, see Beat Brenk, "Spolia from Constantine to Charlemagne: Aesthetics versus Ideology," *Dumbarton Oaks Papers*, XLI, 1987, 103–9; and Joseph Alchermes, "*Spolia* in Roman Cities of the Late Empire: Legislative Rationales and Architectural Reuse," *Dumbarton Oaks Papers*, XLVIII, 1994, 167–78. For their use in medieval Italian buildings, see Greenhalgh, "Discovery," 157–64; and idem, *Survival of Roman Antiquities*.

35 William Hammer, "The Concept of the New or Second Rome in the Middle Ages," *Speculum*, XIX, 1944, 51 (50–62), who observes that in the Middle Ages the terms *Roma nova* and *Roma secunda* were typically applied to cities that sought to rival Rome: Constantinople, Aachen, Trier, Milan, Rheims, Tournai, and Pavia. Cf. Robert Lee Wolff, "The Three Romes: The Migration of an Ideology and the Making of an Autocrat," *Daedalus*, LXXXVIII, 1959, 293 (291–311); and Brown, "*Renovatio or Conciliatio?*" 127–54.

36 Mario Salmi, "La 'Renovatio Romae' e Firenze," *Rinascimento*, I, 1950, 5–24. See also Nicolai Rubinstein, "The Beginnings of Political Thought in Florence. A Study in Mediaeval Historiography," *Journal of the Warburg and Courtauld Institutes*, V, 1942, 198–227; and Charles T. Davis, "Il Buon Tempo Antico," in *Florentine Studies. Politics and Society in Renaissance Florence*, ed. Nicolai Rubinstein, London, 1968, 45–69.

CHAPTER I

1 Giovanni Diacono, *Cronaca Veneziana*, ed. Monticolo, 59, 13; and now in It. transl. with commentary: Giovanni Diacono, *La cronaca veneziana*, ed. De Biasi, Venice, 15: "Due sono le Venezie. Una è quella, di cui si parla nelle antiche storie, la quale si estende dai confini della Pannonia fino al fiume Adda. Ne è capitale la città di Aquileia, nella quale il santo evangelista Marco, illuminato dalla grazia divina, predicò il Vangelo del Signor nostro Gesù Cristo. L'altra è la Venezia che sappiamo esser situata nella zona insulare, nel golfo del mare Adriatico, dove le acque scorrono fra isola e isola, in una splendida posizione, abitata felicemente da una numerosa popolazione. Questa popolazione, per quanto è dato di capire dal nome e dagli annali, trae origine dalla prima Venezia."

2 Giovanni Diacono, *Cronaca Veneziana*, ed. Monticolo, 63, 5–17 (De Biasi ed., 22): "Così diedero a queste isole il nome di Venezia, donde provenivano, e quelli che oggi vivono in queste isole si chiamano Venetici. Eneti, sebbene in latino abbia una lettera in più, è nome che deriva dal greco e significa 'degni di lode'. Dopo che essi ebbero deciso di stabilire in queste isole la sede della loro futura residenza, costruirono alcuni castelli ben fortificati e città, e in tal modo si ricrearono

una nuova Venezia e insieme un'egregia provincia." See also Lorenzoni, "Origini di Venezia," 39–48; Carile, "La formazione del ducato veneziano," 31; Crouzet-Pavan, "Venice and Torcello," 419–21, and Medin, *Storia della Repubblica*, 6–8.

3 Pliny, *Historia Naturalis*, 3.130, cites Cato's claim of Trojan origins for the tribe of Veneti who settled in Este, Asolo, Padua, Oderzo, Belluno, and Vicenza. In ibid., 6.5, he refers to the writings of Cornelius Nepos on the Paphlagonian roots of the Eneti, from whom the homonym Veneti descended and settled in Italy. See also Virgil, *Aeneid*, 1.329–38, for the settlement of Padua by Antenor.

4 Demus, *Church of San Marco*, 165–80, with a summarized chronology on p. 206: San Marco I was begun c.829–32; San Marco II was quickly rebuilt c.976–8 by Doge Pietro Orseolo I after a fire; San Marco III was constructed from the foundations up c.1063–c.1094 under Doges Domenico Contarini, Domenico Selvo and Vitale Falier. Cf. Polacco, *San Marco*, 9–47.

5 Demus, "Renascence of Early Christian Art," 348ff. The ninth-century church can no longer be considered truly visible, although its plan has been adduced from modern excavations.

6 Ibid.; and idem, "Oriente e Occidente." For lingering cultural ties to Byzantium, see Pertusi, "Cultura bizantina," 326–49. For the period in general, see Kitzinger, "The Arts as Aspects of a Renaissance," 637–70.

7 Fasoli, "Nascità di un mito," 452, observing that the image cannot be identified with certainty as the church of San Marco. See also Molmenti, *Storia di Venezia*, 248.

8 Fasoli, "Nascità," 452; Rudt de Collenberg, "Il leone di San Marco," 58–60; and Brown, "Self-Definition of the Venetian Republic", 519. For Venetian seals see G. Bascapé, "Sigilli della repubblica di Venezia: Le bolle dei dogi. I sigilli di uffici e di magistrature," in *Studi in onore di Amintore Fanfani*, I. *Antichità e alto medioevo*, Milan 1962, 93–103. For coins see Papadopoli-Aldobrandini, *Le monete di Venezia*; and G. Castellani, *Civico Museo Correr. Catalogo della raccolta numismatica, Papadopoli-Aldobrandini*, Venice 1925.

9 Demus, *Byzantine Art and the West*, 134–35; and see now Dale, "*Inventing* a Sacred Past," 53–67.

10 Fasoli, "Nascità", 460, citing Petri Damiani, *Opera Omnia*, Paris 1743, 36–7; and Gregory VII in *Monumenta Germaniae Historica*, Epistolae selectae, 5 vols., Weimar 1916–52, II, 175, 341.

11 Laiou, "Observations on the Results of the Fourth Crusade," 47–60.

12 Cessi, *Origo*, with a discussion on dating on pp. XXVII–XXXIII: completed before the dogeship of Sebastiano Ziani (1172–8), with the exception of later updating of imperial, ducal, and episcopal catalogues. Cf. Carile, "La formazione," 44–64, who dates the three versions to 1081–1204.

13 In Cracco Ruggini and Cracco, "Changing Fortunes of the Italian City," 468.

14 Ibid., 468–69, where Cracco states that he was unable to find any reference by a Greek or Roman writer, whether pagan or Christian, who referred to Orpheus as the first founder of cities. Cf. Carile, "La formazione," 59–65.

15 Cessi, *Origo*, 7, 32–3: "Anthenor autem in litore lacum intravit cum septem galeis, ibique civitatem Aquilegia nomine, idest aquis ligata, edificavit."

16 Ibid., 154.

17 Buchthal, *Historia Troiana*, 53–9. See also Yates, *Astraea*, 50–51, 130–33 and passim

18 Cracco Ruggini and Cracco, "Changing Fortunes of the Italian City," 468.

19 Carile, "Il problema delle origini," 94–5: "empio pagano da quella plaga australe, di nome Attila, furiosissimo, con un grande esercito."

20 Although the year 421, later to become the canonical birthdate of the city, was already cited in chronicles of the late twelfth and early thirteenth century, the *Origo* does not take note of it. See De Biasi, "Leggenda e storia," 82.

21 Carile, "La formazione," 64–5. See also idem, "Una 'Vita di Attila'", 369–96.

22 Cessi, *Origo*, 52–3: "In turrem ascendite, ad astra autem videte." See also the legend of Bishop Mauro (or Magno) of Torcello, who had a vision of eight churches to be built on Rialto (ibid., 32–5). Cf. Pompeo Molmenti and Dino Mantovani, *Le isole della laguna veneta*, Bergamo 1904; Giovanni Musolino, "S. Magno," in *Santi e beati venezine. Quaranta profili*, Venice 1963, 87–93; and A. Niero, "Santi di Torcello e di Eraclea tra storia e legenda," in *Le origini della Chiesa di Venezia*, Venice 1987. For the deliberate downplaying of Torcello's historical importance relative to Rialto in later chronicles, see Crouzet-Pavan, "Venice and Torcello," 416–27.

23 Cessi, *Origo*, 146–53.

24 Ibid., 153–4: "Totos namque prenominatos antiquiores et nobiliores Veneticos, quos singilatim nominatos habemus, fuerunt ab antiquis eorum progenie sicuti commemoratos habemus. deinde vero recollegerunt se in antiqua Venecia ex diversis provinciis; edifficantes castra, manserunt ibi."

25 Ibid., 159: "Toti namque isti, quos per nomina recordatos habemus, qui de Eracliana Civitate nova et de Padua exierunt, in Matamauco et in Rivoalto habitare venerunt, et multitudo aliorum hominum cum eis, quam nominare non possumus: fecerunt et constituerunt in insula, que Matamauco modo appellata est, per omnes plateas plurimas ecclesias pulcherrimas sive domos construxerunt in omni ornatu eorum."

26 Ibid., 142: "Valeressi et Pipini multa habentes erant patrocinia de corpore sancti Martini confessoris. isti cum aliis convicinantibus fecerunt ecclesiam ad eius honorem. scolam autem ad honorem sancti Michaelis archangeli et sancti Viti martiris de illorum potentia in hac Dei ecclesia, aurum et argentum ad illorum salutem propter decimam ibique perpetualem constituerunt."

27 Cracco Ruggini and Cracco, "Changing Fortunes," 471.

28 Most notably Marco Barbaro, *Arbori de' patritti veneti* (1536): ASV, Misc. Codici I, Storia Veneta 22. For other references see Grubb, "Memory and identity," 379, nn. 10, 13. For the family in Venice, see Molmenti, *Storia di Venezia*, I, 435–68, and II, 313–56; and Stanley Chojnacki, "In Search of the Venetian Patriciate: Families and Factions in the Fourteenth Century," in Hale, *Renaissance Venice*, 47–90. See also chap. 11 infra.

29 Foscarini, *Della letteratura veneziana*, 199: "Onde sembra, che ai nostri antichi bastasse l'avere degli antenati loro quella sola memoria, che ne conservavano le carte del pubblico, sulle quali poscia in questi ultimi secoli vennero composte le intere genealogie."

30 Schulz, "La piazza medievale," 284–5: the Piazza San Marco measures about 12,500 m², while the largest mainland squares – Bologna, Florence, Siena, Vicenza – measure no more than 9,500 m².

31 Ibid.

32 Silvano Borsari, "Una famiglia veneziana nel Medioevo: gli

33 Sanudo, *Vite*², 302; cf. ibid., 282: "era richo; trovò, si dice, una vacha [vasca?] maziza d'oro in Altim [Altino]." See also Sartor, *Altino Medievale e Moderna*, 56, for the myth of Altinate treasure that the fleeing inhabitants were thought to have buried during the Longobard invasions.

34 See Brown, *Venetian Narrative Painting*, passim, with bibliography; and idem, "Self-Definition," 523–6.

35 For a good summary account, see Kenneth M. Setton, "The Fourth Crusade," in *The Year 1200: A Symposium*, Metropolitan Museum of Art, New York 1975, 33–52. See also Edgar H. McNeal and R.L. Wolff, "The Fourth Crusade," in *A History of the Crusades*, eds. K.M. Setton, R.M. Wolff, and H.W. Hazard, Philadelphia 1962, II, 153–86.

36 See Laiou, "Observations on the Results of the Fourth Crusade," 47–60; and Georgopoulou, "Late Medieval Crete and Venice," 479–96.

37 G.G. Ferrard, "The Amount of Constantinopolitan Booty," *Studi Veneziani* XIII, 1971, 95–104.

38 For the general tendencies of this period see *La coscienza cittadina nei comuni italiani del Duecento*, Convegni del Centro di Studi sulla Spiritualità Medievale XI (Oct. 11–14, 1970), Todi 1972; *Uomini, terre e città nel Medioevo*, ed. Giovanni Cherubini, Milan 1986; and Frugoni, *Distant City*, 54–105.

39 Fasoli, "Nascità," 445–79, who also discusses a counter-myth. For an overview of recent literature, see James Grubb, "When Myths Lose Power: Four Decades of Venetian Historiography," *Journal of Modern History* LVIII, 1986, 43–94. See also the valuable insights in Muir, *Civic Ritual*.

40 See for example, Demus, *Church of San Marco*, 165–83; Wolters, *Die Skulpturen von San Marco*; Weitzmann, "The Genesis Mosaics of San Marco", 105–42; Herzog, *Untersuchungen zur Plastik*; Polacco, *San Marco*, 83–135. See also Cutler, "From Loot to Scholarship."

41 For an illuminating discussion of Venice's dual heritage from both East and West, see Pincus, "Venice and the Two Romes," 101–14.

42 Mango, "Antique Statuary," 55–63. See also Schulz, "La piazza medievale," 134–56 for the urban layout.

43 Choniates, *Annals*, 305–6 (chs. 558–9).

44 Ibid., 353 (ch. 643).

45 Ibid., 306 (ch. 560).

46 Ibid., 357–9 (chs. 648–50).

47 Smith, *Architecture in the Culture of Early Humanism*, 166, with an English translation of the full text, 199–215. Cf. Mango, "Antique Statuary," 70, 75.

48 Choniates, *Annals*, 315 (ch. 573).

49 Ibid., 360 (ch. 652).

50 Perry Caldwell, *Public Display*, 17–21; and Perry, "Saint Mark's Trophies," 48–9.

51 Godfrey Goodwin, "The Reuse of Marble in the Eastern Mediterranean in Medieval Times", *Journal of the Royal Asiatic Society* 1977, 17–18 (17–30).

52 Harrison, *Temple for Byzantium*, 139–43.

53 For example, Choniates, *Annals*, 301–2.

54 As asserted by Greenhalgh, "Discovery of Roman Sculpture," 157–64.

55 Mango, "Antique Statuary," 67–72.

56 BMV, Cod. It. VII 2034, c. 155A, cited in Sanudo, *Vite*², 283: "e voio che voy sapyè che da può che quele cholone fo adute a Venyexia per alguni boni Venyziany li quali algun belo edefizio ho che li podese aver qualche reliquie ho chorpy sancty, lor il aduxeva volentiera alla soa patria . . ."

57 See Hazlitt, *Venetian Republic*, I, 332–7, for an English translation of the complete scenario, including the dialogue of the debate in the Great Council. He writes: "It is perfectly characteristic of what must to a certain extent be called prehistoric history, that the very words used by the speakers in the Venetian Assembly on this important occasion are registered by some of the early Chronicles of the Republic with evident good faith. From what sources their information proceeded is highly uncertain." Cf. Cicogna, *Iscrizioni veneziane*, IV, 552–3.

58 Romanin, *Storia documentata*, II, 208: "i migliori però non ne fanno cenno, ed invero il discorso che viene attribuito al doge sarebbe troppo disdicevole ad un patriotta veneziano. Nondimeno potrebb'essere, che l'idea fosse sorta nella mente di alcuno, e venisse anche discussa nel Consiglio, ma giustamente rigettata . . ." The episode appears in the manuscript chronicles of Daniele Barbaro and Girolamo Savina, who termed the final vote, "il voto della Provvidenza."

59 Cited by Schulz, "La piazza medievale," 148: "Dives, probus, patiens et in cunctis planus/Nulus sibi similis nobilis vel sanus/ Nec si Caesar viveret et Vespasianus."

60 Just when this event took place is uncertain. Although a later chronicle tradition generally dates it to the time of Sebastiano Ziani's dogeship (1172–8), Schulz (ibid., 258 and 309 n. 97) is reluctant to place them there before 1204. Doge Andrea Dandolo, who would conscientiously record the piazza and communal palace projects, did not mention the columns in his *Chronica extensa* (begun *c.*1343), a silence that tends to cast doubt on the reliability of later claims of a late twelfth-century dating. The first to take note of them was Nicolò Trevisan in a chronicle of *c.*1366. Cf. Sanudo, *Vitae*¹, cols. 507–8; *Vite*², 226, 283–4; and Perry Caldwell, *Public Display*, 13–15, who accepts the twelfth-century dating.

61 See Muraro, "La grande scuola di scultura," 31; and Molmenti, *Storia di Venezia*, I, 156–7. For a similar message on the thirteenth-century sculptural decoration of the main portal of San Marco, see Polacco, *San Marco*, 100–104; and idem, "San Marco e le sue sculture del Duecento," 59–75.

62 Perry Caldwell, *Public Display*, 30–33; Perry, "Saint Mark's Trophies." 48–9; Rudt de Collenberg, "Il leone di San Marco," 57–84. See also G. Pavanello, "San Marco nella leggenda e nella storia," *Rivista mensile della città di Venezia* VII, 1928, 293–324; Silvio Tramontin, "San Marco," in Tramontin, *Culto dei santi*, 59–61; and Wolters, *Bilderschmuck*, 231–5.

63 Sansovino, *Venetia città nobilissima*, 1663 edn, I, 317. One wonders if the bronze Colossus of Barletta, part of the Venetian booty from the Fourth Crusade, but abandoned in a shipwreck, had originally been intended as a guardian figure for the column. See Wilton-Ely, *Horses of San Marco*, 163.

64 Luisa Sartorio, "San Teodoro, Statua composita," *Arte Veneta* I, 1947, 132–4: first half fourteenth century. Cf. Giovanni Mariacher, "Postilla al 'S. Teodoro, statua composita'," *Arte Veneta* I, 1947, 230: early fifteenth century. See also Wolters, *Scultura veneziana gotica*, 20, 136; and Pincus, "Venice and the Two Romes," 102.

65 For St. Theodore, see Antonio Niero, "I santi patroni," in Tramontin, *Culto dei santi*, 91–5; and Muir, *Civic Ritual*, 93–5.

66 See above, nn. 42, 47.

67 For the columns see Haftmann, *Italienische Säulenmonument*, 125–7; and Herklotz, *"Sepulcra" e "Monumenta"*, 211–12. Two suggestive parallels in other cities can be cited for these years. An image of St. Michael the Archangel was incised on the wall

68 The figures were positioned in this manner in late fifteenth-century prints. Given the Venetian propensity for keeping things the same, we may conjecture that this was their original orientation.

69 Schulz, "Urbanism in Medieval Venice," 437–40; and idem, "La piazza medievale." Schulz implicitly excludes the monumental columns from the twelfth-century campaign. During that phase he sees relatively modest goals that were essentially intended "to create a meeting space for the citizens of the new commune and a council hall for their elected representatives." Cf. Demus, *Church of San Marco*, 101, who sees the piazza as a huge atrium, or quadriportico, typical of Early Christian schemes.

70 Demus, *Church of San Marco*, 101–3; Howard, *Architectural History*, 35–45; and James S. Ackerman, "Sources of the Renaissance Villa," *Studies in Western Art* II (Acts of the XXth International Congress of the History of Art), Princeton 1963, 6–18. See also Greenhalgh, "Discovery," 161, who suggests that the Doge's Palace might echo the Bukoleon in Constantinople.

71 Demus, *Church of San Marco*, 101.

72 Greenhalgh, "Discovery", 159.

73 Perry Caldwell, *Public Display*, 18–23, who sees the preservation of the horses motivated by political designs rather than by considerations of antiquity or beauty. See also Wilton-Ely, *Horses of San Marco*. For their changing meanings over time, see Perry, "Saint Mark's Trophies," 27–33.

74 Jacoff, *Horses of San Marco*.

75 For the marble reliefs, see Zuliani, "I marmi di San Marco," 68–70, 94–7. For the pilasters, see Harrison, *Temple for Byzantium*, 143, referring to I Kings 7, 13–22; and Deichmann, "I pilastri acritani," 75–89.

76 Perry, *Public Display*, 24–8; and idem, "Saint Mark's Trophies," 39–45.

77 James D. Breckenridge, "Again the 'Carmagnola'," *Gesta* XX, 1981, 1–7; and Jacoff, *Horses of San Marco*, 80–82.

78 See Demus, *Church of San Marco*, 29, 112–14; Muir, "Images of Power," 16–52; and Brown, "Self-Definition of the Venetian Republic," 522.

79 The discussion of these reliefs is based on Demus, *Church of San Marco*, 113–35. Demus cites these dates in Wolters, *Die Skulpturen von San Marco*. Cf. Wladimiro Dorigo, "Sul problema di copie veneziane da originali bizantini," in Traversari, *Venezia e l'Archeologia*, 151–6.

80 Demus, *Church of San Marco*, 125–34.

81 Mango, "Antique Statuary," 63–4, 75.

82 Panofsky, *Renaissance and Renascences*, 64–5 and passim.

83 Demus, *Church of San Marco*, 134ff. Cf. Panofsky and Saxl, "Classical Mythology," 228.

84 Świechowski and Rizzi, *Romanische Reliefs*, 10–11, 17 and 26; Świechowski, "Les courants classicisant," 203–9, who notes at least a dozen *patere* with Hercules that survive from the twelfth to fourteenth centuries; and Rizzi, *Scultura esterna*, 21–40 and passim. See also Perry, *Public Display*, 81–110, for a rich account of spolia and other reliefs set into private buildings. As late as 1509, Doge Leonardo Loredan described a Romanesque relief of a female head as an augury of bad fortune: cited in Chambers and Pullan, *Venice*, 397–8.

85 This interpretation is indebted to the discussion in Settis, "Continuità, distanza, conoscenza," 440–45.

86 Pincus, "Fourteenth-Century Venetian Ducal Tomb," 393–4; and Herzog, *Untersuchungen zur Plastik*, 122–3.

87 Herzog, *Untersuchungen zur Plastik*, 17–55. Cf. Pincus, "Fourteenth-Century Venetian Ducal Tomb," 394–5.

88 Etienne Coche de la Ferté, "Deux camées de Bourges et de Munich, le Doge Ranieri Zeno et la Renaissance paléochrétienne a Venise au XIIIᵉ siècle," *Gazette des Beaux-Arts*, ser. 6, LV, 1960, 273 (257–80): "l'aptitude particulière des Vénetiens à copier, des le moyen âge, les modèles antiques, sans les interpréter (mais non sans erreur parfois) . . ." See also Demus, *Church of San Marco*, 174–83. For the Venetian production of Byzantine-style cameos and other objects, see Laiou, "Venice as a Centre of Trade," 20.

89 Richard Brilliant, "I piedistalli del Giardino di Boboli: spolia in se, spolia in re," *Prospettiva* XXXI, 1982, 2–17.

90 Cf. Lowenthal, *The Past is a Foreign Country*, 74–87, 248; and Settis, "Continuità, distanza, conoscenza," 382, 466–72. Settis observes: "È dunque l'uso delle rovine, dei frammenti, si carica inevitabilmente di una tensione verso l'intero: che sarà, anche verso il recupero del significato originario." See now idem, "Des ruines au musée," 1347–80.

91 Howard, "Venice and Islam," 59–74.

92 Demus, *Church of San Marco*, 104–5.

93 Cited by Sinding-Larsen, "St. Peter's Chair," 42–3.

94 Sinding-Larsen, "Venezia e le componenti artistiche bizantine e cristiano-orientali," 37–43.

95 Canal, *Estoires*, 2–3: "E per questo voglio che gli uni e gli altri, sempre, conoscano le opere dei Veneziani, e chi essi furono e donde vennero e chi sono e come edificarono la nobile città che si chiama Venezia, ch'è oggi la più bella del mondo." See also Fasoli, "La *Cronique des Veniciens*," 42–74.

96 Fasoli, "La *Cronique des Veniciens*," 52

97 Canal, *Estoires*, 6–7.

98 Ibid., 340–41.

99 Demus, *Church of San Marco*, 15. The date of its installation is not documented. Some scholars have argued that the sculpture was originally intended to represent Joachim's Dream.

100 Ibid., 218–19.

101 Canal, *Estoires*, 20–21. See Brown, *Venetian Narrative Painting*, 79–86; and the detailed analysis by Dale, "*Inventing a Sacred Past*," 85–101, who sees "a dynamic process of inventing and reinventing a sacred past that contrasts sharply with the apparent conventionality of medieval hagiography."

102 John White, "The Reconstruction of Nicola Pisano's Perugia Fountain," *Journal of the Warburg and Courtauld Institutes* XXXIII, 1970, 15–83.

103 Le Goff, "L'immaginario urbano," 27.

104 Weiss, *Renaissance Discovery*, 18–19. See Plate 35 *infra*. For more detailed treatments, see Lorenzo Braccesi, *La leggenda di Antenore da Troia a Padova*, Padua 1984; Girolamo Zampieri, ed., *Padova per Antenore*, Padua 1990.

105 Cited by Frugoni, *Distant City*, 75.

106 Carile, "Note di cronachistica veneziana: Piero Giustinian e Nicolò Trevisan," 103: "quod fiat unus liber in quo scribantur omnes iuridiciones Comunis Veneciarum, et specialiter Ducatus, et omnia pacta, et omnia privilegia que faciunt ad iurisdicionem Comunis Veneciarum" (Dec. 18, 1291).

107 Cited in Carile, "Aspetti della cronachistica veneziana," 80, 91–2. See also Le Goff, "L'immaginario urbano," 27.

108 Agostino Pertusi, "Le profezie sulla presa di Costantinopoli (1204) nel cronista veneziano Marco (c.1292) e le loro fonti bizantine (pseudo-Costantino Magno, pseudo-Daniele,

at the Porta Appia in Rome in 1327 as a defense against Ludwig of Bavaria. In 1329 Florence erected new statue of the Virgin and patron saints at the Porta Romana. For both programs see Julian Gardner, "An Introduction to the Iconography of the Medieval Italian City Gate," *Dumbarton Oaks Papers* XLI, 1987, 208–11 (199–213).

pseudo-Leone il saggio)," *Studi Veneziani*, n.s., III, 1979, 13–46. The defensive posture remains to this day: Gallo, *Il Tesoro*, 12, who emphasizes that the French took away much more loot than the Venetians.

109 Polacco, "Porte e cancelli bronzei," 14–23; idem, *San Marco*, 144–8; and Prosdocimi, "Le porte antiche," 529–39.

110 Polacco, "Porte e cancelle," 21–2.

111 Demus, *Church of San Marco*, 140, 180–81. Cf. Prosdocimi, "Le porte antiche," 532–4; and Lazzarini, "La tradizione classica," 23–6, who suggests that the use of classical models indicates a new understanding of the distinction between epochs and styles.

112 ASV, Collegio, Lettere segrete, 1308–1310, fol. 78, cited by Cecchetti, *Documenti*, 13, doc. 99. Cf. Rodolico, *Le pietre*, 197–8. See also the forthcoming study by Debra Pincus, "The Stones of Venice in the Baptistry of San Marco: Eastern Marbles in Western Mosaics," to appear in a volume of memorial essays in honor of Richard Krautheimer.

113 BMV, cod. It. cl. VII 125, *c*.6, cited by Cecchetti, *Documenti*, doc. no. 8: "Ritornato Giustinian da questa impresa vittoriosa, porto con lui molte spolglie della vittoria, colonne bellissime et altre finissime pietre di marmo . . . e nella fabbrica di quella fece metter tutte le pietre e tutte le colonne marmoree che esso già haveva portato di Sicilia . . . ."

114 BMV, cod. It. VII, 794, *c*.58t, "Cronaca di Zorzi Dolfin fino al 1478," cited by Cecchetti, *Documenti*, doc. no. 60.

115 BMV, cod. It. VII, 324, "Cronaca anomina", cited by Cecchetti, *Documenti*, no. 812. Cf. BMV, cod. Lat. X, 74, *c*.58, "Cronaca di Pietro Dolfin"; BMV, Cod. It. VII, 517, *c*.41, "Cronaca Magno"; BMV, cod. It. VII, 1800, *c*.27, "Cronaca anomina."

116 Eusebius, *Vita Constantini*, III, 31, cited by Mango, *Art of the Byzantine Empire*, 11.

117 Procopius, *De aedificiis*, I, i, 23ff, cited by Mango, *Art of the Byzantine Empire*, 72.

118 Cf. Brown, "*Renovatio* or *conciliatio*," 127–54.

CHAPTER 2

1 English translation by Elaine Fantham from Cicogna, *La festa delle Marie*: "Gens devota Deo, Teucrorum clara propago, / Illyrico posuit moenia pulcra salo. / Pergama non fuerant tanto speciosa decore / Cum petiit raptam Graecia tota nurum. / Diva quidem Phrygiam reparans tutela ruinam / Transtulit Iliacos per freta longa Deos, / In Latuim Aeneas Siculis deductus ab undis / Romuleae tandem gentis origo fuit. / Tutus at Adriacas veniens Anthenor in oras, / Providus Illyrici coepit amoena sinus. / Euganeosque fugans, henetos, Troasque locavit, / Et Venetum genti nomen utrique dedit / Pluraque cum starent Venetae fundamina gentis, / Tentavit pelagi subdere jura sibi. / Urbs quoque paulatim mediis fundatur in undis, / Quae caput, et regni summa sit una novi. / Inde tenet nomen multis commune, regensque / Tot populos sceptro, multiplicata sono est. / Iamque adeo crevit *totum* vulgata per orbem / Roma sit ut Veneta viribus urbe minor." Cicogna repeated a paleographical error that led to a misidentification of the author as Pace del Friuli. Cf. Stadter, "Planudes, Plutarch, and Pace of Ferrara", 139–62, who shows that the author is really Pace da Ferrara and dates the poem to 1299–1300. Pace is indebted to the first book of the *Aeneid*: "Antenor potuit, mediis elapsus Achivis/Illyricos penetrare sinus atque intima tutus/regna Liburnorum et fontem superare

Timavi" (Virgil, *Aeneid* 1.242–4). The event is also reported in the opening chapter of Livy.

2 For the Feast of the Maries, see Muir, *Civic Ritual*, 135–56; and G. Musolino, "Culto mariano," in Tramontin, *Culto dei Santi*, 256–60.

3 For the counter-myth, see Fasoli, "Nascita di un mito," 462–4. For the Serrata, see Lane, "The Enlargement of the great council of Venice", in *Florilegium Historiale: Essays presented to Wallace K. Ferguson*, ed. J.G. Rowe and W.H. Stockdale, Toronto 1971, 236–74.

4 Bellavitis and Romanelli, *Venezia*, chap. 5.

5 Dandolo, *Chronica per extensum*, 313, ll.4: "Civitas quoque Rivoltina, que mediacione canalis actenus divisa fuerat, nunc ex lignei pontis constructione unita est." Cf. ibid., 369, l.17. The first bridge had been built on pontoons in 1172, according to Sanudo, *Vite*[2], 286. See Cessi and Alberti, *Rialto*, 163–4; and also Howard, *Architectural History*, 48, who states that the pontoon bridge was replaced only at the end of fourteenth century.

6 Cessi and Alberti, *Rialto*, 29–35, 163–5, noting that a new market, the Rialto Nuovo, was opened in 1281, and a long-term program for renewal of the entire area was finalized in 1288.

7 Bellavitis and Romanelli, *Venezia*, 57–8, state that by 1392 horses were forbidden in the Piazza San Marco even on feast-days. See Sansovino, *Venetia nobilissima*, 1663 edn., 455–6.

8 Stadter, "Planudes," 139–62.

9 See chap. 1 *supra*, at n. 105.

10 Weiss, *Renaissance Discovery*, 17–21. See also Jacks, *The Antiquarian and the Myth of Antiquity*, 43.

11 Weiss, *Renaissance Discovery*, 17–21; Ullman, "Post-Mortem Adventures," 53–77; and Bodon, "L'immagine di Tito Livio," 69–92.

12 Weiss, *Renaissance Discovery*, 22–7; and Luisa Capoduro, "Effigi di imperatori romani nel manoscritto Chig. J VII 259 della Biblioteca vaticana. Origini e diffusione di un'iconografia," *Storia dell'Arte* LXXIX, 1994, 286–325.

13 Brown, *Venetian Narrative Painting*, 79–80.

14 ASV, *Pacta* IV, c. 13, cited by Bartolomeo Cecchetti, *La vita dei veneziani nel 1300*, Venice 1885 (repr. 1980, with intro. by Ugo Stefanutti), 73–4: "Ad aeternam rei memoriam tam personarum nunc vivencium quam futurorum, et quod publice omnibus innotescat . . . dictus leo cognovit carnaliter dictam leonissam, ipsamque prenavit, quemadmodum solita sunt alia animalia se invicem saltari et cognosci atque pregnari, ut per quamplures personas hoc visum fuit, occulata fide . . . dicta leonissa peperit per naturam sicut animalia faciunt, tres leoncinos vivos et pilosos, qui statim nati vivi incoeperunt se movere, & ire circum circa matrem per ipsam cameram, sicut hoc viderant dominus dux predictus et quasi omnes de Venetiis et aliunde, qui dicta die erant Venetiiis, qui cumcurrerunt ad hoc videndum quasi miracolosum." One of the cubs was given to the Signore of Verona; the others remained in Venice and lived for a long period. Cf. Sanudo, *Vite*[1], cols. 594–5.

15 Monticolo, "Poesie latine," 250–51, 270–71.

16 For a discussion of the entire correspondence with transcriptions of the original texts, see Monticolo, "Poesie latine," 244–97. See also Lazzarini, *Paolo de Bernardo*, 4–6; Medin, *Storia della repubblica*, 12–14; and Saxl, "Petrarch in Venice," 141.

17 Monticolo, "Poesie latine," 251–2, 273–4.

18 Ibid., 261, 280–85.

19 Ibid., 265–6, 291–2, who notes the inclusion of several additional verses by a Dominican friar, Fra Pietro.

20 Brown, *Venetian Narrative Painting,* 37–9, 259. For Bonincontro's text, see Sanudo, *Vite*[2] 22:4, 370–411.

21 Brown, *Venetian Narrative Painting,* 37 and *passim,* particularly chap. 5. Zenatti, "Il poemetto di Pietro de' Natali," 123, suggests that there were already paintings of the event in the Palazzo Ducale in the thirteenth century.

22 See Lazzarini, *Paolo de Bernardo*; V. Bellemo, "La vita e i tempi di Benintendi de' Ravagnani Cancelliere Grande della Veneta Repubblica," *Nuovo Archivio Veneto* n.s. XXIII, 1912: 237–84; and XXIV, 1912, 54–95; and the essays in Padoan, *Petrarca, Venezia e il Veneto.*

23 *Familiari* VIII.5, written to Luca Cristiani, 19 May 1349, (in Francesco Petrarca, *Le familiari,* ed. V. Rossi, Florence 1934, II, 172): "Andreas, non minus bonarum artium studiis quam tanti magistratus insignibus vir clarus." See also Pincus, "Andrea Dandolo," 192–3.

24 See Ester Pastorello, Intro. to Dandolo, *Chronica per extensum*; *descripta,* E. Simonsfeld, "Andrea Dandolo e le sue opere storiche," *Archivio veneto* XIV:1, 1877, 1–101; Cracco, *Società e stato,* 399–440; and Arnaldi, "Andrea Dandolo Doge-cronista," 127–268; and C. Ravegnani, "Andrea Dandolo," in *Dizionario Biografico degli Italiani,* Rome 1986, 32, 432–40.

25 Lazzarini, "'Dux ille Danduleus'," 131–2. Burke, *Renaissance Sense of the Past,* 12–13, holds that it is not correct to speak of historical forgery in a period that lacks a "sense of historical perspective."

26 Cadorin, *Notizie storiche,* 188. Cf. Cecchetti, *Documenti,* docc. 102, 103, 830; Pastorello in Dandolo, *Chronica extensa,* VIII. Pincus, "Andrea Dandolo," 194, sees Dandolo's vision of the powerful doge as the motive force of all his patronage in San Marco.

27 For the Greek–Latin ambiguity of the work, see H.R. Hahnloser, "Magister latinitas und peritia greca," in G. von der Osten and G. Kauffmann, eds., *Festschrift für Herbert von Einem,* Berlin 1965, 77–93.

28 Hahnloser and Polacco, *Pala d'oro,* 3–71 and 81–111. Cf. Deer, "Die Pala d'Oro," 308–44; Gallo, *Tesoro,* 157–66; and Fraser, "The Pala d'Oro and the Cult of St. Mark," 273–9.

29 Giovanni Diacono, *Cronaca veneziana,* in Monticolo, *Cronache veneziane antichissime,* 143; and Dandolo, *Chronica extensa,* 180. Gallo, *Tesoro,* 175–8, claims that the upper panel of the present Pala d'Oro was made from Orseolo's silver *tabula.*

30 Dandolo, *Chronica extensa,* 225: "Sequenti MCV anno, dux tabulam auream, gemis et perlis mirifice Constantinopolim fabricatam, pro uberiori reverencia beatissimi Marci evangeliste, super eius altare deposuit; que aliquibus superaucta thesau'ris, usque in hodiernum existit."

31 See the references in n. 28.

32 Dandolo, *Chronica extensa,* 284: "Angelus Faledro solus procurator ducalis capele, tabulam altaris sancti Marci, additis gemis et perlis, ducis iussu, reparavit . . ."

33 Hahnloser and Polacco, *Pala d'Oro,* 9: "Anno milleno cento iungito quinto – tunc Ordelafus Faledrus in urbe ducabat – hec nova facta fuit gemis ditissima pala; que renovata fuit te, Petre, ducante, Ziani, et procurabat tunc Angelus acta Faledrus anno milleno bis centenoque noveno."

34 Ibid. 10: "Post quadrageno quinto post mille trecentos Dandulus Andreas, preclarus honore, ducabat; nobilibusque viris tunc procurantibus almam ecclesiam marci venerandam iure beati de Lauredanis Marco Frescoque Quirino tunc vetus hec pala gemis preciosa novatur."

35 Renato Polacco, "Una nuova lettura della Pala d'Oro (gli smalti, le oreficerie e il ciborio)," in Hahnloser and Polacco, *La Pala d'Oro,* 115–18. Cf. Fraser, "The Pala d'Oro and the

Cult of St. Mark," 277, who argues for its inclusion on the original Pala of 1105; and Deer, "Die Pala d'Oro," 320–40, presents a case for its addition in 1209. Cf. Hahnloser and Polacco, *Pala d'Oro,* cat. 1, 5–7; Demus, "Zur Pala d'Oro," 267ff, and Buchthal, *Historia Troiana,* 55–6.

36 Cf. Pincus, "Andrea Dandolo," 197–8, who stresses Dandolo's focus on the historically central role of the doge: "In the reworking, the Pala d'Oro became a piece that Venice possessed because of its doges, again, in terms of a line of succession that creates a living chain across the face of history." See also idem, "Venice and the Two Romes," 104–6.

37 Muraro, *Paolo da Venezia,* 16–17, 53, 87, 143–144; Pallucchini, *La pittura veneziana del Trecento,* 36–40; and Giuseppe Fiocco and Rona Goffen, "Le pale feriali," in Hahnloser and Polacco, *Pala d'Oro,* 163–84.

38 Katzenstein, "Three Liturgical Manuscripts," *passim.*

39 Wolters, *Scultura gotica,* 160, dates them *c.*1331–50. For a reconstruction, see Hahnloser and Polacco, *Pala d'Oro,* 81–3, pls. LXV–LXVI; and Gallo, *Tesoro,* 189–90.

40 Jacks, *The Antiquarian and the Myth of Antiquity,* 132. For the Marian cult in Venice, see Goffen, *Piety and Patronage,* 138–54.

41 Dandolo, *Chronica extensa,* 53. Dondi was granted citizenship in 1335 or 1339. Carile, "Aspetti," 78, prefers the earlier date. Cf. Lazzarini, "Il preteso documento della fondazione di Venezia," 96–116; E. Franceschini, "La Cronachetta di Maestro Jacopo Dondi," in *Atti dell'Istituto Veneto di scienze, lettere ed arti,* ICIX:2, 1939–40, 969–84; and Crouzet-Pavan, "Venice and Torcello," 424–5. Cf. Anthony Grafton, *Forgers and Critics. Creativity and Duplicity in Western Scholarship,* Princeton 1990.

42 Brown, *Venetian Narrative Painting,* 39–42 and cat. IV, 261–5. See also Pallucchini, *La pittura veneziana,* 106–17; and Banzato and Pellegrini *Da Giotto al tardogotico,* 65–75.

43 Wolters, *Scultura gotica,* 82–8, 244ff.

44 Ibid., 190.

45 Dandolo, *Chronica Extensa,* 234–5. He mentions that the relics were placed in a chapel, perhaps the old church of San Teodoro, supposedly demolished in 1063, but placed precisely in the area of the present Cappella S. Isidoro (Demus, *Church of San Marco,* 73).

46 Raphayni de Caresinis, *Cronica extensa,* in *Rerum Italicarum Scriptores,* n.s., XII:2, Bologna 1939, 8: "Item dux, corpus beatissimi Isidori martyris, diu in ecclesia sancti Marci latitantis, reperit, ipsumque in capella, quam ibidem construi fecit, devotissime collocavit." Raffaino Caresini continued the *Chronica extensa* after Dandolo's death. Cf. Sanudo, *Vitae*[1], col. 617. See also Wolters, *Scultura gotica,* I, 53, 189–90, cat. 79, and II, figs 310, 315, 319; and *La chiesa ducale di S. Marco,* II, 78–80, and III, 34.

47 Polacco, *San Marco,* 273–85.

48 Muraro, *Paolo da Venezia,* 68–9; Demus, *Church of San Marco,* 46–7, 79; Degenhart and Schmitt, *Corpus, Teil II. Venedig,* I, 101; and Rona Goffen, "Paolo Veneziano e Andrea Dandolo. Una nuova lettura della pala feriale," in Hahnloser and Polacco, *Pala d'Oro,* 173–84.

49 See Brown, *Venetian Narrative Painting, passim.*

50 Dandolo, *Chronica extensa,* 232: "lapidem super quem Christus extra civitatem sedit."

51 Ibid., 280. See Pincus, "Christian Relics and the Body Politic," 39–57.

52 Dandolo, *Chronica extensa,* 92–3: "Detulit ecciam secum de Alexandria kathedram, in qua beatus Marcus evangelista in eadem urbe pontificium tenuit, que, subsequenti patriarcha, Venecias portata est." The seat was first recorded in the basilica

in 1534 when it was moved from behind the high altar to the baptistery. The date of its arrival in Venice is unknown. Although some have suggested that it was brought from Alexandria with Mark's relics in 828, others propose that it came from Grado, where thrones of both St. Mark and St. Hermagoras are recorded in early sources. See Danielle Gaborit-Chopin's catalogue entry in *The Treasury of San Marco, Venice*, Milan 1984, 105, no. 7.

53 Andre Grabar, "La 'Sedia di San Marco' à Venise," *Gazette des Beaux-Arts*, 7, 1954, 19–34. Hahnloser, *Tesoro*, II, 9, cat. 10, observes that the chair was too small to serve as a real throne. While it would have served as a reliquary, it may also have been used as an evangeliary in an early Christian church. See also Buchthal, *Historia Troiana*, 54.

54 Staale Sinding-Larsen, "St. Peter's Chair in Venice," in *Art the Ape of Nature. Studies in Honor of H.W. Janson*, ed. Moshe Barasch and Lucy Freeman Sandler, New York 1981, 35–50.

55 As observed by Glenn Most.

56 Pincus, "Andrea Dandolo and Visible History," 200.

57 Buchthal, *Historia Troiana*, 60: "Veneciarum urbem inhabitaverit ille Troyanus Anthenor."

58 Dandolo, *Chronica extensa*, 59–60; and idem, *Chronica brevis*, in ibid., 351. Cf. Buchthal, *Historia Troiana*, 60.

59 Buchthal, *Historia Troiana*, 1971, 24. Cf. Degenhart and Schmitt, *Corpus, Teil II. Venedig*, 2, p. 101.

60 Cf. the review of Buchthal, *Historia Troiana*, by Silvana Ozoeze Collodo, in *Archivio Storico Italiano* CXXX, 1970, 553–61. See chap. 3 *infra* for two other illuminated manuscripts of the *Historia Troiana* made in Venice about 1370.

61 Ludolf von Suthem (Südheim), *De Itinere Terrae Sanctae Liber*, cited by Paton, *Chapters on Mediaeval and Renaissance Visitors*, 26–9: "ubi quondam illa nobilissima civitas Troia fuit sita, cuius aliquod vestigium non apparet, nisi aliqua fundamenta in mari sub aqua et in aliquibus locis aliqui lapides et aliquae columnae marmoreae subterratae, quae tamen dum inveniuntur, ad alia loca deportantur. De quibus est sciendum, quod in civitate Venetiae non est aliqua columna lapidea vel aliquod bonum opus lapideum sectum, nisi de Troia ibidem sit deportatum." Cf. J.P.A. Van der Vin, *Travellers to Greece and Constantinople. Ancient Monuments and Old Traditions in Medieval Travellers' Tales*, Leiden 1980, I, 32–3.

62 Paton, *Chapters on Mediaeval and Renaissance Visitors*, 29: "Nam ea civitate ianuensi non est aliqua columna marmorea vel aliquod opus bonum lapideum sectum, nisi sit de Athenis ibidem deportatum et totaliter ex Athenis civitas est constructa, sicut Venetia ex lapidibus Troiae est aedificata."

63 Raphayni de Caresinis, *Cronica*, 8: "iuxta Sanctum Marcum quiescit, in capella baptismali, quam nobili opere musaico decoravit."

64 Muraro, *Paolo da Venezia*, 33, 121. Cf. Tozzi, "I mosaici del battistero," 418–32; and Pallucchini, *La pittura veneziana del Trecento*, 75–8.

65 Cf. Muraro, "Petrarca, Paolo Veneziano e la cultura artistica," 161–2, who dates the mosaic to *c*.1330 on the basis of style and makes the unconvincing suggestion that the portrayed doge is Francesco Dandolo.

66 According to Arnaldi, "Andrea Dandolo, Doge-Cronista," 154, 205 n. 4; Tozzi, "I mosaici del battistero," 426; Pertusi, "Quedam," 46–7; and Saxl, "Petrarch in Venice," 43. Cf. Muraro, *Paolo da Venezia*, who suggests Nicolò Pistorini, Cancelliere Grande from 1323 to 1347. To be excluded is Raffaino Caresini (suggested by Demus, *Church of San Marco*, 79) who took office only in 1365.

67 A similar costume, excepting the headgear, is seen in the miniature of the Capitolare of Paolo Belegno, Procurator of San Marco (1367), illustrated in Molmenti, *La Storia di Venezia*, 86, who identifies the figure in the mosaic as the Cancellier Grande. Tozzi, "I mosaici del battistero," p. 426, refers to him as "un altro personaggio sconosciuto, certo un magistrato." Cf. Testi, *La storia della pittura veneziana*, 514, for a *consigliere* in the same costume.

68 Pincus, "Andrea Dandolo and Visual History," 196. Cf. Arnaldi, "Andrea Dandolo Doge-Cronista," 205, who defines the mosaic as a "sintesi figurativa del suo Dogado."

69 Dandolo, *Chronica extensa*, p. CIII: ". . . si que inter mortales ullum laudis locum teneat beneficii gratitudo, illas honorificentias intactas servare, quas nobis iugi solicitudine paravit antiquitas, nichilo minoris quam novas edere censeamus, in quo et nostra sublimatur autoritas, posterorum providetur utilitas, et accepti muneris grata memoria commendatur . . ." (Eng. trans. from Katzenstein, "Three Liturgical Manuscripts," 250–51).

70 For the Florence campanile, see Marvin Trachtenberg, *The Campanile of Florence Cathedral*, New York 1971. For analogous programs, see John White, "The Reconstruction of Nicola Pisano's Perugia Fountain," *Journal of the Warburg and Courtauld Institutes* 33, 1970, 70ff; and C.G. Mor, ed., *Il Palazzo della Ragione di Padova*, Vicenza, 1963.

71 See *infra*, Prologue to Part II.

72 Settis, *Giorgione's Tempest*, 119–21. Cf. Didron and Burges, "Iconographie du Palais Ducal," 68–88, 193–216; and Sinding-Larsen, *Christ in the Council Hall*, 167–74.

73 Sinding-Larsen, *Christ in the Council Hall*, 48–55; Martindale, "The Venetian Sala del Gran Consiglio," 76–124.

74 Sanudo, *Vita*[1], 109–10, recording the name Carolus instead of Pipinus. Cf. Monticolo's note, p. 110 n. 2, observing that other writers recorded the name Pipinus.

75 Dandolo, *Chronica extensa*, 128–40, whose identification of Agnello Participazio (the family surname was later changed to Badoer) as the first doge at Rialto is accepted by modern scholars.

76 BMV, Cod. It. VII, 519 (8438), c. 23A, cited by Monticolo, in Sanudo, *Vite*[2], 22:4, 109 n. 8: "questo ancora una pitura plechlara [sic] e insegna dechiara." Cf. Sanudo, *Vite dei dogi*, in ibid. for the same use of the painting. For Trevisan, see Carile, "Note di cronachistica veneziana," 119–25.

77 Sanudo, *Vite*[2], 110–12. Francesco Sansovino, writing in 1581 (*Venetia nobilissima*, 1663 edn., II, 538), is more cautious. He notes that the two brothers, "secondo alcuni, portarono il Trono Ducale in Rialto," but only because of the portrait and *titulo* painted in the Great Council Hall.

78 Brown, *Venetian Narrative Painting*, 39–41. See also a detailed discussion and an argument for a preceding cycle of history paintings in Martindale, "The Venetian Sala del Gran Consiglio," 76–124.

79 See Schmitt, "Der Einfluss des Humanismus," 215–57; idem, "Zur Wiederbelebung der Antike," 167–218; Donato, "Famosi Cives," 27–42; and idem, "Gli eroi romani," 95–152.

80 Mommsen, "Petrarch and the Decoration of the Sala Virorum Illustrium", 113–14; and Gasparotto, "La Reggia dei Da Carrara," 95–109. See also chap. 3 *infra*.

81 Martindale, "Venetian Sala del Gran Consiglio," 96–7, who suggests a French precedent.

82 See Giandomenico Romanelli, "Ritrattistica dogale: ombre, immagini e volti," in *I Dogi*, ed. Gino Benzoni, Milan, 1982, 125; Giulio Lorenzetti, "Ritratti di dogi in Palazzo Ducale," *Rivista di Venezia* 12, 1933, 387–98; and Jürg Meyer zur Capellan, "Zum venezianischen Dogenbildnis in der zweiten

Hälfte des Quattrocento," *Konsthistorisk Tidskrift* 50, 1981, 70–86.

83 Wolters, *Scultura gotica*, 62–7, 146, 213–14, 223.

84 Ibid., 67, 223.

85 Ibid., 67, 146, 223: "MCCCXCIIII. HOC OPVS FACTVM FVIT TEMPORE EXCELSI DOMINI ANTHONII VENERIO DEI GRATIA DVCIS VENETIARVM AC NOBILIVM VIRORVM DOMINORVM PETRI CORNERIO, ET MICHAELIS STENO HONORABILIVM PROCVRATORVM. IACHOBELLVS ET PETRVS PAVLVS FRATRES DE VENECIIS FECIT HOC OPVS."

PART II

PROLOGUE

1 Petrarca, *Fam*, VI.2, trans. Bernardo, 294. Cf. Mommsen, "Petrarch's Conception," 232.

2 Petrarca, *Africa*, IX, 451–7, cited by Mommsen, "Petrarch's Conception," 240.

3 Ibid., 228.

4 Quinones, *Renaissance Discovery of Time*, 3, whose telling insights inspired much of the discussion that follows. For the Torcello reliefs, see the Prologue to Part I *supra*.

5 See Le Goff, "Merchant's Time and Church's Time," 29–42. For another view, see Gerhard Dohrn-van Rossum, *Die Geschichte der Stunde*, Munich 1992.

6 L.T. Belgrano, "Degli antichi orologi pubblici d'Italia," *Archivio Storico Italiano* ser. 3, VII:1, 1868, 31–3 (28–68). See also Le Goff, "Labor Time," 43–52. For the debate on when the mechanical clock was invented, see Lynn White, *Medieval Technology and Social Change*, Oxford 1962, 122ff.

7 Molmenti, *Storia di Venezia*, 322.

8 See *supra*, chap. 2, nn. 39–40.

9 Carlo Cipolla, *Clocks and Culture, 1300–1700*, London 1967, 52.

10 For the planetarium, see Giovanni Dondi dall'Orologio, *Tractatus Astrarii (Biblioteca Capitolare di Padova, cod. D. 39)*, ed. A. Barzon, E. Morpurgo, A. Petrucci, G. Francescato, Vatican 1960. Cf. D.S. Bedini and F.R. Maddison, "Mechanical Universe: The Astrarium of Giovanni de' Dondi," in *Transactions of the American Philosophical Society*, n.s. LVI, 1966; and Derek J. De Solla Price, "On the Origin of Clockwork, Perpetual Motion Devices and the Compass," *Contributions from the Museum of History and Technology* IX (United States National Museum, Bulletin 218), Washington, D.C. 1959, 82–112.

11 Mommsen, *Petrarch's Testament*, 84 f; and Rose, "Petrarch, Dondi and the Myth," 102.

12 Cessi and Alberti, *Rialto*, 49–51: "leggieri contrappesi, di bello e grande magistero, che batteva le ore senza difficoltà con una sonorità tripla del predecessore." See also Brown, "Committenza e arte di stato."

13 Molmenti, *Storia di Venezia*, 52, citing Milanesi, *Documenti per la storia dell'arte senese*, Siena 1854, I, 326, doc. 108: "sona le ore, et vene fora uno galo, el qual canta tre volte per ora."

14 Cf. Wilcox, *Measure of Times Past*, 153–8: and Burke, *Renaissance Sense of the Past*, 19. Le Goff, "Merchant's Time and Church's Time," 34–9, speaks of the new conjunction of natural time, professional time, and supernatural time as "a decisive change in Western man's mental structures that began in the twelfth century."

15 Cosenza, *Petrarch's Letters*, 4: *Fam*. XXIV, 3.

16 Ibid., 89: *Fam*. XXIV, 7.

17 Petrarca, *Fam*., trans. Bernardo, 239 (*Fam*. V, 4): "agli uomini grandi ogni luogo sia patria."

18 Cosenza, *Petrarch's Letters*, 101: *Fam*., XXIV, 8.

19 Bevilacqua, "Geografi e Cosmografi," 325–74; Schulz, "Jacopo de' Barbari's View," 442–67; and idem, "Maps as Metaphors."

20 Degenhart and Schmitt, "Marino Sanudo und Paolino Veneto," 1–134.

21 Ibid., partic. 17–18, 25–6.

22 Ibid.; and Bevilacqua, "Geografi e Cosmografi," 356–8. Cfr. Bellavitis and Romanelli, *Venezia*, 53.

23 Bevilacqua, "Geografi e Cosmografi," 356–8; and Degenhart and Schmitt, "Marino Sanudo und Paolino Veneto," 60–87.

24 Cessi and Alberti, *Rialto*, 29–35, 163–5; and Brown, *Venetian Narrative Painting*, 268 and *passim*, particularly chap. 5.

25 Cessi and Alberti, *Rialto*, 39, 312–15. Cfr. Brown, *Venetian Narrative Painting*, 83–4, 261, 268.

26 Burke, "Historical Perspective," 617; and idem, *Renaissance Sense of the Past*, 1–6.

27 Petrarca, *Fam*. VI, 2, trans. Bernardo, 293.

28 Burke, *Renaissance Sense of the Past*, 7–13.

29 Petrarca, *Fam*. VI, 2, trans. Bernardo, 293.

30 Burke, *Renaissance Sense of the Past*, 13–20.

31 As evidenced by legends about prophetic mosaic images in San Marco that were said to have been devised by Joachim da Fiore (c.1135–1202), the Abbot from Calabria whose Trinitarian model of history had great appeal in the fourteenth and fifteenth centuries. See Reeves, *Influence of Prophecy*, 96–7; Niccoli, *Prophecy and People*, 23–5; and chap. 12 *infra*.

32 Burke, "Historical Perspective," 627; and idem, *Renaissance Sense of the Past*, 1–6. See also Le Goff, "Merchant's Time and Church's Time," 36–7; and Pierre Francastel, *Peinture et Société. Naissance et destruction d'un espace plastique. De la Renaissance au Cubisme*, Paris 1951.

CHAPTER 3

1 Vatican Library, cod. Vat. Lat. 1960, f. 13, cited with English trans. by Juergen Schulz, "Jacopo de' Barbari's View of Venice," 452: "Sine mapa mundi ea, que dicitur de filiis ac filiis filiorum Noe et que de IIII^or monarchiis ceterisque regnis atque provinciis tam in divinis quam humanis scripturis, non tam difficile quam impossibile dixerim ymaginari aut mente posse concipere. Requiritur autem mapa duplex, picture ac scripture. Nec unum sine altero putes sufficere, quia pictura sine scriptura provincias seu regna confuse demonstrat, scriptura vero non tamen sufficienter sine adminiculo picture provinciarum confinia per varias partes celi sic determinat, ut quasi ad oculum conspici valeant." Cf. Jacks, *The Antiquarian*, 50–52. For a detailed discussion of the manuscript, see Degenhart and Schmitt, "Marino Sanudo und Paolino Veneto," 60–87.

2 Degenhart and Schmitt, "Marin Sanudo und Paolo Veneto," 17. One is reminded of similar descriptions made of the Florentine humanist Niccolò Niccoli of a century later. See Alsop, *Rare Art Traditions*, 324–5, with primary source references.

3 Degenhart and Schmitt, "Marin Sanudo und Paolo Veneto," 16–20.

4 Petrarca, *Fam*., V, 4 (Nov. 22, 1343), trans. Bernardo, I, 238.

5 BMV, cod. Lat. Zan. 399 (1610), f. 98 recto. For the plan of Venice, see T. Temanza, *Antica pianta dell'inclita città di Venezia*, Venice 1781; and Schulz, "Jacopo de' Barbari's View," 445.

6 Biblioteca Vaticana, cod. Vat. Lat. 1960, f. 270 verso. A map

of Rome was also begun in a third codex now in Paris, but only the walls were drawn: Paris, Bibliothèque Nationale, Parisin lat. 4939, f. 27r. See Degenhart and Schmitt, "Marin Sanudo und Paolino Veneto," 86–7; Benocci, "Le figurazioni", 69–72; and Jacks, *The Antiquarian*, 44–54.

7 W. Holtzmann, "Der älteste mittelalterliche Stadtplan von Rom," *Jahrbuch des Deutschen Archäologischen Instituts* XLI, 1926, 56–66; and Jacks, *The Antiquarian*, 54.

8 Onorio d'Autun, *De imagine mundi*, cited by F. Finzi, "Di un inedito volgarizzamento dell'Imago mundi di Onorio d'Autun, trato dal codice estense VII. B. 5," in *Zeitschrift für romanische Philologie* XVII, 1893, 519–20 (490–543); and ibid., XVIII, 1894, 1–73): "Antiqui civitates secundum precipuas feras ob significationem formabant. Unde Roma formam leonis habet, quia ceteriis bestiis quasi rex preest." Cf. Benocci, "Le figurazioni," 63.

9 "In Ymagine mundi [Rom]a habet formam leonis," cited by Benocci, "Le figurazioni," 71.

10 Degenhart and Schmitt, "Marino Sanudo und Paolino Veneto," 87.

11 As proposed by Jacks, *The Antiquarian*, 45, who notes that few of the monuments inside the walls are oriented correctly.

12 Cf. Benocci, "Le figurazioni," 70, whose political interpretation of the animals is not convincing. Richard Krautheimer, *Rome. Profile of a City, 312–1308*, Princeton 1980, 209, 233, identifies the area as a deer park serving the adjacent Vatican palace.

13 Cf. Jacks, *The Antiquarian*, 48–50.

14 See A. Michaelis, "Storia della collezione capitolina di antichità fino all'inaugurazione del Museo (1738)," *Mitteilungen des Kaiserlich deutschen archaeologischen Instituts. Römischer Abteilung* VI, 1891, 12–16; William S. Heckscher, *Sixtus IIII Aeneas Insignes Statuas Romano Populo Restituendas Censuit*, The Hague n.d.; and *Da Pisanello alla nascità dei Musei Capitolini*, 207ff.

15 Degenhart and Schmitt, "Marino Sanudo und Paolino Veneto," 86ff. Cf. Schulz, "Jacopo de' Barbari's View of Venice," 456–7, 462–3.

16 Benocci, "Le figurazioni," 72, states that Leonardo was the artist, but see Wilhelm Erben, *Rombilder auf kaiserlichen und päpstlichen Siegeln des Mittelalters*, Graz, Vienna, Leipzig 1931, 55–6, 81–2, 110–11, and tables III–IV, who cites a document naming a certain Lionardo from Venice as the artist who designed the golden bull of Henry VI in 1312 that also included identifiable Roman monuments. Noting its stylistic similarities to the bull of Ludwig IV, Erben attributes the latter to a follower of Lionardo. It is possible, however, that the same artist was responsible for both bulls. A Venetian goldsmith named Leonardo is cited in documents in 1338 and 1342. See *infra* n. 37.

17 In addition to the citations in the previous note, see Dorothy Scherer, *The Marvels of Ancient Rome*, New York 1955, no. 6; G.B. De Rossi, *Piante iconografiche e prospettiche di Roma anteriori al sec. XVI*, Rome 1879, III, 87–9; V. Capobianchi, "Le immagini simboliche e gli stemmi di Roma," *Archivio della Società Romana di Storia Patria* 19, 1897, 354–5 (347–417); and C. Cecchelli, *La vita di Roma nel Medio Evo*, I, Rome 1951–2, 112–14, 127.

18 According to tradition, Brennus was a Gallic king who captured Rome *c*.390 B.C. and said "Vae victis." See Brennus, s.v., *The Oxford Classical Dictionary*, ed. N.G.L. Hammond and H.H. Scullard, 2nd edn., Oxford 1970, 179.

19 Fra Paolino, map of Venice: BMV, MS Lat. Zan. 399 (1610), f. 98r: "Roma suos cineres vidit sub duce Breno. Incendium suum oruit sub Alarico. Successivos atque cotidianos runiarum defectus deplorat. Et more senis decrepiti vix potest alieno baculo sustentari nil habens honorabilis vetustatis preter antiquatam lapidum congeriem et vestigia runiosa. Ex gestis beati Benedicti antistiti Canusie dicti quia per Totilam Roma destrueretur ait Roma a gentibus non exterminabitur sed tempestatibus coruscis et turbinibus ac terremotu fatigata marcescet in semetipsa."

20 Rome, Vat. Lat 1960. According to Degenhart and Schmitt, "Marino Sanudo und Paolino Veneto," 84–5, this is probably the presentation copy given to King Robert of Naples.

21 Ibid., 20, 87.

22 Petrarca, *Fam.* II, 12 (Letter to Cardinal Giovanni Colonna, Feb. 13, 1337): cited by Anthony Luttrell, "Capranica before 1377: Petrarch as Topographer," in *Cultural Aspects of the Italian Renaissance*, ed. C. Clough, Manchester 1976, 9 (9–21).

23 Biondo, *Italia illustrata*, 353: "pictura Italiae quam imprimis sequimur Roberti Regis Siciliae et Francisci Petrarcae ejus amici opus," cited by Degenhart and Schmitt, "Marin Sanudo und Paolino Veneto," 20. See also Mori, "Le carte geografiche," 268ff.; and Jacks, *The Antiquarian*, 48–51. For a drawing of Castel Sant'Angelo (probably by another hand) in Petrarch's copy of Pliny (Paris, Bibliothèque Nationale, MS Par. Lat. 6802, f. 266v), see Chiovenda, "Zeichnungen Petrarcas," 31.

24 See *supra*, chap. 1, n. 33.

25 See, for example, Frugoni, "L'antichità," 5–21; and Greenhalgh, "'Ipsa ruina docet'," 129–32.

26 Laiou, "Venice as a Centre of Trade," 15–16.

27 Sanudo, *Vite*[1], col. 534.

28 Perry, "Pride of Venice," 798.

29 Perry Caldwell, *Public Display*, 84–6.

30 Ristoro d'Arezzo, *Mappa mundi. Destinazione ottava*, IV: *Delle vasa antiche*, in V. Nannucci, *Manuele della letterature del primo secolo della lingua italiana*, 3rd edn., Florence 1874, 201–3; cited by Dacos, "Arte italiana e arte antica," 9: "che li conoscitori, quando le vedeano, per lo grandissimo diletto raitieno e vociferavano de se, e deventavano ad alto e uscieno de se, e deventavano quasi stupidi; e li non conoscenti la voleano spezzare e gettare. Quando alcuno de questi pecci venia a mano a scoplpitori o a disegnatori, o ad altri conoscenti, tenelli in modo de cose santuarie, maravigliandosi che l'umana natura potesse montare tanto alto." See also Cantino Wataghin, "Archeologia e 'archeologie'," 187–8; and Weiss, *Renaissance Discovery*, 13–14.

31 Transcribed and discussed in detail by Gargan, *Cultura e arte*, 34–65, who also provides rich background information on Forzetta and his family. See also idem, "Oliviero Forzetta e le origini del collezionismo veneziano," 13–21, for a summary and updating of his research on this topic.

32 Gargan, *Cultura e arte*, 37, n. 10, defines them as antique heads; and Alsop, *Rare Art Traditions*, 299–300, as cameos. Muraro, *Paolo da Venezia*, 74, n. 56, proposes bronze medals. They may well have been a mixture of genres.

33 Gargan, *Cultura e arte*, 42–3. Sanudo later noted that Jacopo Sansovino was ordered by the Signoria to remove them for installation in the Libreria di San Marco then under construction. For reasons unknown they were moved instead to the church of Santa Maria dei Miracoli where they remained until 1811, when they entered the museum.

34 Idem, "Oliviero Forzetta e la diffusione dei testi classici," 73–80. Cf. idem, "Oliviero Forzetta e le origini del collezionismo veneziano," 13, which cites 136 volumes and 24 fascicules of loose leaves.

35 Ibid., 46–53.

36 Gargan, *Cultura e arte*, 38: "Item queras exigere omnia designamenta, que condam fuerunt Perenzoli, filii magistri Angeli, pignorata penes magistros Franciscum et Stephanum de Sancto Iohanne Novo, et quaternum suum, in quo sunt omnia animalia et omnia pulcra, facta manu dicti Perenzoli et omnes eius taglos pariter et designamenta, ubicumque pignorata et deposita etc. . . . Item de testa, leonibus, anera, equis depictis quos habet Anna soror condam Ioachini, que testa habet super caput gislandam de rosis cum una infula . . . Item de puero condam Guillielmi Zaparini lapideo et multis aliis designamentis Perenzoli quas uxor condam ipsius habet etc. Et nota quod Marinus de Gallera habet leones, equos, boves, nudos homines, caelaturas hominum et bestiarum et aves condam Perenzoli."

37 Gargan, *Cultura e arte*, 46–55; and Muraro, "Varie fasi dell'influenza bizantina," 182–4.

38 See, for example, Sanudo, *Itinerario*, 86–8, discussed in chap. 7 *infra*.

39 Gargan, *Cultura e arte*, 39–40.

40 Favaretto, *Arte antica*, 33–4.

41 Gargan, *Cultura e arte*, 6–33.

42 Urbani de Gheltof, *La collezione del Doge Marin Faliero*, 1–9. The inventory is cited as genuine by Levi, *Le collezione veneziane d'arte e d'antichità*, XXXVI; Simona Savini Branca, *Il collezionismo veneziano nel '600*, Florence 1965, 11; Alsop, *Rare Art Traditions*, 301–2; Gargan, *Cultura e arte*, 62. It is dismissed as a *falso* by G.B. Cervellini, "Per una revisione di G.M. Urbani de Gheltof," *Civiltà moderna* XI, 1939, 291–301; and Zorzi, *Collezioni di antichità*, 112–13. The middle road, which I follow as well, is taken by Favaretto, *Arte antica* 37–9, who states "con le dovute perplessità e cautele, è doveroso qui ricordare il documento in questione che, per certi versi, presenta molte affinità con la 'nota' di Oliviero Forzetta."

43 Urbani de Gheltof, *La collezione del Doge Marin Faliero*, 8: "Item una tabula cum figuris diversarum nationum manu m. thomae pictoris."

44 Ibid.: "Item unum speram munai aeneam quam fuit magistri antonii astrologi."

45 Ibid.: "unum anulum cum inscriptione que dicit Ciuble Can Marco Polo . . ."

46 Ibid., 9: "Item de itineribus Marci praedicti liber in corio albo cum multis figuris. Item aliud volumen quod vocatur de locis mirabilibus tartarorum scriptum manu praedicti marci."

47 Ibid., 8: "Item una capseleta cum quinquaginta nummis mire antiquitatis."

48 Ibid., 9: "Unum gladium mire antiquitatis cum inscriptionibus."

49 Ibid., "Item gladium aeneum padue inventum."

50 Ibid., "Item tres inscriptiones in marmore invente tarvixii."

51 Favaretto, *Arte antica*, 37–9, gives the most even-handed account of the inventory. For Falier see Vittorio Lazzarini, *Marino Faliero*, Florence 1963; and Brown, "Committenza e arte di stato."

52 Lino Moretti, in *Pitture murali nel Veneto e tecnica dell'affresco*, Venice 1960, 53. Pallucchini, *La pittura veneziana*, 81, 91; and R. Longhi, *Viatico per cinque secoli di pittura veneziana*, Florence 1946, 7, date them to the first half of the fourteenth century. Cf. Toesca, *Storia dell'arte italiana*, II: *Il Trecento*, 699, who dates them to the second half of the fourteenth century.

53 Cf. the paintings by Paolo and Giovanni Veneziano, *Coronation of Virgin* in the Frick Collection, New York (cat. 124), with the moon beneath Madonna's foot; and Lorenzo Veneziano: *Marriage of St. Catherine*, Accademia, Venice, with

sun and moon beneath the feet of Madonna; and also several paintings by Catarino Veneziano of the Madonna and Child, with the moon on the Madonna's breast. See Pallucchini, *La pittura veneziana*, figs. 605–7.

54 See Mariacher, *Il Museo Correr*, 159–61. For virtues in medieval art, see Emile Mâle, *The Gothic Image. Religious Art in France of the Thirteenth Century*, New York 1913 (1958 edn.), 98–130.

55 Saxl, "Jacopo Bellini and Mantegna," 151.

56 Cf. the frescoes in the lower church of San Francesco in Assisi, painted by Pietro and Ambrogio Lorenzetti, where the pinnacle figures are either clothed or are conventional winged nude putti – survivals of classical genii.

57 See Camille, *The Gothic Idol*, 74–9, who refers to similar representations in medieval manuscripts: "What better way might the power of ancient pagan deities be neutralized than by viewing them through the ideology of the aesthetic, as 'art'."

58 From Petrarch's *De Remediis Utriusque Fortunae*, I, 118 in *Opera Omnia*, Basel 1554. Cf. Buddensieg, "Criticism and Praise of the Pantheon," 259–67; and idem, "Gregory the Great," 44–65. For Petrarch's actual knowledge of ancient monuments, see Weiss, "Petrarch the Antiquarian," 199–209.

59 Bettini, "Tra Plinio e sant'Agostino," 219–67; and, in particular, Baxandall, *Giotto and the Orators*, 53–8. For Petrarch's interest in Pliny, see Marjorie Chibnall, "Pliny's *Natural History* and the Middle Ages," in *Empire and Aftermath*, ed. T.A. Dorey, London 1975, 74 (57–78).

60 Petrarca, *Fam.* XIX, 3 (to Lello di Pietro Stefano dei Tosetti, 25 Feb. 1355), trans. Bernardo, III, 79.

61 Petrarca, *Senili* IV, 3, cited in Perry, "Saint Mark's Trophies," 29.

62 Petrarca, *Fam.* V, 4 (to Cardinal Giovanni di Stefano Colonna, Nov. 23, 1343), trans. Bernardo, I, 239.

63 Petrarca, *Fam.* III, 18 (to Giovanni Anchiseo [Giovanni dell'Incisa], 1342 or 1346), in Petrarca, *Opere*, I, 372: "l'oro, l'argento, le gemme . . . le tavole dipinte . . . tutte le cose di questo genere danno un piacere muto e superficiali: i libri dilettano invece profondamente, parlano, consigliano, e sono congiunti a noi da una consuetudine viva e parlante." Cf. Petrarca, *Fam.*, trans. Bernardo, I, 157.

64 Bettini, "Tra Plinio e sant'Agostino," 227: "Ecco il punto. Con i libri Petrarca può parlare, con le immagini no."

65 See Chiovenda, "Zeichnungen Petrarcas," 56–8.

66 Petrarca, *Fam.* VIII, 5 (May 19, 1349), cited by Wilkins, *Petrarch's Later Years*, 41: "E sarà a noi vicina Venezia, la più meravigliosa città c'io abbia mai visto – e ho visto quasi tutte quelle di cui va superba l'Europa."

67 ASV, Maggior Consiglio, Deliberazioni, Reg. 19 (Novella) 1350–84, f. 85r (Sept. 4, 1362), cited by Wilkins, *Petrarch's Later Years*, 34–7. See also idem, *Studies on Petrarch and Boccaccio*, 104–5.

68 Manlio Pastore Stocchi, "La biblioteca del Petrarca," in *Storia della Cultura Veneta 2. Il Trecento*, 536–65.

69 Translated by Hans Nachod: "On His Own Ignorance and That of Many Others," in *The Renaissance Philosophy of Man*, ed. Ernst Cassirer, Paul Oskar Kristeller, and John Herman Randall, Jr., Chicago and London 1948, 47–133; see also 29–31.

70 As defined by Kristeller, "Petrarch's 'Averroists'," 59–65. For this episode, see also Wilkins, *Petrarch's Later Years*, 92, 180; and Saxl, "Petrarch in Venice," 143–4.

71 Both passages are cited in Cicogna, *Iscrizioni veneziane*, III, 364–5: "Ilii erant dominus Leonardus Dandalus, Thomas Talentus: Dominus Zacharias Contareno omnes de Venetiis: quartus

magister Guido de Bagnolo de Regio. Primus miles. secundus simplex mercator. tertius simplex nobilis. quartus medicus physicus"; and "Ita tamen ut primus literas nullas sciat, nota tibi loquor; secundus paucas; tertius non multas; quartus vero non paucas fateor sed perplexas adeo tamque incompositas et, ut ait Cicero, tanta levitate et jactatione ut fortasse melius fuerit nullas nosce." I owe the English translation to Elaine Fantham.

72 Wilkins, *Petrarch's Later Years*.

73 Ugo Foscolo, *Essays on Petrarch*, London 1823, 205 (orig. publ. in English). Foscolo's source was Iacobi Philippi Tomasini, *Petrarcha redivivus*, Padua 1635, 188–93, who reported such an incident in 1630, when three miscreants were punished with exile from Venetian territories.

74 See chap. 2 *supra*.

75 Degenhart and Schmitt, *Corpus, Teil II: Venedig*, cat. 640, 79–86, 116, who pronounce it "Venezianisch um 1350." See also Billanovich, "Disegni italiani del Trecento," 365–74; and Serafino Prete, *I codici della Biblioteca Comunale di Fermo. Catalogo*, Florence 1960, 110–14.

76 Degenhart and Schmitt, *Corpus, Teil II: Venedig*, cat. 640, 79–86. Ibid., cat. 697: another manuscript of the text with emperors' portraits had been started in Naples about 1340, but its illustrations were never completed. Adopting the Roman coin format introduced by Giovanni Mansionario in his *Historia imperialis*, the Naples codex featured a double circle drawn next to the description of each emperor. However, only Claudius was actually portrayed, and the other frames remained empty, presumably awaiting coins to serve as prototypes for the relevant figures.

77 Schmitt, "Wiederlebung," 190–94, holds that the Fermo portraits were probably copied from pattern books rather than directly from coins.

78 Degenhart and Schmitt, *Corpus, Teil II: Venedig*, 83–4, 116.

79 Ibid., 85.

80 Billanovich, "Disegni italiani del Trecento," 365–74.

81 Ambrosiana, Milan, cod. c. 214 inf. (35.4 × 28.0 cm., 206 pages). See Degenhart and Schmitt, *Corpus, Teil II: Venedig*, 106–16.

82 Cited by Degenhart and Schmitt, *Corpus, Teil II: Venedig*, 107: "Io non so[no] bene per certo se io farò alchuna utilita scrivendo le storie del popolo de Roma . . ."

83 Fogolari, "La prima deca," 330: "Et Jo zianin chatanio fio che fo de Andriol che fo de ser zian chatanio de S. crosie il dito libro trasy adnistancia del delecto mio e de certy mie bony amisy et ecc."

84 Degenhart and Schmitt, *Corpus, Teil II: Venedig*, 116–17, who characterize it as "einem gemeinsamen Band immanenter venezianischer Wesensart." See also Brown, *Venetian Narrative Painting*, passim.

85 Fogolari, "La prima deca," 336: "Nessuna precisa conoscenza dell'antichità, tratta dai monumenti, turba i nostri buoni veneziani nelle visioni."

86 Degenhart and Schmitt, *Corpus, Teil II: Venedig*, 116, point out the similarities between the Ambrosiana Livy and Semitecolo's Saint Sebastian cycle, which consists of four panel paintings.

87 See chap. 2 *supra*; and Brown, *Venetian Narrative Painting*, 39–41.

88 See Levi d'Ancona, "Giustino del fu Gherardino da Forlì," 34–44.

89 Buchthal, *Historia Troiana*, 60.

90 Ibid., 32–41.

91 Cf. Saxl, "Jacopo Bellini and Mantegna," 152–3.

92 Lazzarini, *Paolo de' Bernardo*, 228–9: "Nota quod ab Etruscis habuerunt Romani lictores, sellam curulem, togam pretextam, ut hic, et signa militaria secundum Salustium", and "Nota his et alibi, quod Ianiculum est templum Iani et hic Ianiculus est quidam mons apud Romam."

93 In addition to the references in chap. 2, n. 79 *supra*, see Von Schlosser, "Ein veronesisches Bilderbuch"; and Andrew Martindale, "Painting for Pleasure – Some Lost Fifteenth Century Secular Decorations of Northern Italy," in *The Vanishing Past. Studies of Medieval Art, Liturgy and Metrology presented to Christopher Hohler*, eds. A. Borg and A. Martindale, Oxford 1981, 109–15 (109–31).

94 Schmitt, "Wiederlebung," 173–8; Mommsen, "Petrarch and the Decoration," 108–13; and Gasparotto, "La reggia dei da Carrara," 104–5.

CHAPTER 4

1 From *Chronicles of the Kings of England*, ed. J.A. Giles and trans. John Sharpe, London 1847, cited in Thompson, *Idea of Rome*, 160–61. The poem was composed following a visit to Rome during the pontificate of Paschal II (1099–1118). See also James Bruce Ross, "A Study of Twelfth-Century Interest in the Antiquities of Rome," in *Medieval and Historiographical Essays in Honor of James Westfall Thompson*, eds. J.L. Cate and E.N. Anderson, Chicago 1938, 302–21; Mortier, *La Poétique des ruines*, 23–6; and Herbert Bloch, "The New Fascination with Ancient Rome," in Benson and Constable, *Renaissance and Renewal*, 615–36.

2 Cited with English translation by Mango, "Antique Statuary," 69.

3 Petrarca, *Fam.* VI, 2, trans. Bernardo, I, 291.

4 Heckscher, *Die Romruinen*, 15–29; Mortier, *Le Poetique des ruines*, 21–32. See also Greene, *Light in Troy*, 88–93. I have also benefited from the unpublished typescript of Giancarlo Maiorino, "Ruins of Unremembered Antiquities."

5 Petrarca, *Fam.* VI, 2, trans. Bernardo, I, 291. Cf. Mortier, *Le Poetique des ruines*, 21–32.

6 Lowenthal, *The Past is a Foreign Country*, 85–7. See also Greene, *Light in Troy*, 92; Mazzocco, "Antiquarianism of Francesco Petrarca," 203–24; idem, "Petrarca, Poggio, and Biondo," 353–7; and Burke, *Renaissance Sense of the Past*, 21–5.

7 See references in chap. 1, n. 90 *supra*.

8 Petrarca, *Fam.* XVIII, 8 (1355, written from Milan to Francesco Nelli, prior of SS. Apostoli), trans. Bernardo, III, 57.

9 Cantino Wataghin, "Archeologia e 'archeologie'," 183–6.

10 "In arcu triumphali qui dicitur vulgo *arco de trassi* sunt multae literae sculptae, sed difficiliter leguntur . . .": Giovanni Dondi, "Iter Romanum," in Valentini and Zucchetti, *Codice Topografico*, IV, 70. Cf. Smith, *Architecture in the Culture of Early Humanism*, 173–4.

11 Cantino Wataghin, "Archeologia e 'archeologie'," 191.

12 R. Valentini and G. Zucchetti, *Codice Topografico della città di Roma*, Rome 1946, IV, 73: "Notabilia paganorum quae adhuc sunt Romae in parte et indicant quam magna fuerunt, quibus paria non cernuntur alibi, ultra quae sunt eclesiae christianorum et reliquiae sanctorum et innumerabilia veneranda nostrae legis."

13 Cited by Krautheimer, *Lorenzo Ghiberti*, 296–7.

14 *The Life of Cola di Rienzo*, trans. John Wright, Toronto 1975, 1. Cf. Krautheimer, *Lorenzo Ghiberti*, 295.

15 Cantino Wataghin, "Archeologia e 'archeologie'," 191. Sylloges of epigrams are known from antiquity, as well as from the Middle Ages, if the *Mirabilia* are included under that rubric.

16 For a cogent summary of Chrysoloras's impact on Italian humanists see Paul Grendler, *Schooling in Renaissance Italy. Literacy and Learning, 1300–1600*, Baltimore and London 1989, 124–5. For a fuller discussion, see Smith, *Architecture in the Culture of Early Humanism*, 133–97.

17 Smith, *Architecture in the Culture of Early Humanism*, 158. See also Baxandall, *Giotto and the Orators*, 78–83.

18 Cited in Smith, *Architecture in the Culture of Early Humanism*, 201–2; see also 159–60. Cf. Settis, "Continuità," 456–63 for Buondelmonte's use of the terms *autopsía*: "osservazione diretta e personale"; and *parousía*: "viva presenza."

19 See, in particular, Krautheimer, *Lorenzo Ghiberti*, 294–305; and Weiss, *Renaissance Discovery*, 48–72.

20 Beschi, "Collezioni d'arte Greca," 258–9; idem, "La scopertà dell'arte greca," 326–33; and Favoretto, *Arte antica*, 45–55.

21 Cited in King, *Venetian Humanism*, 5–6.

22 Weiss, *Un umanista veneziano*.

23 As characterized by Weiss, "Un umanista antiquario," 116.

24 Weiss, "Un umanista antiquario," 110–11; idem, *Renaissance Discovery*, 135–7; and Sabbadini, *Le scoperte dei codici*, 43–71. See *The Hieroglyphics of Horapollo*, trans. George Boas, Princeton 1993.

25 Buondelmonti, *Descriptio*, 41–51.

26 Cristoforo Buondelmonti, *Liber Insularum Archipelagi*, ed. G.R.L. De Sinner, Lipsiae et Berolini 1824.

27 BMV, Cod. Lat. X, 124 (3177). Cf. BMV. Cod. Lat. XIV, 45 (4595).

28 Beschi, "La cultura antiquaria," 20. The fundamental work is Gerola, *Monumenti Veneti dell'isola di Creta*. See also Hemmerdinger Iliadou, "La Crete sous la domination venitienne."

29 The island was purchased by Venice in 1204 from Boniface di Monserrat, who had received it from the Greek Emperor Alexius Paleologus. It was under Genoese occupation until 1210 when the Venetians actually took possession. See Giuseppe Gerola, "I rapporti tra Venezia e la Grecia nell'ambito del predominio della Serenissima nel bacino orientale del Mediterraneo," in Spiridione Alessandro Curuni and Lucilla Donati, *Creta veneziana. L'Istituto Veneto e la Missione Cretese di Giuseppe Gerola. Collezione fotografica 1900–1902*, Venice 1988, 15–34. Gerola's essay is taken from an unpublished typescript, datable to *c*.1931, and provided with an extensive updated bibliography.

30 Freddy Thiriet, "Candie, grande place marchande dans la première moitié du XVe siècle," in *Etudes sur la Romanie greco-vénitienne (Xe–XVe siècles)*, IX, 338–51.

31 Laiou, "Venetians and Byzantines," 29–43. See also Georgopoulou, "Late Medieval Crete and Venice," 479–96.

32 Buondelmonti, *Descriptio*, 150, 254–5: "A quo per unum miliare Candia civitas in muris albescit que a Grecis Ghandacha dicta est; in qua portus manu artificiose compositus, meniis turribusque septus ac tutus, a ventis omnibus convalescit, licet aliquando in eum ex ventorum impetuosis flatibus nauium difficilis sit ingressus."

33 Ibid., 151–2, 255–6: "in qua via ad eius dexteram in eminenti loco gradibus porticum minantem aspexi in quo societas plurium civium resedebat ac in eorum medio gubernatores totius insule, sed pro imperio eminebant qui ab inclita urbe Uenetiarum fuerant destinati. Coram quibus notarius Bonaccursius ex omnibus beneuolus, dulcibus uerbis ita fatur: 'Si tantus amor, frater optime, est hanc insulam uisitare, fare,

oro, ut possim te meis opibus adiuare.' Cui brevibus uerbis omnia reseraui. Qui deinde totam demonstrare ciuitatem incepit. 'Hec non ex antiquis ciuitatibus fuit sed nunc ubi portus eminet in orientali latere oppidum paruum extitit, quod ciuitati propinquiori illis temporibus seruiebat. Denique postquam Romani illam desolauerunt urbem ciuium residuum huic adhesit oppido atque ghandacum, id est uallum, circum circa domos conglutinatas instruxit. Et tandem, revolutis seculis non sine multis desolationibus, Veneti totam ementes insullam, ipsam Candiam amplis cinxere meniis . . .'"

34 Gerola, *Monumenti Veneti*, III, 35–6.

35 Buondelmonti, *Descriptio*, 255–6. For Lorenzo de Monacis, see Poppi, "Ricerche," 153–86, who observes that the office of Cancelliere was reserved to *cittadini originari* (p. 153, n. 1). For Bonaccorsi Grimani, who was elected chancellor of the island in 1436, see Freddy Thiriet, *Délibérations des assemblées vénitiennes concernant la Romanie*, Paris 1971.

36 Buondelmonti, *Descriptio*, 155–6, 257–8: "usque ad montem lucta hodie applicamus ad quem per periculosissimam ascendimus uiam, usque ad summitatem dicti montis; a quo omnia rura et uirentia uineta circum circa patescunt. Effigiem ibi a longe faciei habet, in cuius fronte templum Iouis usque ad fundamenta deletum cognoui. In circuitu eius infinitas ymagines seriatimque moles reperimus, quarum fabricatorem non humanum fuisse censemus. In nasum, post frontis inquisitionem, deuenimus, in quo congestas tres Ecclesias connumeramus. Prima harum, quia in tali monte principaliter Iuppiter colebatur, Ecclesiam Saluatoris hic posuerunt. Secunda, quia per multos deos mundus regebatur, Pandon Aghion dicta fuit, hoc est ecclesia Omnium Sanctorum. Tertia, quia sceptrum domini Cretensium antiquis temporibus per ensem acquisiuerunt, ideo Sancto Georgio dedicauerunt."

37 Ibid., 116, 232: "A qua fontem nobilissimum collaudaui cum amplis marmoreis lapidibus prosternatis. Iuxta quam planum amplum et fecundissimis montibus cupressorum circumdatum enumeraui; in quo greges florentem pratum tondunt . . ."

38 Buondelmonti, *Descriptio*, 117–18, 232–3: "intrauimus et destructam ciuitatem uetustissimamque cum columpnis prostratam uidemus. Inter eas candidissimi marmoreis sepulcra, prope casa illorum rusticorum, inueni; in quibus sues polentum comedebant et sculpturas circum nobilissimas laniabant. Lacerata et fracta multa uidi busta ydolorum et, intra marmorum hedifitia, sparsa iacebant. Dimicto, postquam uidi amplas catacumbas atque infinitas, locum et uersus terram rura ampla procuro, in quibus sex antiquorum nobilium Romanorum reliquias inuenies, que titulum et arma in scutis eorum in hodiernum seruare delectant."

39 For Venetian visitors to the Gortyn labyrinth in the early fifteenth century, see A.M. Woodward, "The Gortyn 'Labyrinth' and its Visitors in the Fifteenth Century," *The Annual of the British School at Athens* XLIV, 1949, 324–5.

40 Buondelmonti, *Descriptio*, 171–2, 276–8: "Ibique prope eam Pidiata oppidum in fetrilissimo [sic] campo apparet. Ad septentrionem autem in rure quodam Chirsonensem episcopatum prospicimus ac etiam uisitamus; quo uiso ad austrum Archadensem Episcopatum procurauimus ab alto. Post hec ad orientem uergens, in ualle quadam nobilem et scientificum dominum Nicolaum ex origine Scipionum ortum inuenio qui sine prole uiridiarium simile paradiso sculpturis marmoreis antiquissimis adornauit et edificari fecit ibique quisquid corpus in arboribus delectamini sumit reperitur habunde. Ipse in latinis delectatur libris et Dantem in manibus aliquando tenet. De ore marmoris hominis uiuus emanat fons. Ad dexteram atque levam Marci Antoni caput et Pompei

patres posuere. Ibi marmora pulchra cognovi, que ab aliis
hedifitiis translata fuere."

41 Although genealogical charts are notoriously unreliable for this
period, Scipion appears to have been the grandson of Nicolas's
brother Pietro. Charts for this branch of the Cornaro family
can be found in Stergios Spanakis, in *KPHTIKA XPONIKA*,
Heraklion 1955; and MCV, cod. Cicogna 3662, 102-4.

42 Buondelmonti, *Descriptio*, 278. See also Corner, *Creta sacra*, 1,
47, 119.

43 See, in particular, Ashmole, "Cyriac of Ancona," 25-41;
Bodnar, *Cyriacus of Ancona and Athens*; Mitchell, "Archaeology
and Romance," 468-483; Weiss, *Renaissance Discovery*, 131-44;
Chiarlo, "'Gli fragmenti dilla sancta antiquitate'," 271-97; and,
with caution, Colin, *Cyriaque d'Ancône*.

44 As observed by the Veronese antiquarian Jacopo Rizzoni in a
letter to Cyriacus: G. P. Marchi, "Due corrispondenti veronesi
di Ciriaco d'Ancona," *Italia medioevale e umanistica* XI, 1968,
322. See also Chiarlo, "'Gli fragmenti'," 271-2.

45 Scalamonti, *Vita*, 72: "At et cum maximas per urbem tam
generosissimae gentis reliquias undique solo disjectas aspexisset
lapides et ipsi magnarum rerum testarum majorem longe quam
ipsi libri fidem et notitiam praebere videbantur." See n. 49
infra.

46 For the date of Cyriacus's death, see Michael Vickers, "Cyriac
of Ancona at Thessaloniki," *Byzantine and Modern Greek Studies*
II, 1976, 75 n. 2 (75-82); Sabbadini, *Miscellanea Ceriani*, 193,
243. See also Julian Raby, "Cyriacus of Ancona and the
Ottoman Sultan Mehmed II," *Journal of the Warburg and
Courtauld Institutes* XLIII, 1980, 242-6, who proves conclusively
that Cyriacus did not act as tutor to the Ottoman Sultan
Mehmed II in 1452-53, as had been argued by E. Jacobs,
"Cyriacus von Ancona und Mehemmed II," *Byzantinische
Zeitschrift* XXX, 1929-30, 197-202, and followed by Bodnar
and most other scholars.

47 The surviving section of the *Commentaria* is part of Cod.
Ambrosiano-Trotti 373, ff. 101-24. See Bodnar, *Cyriacus of
Ancona and Athens*, 55-64, 117-18 and *passim*. For the prob-
ability that the *Commentaria* were destroyed by fire rather than
simply disassembled and dispersed to various collectors, see
ibid., 69-72; and Sabbadini, *Miscellanea Ceriani*, 240-42.

48 See in particular Bodnar, *Cyriacus of Ancona and Athens*, 73-
120; and Carlo Claudio Van Essen, *I Commentaria di Ciriaco
d'Ancona*, in *Il mondo antico nel Rinascimento* (Atti del V
Convegno Internazionale di studi sul Rinascimento), Florence
1958, 191-4. See also Brown, "The Antiquarianism of Jacopo
Bellini," 65-84.

49 Scalamonti, *Vita*, is an autograph manuscript of Feliciano's that
includes letters and a selection of Latin and Greek inscriptions.
It is published without the inscriptions by Colucci, *Antichità
Picene*, 45-155 (commentary 1-44). Based on personal conver-
sations and correspondence with Cyriacus, it can be considered
a reasonably accurate reflection of his attitudes and activities.

50 Mehus, *Kyriaci Anconitani Itinerarium*, 54-5: "O magnam vim
artis nostrae, ac penitus divinam! Siquidem dum vivimus quae
/ diu vivis viva, & praeclara fuere, & longi temporis labe,
longaque semivivum injuria obstrusa penitus, & defuncta
jacebant, ex ea demum arte diva iterum vivos inter homines
in lucem ab orco revocata vivent felicissima temporis
reparatione." Cf. Mitchell, "Archaeology and Romance,"
470-83.

51 Cited in L. Bertalot and A. Campana, "Gli scritti di Iacopo
Zeno e il suo elogio di Ciriaco d'Ancona," *La bibliofilia* XLI,
1939-40, 356 (356-376). See also King, *Venetian Humanism*,
10-11, whose English translation is used here.

52 Scalamonti, *Vita*, 50-51: "ut saepe suo audivimus ore,
quicquid in orbe reliquum est ad extrema Oceani pro-
montoria, et ad Tylem usque insulam, et abmotas quascunque
alias mundi partes videre, scrutarique indefesso nempe animo
proposuerat suis quibusque incomodis, laboribusque, atque
vigiliis omnibus expertis posthabilitisque . . ." For the island of
Thule or Thyle (It: Tule), see Pliny, *Natural History*, 2.187,
who writes that it is a six-day voyage north of Britannia.

53 Scalamonti, *Vita*, 50. For Cyriacus's relation to Venice, see in
particular Howard, "Responses to Ancient Greek
Architecture," 29-32.

54 Ibid., 66: "quam magna ex parte diruptam vetustate
conspexerat. Sed nobilia pleraque suae antiquitatis vestigia
vidit. Et Salvie postumie Sergi II vir. aed CL. filiae egregias
portas et aedificia pleraque ingentia viderat. Et nobile ac
magnis editum lapidibus amphitreatum, quod Polenses voti
sui compotes L. Septimio Severo et Antonino divis et caesareis
fratribus dicavere, viderat; et innumera per urbem et extra ad
mare usque lapidea sepulchra, quorum pleraque nobilia
exceperat epigrammata . . ."

55 Augusto Campana, "Giannozzo Manetti, Ciriaco e l'arco di
Traiano ad Ancona," *Italia medioevale e umanistica* II, 1959, 483-
504.

56 Transcribed in Scalamonti, *Vita*, 70-71. See also Bodnar,
Cyriacus of Ancona and Athens, 20.

57 Bodnar, *Cyriacus of Ancona and Athens*, 21-2.

58 Ibid., 18-23; and Colin, *Cyriaque*, 179-80.

59 Favaretto, *Arte antica*, 49; and Bodnar, "Athens in 1436," 103.

60 Colin, *Cyriaque*, 212.

61 *Inscriptiones seu Epigrammata*, p. IIII, no. 37. See also Colin,
Cyriaque, 152.

62 *Inscriptiones seu Epigrammata*, p. XXII.

63 Ibid., p. XXXXIII.

64 Favaretto, *Arte antica*, 47; and Ashmole, "Cyriac," 38-9. Cf.
Colin, *Cyriaque*, 107, 556-9, who makes an unconvincing case
that the episode involved Bertuccio and not Giovanni Dolfin.

65 Traversari, *Hodoeporicon*, 65-6: "Adiit nos inter caeteros &
Cyriacus Anconitanus, multaque nobis ostendit antiquitatis,
cujus studiosissimus indagator erat, tum monumenta, tum
epigrammata vetusta, tum signatos nummos argenteos &
aureos, tum signa."

66 Traversari, *Latinae Epistolae*, coll. 411-13. Epistola no. 314
(May 3, 1432) to Niccolo Niccoli: "Offendi Cyriacum
Anconitanum antiquitatis studiosum. Ostendit aureos &
argenteos nummos, eos scilicet, quos ipse vidisti: Lisymachi,
Philippi, & Alexandri ostendebat imagines: sed an Macedonum
sint, scrupulus est. Scipionis Iunioris in lapide onychino, ut
ipse aiebat, effigiem (nostrae literae auro tegebantur) vidi
summae elegantiae; adeo ut nunquam viderim pulchriorem."
See also Zorzi, ed., *Collezioni di antichità*, 15-18, with further
bibliography.

67 Traversari, *Latinae Epistolae*, coll. 416-17. Epistola no. 317
(July 3, 1433): "Multa enim id genus numismata Venetiis
haberi apud plerosque Nobilium, quae videnda mihi
adtulissent."

68 Weiss, *Un umanista veneziano*, 83-90; Müntz, *Les arts à la Cour
des Papes*, II, 2-3, 11, 171-2; and Zorzi, *Collezioni di antichità*,
16.

69 *Inscriptiones seu Epigrammata*, p. XXV. Cyriacus's inscription is
found on the raised right hoof of the left-hand horse as one
faces the church. He missed several similar marks on the other
horses. See Anna Guidi Toniato, "A Descriptive Analysis of
the Horses of San Marco," in Wilton-Ely, *Horses of San Marco*,
147-50, fig. 195.

70 Mehus, *Kyriaci Anconitani Itinerarium*, 33: "Ac inde postquam per triduum omnia tantae civitatis vestigia oculis obversata perspeximus, ad sacram, & ornatissimam Leonidei Marci aedem perreximus. Aeneos primum illos, & arte conspicuous quadrijugales equos Phidiae nobile quidem opus, & insigne olim in Urbe belligeri Jani specimen Delubri non semel, sed dum placuerat, inspectare licuit." The English translation is taken from Perry, "Saint Mark's Trophies," 33. See also Licia Borrelli Vlad and Anna Guidi Toniato, "The origins and documentary sources of the Horses of San Marco," in Wilton-Ely, *Horses of San Marco*, 128 (an extract of Perry's article appears in the same volume, 104–10).

71 Mehus, *Kyriaci Anconitani Itinerarium*, 33: "Secreta vero deinde intus, & delubri penetralia, sacra nobis relicta monumenta Divum, & pretiosa vidimus auri, atque lapidum, unionumque ingentia, & speciosissima gaza. Inter ostentantes egregia quaecumque, nonnulla preciosa vasa graecis insignita litteris Princeps ipse Franciscus Francisco Barbaro, mihique manu manibus, ut lectitaremus, exhibuerat . . ."

72 King, *Venetian Humanism*, 42–5, 92–8, 323–5 and *passim*.

73 Degli Abati Olivieri, *Commentariorum*, 24–5: "insigne scilicet animal, ac breve sub eo aliquid, & memorabile dictum, quin aemularier quoad posse videretur, illius nostri clarissimi Francisci Barbari equitis, qui Hermellinum pro insigne gerens praeclarum illud apposivit hypogramma POTIVS MORI QVAM FOEDARI." The letter was written to a certain "Jacobus adolescens" from Ferrara in the eighth year of the pontificate of Eugenius IV, i.e., c.1440.

74 See, for example, Ashmole, "Cyriac," 26–32, who stresses Cyriacus's desire for accuracy; and Lehmann-Hartleben, "Cyriacus of Ancona, Aristotle and Teiresias in Samothrace," 115–34. Cf. Bodnar, *Cyriacus of Ancona and Athens*, 121–42, who points out a number of errors in Greek transcriptions, with the line divisions almost always incorrect.

75 Bodnar, "Athens in April 1436," 100, with an English translation. For the Latin text see Berlin, Cod. Hamilton 254, f. 85r: "Et quod magis adnotari placuit, extat in Summa Ciuitatis arce ingens, & mirabile Palladis Diuae marmoreum Templum, ex Phidia. divum quippe opus quod LVIII. sublime columnis lagnitudinis p. VII. diametrum habens, ornatissimum praeclaris imaginibus in frontespiciis ambobus & intus in summis parietum listis ac epistiliis ab extra vndique & centaurorum pugna mira fabrefactoris arte conspicitur." Cf. Bodnar, *Cyriacus of Ancona and Athens*, 35, with a slightly different text.

76 As observed by Bodnar, "Athens in April 1436," 100.

77 See chap. 3, n. 58 *supra*.

78 As observed by Bodnar, "Athens in April 1436," 100; and Chiarlo, "'Gli fragmenti'," 274.

79 Bodnar, "Athens in April 1436," 100. See also Beschi, "La scoperta," 318, who observes that Niccolo Niccoli had obtained the first codex of Pausanias to reach the west in 1418 and finds it surprising that Cyriacus did not make use of a copy to identify Greek sites and iconography.

80 Lehmann, "Cyriacus of Ancona's Visit to Samothrace," 4, 9.

81 For the gem, see *Antike Gemmen in deutschen Sammlungen. Staatliche Museen Preußischer Kulturbesitz Antikenabteilung Berlin*, ed. Erika Zwierlein-Diehl, 1969, no. 456, 169–71, who identifies Cyriacus's host as Bertutius Delphinus and not Johannes, as Colin, *Cyriaque*, 556–9.

82 Colin, *Cyriaque*, 557: "Eug. P. a. xv [Eugenii Papae anno XV, i.e. 1445], Venetum seu ab urbe condita m. XXIII." By this time the year of Venice's birth was generally accepted as 421.

83 Cited with English translation by Ashmole, "Cyriac," 39, from Cod. Vat. Lat. 5237, f. 515v–516r.

84 Cyriacus's text is published along with the drawings in Sabbadini, "Ciriaco d'Ancona e la sua descrizione," 183–247. The manuscript was owned by Leonardo Botta, a passionate bibiophile and collector of epigrams and epigraphy. According to Sabbadini (233), he would have obtained the section of the *Commentaria* in 1471 when he was in the service of Alessandro Sforza, Lord of Pesaro. He was also Milanese ambassador to Venice between 1470–80. See Molmenti. *Storia di Venezia*, II, 437; and Alexander, *The Painted Page*, 178.

85 See Bodnar, *Cyriacus of Ancona and Athens*, 55–64 for a good account of this trip.

86 Ibid.; and Sabbadini, "Ciriaco d'Ancona e la sua descrizione," 238.

87 Sabbadini, "Ciriaco d'Ancona e la sua descrizione," 210: "Ad villam dryeam et eiusdem nautae Lares venimus. Ubi per diem morantes plerasque alias lata in planicie villas inspeximus. cultis agris vinetisque et oliveis arboribus uberes. Quas inter non nulla conspeximus antiqua taenariae almae nobilitatis monumenta et eadem ipsa dryea in villa antiqui colonum habitus marmoream imaginem huiusmodi figurae comperimus."

88 Sabbadini, "Ciriaco d'Ancona e le sue descrizione," 228–9: "Polycleti opus ex antiquo et diu iam deleto Argive myceneaeque Iunonis delubro. et Argivo in campo ad sacram b. Virginis aedem aposteris et nostrae religionis hominibus ornamento deductum."

89 Bodnar, *Cyriacus of Ancona and Athens*, 95–106; Erich Ziebarth, "De antiquissimis inscriptionum syllogis," *Ephemeris epigraphica* IX, 1913, 197–8 (188–322); Theodor M. Mommsen, *Inscriptiones Asiae Provinciarum Europae Graecarum Illyricae Latinae, Corpus Inscriptionum Latinarum*, Berlin 1873, III, 271–3.

90 Staatsbibliothek zu Berlin, Cod. Hamilton 254, ff. 81–90v. See H. Boese, *Die lateinischen Handschriften der Sammlung Hamilton zu Berlin*, Wiesbaden 1966, 125–30; and Bodnar, *Cyriacus of Ancona and Athens*, 84–5, 213–14 and *passim*. The pages measure 25 × 17 cm.

91 Bodnar, *Cyriacus of Ancona and Athens*, 51–2, n. 2.

92 Scholarly opinion remains divided as to the authorship of the drawings. Cyriacus autograph: A. Michaelis, "Ein Originalzeichnung des Parthenon von Cyriacus von Ancona," *Archäologische Zeitung* XL, 1882, 367–84; Mitchell, "Ciriaco d'Ancona," 114; Brown and Kleiner, "Giuliano da Sangallo's Drawings after Ciriaco d'Ancona," 326–27; and Bodnar, *Cyriacus of Ancona and Athens*, 84–5.

By the hand of one or more unknown artists: Ashmole, "Cyriac of Ancona," 29–34; Bodnar, "Athens in April 1436," 101; and Degenhart and Schmitt, *Corpus: Jacopo Bellini*, V, 194, whose analysis convinces me that Cyriacus could not have been the artist. When compared to his indisputably autograph drawings in the Trotti codex, the Parthenon drawing is simply too professional.

93 See, in particular, Mitchell, "Ciriaco d'Ancona," 111–23; and Brown and Kleiner, "Giuliano da Sangallo's Drawings," 321–35; and Howard, "Responses to Ancient Greek Architecture," 29–31.

94 As argued by Brown and Kleiner, "Giuliano da Sangallo's Drawings," 321–35.

95 For the most extensive arguments, see Lehmann, "Theodosius or Justinian?," 39–57, who proposes that the drawing was copied after a lost medallion of Theodosius; and her exchange of letters with Cyril Mango, *op. cit.*, 351–8, who makes a stronger case that the model was the statue of Justinian in the Augusteion of Constantinople, with the Theodosian inscription indicating a reused statue; see the concurring view of

Giuseppe Bovini, "Giustiniano sul cavallo di Teodosio," *Felix Ravenna*, ser. 3, fasc. 36 (LXXXVII), June 1963, 132–7. My thanks to Elaine Fantham for help with this translation.

96 Degenhart and Schmitt, *Corpus: Jacopo Bellini*, V, 211–13.

97 See Babinger, "Johannes Darius, 75–8; idem, "Notes on Cyriac of Ancona and Some of His Friends," *Journal of the Warburg and Courtauld Institutes* XXV, 1962, 321–3; idem, "Veneto-Kretische Geistesstrebungen um die Mitte des XV. Jahrhunderts," *Byzantinische Zeitschrift* LVII, 1964, 62–77; Brown, *Venetian Narrative Painting*, 64–7 and 241–2; and Giovanni Dario, *22 dispacci da Costantinopoli al Doge Giovanni Mocenigo*, transl. and commentary by Giuseppe Calò, Venice 1992. For the inscription see chap. 11 *infra* at n. 115.

98 J.J.G. Alexander, "The Illustrated Manuscripts of the Notitia Dignitatum," in *Aspects of the Notitia Dignitatum*, ed. R. Goodburn and P. Bartholomew, BAR Supplementary Series 15, 1976, 13–17 (11–25). For a succinct definition of the *Notitia Dignitatum*, see q. v., *The Oxford Classical Dictionary*, ed. N.G.L. Hammond and H.H. Scullard, 2nd edn., Oxford 1970, 738.

99 Scalamonti, *Vita*, 81: "vidit vetustatum nobilia monumenta antiqua, moenia, Columnas, statuas, bases & doricis litteris epigrammata . . . Viderat ibi praeterea locis ejusdem amoena pleraque & dulcissima visui prata virentia ac fructiferos regios paradiseosque cedros, & florentissimos hortos dignum quarti dimatis in orbe specimen & aecumeniae latitudinis medium." Cf. Chiarlo, "'Gli fragmenti dilla sancta antiquitate'," 281.

100 Scalamonti, 61: "Sì suave Harmonia tua voce rende/Che quasi Orpheo, Apollo, & Amphione/Le labra a più bel canto mai non sciolse." See also Colin, *Cyriaque*, 431. For Leonardo Giustiniani (*c.*1389–1446), father of Bernardo, see King, *Venetian Humanism*, 383–5; and Manlio Dazzi, "Leonardo Giustinian (1388–1446)," in Branca, *Umanesimo europeo e umanesimo veneziano*, 173–92.

101 Ashmole, "Cyriac," 40–41.

102 Chr. Hülsen, *Il libro di Giuliano da Sangallo: Codice Vaticano Barberiniano Lat. 4424*, Rome 1910, compiled by Giuliano and his son Francesco about 1500.

103 Bodnar, "Athens in April 1436," 104–5.

104 Ashmole, "Cyriac," 40–41. See also Colin, *Cyriaque*, 145, 285.

105 Mitchell, "Archaeology and Romance," 472–3. Cf. idem, "Ex Libris Kiriaci Anconitani," *Italia medioevale e umanistica* 5, 1962, 283–99; and Lehmann in *Samothracian Reflections*, 125–31.

106 Bodnar, *Cyriacus of Ancona and Athens*, 20–21.

107 Gasparrini Leporace, *Il Mappamondo di Fra Mauro*, 5–7. The map in Venice is a circle, *c.*195 cm. in diameter, inscribed in a square, measuring 223 cm. to the side, drawn on parchment and painted with colors. It was completed on August 26, 1460, according to an inscription on the reverse. Allowing that it is usually held to be a copy of a map sent to Alfonso V, King of Portugal, in 1459 and now lost, Gasparrini proposes instead that the Marciana map came first. A third *mappamondo* survives in the Vatican Library.

108 Ibid., "Del numero de hi cieli secondo i auctorita de hi sacri theologi."

109 Ibid., 39 (pl. XXIII), no. 62 (i17): "Circa i confini over termini de queste p[ro]vincie, çoè cirenaica e libia marmarica i[n]sieme cu[m] egypto, no[n] se può hora p[ar]lar coretam[en]te, p[er]chè ce[r]to altram[en]te se pratica se q[ue]llo che scriveno autori, p[er] ess[er] ca[m]biadi nomi e destrute le citade famose de le q[u]al i[n] q[ue]sta affrica apar gra[n] ruine, no[n] de me[n] a dechiaratio[n] de q[ue]ste provi[n]cie . . ."

PART III
PROLOGUE

1 Zenatti, "Il poemetto," 161: "Poscia, cercando le antiche e le nove / croniche, e releggendo ognun istoria / di quella terra che Neptuno fove, / non trovo alcuna, che faza memoria / che mai la nobel patria di Rialto / fosse exaltata da cotanta gloria!"

2 See chap. 2 *supra*. Cf. the miniatures in Museo Correr, Cod. I, 383; they are datable to *c.*1370 on the basis of style. See a summary of the literature in Brown, *Venetian Narrative Painting*, 260.

3 Zenatti, "Il poemetto," 120.

4 King, *Venetian Humanism*, 208–14; and Lazzarini, *Paolo da' Bernardo*, 121–9.

5 According to Lazzarini, *Paolo de' Bernardo*, 121–3, De' Natali began the poem during the dogate of Andrea Dandolo 1342–54). Cf. Robey and Law, "The Venetian Myth and the 'De Republica Veneta'," 7–15.

6 See Cozzi and Knapton, *Storia della Repubblica*; Cessi, *Storia della repubblica*, 333–49; and Romanin, *Storia documentata di Venezia*, III 300–71.

7 For the Serrata of 1297 and its consequences, see Lane, "The Enlargement of the Great Council of Venice," 236–74; Stanley Chojnacki, "In Search of the Venetian Patriciate: Families and Factions in the Fourteenth Century," in Hale, *Renaissance Venice*, 47–90; Dennis Romano, *Patricians and Popolani. The Social Foundations of the Venetian Renaissance State*, Baltimore and London 1987; and the revisionist view of Donald Queller, *The Venetian Patriciate. Reality versus Myth*, Urbana and Chicago 1986.

8 Cessi, *Storia della repubblica*, 333–49.

9 King, *Venetian Humanism*, 206–16.

10 Ibid., 219–25.

11 Ibid., 186–7.

12 Ibid., 18–23, 217–25; and Robey and Law, "The Venetian Myth and the 'De Republica Veneta'," 3–59.

13 Hill, *Corpus*, I, 1–4; Roberto Weiss, "The Study of Ancient Numismatics During the Renaissance (1313–1517)", *Numismatic Chronicle*, ser. 7, VIII, 1968, 177–87; and L. Rizzoli, "Ritratti di Francesco il Vecchio e Francesco Novello da Carrara in medaglie ed affreschi padovani del secolo XIV," *Bollettino del Museo Civico di Padova*, XXV, 1932, 104–14. Cf. Jones, *Art of the Medal*, 7–8; and Donato, "Gli eroi romani tra storia ed 'exemplum'," 122–3.

14 Von Schlosser, "Die ältesten Medaillen und die Antike," 64–108; Jones *Art of the Medal*, 9–11; Weiss, "La medaglia veneziana," 337–40; and idem, *Pisanello's Medallion of the Emperor John VIII Palaeologus*, London 1966, 20, 31. For medals of Constantine and Heraclius that may have been Venetian forgeries, see also *The International Style. The Arts in Europe around 1400*, exh. cat., Walters Art Gallery, Baltimore 1962, 144–7; and Krautheimer, *Lorenzo Ghiberti*, 59 n. 28.

15 See chap. 1 *supra*.

16 Rosand, "Venetia Figurata," 180. For a detailed discussion of the medal, see Stahl and Waldman, "The Earliest Known Medallists." Jones, *Art of the Medal*, 8, identifies the wheel as part of the Carrara *carro* and suggests that it refers to a Venetian defeat of Francesco II Novello in 1393. This interpretation seems unlikely.

17 See the Prologue to part 1 *supra*.

18 Panofsky, "Father Time," 72.

19 Wittkower, "Chance, Time and Virtue," 100–2. See Petrarch, *De remediis utriusque fortunae*, Introduction.

20 Although Rosand, "Venetia Figurata," 180, likens the figure to Dea Roma, its symbolism deriving from Roman insignia of state, he allows that Venetians considered their state superior to Rome.

21 Weiss, "La medaglia veneziana," 338. See also Giovanni De Lorenzi, *Medaglie di Pisanello e della sua cerchia*, Florence 1983, 9; and Wolters, *Storia e politica*, 230.

22 Stahl and Waldman, "The Earliest Known Medallists," 167–88. Cf. Weiss, "La medaglia veneziana," 338.

23 Stahl, "A Fourteenth-Century Venetian Coin Portrait," 211–14.

24 Cited in ibid., 211–12. See also Papadopoli, *Le Monete di Venezia*, II, 19.

25 The latter possibility is suggested by Stahl and Waldman, "The Earliest Known Medallists," 167–88. See also Jones, *The Art of the Medal*, 9; Weiss, "La medaglia veneziana," 338; and idem, *Renaissance Discovery*, 54.

26 Molmenti, *Vita privata*, I, 207, includes a photograph of a medal of Doge Michele Steno (1400–13). The bearded doge is shown in profile with a sumptuous ermine cape and corno and is surrrounded by the inscription: "MICH. STENO DVX VEN." The piece is not discussed in the text and appears to be undocumented. It likely dates to a much later period, probably the sixteenth century.

27 Weiss, "La medaglia veneziana," 341; and idem, *Pisanello's Medallion*. A few other Renaissance medals are known from this period, but none can be placed in Venice. See Weiss, "The Medieval Medallions of Constantine and Heraclius," 129–44. Cf. Krautheimer, *Lorenzo Ghiberti*, 59.

28 Sanudo, *De origine*, 75–9. For an important study of Venetian rule in one city, see James S. Grubb, *Firstborn of Venice. Vicenza in the Early Renaissance State*, Baltimore and London, 1988.

29 King, *Venetian Humanism*, 212–13, 225.

30 Arnaldo Segarizzi, *La Catinia, le orazioni e le epistole di Sicco Polenton*, Bergamo 1899, 79: "quod fuerat tot seculis terrae visceribus conservatum, is homo trivit." Cf. Buddensieg, "Gregory the Great," 52; and Ullman, "The post-mortem Adventures of Livy," 53–77.

31 Frey, "Apokryphe Liviusbildnisse," 132–3.

32 Ibid., 150–51.

33 Sabbadini, "Storia e critica di alcuni testi Latini," cols. 323–4; and Degli Agostini, *Notizie istorico-critiche*, I, 140. Cf. Labalme, *Bernardo Giustiniani*, 249; and Bodon, "L' immagine di Tito Livio," 69–92.

34 King, *Venetian Humanism*, partic. 244–51.

CHAPTER 5

1 "Quartine in dialetto veneziano," published by Gamba, *Raccolta di poesie*, 3–4: "Inchoronato regno sopra i regni / De luniverso dove al christianismo / In el santo batesmo / Simel a te al mondo non se trova. / . . . / Tu sei nel mondo una viva fenize / Che se renovi e mai non muti forma / Simel la tua norma / Me par tramutata in quel chio parlo. / Qual Alesandro Sepione e Charlo / Che zia segnorizo chome se trova / Tu ne vedi la prova / Chome son ziti i lor sezi e maxone. / Chome ian fato del bon lione / Tranfigurato a Marcho evanzelista / De chui parla mia vista / Sempre piu brama dir che quel vero sona. / . . . / Io dico el vero io dico quel chio amo / Che Troya non fo mai sì posente / Ne Roma antichamente / Quanto e Veniexia e dezo chiaro el mostro. / Tu signorizi in Tramonta e in Ostro / Garbin Grego Levante

e Ponente / Siroco veramente / Vento maistro senza lei non varga. / Pizola fosti e mo sei tanta larga / A torno el mondo se inchina / Tu sola sei Raina / Sopra ogni regno nel mondo creato. / El gran lion un pe tien in sul prato / Laltro nel monte el terzo in piana terra / El quarto al mar saferra / Per modo che la fato un largo vargo."

2 The poet has been identified by some writers as a Jacopo Sanguinucci. See Moschetti, *Due cronache veneziane*, 99–102 (which I have not seen); and a review of ibid. by Francesco Flamini in *Giornale storico della letteratura italiana* XXXII, 1898, 200–2. See also Medin, *Storia della Repubblica*, 490–91.

3 As brilliantly formulated by Tafuri, *Venice and the Renaissance*, 1–13. See also Brown, "Renovatio or Conciliatio," 127–54; as well as chap. 1 *supra* and chap. 12 *infra*.

4 Poppi, "Ricerche," 153–86.

5 Poppi, "Un'orazione," 464–97, with a transcription of the text; and Marx, "Venezia – altera Roma?," 3–18. Poppi notes that Flavio Biondo, who believed that the city had actually been founded in 456, urged Doge Foscari to celebrate a millenary in 1456. The celebration never took place because of problems of the later Foscari dogate. See Romanin, *Storia*, IV, 265–301.

6 See Brown, "City and Citizen," 96. Cf. Jacks, *The Antiquarian*, 133.

7 See the fundamental study, Medin, *Storia della Repubblica*.

8 My understanding of the term *Juventus* is based on Trompf, *Idea of Historical Recurrence*, 188–92 and 212–14. See also Sears, *The Ages of Man*, 54–79.

9 Poppi, "Un'orazione," 488–91: "que iam annis sexcentis et ultra in Rivoalto feliciter inchoata in augmento" (488). The golden-age imagery of the first period derives from the sixth-century account of Cassiodorus, *Variarum libri XII*, XII, no. 24. Cf. Buck, "'Laus Venetiae' und Politik," 186–94. Seneca the Elder and Florus also conceived a biological conception of history but concluded the cycle with decaying old age. De Monacis seems to have followed the model used by Gregory the Great in his *Moralia in Job*. It was an adaptation created especially for the church, which presumably would not decline into senility. See Trompf, *Idea of Historical Recurrence*, 214.

10 Rosand, "Venetia Figurata," 182–4.

11 See Wolters, *Storia e politica*, 230, for the inscriptions. Gabriel: "VIRGINE PARTUS HUMANE NUNCIA PACIS/VOX MEA VIRGO DUCEM REBUS TE POSCIT OPACIS"; Michael: "SUPLICIUM SCELERI VIRTUTUM PREMIA DIGNA/ET MICHI PURGATAS ANIMAS DA LANCE BENIGNA"; Venetia-Justice: "EXEQUAR ANGELICOS MONITUS SACRATAQUE VERBA/BLANDA PIIS INIMICA MALIS TUMIDISQUE SUPERBA." See also Sinding-Larsen, *Christ in the Council Hall*, 56, 175.

12 Poppi, "Ricerche," 183–4, citing Book I, 3 (written after 1421): "Questa sola città fra tutte quelle fondate prima e dopo di lei è l'unica, e ciò che è ammirevole senza campi, prati e vigne, ad aver conservato integra la libertà nella quale fu fondata per più di mille anni, senza che sia mai stata mutata la maniera di governo . . . Pochissime città giunsero perdere le loro libertà dopo due o trecento anni. Quale mai la protrasse di mille in mille?"

13 Poppi, "Un orazione," 472.

14 See, for example, Goldner, "The Decoration of the Main Façade Window of San Marco," 13–34, for a cycle of nine Genesis reliefs and figures of prophets and evangelists, based on Tuscan prototypes.

15 Wolters, *La scultura veneziana gotica*, 70–71, 222; Arslan, *Venezia Gotica*, 149–50; Paoletti, *L'architettura* I (testo), 2–3; and Lorenzi, *Monumenti*, nr. 126.

16 Brown, *Venetian Narrative Painting*, 41, 261–5.

17 Cadorin, *Notizie storiche*, 12–13.

18 For an overview see Howard, *Architectural History*, 79–85, 102–12. See also Franzoi et al, *Il Palazzo Ducale*.

19 See chap. 8 *infra*.

20 Alberti, *On the Art of Building*, 265 (Book VIII, chap. 6). Cfr. Pincus, *Arco Foscari*, 156–7.

21 Marx, "Venezia – altera Roma?," 7–8.

22 Ibid., 14.

23 Gilbert, "The Venetian Constitution," 468–9.

24 King, *Venetian Humanism*, 44–5.

25 Ibid.

26 Chiarelli, *L'opera completa del Pisanello*, 96–101, depicts twenty-four securely attributed medals made between 1438 and 1449.

27 Rosand, "Venetia Figurata," 180; and Wolters, *Storia e politica*, 230. See also Hill, *Corpus*, 108; and Pollard, *Italian Renaissance Medals*, 245. Cf. Weiss, "La medaglia veneziana," 341.

28 Weiss, "La medaglia veneziana," 341. See also Hill, *Corpus*, 108; and Pollard, *Italian Renaissance Medals*, 245.

29 Ziliotto, *Raffaele Zovenzoni*, 20–21, 150–54 (no. 247): "Epaenodia in inclytum atque potentissimum dominium venetorum per summum poetam raphaelem jovenzonum edita" (excerpt): "Quid loquar urbis opus mirum cui sparsa per aequor / stant loca sancta patrum? pro moenibus inde columnae / Herculis occurrunt subeuntibus ostia nautis. / Cernis et augustas hinc divi Principis aedes, / hinc turrim aurato tangentem vertice coelum / hicque micat Pario structum de marmore templum, / Marce tibi, foribus fulget cui limen aenis: / intus ebur vivens, simul aera loquentia credas: / hinc Scopae dea facta manu simulacraque magni / Zeusis et antiqui Polycleti opera alta renident. / Hic pallam insignem gemmis auroque rigentem, / hic, monocorne, tuum specimen mitramque ducalem / praetereo solidoque graves adamante coronas."

The *corno* refers to the doge's distinctive headgear, which features a "horn."

30 Muraro, "Statutes of the Venetian *Arti*," 264. Sanudo, *Vite*[1] (1733), cols. 1006–7, reports such an attempt in February 1430 *more veneto*, that is, 1431. The chapel was given its present name in 1618.

31 See also Brown, *Venetian Narrative Painting*, chap. 7.

32 For a summary of the various arguments on attributions and dating, see Hartt, "The Earliest Works of Andrea del Castagno," 225–36. To this should be added Muraro, "Statutes of the Venetian *Arti*," 263–74; Merkel, "Un problema di metodo," 65–80; idem, "Venezia, 1430–1450," 59–65; Degenhart and Schmitt, *Corpus: Jacopo Bellini*, II-5, 137–44; and Bertelli, "The Tale of Two Cities," 373–97.

33 Cf. Bertelli, "The Tale of Two Cities," 387–90, for a proposal for the Sienese artist Vecchietta's responsibility for the *Birth* and the *Visitation*.

34 For Castagno's work in Venice, see Horster, *Andrea del Castagno*, 18–20, 171–3.

35 Cf. Polacco, *San Marco*, 287–303, who postulates two campaigns: an earlier one directed by an International Gothic style artist – perhaps Zanino di Pietro, but in any event not Giambono – that was completed and then suffering some kind of catastrophic damage that necessitated a second campaign to repair the damage. Following this line of argument, Castagno would have been called back from Florence in 1448–9 to re-design the *Dormition*, while preserving the figures at the right that remained from the first program. Cf. also Bertelli, "'A Tale of Two Cities," 373–97, who finds Uccello's intervention in the medallions of the vault and in the early phases of

the *Dormition*. A number of scholars, including Polacco, assign three or four apostles in the *Dormition* to Jacopo Bellini as well as the upper portion of the *Visitation*, a work for which others give him full credit. See the following note.

36 As noted by Degenhart and Schmitt, *Corpus: Jacopo Bellini*, II-5, 137–43, although the figures are similar in style to those in the *Birth* and the *Presentation*, their placement inside and not in front of the centralized architecture is one of Jacopo's most typical compositional strategies.

37 See for example, Botticelli's many Adorations that featured crumbling Roman arches. For the symbolism of Romanesque, Gothic and Classical architecture in this period, see the references in chap. 6, nn. 90–91.

38 As observed by Polacco, *San Marco*, 288–91.

39 See Pincus, *Arco Foscari*, 75, for the term "via triumphalis."

40 See ibid. for a meticulous examination of the stylistic evolution of the arch, with an overview on 34–75. See also McAndrew, *Venetian Architecture*, 82ff.

41 For the dependence of the Porta della Carta on tabernacle forms, see Pincus, *Arco Foscari*, 48. Both the Porta and the Arco dei Foscari lost their marble ensembles of the doge and the lion of San Marco in the iconoclastic outbursts that followed the fall of the republic in 1797. Only that on the Porta della Carta was replaced with a copy; the space on the balcony of the Arco remains empty.

42 Ibid., 54–58. See Onians, *Bearers of Meaning*, 119–23, for the introduction of putti into Gothic architecture.

43 Concina, *Arsenale*, 56–68, who makes a persuasive argument against the attribution to Gambello and proposes three other possibilities: Bartolomeo Buon, the Dalmatian architect Luciano Laurana, and Filarete. See also McAndrew, *Venetian Architecture*, 17–23; and Pincus, *Arco Foscari*, 133–4, n. 25. Cf. Lieberman, *Renaissance Architecture*, Plate 70; and, with less certainty, Howard, *Architectural History*, 104–6 and 126, who maintain the Gambello attribution.

Bartolomeo Buon designed new classical portals for the churches of Madonna del Orto (1460–62) and SS. Giovanni e Paolo (1459–63) that were also modeled after the Arco dei Sergii. For a succinct analysis, see Lieberman, *Renaissance Architecture*, Plate 1.

44 Ibid., 58–63.

45 Lieberman, "Real Architecture, Imaginary History," 117–26, who notes that winged victories were added to the spandrels in 1571 after the victory at Lepanto and that Santa Giustina was installed on the gable a few years later. The front terrace with its statuary was built at the end of the seventeenth century. It was soon augmented by a new set of bronze doors and booty – three lions taken from Piraeus and Delos – to commemorate Venetian reconquests of the Morea and Corfu. See also Tafuri, "La 'nuova Costantinopoli'," 25ff, for an earlier statement of the principal of continuity. Cf. Onians, *Bearers of Meaning*, 119–23, for another argument for a case of conscious architectural historicism.

46 Jacks, *The Antiquarian*, 129–33. See also n. 5 *supra* and chap. 8 *infra*.

47 As analyzed in the fundamental study of Pincus, *The Arco Foscari*. See also Ugo Franzoi, "Architettura," and Wolfgang Wolters, "Scultura," both in Franzoi et al, *Il Palazzo Ducale*, 57–64, 142–53, respectively.

48 Pincus, *Arco Foscari*, 92–5, suggests a sixteenth-century date for the antique-looking winged putto on the keystone of the arch. She also points to analogous statements in the mosaic decoration of the Cappella Mascoli in San Marco and in the drawings of Jacopo Bellini. We will return to them in chap. 6.

49 Ibid., 104–7.

50 Ibid., 144ff.

51 Ibid., 169–88.

52 Ibid., chaps. VI and VII.

53 Huse and Wolters, *Art of Renaissance Venice*, 138–9.

54 Pincus, *Arco Foscari*, 207–48.

55 Ibid., 193 n. 21.

56 Pope-Hennessy, *Italian Renaissance Sculpture*, 335, 367, soon after 1457; Seymour, *Sculpture in Italy, 1400–1500*, 198, ? *c*.1460; McAndrew, *Venetian Architecture*, 8–12, 1466–70, noting that the east end of the Frari was not completed until 1468; Huse and Wolters, *Art of Renaissance Venice*, 134, ? early 1460s; Pincus, *Arco Foscari*, 193–4, n. 21, 412–14, middle to late 1480s, with further revision in the sixteenth century, adding that "The Foscari tomb should be considered as standing outside the Venetian tradiiton of Renaissance monuments."

57 See McAndrew, *Renaissance Architecture*, 8–12; and Pincus, *Arco Foscari*, 193–4 n. 21, 402–38. For the Coscia (or Cossa) tomb, see Lightbown, *Donatello and Michelozzo*, I, 24–51.

58 Onians, *Bearers of Meaning*, 119–28.

59 McAndrew, *Venetian Architecture*, 63–6, with the tomb of Pietro Mocenigo discussed on 123–6.

60 Usually interpreted as the Venetian entry into Scutari and the surrender of the keys of Cyprus to Caterina Cornaro. See also Pope-Hennessy, *Italian Renaissance Sculpture*, 339, 368, who reports Debra Pincus's unpublished proposal that the first relief actually represents Mocenigo's restoration of the kingdom of the Lords of Karaman after its liberation from the Turks.

61 McAndrew, *Venetian Architecture*, 123.

62 See chap. 1 *supra*.

63 The tomb of Tommaso Mocenigo (1414–23), in SS. Giovanni e Paolo offered an abbreviated version of age imagery, with two warrior figures of different ages at the corners of the sarcophagus. See Pincus, "The Tomb of Doge Nicolò Tron," 130, who sees only three ages represented on the tomb of Pietro Mocenigo.

64 See above for Lorenzo De Monacis's three-age system for the republic, ending with Juventus.

65 Pincus, "The Tomb of Doge Nicolò Tron," 139.

66 Cf. Pincus, *Arco Foscari*, 198–202.

67 Pincus, "The Tomb of Doge Nicolò Tron," 127.

68 Molina, ed., *Orazioni, elogie e vite*, 78.

69 See the Prologue to part III *supra*.

70 As interpreted by Pincus, *Arco Foscari*, 180 n. 10, who suggests that the painting was a homage to Tron on his death in 1473. The magistrates are Paolo Corner, N. Vitturi, and Antonio Venier. See also Nepi-Scirè and Valcanover, *Gallerie dell'Accademia*, 169, cat. no. 272; and Moschini Marconi, *Gallerie dell'Accademia*, 151.

71 I owe the term to Degenhart and Schmitt, "Ein Musterblatt," 153.

CHAPTER 6

1 Modena, Biblioteca Estense, MS IX, A, 27, published in Testi, *La storia della pittura veneziana*, II, 159 n. 2 (cited and translated by Eisler, *The Genius of Jacopo Bellini*, 512): "Quanto che gloriar te puoy bellino / che quel che sente il tuo chiaro Intellecto / la mano industriosa il proprio effecto / mostra di fuora gaio et pelegrino, / Siche ad ogni altro insegni il ver camino / del divo Apelle et nobel policlecto / che se natura ta facto perfecto / questa e gratia dal ciel e tuo destino . . ."

2 For example, Saxl, "Jacopo Bellini and Mantegna as Antiquarians," 150–60.

3 Degenhart and Schmitt, *Corpus: Jacopo Bellini*, II-5, 200–201.

4 The discussion that follows is an evolved version of an argument first proposed in Brown, "The Antiquarianism of Jacopo Bellini," 65–84.

5 The number tends to fluctuate in scholarly citations, across a range of 200–230, according to different definitions of what constitutes a single drawing. The figure here is taken from Degenhart and Schmitt, *Corpus: Jacopo Bellini*, II-5, 10. Technical information for each drawing can be found in ibid., II-6; and in Albert J. Elen's discussion in Eisler, *The Genius of Jacopo Bellini*, 454–79.

6 Ames-Lewis, *Drawing in Early Renaissance Italy*, 64. See also Robert Scheller, *A Survey of Medieval Model Books*, Haarlem 1963, partic. 171–215.

7 See Degenhart and Schmitt, "Gentile da Fabriano in Rom," 59–151; and Cavallaro, "Studio e gusto dell'antico nel Pisanello," 89–100.

8 Joost-Gaugier, *Jacopo Bellini*, ix, n. 7: The pages of Jacopo's British Museum album measure *c*.41.5 × 33.6 cm. and those of the Louvre album *c*.42.7 × 29 cm. Leaves of surviving model and sketch books range from *c*.9 × 9.5 cm. to *c*.23.5 × 17.7 cm.

9 Paoletti, *Raccolta*, 11. Degenhart and Schmitt, *Corpus: Jacopo Bellini*, II-5, 16–17, argue persuasively that the *quadros dessignatos* are the drawings in the Louvre and BM albums.

10 Degenhart and Schmitt, *Corpus: Jacopo Bellini*, II-5, 105–25, 218–27 (with a full summary of earlier views on 252–3). Their chronology is first adumbrated in idem, *Jacopo Bellini*, New York 1984, 12–21. See the concurring views of Merkel, "Venezia, 1430–1450," 63; Brown, *Venetian Narrative Painting*, 108–18; and in reviews of the *Corpus* by Peter Humfrey in *Renaissance Studies* VI, 1992, 217–20; and by Patricia Fortini Brown in *Biography* XV, 1992, 290–94. For contrary opinions see, in partic., Rothlisberger, "Studi su Jacopo Bellini," 43–89 (both albums 1450–55, with London album the earlier); Eisler, *The Genius of Jacopo Bellini*, 99–104 (both albums made simultaneously from the 1440s through the 1460s); and Keith Christiansen in *Andrea Mantegna* (1992), 113 n. 54 (anywhere between *c*.1440 and *c*.1460, with the London album earlier, but possibly overlapping with the Paris album).

11 Paoletti, *Raccolta*, 11: "omnia laboreria de Zessio, de marmore et de relevijs, quadros dessignatos et omnes libros de dessignijs et alia omnia pertinentia pictorie et ad depingendum que fuerunt quondam prefati magistri Iacobij bellino veri mei."

12 Ziliotti, *Raffaele Zovenzoni*, 109, no. 135: "Qui Paphiam nudis Venerem vidisse papillis / optet in antiquo marmore Praxitelis, / Bellini pluteum Gentilis quaerat, ubi stans, / trunca licet membris, vivit imago, suis."

13 Reported by Piero Valeriano and cited by Brown, "'Una testa de Platone antica'," 372ff.

14 Modena, Biblioteca Estense, MS IX, A, 27, cited by Testi, *Storia*, II, 159 n. 2; English transl. by Roger Fry, "A Note on Jacopo Bellini," *The Dome*, Feb. 2, 1899, 126 (repr. in Eisler, *The Genius of Jacopo Bellini*, 512). For the importance of the Ferrara experience in the formation of Jacopo Bellini and his exposure there to Alberti's theories, see Christiansen, "Venetian Painting of the Early Quattrocento," 170–72.

15 Baxandall, "A Dialogue on Art," 304–26, who dates the work to *c*.1450.

16 Degenhart and Schmitt, *Corpus: Jacopo Bellini*, II-5: Text, 220–26.

17 See ibid., 218–19; and chap. 4 *supra*.

18 See Lightbown, *Mantegna*, 28, 40, who suggests that Mantegna

would have first met Bellini in Venice, perhaps in 1447 when the younger artist was living there for a time with his master, Francesco Squarcione.

19 Zeno, *Dissertazioni Vossiane*, I, 143–4: "Cum omnibus in rebus sanctam vetustatem admiremur, ac veneremur, ejusque studiosos & diligentes inquisitores praecipua quadam laude dignos censeamus: Vt videas antiqua virum monumenta priorum, / Quid maris & terrae, multa pericla subis? / Ecce quod ut videas, totus peragrabitur orbis, / Pagina nunc oculis subijcit una tuis. / Quae si fortè tuae ferat oblectamina menti, / Auctori gratis dicere ne pigeat." Cf. Scardeone, *De antiquitate urbis patavii*, 239–40.

20 Bern, Burgerbibliothek, MS B 42, with a note that the work was begun in Padua, finished in Cesena and put into its final form in Bologna.

21 For the Modena codex (Bibl. Estense, Cod. L. 5. 15 [Lat. 992]), see Alexander, *The Painted Page*, 143–4; Huelsen, *La Roma antica*; Mardersteig, *Alphabetum Romanum*, 22–3; and Danesi Squarzina, "Eclisse del gusto cortese," 28–31, and 38–45.

22 Princeton University Library, MS Garrett 158; and Paris, Bibliothèque Nationale, MS Lat. 5825 F. For the Princeton codex, which includes fifteen full-page drawings of ancient Rome, see Alexander, *The Painted Page*, 144–5; and Sheard, *Antiquity in the Renaissance*, cat. no. 4.

23 Mardersteig, *Alphabetum Romanum, passim*. Cf. Meiss, "Toward a More Comprehensive Renaissance Palaeography," 97–112, who credits Mantegna with the revival.

24 See in particular, Mardersteig, *Alphabetum Romanum*, 9–30; Mitchell, "Felice Feliciano *Antiquarius*," 197–221; Pozzi and Gianella, "Scienza antiquaria," 459–77. For a complete bibliography of his works, see Serena Spano Martinelli, "Note intorno a Felice Feliciano," *Rinascimento*, 2nd ser., XXV, 1985, 221–8.

25 Treviso, Biblioteca Capitolare, MS I, 138. See Fiocco, "Felice Feliciano amico degli artisti," 192; and Chiarlo, "'Gli fragmenti'," 280–283. For the passage from Scalamonti, see chap. 4 *supra*.

26 It was included in the Treviso manuscript along with the *Vita* of Scalamonti and a collection of epigrams. For an argument stressing its largely imaginary character, see Billanovich, "Intorno alla 'Iubilatio'," 351–8; and the comments by Michael Hirst in his review of the Mantegna exhibition at the Royal Academy of Arts in *Burlington Magazine* CXXXIV, 1992, 318–21.

27 Chiarlo, "'Gli fragmenti'," 282.

28 The Latin text is found in Mitchell, "Archaeology and Romance," 477; and with minor differences in Billanovich, "Intorno alla 'Iubilatio'," 351 n. 3 (Eng. trans. from Mardersteig, *Alphabetum Romanum*, 20).

29 Mardersteig, *Alphabetum Romanum*, 20–21. Lightbown, *Andrea Mantegna*, 40, 94–6, rejects the identification of Giovanni Antenoreo as Marcanova, but his arguments are not convincing. Billanovich, "Intorno alla 'Iubilatio'," 352, notes that the nickname may have alluded to the fact that Marcanova, born in Venice, had made Padua his second home, just like the Trojan Antenor.

30 In the codex in Venice, (Biblioteca Marciana, Cod. Lat. X, 196 [3766]), the IVBILATIO and twenty-three inscriptions from the Garda region are recorded on ff. 44–8. The two inscriptions on the campanile are cited on f. 46: "In ecclesia sancti petri thusculani" and "ad Protomartyriis aedem." They are located on the campanile by Bettoni, *Storia della Riviera di Salò*, 318, 320, nos. XXXVII and XLI. Cf. *C.I.L.*, V, nos. 4852–87, 8889.

31 "Ad splendidissimum virum Andream Mantegnam Patavum pictorem incomparabilem." The original manuscript made for Mantegna is lost, but it exists in two copies: Verona, Biblioteca Capitolare, Cod. 269, dated 1463; and Venice, Biblioteca Marciana, Cod. Lat. X, 196 (3766), dated 1464. In the Marciana codex, the IVBILATIO and twenty-three inscriptions from the Garda region are recorded on ff. 44–48. Cf. Romano, "Verso la maniera moderna," 9–13.

32 The English text is taken from Mardersteig, *Alphabetum Romanum*, 19.

33 Degenhart and Schmitt, *Corpus: Jacopo Bellini*, II-5, 192–213, II-6, 370–73.

34 Degenhart and Schmitt, "Ein Musterblatt des Jacopo Bellini," 146; Rothlisberger, "Studi su Jacopo Bellini," 70–71; and Eisler, *Genius*, 207–8. See also Billanovich, "Una miniera di epigrafi e di antichità," 242–4, who thought that Mantegna obtained his epigrams from Jacopo; and Testi, *La storia della pittura veneziana*, I, 460, and II, 641, who held that Jacopo worked from other drawings rather than from the original monuments.

35 As observed by Degenhart and Schmitt, *Corpus: Jacopo Bellini*, II-5, 207–11, with an example from a Paris redaction of the manuscript.

36 Princeton University Library, MS Garrett 158, f. 127. Cf. Mitchell, "Felice Feliciano *Antiquarius*," 216–19.

37 Ibid.; and E. Lawrence, "The Illustrations of the Garrett and Modena Manuscripts of Marcanova," *Memoirs of the American Academy in Rome* VI, 1927, 127–31. Huelsen, *La Roma antica*, reproduces the full set from the Modena codex; Danesi Squarzina, "Eclisse del gusto cortese," 40–44, illustrates nine of the pages. See also Christine Smith, "The Winged Eye: Leon Battista Alberti and the Visualization of Past, Present, and Future," in Millon and Lampugnani, *The Renaissance from Brunelleschi to Michelangelo*, 459–60.

38 Chiarlo, "'Gli fragmenti dilla sancta antiquitate'," 286, attributed it to Cyriacus and judged it comparable to the Marcanova illustrations and those depicted in Colvin, *A Florentine Picture-Chronicle*.

39 See also ff. 9v–10r, 11v–12r, 28v–29r, 50v–51 in the London album.

40 Saxl, "The Classical Inscription," 24.

41 Cf. Rothlisberger, "Studi su Jacopo Bellini," 50ff; idem, "Notes on the Drawing Books of Jacopo Bellini," 359–64; and Degenhart and Schmitt, *Corpus: Jacopo Bellini*, II-5 and II-6.

42 Malatesta died before receiving the Modena codex from Marcanova. Upon the latter's death in 1467 it passed in accordance with his testament to the Canons Regular of the Augustinian monastery of San Giovanni in Verdara in Padua.

43 Princeton, MS Garrett 158; and Saxl, "The Classical Inscription," 38.

44 The British Museum album was left by Gentile Bellini in his will of Feb. 18, 1507, to his brother Giovanni Bellini. Marcantonio Michiel observed it in the house of Gabriele Vendramin in 1530. For a detailed account of the peregrinations of both albums, see Tietze and Tietze-Conrat, *The Drawings of the Venetian Painters*, 107; and Degenhart and Schmitt, *Corpus: Jacopo Bellini*, II-5, 16–17.

45 Now lost. See L. Vagnetti, "Lo studio di Roma negli scritti albertiani," in *Convegno internazionale indetto nel V centenario di Leon Battista Alberti*, Accademia Nazionale dei Lincei, Quaderno no. 209, Rome 1974, 73–137; and Gabriella Befani Canfield, "The Florentine Humanists' Concept of Architecture in the 1430s and Filippo Brunelleschi," in *Scritti di Storia dell'arte in onore di Federico Zeri*, Milan 1984, I, 112–21. For a

map that may reflect it, see Gustina Scaglia, "The Origins of an Archaeological Plan of Rome by Alessandro Strozzi," *Journal of the Warburg and Courtauld Institutes* XXVII, 1964, 136–63, who suggests, however, that the Strozzi plan is related to Flavio Biondo's *Roma instaurata*. For an extensive bibliography on Alberti, see Franco Borsi, *Alberti: Opera Completa*, Milan 1984. See now Brian Curran and Anthony Grafton, "A fifteenth-century site report on the Vatican obelisk," *Journal of the Warburg and Courtauld Institutes*, LVIII, 1995, 234–48.

46 For the Latin text and an Italian translation, see D'Onofrio, *Visitiamo Roma nel Quattrocento*, 65–90.

47 Ibid., 78: "Di fronte, al di là della strada, ci sono numerose colonne marmoree, parte del portico di un tempio detto di Giove, il cui settore circolare è occupato da nuovi edifici, ed internamente da orticelli. (Ex adverso, via intermedia, sunt plures columnae marmoreae, pars porticus templi, ut aiunt, Iovis, cuius portio rotunda novis aedificiis, interius vero hortulis est occupata)."

48 Ibid., 78: "con un lato in mattoni, presso la chiesa Hierusalem, inserito con queste nuove mura forma parte della cerchia di mura della città (Tertium ex latere cocto iusta ecclesiam, quam *Hierusalem* appellant, his novis insitum moeniis partem efficit ambitus murorum urbis)."

49 Mortier, *Le poétique*, 32. Cf. Mazzocco, "Petrarch, Poggio, and Biondo," 357–9.

50 Angelo Mazzocco, "Rome and the Humanists: The Case of Biondo Flavio," in A. Ramsay, ed., *Rome in the Renaissance: The City and the Myth*, Binghamton 1982, 185–95; Denys Hay, "Flavio Biondo and the Middle Ages," *Proceedings of the British Academy* XLV, 1959, 97–128 (with an appendix giving dates of composition and publication of Biondo's writings); and Dorothy M. Robathan, "Flavio Biondo's *Roma Instaurata*," *Medievalia et Humanista* I, 1970, 203–16. For the Latin version of *Roma instaurata* and an Italian translation see D'Onofrio, *Visitiamo Roma nel Quattrocento*, 93–266.

51 Biblioteca Nazionale Marciana, Venice: Cod. Gr. Z. 388 (=333), f. 6v. See Jay A. Levenson, ed., *Circa 1492. Art in the Age of Exploration*, National Gallery of Art, Washington, D.C., New Haven and London, 1992, 226–7: cat. 126; Maria Cecilia Ferrari, "La Geografia del Tolomeo fatta miniare dal Cardinale Bessarione," *La Bibliofila* XL, 1939, 23–37; Fiaccadori, *Bessarione e l'Umanesimo*, 423, cat. 39; and Zorzi, *Biblioteca Marciana, Venice*, 122–3.

52 Millon and Lampugnani, *The Renaissance from Brunelleschi to Michelangelo*, 459–60.

53 See references in nn. 59–60 *infra*.

54 Degenhart and Schmitt, "Gentile da Fabriano in Rom," 115–17. See also Baxandall, *Giotto and the Orators*, 78–96, 130, whose discussion of Pisanello can be applied in good part also to Gentile da Fabriano.

55 For a full analysis, see Degenhart and Schmitt, *Corpus: Jacopo Bellini*, II-5, 192–214, and II-6, 370–73, who conclude that Jacopo's exactitude in rendering both the epigraphy and the form of the monuments is based on eye-witness viewing of the original objects.

56 For Jacopo's architectural syntheses, see ibid., II-5, 34–58. See also the notion of a "compromise style" and "arte decorativa" of Filarete, developed in the Venetian ambient, as discussed by Spencer, *Filarete's Treatise on Architecture*.

57 Further discussed and dated, respectively, to 1435–40 and *c*.1440 by Degenhart and Schmitt, *Corpus: Jacopo Bellini*, II-6, 313–15, and 356–7. They identify the subject of f. 35 as *Christ Before the High Council*. Cf. Eisler, *The Genius of Jacopo Bellini*, 327, for both drawings. For the Arco dei Sergii, see

Lieberman, "Real Architecture, Imaginary History," 117–26; and chap. 5 *supra*.

58 Ernst Gombrich, *Art and Illusion: A Study in the Psychology of Pictorial Representation*, Princeton 1972, 87–8. See also chap. 4 *supra*, nn. 93–4.

59 *C.I.L.*, V, no. 2528; Degenhart and Schmitt, *Corpus: Jacopo Bellini*, II-5, 203–4. The original inscription was recorded in Montebuso, south of Padua and halfway between the towns of Este and Monselice. Cf. Moschetti, "Le Inscrizioni lapidarie romane," 227–39, who argues that Mantegna would have seen the stone at first hand even though he errs by adding an extra "I" to the number that begins the third line of the epigram. Meiss, "Renaissance Palaeography," 104–5, notes the greater accuracy of Jacopo Bellini and suggests that he was Mantegna's source for the inscription of T. Pullius Linus.

60 For a detailed iconographical study of this work, see Knabenshue, "Ancient and Mediaeval Elements in Mantegna's *Trial of St. James*," 59–73. Cf. Eisler, *The Genius of Jacopo Bellini*, 58 and 207, who suggests that Mantegna might have married Nicolosia Bellini to gain access to her father's drawings.

61 See Banzato and Pellegrini, *Da Giotto al tardogotico*, 13–17; and L. Grossato, *Da Giotto al Mantegna*, Milan 1974.

62 Banzato and Pellegrini, *Da Giotto al tardogotico*, 18.

63 For a full discussion see Lightbown, *Mantegna*, 15–29; and *Andrea Mantegna*, exh. cat., 1992, 8–30 and 94–114.

64 Scardeone, *De antiquitate urbis patavii*, 370: "Quo circa annavigavit in Graeciam, & totam illam provinciam pervagatus est: unde multa notatu degna, tum mente, tum chartis, quae ad eius artis peritiam facere visa sunt, inde domum secum detulit . . . Signa autem pictasque tabellas plurimas habuit, quarum magisterio & arte Andream & reliquos condiscipulos instruxerat, magisquam editis à se archetypis, aut ditatis, seu novis exemplis ad imitandum praebitis." On Scardeone's credibility, see Boskovits, "Una ricerca su Francesco Squarcione," 40–70; and Bernard Aikema, "The Fame of Francesco Squarcione," *Ateneo Veneto*, n.s., XV:1–2, 1977, 33–7. On Squarcione's drawings see Schmitt, "Francesco Squarcione als Zeichner und Stecher," 205–13.

65 Vasari, *Vite*, I, 487–92.

66 Lightbown, *Mantegna*, 18–19.

67 Ibid.

68 Lightbown, *Mantegna*, 29, emphasizes Mantegna's debt to Jacopo Bellini. See also Keith Christiansen's observations in *Andrea Mantegna* (1992), 107–8.

69 See, for example, King, *Venetian Humanism*, 186–7; and the Prologue to part II *supra*.

70 Demus, *The Mosaics of San Marco*, I:Text, 219–30. The other two scenes depict SS. Simon and Judas Thaddeus, who topple Sol and Luna.

71 Buddensieg, "Gregory the Great," 44–65. See also, in general, Camille, *The Gothic Idol*.

72 Amalricus Augerius, *Actus pontificum Romanorum usque ad . . . annum 1321*, in J.G. Eccardus, *Corpus Hist. med. aevi*, II, 1743, col. 1684, cited by Buddensieg, "Gregory the Great," 45, who notes that the passage is taken directly from Martinus Polanus's (d. 1278) *Chronicle of the Emperors and Popes*, "the most widely read historical work of the late Middle Ages": "statuit et ordinavit, ut omnes imagines daemonum, capita et membra ipsorum, quae tam in urbe Romana quam extra inveniri possent, amputari et dilaniari penitus deberent, ut propter hoc exstirpata haereticae pravitatis radice, ecclesiasticae veritatis palma plenius exaltaretur."

73 See the Prologue to part III *supra*.

74 Polenton, *Scriptores illustres latinae linguae*, Book VI, 181f. The second edition was completed in 1437.

75 Buddensieg, "Gregory the Great," 51, n. 23, citing Paris, Bibl. Nat., MS Ital. 81, f. 69v: "Gregorio papa deffece le statue in Roma che oggi quasi tucte si vedono sanca teste. Preterea molti libri historici fece brusare come furono le opere overo deche di Tito Livio, li quali conteneano li animosi et alti gesti di romani antiqui per che non erano stati christiani." Lorenzo Ghiberti would change the terms of the debate in the second book of his *Commentarii* (written 1447–55). Here he antedated the destruction to the time of the Emperor Constantine and Pope Sylvester, charging that the triumph of Christianity had been made at the expense of art. See ibid., 44; Von Schlosser, *Lorenzo Ghiberti's Denkwürdigkeiten*, I, 35; Camille, *The Gothic Idol*, 341–3; and Krautheimer, *Lorenzo Ghiberti*, I, 309.

76 Degenhart and Schmitt, *Corpus: Jacopo Bellini*, II-6, 429.

77 Ibid., II-6, 367–70.

78 See Brown, *Venetian Narrative Painting*, 79–97 on this general issue. Cf. Joost-Gaugier, "Jacopo Bellini's Interest in Perspective," 1–28.

79 Cf. Camille, *The Gothic Idol*, 338–49.

80 See ibid., 375–6.

81 The attribution to Vivarini is not entirely convincing, but no better one has been proposed. See Fabio Bisogni, "The Martyrdoms of St. Apollonia in Four Quattrocento Panels," *Studies in the History of Art* VII, 1975, 41–7, who identified the text informing the subject matter of the panels and proposes a Paduan provenance; and Shapley, *Catalogue of the Italian Paintings* I, 537–8, who remains with the Vivarini attribution. See also Federico Zeri, "Un 'San Girolamo' firmato di Giovanni d'Alemagna," in *Studi di Storia dell'Arte in onore di Antonio Morassi*, Venice 1971, 47–8, who suggests that Giovanni d'Alemagna, the brother-in-law of Antonio Vivarini, is the author of the paintings.

82 See Onians, *Bearers of Meaning*, partic. chap. VIII.

83 *Katalog der Staatsgalerie Stuttgart*, 309–10, inv. nr. 90: "Tenplum pacis in eternum [aedificatum] coruit quando virgo f[ilium] p[eperit]." The dimensions of the work (95 × 79 cm.) suggest that it is an altarpiece. None of the attributions cited thus far are truly convincing: Jacobello del Fiore or his circle, Jacobello di Bonomo, Maestro Stefano, someone other than Jacobello del Fiore, a terraferma painter connected to Giusto di Menabuoi. The most prudent judgment is given by Robert Oertel: "venezianisch, um 1400." See also Settis, "Continuità, distanza, conoscenza," 375–82.

84 See also Degenhart and Schmitt, *Corpus: Jacopo Bellini*, 338–40, who demonstrate that the *Baptism* (f. 24) was originally the right-hand side of a double-page composition with *St. Jerome in the Desert* on the left (f. 22v). At some point after its execution, another leaf depicting the Presentation of the Virgin (f. 23r) was inserted between them.

85 Settis, "Continuità, distanza, conoscenza," 382; and idem, "Des ruines au musée," 1347–80.

86 Degenhart and Schmitt, *Corpus: Jacopo Bellini*, II-6, 328–30.

87 Cf. Arnold Esch, "Mauern bei Mantegna," *Zeitschrift für Kunstgeschichte* XLVII, 1984, 307 (293–319), who has a different view.

88 Jacopo depicted three other drawings with significant elements of classical ruins or sculptural fragments: Paris, f. 18v, *St. Jerome in the Desert*; and f. 34, *Deposition of Christ from the Cross*; and London, ff. 1v–2r, *Crucifixion with view of Jerusalem*.

89 Most notably Maso di Banco's fresco of *St. Sylvester in the Roman Forum* (c.1336–9) and Agnolo Gaddi's fresco of *The Temptation of St. Anthony* (1390s), both painted in Santa Croce, Florence.

90 For Squarcione's painting see Boskovitz, "Una ricerca su Francesco Squarcione," 40–70; and Banzato and Pellegrini, *Da Giotto al tardogotico*, 104–6. For Mantegna's work, see Lightbown, *Mantegna*, 47–57; and Cieri Via, "L'antico in Andrea Mantegna fra storia e allegoria," 69–91. Another painting with classical ruins from the same period is a tondo of the *Adoration of the Magi* probably begun by Fra Angelico and completed by Fra Filippo Lippi shortly after 1453, now in the National Gallery, Washington. See Shapley, *Catalogue of the Italian Paintings, National Gallery of Art*, I, 10–13.

91 On ruins in paintings, see also Erwin Panofsky, *Early Netherlandish Painting: Its Origins and Character*, New York 1971, I, 134–40; Burckhardt, *The Civilization of the Renaissance in Italy* I, 183–95; and Rab Hatfield, *Botticelli's Uffizi "Adoration": A Study in Pictorial Content*, Princeton 1976, 56–67, who cites two ruined buildings in Adoration altarpieces prior to the Washington tondo: Gentile da Fabriano's Strozzi altarpiece of 1423, and a work by Francesco d'Antonio in Santa Felicità, Florence. However, neither depicts identifiably *classical* ruins.

92 Zeri, *Catalogue of the Walters Art Gallery*, 212–13; Armstrong, *The Paintings and Drawings of Marco Zoppo*.

93 See Prologue to part V *infra*.

94 L. Sighinolfi, "La biblioteca di Giovanni Marcanova," in *Collectanea variae doctrinae Leoni S. Olschki oblata*, Munich 1921, 218ff, nos. 498 and 517, citing an inventory of 1467: "liber Blondi de Roma instaurata in papiro, liber Pogii de varietate fortune in papiro." See Esch, "Mauern bei Mantegna," 313–18; Jones, "Mantegna and Materials," 71–90; Vickers, "Mantegna and Constantinople," 680–87.

95 Cf. Esch, "Mauern bei Mantegna," 318.

PART IV

PROLOGUE

1 BMV, Cod. Lat. XIV 14 (=4235), trans. Martin Lowry in Chambers and Pullan, *Venice: A Documentary History*, 357–8. For the manuscript of the act of donation, see Fiaccadori, *Bessarione e l'Umanesimo*, 381–2; Zorzi, *Biblioteca Marciana Veneziana*, 54 and pl. II.

2 For Bessarion's bequest, see Labowsky, *Bessarion's Library*, and Zorzi, *La Libreria di San Marco*. For many aspects of Bessarion's life and a comprehensive and up-to-date bibliography, see Fiaccadori, *Bessarione e l'Umanesimo*.

3 ASV, Senato, Secreto, reg. 19, ff. 202r–203v, published in Pertusi, *La caduta di Costantinopoli*, 22–23: "se il Dio nostro misericordioso, vostra Santità e le altre Potenze cristiane non offrono al più presto il loro aiuto contro questo male pestilenziale, graverà su tutta quanta la religione cristiana la minaccia di un totale annientamento . . ."

4 See Setton, *The Papacy and the Levant*, II, 231–70; and Stinger, *Renaissance in Rome*, 106–19. For Bessarion, see Zorzi, *La Libreria di San Marco*, 28–37.

5 Lane, *Venice*, 242.

6 *Atila flagellum Dei*, Maestro Philippo de Piero da Venetia: October 1477, Venice [BMV: Inc. Ven. 734]: "Atila persecutor della christiana fede . . . La quale Città [Aquileia] insieme con molte altre Città Castelli e fortezze ne la fertile et bella Italia destrusse. Li habitatori de li dicti luoghi fugiendo la sua

canina rabia ad modo che nel presente tempo: Cioé del summo pontifice Papa Sixto de federico imperatore et del inclyto Duce Andrea Vendramin in Venetia imperante: ne li anni del signore. MCCCLXXVII. se fuge la crudele et abhominabile persecucione del perfido cane Turcho el quale come dicto di sopra abandonando le loro dolce patrie pervenneno a le prenominate isole. ne le quale fo edificati la potentissima famosa et nobile citta de Venetia . . ."

7 Donato Contarini, *Cronaca veneta sino al 1433*, Vienna, Österreichischen Nationalbibliothek, Cod. 6260 (Fosc. 70), f. 17v.

8 Huszár, "Attila dans la numismatique," 5–21. A similar image appeared as a sculpted relief on the façade of the Certosa of Pavia, designed by Giovanni Antonio Amadeo before 1498. See also Münsterberg, "Attila als Faunus ficarius," 62–6; Haskell, *History and Its Images*, 46; and Klinger, "The Portrait Collection of Paolo Giovio," I, 173, 210, and II, 17–18.

9 See, in particular, Geanakoplos, *Greek Scholars in Venice*; idem, "Italian Humanism and Byzantine Emigrés," 350–81; Nicol, *Byzantium and Venice*, 381–422; and Wilson, *From Byzantium to Italy*, partic. chaps. 8 and 14. See also *infra*, chap. 12.

10 Brown, *Venetian Narrative Painting*, cat. XIII, 272–9. The cycle would be completed with seven paintings on the south wall in a second campaign that began in 1537. All the canvases were destroyed by a devastating fire on Dec. 20, 1577.

11 Sansovino, *Venetian nobilissima*, 1663 edn, I, 334.

12 Ibid., 335. Very few of the lost Great Council paintings can be dated with certainty. Gentile's name does not appear on a salary list dated Dec. 1495. Since he was heavily involved during that period with commissions for the Scuole Grandi, his participation in the Great Council Hall cycle may have ceased by that time. See Brown, *Venetian Narrative Painting*, 275, doc. XIII.11, and Huse, *Studien*, 56–71.

13 Sansovino, *Venetia*, 1663 edn., I, 335: "Dopo a' quali seguiva un drapello di personaggi tutti singolari nelle lettere Greche & Latine, & di conosciuta dottrina: & questi erano, Giovanni Argiropolo, Theodoro Gaza, Emanuello Chrisolora, Demetrio Calcondile, & Giorgio Trapesuntio, vestiti ugualmente alla greca con capelli in capo, quasi in foggia Albanese." The painting is faintly commemorated in two surviving preparatory drawings. See Brown, *Venetian Narrative Painting*, 84–5.

14 Wilson, *From Byzantium to Italy*, 95.

15 See King, *Venetian Humanism*, 3.

16 Wilson, *From Byzantium to Italy*, 86–95.

17 Ibid., 58–60; 76–85. See also chap. 5 *supra*.

18 Ibid., 76–85.

19 Ibid., 95–8.

20 Sansovino, *Venetia*, 1663 edn., I, 335. For a probable date before 1495, see n. 12 *supra*.

21 Sansovino, *Venetia*, 1663 edn., I, 334. For Amaseo, see Gilbert, "Biondo, Sabellico, and the beginnings of Venetian official historiography," 282–3; and Gaeta, "Storiografia, coscienza nazionale e politica culturale," 75–6. For Merula, see King, *Venetian Humanism*, 400–2. For Sabellico see chap. 8 *infra*.

22 Sansovino, *Venetia*, 1663 edn., 335–6.

23 Cited by Lepori, "La scuola di Rialto," 576–88: "Hic Cornelius ille quem solebant / rerum principia et Deos docentem / olim Antenoreae stupere Athenae . . ." For Ermolao Barbaro (1453/4–92), Poliziano (1454–94), and Girolamo Donato (c.1456–1511), see Branca, "Ermolao Barbaro e l'umanesimo veneziano"; King, *Venetian Humanism*, 322–3, 366–8; and Wilson, *From Byzantium to Italy*, 101–13.

24 See chap. 13 *infra* for further discussion of portraits in the Great Council Hall paintings.

25 Tenenti, "The Sense of Space and Time," 17–46.

CHAPTER 7

1 Malipiero, *Annali veneti*, I, 73: "et è passada a Delos, isola famosa per el tempio d'Apoline, e per la fiera che anticamente se soleva far là, a la qual ghe soleva concorrer zente da lontanissimi paesi a vender e comprar diverse sorte de merce preciose. Se vede molti vestigii del tempio e del anfiteatro, i quali è de marmo bianchissimo e finissimo; alcune colonne bellissime, e gran numero de statue de marmo antichissime, e un colosso de 15 cubiti."; and ibid., 78: "Fo trovado in questo luogo [Smyrna], tra le altre notabele antichità, la sepoltura d'Homero, e la soa statua in beliisima forma."

2 Milan, Ambrosiana, Cod. C 61 inf., ff. 88–97, with brief descriptions of Corinth, the gulf of Patras, Malvasia, Sparta, Mistra, and Constantinople. The excerpt is transcribed in Ziebarth, "Ein griechischer Reisebericht," 72–88, who proposes a date around 1470 but was unable to name the author (82). The work is convincingly ascribed to Bolzano, however, by Beschi, "L'Anonimo Ambrosiano," 3–22, who suggests c.1475–85 as the most plausible time frame for Bolzanio's trip. Cf. Paton, *Chapters on Medieval and Renaissance Visitors*, 173–7; Weiss, *Renaissance Discovery*, 142–4; and Howard, "Responses to Ancient Greek Architecture," 24–6.

3 Cited in Ziebarth, "Ein griechischer Reisebericht," 73–4, §2: "e in summità del monte è aedificata la fortezza, et è un fortissimo castello e muri antiqui con sassi quadrati, et è longo el ditto castello circa u[n] 4° [di] miglia, et estendisse la longezza ab occidente in levante aedificio molto bello da veder, et è nel detto castello una chiessia che già fu tempio antiquo de romani molto mirabile tutto de marmore con col[on]ne a torno, et è oblongo pur ab occidente in orientem, et la fazza davanti nel fronto sono inifiniti imagini di marmoredi tutto rilievo et copert[i] tutti di marmori . . . ancora nel detto castello un dignissimo palazzo antiquo apresso la detta chiesia, et è tutto di marmore fatto alla romana." Beschi, "L'Anomimo Ambrosiano," 20, identifies the latter monument as the Propylaeum.

4 Ziebarth, "Ein griechischer Reisebericht," 74, §4.

5 Ibid., 75, §8: "perchè è in f[orm]a de portico aperto da ogni banda, ma parre, come è detto, che fusse coperto di marmore et non è alcuna scraja del muro." Cf. Beschi, "L'Anomimo Ambrosiano," 20, who notes that neither location is correct.

6 Ziebarth, "Ein griechischer Reisebericht," 75, §9: "a che proposito fusse fatto tal aedificio non ho potuto comprender."

7 Ibid., 77, §15: "Dentro la terra e primieramente un edificio non molto grande tutto intiero in 8 fazze con una bella cuba et immediate soto el corniso sono 8 imagine da mezzo rilievo mazzor che statur d'homo, e sono distese con diversi atti: gittano vento, chi con un corno, chi con el gremio, chi con la bocca e sopra ciascuno è scritto el nome suo βορρα etc.; al presente è una chiesia dei greci et è opera molto degna, tutta di marmoro." Cf. Beschi, "L'Anomimo Ambrosiano," 23.

8 The following account of Barbaro's travels appears in an abbreviated version in Brown, "Ancient Artifacts and the Mercantile Mentality."

9 See, for example, Tucci, "Mercanti, viaggiatori, pellegrini," 317–53; and Brown, *Venetian Narrative Painting*, 125–32.

10 Barbaro's narrative was first published only in 1543 in the collection of *viaggiatori* compiled by Giambattista Ramusio. It has since been republished several times. The version used here is Giosafat Barbaro, *Viaggi in Persia*, in L. Lockhart, R. Morozzo della Rocca, M.F. Tiepolo, eds., *I viaggi in Persia degli ambasciatori veneti Barbaro e Contarini*, Rome 1973 [Barbaro, *Viaggi*]. For a version that replaces Barbaro's Venetian dialect with modern Italian, see Ramusio, *Navigazioni e viaggi*, III, 481–576. Cf. Di Lenna, "Giosafat Barbaro," 5–105; and Brown, *Venetian Narrative Painting*, 126, 130, 196.

11 Barbaro, *Viaggi*, 68.

12 See, for example, Stussi, *Zibaldone da Canal*; and Cotrugli, *Il libro dell'arte di mercatura*.

13 For Tana, see Skržinskaya, "Storia della Tana," 3–45; and Verlinden, "La colonie vénitienne de Tara," 1–25.

14 Barbaro, *Viaggi*, 69. Similar tombs were described in the nineteenth century by Baron von Haxtahusen, *The Russian Empire, its People, Institutions, and Resources*, London 1856, II, 79–90.

15 For the Alani, see Minns, *Scythians and Greeks*, 37. He places the Venetian colony of Tana at Azov on the Don delta and describes a four-mile area covered with barrow tombs (566).

16 See ibid., 149, stating that most of the surviving tombs postdate the Scythian period; and also Rolle, *The World of the Scythians*, 19–20, who describes a variety of burial mounds in the region north of the Black Sea. Cf. A.I. Melyukova, "The Scythians and Sarmatians," in *The Cambridge History of Early Inner Asia*, ed. Denis Sinor, Cambridge 1990, 97–117.

17 Barbaro, *Viaggi*, 70: "che fu quasi cosa mirabile, la qual lassarò per adesso."

18 See ibid., 69, 70, 245, n. 32.

19 Ibid., 245, n. 35: One *miglio veneto* equals 1.739 kilometers.

20 Ibid.: one *passo veneziano* equals 1.739 meters.

21 Ibid., 70.

22 Rolle, *The World of the Scythians*, 19–20, cites Scythian kurgans that are often taller than three-story buildings, with bases of more than 100 meters in diameter. For eighteenth- and nineteenth-century explorations of the area see Boris Piotrovsky, "Excavations and Discoveries in Scythian Lands," in *From the Lands of the Scythians. Ancient Treasures from the Museums of the U.S.S.R. 3000 B.C.–100 B.C.*, a special issue of *The Metropolitan Museum of Art Bulletin* XXXII, no. 5, 1973/74, 26–31,

23 Barbaro, *Viaggi*, 71: "el terren era sì duro et agiazato che nè con zape, nè con manare el potevamo rompere."

24 Ibid., 71–2: "La maraveglia grande che havessemo fu che prima de sopra el terreno era negro per le herbe, da poi erano li carboni per tutto, e questo è possibile conzosia che avendo arente i boschi de salesi potevano far foco su tutto el monte. Da poi erano cenere per una spana, e questo anchora è possibile conzosia che havendo arente el canedo e potendo far focho de canne, potevano haver cenere. Da poi eravi scorze de meglio per un'altra spana e (perchè a questo el se potria dir che manzavano panizo fatto de meio et havevano salvati li scorzi da metter in quel logo) vorrei sapere quanto meglio bisognava che havesseno a voler compir tanta largeza, quanta era quella dil monticello, de scorzi de meglio alti una spana. Da poi eravi squame de pesce, zoè raine et altri simili, per un'altra spana e (perchè el se potria dir che in quel fiume el se catano raine e pesce assai, dei quali el se poteva coprir el monte) io lasso considerar a quelli che lezerano quanto questa cosa è possibile o verissimile. Certo è che è vera . . ."

25 Ibid.: "Havendo fatta questa tagliata et non ritrovandosi fin lì el thesoro, deliberassemo de far due fosse intra el monticello masizo, le qual fossero quatro passa per largo e per alto et

(facendo questo) trovassemo un terren bianco e duro in tanto che fessemo scalini in esso su per i qual portevamo le ziviere. Andando sotto circa passa .5. trovassemo in quel basso alcuni vasi di pietra, in alcuni di quali era cenere et in alcuni carboni; alcuni erano vacui, et alcuni pieni de ossi de pesce de la scena. Trovassemo etiam da .5. in .6. paternostri grandi como naranzi, i quali erano di terra cotta invidriata, simile a quelli che se fanno in la Marcha i quali se mettono a le tratte. Trovassemo etiam mezo manego de un ramin d'arzento picholino, che haveva de sopra al modo de una testa de bissa." For the *paternostri*, a term used in the Veneto and the Marche for weighted spheres tied to the edges of trawl nets to keep them from floating, see ibid., 245 n. 38; and Ramusio, *Navigazioni e viaggi*, 490, n. 2.

26 Ibid., 72: "El logo per avanti se chiamava le Cave de Gubledin e da poi che nui chavassemo è sta" chiamato per insina a questo zorno la Cava de i Franchi . . . imperochè è tanto grande el lavor che fessemo in pochi zorni ch'l se potria creder che'l non fusse sta' fatto in quel pocho tempo da mancho de un migliar de homini. Non habbiamo altra certeza de quel thesoro, ma (per quanto intendessemo) se thesoro era lì, la cason che'l fece metter lì sotto fu, perchè el ditto Indiabu signor de questi Alani intese che l'imperator di Tartari li veniva incontra, e deliberando de sepelirlo (a zò che niuno se ne adesse) finse de far la sua sepultura secondo el lor costume et secretamente fece metter in quel logo prima quello che a lui pareva e poi fece far quel monticello." All Europeans, even Italians, were frequently called Franchi [Franks] in the East.

27 See ibid., 242 n. 6, 245 n. 37.

28 Barbaro, *Viaggi*, 19–21, 47–8. Cf. Ugo Tucci, "Il viaggio di Giosafat Barbaro in Persia," a paper presented at *Una famiglia veneziana nella storia: i Barbaro*, a Convegno sponsored by the Istituto Veneto di Scienze, Lettere ed Arti, Nov. 4–6, 1993. The paper, which I did not hear, is to be published in the Atti del Convegno.

29 Barbaro, *Viaggi*, 155: "terra (como se dice) edificata da Alexandro, la qual è sul Mar de Bachu."

30 Ibid.: "im mo' che le teste de i muri sonno do passa sotto aqua . . . I muri de la qual sonno de szi grandi alla romana."

31 Ibid., 110: "ha su le porte maestre certe inscription de lettere le qual mostravano d'esser belle e simel a le armenie, pur in altra forma de quella che usano li Armeni de presenti, conciosia che li Armeni ch'io havea con mi non le sapevan lezer." For Curico, see Hild and Hellenkemper, *Kilikien und Isaurien*, I, 315–20.

32 Ibid., 149: "le quale se chiamano Cilmynar, che vol dir in nostra lengua .40. colonne, ciascuna de le qual è longa braza .20., grossa quanto abracia .3. homeni; de le qual perhò parte ne son ruinate; per quello si vedeva è stato zà un bello edificio." Cf. Schmidt, *Persepolis*.

33 Barbaro, *Viaggi*, 149: "In su questo piano è un pezo de saxo, sul quale sonno sculpite figure de homeni assai, grandi como ziganti, e sopra di tutte è una figura simile a quelle nostre che nui figuramo Dio Padre, in uno tondo, la qual ha un tondo per mano e sotto la qual sono altre figure picole; davanti, la figura de un homo apogiato ad un arco, la qual se dice esser figura di Salomon." See ibid., 292 n. 327, for the probable identification of this image as a bas-relief of the Roman emperor Valerian who was defeated by King Shapur I at the battle of Edessa in 260.

34 Ibid.: "Più sotto ne sonno molte altre le qual par che tengono li sui superiori di sopra, e di questi minori uno è lo qual par che habbia in capo una mitria di papa, e tien la man alta aperta, mostrando di voler dar la benedition a quelli li son di sotto, li

quali guardano ad essa e par che stagano in certa expectation de dicta benediction. Più avanti è una figura grande a cavallo che par che sia d'un homo robusto; questa dicono esser de Sampson, apresso la qual son molte altre figure vestitte alla francese, o hanno capelli longi. Tutte queste figure sonno de uno mezo relievo."

35 Ibid., 150.

36 Sanudo, *Itinerario*, 21 (Incipit to his *Itinerarium cum Syndicis Terre firme*): "A comenciar a descriver le terre, castelli, borgi, ville, lagi, fiumi, fonti, campi, prati et boschi ene soto l'imperio Veneto da la parte di terra, bisogneria ingegno, lectori doctissimi et optimi, di più speculatione et maturità dil nostro imbecille; ma pur, havendo desiderato più et più volte l'andar el veder et quello con gi ochij ho visto possi scriver, accio descrivando sia dotato, et la memoria sia eterna, piaque al Redemptor superno, mediante colui ogni cossa ene . . ."

37 For Sanudo's dependence on Biondo's treatise, published in 1474, see Cozzi, "Marin Sanudo il Giovane," 336–7.

38 In Greek mythology, Pylades was the companion of Orestes, son of Agamemnon and Clytemnestra and brother of Iphigenia.

39 Sanudo, *Itinerario*, 14: "Ne la cita si bella et felice/ Pri' arivam che Antenor Troian/ Edificò et fu de noi radice."

40 Ibid., 26–7: "et il tempio di S.ta Justina vergene è posto sopra il Pra di la Valle, el qual è grande ne la terra, et si fa le fiere ivi; ma la chiesa che fusse anticha par vestigie, *propterea quod* quando fo redificà fu trovato in una capsula de plumbo le osse de Tito Livio, et poste nel Palazo."

41 See chap. 2 and the Prologue to Part III *supra* and Jacks, *The Antiquarian*, 130–31, for the longstanding belief that the Basilica of S. Giustina stood on the site of an ancient Roman temple dedicated to Concordia. The inscription was: "V. F./T. Livius/Liviae T. F../ Quartae L./ Halys/ Concordialis/ Patavi/ sibi et suis/ omnibus" (*C.I.L.*, V, 2865).

42 Sanudo, *Itinerario*, 27: "E in questa caxa sacra di Justina el suo corpo, di S. Maximo secundo Episcopo di Padoa, di S.ta Foelicita, S. Luca evangelista, S.to Mathia Apostolo, S. Maximino, S. Brunaldo et S.to Prosdocimo cum altri corpi di Santi. Ma *si credere liceat*, era el tempio di Jove, *in quo Livius in X.mo narrat, spolia de Cleomini Lacedaemonis piratae victoria Patavium reportata fuisse.*"

43 Ibid., 26: "mostra vestigia fusse anticha et bella."

44 Ibid.: "dà ducati 100 de *jus patronatus*."

45 Ibid.

46 Ibid., 29, citing Martial, *Epigrams* 10.93: "Si prior Euganeas, Clemens, Helicaonis oras/Pictaque pampineis videris arva jugis." Euganei is an old name for the inhabitants of Venetia. Heliacaon was the son of Antenor, founder of Patavium.

47 Sanudo, *Itinerario*, 29.

48 Ibid., 28: "loco ameno et soave."

49 Ibid., 28: "et ivi componeva, et fin or a dura il suo desiato lauro, et mai da quel in qua fin non è morto."

50 Ibid., 22: "passato uno ponte alquanto pericoloxo di Noventa, poi quello nuncupato di Graizi, overo è corupto il vero vocabullo perchè Greci ivi vegniva, vel pur per esser di graizi *licet* mostra vestigia di marmo."

51 Ibid., 33–4: "Monte Richo: è alto, jucundissimo et pieno di soavità et gaudio, et perchè ogni cossa, sì erba qual fruto, olivari et vigne perfectissime vi nasse et lì trovasse, è dicto Monte Richo, *etiam* perchè, ut multi asserunt, ne è trovado et si trova ivi pecunia di auro et argiento. Di questo Plinio in Natural Historia, nel libro 13.mo et 14.mo, molto ne dice; Theofrasto *di erbibus*; Herodoto, et Apollodoro, *qui de odoribus scripsit*, nomina questo monte di miribilli dil mondo."

52 Herodotus *History* 3.115–16, doubts the existence of a river called the Eridanus (usually identified with the Po) and states: "This only we know, that our tin and amber come from the most distant parts. This is also plain, that to the north of Europe there is by far more gold than elsewhere."

53 Pliny *Natural History* 3.18–19, 130, 133–4. The Veneti are also cited in 4.107 and 6.5. In his index in Book 1, Pliny cites Theophrastus as a source for Book 3, without further detail. He cites him again, along with Herodotus and Apollodorus for Book 13, and again for Book 14, where he discusses vines and winemaking in detail, but does not mention this area. He also cites Theophrastus and Apollodorus for Books 33 and 34 on metals and Books 36 and 37 on precious stones. Sanudo may have confused Eugeneus, a variety of grape cited in *Nat. Hist.* 14.25, 26, 46, with the Euganei.

54 Sanudo, *Itinerario*, 29: "adornata de caxe de Venitiani nostri . . . Antiquissimi epithaphij quivi ene, tuti i' vidi et lexi, et ne la opera nostra *de antiquitatibus et epithafia* son posti: *lege tu si vis.*" Aricò, "Una testimonianza," 32–4, asserts that this codex survives in the Biblioteca Capitolare in Verona.

55 Sanudo, *Itinerario*, 101: "in letere perfecte et bone antiche: *Lucius Vitruvius L. L. (id est Lucij liberti) F. Cerdo Architectus; unde* apar Lucio Vitruvio, che scrise di architectura, fu veronese et auctor celeberimo, edificasse l'Arena, et di quella fusse *conditor.*" For the arch, see also ibid., XXXVIII; and Pirro Marconi, *Verona Romana*, Bergamo 1937, 95–101, with the inscription recorded as L. VITRVVIVS . L . CERDO . ARCHITECTVS. Much admired and copied by artists and architects in the Renaissance, the structure was dismantled by the French in 1805 and reassembled on the present site only in 1932. According to current views, it dates to the first century A.D. and was erected in honor of the family of the Gavii.

56 See the comments in Sanudo, *Itinerario*, p. XXXVIII n. 59; and Weiss, *Renaissance Discovery*, 117–18.

57 Sanudo, *Itinerario*, 67–68: "patria di Catulo veronese, cantator de verssi erotici. Fu poeta lasciviuscullo aliquanto: amò una fanziulla nominata Clodia et apelola Lesbia: morì di 30 anni. Scripse lo epitalamio de Manlio; et qui è le suo caverne dove stava."

58 Sanudo, *Itinerario*, 86: "Qui è zardini de zedri, naranzari, et pomi damo [sic] infiniti: lochi, concludendo, amenissimi, gentili et soavi, da sir habitati sempre."

59 Ibid., 88: "Benaco dove è una chiesia antiqua se apella S.ta Maria de Benaco. Lì è molte antigità; si trova soto terra epitafij di perfete letere et antiqui; et qual i' vidi, è posto, nel intrar di la porta, questo *noviter* trovado: *Antonini Pij Hadriani filij*, et siegue la sua geneologia; et si cava molti musaichi . . ."

60 Ibid., "et è l'altar grando in mexo la chiesia con quatro collone, e di sopra uno capitello con ydolo, zoè Jove Amone in forma de ariete, con uno buso nela cuba, andava el fumo de li sacrificij suso: ma sopra l'altar è una piera, la qual, *ut dicitur*, suda tre volte al anno, di Nadal, Venere Sancto, et la Nostra Donna di febrer . . ."

61 Bettoni, *Storia della Riviera di Salo*, I, 57, 217–19. Borromeo also had the bones of S. Ercolano removed from a Roman urn in Sant'Andrea in Maderno and ordered the pagan reliefs that decorated it to be destroyed.

62 Sanudo, *Itinerario*, 143: "Aquileia città antichissima . . . *olim* potentissima et grande città, *nunc pene derelicta est*, et habitata da Canonici numero XXIIII, i quali officiano la chiesa cathedral, et da alcuni pescatori . . ."

63 Ibid., 145: "uno ephithaphio antiquissimo atorno il coro . . . con gran fadicha."

64 Ibid., 154: "Ne sono infeniti epithafij, qual ne la mia opereta *De antiquitatibus Italiae* ho scripto."

65 Ibid., 25: "non chome le altre *imo* più felice"; and ibid., 27: "Al gimnasio celeberimo de Italia i' vo, nel qualle è molti studenti in tute facultà, et di ogni natione quivi veneno, et molti Sygnori ultramontani; con grande spesa di Venetiani se tiene . . ." The university is still called the "Bo".

66 Ibid., XXXIV, n. 53, cites the following place names in the mountainous area to the northwest of the city: Valdomia (=Vallis dominica), Calvaria (Monte di San Rocco). Inside the walls are Nazaret and Betlemme, and Monte Oliveto (Monastery of SS. Trinità).

67 Ibid., 96: "Verona, a scriptori Hebraici nominatissima et a Sem filgio di Noè edificata, et *Hierusalem menor* vocitata, perchè in questo zorno el monte Oliveto, la valle Calvaria, Nazareth et Bethlen dura et è denominati, dimonstrando l'antigità sua. A Breno Capitano di Galli, gente feroce et belicosa . . ." A similar quotation appeared in the Proemio to the city statutes in 1450. Sanudo would also have been aware of a new seal of the city, approved by the Consiglio of Verona in 1474. It bore the inscription: VERONA MINOR HIERVSALEM DI ZENONI PATRON. See Nino Cenni and Maria Fiorenza Coppari, *I segni della Verona veneziana (1405–1487)*, Verona 1989, 43–7; and G.P. Marchi, "Verona Minor Jerusalem. Contributo alla storia dell'urbanistica carolingia," in *Architetti Verona*, no. 13, July–August 1961, 25–34.

68 Sanudo, *Itinerario*, 97: "con gran calamità et intolerabille dano."

69 Ibid., 97: "*Sed demum* del M.C.C.C.C.IV venuta soto l'imperio veneto, per suo benificio et libertà, in mirabille è venuta incressimento et opulenta, e di giorno in giorno melgio si rinova."

70 Ibid., 70: "Fu edificata avanti Roma cinquecento anni, et si chiamava *civitas herculei*, et herculle vi habitò; et nela citadella vechia è uno palazo antiquo dove è molte antigità che dura ancora; alcune collone marmorea da do bande dove era una via in mexo, e sono molti epithafij per i qual se dimostra la sua antigità; ma in questo tempo, zoè del 1440 in qua, che vene soto el Dominio Veneto, è in mirabille cressimento, et opulenta."

71 Ibid., 94: "Securi dormite omnes; custodiet urbem Pervigil hanc, cives, aliger ipse Leo."

72 Cf. Aricò, "Una testimonianza," 32–4, who points out that he was recognized as such in his own time. Aldus Manutius dedicated editions of Ovid's *Metamorphosis* and *Eroidi* to him, as well as the complete works of Angelo Poliziano (1498). Mommsen, moreover, used Sanudo's sylloges as primary sources for the *Corpus Inscriptionum Latinarum* for otherwise unknown inscriptions.

73 See Brown, *Venetian Narrative Painting*, partic. chap. 8; and Morelli, *Dissertazione*, 19–28, with the account of Giovanni Bembo, who described antiquities seen on a voyage along the north African coast, c.1505–6.

74 BMV, Cod. It. IX, 188 (=6286), Bartolomeo dalli Sonetti, *Isolario*, fol. 2r: "Adoperato lo desioxo core / per me bon venetian bartholomeo / dali soneti ver compositore / E havendo el spirto prompto col desio / e con lochio vedute ad una ad una / e calcate col piede al voler mio / Con le mie proprie man picta o ciascuna / e in sto picol volume le agio poste / come ha piaciuto ala bona fortuna / Con soi soneti in settandoe poste / Ahonor de christo e de quei soi scholari / che predico il suo nome in piane e in coste. Et a contemplation de marinari / et a piacere de tutti coloro / che legerano i mei bassi vulgari."

See also Zorzi, *Biblioteca Marciana Venezia*, Venezia 1988,

174–5. Another copy of the manuscript is in Paris, Bib. Nat. in f° Jq 13, cited in Buondelmonte, *Descriptio*, pls. XIXa–XXXI, who attributes it to a Bartolomeo Zamberti. It was published in Venice in 1485 and 1486 by the printer Guglielmo Anima Mia.

75 BMV, Cod. It. IX, 188 (=6286), c. 1r: Quante insule vi son picole e grande / Et scogli et seche e citate e Castella / Li luochi i quali le dolce aque spande / Come gia furno e come hora si trova / E qual venti contra stan le lor bande. / Qual mure sono in piede e qual giu cova / Tutte precise a voi sia manifesto / Ne vo che altri cha effeto sia mia prova . . . / Potrasi anchor veder come appellade / Fun dagli antiqui e como hora se chiama / E da cui funo et e signorizade."

76 Ibid., 4v–5r: "Linsula del gran Jove tenito degna / La qual si siede vasta in mezo el mare / con il monte ideo e cento Cita apare / in lei gia grande et vberima regna . . . / Quivi regno Saturno sapientissimo / fiol de uriano che vol dir cielo / che stampar la moneta fu primo e lo / e in coltivar e seminar doctissimo."

77 Ibid.: "tanti musaichi edifici se vede e de litera greca che in latina."

78 Ibid.: "I lochi el monte dove e laberinto / che stava il minotauro e tante cose."

79 Ibid., c. 5v: "Cha nela sumita uno edificio / Dove Saturno facea sacrificio."

80 Ibid., c. 22v: "Tine questa si chiama e si chiamo / da aristotile greco prima idrosa / e demostene gli disse ophiosa / Ogniun di lor gli disse el parer so." See Pliny, *Nat. Hist.* 4.65; the word comes from the epithet *hydróeis*, meaning "rich with water."

81 BMV, Cod. It. IX, 188 (=6286), c. 22v: "Sopra lun di duo monti e il castel po / e in mezo una gran vale fructuosa / che al tempo de alexandro fu famosa / e de romani quasi la ruino."

82 Ibid., cc. 24v–25r: "Se lecito me qui chiamar apollo / per observar il poetico stile / a dir de linsulete dele schile / dove fu el tempio suo sopra dun collo."

83 Ibid., cc. 24v–25r: "Quivi un gran tempio apollo fu adorato / con doni e sacrificij magni e degni / di diversi paesi armati legni / venia et da nobel gente frequentato. / Chi virgine fanciulle havea portato / chi imagine de marmi et altri ingegni / al tempio suo monstrandosi benegni. / Per saper dil futuro lo suo stato / Quivi se dice che nacque diana / cinthia chiamata dalo cinthia monte. / apresso il quale iace una fontana / Che quando cresce il nilo cresce il fonte / da cinthio in fuori tutta laltra e piana."

84 BMV, Cod. Lat. XIV, 267 (4344), f. 1: "In uno di questi e ritrovata una giovanita integer con tute le suo member aromatizata cum una scorzà de pusta grossi . . . Ge se existima fosse de myrrha incenso et aloe et alter compositione degna. Si scopersse uno viso cossi grato recepto & venusto, che quant uosse su conjectura sin de anni M°CCCC, zoe 1500, e piu: Parea fosse mandata: questo giorno medesimo cum li soi capelli e collecto in capo more romano." See also Lanciani, *Storia degli scavi*, I, 84; Saxl, "The Classical Inscription," 26–7 and 44–5, pl. 5b; and Franzoni, "Girolamo Donato," 28.

85 BMV, Cod. Lat. XIV, 267 (4344), f. 1: "tuta roma mascoli & femine andorono an detta cum admiratione & stupor grandissimo . . . intendente quanto li antiqui nostri studiavano li animi gentil farli immortali ma ancora li corpi neli quali la natura per farli belli haver posto ogni suo inzegno che invero se havessa veduto questo viso saresti non meno innamorato ossia maravelgiato e credo se tegnira sopra la terra tanto che ciascuno sara dil veder satisfatto." Weiss, *Renaissance Discovery*, 102, notes that Pope Innocent VIII put an end to the (pagan) pilgrimage by having the body spirited away at night. The

episode recalls the excitement provoked by the supposed discovery of Livy's bones in Padua in 1414 (see *supra*).

CHAPTER 8

1 Cited by Labalme, *Bernardo Giustiniani*, 258–9 with original Latin and Eng. trans.

2 Pertusi, "Gli inizi," 292–304; and Gilbert, "Biondo, Sabellico, and the Beginnings," 275–93. Aiming to induce Venetians to support the crusade of Nicholas V against the Turks, Biondo wrote a short treatise entitled *De origine et gestis Venetorum* (1454). Inserted in his *De Roma instaurata libri tres de Italia illustrata*, it was first published in Verona *c.*1481–2 and in Venice in 1503 by Bernardinum Venetum de Vitalibus. See J.B. Graevius, *Thesaurus antiquitatum et historiarum Italiae*, V:1, Lugduni Batavorum 1722, coll. 1–26. Biondo also began *Populi Veneti historiarum liber I*, but it remained unfinished at the time of his death in 1463 (published in B. Nogara, *Scritti inediti e rari di Biondo Flavio*, Rome 1927, 77–89).

3 Giustiniani, *De origine*. Pertusi, "Gli inizi," 306–18, posits the beginning of the work in 1477. But cf. Labalme, *Bernardo Giustiniani*, 256, who dates the writing to *c.*1484–9.

4 Cited by Labalme, *Bernardo Giustiniani*, 260 (with Eng. trans.): "Quae sententiae licet diversae sint, non tamen a vero sunt alienae: Siquidem omnium rerum, quae aut natura gignuntur, aut arte constant, plura fere semper principia videmus . . . Sumere etenim licet civitatum initia, vel altiora, vel absolutiora, ut cuique magis videtur. Arbitraria enim res omnis posita in populorum principumque voluntate."

5 Cozzi, "Cultura politica," 221.

6 Sabellico, *Dell'historia venetiana*, 1 (Eng. trans. from Chambers and Pullan, *Venice*, 359). See also Cozzi, "Cultura politica," 219–22; and idem, "Marin Sanudo il Giovane," 338–42.

7 Sabellico, *Croniche che tractano de la origine de veneti*, c. vii verso: "Li aquiliensi furono habitatori latini. I concordiensi furono romani: Questi mescoladi con li antiqui veneti steteno a Grado: e Caorli: quando el tumulto Hunicho guasto la terra de quelli. Da tute queste parte in processo de tempo: como e manifesto: se vene habitar in la cita: che adesso se vede: per laqual cossa la origine veneta. Da Roma: da Italia: e da Troia piu vero e descesa: cha de Paphlagonia: na Galia: e questo e quanto ho possuto piu breve narrare del suo principio: e antiquita."

This is the first vernacular translation of Sabellico's *Rerum venetarum*, published in 1487. See E.A. Cicogna, *Saggio di bibliografia veneziana*, Venice 1847 (repr. New York 1976), I, 77. For Sabellico, see Gaeta, "Storiografia, coscienza nazionale e politica culturale," 65–75; and Cozzi, "Cultura politica," 221 n. 12.

8 Sanudo, *De origine*, 13–14: "Questi – come ho scritto che fuggiteno la persecution barbarica, veneno primo ad habitar in queste isole per sua cautione et segurtà a torno Rivoalto, et così de tempo in tempo veniva zente nuova, et di qui la vien la varietà del principio. Questi habitanti attendevano a far mercadantie con loro barchette alli liti vicini portando sal et pesse; non erano superbi né stimavano ricchezza, benché ricchi fossero, ma pietà, et innocenza; non vestivano ornatamente nécercavano honore, ma *coacti, et electi* per ben del Commun intravano al governo; non era differentia alcuna, et scrive Cassiodoro in la sua epistola questo: 'Paupertas ibi cum divitibus sub aequalitate vivit' . . ."

9 Sanudo, *De origine*, 20: "Questa città de Veniesia, commun

domicilio di tutti, terra libera né mai da niuno subiugata come tutte le altre, edificata per Christiani non per volontà, ma per timor, non per conseglio, ma necessitade, et non da pastori come Roma, ma da populi potenti, et ricchi, et quellhoro che da indi qua sono stati sempre obstaculo a' Barbari, et oppugnatori per la fede de Christo . . ." (Eng. trans. from Chambers and Pullan, *Venice*, 4).

10 Pertusi, "Gli inizi," 269–332; and Cozzi, "Cultura politica," 220–36.

11 For the program as a whole, see Schulz, *Antonio Rizzo*, 98–113. Cf. Lieberman, *Renaissance Architecture*, pls. 79–80, who suggests that it replaced an older less splendid staircase; Muraro, "La Scala senza Giganti," 350–70; and Franzoi, Pignatti, and Wolters, *Palazzo Ducale*, 71–5, 153–7.

12 Muraro, "La Scala senza Giganti," 352–3.

13 For the coronation ritual, see Muir, *Civic Ritual*, 282–9; and Schulz, *Antonio Rizzo*, 98–9, who shows that the public coronation was a new practice, first used in 1485 for Marco Barbarigo, probably on the older staircase that led to the Sala del Maggior Consiglio.

14 Muraro, "La Scala Senza Giganti," 351–3.

15 Ibid.

16 Sansovino, *Venezia città nobilissima*, 1663 edn., 320.

17 Cf. Schulz, *Antonio Rizzo*, 99.

18 Muraro, "La Scala Senza Giganti," 352; and Lieberman, *Renaissance Architecture*, Plate 79.

19 Muraro, "La Scala Senza Giganti," 359.

20 Ibid., 361.

21 Schulz, *Antonio Rizzo*, 103–5.

22 See *infra*, part V.

23 Muraro, *La Scala senza Giganti*, 360. Cf. chap. 5, n. 28.

24 Wolters, "Scultura," 153–4.

25 Ibid.; and Huse and Wolters, *Art of Renaissance Venice*, 140–41. For a thoughtful assessment of the Victories program, see Schulz, *Antonio Rizzo*, 109–13.

26 Antonio Medin, "La visione Barbariga di Ventura da Malgrate," *Atti del Istituto Veneto di Scienze, Letttere ed Arti* LXIV, 1904–5, 1667–82: "sereno duce et principe della nuova Roma . . . Io dico di Venetia unica luce / Et specchio al mondo di giustitia et fede / La cui gloria crescendo ognhor più luce / Che se a spirto prophetico si crede, / Ella fia anchor com'era Che se a spirto prophetico si crede, / Ella fia anchor com'era Roma, quando / Rimase del magior Cesare heredi."

27 Cited by Muraro, "La Scala senza Giganti," 356: "Barbadico postes auro spoliisque superbi."

28 Pincus, *Arco Foscari*, 377–83. Schulz, *Antonio Rizzo*, 103, sees in the relief program "no more specific meaning attached than allusions – possibly unintentional – to the glories of ancient Rome as an antique parallel to Venice."

29 Sheard, "'Asa Adorna'." 117–56: "la qual archa [sia posto] sopra uno apresso [la] deta capella [as] a [assai] grande e ben f[ato] e asa adorna in laqual voglio sia messo il mio corpo."

30 Sheard, "Tomb of Doge Andrea Vendramin," 142–6, 418–21; and idem, *Antiquity in the Renaissance*, cat. 118.

31 Marine motifs were often used in tomb decoration. See, for example, the sarcophagus of Bishop Zanetti in the Duomo of Treviso, by Tullio and Antonio Lombardo (dated before Sept. 1486: Sheard, "'Asa adorna'," 129, 148–9).

32 Eve is lost and the Ephebes were badly damaged during World War II. See Sheard, "Sanudo's List," 242 n. 3.

33 Sheard, "Tomb of Doge Andrea Vendramin," chaps. 4, 6, 7. See also Wilk, *Sculpture of Tullio Lombardo*, 21.

34 Sheard, "Tomb of Doge Andrea Vendramin," chaps. 4, 6, 7. See also Wilk, *Sculpture of Tullio Lombardo*, 21.

35 Sheard, "Tomb of Andrea Vendramin," 511f, n. 74; and idem, "*Asa adorna*", 144 n. 68.

36 Vitruvius, *De architectura libri decem*, Como 1521, c. XLVIIIr, cited by Sheard, "'*Asa adorna*'," 149 n. 85. In 1504, Tullio was praised by Pomponius Gauricus, presumably for work in the Santo in Padua, as the greatest sculptor of his time and one who had brought back the genius and the miracles of the past. See McHam, "La ridecorazione della Cappella dell'Arca," 195–8.

37 Cited by Huse and Wolters, *Art of Renaissance Venice*, 142–3, who identify the tombs as those of Pietro Mocenigo and Andrea Vendramin.

38 Sheard, "Sanudo's List of Notable Things," 219–68: "la più bella di questa terra p[er] li degni marmi vi sono."

39 *Una città e il suo museo*, 150, cat. IV.20: MCV, Cod. cl. III, 313 (formerly Cicogna 829).

40 *Una città e il suo museo*, 151, cat. IV.22: MCV, Cod. cl. III, 33 (formerly Cicogna 2266).

41 Labalme, *Bernardo Giustiniani*, 265.

42 Ibid., 296, citing Giustiniani's "Responsio ad sacrum collegium" (28, May 1483), *Orationes*.

43 Ibid., 272, 304.

44 Goffen, "Icon and Vision," 487–518.

45 Ackerman, "Observations on Renaissance Church Planning," 287–307. Ackerman was building on earlier studies by John McAndrew, "Sant'Andrea della Certosa," *The Art Bulletin* LI, 1969, 15–28; and W. Timofiewitsch, "Genesi e struttura della chiesa del rinascimento veneziano," *Bolletino del Centro internazionale di Storia de'Architettura "Andrea Palladio"* VI, 1964, 271–82. See also Plant, "Mauro Codussi," 9–22.

46 Ackerman, "Observations on Renaissance Church Planning," 289–90. Other churches featuring significant aspects of the revival plan include San Mattio di Rialto (destroyed), Santa Maria Formosa (begun 1492), San Giovanni Crisostomo (1497), San Gemignano (1505) (destroyed), San Salvatore (1506/7).

47 As observed by Wilk, *Sculpture of Tullio Lombardo*, 85–144, particularly 119ff.

48 Ackerman, "Observations on Renaissance Church Planning," 288–9.

49 Ibid., 290–93.

50 Tafuri, *Venice and the Renaissance*, 33. Cf. Ackerman, "Observations on Renaissance Church Planning," 293.

51 Puppi, *Verso Gerusalemme*, 62–76; idem, "Venezia come Gerusalemme nella cultura figurativa," 117–36; and idem, *Nel mito di Venezia*, 17–40. See also the illuminating study of Crouzet-Pavan, "Récits, images et mythes," 489–553. Cf. Meredith J. Gill, "Antoniazzo Romano and the Recovery of Jerusalem in Late Fifteenth-Century Rome," *Storia dell'Arte* LXXXIII, 1995, 28–47.

52 Fabri, *Venezia nel MCDLXXXVIII*, 66.

53 See Puppi, "Venezia come Gerusalemme," 117–36; and Brown, *Venetian Narrative Painting*, passim. See also Rosand, *Painting in Cinquecento Venice*, 124–30. The staging of biblical scenes in contemporary settings was, of course, quite common in the art of the period and was not unique to Venice.

54 See Lieberman, *Renaissance Architecture*, pl. 81; and McAndrew, *Venetian Architecture*, 144–9.

55 The concept and term comes from Sheard, "The Birth of Monumental Classicizing Relief," 149–74, who attributes *St. Mark Baptizing Anianus* to Tullio and *St. Mark Healing Anianus* to Antonio. See also McHam, *Chapel of St. Anthony*, 96–7, who notes a similar illusionistic effect in Tullio's *Coronation of the Virgin* relief in San Giovanni Crisostomo (1500–2), as well

56 as in the Chapel of St. Anthony in the Basilia del Santo in Padua.

56 Sheard, "The Birth of Monumental Classicizing Relief," 161.

57 Beautifully argued by Sheard in ibid., 149–74.

58 Jacks, *The Antiquarian*, 135–40: Padua, Bibl. Universitaria cod. 2557 (dated 1466).

59 Jacks, *The Antiquarian*, 319–20.

60 For the horoscope see ibid., 135–8. For a connection between Venice and Venus already in 1486, see Rosand, "Venetia Figurata," 189–90. The Venetian year began on the first of March.

61 Sabellico, *Croniche che tractano de la origine de veneti*, c. vi verso: "e tuti quasi in questo se acordeno che a. xxv. de Marzo comenzono iprincipii dela cita. Per laqual cossa se noi volemo considerare alchune opere excelente in tal zorno esser sta facte: non sara dubio creder: niente in quel zorno principiar: qual non sia amplo e magnifico: e perpetua gloria dele cossehumane (le sacre scripture questo affirmano) in quel medesimo zorno lomnipotente Dio haver formato el nostro primo Parente. Similmente esso figliol de Dio nel ventre dela Verzene concepto. Elqual dignissimo mysterio: per humano ingegno non pol con parole esser dechiarito: ma solamente con lintellecto comprehendere. Come noi sapientemente con amor crediamo: e constantamente confessiamo la divinita con la humanita conzonta: e che leternal secreto incomprehensibile: sia con il corruptibile & comprehensibile insieme copulato . . . Ma schernira forsi questo alchuno quasi come vana observatione: pensando da non creder el sia differente: piu uno: chaunaltro zorno. Noi veramente stimamo tal di esser idoneo. Vedendo quanto la natura non una ma piu volte in quello nobilissimamente havia operato."

62 Unlike Sabellico, Giustiniani rejected the old legend of Venice's foundation by Paduan consuls. See Labalme, *Bernardo Giustiniani*, 267–8.

63 Sabellico, *Croniche che tractano de la origine de veneti*, c. vi verso: "Dicono alchuni: che dove e adesso la ghiesia de s. Marco gli prima fu comenzato edificar." For Renaissance similitudes, see Michel Foucault, *The Order of Things*, New York 1973, 17–34.

64 Sanudo, *De origine*, 12–13: "Ma altri cronici, scrivendo questa origine, voleno – e questa è la verità – che questa città in lisola de Rialto fo comenzata a edificar, et fatto li primi fondamenti della chiesa de San Giacomo – che è ancora al presente in Rialto – del 421, adì 25 Marzo in zorno di Venere cercha l'hora di non ascendendo, come nella astrologica apar, gradi 25 del segno del Cancro . . . et secondo l'opinione theologica fo in quel medesmo zorno da Zudei crucefisso, et posto su la† granda; era zorno de grande cerimonia, et cusì nostri progenitori volsero ellezzer ditto zorno a tal e tanta edificatione." Repeated almost verbatim in his *Vite dei Dogi* (*Vite*[1], col. 406).

65 Sanudo, *Diarii*, 53, col. 72 (March 25, 1530): "A dì 25, venere, fo il zorno di l'Anonciation di la madona, nel qual zorno, del 421, fo principià la città di Rivoalto et messa la prima piera, nel qual zorno fo formà il mondo, fo crocefixo missier Jesu Christo, secondo Santo Augustin; fo del 1507 in tal zorno posto la prima piera a la nuova redification di la chiexa di San Salvador in questa terra. Sichè è zorno molto celebrado." Cf. Tafuri, *Venice and the Renaissance*, 22.

66 On this general issue, see Tafuri, *Venice and the Renaissance*, 1–50; and Puppi, "Venezia come Gerusalemme," 120.

67 Sanudo, *Diarii*, 2, col. 396: "In questo zorno primo di fevrer, a hora andava el principe per piaza per andar a vespero a Santa Maria Formoxa, fo aperto et scoperto la prima volta lo

Modern Origin of the Self and History," 6–8, observes that only two of the temples described by Polifilo are in ruins.

44 For the meaning of "lineamento" see Onians, *Bearers of Meaning*, 208.

45 Colonna, *Hyp. Pol*, I, 14–15 (a7v-a8r); II, 58–9: "Quivi dunque tanta nobile columnatione io trovai de ogni figuratione, liniamento et materia, quanto mai alcuno el potesse suspicare, parte dirupte, parte alla sua locatione et parte riservate illese, cum gli epystilii et cum capitelli, eximii de excogitato et de asperea celatura, coronice, zophori overo phrygii, travi arcuati, di statue intente fracture, truncate molte degli aerati et exacti membri, scaphe et conche et vasi et de petra numidica et de porphyrite et de vario marmoro et ornamento; grandi lotorii, aqueducti et quasi infiniti altri fragmenti, de sculptura nobili, de cognito quali integri fussaron, totalmente privi et quasi redacti al primo rudimenti, alla terra indi et quindi collapsi et disiecti. Sopra le quale et tra le quale confragose ruine germinati erano molti selvatici virgulti et praecipue de anagyro non quassabondo cum le teche fasselacie et uno et l'altro lentisco et la ungula ursi et cyncephalo et la spatula fetida et el ruvido smylace et la centaurea et molte altre tra ruinamenti germinabonde..." The anagre, after *anagyros* – a Latin adaptation from the Greek – is a thorny leguminous shrub featuring recurred pods.

46 Casella and Pozzi, *FC*, II, 138–43. For the herbal (Biblioteca Nazionale Marciana, Cod. Lat. VI, 59 [=2548]), see Zorzi, *Biblioteca Marciana*, 146.

47 Colonna, *Hyp. Pol.*, I, 51 (d2r): "Insaturabilmente dunque speculando mo' una mo' l'altra bellissima et molosa opera, tacitamente diceva: 'Si gli fragmenti dilla sancta antiquitate et rupture et ruinamento et quodammodo le scobe ne ducono in stupenda admiratione et ad tanto oblectamento di mirarle, quanto farebbe la sua integritate?'"

48 Ibid., I, 57–60 (d54-d6v); and Michael Greenhalgh, "The monument in the Hypnerotomachia and the Pyramids of Egypt," *Nouvelles de l'estampe* XIV, 1974, 13–16.

49 Ibid., I, 15 (a8r): "adamantineamente fastigiata et portentosissima pyramide: diqué ragionevolmente iudicai che non sencia inaestimabile impensa, tempo et maxima multitude de mortali se havesse unque potuto excogitare et ridriciare tale incredibile artificio...uno ingente et solido plintho over latastro."

50 Ibid., I, 16 (a8v): "nelle facie del quale erano hieroglyphi aegyptici egregiamente insculpti."

51 Ibid., I, 20 (b2v).

52 Ibid., I, 17 (b1r): "Questa statua dunque ad qualunque aura flante facile gyravasi, cum tale fremito dil trito dilla vacua machina metallina, che tale nunquam dal romano aerario se udite; et ove il figmento posava cum pedi sopra la subiecta arula, fricantise, che cusì facto tinnito non risonava il tintinabulo alle magnifiche therme di Hadriano, né quello dille cinque pyramide sopra il quadrato stante." See also ibid., II, 61, for the literary sources.

53 For the fresco in Mantua, now detached, see Lightbown, *Andrea Mantegna*, 470–71, cat. no. 143 (pl. 173); and Wittkower, "Chance, Time and Virtue," 97–106. For the relief at SS. Giovanni e Paolo, see Chiarlo, "'Gli fragmenti'," 291.

54 Casella and Pozzi, *FC*, II, 63–4. See also Edgar Wind, *Pagan Mysteries in the Renaissance*, Harmondsworth, 1967, 101–3.

55 Casella and Pozzi, *FC*, II, 49–51.

56 *De Architectura*, I, 6, 4, describing the figure of Andronicus Cirreste. Casella and Pozzi, *FC*, II, 49–52, cite at least three structures in Filarete's treatise in addition to the weather vane

as possible inspirations for Colonna: the palace of Vices and Virtues, the water labyrinth that surrounds the citadel of Galisforma, and the antique ship found in the port.

57 Onians, *Bearers of Meaning*, 208. Cf. Parronchi, "Polifilo e la 'perspettiva'," 267–74; and Goebel, *Poeta Faber*, 38–68.

58 As argued by Onians, *Bearers of Meaning*, 210–14.

59 As proposed by ibid., 215.

60 Lefaivre, "Eros, Architecture, and the Hypnerotomachia Poliphili," 17–20.

61 For Colonna's literary sources, see Casella and Pozzi, *FC*, II, 81–122. For his dependence on Boccaccio, see Saxl, "Pagan Sacrifice," 359–61.

62 Colonna, *Hyp. Pol.*, I, 188: "Sopra la plana della dicta veneranda ara, rigidamente rigoroso, promineva el rude simulachro del'hortulano custode cum tutti gli sui decenti et propriati insignii." See Casella and Pozzi, *FC*, II, 27; and Saxl, "Pagan Sacrifice," 361–3.

63 Painter, *Hypnerotomachia Poliphili*, 10–11.

64 Casella and Pozzi, *FC*, II, 70: The woodcut is based on an illustration in an edition of Petrarch published in Venice in 1488, where the dragons draw the chariot of Time.

65 Colonna, *Hyp. Pol.*, I, 63–5 (d8r–e1r): "vidi inscalpto questo mysterioso dicto di egregio charactere atthico: ΠΑΝΤΩΝ ΤΟΚΑΔΙ" (d8v). See the comments in ibid., II, 93–4. See, in particular, Meiss, "Sleep in Venice," 350–51, who notes that the phrase is repeated in the text as ΠΑΝΤΑ ΤΟΚΑΔΙ (All Things to the Parent). Pozzi and Ciapponi in Colonna, *Hyp. Pol.*, II, 95, interpret this as a typographical error. On the life-force of nature, see Bialostocki, "The Renaissance Concept of Nature and Antiquity," 19–30.

66 See *supra* chap. 4, n. 88. The similarity was noted independently by Wendy Stedman Sheard in a paper presented at the annual meeting of the Renaissance Society of America in 1995. Cf. Calvesi, "Il gaio classicismo," 99; and Madlyn Kahr, "Titian, the 'Hypnerotomachia Poliphili' Woodcuts and Antiquity," *Gazette des Beaux-Arts* LXVII, 1966, 121–2 (119–27).

67 Colonna, *Hyp. Pol.*, I, 40–41 (c4v–c5r); Jacobsen, "Vulcan Forging Cupid's Wing," 425, with the text in English.

68 Jacobsen, "Vulcan Forging Cupid's Wing," 422.

69 Ibid., 418–29; and Pope-Hennessy, "Italian Plaquettes," 206–213.

70 Jacobsen, "Vulcan Forging Cupid's Wing," 418–20.

71 Ibid., 422.

72 Colonna, *Hyp. Pol.*, I, xii.

73 Casella and Pozzi, *FC*, II, 11–31; and Pozzi and Gianella, "Scienza Antiquaria," 480–81.

74 Casella and Pozzi, *FC*, II, 18–24.

75 Ibid., 11–30; and Saxl, "Pagan Sacrifice," 361.

76 Casella and Pozzi, *FC*, I, 153. However, it enjoyed great fortune in France. Francis I owned a copy of the 1499 incunabulum, and a French edition published in 1546 made the challenging text accessible to a large readership. Its influence is seen particularly in the works of Rabelais. See Anthony Blunt, "The Hypnerotomachia Polifili in 17th Century France," *Journal of the Warburg and Courtauld Institutes* I, 1937–8, 117–37; and Hieatt and Prescott, "Contemporizing antiquity," 291–319.

77 Blass-Simmen, "'Povero Giopo'," 111–28, convincingly relates this work to a reconstruction campaign for the Scuola di San Giobbe in 1504, along with Carpaccio's *Meditation on the Passion*. She argues that the latter painting, which is considerably smaller, would have been the altarpiece in the small meeting room, and that the *Entombment* would have covered

the right-hand wall. She further suggests that the original campaign included a third painting, of which there is no record. See also Frederick Hartt, "Carpaccio's Meditation on the Passion," *Art Bulletin* XXII, 1941, 22–35.

78 See the fine iconographical study of Mori, "L'iter salvationis cristiano," 164–200, who emphasizes the theological message of the painting.

79 As also observed by Blass-Simmen, "'Povero Giopo'," 113.

80 For the notion of "contemporizing antiquity" applied to the *Hypnerotomachia*, see Hieatt, "The Alleged Early Modern Origin of the Self and History," 5–6. Blass-Simmen, "'Povero Giopo'," 113, defines the episode as a pastoral idyll that exists in a timeless "third world" of Arcadia, a Golden Age of interconnectedness with nature, that is outside the epochs of biblical and pagan history. Mori, "L'iter salvationis cristiano," 194, stresses the message of continuity inspired by cultural syncretism in the painting, and interprets the pastoral episode as a calling of the Christian faithful, symbolized here by the sheep.

    The Vicentine painter Marcello Fogolino used a similar motif in an *Adoration of the Magi*, painted 1511–12 (Pinacoteca di Vicenza, Inv. A-34).

PART VI

PROLOGUE

1 Aretino, *Opera nova*, ff. 4v–5v. There are five *strambotti* under the rubric *De tempore*. Only one copy of the book appears to survive; and since the verses have not, to the best of my knowledge, been reprinted in their entirety, a transcription is provided in Appendix 2.

2 G. Innamorati, "Pietro Aretino," in *Dizionario Biografico degli Italiani* 4, Rome 1962, 90 (89–104): the book was published in Perugia, but printed in Venice. Aretino, who had been leading an itinerant existence and living in Perugia at the time, went on to Rome in 1517 where he charmed his way into the circle of Agostino Chigi and Pope Leo X. Anticipating the sack of Rome, he moved to Venice in 1527 and resided there more or less permanently, until his death in 1556.

3 Mortier, *La poétique des ruines*, 42.

4 Ibid., 41–2. See also J. Hösle, *Pietro Aretinos Werke*, 1969, 38. Mortier points out that the verse cited here is the first of five *strambotti* on the theme *De Tempore* and not simply the first strophe of a single poem, as Hösle thought. This group is followed by eighteen verses on the theme *De Morte*.

5 This brief summary of Venice's economic and political situation in this period is based upon Ugo Tucci, "I tempi di Giorgione," 19–24; Tenenti, "Sense of Space and Time," 17–46; and Lane, *Venice*, 225–49.

6 Tenenti, "Sense of Space and Time," 17–46.

7 Priuli, *Diarii*, II, 269, cited by Tenenti, "Sense of Space and Time," 26.

8 Priuli, *Diarii*, III, 136 (cf. ibid., 367), cited by Tenenti, "Sense of Space and Time," 45 n. 120, "Considerando ettiam che ogni chossa facta over procreatta he necessario che tandem habia il fine, pensando ettiam ali grandi signori Romani che furono signori del mondo et tandem anchora loro hanno habuto fine dipoj molte persequctione et travagli."

9 Priuli, II, 267, cited by Tenenti, "Sense of Space and Time," 45, n. 129.

10 Priuli, III, 203, cited by Tenenti, "Sense of Space and Time,"

45 n. 126: "Bisognava fare come se poteva, ponendo tempo de medio, et lassare scorrerre queste influentie celeste contrarie et liberare una volta la republica veneta da pericolo et sperando cum il tempo che tutto dovesse prendere qualche bonno setamento et partito."

11 Priuli, III, 396, cited by Tenenti, "Sense of Space and Time," 45 n. 125: "Et in fine se die fare ogni chossa, sia quale se voglia, per non morire et vivere, se l'he possibelle, perché chui ha tempo ha vita."

12 Tucci, "I tempi di Giorgione," 22; but cf. Lane, *Venice*, 328, who states that only the Pisani bank survived the crisis of 1499.

13 See the discussion in Brown, *Venetian Narrative Painting*, chap. 1.

14 Aretino, *Opera nova*, ff. 4v–5v, as in Appendix 2 *infra*.

15 Cf. Battisti, *Rinascimento e Barocco*, 156, who notes the use of the phrase in poems by Cesare Nappi (*Egloga Pastorale*, 1508) and Panfilo Sasso; and Thomas Caldecot Chubb, *The Letters of Pietro Aretino*, n.p. 1976, 6, who states that the verses echo those of the "short, ugly popular Florentine poetaster, Sarafino Aquilano." See also Curtius, *European Literature*, 289–90, who cites a similar sonnet by Panfilo Sasso and characterizes the poetic form as a "summation schema."

16 Sanudo, *De origine*, as cited by Vescovo, "'Col tempo'," 58.

17 M.T. Muraro, "La festa a Venezia," 320. The motto has also been read as "Con Tempo." See Anguissola, "Da Proust al *Polifilo* attraverso Carpaccio," 47–52; and Bernardo Giustinian, *Historie cronologiche dell'origine degli ordini militari e di tute le religioni cavalleresche infino ad hora instituite del Mondo*, Venice 1692, 116.

18 Anguissola, "Da Proust al *Polifilo* attraverso Carpaccio," 66–7, who notes that bronze or wrought-iron lamps in the form of sirens were popular items in fifteenth-century Germany. Their implied message was that the pleasures of the flesh made the oil of human life burn more rapidly. Anguissola also observes that Polifilo described such a lamp in the Temple of Venus in the *Hypnerotomachia Poliphili* (Colonna, *Hyp. Pol.*, 200–2). Fueled with "liquore inconsumptibile," it would appear to subvert the tradition, for it suggests that love will endure for an infinite time.

19 Pignatti, *Giorgione*, 112.

20 Panofsky, *Problems in Titian*, 90–91, whose attribution of the work to Titian is not convincing. As Nepi Sciré and Valcanover, *Gallerie dell'Accademia*, 121, point out, the present attribution to Giorgione c.1510 is now generally accepted, and the artist may very well have been influenced by the realism of the young Titian.

21 Vescovo, "'Col tempo'," 47–61, who provides a fine overview and a sound analysis of the question. For Giorgione's exploration of the theme of transience, see Holberton, "Varieties of *giorgionismo*," 36.

22 Indeed, X-rays have shown that *La Vecchia* was originally painted with a bare breast: Meller, "La 'madre di Giorgione'," 110, whose interpretation of the work as a political allegory of "povera Italia" is well argued but ultimately not convincing.

23 To the attributions cited in Pignatti, *Giorgione*, 143–4, should be now added that of idem, "Giorgione's pre-Venetian beginnings: A new proposal," in *War, Culture and Society in Renaissance Venice. Essays in Honour of John Hale*, London 1993, 191 (Giorgione himself); and S.J. Freedberg, "The Attribution of the Allendale *Nativity*," in Manca, *Titian 500*, 69 (51–71), who ascribes the work to the juvenile Titian c.1506.

24 Rosand, "Giorgione, Venice and the Pastoral Vision," 56.

25 See, in partic. Bialostocki, "The Renaissance Concept of Nature and Antiquity," 19–30.

26 The most stimulating discussion of the work, with a comprehensive survey and analysis of prior scholarship, is Settis, *Giorgione's Tempest*, but see now Paul Holberton, "Giorgione's *Tempest* or 'little landscape with the storm with the gypsy': more on the gypsy, with a reassessment," *Art History* XVIII, 1995, 383–407. For proposals linking the painting to Venetian concerns about the Wars of Cambrai, see Deborah Howard, "Giorgione's *Tempesta* and Titian's *Assunta*, in the Context of the Cambrai Wars," *Art History* VIII, 1985, 271–9; Paul Kaplan, "The Storm of War: The Paduan Key to Giorgione's *Tempesta*," *Art History* IX, 1986, 405–27; and Linda L. Carroll, "Giorgione's *Tempest*: Astrology is in the Eyes of the Beholder," in *Reconsidering the Renaissance*, ed. Mario A. Di Cesare, Binghamton, 125–40.

27 Cf. Arthur Steinberg, "Blurred Boundaries, Opulent Nature, and Sensuous Flesh: Changing Technological Styles in Venetian Painting, 1480–1520," in Manca, *Titian 500*, 199–220.

28 Hill, *Corpus*, no. 529. Dedo's identity is uncertain. No person by this name is cited in Sanudo's *Diarii* during this period. However, a "Polo Diedo, canonico de modon," appears on the membership rolls of the Scuola Grande di San Marco in 1500 as exempt from the discipline, and may be the same person (ASV, Scuola Grande di San Marco, reg. 4, f. 133). For the *tricipitium*, see Tafuri, *Venice and the Renaissance*, 11–12. For an earlier reflection on the same theme, see Colonna, *Hyp. Pol.*, 25–7, with interpretation by Anguissola, "Da Proust al Polifilo attraverso Carpaccio," 69–71.

29 Vasari, *Lives of the Artists*, trans. George Bull, 448.

30 Panofsky, *Problems in Titian*, 94–6. See also Rosand, "Giorgione, Venice and the Classical Vision," 30–45; Mauro Lucco, "Le cosidette 'Tre età dell'uomo' di Palazzo Pitti," in *Le tre età dell'uomo della Galleria Palatina*, Florence 1989; and Holberton, "Varieties of *giorgionismo*," 37–41.

31 Cf. the different view of Claudia Cieri Via, "Allegorie morali dalla bottega belliniana," *Giorgione e la cultura veneta tra '400 e '500. Mito, Allegoria, analisi iconologica*, Rome 1981, 129 (126–45) who sees the amphorae as both about to be emptied, implying only *Mala Fortuna*.

32 Ibid.; and Rona Goffen, *Giovanni Bellini*, 237. Cieri Via's dating of the work to 1504–5 is tenable. See also Gustav Ludwig, "Restello, Spiegel und Toilettenutensilien in Venedig zur Zeit der Renaissance," *Italienische Forschungen* I, 1906, 185–361.

33 As observed by Shapley, *Catalogue of the Italian Paintings*, I, 480 (cat. no. 324).

34 Wilhelm Suida, *Le Titien*, 1935, 71, cited by Shapley, *Catalogue of the Italian Paintings*, I, 480. Cf. Wind, *Pagan Mysteries*, 104–5.

CHAPTER 11

1 Michele Orsini, *Francisci Philelphi opinio de summa venetorum origine . . . improbata* (March 1462), cited by King, *Death of the Child*, 75: "Marcellus et Romane probitatis et nominis et gentis, vel domi vel foris, vel paci vel bello clarus, maiorum suorum facinora memoranda renovasse videtur; dicereque fas est quicquid fortune virtutis et probitatis in omnibus Marcellis olim apud romanos emicuit nunc apud Venetos in uno Iacobantonio fulgere." King's book is an outstanding contribution to our understanding of family relationships and of the interaction between the public and the private in Venetian life

in this period. The following discussion on Marcello is largely drawn from it.

2 King, *Death of the Child*, 42–3, noting that Orsini later dealt with the subject at length in a full scale history of Venetian origins: *De antiqua venetorum origine*, Biblioteca Apostolica Vaticana, Cod. Vat. Lat. 5280.

3 See *supra*, chap. 1 at nn. 23–7.

4 For Marcello's art patronage, see King, *Death of the Child*, chap. 4, esp. 122–5, 314–15; Alexander, *The Painted Page*, 87–90; Millard Meiss, *Andrea Mantegna as Illuminator: An Episode in Renaissance Art, Humanism and Diplomacy*, New York 1957; and Martineau, *Andrea Mantegna*, 131–4.

5 King, *Death of the Child*, 69, citing Janus Pannonius, *Poëmata* and *Opusculum pars altera*, 2 vols., ed. Sámuel Teleki, Utrecht 1784, 1:61: "Nempe togatorum generosus stirpe Quiritum / Marcellus, Venetae firma columna rei."

6 King, *Death of the Child*, 74, 214.

7 Ibid., 69, citing Janus Pannonius, *Poëmata* and *Opusculum pars altera*, 1:473: "Si Marcellorum componas facta duorum, /Romani Venetus, vincet avi acta nepos." Cf. *Janus Pannonius: The Epigrams*, ed. and transl. Anthony Barrett, Covina Kiadó, Hungary, 1985.

8 Molina, *Orazioni, elogie e vite*, 130.

9 Romanin, *Storia*, IV, 420 n. 1, lists *i lunghi*, or the old houses as: Badoer, Basegio, Barozzi, Bembo, Bragadin, Contarini, Corner [Cornaro], Dandolo, Dolfin, Falier, Gradenigo, Memmo, Michiel, Morosini, Polani, Querini, Salomon, Sanudo, Soranzo, Tiepolo, Zane, Zen, Zorzi, Zustinian [Giustiniani]. The last of this group to serve as doge had been Michele Morosini in 1382; in 1450, the sixteen "new houses" – *i curti* – made an agreement to prevent any member of an old house from ascending to the dogate. These families were: Barbarigo, Donà [Donado], Foscari, Grimani, Gritti, Lando, Loredan, Malipiero, Marcello, Mocenigo, Moro, Priuli, Trevisan, Tron, Vendramin, and Venier. The ban remained in force until the election of Marcantonio Memmo in 1620. See also Labalme, *Bernardo Giustiniani*, 5, n. 1.

10 BMV, It. VII 925 (8594), Marco Barbaro, *Genealogia*, f. 7, who notes that there were also "some Coroneli or Coronelli, because in their arms they carried a crown, who came from Rimini, and being of one blood these latter were accepted as citizens and then in the Council." Cf. Giovanni Pozzi, "Conegliano – Corneliano," *Italia Medioevale e Umanistica* II, 1959, 505–7.

11 BMV, Cod. It. VII 925 (8594), f. 268.

12 BMV, Cod. It. VII 366 (=7660), Discorso della Fameglia Dardana, f. 2: "Per la qual cosa è da sapere, come la gente, e Familgia Dardana: la qual tra le famiglie de cittadini vinitiane, ben si puo dir, ch'essa di nobeltà, et antiquità tenga il primo luoco, è discesa, si come si può dal nome conietturare, et ha havuta origine da quelli Troiani, che con Antenore dopo l'occidio di Troia venero a edificar Padoa, et – furno di quelli, che discesero da Dardano. Il qual si come conferma Virgilio, fu primo Re di Troia." The word preceding "furno" is scratched out and replaced by a line, but cf. an eighteenth-century copy of the manuscript, BMV, Cod. It. VII 351 (8385), f. 238, where the word appears as "forse."

13 Scher, *Currency of Fame*, 102–3; Pollard, *Italian Renaissance Medals in the Bargello*, I, 246–7; and Weiss, "La medaglia veneziana," 341–4.

14 Vermeule, "Graeco-roman Asia Minor to Renaissance Italy," 268–9.

15 Scher, *Currency of Fame*, 103; and H.W. Janson, "The Putto with the Death's Head," *Art Bulletin* XIX, 1937, 428–9 (423–

49). Cf. Seznec, "Youth, Innocence and Death," 300, who identifies the winged figure as Spes wearing the forelock of Occasio and the figure with the scourge as Metanoia. He finds in the scene the idea of repentence over missed opportunity, but allows that it carries religious overtones.

16 See Vermeule, "Graeco-roman Asia Minor to Renaissance Italy," 268–9; Seznec, "Youth, Innocence and Death," 298–303; and Sheard, *Antiquity in the Renaissance*, cat. no. 80.

17 Seznec, "Youth, Innocence and Death," 301.

18 Hill, *Corpus*, 115.

19 Janus Pannonius, *Poèmes Choisis*, ed. Tibor Kardos, Budapest 1973, 50–51: Epigram I. 130 (written *c.*1454–8): 'De Immutatione sui nominis /Joannes fueram, Janum quem pagina dicit, /Admonitum ne te, lector amice, neges. /Non ego per fastum sprevi tam nobile nomen, /Quo nullum toto clarius orbe sonat. /Compulit invitum mutare vocabula, cum me /Lavit in Aonio, flava Thalia, lacu."

20 Ibid., 52–3, Epistle I. 192: "De vitae mutatione / Sat cuivis semel est habitum mutare priorem; / Felices! quibus id contigit in melius." See also the commentary on p. 126 on the paired meaning of the two epigrams.

21 Hill, *Corpus*, I, 115; and Scher, *Currency of Fame*, 103–4.

22 Hill, *Corpus*, no. 448. The portrait has also been identified as Augustus.

23 Sheard, *Antiquity in the Renaissance*, cat. 84; and Hill, *Corpus*, 446.

24 See Goffen, *Giovanni Bellini*, 191–2, for two atypical painted portraits of young men in classical dress coming out of the circle of Giovanni Bellini and datable to the late 1470s.

25 Rosand, "The Portrait, the Courtier, and Death," 104.

26 For parapet inscriptions, see De Grummond, "VV and Related Inscriptions," 346–56.

27 This interpretation is indebted to Rosand, "The Portrait, the Courtier, and Death," 104–7. Observing that X-rays show that the raised parapet was not part of the original composition, he hypothesizes that the sitter died during the course of its execution and that the relief is already a monument of the deceased. Cf. S. Caroselli, "A Portrait Bust of Caterina Cornaro," *Bulletin of the Detroit Institute of Arts*, Summer 1983, 45–57, who proposes an identification of *La Schiavona* as Caterina Cornaro.

28 For the patronage of tombs and family chapels in churches, see Goffen, *Piety and Patronage*, 22–9 and *passim*.

29 Cited and translated by Patricia H. Labalme, "Secular and Sacred Heroes: Ermolao Barbaro on Worldly Honor," in a lecture delivered at the convegno, *Una famiglia veneziana nella storia: I Barbaro*, held Nov. 4–6, 1993, at the Istituto Veneto di Scienze, Lettere ed Arti, Venice, and now in press. I am grateful to the author for allowing me to read her paper in typescript.

30 See Goffen, *Piety and Patronage*, 24; and Schulz, *Niccolò di Giovanni Fiorentini*, 6, who dates the Cornaro monument to the mid 1450s. But cf. Pincus, *Arco Foscari*, 349, who more convincingly suggests a dating after 1460.

31 For the Diedo tomb, that is located directly in front of the present Cappella dell'Addolorata, once dedicated to Sant'Alvise, see Mariacher, "Pietro Lombardo a Venezia," 38–9.

32 As suggested by ibid. See also Pozzi and Ciapponi, "La cultura figurativa di Francesco Colonna," 158–9; and Puppi, "Il tempio e gli Eroi," 44–5.

33 "LUDOVICUS DIEDO X. VIR./ OPT. BIZANTIO CAPTO/ET EX BRITANNIA FILIO REI/P CAUSA IN VINCULIS RE/LICTO, VENETORUM CLASSEM PER MEDIOS HOSTES TUTO IN PATRIAM EREXIT. TAMD/EM IADERE PRAETOR MORTA/LES EDOCUIT, PULCRUM ESSE/ PRO RE P MORI / SIBI ET SUIS."

34 For the most complete eyewitness account by a Venetian, see Nicolò Barbaro, "Giornale dell'assedio di Costantinopoli," in *La caduta di Costantinopoli: Le testimonianze dei contemporanei*, ed. Agostino Pertusi, Verona 1976. For summaries of the events, see Nicol, *Byzantium and Venice*, 395–407; and Setton, *The Papacy and the Levant*, II, 131–2.

35 Puppi, "Il tempio e gli Eroi," 45. Alvise's biography is difficult to sort out, and the only certain document is the tomb inscription that presently bears no date. G. Tournoy, "Francesco Diedo, Venetian humanist and politician of the Quattrocento," *Humanistica Lovaniensia* XIX, 1970, 201–4, claims that the father of the well-known humanist Francesco Diedo was the same Alvise who led the flight from Constantinople in 1453. However, King, *Death of the Child*, 55, cites a letter of consolation written to the humanist Francesco Diedo in 1463 on the death of his father (cf. King *Venetian Humanism*, 361–3), a date that precedes by three years the dating of the tomb (1466), cited by Lorenzetti, *Venice and its Lagoon*, 348. No date is presently visible on the tomb. To complicate the matter even further, Cappellari, *Campidoglio Veneto*, II, f. 25v, appears to have combined the lives of two men with the same name. It describes Alvise Diedo, the hero of the sack of Constantinople in 1453, as still living in 1480, long after the inhabitant of the tomb would have died.

36 Lorenzetti, *Venice and Its Lagoon*, 597.

37 Sansovino, *Venetia nobilissima*, 1581 edn., 66r, attributed the monument to "Iacomo Padovano," a label that still holds. See Goffen, *Piety and Patronage*, 24; and also Schulz, *Niccolò di Giovanni Fiorentini*, 6, who appears to accept the attribution of the fresco to Mantegna made by Giovanni Fiocco, *The Art of Andrea Mantegna*, Bologna (1927) 1959, 115ff. Cf. Pincus, *Arco Foscari*, 349–52, who assigns the angel to a Master of the Giustiniani Tomb, with a date of *c.*1465–9.

38 Goffen, *Piety and Patronage*, 62–9.

39 Ibid., who suggests that the closed book indicates a time of war.

40 Jestaz, *La Chapelle Zen*, 117.

41 Chavasse, "Humanism Commemorated," 455–61.

42 See chap. 5 *supra*, for Lorenzo de' Monacis's use of the same metaphor for the Venetian republic.

43 Chavasse, "Humanism Commemorated," 455–61.

44 Ibid., 456.

45 Lightbown, *Mantegna*, cat. 62, 131–2, 455–6, whose analysis serves as the basis for this discussion.

46 Sheard, "Giorgione's Portrait Inventions," 151–2.

47 Wilk, *Sculpture of Tullio Lombardo*, 58. See also Giovanna Nepi-Scirè's catalogue entry for the Ca' d'Oro relief in *Giorgione a Venezia*, 203–5. Another exception is the bust of a youth in the Correr Museum, sometimes attributed to Antonio Rizzo. On the low priority accorded personal commemoration in Venice, see Grubb, "Memory and identity," 384–5.

48 Wilk, *Sculpture of Tullio Lombardo*, 83–4.

49 Luchs, "Tullio Lombardo's Ca' d'Oro Relief," 230–36; and Wilk, *Sculpture of Tullio Lombardo*, 58, who shows that Tullio fused together three artistic traditions: the romantic antiquarianism of late fifteenth-century north Italy, Netherlandish and German marriage portraits of the same period, and Roman tomb portraits. For reservations on the attribution, see Pincus, "Tullio Lombardo as a Restorer of Antiquities," 42 n. 20.

50 Huse and Wolters, *Art of Renaissance Venice*, 158–9.

51 Meller, "Marmi e bronzi," 199–210. Cf. Schlegel, "Simone Bianco," 187–96.

52 See chap. 7 *supra*.

53 Sanudo, *I diarii*, 40, col. 758 (Feb. 1, 1526).

54 Francesco Guicciardini, *Storia d'Italia*, VIII, 16, cited by Franzoni, "Girolamo Donato," 28. See also Degli Agostini, *Notizie*, II, 201–39; Cicogna, *Inscrizioni veneziane*, I, 89–91; Paola Rigo, "Catalogo e tradizione degli scritti di Girolamo Donati," *Rendiconti dei Lincei, scienze morali*, ser. 8, XXIX, 1974, 49–80; and King, *Venetian Humanism*, 366–8.

55 Baldessare Castiglione, *The Book of the Courtier*, trans. Charles S. Singleton, New York 1959 (Book II, 61), 159, 364 n. 26: the first quotation is taken from Ovid, *Ars amatoria*, I, 59; the second is presumably Donato's own invention.

56 Franzoni, "Girolamo Donato," 29.

57 All the reliefs are now in Ca' d'Oro. See the catalogue entry of Anthony Radcliffe in Martineau and Hope, *Genius of Venice*, cat. S16, 371–2; and *Natur und Antike*, cat. 62, 361–3. Both date the bronzes to 1495–1500. See also Luchs, *Tullio Lombardo and Ideal Portrait Sculpture*.

58 Cicogna, *Iscrizioni veneziane*, I, 202–203: "LIGNVM EX CRVCIS TITVLO QVI IN TEMPLO S. † IN HIERVSALEM ROMAE SERVATVR QVOD HIER. DONATVS ORATOR VENETVS SIBI AB INNOCEN. VIII. PONT. MAX. MIRAE CLEMENTIAE DONO CONCESSVM PRECIOSO OPERE CONCLVSIT. ET IN SACRARIO SERVORVM DIVAE VIRGINIS DEDICAVIT ANNO SALVTIS ET GRATIAE MCCCCLXXXXII."

59 See Fontana, "De instauratione Urbis Ravennae," 295–320.

60 See ibid., 302, who uses the term "*pietas* umanistica'; and Mattaliano, "La scultura a Ravenna," 362.

61 Fontana, "De instauratione Urbis Ravennae," 297–8; Mattaliano, "La scultura a Ravenna," 334; and Wladimiro Bendazzi and Riccardo Ricci, *Ravenna. Guida Turistica*, Ravenna 1977, 80–81.

62 Fontana, "De instauratione Urbis Ravennae," 302.

63 Franzoni, "Girolamo Donato," 30 n. 7.

64 Fontana, "De instauratione Urbis Ravennae," 302; and Franzoni, "Girolamo Donato," 27–9. The Ravennate statue remained in place for nearly a century, only to be destroyed in an earthquake in 1591. Today only the base and part of a foot remain.

65 Franzoni, "Girolamo Donato," 29. See also the Prologue to part IV, *supra*. For the inscriptions, see *CIL*, v, 127★; they were thought by Mommsen to be fakes, but shown by Huelsen to be genuine antiques.

66 Franzoni, "Girolamo Donato," 28. For the full inscriptions see Degli Agostini, *Notizie*, 208; and *CIL*, v, 2937, 2248.

67 Ibid., 30; and Pope-Hennessy, "Italian Plaquette," 209.

68 See Favaretto, *Arte antica e cultura antiquaria*, 49–71; P. Jane Low (now Jane Roberts, to whom I am indebted for making a copy of her thesis available to me), "The Knowledge and Influence of Classical Sculpture in Venice and Padua, c.1460–1530," M.A. Report, Courtauld Institute of Art, London 1973; Beschi, "Collezioni d'antichità a Venezia ai tempi di Tiziano," 2–44; and Zorzi, *Collezioni di antichità a Venezia*, 19–24. For Isabella d'Este's contacts with the art market in Venice, see Brown, "An art auction in Venice," 123–7; idem, "'Lo insaciabile desiderio nostro'," 324–53; and idem, "'Una testa de Platone antica'," 372–7.

69 The painting was originally in San Giovanni Battista on the Giudecca, since destroyed. See Mariacher, *Il Museo Correr,* 52; and Zorzi, *Venezia Scomparsa*, 230–31. For the doge see Hazlitt, *Venetian Republic*, 87–93.

70 As implied by Fletcher, "Harpies, Venus and Giovanni Bellini's Classical Mirror," 171.

71 Franzoni, "Girolamo Donato," 28.

72 Beschi, "Collezioni d'arte Greca," 253–5; idem, "La scoperta dell'arte greca," 326–31; and idem, "Antichità Cretesi a Venezia," 479–502.

73 Branca, *Poliziano e l'umanesimo*, 145: "un bellissimo vaso di terra antiquissimo mi mostrò stamattina detto messer Zaccheria, el quale nuovamente di Grecia gli è stato mandato . . . Credo non ne abbiate uno sí bello in eo genere: è presso che tre spanne alto e quattro largo." See also Zorzi, *Collezioni di antichità*, 19.

74 See above, chap. 6, n. 13; and Brown, "'Una testa de Platone antica'," 372–7.

75 Pincus, "Tullio Lombardo as a Restorer of Antiquities," 29–42, who dates the intervention to the 1490s.

76 As cited in the forthcoming book of Alison Luchs, *Tullio Lombardo and Ideal Portrait Sculpture in Renaissance Venice, 1490–1530* (working title), chap. 1. I am grateful to the author for making available to me the typescript of the section entitled "Private Collecting of Sculpture."

77 See Panofsky, *Renaissance and Renascences*, 41; idem, *Meaning in the Visual Arts*, 294; and Otto Kurz, *Fakes. A Handbook for Collectors and Students*, London 1948, 117. For Michiel, see *infra* n. 85.

78 The trip is described in BMV, Cod. It. XI, 67 (=7351), published by E. Müntz, "Les Monuments Antiques de Rome a l'Epoque de la Renaissance," *Rèvue Archèologique*, 1884. According to Zorzi, *Collezioni*, 1988, 23–4, previous attributions of the text to Bembo or to Donato are now held to be unfounded. An account written by Rainerio de Fideli to Alessandro Calcedonio and dated March 16, 1505, appears in Sanudo, *Diarii* 6, cols. 171–5.

79 See, in particular, Perry, "Cardinal Domenico Grimani's Legacy, 215–44; Favaretto, *Arte antica e cultura antiquaria*, 84–93; and Zorzi, ed., *Collezioni di antichità*, 25ff.

80 Sanudo, *Diarii*, 6, col. 172.

81 Ibid., cols. 172–3: "e li mostrò a presso a quella la sua libraria, fornita di grandissima quantità di libri bellissimi, et de gran copia de figure de marmoro, et molte altre cosse antiche, tutte trovate a la sua vigna, sotto terra, cavando per la fabricha dil palazo, che 'l fa edifichare in essa."

82 For the vineyard, see Perry, "Cardinal Domenico Grimani's Legacy," 217, n. 13; and Christian Huelsen, "Römische Antikengärten des 16. Jahrhunderts," *Abhandlungen der Heidelberger Akademie*, 1917, figs. 29, 30, 34, 61; and Rodolfo Lanciani, *Storia degli scavi di Roma*, Rome 1902, I, 138–9.

83 See Brown, *Venetian Narrative Painting*, 154–6, 281. The figure of the water carrier on the door lintel in the left background of Carpaccio's *Dream of St. Ursula* is based upon a drawing by Mantegna. See Popham and Pouncey, *Italian Drawings*, no.164, pl. CLI; and Zorzi, "L'immagine di Roma," 448–58.

84 Favaretto, "Lo studio dell'antichità," 1–7; Wazbinski, "Portrait d'un amateur d'art," 21–9; and Brown, "*Sant'Agostino nello studio* di Carpaccio," 303–19.

85 Frimmel, *Der Anonimo Morelliano*, 81; and Luchs, *Tullio Lombardo and Ideal Portrait Sculpture*. For Michiel, see Fletcher, "Marcantonio Michiel's Collection," 382–5; idem, "Marcantonio Michiel: His friends and collection," 453–67; and idem, "Marcantonio Michiel, 'che ha veduto assai'," 602–8.

86 Frimmel, *Der Anonimo Morelliano*, 82: "El piede marmoreo intiero sopra una base fu de mano de Simon Biancho." See also Luchs, *Tullio Lombardo and Ideal Portrait Sculpture*. Michiel notes that Tullio once owned one of Odoni's marble busts and that he had reproduced it several times in his works. For Odoni, see Battilotti and Franco, "Regesti di committenti," 79–82.

87 Cited by R. Fulin, *Diarii e diaristi veneziani*, Venice 1881.

88 Castiglione, *Ricordi*, 56v (English transl. from Klein and Zerner, *Italian Art, 1500–1600*, 23–5). See also Luchs, *Tullio Lombardo and Ideal Portrait Sculpture*; and Alsop, *Rare Art Traditions*, 422–6.

89 Castiglione, *Ricordi*, 58v–59r (English transl. from Klein and Zerner, *Italian Art, 1500–1600*, 23–5).

90 Ridolfi, *Le maraviglie dell'arte*, 72: "In Venetia in casa Grimana à Santa Ermacora dipinse nella Sala due gran quadri di Cosmografia con le figure di Tolomeo, Strabone, Plinio e Pomponio Mella, e v'iscrisse il nome suo." Cf. Goffen, *Giovanni Bellini*, 225. The subject matter recalls Bramante's frescoes originally painted in Casa Panigarola, Milan, *c.*1480–90 (now in the Brera). One scene depicts a weeping Heraclitus and a laughing Democritus who flank a terrestial sphere and presumably illustrates Ficino's evocation of the Platonic Academy. See Bruschi, *Bramante*, 39–41 and 179.

91 Knox, "The Camerino of Francesco Corner," 84, n. 13, cites two additional friezes that survive from the sixteenth century: in Palazzo Morosini at San Stefano and in the Sala del Fregio of the Palazzo Vendramin-Calergi. A frieze painted by Marcello Fogolino removed from Villa Trissino-Muttoni near Vicenza is now in Ca' d'Oro: Guenther Schweikhart, "Antikencopie und -verwandlung in fries des Marcello Fogolino aus der Villa Trissino-Muttoni (Ca' Impenta) bei Vicenza. Ein Beitrag zur Geschichte der Villendekoration des frühen 16. Jahrhunderts im Veneto," *Mitteilungen des Kunsthistorishes Institutes in Florenz* XX, 1976, 351–8.

92 Hieronymus Avantius, *Marco Cornelio. S. M. in porticu Cardinali Veronae Episcopatum Ineunti gratulatur*, Venice 1504, f. Av (English transl. by Lightbown, *Andrea Mantegna*, 214–15).

93 Lightbown, *Mantegna*, 213–18, 451–2. See also Davis, *The Earlier Italian Schools*, 330–34; Braham, "A reappraisal," 456–63; Brown, "Andrea Mantegna and the Cornaro of Venice," 101–3; Dunkerton, et al, *Giotto to Dürer*, 372–5, cat. no. 64; and Martineau, *Andrea Mantegna*, 414–16, cat. no. 135 (catalogue entry by Keith Christiansen).

94 The work is also known as *An Episode from the Life of Publius Cornelius Scipio*. See Robertson, *Giovanni Bellini*, 132–3; Shapley, *Catalogue of the Italian Paintings*, 52–4; and Goffen, *Giovanni Bellini*, 238–42. Braham, "A reappraisal," 458; and Knox, "The Camerino of Francesco Corner," 79–84, associate two smaller panel paintings representing *Tuccia* and *Sophonisba* with the program. But cf. Christiansen's assessment in Martineau, *Andrea Mantegna*, 414. The two panel paintings are assigned to a "follower of Mantegna" by Davies, *Earlier Italian Schools*, 340–41.

95 Lightbown, *Andrea Mantegna*, 216.

96 Recounted by a number of classical writers. See Lightbown, *Andrea Mantegna*, 267 n. 19: Valerius Maximus (VIII, 15); Martineau, *Andrea Mantegna*, 414: Livy (XXIX, xiv), Ovid (*Fasti*, IV, 247–348), Appian (*Roman History*, IX, 56).

97 Although some scholars identifiy the kneeling figure as Claudia Quinta, symbolizing female chastity, the unmistakable profile of an Adam's apple makes the designation untenable: noticed by Lightbown, *Andrea Mantegna*, 217; and affirmed by Christiansen in Martineau, *Andrea Mantegna*, 415. The proponents of Claudia Quinta are Braham, "A reappraisal," 461; and Davies, *Earlier Italian Schools*, 331–3.

98 Goffen, *Giovanni Bellini*, 238. For Bembo's letter, see Gaye, *Carteggio inedito*, II, 71–3.

99 Goffen, *Giovanni Bellini*, 239.

100 Ibid., 242–7, who observes that a similar mindset informs Giovanni's *Feast of the Gods*, completed for the Duke of

Ferrara, Alfonso d'Este, in 1514. Although much has been written on this work, see now the well-argued proposal by Anderson, "The Provenance of Bellini's *Feast of the Gods*," 265–87.

101 The discussion that follows is primarily based upon the pioneering study of Mariuz, "Appunti per una lettura del fregio giorgionesco," 49–70. See also Sgarbi, "Il 'fregio' di Castelfranco," 273–84; and Martin, *Giorgione negli affreschi di Castelfranco*, 97–116.

102 Sgarbi, "Il 'fregio'," 273–7.

103 Mariuz, "Appunti," 51–66.

104 Martin, *Giorgione negli affreschi*, 99. Pignatti, *Giorgione*, 103–4, cat. no. 16a–c, accepts the east wall frieze as autograph and the west wall as autograph with assistance. Cf. Sgarbi, "Il 'fregio'," 273–80, who rejects the Giorgione attribution and stresses the Lombard character of the work. He provides a summary of earlier views.

105 Mariuz, "Appunti," 59, citing *Wisdom*, II, 5: "Umbre transitus est tempus nostrum'; and Sallust, *Bellum Catilinae*, I, 4: "Sola virtus clara aeternaque habetur."

106 Mariuz, "Appunti," 59, 62–3.

107 Ibid., 66, stating that *territ* seems to be an incorrect form of *terit*: "Territ omnia tempvs," and "Virtus vincit omnia."

108 Publilius Syrus, *Sententiae*: Mariuz, "Appunti," 60, 66–7, "Amans quid cupi[a]t s[c]it quid sapiat non videt." Mariuz notes that two words are copied incorrectly in the frieze: *cupit* should be *cupiat*, and *sit* should be *scit*.

109 Mariuz, "Appunti," 67, noting that the inscription is incomplete because of damage to the fresco: "Omnium rerum respicien [da finis]."

110 Ibid., 69: "A differenza della natura, che perpetuamente si rinnova in una molteplicità inesauribile di forme, l'uomo è autore di opere effimere e tuttavia solo grazie ad esse egli può sperare di sopravvivere a se stesso." Cf. Sgarbi, "Il 'fregio'," 281, who interprets the program as a celebration of the moral virtues over the military, civil, and political virtues and of the contemplative over the active life.

111 Cicogna, *Della famiglia Marcello*, 9; De Minerbi, *La Tempesta di Giorgione e l'Amore profano di Tiziano*; Anderson, 'Giorgione, Titian and the Sleeping Venus," 341; and Goffen, "Renaissance Dreams," 697–701. For other pastoral paintings of the period, see Rosand, "Giorgione, Venice, and the Pastoral Vision"; and the essays in Manca, *Titian 500*, particularly Holberton, "The *Pastorale* or *Fête Champêtre*," 245–62. Also essential is Hunt, *The Pastoral Landscape*.

112 Sanudo, *De origine*, 13–14: "Questi habitanti attendevano a far mercadantie con loro barchette alli liti vicini portando sal et pesse; non erano superbi né stimavano ricchezza, benché ricchi fossero, ma pietà, et innocenza; non vestivano ornatamente nécercavano honore, ma *coacti, et electi* per ben del Commun intravano al governo; non era differentia alcuna, et scrive Cassiodoro in la sua epistola questo: 'Paupertas ibi cum divitibus sub aequalitate vivit' . . ."

113 Powerfully stated by Tafuri, *Venice and the Renaissance*, chap. 1; and Concina, "Fra Oriente e Occidente," 265–90. For a fine summary of Venetian architecture in this period, with essential bibliography, see Lionello Puppi and Loredan Olivato, "L'architettura a Venezia: 1480–1510," in Maschio, *I tempi di Giorgione*, 40–54.

114 Jacks, *The Antiquarian*, 134–5. See also Cicogna, *Inscrizioni veneziane*, I, 288–9; and Tassini, *Curiosità veneziane*, 367–8: Dorsoduro no. 3604 (Fondamenta Bembo detta Malcanton). Zorzi, *Venezia Scomparsa*, 295, identifies the building as the Palazzo Falier-Dandolo that rose at the head of Rio Malcanton